PENGUIN BOOKS

BRITAIN UNWRAPPED

Hilaire Barnett is a Senior Lecturer in Law at Queen Mary, University of London, where she teaches Constitutional Law, Jurisprudence and Legal Theory and Family Law. She is also actively involved with the University of London's LLB Programme for External Students. She is the author of the *Textbook on Constitutional and Administrative Law* (Cavendish Publishing Ltd), now in its third edition with a fourth edition forthcoming in 2002, *Sourcebook on Feminist Jurisprudence* (Cavendish, 1997) and *Introduction to Feminist Jurisprudence* (Cavendish, 1998).

BRITAIN

Government and Constitution Explained

UNWRAPPED

Hilaire Barnett

PENGUIN BOOKS

PENGUIN BOOKS

Published by the Penguin Group
Penguin Books Ltd, 80 Strand, London WC2R 0RL, England
Penguin Putnam Inc., 375 Hudson Street, New York, New York 10014, USA
Penguin Books Australia Ltd, 250 Camberwell Road, Camberwell, Victoria 3124, Australia
Penguin Books Canada Ltd, 10 Alcorn Avenue, Toronto, Ontario, Canada M4V 3B2
Penguin Books India (P) Ltd, 11, Community Centre, Panchsheel Park, New Delhi – 110 017, India
Penguin Books (NZ) Ltd, Cnr Rosedale and Airborne Roads, Albany, Auckland, New Zealand
Penguin Books (South Africa) (Pty) Ltd, 24 Sturdee Avenue, Rosebank 2196, South Africa

Penguin Books Ltd, Registered Offices: 80 Strand, London WC2R 0RL, England

www.penguin.com

First published 2002
6

Copyright © Hilaire Barnett, 2002
All rights reserved

The moral right of the author has been asserted

Set in 9.75/12.5 pt Adobe Minion
Typeset by Rowland Phototypesetting Ltd, Bury St Edmunds, Suffolk
Printed in England by Clays Ltd, St Ives plc

CONTENTS

PREFACE

Britain Unwrapped aims to provide an overview of the constitution, government and legal system. British government is founded on a constitution which is, contrary to that of the majority of modern democratic states, largely unwritten. At no point in history has a comprehensive document been drafted which details the legal and non-legal rules which comprise the constitution. As a result, the contemporary system of government is one which has evolved through practical experience rather than one which has been consciously and systematically designed. Pragmatism rather than principle has long been a dominant theme in British governance. Changes to the constitution, government and law have reflected this steady evolutionary movement, being piecemeal and reactive rather than proactive.

Since the election of the Labour government in 1997 the framework of government and the constitution has undergone significant change. Devolution to national assemblies has been accomplished as has the introduction of a new system of government for London. The composition of the House of Lords has been reformed, albeit, by early 2002, incompletely. The Human Rights Act 1998 has made the European Convention on Human Rights enforceable within the domestic legal system. Changes in the voting system for general elections are under consideration and the funding of political parties has been subjected to legal controls. Never before has a programme of such magnitude – and with so little coherence and thought to the overall consequences for

British governance – been attempted in so short a span of time. The system is in a state of constitutional flux, the long-term consequences of which are by no means certain.

For readers unfamiliar with British history, a brief sketch of the past outlining major constitutional and governmental developments – without which the contemporary system is difficult to understand – is provided in Chapter 12. For easy reference, Appendices I and II list the monarchs and Prime Ministers and their years of reign and office.

Hilaire Barnett
Department of Law
Queen Mary, University of London
June 2002

INDEX OF CASES

INDEX OF LEGISLATION

THE CONSTITUTIONAL FRAMEWORK

INTRODUCTION

The constitution of a state – which forms the backcloth of government and its powers – is a set of rules, written or unwritten, which identifies the principal institutions of the state, their powers and relationships with other state institutions and the relationship between government and citizen. In the United Kingdom the constitution is best described as 'largely unwritten', the product of gradual historical evolution. At no point in time has the process of government and the rights and freedoms of citizens been set down in an authoritative text. The system of government is a mix of structures and institutions inherited from the past, adopted and adapted in seemingly haphazard fashion to meet the needs of contemporary society. Pragmatism and experience rather than principle or theory have shaped the system. By contrast, where a written constitution exists – as is the case in the vast majority of contemporary states – the powers of differing institutions of the state are set down, their limits defined. Individual citizens will also generally have a Bill of Rights enshrined within the constitution which clarifies their freedoms and rights which are enforceable even against government. As a general rule, it is the constitution interpreted and enforced by a Supreme Court which reigns supreme.

Britain, having one of the world's oldest and most stable constitutions, formerly a vast imperial power, now a small but relatively influential democratic state, exhibits the hallmarks of internal peace and security.[1] But while the physical manifestations of government – the Crown, Prime Minister and Cabinet, Parliament, Whitehall and the court system – are readily visible, the foundations of the system of government – the constitutional infrastructure – are far from apparent. To understand the system of government and the underlying constitution is accordingly a more complex task than where a written constitution exists. The system operates at differing levels of visibility, the legal rules being supplemented by non-legal, but obligatory, conventional rules. In addition, the constitution is guided by three basic principles – the sovereignty of Parliament, the separation of powers and the rule of law.

There are anomalies in the system. The United Kingdom is regarded as a 'parliamentary democracy', and yet the head of state is a hereditary monarch and Britain a 'constitutional monarchy'. The Queen appears to exercise little practical political power, and yet in strict legal terms the powers of the Crown – prerogative powers – are considerable and fundamentally important. The Crown is the 'fountain of justice', the head of government and a constituent part of Parliament. Parliament itself has two chambers, the Commons and the Lords.[2] While the Commons is elected, the House of Lords – or Upper House – still reflects its medieval origins. It remains unelected by the people for whom it makes laws – and, until recent reforms, comprised a majority of members who inherited their titles and held their seats as of right of birth.[3]

Under any constitution, it is generally understood that citizens have numerous freedoms and rights, and yet in Britain there is no indigenous Charter or Bill of Rights setting out the basic rights and freedoms to which individuals are entitled.[4] Traditionally, the emphasis under domestic law has been that citizens enjoy freedoms, rather than rights: that any conduct which is not prohibited is lawful. While Britain is a signatory to the European Convention on Human Rights[5] which pro-

---

[1] Save for the intractable problem of Northern Ireland.   [2] See Chapter 3.
[3] Under the House of Lords Act 1999 the right of all but 92 of the hereditary peers to sit and vote in Parliament was removed; this is but a first stage of the reform which is unlikely to result in a fully elected Upper House.   [4] See Chapter 7.
[5] Introduced in 1950 under the aegis of the Council of Europe.

vides for the protection of rights on a European-wide basis, it was not until the introduction of the Human Rights Act 1998 that Convention rights became enforceable before the domestic courts of law rather than through an application to the European Court of Human Rights in Strasbourg.

Since the British constitution has never been committed to writing, to understand its elements the various sources of power and the rules which regulate the exercise of power by the principal organs of the state – the executive, legislature and judiciary – must be examined. Sources of power include written documents, ancient and modern, Acts of Parliament, the prerogatives of the Crown, unwritten but binding 'constitutional conventions' and judicial case law. The basic principles – parliamentary supremacy, the separation of powers and the rule of law – on which the constitution rests also require explanation.

SOURCES OF THE CONSTITUTION

Legal sources

Acts of Parliament

In terms of formal sources of the constitution, there exists a mixture of formal written documents, ancient and modern, which provide the most visible structural outline.[6] Magna Carta, for example, signed in 1215 between the Barons, representing the upper classes and landowners, and King John, provides an early claim of citizens' rights against the near-absolute power of the Crown. Magna Carta, although now largely redundant, asserted the right of freedom of the people from unlawful arrest, seizure of property, and the right if accused of a crime to be tried in the courts by a jury of fellow citizens. In 1628, as a result of Charles I's years of rule without Parliament and his abuse of power in relation to civil liberties, Parliament presented to the King the Petition of Right denying the King the right to raise revenue through forced loans or taxation without Parliament's consent. Most importantly, and still

---

[6] Many of the ancient documented sources are discussed in Chapter 12.

relevant today, is the Bill of Rights 1689. The Bill of Rights finally settled the question of the King's power against Parliament's, in Parliament's favour. The offer of the Crown to Prince William of Orange, following the flight of James II to France, was one based on conditions, conditions designed to remove certain rights which the King had periodically claimed through personal rule and the relative weakness of Parliament in the face of royal abuse of power. From this date it is realistic to talk of the supremacy of Parliament as the principal law-making body. The Bill of Rights was not an exhaustive document by any means, and future Acts were to clarify further issues such as the independence of the judges in the exercise of their duties, and the succession to the Crown. The Bill of Rights was a culmination of the long conflict between the Crown and Parliament, a conflict fuelled and refuelled by the question of religion which Henry VIII had originated through his break with Roman Catholicism in the sixteenth century. Its more important provisions included the statement that the king no longer enjoyed the right to dissolve Parliament and to rule in his own right, nor could the Crown raise taxation without Parliament's approval, or keep an army in peacetime unless Parliament consented. It provided also for free elections to Parliament, for regular meetings of Parliament and for the rights and immunities enjoyed by Members of Parliament, for example freedom of speech in Parliament and freedom from arrest for a civil matter. The Bill of Rights reaffirmed the right to trial by jury and made clear that excessive punishments should not be inflicted on citizens.

In 1701 the question of judicial independence and royal succession were covered in the Act of Settlement. To stop the Crown from exercising any purported right to dismiss judges the Act provided for judicial security of tenure during 'good behaviour', and that should there be claims of abuse of power by judges it would be Parliament and not the King which would exercise any power of dismissal. To prevent for all time the possibility that Roman Catholicism would find its way back to the Crown the Act of Settlement also stipulated that only Protestant heirs through the male line could inherit the Crown, and moreover, that no heir to the throne could marry a Roman Catholic and still inherit.

As will be discussed in Chapter 5, the formation of the United

Kingdom as we know it today was a slow process, starting with the conquest of Wales in 1254. Scotland became constitutionally and politically united with the United Kingdom in 1707 through the Act of Union 1707. The Act provided for the Union to be everlasting – or in the flowery language of the eighteenth century – 'in all time being'. To many Scottish constitutional lawyers the Act of Union represents a basic written constitution for the nation, a view generally disputed south of the border. The claim to a basic written constitution arises from the fact that following centuries of conflict between Scotland and England – both independent sovereign states – and years of negotiations to find a lasting peace, the Act of Union provided for the demise of both the Scottish and English Parliaments and their coming together in a united Parliament representing Great Britain. In 1800 the Act of Union with Ireland was signed between Ireland and England, and although the language of the Treaty suggested permanence of the Union, it was not to survive Irish demands for freedom from Britain. Ultimately Ireland was divided, with the mainly Protestant counties of Ulster remaining part of the United Kingdom.

In terms of written sources of the constitution, in addition to those Acts which have brought the United Kingdom into being we must now also add the Scotland Act 1998, the Northern Ireland Act 1998 and the Government of Wales Act 1998, each of which in its different way grants greater self-governance to the countries of the United Kingdom, without destroying its unity.[7] The system of local government is closely regulated by Act of Parliament, and all powers devolved to local authorities are contained in statutes.

Acts of Parliament which regulate Parliament itself are also constitutionally important. Parliament comprises the Queen, the House of Lords and the House of Commons, of whom only the last is elected, the position of the Crown being hereditary and membership of the House of Lords being (until 1999, see below) largely hereditary, but also comprising a significant proportion of members awarded life peerages.[8] While the Bill of Rights 1689 regulated and controlled the powers of the Crown, it was not until early in the twentieth century that the respective powers of the Lords and Commons were regulated. Prior to 1911 the

---

[7] On devolution see Chapter 5.   [8] Under the Life Peerage Act 1958.

House of Lords enjoyed equal powers with the Commons in terms of law-making. A constitutional and political crisis arose between 1908 and 1910 when the Lords exercised its lawful powers, contrary to established conventional practice, to reject the financial budget of the government. Following this act of defiance of the will of the Commons, the powers of the House of Lords were curtailed under the Parliament Act 1911, and further limited by the Parliament Act 1949, which set strict limits on the right of the Lords to delay legislation and removed the right to reject financial legislation. The undemocratic composition of the Lords, however, remained. That position only changed with the House of Lords Act 1999. As will be discussed further in Chapter 3, a democratic deficit remains in Parliament, the majority of peers now being nominated life peers with the control over appointments remaining in the hands of the Prime Minister.

Beyond the shores of Britain throughout history, and particularly from the reign of Elizabeth I (1558–1603), British imperial power and influence reached far and wide. While British power reached its height in the nineteenth century, the demands of colonies for a greater measure of self-governance grew more insistent. The Colonial Laws Validity Act 1865 clarified the legal relationship between the British Parliament and law-making bodies of the colonies. By the end of the First World War in 1918 it became apparent that Britain could no longer sustain its power. While the original thirteen colonial states of America threw off the yoke of the British in 1776, it was in the twentieth century that decolonization and freedom were achieved by many formerly dependent states. In an effort further to clarify and strengthen colonial self-government, the Act of Westminster 1931 was passed to extend the scope of colonial legislative power. But even that move could not quell the increasing demands for independence from Britain as ideas of self-determination and nationalism took firm hold throughout the world following the Second World War. Imperialism had had its day, and by the 1960s much of Britain's former empire had disappeared. Remnants of it remain, but nowadays in the form of relationships within the Commonwealth of Nations – many members of which were formerly under British rule – regulated not by law but by the mutual self-interest of its fifty-four member states.

The birth of the European Communities in 1957,[9] however, changed many of the trading relations of Britain with the rest of the Commonwealth and signalled, when Britain finally joined the Community in 1973, through the Treaty of Accession and the European Communities Act 1972, a redirection of British commercial, trading and financial dealings. Today, as the Community has gradually expanded its original aims and objectives, and particularly from 1992 with the birth of the European Union, the system of British government cannot be understood in isolation from the Community and Union. Not only does the Union, now with fifteen member states, have its own form of government in which the British government participates but which it cannot control, but the law of the Community has far-reaching implications for Parliament and what it can lawfully do within the terms of membership of the Community and Union. Put shortly, the supremacy of Parliament, discussed below (pages 24 ff.), has shrunk. While before membership of the Community it was accurate to say that Parliament could make laws on any subject whatsoever and that no one or nobody, including the highest court in the land, could invalidate an Act of Parliament, nowadays Parliament can only act within the diminishing sphere of matters left immune from Union and Community control and regulation.

Constitutional statutes – Acts of Parliament – also include those which regulate the relationship between citizens and the state. Nationality law determines citizenship, and Immigration Acts regulate the right to enter and remain in Britain, and regulate asylum, deportation and extradition. The right to participate in the democratic process through the vote is regulated by Representation of the People Acts. Rights to non-discrimination on grounds of race and gender are contained in the Race Relations Act 1976, the Sex Discrimination Act 1965 and the Equal Pay Act 1970. Under the Human Rights Act 1998, most of the rights formerly guaranteed under the European Convention on Human Rights are incorporated into domestic law and enforceable before the domestic courts. These Convention rights – among them the right to life, right

[9] On which see Chapter 4. Originally there were three Communities, subsequently amalgamated into the single Community. In 1992 the European Union came into being, of which the EC is a constituent part.

to freedom from torture and inhuman treatment, right to fair trial, right to marry and found a family – both extend and supplement British statutes and the common law.

The royal prerogative

Actions of government may be exercised under the royal prerogative, which remains an important source of power, notwithstanding the Bill of Rights 1689 which curtailed the powers of the Crown. Two constitutional authorities have provided classic definitions of the prerogative. The first, Sir William Blackstone, in *Commentaries on the Laws of England* (1765–9),[10] defined the prerogative as the 'special preeminence which the King hath over and above all other persons'. This power is 'singular and peculiar' to the Crown and cannot be enjoyed by anyone else – if it is, it is not a prerogative power. The nineteenth-century constitutional authority, Albert Venn Dicey, in his *Introduction to the Study of the Law of the Constitution*,[11] states that the prerogative is the 'residue of discretionary or arbitrary authority, which at any time is legally left in the hands of the Crown' and goes on to state that 'every act which the executive government can lawfully do without the authority of an Act of Parliament is done in virtue of this prerogative'.

One of the outstanding features of British government, when compared to governments operating under written constitutions, is the extent to which the residual prerogatives of the Crown are used – now by the government rather than the Crown – and remain largely uncontrolled either by the courts or by Parliament itself. Most of these powers in the modern state are devolved to the government of the day. The powers which theoretically remain with the Crown are, however, significant. Under the royal prerogative the Crown has the legal power to enter into treaties with other nations. Treaties are governed by international law and when the United Kingdom signs a treaty – such as the Treaty of Rome, which enabled the United Kingdom to enter the European Community – the provisions of the treaty do not alter national law unless and until an Act of Parliament, or statute, is passed by the House of Commons and the House of Lords. The power to declare war

---

[10] Chicago: Chicago University Press.
[11] 1885 (London: Macmillan, 10th edn., 1959).

and peace also lies under the prerogative. This enables the government (in the name of the Crown) to act with speed in relation to the despatch of armed forces where circumstances dictate without first having to seek parliamentary approval for the action. Aside from the delay involved in seeking that approval, the publicity attracted would adversely affect the operation in question. This happened, for example, in relation to the Falkland Islands, when in 1982 Prime Minister Thatcher despatched the navy to the South Atlantic several days before Parliament debated the matter; and again in relation to the NATO action in the former Yugoslavia in the 1990s. The recognition of foreign states and diplomatic relations are also conducted under the royal prerogative.

To a limited extent the immunity from prior parliamentary scrutiny is an essential aspect of the prerogative, and one which exists under all constitutions. In relation to the power to make declarations of war and peace for example, it would hardly have been prudent to have expected the Prime Minister to hold a debate in Parliament before despatching the troops to the Falklands to defend the islands from the invading Argentinians. The despatching of troops and their operational orders, weaponry and manoeuvres, being fundamental to the security of the state, are not matters for advance publicity and debate but must be left to those in whom, rightly or wrongly, the people have entrusted power. Only after the event can public and parliamentary debate be entered into to test the soundness of the government's action.

The prerogative also operates in relation to domestic affairs. Parliament is summoned to meet, and is dissolved before a general election under the prerogative. The Crown must assent to all legislation, and once a Bill has passed through the Houses of Commons and Lords, this assent, which marks the formal transition from a legislative proposal (or Bill) to an Act of Parliament, is granted under the prerogative. The appointment of the Prime Minister is also a prerogative power, as is the regulation of the civil service. The granting of honours, that peculiarly British system of recognizing contributions to public life, also falls within the prerogative. The prerogative also functions within the criminal justice system, operating as the prerogative of mercy in the commutation of sentences and the pardoning of offenders. There is also the prerogative power of *nolle prosequi* – the power to order that a criminal prosecution be stopped in the public interest.

While these are wide and diverse powers, theoretically in the hands of the Crown but for practical purposes exercised by the government, there are numerous non-legal conventional rules which regulate the exercise of prerogative power. To give just one example, the Crown has never refused to assent to a Bill since the early eighteenth century. The unwritten rule requires that royal assent be given if the government demands it. Prerogative powers are also subject to limited judicial control. The courts can determine, for example, whether a prerogative power exists, and its extent. If the courts find that the government has acted outside the proper scope of the prerogative and misused or abused its power, the courts can nullify the decision. One firm rule is that if there is an Act of Parliament which regulates a matter formerly controlled by the prerogative, the Act of Parliament must be used as the correct source of power – not the prerogative. Two cases illustrate this. The first is *Attorney General v. de Keyser's Royal Hotel Ltd.*,[12] in which following the First World War, during which the plaintiff's hotel had been taken over for the housing of troops, compensation was sought. The government argued that compensation was payable under the royal prerogative, which would have given the government scope to offer lower compensation than that which would be awarded under the Defence of the Realm Act 1914. The court ruled that the government could not simply ignore an Act of Parliament and legitimately use a former prerogative. The same principle was applied in the more recent case of *R v. Secretary of State for the Home Department ex parte Fire Brigades' Union and Others*.[13] Here, the Criminal Justice Act 1988 regulated compensation tariffs awarded for those injured through the criminal actions of others. The original Criminal Injuries Compensation Scheme had been established under the royal prerogative. The then Home Secretary, Michael Howard QC, decided that he would attempt to introduce a new tariff under the prerogative rather than the Act of Parliament. The House of Lords ruled that this was beyond his powers: the only legitimate source of power was the Criminal Justice Act 1998.

However, because of the principle of separation of powers – that one institution of the state, here the judges, should not encroach on the power of another, usually the executive – and because of the requirement

[12] [1920] AC 508.   [13] [1995] 2 WLR 1.

that the judges stay out of matters of politics, many areas are immune from the court's control. Within this category of unreviewable matters fall the most important prerogative powers: the signing of treaties, declarations of war and peace, disposition of the armed forces, the appointment of ministers, the summoning and dissolution of Parliament and the granting of honours.

The constitutional system of checks and balances includes the conventional rules controlling the way in which the prerogative operates, the way that the judges rule – albeit in limited manner – on the exercise of the prerogative, and Parliament's right to abolish a prerogative power. However, there is a split in the appearance of things and their constitutional and legal significance. For example, while the Queen will by convention (one of the important non-legal sources of the constitution) always grant a dissolution of Parliament which precedes a general election on the request of the Prime Minister, in strict law the Queen retains the right to refuse that request, or in an even more extreme case, to decide to end the life of a Parliament on her own initiative. Also, by way of example, the Queen has the legal right to appoint as her Prime Minister any person she chooses, irrespective of their party political support or the wishes of the electorate. Of course, in practice it has been established – again by convention rather than legal rules – that the Queen will appoint as Prime Minister the leader of the political party which can command a majority in the House of Commons following a general election and thus lead the country. It would be contrary to the whole idea of democratic government for the position to be otherwise.

While the general rule has been in operation since the 1960s – by which time all major political parties had adopted a system for the election of the leader of the party – it is only relatively recently that the Queen has had no discretion over whom she should appoint. Before the major political parties adopted procedures for the election of their leaders, the Queen did have a measure of choice of Prime Minister. In 1957 the Conservative Prime Minister, Anthony Eden, resigned office because of ill-health, as did Harold Macmillan in 1963. There being no election procedure at the time for the leader of the Conservative Party, the Queen had to decide who should become Prime Minister and leader of the party. In 1957, having taken soundings from senior party figures, the Queen chose Harold Macmillan over the other contender, R. A. Butler. When Macmillan resigned in 1963 three possible successors waited in the wings: Butler, Reginald Maudling and Lord Home, the Foreign Secretary. Macmillan advised the Queen to send for Lord Home who then relinquished his peerage and seat in the Lords to become leader. Such involvement in the political process can be dangerous for the monarch, since it brings him or her into the political limelight (rather than remaining above and outside politics), and inevitably gives rise to controversy. However, since the Conservative, Labour and Liberal Democrat parties all now elect their leaders, albeit by different processes, the opportunity, or need, for the monarch to exercise any discretion is largely removed, barring one possible circumstance. As will be seen in Chapter 6, while the Conservative and Labour parties since the 1920s have represented the two main political parties in terms of election to government, the Liberal Democrat Party also retains considerable electoral support across the country. That this popular support does not translate itself into the proportional number of seats in Parliament is the consequence of the voting system. However, if the voting system were to change, a general election might well result at some time in a 'hung parliament', one in which there is no clear overall majority for any one party. In that situation, the Queen would again have to exercise discretion.

Some minor prerogatives remain personal to the Crown, however, such as the right to confer the Order of Merit and Orders of the Garter and Thistle. The Queen is also immune from prosecution in courts of law, on the basis that she is the fountain of justice, and cannot therefore be tried by herself, by her own judges. Beyond this, it remains the position that while the Crown does not in fact exercise these powers directly and personally, the Crown *could* exercise the powers should a situation arise where protection of the constitution so demanded. For example, if the government of the day demanded that the Crown assent to a Bill which would fundamentally undermine the rights of citizens against all precedent, it is arguable that the Queen would have not only the right to refuse her assent, but also the constitutional duty to refuse it. Likewise, although it is a convention that the Crown will agree to a dissolution of Parliament for the purposes of holding a general election and allowing the people to express their sovereign will, should a government seek a dissolution purely for party political advantage (say to obtain a more secure majority following promises to the electorate which would guarantee that outcome), the Queen would be within her legal rights to refuse. Such a refusal would, however, put the continuance of the monarchy in supreme danger.

The power of the government under the prerogative is capable of conflicting with individual freedoms and liberties. For the exercise of power to be legitimate there must be processes in which this can be tested. Two forums exist for this purpose: Parliament and the courts of law (both domestic and European). Ministers are accountable to Parliament and to the courts. In relation to Parliament the difficulty with the prerogative is that any scrutiny is necessarily *ex post facto*, with the minister justifying his or her actions and answering questions on the exercise of power. But this is not always possible: there exist a number of categories of information which, under conventional rules, are immune from parliamentary scrutiny. Ministers may decline to answer questions in relation to, among other matters, the dissolution of Parliament, the granting of honours, defence and national security: all prerogative issues.

Judicial decisions

Among the legal sources of the constitution are the decisions of the judges. The judges have over the centuries developed common law. The English legal system was highly centralized by the reign of Henry II (1154–89), with judges developing the law on a consistent nation-wide basis. Until the nineteenth century, when an explosion of parliamentary activity took place, largely as a result of the industrial revolution and the need for state intervention across a range of economic and social issues, the principal source of law was common law. The courts have jurisdiction to rule on the interpretation of Acts of Parliament, and to develop the common law of the land, subject to Parliament's right to overrule their decisions.[14] In addition to its evolution of common law, it is the courts which interpret the scope of government powers and keep government and its many subordinate bodies (such as local authorities and quasi-autonomous government bodies) within the

[14] On the rules of statutory interpretation and the doctrine of precedent see Chapter 9.

limits of power conferred by Parliament. In addition, from the point of view of the individual citizen, the courts' powers to rule on rights and freedoms, either through common law (judge-made law) or through the interpretation of Acts of Parliament, are of crucial importance.

The subordination of British judges to Parliament, however, does not mean judicial impotence nor that Parliament will be quick to exercise its supreme power. Parliament does not always choose to legislate nor will it frequently overturn judicial decisions. Furthermore, although Acts of Parliament became a major source of law around the end of the nineteenth century, even so, when enacting law, Parliament will often base its statute on the common law, rather than overturn the whole *corpus* of law which the judges have developed. To this extent, judicial decisions form the basis and content of substantial areas of law.

An area of law which has particular significance to the constitution is that of judicial review. The constitutional position of judges is such that no Act of Parliament may be declared void on any basis, and accordingly judges have no power to question the validity of an Act of Parliament. They are, however, frequently called upon to rule on the validity of delegated legislation – detailed rules drafted by ministers, government departments and other public bodies under the authority of an Act of Parliament. Acts of Parliament may, in order to promote more efficient rule-making, grant power to the executive, to draft the minutiae of rules which supplement the 'parent Act'. Parliamentary procedures for examining these detailed rules are inadequate, although mechanisms do exist for both scrutinizing the rules and challenging their legality in Parliament.[15] The problem is in part the sheer volume of secondary or delegated legislation: while in any parliamentary year about fifty or sixty Acts of Parliament will be passed, over two thousand pieces of delegated legislation are likely to be drafted and come into effect.

The judges play an active role in ensuring that delegated legislation is valid, that it conforms to the powers granted by the parent Act and does not go further than the power granted. For example, if an Act of Parliament gives power to a minister to 'give guidance to' a particular

[15] See further Chapter 3.

regulatory body such as the Civil Aviation Authority, and the minister *orders* the authority to do something, the question arises as to whether the minister exceeded his power.[16] Should a person be adversely affected by the minister's order, he or she may apply to the courts for a ruling as to the legality (or *vires*) of the minister's action, by an application for judicial review. The court has the power to determine whether or not the minister acted inside or outside his or her powers, and, if he or she acted outside the powers given, to declare that action unlawful. Here the independence of the judiciary in relation to the executive is critically important, and shows the manner in which the separation of powers – by guaranteeing that independence – upholds the principle of government under law, and in so doing protects citizens against abuse of power.

The most frequent 'defendants' in judicial review proceedings are local authorities. Local authorities are granted power by Act of Parliament to make detailed rules (by-laws) for their areas. One example is the power of a local council to draft rules relating to cycling and other vehicular access to tow-paths along rivers. Local authorities also have important powers in relation to planning applications, whether for new buildings or for loft extensions and so on for existing buildings. An Act of Parliament may stipulate procedures which a local council must follow in order to achieve some objective under the Act. Typically, for example, if a new development of houses is being considered, a local council must notify members of the local community who would be affected by the grant of planning permission, and provide them with opportunities to oppose that grant. If, in contravention of the notification and consultation procedures, a local council granted permission, then those affected by its unlawful action may seek judicial review and attempt to have the council's decision nullified (quashed or set aside).[17] Where this happens, the local council is then under a duty to remake its decision, following the correct procedures. By this means, the judges keep public bodies within the powers given to them by Parliament.

[16] *Laker Airways v. Department of Trade* [1977] QB 643.
[17] It should be noted, however, that when it comes to decisions which entail considerable expenditure, Parliament may limit the availability of judicial review by way of placing strict time limits on when applications may be brought.

The courts also have the power to review the exercise of the royal prerogative, discussed above. Here, however, difficulties are encountered as the judges – ever mindful of the need to remain outside the realm of politics and matters of high policy – limit the extent to which they can exercise their jurisdiction. Aside from that restriction, which is significant but perhaps an inevitable consequence of an unwritten constitution, the courts will be astute to ensure that governments do not either claim powers under the prerogative which do not in fact exist, or attempt to avoid using an Act of Parliament by resorting to the prerogative.

Judicial review is thus crucial to keeping government and other public authorities within the confines of the powers which Parliament has conferred upon them. A citizen, or an organization representing the interests of its members or supporters, may apply to the High Court for judicial review of administrative decisions. There is no *right* to judicial review, and in order to balance the requirements of certain administrations against the rights of individuals the courts require that the applicant have 'standing', or *locus standi*, or *sufficient interest* in a matter to seek review. An application must also be brought within three months of the relevant decision, although the court has a discretion to extend this time in the interests of justice.[18] Furthermore, the matter must be a matter of public, as opposed to private, law and relate to the exercise of powers by a public body, or a body which while under private control is exercising powers that otherwise a government body would exercise.[19] Where an application is granted, the High Court will then proceed to examine the case. Where the court finds that a public body has acted outside its powers – *ultra vires* – the court will quash, or nullify, the decision made and require the decision-maker to re-decide the matter in accordance with law. The court is not concerned with the justice or otherwise of the rules in question, or the merits of

[18] Supreme Court Act 1981, section 31, and Civil Procedures Rules 1998.
[19] See *R v. City Panel on Takeovers and Mergers ex parte Datafin Ltd.* [1987] 2 QB 815, in which the Panel was ruled to be a public body, and compare *R v. Disciplinary Committee of the Jockey Club ex parte Aga Khan* [1993] 1 WLR 909, in which the court ruled that the matter was regulated by the private law of contract and that the Jockey Club was not a public body within the meaning required for judicial review.

the case, but solely with the question of whether or not the public body has acted inside – *intra vires* – or outside its powers. As quoted above, however, mindful of the need for separation of powers, judges are cautious about straying into areas of high policy which are more appropriately decided by the executive.

Non-legal sources

Constitutional conventions

To operate effectively, all governments require a degree of flexibility. Strict rules of law cannot cover every scenario. Underlying the law and its operation are conventional rules which develop and change over time to meet new requirements. Lacking a written constitution, these conventional rules assume special importance in Britain and operate as a web of largely unseen and little understood non-legal rules. Constitutional conventions may be defined as those unwritten, binding rules which regulate the conduct of the institutions and personnel of government. Conventions lurk in the shadows of the constitution, rarely obvious but always influential. Nowhere are these written down in any authoritative document. But rules they are, and in terms of understanding government they are at least as important as, and in some cases more important than, the legal rules which they underpin. To breach a convention, without justifiable cause, is to act *unconstitutionally*, but since the rules are not legal rules this does not mean that the action will be *unlawful*. This split between *constitutionality* and *legality* is one of the paradoxes of the British system. Under a written constitution this split would not be possible, for unless conduct falls within the limits of power allowed by the law (and adjudicated on by the courts) it is both unconstitutional and unlawful. In Britain, unconstitutional conduct may lead to a political crisis of sorts but not, for the most part, to legal action, although it may lead to new laws being introduced to avoid any future breaches of the conventional rule. Conventions have an inherent flexibility. They change over time. Quite how and when they change is difficult to see at the time, and becomes apparent only with hindsight.

This conundrum requires unravelling. For this it is helpful to look at some of the specific conventions and see how they operate. In terms of who is bound by these rules, all organs of government are affected. As noted already in discussing the prerogative, the Queen's powers to give or refuse the royal assent to Bills and to dissolve Parliament are controlled by conventional rules. To breach the conventions would be to challenge the democratically elected government and suggest a return to the pre-1689 days of absolute Crown powers.

Conventions also regulate the workings of Parliament. Until 1911, when the Parliament Act was passed, the relationship between the House of Commons and the House of Lords was entirely governed by convention. Since the Commons had become fully representative of the people through the extension to all adult males of the right to vote, the convention was that the House of Lords would not reject a financial Bill passed by the Commons, and would be cautious about delaying any other Bill unduly. But between 1908 and 1910 the House of Lords flexed its muscles, rejecting the Bill that was intended to give effect to the government's annual budget. Frustrated by the Lords and unable to bring in the financial programme, the Prime Minister asked the King to create sufficient new peers to overcome the opposition. Meanwhile two general elections were fought to establish the supremacy of the Commons. In the event, threatened by the King, the Lords passed the Bill, promptly to have their powers curtailed by the Parliament Act 1911. Convention still operates between the two Houses. Now, although Acts of Parliament have ensured that 'money bills' are not delayed by the Lords for more than a month and other bills for not more than about a year over two parliamentary sessions (years), by convention (the 'Salisbury convention') the Lords will not block any Bill giving effect to the election manifesto of the elected government.

One of the most important conventions operating is that of the responsibility of ministers to Parliament and through Parliament to the electorate. Of all the conventional rules, ministerial responsibility reveals the strengths and weaknesses of these non-legal rules. It operates in two main ways. First there is the collective responsibility of the Cabinet, the heart of the executive. The rule is that discussions in Cabinet are secret and may not be revealed to the outside world. Furthermore, once a decision has been reached in Cabinet, that decision is binding on all members of the Cabinet and other government ministers who are not in the Cabinet.[20] The idea behind the rule is that government must maintain its support and that this can only be achieved if the government presents a strong united face to the public and Parliament. Secondly, there is the individual responsibility of ministers to account for the workings of their government departments and to take responsibility not only for their department but also for their own personal conduct. This is the trickiest aspect of responsibility and one which sometimes appears to be so uncertain in its meaning and scope that it is not a rule at all.

On occasion, collective responsibility has changed in the way it operates. In 1975, for example, the Labour government was split over Britain's continued membership of the European Community. A referendum was planned in which the people would express their wishes – although the government made it plain that it would not be bound by the result of the referendum, which made something of a nonsense of the 'will of the people'. When it became clear to the Prime Minister that ministers would not toe the line consistently on membership, and were threatening to reveal deep divisions in government and the Labour Party, he announced that the convention would be set aside for the limited purposes of public debate on the future of Britain in Europe, but not for any other issue about which ministers might privately disagree. As a temporary expedient it worked: full and frank debate took place; the people obligingly declared that they wished to stay in Europe, and the government agreed with them. Once that decision was taken, collective responsibility returned in full.

The power of the Prime Minister also to dictate the agenda for Cabinet causes disquiet. Notorious as an example of how not to run Cabinet is the saga over the rescue of an almost unheard-of British helicopter manufacturer, Westland, which arose in 1986. Westland was in dire financial straits. Since it was the only manufacturer of helicopters in Britain the government wanted it rescued. But by whom? The then President of the Board of Trade, Michael Heseltine, had been negotiating with a European consortium. The Prime Minister, however, favoured a rescue bid by the American-based Sigorski company, a view imposed on Cabinet allegedly before Heseltine had had the opportunity to put

[20] For the structure of government and the Cabinet, see Chapter 2.

the case for the European consortium. Heseltine requested a further meeting of Cabinet to put his proposals. Accounts differ, but one interpretation of events is that before the scheduled meeting took place, the Prime Minister cancelled it. Furious, Heseltine resigned from Cabinet in order publicly to express his dissent from the Cabinet's decision. Nor did the story end there. Leon Brittan, then Secretary of State for Trade and Industry, was found by a parliamentary Select Committee which subsequently inquired into the whole business to have authorized the leak of advice given to the government by the Attorney-General, advice which by convention must never be disclosed. Neither Brittan nor his civil servants proved helpful to the Select Committee in its inquiries – thus furthering allegations of a cover-up and of government secrecy. Brittan also eventually resigned.

The difficulties with maintaining collective responsibility pale into insignificance when attention is turned to individual responsibility. In recent years, in particular, a wealth of evidence has been revealed which raises basic questions as to its meaning and relevance. The 1950s provided the classic scenario of how the convention should work. In what became known as the Crichel Down affair, the Minister of Agriculture resigned after a series of blunders by his department over a piece of land in Devon which had been taken over by the government in wartime for use of the forces. The former owners tried to get 'their' land back. Meanwhile, it had been disposed of to others. It took a full public inquiry to unravel the facts and the question of who was responsible for what. Despite the fact that Thomas Dugdale, the minister, had no personal knowledge of or involvement in the debacle, he resigned. Later it became clear that Dugdale resigned not out of a developed sense of constitutional propriety but because he had lost the support of colleagues: but this has done little to prevent it being cited as the classic example of the principle of individual responsibility in action.

Curiously, there were to be no further resignations on the basis of individual responsibility for departmental blunders, as opposed to personal conduct, until the Falklands War in 1982 which claimed the resignations of the Foreign Secretary, Lord Carrington, and two junior ministers in the Foreign Office. Gradually and increasingly, the concept of responsibility had changed over the years. No longer were accountability, responsibility and its consequence – resignation – inextricably linked.

The change in practice originated in 1983 when there was a mass break-out of prisoners from the Maze prison in Belfast. A subsequent report on security arrangements found that there were weaknesses in both management and the security of the prison. Responsibility lay with the prison governor, but there was criticism of the Northern Ireland Office in its handling of the supervision of prison security. The Secretary of State for Northern Ireland, James Prior, did not resign despite his overall responsibility. In debate in the Commons, the minister denied that there was a clear convention linking responsibility to the requirement of resignation. Instead he laid the blame firmly on the governor, who by now had resigned. A subsequent lapse in prison administration occurred under Home Secretary Michael Howard. In 1991 IRA prisoners escaped from Whitemoor prison: Howard cited the Prior precedent as justification for not resigning, having dismissed Derek Lewis from his position as Director-General of the Prison Service Agency.

The most blatant challenge to any linkage between individual responsibility and resignation as a consequence comes with the arms to Iraq affair. Company directors faced prosecution for breaching export regulations in relation to machine parts capable of being used as weapons components. The government had changed its export policy without advising Parliament, and when faced with requests for evidence for the court proceedings issued Public Interest Immunity Certificates to prevent that evidence coming before the court. When a junior minister let it be known that the evidence would exonerate the defendants, the prosecution's case collapsed. The then Prime Minister, John Major, immediately announced a major judicial inquiry into the affair. The inquiry, headed by Sir Richard Scott, was to produce the most wide-ranging analysis of ministerial accountability and responsibility. One of Scott's most telling findings was that while no minister had deliberate lied to Parliament, ministers had however been guilty of telling less than the full truth. As Scott expressed the matter:

the proposition that it is acceptable for a Minister to give an answer that is deliberately incomplete is one which, in my opinion, is inconsistent with the requirements of the constitutional principle of ministerial responsibility. Half the picture can be true . . . but the audience does not know that it is seeing only half the picture. If it did know, it would protest.[21]

The position which emerges from the arms to Iraq affair is that there is now a recognized distinction between ministerial accountability to Parliament which is absolute, and resignation as a consequence of a failure in accountability. A further problem with the doctrine of responsibility also lies with the position of civil servants. Where a civil servant is within a government department he or she is accountable to the minister, not to Parliament. He or she may be permitted to give evidence to Commons' committees but only express views which are consistent with the minister's policies. It is no defence to argue, as did Clive Ponting in the 1980s, that a civil servant's first duty is to Parliament.[22]

How then can the doctrine of ministerial responsibility for administration be evaluated? Some matters are clear, others less so. On the side of clarity, particularly after the Scott Inquiry, is the fact that ministers are under a duty to account to Parliament, either in debate on the floor of the House or through Select Committees, for the working of their departments, and this duty includes a duty not to withhold information from Parliament or to paint 'half the picture'. This does not mean, however, that resignation is a sanction which will necessarily follow an acceptance of responsibility when matters go wrong. A resignation may be expected if a minister is personally culpable of wrongdoing, and if that wrongdoing loses him or her the confidence of the Prime Minister, Cabinet, Parliament or the party. On the other hand, if a minister claims that administrative failure is less to do with policy or his or her own actions and lies within the responsibility of the head of a government service, it may well be the case, as with Michael Howard and the problems in prisons, that it will be the governor of the prison who will face loss of office, not the minister. Here, the minister's responsibility

---

[21] (Sir) R. Scott, 'Ministerial responsibility' [1996] PL 410, at p. 424.
[22] However, given that the jury acquitted him of offences under the Official Secrets Act 1911 for disclosing official documentation relating to the sinking of the *General Belgrano* in the Falklands War, the public might well have preferred Ponting's view of the position.

is confined to accounting to Parliament for the administrative failings. This is an absolute requirement; resignation is not.

A further aspect of ministerial responsibility relates to personal conduct. It is expected, realistically or not, that ministers will conduct their private lives in a manner which does not attract criticism that could lower the standing of government in the eyes of the public. Strict rules apply to financial matters. On taking office, a minister is required to divest him- or herself of any other office, such as directorships, in order to avoid any suspicion of dual- or self-interest. All Members of Parliament are required to register their outside financial interests. In relation to sexual matters the control over ministers has become more stringent, especially since the last years of Conservative government when repeated allegations of sexual impropriety were made. What was formerly a curious ambivalence over sexual matters hardened into a moralistic attitude demanding resignation for personal 'misconduct'.

Over the past decades numerous ministers have fallen victim to the requirement of high standards in public life. In 1963 the Minister for War, John Profumo, was found to have been having an affair with a prostitute who was herself in a relationship with a junior attaché at the Russian Embassy. Profumo was forced to resign, less because of his adultery than because when challenged in Parliament he lied about the matter. Lords Lambton and Jellicoe resigned office in 1973 following allegations of involvement with prostitution and drugs. In 1983 Cecil Parkinson, then Secretary of State for Trade and Industry and Chairman of the Conservative Party, was forced to resign following an affair with his secretary, who was carrying his child. In 1992 David Mellor, Heritage Secretary, resigned over an affair with an actress and allegations that he had received gifts from inappropriate quarters. While he might have survived the affair, the tabloid press using surveillance techniques were able to ridicule Mellor to such an extent that his position became untenable and he had to resign. More recently, in 1998, Ron Davies, the Welsh Secretary, resigned immediately after being discovered in still unexplained but curious circumstances on Clapham Common. Also during the Labour government's first term of office (1997–2001), Peter Mandelson – a member of Cabinet and close friend of the Prime Minister – resigned not once, but twice. The first resignation revolved around an undisclosed loan from another minister. The second occasion, in 2001, concerned allegations that Mandelson had improperly intervened in the passport application of a foreign businessman who had contributed funds to the Millennium Dome project, for which Mandelson was, at the time, responsible. The contemporary message is that if you are caught out doing something which is clearly wrong, or even possibly wrong, you should resign sooner rather than later in order to spare the government embarrassment and loss of public confidence.

CONSTITUTIONAL PRINCIPLES

In the United Kingdom three major concepts underpin the constitution and guide its working: parliamentary supremacy, the separation of powers and the rule of law. In essence, parliamentary sovereignty (or legislative supremacy) means that Parliament is free to make laws on any subject whatsoever, while the separation of powers requires that the three major institutions of the state, the legislature, executive and judiciary, have different personnel and exercise separate functions. The rule of law demands that all acts of government be conducted according to law and that public officials are accountable to the courts of law. Each of these three principles entails ambiguities, but nevertheless remains of fundamental importance.

The sovereignty, or legislative supremacy, of Parliament

The supremacy of the United Kingdom Parliament (or Westminster) represents the fundamental rule of the constitution. In 1885 England's then leading constitutional authority, Albert Venn Dicey, set out what was to become accepted as the classic legal definition of parliamentary sovereignty. In Dicey's view, Parliament's power to make law was unlimited. Parliament could make law on any subject-matter whatsoever, and no one – including the courts of law – could challenge the legality of an Act of Parliament. Further, the power of one Parliament could not be limited by Acts of a former Parliament, and conversely no one Parliament could restrict the power of a future Parliament.

Sovereignty therefore has both positive and negative aspects. Dicey drew a clear distinction between the *political fact* of the sovereignty of the people over government and the *legal power* of Parliament to make valid and unchallengeable law. He recognized that political sovereignty is 'fully as important as the legal sense or more so', but the two concepts are 'essentially different',[23] but it was with the ultimate *legal power* within the state that Dicey was concerned.

One consequence of sovereignty is that any proposal for legislation contained in a Bill passed by Parliament and given the royal assent (the formal approval of the Crown), however morally sound or morally repugnant, is valid law. To take some often-cited if improbable examples of this omniscient power, Parliament could ban smoking on the streets of Paris,[24] regardless of the ineffectiveness of the Act, or could order that all blue-eyed babies be put to death.[25] Equally contentiously, just as Parliament may grant independence to a formally dependent territory, Parliament could in theory repeal that grant of independence: the freedom which Parliament gives may be taken back. On the other hand, any attempt to restore Parliament's supremacy over a now-independent state would prove an act of futility, ignored by the state in question and the world at large.[26] Parliament can also legislate extra-territorially – that is to say, make laws for areas outside the territory of the United Kingdom which are enforceable before the United Kingdom courts. An example of such an Act is the Aviation Security Act 1982 which enables the United Kingdom courts to try charges of hijacking of aircraft, irrespective of the nationality of the hijacker and where the hijacking occurs.

While theoretically Parliament has the power to make offensive, ineffective and plain bad law, and the courts have no power to rule that law invalid, in practical terms no government – mindful of its continued

---

[23] Dicey, *Introduction*, pp. 73–4.

[24] According to Sir Ivor Jennings. See I. Jennings, *The Law and the Constitution* (London: Hodder & Stoughton, 5th edn., 1959).

[25] According to Sir Leslie Stephen. See L. Stephen, *The Science of Ethics*, 1872 (Newton Abbot: David and Charles, 1972).

[26] The position would be different if, for some reason, a formerly independent state became subject to British rule through the military overthrow of the government in that state. Such actions are however, while not impossible, highly unlikely in a post-imperialist age.

authority and existence – would deliberately propose legislation that would prove unworkable or unenforceable. The reason for this is that while Parliament is legally supreme, this legal supremacy is dependent upon the will of the people, expressed most clearly at general elections but also in the process of interactive government and through Members of Parliament as their representatives. While *legal* sovereignty lies in Parliament, *political* sovereignty lies with the people. On occasion, however, laws may be passed which prove unworkable. A prime example is that of the poll tax. During the 1980s the Conservative government decided that the system of local taxation – then a rating system based on property values – required reform. The preferred option was a system of taxation which levied a flat rate of tax on each person within a local government area, irrespective of property values.[27] The system was first introduced in Scotland and proved unacceptable and unenforceable. As public protest grew the government was forced to reconsider and the system was once again reformed. The relevant Act of Parliament was perfectly valid and unchallengeable in the courts, but the people rejected the law and its ineffectiveness created a political reason why the law should be repealed.

As noted above, in Dicey's view Parliament's supremacy is one which has continuity over time: no single Parliament at any fixed point in time can exercise power which limits the power of a future Parliament, nor, it follows, can any Parliament be restricted by Acts of a former Parliament. Since sovereignty is an all-or-nothing concept, this is a logical implication of the term. Sovereignty entails absolute and unlimited law-making power. However, the idea of parliamentary continuity gives rise to difficulties and has formed the basis of numerous challenges to Dicey's thesis. The most commonplace illustration is where one Parliament passes a law which appears to limit or 'bind' a future Parliament as to what it can and cannot do. This can work in different ways. An Act of Parliament may provide, for example, that any future law on a particular subject must be interpreted in a manner which is consistent with the provisions of the earlier Act. Alternatively, Parliament may decree that in future an Act of Parliament – whether of the United Kingdom Parliament or (in earlier times) an Act of a colonial

[27] Under the Local Government Finance Act 1988.

territory – may only be passed under a certain procedure. Such attempted limitations offend against the principle of continuing and equal sovereign power. When a dispute arises it is for the courts to decide.

In relation to Acts of Parliament which appear to require the interpretation of subsequent laws in line with the earlier Act, the courts use the doctrine of implied repeal to resolve the difficulty. The judges will rule that the later Act is to prevail: it is the task of the judges, in upholding continuous sovereignty, to ensure that the latest expression of Parliament's will is given effect. Accordingly, a later Act of Parliament will by implication repeal any inconsistent previous provisions in the earlier Act.[28]

More difficult is the situation in which an Act of Parliament lays down procedures to be followed by a subsequent Parliament in the exercise of its law-making powers. In colonial times this issue raised its head in several cases. What is clear, however, is that where powers were granted to subordinate colonial parliaments by Westminster, they derived from a superior sovereign legislature and were accordingly obliged to comply with the rules laid down by that legislature.[29] A contemporary example is provided by legislation relating to the position of Northern Ireland and its continued union with the rest of the United Kingdom. Successive Acts have provided that the constitutional position of Northern Ireland will not be changed by Parliament unless and until a majority of the people of Northern Ireland, in a referendum, vote for change.[30] This is a clear attempt to limit the power of Parliament, making its power dependent upon the will of the people. However, although the requirement of the consent of the people is required, that requirement, being contrary to the concept of sovereignty, can carry only moral but not legal authority. If, following some unforeseeable event, a government chose to ignore the referendum requirement and passed another Act, no court of law would rule that Act invalid.

[28] See *Vauxhall Estates Ltd. v. Liverpool Corporation* [1932] 1 KB 733 and *Ellen Street Estates Ltd. v. Minister of Health* [1934] 1 KB 590.
[29] See e.g. *Attorney General for New South Wales v. Threthowan* [1932] AC 526; *Harris v. Minister of the Interior* (1952) (2) SA 428 (South Africa); *Bribery Commissioner v. Ranasinghe* [1965] AC 172 (Sri Lanka, formerly Ceylon).
[30] See most recently the Northern Ireland Act 1998.

Theoretically, no Act of Parliament has any special constitutional status: all – whether they regulate fundamental organization of the state or a mundane matter such as road traffic – have the same status. None, under the doctrine of sovereignty, is immune from amendment or repeal, or subject to special procedural requirements. However, there have been claims that some Acts of Parliament are of such fundamental constitutional significance that they do control the manner in which Parliament exercises its power in the future. One frequently cited example is the Act of Union with Scotland 1706, discussed in Chapter 5. Prior to 1707, when the Act came into force, England and Scotland were independent states, each having its own law-making body and separate legal system. By the Treaty the two countries were united under a single Parliament. The Treaty laid down guarantees for the continuance of the Scottish legal system, the education system and for the Presbyterian Church. The new Parliament to be established came about by the conceptual 'abolition' of the existing Scottish and English Parliaments and the creation of the Parliament of Great Britain. The Treaty also stated categorically that the Union between Scotland and England was to be 'in all time being', that is to say permanent and unalterable.

When the present Queen acceded to the throne she adopted the title Queen Elizabeth II under the Royal Titles Act 1952. This was objected to by the Scottish constitutional lawyers on the basis of historical inaccuracy and was argued to be in breach of the Acts of Union, and the claim was made that the Royal Titles Act was accordingly invalid. The court (the Scottish Inner House) disagreed: the Acts of Union did not deal with royal titles and the argument accordingly failed on the basis of relevance. However, the Lord President of the court proceeded to discuss the concept of sovereignty, and to draw distinctions between the Diceyan English view and the Scottish approach. From the Scottish point of view it was clear that Dicey's notion of Parliament's unlimited law-making power had no counterpart in Scotland, where the only notion of sovereignty was the sovereignty of the people. At the root of the problem was the question of whether the Act of Union represented a form of early written constitution which bound all future Parliaments of Great Britain. The court, however, ruled that while English and Scottish notions of sovereignty were undoubtedly different, Parliament had the sovereign power to pass the Royal Titles Act.[31]

The theoretical arguments about Parliament's sovereignty were resurrected in relation to Britain's membership of the European Communities. In 1972 the British government successfully negotiated terms for Britain's entry into the Communities, and acceded to the Treaty of Rome which governed the Communities. In order for Community law to have effect in the domestic courts it was necessary for Parliament to pass a statute, the European Communities Act 1972, which took effect in January 1973. From that time, in matters regulated under the Treaty (freedom of movement of persons, capital, services and goods under the Common Market), Community law entered the domestic legal system and created rights and duties enforceable in the national courts.

The question which arose in debate in the United Kingdom was whether the United Kingdom Parliament retained its sovereignty to legislate as it wished, or whether its sovereignty was in some sense limited by Community membership. Was the former power to legislate *delegated* or *transferred* from Westminster to the European institutions? Was there to be a form of shared sovereignty (notwithstanding that sovereignty is traditionally understood to be 'indivisible' or inseparable), or had Parliament, through the European Communities Act 1972, relinquished for all time its power to legislate over matters covered by the Treaty of Rome? At the time of British accession to the Community these fears were very real and went to the heart of the meaning of legal and political independence and British sovereignty.[32] Nor have the concerns abated with the passage of time, especially in the light of repeated assertions of the supremacy of Community over national law.[33]

How, then, can the issue of parliamentary sovereignty and Europe be understood? By distinguishing between legal and political sovereignty,

---

[31] *MacCormick v. Lord Advocate* 1953 SC 396. For similar arguments see also *Gibson v. Lord Advocate* [1975] 1 CMLR 563 and *Sillars v. Smith* 1982 SLT 539.

[32] Although the concerns were also tinged with the little-island mentality of a country which had always existed in constitutional isolation and fought off any attempts to subject Britain to a foreign power.

[33] In 1992 the European Union was born when the Treaty on European Union, the Maastricht Treaty, was signed and ratified; in 1997 the second Treaty on European Union, the Amsterdam Treaty, further consolidated and rationalized the basis of the Community and Union. See Chapter 4.

an answer can be found which – although politically increasingly unrealistic – satisfies the conventional concept of sovereignty as propounded by Dicey over a century ago. Under British law, the signing of a treaty, no matter how significant its impact, has no legal effect unless and until Parliament passes an Act which gives effect to the provisions of the Treaty. The Treaty of Rome – the original treaty – accordingly had no status in domestic law unless and until Parliament enacted the European Communities Act 1972. Once the Act was passed and came into effect, all Community law which is directly effected without any further parliamentary action, comes into effect *under* and *by virtue of* the European Communities Act. Joining Europe was a voluntary political act, endorsed by the people in a referendum. All European law enters Britain not as a direct consequence of this political act, but as a consequence of Parliament passing an Act to give effect to the original treaty. It follows from this that, whatever the possible consequences of attempting to withdraw from Europe – which it is generally but not unanimously agreed would result in economic disaster – continued membership is the result of an ordinary Act of Parliament which *could* in theory be repealed tomorrow.

This conventional view, while theoretically sound, is unsatisfactory in some respects. In order to be consistent with the obligations undertaken once membership was effected, it is necessary that the Westminster Parliament passes no law which contradicts, intentionally or unintentionally, European law. Furthermore, when questions arise on the compatibility of British law with Community law, it is ultimately for the European Court of Justice of the Community (in Luxembourg) to adjudicate.

Several consequences flow from an adverse ruling from the European Court of Justice. First, in the Court's view, member states through joining the Community (and now Union) have committed themselves to do everything in their power to comply with the objectives laid down in the treaties, and to refrain from any action which might impede Community objectives. Any action, or failure to act when required, which has the effect of undermining Community objectives places the member state in breach of its Community obligations, and liable to the penalties provided by the treaties. As Europe expands its sphere of operation into such matters as justice and home affairs, common policy and defence, border controls and immigration, so the right of the individual member state to regulate these matters, outside the European framework, diminishes. The domestic courts are under a duty to ensure that in interpreting and applying domestic law, they do so in accordance with European law. The effect of this is that the courts must interpret an Act of Parliament, not as a single self-contained authoritative document, but as a document to be interpreted in the light of Community law. Where the judges cannot reach such an interpretation, perhaps because it is unclear whether or not compatibility exists, the issue is referred to the European Court of Justice for consideration. The decision which emerges from Luxembourg is then the authoritative ruling which the domestic courts must apply to the particular case. Moreover, once it is clear that European law has been breached, the government of the relevant member state is obliged to take action to eliminate any incompatibility, or face the consequence of ultimately being taken to the Court for a breach of the treaties.

From the perspective of the citizen, the rights conferred under Community law 'trump' any rights or duties under domestic law. The citizen, on feeling aggrieved about an issue such as equal terms of employment or equal pay, may go to court to seek enforcement of Community law rights, over and above any rights which domestic law may grant but which do not achieve the European standard. These Community rights also apply to commercial organizations. If domestic policy conflicts with Community requirements, the government may be held accountable for redress. Not only must the law be changed to bring domestic law into line with Community law, but where a breach of Community law occurs in relation to a clear and unconditional duty to Community law, the state may – and will – be held liable in damages for any loss directly sustained as a result of the offending policy. Nowhere was this more apparent than in the *Factortame cases*.[34] Here, in violation of Community law, the British government had restricted access to British fishing waters to foreign-owned fishing companies. The terms and conditions for eligibility to fish in British coastal waters resulted in Spanish companies suffering severe losses in revenue. At the end of protracted

[34] Of which there were ultimately seven. See principally *R v. Secretary of State for Transport ex parte Factortame (No. 1)* [1989] 2 CMLR 353; *(No. 2)* [1991] AC 603.

litigation, which the British government lost, the Spanish companies were ruled to be entitled to compensation for their loss.

Some of the arguments about parliamentary supremacy considered above, and most particularly membership of the European Union, indicate the difficulties the concept poses. From a legal-theoretical approach it remains undoubtedly correct to argue that Parliament retains absolute supreme power to legislate as it wishes. That continuing power includes the power to delegate some of its law-making functions to other institutions, most importantly to the institutions of the European Union but also to devolved national and regional bodies such as the Scottish Parliament, Northern Ireland Parliament and Welsh Assembly. Power which is devolved can equally be taken back. While such powers remain devolved, however, Parliament's law-making powers are diminished in direct proportion to the power devolved to others. Legal theory, however, cannot exist in a conceptual vacuum divorced from economic, political and social reality. In the last analysis it is the people who hold political sovereignty and who have the power to control what Parliament does. If in a referendum the people expressed the view that they wished to be divorced from the European Union, and if the government accepted that the wishes of the people should be respected, the government would be obliged to put to Parliament a bill withdrawing Britain from Europe.

The separation of powers

For any state to conform to democratic principles it is imperative that power is divided between the major institutions – the executive, legislature and judiciary – so that there is no concentration of power in one set of hands. In addition, it is necessary that there be a system of checks and balances built into the system so that no institution operates in total isolation from the other and a balance of power can be maintained. This is the concept of the separation of powers. The doctrine is of great antiquity, Aristotle in the sixth century BC stressing the need for the institutions of the state to operate in separated spheres. The concept was analysed in more detail by both Viscount Henry St John Bolingbroke and Baron Montesquieu writing in the eighteenth century, the former emphasizing the need for the division of power to protect the constitution: 'the safety of the whole depends on the balance of the parts.'[35] Montesquieu's assessment of the British system was inaccurate at the time, yet has become a classic statement of the principle. Montesquieu emphasized the importance of the independence of the judiciary from both the legislature and the executive, stating that 'there would be an end to everything, if the same man, or the same body . . . were to exercise those three powers' (those of enacting laws, executing public affairs and of trying crimes or individual causes).[36] First and foremost there is the need to prevent the *concentration of power* in any one institution, and to provide for a *balance of power* between the three in order to prevent tyranny and the potential threat to the individual rights and freedoms of citizens. In order to understand the British arrangement, it is necessary to look at the different relationships between the institutions. It will be seen from this analysis that there are a number of anomalies in the British system.

The executive and legislature

The most glaring ostensible breach of separation of powers relates to the close relationship between the executive and legislature. The executive is firmly *inside* rather than separated from the legislature, a feature which Walter Bagehot writing in 1867 labelled the 'efficient secret' of the constitution.[37] This arrangement raises the very real question of where power lies and whether the British governmental system is one most accurately portrayed as 'parliamentary government', 'Cabinet government' or 'Prime Ministerial government'. When the idea of 'parliamentary sovereignty' was considered, no analysis was made of the composition of Parliament nor the actual machinery through which Parliament operates:[38] Parliament was portrayed in the abstract as an institution which masks the reality of the respective components within Parliament and the relationship between them.

[35] H. Bolingbroke, *Remarks on the History of England* (London: Francklin, 3rd edn., 1748).
[36] C. Montesquieu, *De l'esprit des lois*, first published 1748 (Cambridge: Cambridge University Press, 1989).
[37] W. Bagehot, *The English Constitution*, 1867 (London: Fontana, 1993).
[38] On which see Chapter 3.

Looking first at the House of Commons, which is the dominant and democratically elected chamber, it can be seen that the membership, currently 659, is divided between the political party which won a majority at a general election and which forms the government, the largest minority party which forms Her Majesty's Loyal Opposition, and other minority parties which may from time to time have more influence than their numbers suggest in a situation where the government of the day lacks a secure majority. The leader of the majority party will be appointed Prime Minister and appoints his or her ministerial team, the majority of whom will be in the Commons. Law restricts the number of ministers who are salaried to ninety-five, in order to prevent a distortion in power between the Commons as a whole and the executive.[39] Without such restrictions, it would be theoretically possible, though undeniably unconstitutional, for the Prime Minister to appoint every member of his party in Parliament to ministerial office, thereby stifling debate and dissent through the doctrine of ministerial responsibility which ensures that the government 'speaks with one voice' in Parliament.

Law also prohibits certain classes of person from standing for election to Parliament, again to preserve an appropriate separation of powers. The House of Commons Disqualification Act 1975 bars judges, civil servants, chief executives of government agencies, members of the armed forces, police officers, stipendiary (full-time, salaried) magistrates, and holders of other assorted offices from membership of Parliament. The justification for these disqualifications harks back to former centuries and the power of the Crown to control and manipulate the composition of the Commons in favour of the Crown by the appointment of 'placemen'. The contemporary rationale relates not to the Crown but to ensuring that holders of certain offices are excluded from Parliament in order to avoid a conflict of interest between that office and the duties of a Member of Parliament.

Subject to these legal limitations and restrictions, however, the Prime Minister is entitled to the loyal support of up to ninety-five ministers, a minority of whom will be in the House of Lords, and the support of their parliamentary private secretaries, which swells the number of

[39] Ministerial and Other Salaries Act 1975.

government supporters in the Commons to around 120, out of a total of 659 members. Through the use of the party whip system,[40] the parties control the activities of their members. On the government side, government whips will ensure, through their disciplinary procedures, that government supporters are present for important debates and votes in the House: to defy the whip is to put in peril any possible political advancement. The political power which the Prime Minister can wield over Parliament, through efficient use of government supporters, will depend on a number of factors. First and foremost is the personality and style of the Prime Minister, and how he or she controls both government members and ordinary Members of Parliament on the government side. Margaret Thatcher's early years of premiership were characterized by her strict control of Cabinet and the party: her political downfall came when she lost party political support and her leadership was successfully challenged. The style of John Major's premiership, during which his government in the 1992–7 Parliament never enjoyed such a secure majority in Parliament as his predecessor, was less stridently personal or 'presidential' than Mrs Thatcher's. By contrast, Tony Blair has been repeatedly criticized for exhibiting presidential characteristics.

Any government's power in relation to Parliament as a whole but most particularly the Commons depends on the size of its electoral majority. Membership of the Commons' committee system is directly proportionate to party political membership of the Commons. The effectiveness of both Standing Committees which scrutinize legislative proposals and Select Committees which scrutinize government administration is related to the committees' composition. A government with a strong majority in the Commons will have an equally strong majority in committee. For there to be an adequate separation of powers between the executive and legislature it is essential that parliamentary procedures provide adequate checks and balances to prevent executive domination. Given a strong parliamentary majority and an elected government's legitimate right to control the parliamentary timetable to ensure that its policies are translated into the necessary legislation, it is difficult to avoid the initial impression that strong parliamentary majorities

[40] On which see Chapter 3.

emasculate parliamentary control of the executive. This was the thrust of former Lord Chancellor Lord Hailsham's critique of the British system when he wrote of an 'elective dictatorship'.[41] However, such an assumption is not necessarily true.

It is a usual, but not inevitable, consequence of the voting system employed for general elections that the winning party secures a workable majority. Exceptions exist, as in 1974 when the Labour government under Harold Wilson had a majority of just three seats in the Commons, and in the closing years of John Major's government, when an electoral majority was reduced to a bare majority prior to the May 1997 election. In terms of the balance of power between the executive and Parliament, clearly where a weak government has a small majority the scales tip towards the opposition parties and to Parliament as a whole. Where a majority is slim, a government may need to rely too heavily on the support of minority parties to sustain office. This was seen in 1974 when the Conservative Party under Prime Minister Edward Heath lost the general election and sought to remain in office by negotiating with the Liberal Party – unsuccessfully as it turned out – for parliamentary support for its programmes, and in the 1992–7 Parliament when John Major's government was forced to rely on the support of the Ulster Unionists.

'Weak government', however, while tilting the balance of power in Parliament's favour, does not necessarily lead to the conclusion that it is 'good' government, nor that an all-powerful Parliament *vis-à-vis* the government is advantageous to the country. Recalling John Stuart Mill's nineteenth-century analysis of Parliament, Parliament is not there to govern. It is 'radically unfit' to do so. Parliament's role is to act as the 'sounding board' of the nation, to scrutinize the actions of government and to legitimize government policies through the parliamentary law-making process. From the perspective of the government, the people have mandated it to govern, not to be constantly defeated in its implementation of policy and law, and the elected government has the legitimate right to govern: anything less would signal democratic deficiency. The checks and balances which exist ensure, or should ensure, that government is able to act effectively, yet be scrutinized to

[41] Lord Hailsham, *The Dilemma of Democracy* (London: Collins, 1978).

ensure that its legislative proposals and administration are in accordance with constitutional principles and law. Despite the constitutional anomaly of an executive residing at the heart of the legislature, and the violation of the separation of powers that this represents, the arrangement facilitates scrutiny and openness, ensuring to the best degree possible that government remains under law and accountable to the people it represents.

Executive, legislature and judiciary

In the relationship between the legislature and judiciary, a number of factors affect the extent to which separation of powers applies. It is a long-held and clearly established principle that for rights and freedoms to be protected adequately the judiciary must be independent of both the executive and Parliament. When it comes to the senior judges who staff the highest domestic appeal court, the House of Lords, they are selected by the Lord Chancellor (who is head of the judiciary and also a member of Cabinet) for formal appointment by the Queen. The Law Lords, or more properly the Lords of Appeal in Ordinary, not only determine judicial cases which rise through the appeal structure to the House of Lords, but also sit and vote in the House of Lords as legislators. The role of the Lord Chancellor is particularly difficult to reconcile with the idea of separation of powers. The appointment of Lord Chancellor is a political one: the Lord Chancellor is a member of the inner circle of government, the Cabinet. The Lord Chancellor, however, is also the Speaker in the legislative forum of the House of Lords, required in this position to be absolutely impartial, and, to complete the triumvirate, he is the head of the judiciary, in which position he must also be politically impartial when exercising his powers of appointment of judges. At the heart of the British system of government is one office-holder playing crucial roles in relation to the executive, legislature and judiciary.

The office of Lord Chancellor appears to be fundamentally unconstitutional, violating every aspect of separation of powers. Increasingly, demands are heard for a reform of the office of Lord Chancellor on the basis that this concentration of power is constitutionally unacceptable and dangerous, representing the very concentration of power in the hands of one man which the separation of powers is designed to prevent.

As with so much of the British system, however, all is not what it seems at first sight. Here, the non-legal conventional rules come into play to prevent abuse of power or even the appearance of abuse of power. When the Lord Chancellor is acting as Speaker in the Lords, he sits on the 'woolsack'. When he speaks in the Lords on behalf of government, he moves from the woolsack to a position stipulated in the reign of Henry VIII. This simple movement indicates that he has ceased for the time being to be the impartial Speaker, and is now adopting his role as a government Cabinet minister. In relation to his role as the senior member of the judiciary, the Lord Chancellor has the power to appoint judges (discussed below), and also the right to participate in appeals reaching the judicial wing of the House of Lords. Again, at first sight this appears unacceptable. What prevents the potential abuse of a political appointee sitting judicially is the conventional rule that the Lord Chancellor will refrain from participating in appeals which have political overtones, and is prohibited from sitting on appeals involving the government as a party.

Regarding the basic requirement of separation between the executive, legislature and judiciary, judges may not, as noted above, stand for or be elected to Parliament. On the other hand, Members of Parliament are not permitted to criticize judicial decisions. Judges' salaries are paid out of the Consolidated Fund, a pool of money set aside each year, and not debated in Parliament, out of which expenses that might entail political controversy are met. Since the Act of Settlement 1701, judges have enjoyed security of tenure: they cannot be dismissed at the whim of the Crown or executive, however inconvenient their decisions prove to be. A senior judge can only be removed from his or her post if an 'address' is successfully made to both the House of Lords and House of Commons. Magistrates and Circuit Judges who sit in the County Courts and Crown Courts are removable by the Lord Chancellor 'on the grounds of incapacity or misbehaviour or failure to comply with their terms of appointment'.

The role of the Lord Chancellor in relation to judicial appointments is not free from criticism. Unlike France, where law graduates elect to train for a judicial career and ascend the ladder according to their abilities, or the United States where there is a mix of elected and appointed judges, all judges in Britain are selected from the legal profession. The power of appointment lies with the Lord Chancellor, the highest figure in government after the Prime Minister. Appointment to the Lord Chancellorship is within the gift of the Prime Minister, on whose recommendation the Crown makes the appointment. That this office violates any interpretation of separation of powers is without argument.

There have long been arguments for reform of the process of judicial appointment and for a widening of the pool of eligible candidates for the bench that would break the Bar's stranglehold on appointments to senior judicial posts. From the perspective of the separation of powers, however, it is the role of the Lord Chancellor which attracts most attention. Promotion to the bench normally follows a set pattern: success as a junior barrister, elevation to the status of Queen's Counsel, or 'silk', and subsequent appointment as a judge. The process of appointment is neither open nor subject to independent scrutiny. The system is criticized for its secrecy, and the power of patronage which this gives to the head of the judiciary and close Cabinet colleague of the Prime Minister. Whether or not the Lord Chancellor's powers are exercised in the interests of an independent judiciary is not the central issue. The key question is how an appointments system can be justifiable when it rests solely on the decision of a judicial-political figure and is not subject to outside scrutiny, nor challengeable in any forum. Repeated calls for reform of the system have been made, including one by the Law Society. Little is known about the actual working of the process of judicial appointment, save that it all depends on widespread consultation and 'secret soundings' as to the suitability of possible candidates. Some reform has been introduced, with advertisements placed in the press for vacancies for High Court judges.

The system has its defenders, however, including the Lord Chief Justice, Lord Bingham of Cornhill. In 1999, though agreeing that an independent 'watchdog' appointed to monitor the system would be perfectly acceptable, he also argued that the current system 'is extraordinarily thorough and comprehensive and extraordinarily successful'.[42] The current Lord Chancellor, Lord Irvine of Lairg, rejected proposals for an Appointments Commission, but has introduced an Appointments

---

[42] Annual Press Conference, 1999, reported in *The Times*, 5 November 1999.

Commissioner with power to supervise the process of selection – but not to have the ultimate say in appointments.[43]

The relationship between legislature and judiciary is expressed in the traditional view that 'Parliament makes law and the judges apply the law'. Under the doctrine of parliamentary sovereignty, however, judges remain subordinate to Parliament: should a judicial decision usurp Parliament's law-making role, Parliament may overturn that decision. In defence of this position it is argued, albeit by governments in power, that Parliament alone – or more accurately, the House of Commons – is the democratically elected law-making body. The composition of the House of Commons, and the government of the day, is determined by the people in regular general elections and occasional by-elections in between. Judges are appointed, nominally by the Crown: they are elected by no one and not accountable to an electorate. Judicial law-making does, however, raise the question of the appropriate role of the courts. Until quite recently judges adhered to the conventional theory that Parliament makes the law, judges interpret it, and that the judges do no more under common law than 'declare' what the law is. This 'declaratory theory' was always a fiction – one designed to protect the judges from the charge that they are interfering in the law-making process which constitutionally is within Parliament's power. The theory has long been abandoned, but the underlying caution about judicial activism has not.

Although subordinate to Parliament, judges are independent of government and jealously preserve that independence. Nonetheless, the judiciary is part of the apparatus of the state, interpreting and upholding the law and developing the law through statutory interpretation and the common law – subject always to Parliament's approval. Three cases illustrate the interaction of the courts and Parliament. The first is that of *Burmah Oil v. Lord Advocate*.[44] In this case, to prevent oil installations falling into Japanese hands in wartime, the government ordered the destruction of oil refineries. The Burmah Oil Company had its property destroyed and duly claimed compensation from the British government. The case reached the House of Lords which ruled in the company's

[43] The system is to be operational by the end of 2001: evidence of the Lord Chancellor to the Select Committee on Home Affairs, 23 January 2001.   [44] [1965] AC 75.

favour. The government, however, realizing that several other oil companies would rely on this decision to base their claims for compensation, quickly introduced the War Damage Bill into Parliament, which when passed had the effect of reversing the House of Lords' decision.

Conversely, in *Shaw v. Director of Public Prosecutions*,[45] the House of Lords reached an innovative decision which Parliament did not seek to reverse. In *Shaw* the defendant had published a directory of prostitutes' names and their services. At the time, overt prostitution was unlawful. A Director of Public Prosecutions decided to prosecute, alleging that Shaw was guilty of a 'conspiracy to corrupt public morals': an offence hitherto unknown to law. Surprisingly or not, the House of Lords upheld Shaw's conviction, ruling that as the highest court, as it then was before membership of the European Community, it was custodian of public morals and could recognize a previously unrecognized criminal offence. Parliament took no action to reverse this decision. Thirdly, the case of *R v. R*[46] provides an illustration of a situation where Parliament expressly approves a decision and incorporates it into an Act of Parliament. In *R v. R* the former right of husbands to rape their wives was removed by the House of Lords. This immunity from the law of rape had endured as an anomaly in law for centuries. The House of Lords declared that at a time of sexual equality the law could no longer recognize the ancient right of a husband to demand sex whenever he so chose, and irrespective of a wife's consent. The Criminal Justice and Public Order Act 1994 incorporated a new definition of rape which removes the former immunity.

One aspect of the judges' role which does cause some disquiet from the point of view of the separation of powers is in relation to tribunals of inquiry. It is commonplace for governments to establish inquiries, under the chairmanship of a senior judge, to inquire and report into allegations of wrongdoing or following disasters. Recent examples include the inquiry into the Hillsborough Football Club disaster chaired by Mr Justice Popplewell, the arms to Iraq inquiry chaired by Sir Richard Scott, an inquiry into the Dunblane shootings chaired by Lord Cullen and the inquiry into BSE in cattle chaired by Lord Phillips. While judges are uniquely qualified to scrutinize facts impartially, the

[45] [1962] AC 220.   [46] [1991] 3 WLR 767.

danger is that – irrespective of their findings and recommendations – their political impartiality will be called into question in one quarter or another, damaging the image of the judiciary.

The rule of law

The rule of law is one of the most nebulous concepts employed in political and constitutional thought. As with separation of powers, the rule of law is of great antiquity. Aristotle opens the discussion: 'where laws do not rule there is no constitution.'[47] The essence of the rule of law is that government and individuals alike should be under, rather than above, the law. Quite what this apparently clear-cut statement means is complex and not free from controversy. In order to unravel key strands of thought about the rule of law, differing approaches can be made. One is to view the rule of law as an aspect of legal and political philosophy. Here immediately three conflicting perspectives clash: the Western liberal conception of the rule of law, Marxist ideas and ideas stemming from orthodox oriental thought.

Western liberalism places the individual centre-stage. The individual adult and legally competent citizen is entitled to enjoy the maximum sphere of personal civil and political liberty which is consistent with the protection of others. Only where individual action would cause harm to others in society can that action be restrained by law. This is the classic philosophy expounded by John Stuart Mill in *On Liberty*, first published in 1859. The role of law in society is to provide for the security of the nation as a whole and to proscribe those actions which are injurious to others. Individual freedom is maximized, in order to secure as great a sphere of freedom as possible for all in society. From Mill's perspective, there is a private sphere of life into which the law cannot intrude, save to prevent harm to others. There exist intractable problems with the interpretation of Mill's harm principle. To what extent, for example, is the state justified in interfering in the life of an alcoholic other than where he or she resorts to criminal activity: does alcoholism 'harm' society? Can the liberty of a mentally ill person who is considered

---

[47] Aristotle, *Politics*, tr. T. A. Sinclair (London: Penguin, 1962).

potentially dangerous be curtailed to ensure that proper medication and treatment be received in order to remove the potential danger to society which the individual poses but which has not yet occurred? There are equally serious difficulties with the concept of a 'private sphere' of life, and on one analysis all actions in the private sphere, most notably within the family unit, are political and impact on society as a whole.

Notwithstanding the complexities, the liberal concept remains the dominant Western ethos. A society living under the rule of law will be one with limited government and maximum individual freedom. Government must be representative, responsive, limited and accountable. Democracy is implicit. Government needs to be limited and accountable – both directly to the people and to the law – in order to ensure that no arbitrary action restricts individual freedom. Since individual freedom is prioritized, governments must also serve the need of the people to realize whatever rational life-plan they choose for themselves. This in turn implies a measure of equality between individuals to pursue their own goals, subject only to the interests of society. To secure real individual freedom and opportunity, equality and nondiscrimination must also be ensured. To protect the individual from the 'tyranny of the majority', governments must provide protection and representation for minority groups in society: a racist majority must not be allowed to restrict the equally entitled freedom of minorities to pursue their own lifestyles and life-plans. Social benefits such as health, education and welfare must be available equally to all, as must be the opportunity to compete on the basis of equality for employment, both in the public and private sectors of the work-place.

If a society is ordered upon these principles, that society will conform to liberal ideals. The system of government will be accepted by the people, the laws reflecting these principles will be obeyed. The institutions of the state, such as the police and the courts of law, must operate within the law, under the carefully defined principles and rules laid down by law. Under these conditions, citizens will obey and respect the law which in large measure, by virtue of its fairness and acceptability and its powers of enforcement, will be seen to be upholding a fair system of government. The rule of law will prevail.

Where powers are given to agencies of the state which are over and above those of ordinary citizens these powers must be seen to be adequately controlled by the law. Corruption in the enforcement agencies, or more general racism or sexism, undermine the security of the state by acting arbitrarily or according to prejudice and thus discrediting the carefully constructed system. The now well-documented failures of the police to act according to law, in relation to the Birmingham Six, the Maguire Seven, the Guildford Four, the Stephen Lawrence murder investigation and other such cases, represent aberrations which threaten not only the liberties of the individuals whose lives are wrecked by wrongful police action, but society as a whole as they contribute to a loss of confidence and respect for the system.[48] Equally, judges must be seen to be impartial and unprejudiced in their handling of cases. Not only must justice be done, it must manifestly be seen to be done.

It will be apparent from the above brief discussion that in a Western liberal democracy the law plays a central role in ensuring that the conditions of freedom and security are maintained, albeit with the tensions apparent in the individual–collective dynamic. From alternative perspectives, however, the centrality of law represents not so much a strength in society as a defect. This is the view taken by traditional oriental societies. From this perspective, society is held together by shared bonds, by a system of give and take and mutual respect for others, rather than by law. To have recourse to law is to demonstrate the failure of the conventional non-legal practices which regulate interpersonal and business relationships. In this view, the rule-of-law ethos of Western society represents not so much its strength but the failure of traditional means of dispute-resolution to work.

Rather different is the Marxist approach, which views the centrality of the rule of law in Western liberal democracies not so much as a failure of social mechanisms as a device employed to mask inequalities and the realities of power. Western capitalist society, Marxists argue, evolves and thrives on the exploitation of the masses by those with economic and industrial power. The individual citizen is forced into a contract of employment with a more economically powerful employer who can not only set the (non-negotiable) terms and conditions of pay and employment, but also profits from the worker's labour by

---

[48] See further Chapter 10.

compensating the worker at a lesser rate than the market price of the goods and taking the profit for himself, rather than passing it down to the employee. The rule of law presents itself as a protective mechanism for ensuring legality: the law of contract implies that there is an equality in bargaining power; employment law implies the protection of the employee from exploitation. From a Marxist perspective this is a fraud: the rule of law provides the legal framework in which exploitation and inequality may thrive without being noticed by the individual, who is encouraged or indoctrinated to believe that the system under which he or she exists is one which is fair and rational rather than the expression of the capitalist ideology which is inherently exploitative.

One view of the rule of law – which is both limited and potentially dangerous to individual liberties and freedoms – is that the rule of law means the dominance of law over all, imposing on individuals an absolute obligation to obey the law, irrespective of its content. It is certainly true that if law is not generally respected and obeyed a society may disintegrate into chaos and anarchy. The view also highlights the need for disputes in society to be resolved, not through recourse to aggression or violence but through the normal processes of law adjudicated in the courts. However, where obedience to law alone is raised as the highest standard of civilization, as it is most notably by right-wing authoritarian politicians, there are dangers. Even in a democratic state which adheres to the ideal of the law applying fairly and equally to all, situations arise where individuals and groups will be dealt with harshly. Societies admitting new minority groups will face the dilemma of how to treat its members fairly, requiring both compliance with law while at the same time respecting cultural differences under the law. Dilemmas also arise with social change or when groups in society seek to alter the dominant mores. The struggle for women's suffrage is an example. In 1918 women over the age of thirty were given the right to vote. It 1928 this was extended to all women over the age of majority, on the basis of equality with men. To achieve the vote, however, women resorted to civil disobedience in order to raise the public profile of their cause. They were breaking the law in order to achieve social justice. Was this compatible with any interpretation of the rule of law? It was certainly not compatible with the 'law and order' version of it.

The rule of law has also been seen as a manifestation of natural law. Natural lawyers, in brief, argue that there is a system of law over and above that of humankind, which lays down fundamental precepts that human law must respect and accord to. This natural law was, until the Enlightenment, predominantly theological: the idea that God hands down to humankind the basic laws which must regulate human conduct. Natural law also gives to individuals certain inalienable rights, such as the right to life, to equality and freedom. These rights cannot be limited or removed by government, and any government which fails to respect these fundamental rights exceeds its power. Following on from theological natural law theory, which proved contentious, came the secular view of natural law, the idea that human beings, by virtue of their superior rationality (compared with the rest of the animal kingdom), could determine through that rationality the principles and rights which govern society. Irrespective of its source, natural law theory has a long pedigree but has also long been controversial. In the eighteenth century, the lawyer and law reformer Jeremy Bentham attacked the idea of innate individual rights: rights to Bentham were not just 'nonsense' but 'nonsense on stilts'. In the nineteenth century, legal theory became dominated by the positivist school of thought, which rejected the metaphysics of natural law and sought to explain law in an objective rational scientific manner. Any rights which human beings had, derived not from God nor from the secular rationality of ordinary individuals, but from law – the law of 'man' made for 'man'.

While natural law theory gave way to positivism, it nevertheless retained its powerful appeal. It also provided the rationale for an interpretation of the rule of law which has proved remarkably influential in the twentieth century. The late Professor Lon Fuller [49] argued that since law and government must serve the needs of the people, as opposed to being self-validating, a legal system must comprise laws designed to facilitate people's aspirations. In short, Fuller injected morality into law. A legal system either conforms to moral principles or not. If it does, it is valid. If it does not, it is not a legal system but a form of arbitrary regulation which does not deserve the name of law.

[49] L. Fuller, *The Morality of Law* (New Haven: Yale University Press, 1964).

Fuller cites the German Nazi regime and the South African regime under apartheid. In both cases, and to differing degrees, government and law discriminated against entire sections of the population, in the case of the Nazis a minority, in the case of South Africa the majority of the population. Neither regime bore any relation to what is required by the rule of law and Fuller rejects the idea that the system amounted to a valid legal system. This is a morally appealing approach, but one which lends itself to all sorts of intractable moral debates, not least about the amount and type of discrimination (or other unacceptable feature) which is required before condemning that state as being outside the rule of law.

One conundrum illustrating differing perceptions about the rule of law and justice on an international scale relates to the problem of how to deal with those who have violated individual and collective rights and freedoms in pursuit of discriminatory ideology. Following the Second World War, the Western allies decided to put Nazi leaders on trial before an international war crimes tribunal specially established for the purpose of giving legal judgment on the responsibility for the atrocities and the attempted and actual extermination suffered by Jews and other minorities under the Nazis. The question as to 'what to do' with Nazi war criminals had been asked throughout the war. Churchill was in favour of summary execution of Nazi leaders but the other leaders of the allied forces were not. Agreement was reached to establish the Nuremberg tribunal, to try Nazi leaders with the full and due process of law. The Nuremberg Charter, signed by the allied powers in 1945, by Article 6(c) provided that agents of the state were criminally responsible for crimes against humanity (among other offences) which would render them liable to trial and punishment by any court before which they were brought. Procedures at the trial were rigorously fair: the whole process was stamped with legality.[50] Twelve defendants were

---

[50] A number of questionable practices did attend the proceedings, not least the refusal to examine the evidence of alleged war crimes by allied forces, and the fact that the prosecutors and judges were all allied nationals, while defending lawyers were all German. There was also a fundamental difficulty in the idea of prosecuting for crimes not previously known to law, offending against the principle of nonretrospectivity. See G. Robertson, *Crimes Against Humanity* (London: Penguin, 1999); W. Morrison, *Jurisprudence: From the Greeks to Postmodernism* (London: Cavendish, 1997).

sentenced to death, three defendants acquitted and seven spared the death penalty. What has all this to do with the rule of law? The answer to that depends upon interpretation. The Nuremberg Charter established for the first time that any officer of a state may be held personally and criminally liable for actions against citizens of that state. There could be no defence of having acted on 'superior orders'. Citizens who suffered and survived could demand justice from an international court. The Western allies seeking victor's justice did not, as Churchill favoured, simply take the leaders out and shoot them. A full public trial with rigorous rules of evidence was undertaken, which – whatever its defects and whatever its motives – showed to the world a form of justice being conducted, not in the name of revenge (which undeniably motivated the trials), but in the name of law and under the authority of law. Nevertheless, problems remain, not least in justifying the imposition of retrospective liability for actions taken under orders, and in the political motivations behind the use of law to bring justice.

For reasons and doubts such as these, others choose to place the rule of law in less rarefied terms than those of morality and philosophy. Dicey offered an analysis of the rule of law which is practical rather than philosophical. For him, the rule of law required three principal features. The first was that no one may be punished except for a clear breach of the law. What he meant by this was that the law must be clear and certain if individuals are to be capable of obeying it. Secret laws would be a breach of this requirement, as would retrospective laws which made conduct that was legal at the time subsequently unlawful through a backdated law. The second requirement was that of equality before the law. In this Dicey was not making the unrealistic demand that each individual in society has equal rights and powers and duties. The Crown, police, judges and magistrates, diplomats, adults and children each have necessarily differing powers and rights. What Dicey was arguing was that, irrespective of rank and status in society, each individual is equally accountable to the law. There are still exceptions: the Crown has special immunities, as have diplomats; children are not treated as fully criminally responsible until the age of fourteen, whilst the insane will be treated differently from the sane in relation to the issue of punishment for crimes. That aside, there is equal accountability under law. Any police officer breaking the law is answerable to the law.

Any government minister reaching decisions and taking action which is outside his or her power to do so, as defined in law, will find his or her actions set aside, ruled to be *ultra vires*, by the courts. While the law recognizes, as a first principle of justice, that like must be treated alike, it also respects the notion that different cases must be treated differently. To treat a child of the age of eight in the same manner as an adult would not respect justice or equality. Absolute equality is neither viable nor just.

Dicey's equality principle also suggests a number of concrete requirements for a legal system. If law is to be equal, there must be equality between the parties in a court of law. This implies that the defendant, irrespective of his or her means, must be eligible for financial assistance from the state in order to place him or her in a position of equality with the might and expertise of the prosecution. Legal aid is thus required to enable a defence lawyer to be appointed to conduct the case. Equally, there must be strict rules of evidence in court proceedings to ensure that evidence obtained unlawfully, and particularly through oppression of the defendant leading to a false confession, must be excluded from the proceedings. Equality between the parties cannot be achieved if a judge sitting on a case is biased in favour of one party or the other, for financial or other reasons. Justice and equality require absolute judicial impartiality.

Dicey's third requirement of the rule of law was one about which nowadays most doubts may be raised. In Dicey's view, individual rights and freedoms are best secured by the judges under the common law in the ordinary courts, rather than under some written constitutional Bill of Rights adjudicated before a special tribunal. As will be discussed in Chapter 7, the record of British judges – not least because of their subordination to Parliament, which restricts their freedom of action in interpreting statutes – in protecting rights and freedoms is at best equivocal. Until the Human Rights Act 1998 was implemented, there was no definitive 'charter' of rights which could be applied in the domestic courts, and judges were only able to use the European Convention on Human Rights (to which Britain was a founding signatory) as a guide to interpretation where domestic law was ambivalent; thus their hands were tied. But Dicey was writing in 1885, in an age before statutes became the dominant source of law in place of the judge-made common law, and before international standards and charters of rights were introduced, and before issues such as racial and gender equality came to the fore. Small wonder that he did not foresee the problems which would arise in the multi-racial, multi-cultural society that Britain became in the twentieth century, or foresee that equality between citizens, irrespective of race, colour or gender, would become one of the main guiding principles of the twentieth century.

The concept of 'government under law' is central to the rule of law. Given that the constitution is largely unwritten, a mixture of law and constitutional convention comes into play to ensure that the conduct of government is exercised both under the law and according to conventional rules. In relation to the latter, the doctrine of ministerial responsibility, discussed above, is crucial. Ministers are accountable and responsible to the electorate, through Parliament, for their personal conduct and for the administration of their departments. In judicial review proceedings judges may ensure that ministers, and other public authorities, act under the law by complying with specified procedures, by restricting the use of their power to the actual power granted and by employing the rules of natural justice and fairness. Judicial review is a prime example of the courts insisting that governments act under the rule of law. By controlling any abuse in the exercise of power, judges are both upholding the will of Parliament and ensuring that government acts *under* and not *above* the law. Notwithstanding its limitations – of which the concept of justiciability is the most significant, explained by the judges' unwillingness to be drawn into the political arena and matters of high policy – judicial review remains an increasingly important safeguard for the individual in relation to the powers of the state.

CONCLUSION

The constitutional structure and form of British government is a myriad web of intersecting sources: Acts of Parliament, judicial decisions, the royal prerogative and conventional rules. While the majority of these sources are *legal*, the conventional rules underpin the system, providing a degree of flexibility, and with it uncertainty. The merit of a written constitution – enjoyed by all but three countries in the world – is said to be its clarity and certainty. Studying a written constitution involves analysis of the primary source, the constitutional document itself, and analysis of the decisions of the Supreme Court which has the power to rule on the constitutionality of any legislation and government action: the *legal* and the *constitutional* coalesce. The relationship between the executive, legislature and judiciary will be clearly set out. Usually, the rights of citizens will be stated in a Bill of Rights, and these rights will be enforceable against the government of the state. In a federal state, the respective powers of the federal government and state governments will be laid down. Equally, the constitution itself will prescribe how any amendments may be made, and the extent to which states are to be involved in any structural changes to the constitution, or to changes in the law relating to fundamental rights. This all leads to certainty, and in many instances to rigidity.

Constitutional change is a natural evolutionary process which reflects changes in society and its standards: no constitution founded in the 1700s is likely to meet the needs of society in the early 2000s. Nothing marks so clearly the difficulties entailed in such constitutional certainty as the problem of the right in the United States to 'bear arms'. In the United States all citizens are entitled to purchase and keep guns for their personal protection. While in the uncertain times of the nation's birth such a right may have been justified, in contemporary society this fundamental right is too often abused by the sick and simply criminal, leading to massacres of the innocent. In Britain, there was a swift response to the shootings in a school in Dunblane, Scotland, in which many children died or were injured: an ordinary Act of Parliament was passed in near-record time to produce a system of gun control which is one of the strictest in the world. Under the United States constitution, however, the issue of gun control becomes impossible to address: the power of the 'gun lobby', and the need for the consent of a majority of the States before legislative reform can be undertaken, condemn the citizens of the United States to the fate of largely unregulated gun control.

On the other hand, a written constitution ensures that the people know their rights, ensures that when a right is infringed there is access to a court of law – ultimately to the Supreme Court – to challenge the constitutionality of any executive action or government practice. As a result of this, black minorities have secured equality, women have secured the right, albeit fragile, to abortion. Freedom of the press guarantees that allegations of impropriety in government will be rigorously pursued, to the point, as Presidents Nixon and Clinton found, of attempted impeachment of the President. In the United Kingdom, however, save where the European Convention on Human Rights comes into play and now under the Human Rights Act 1998 which incorporates the Convention into domestic law, rights are at best regarded as freedoms, or loosely freedom-rights. These rights, notwithstanding the Human Rights Act 1998, will be interpreted by a judiciary subordinate to Parliament, and reforms to the law will be in the hands of the government.

The constitution of the United Kingdom is the product of the country's long and winding history: the product of the past, adapted and modified as government and society change. The interweaving of law and convention provides the structure, which is inherently flexible. Notwithstanding the influence of fundamental principles, the British system of government remains a near-unique phenomenon. Israel and New Zealand are the only other states sharing the feature of an unwritten constitution. While many of the sources of power within the British constitution are written, albeit in disparate texts, and many are clear in their meaning and scope, much of the substance of the contemporary constitution remains shrouded in uncertainty. The three principal components of this lack of transparency are the royal prerogative, constitutional conventions and the conventional attitude towards individual rights and freedoms. The European Convention on Human Rights, and the Human Rights Act 1998, discussed in detail in Chapter 7, go a long way towards providing a charter of overriding rights, although even here there is great discretion left to the state in its interpretation of rights and the legitimate restrictions which may be placed on rights through law. In relation to the prerogative, proposals have been made that it be placed under statutory authority: in 1988 Tony Benn unsuccessfully introduced a Private Member's Bill[51] into

---

[51] The Crown Prerogatives (House of Commons Control) Bill 1988.

Parliament which would have had the effect of bringing the residual, but substantial, Crown powers under Parliament's control. Paradoxically, while Parliament went to war with the Crown in the seventeenth century in order to establish Parliament's supremacy over the Crown and its prerogatives, in more recent times there has been no concerted effort even to clarify, let alone control, the prerogative. While reform of powers may be attractive to political parties when they are out of office, once power is gained any willingness to control this wide-ranging, opaque source of power melts away. In addition to the lack of political will, there are problems in any proposal to control the prerogative. Not least among these is the difficulty of identifying the number of prerogatives which exist. It is clear that no new prerogative powers can be created, and those which remain are those which existed before the constitutional settlement of 1689.[52]

The supremacy of Parliament, the separation of powers and the rule of law are the basic principles underlying and running through the system of government in Britain. Each concept interacts with the others and impacts on them. Without judicial independence, and a degree of separation of power between the executive and the legislature which enables the legislature to control the executive, there can be no guarantee that government is conducted both under law and under the established principles of constitutional practice. The supremacy of Parliament, and the related supremacy of the Commons over the Lords, ensures that it is the democratically elected body which makes law for the people rather than the unelected and democratically unaccountable judiciary. The rule of law requires that governments respect liberal values in society, and act only within the remit of both law and constitutional principles. Any government, irrespective of its majority in Parliament, finds itself vulnerable to electoral rejection if it oversteps the boundaries of legitimacy and the vague and largely unarticulated principles which have emerged through the long process of evolution of the British system. While Parliament's supremacy poses challenges to the rule of law, especially in matters deemed to relate to national security where the 'greater good' may override the freedom of the individual, the

---

[52] See *BBC v. Johns* [1965] Ch 32, in which Diplock LJ stated that it was then '350 years and a civil war too late for the Queen's courts to broaden the prerogative'.

rule of law also provides protection for the individual through the democratic and judicial process. The legal liability of government institutions, the role of judicial review and its availability to test the lawfulness of government administration – albeit with the exceptions discussed – aim to ensure that government action remains within the law.

THE STRUCTURE OF
CENTRAL GOVERNMENT

Consistent with the evolutionary nature of the constitution is the organization of central government. Never rationally planned, and little regulated by law, the central offices of Prime Minister and Cabinet emerged out of historical forces which marked the transition from personal rule by monarchs to representative democracy and accountable government. However, as discussed below, the United Kingdom remains a 'constitutional monarchy' and accordingly the Crown cannot be left out of the picture. In this chapter the Crown, the office of Prime Minister and the role of Cabinet, together with the civil service which translates policy into administration, are discussed.

THE CROWN

All acts of government – whether executive or legislative and including the courts and administration of justice – are carried out in the name of the Crown. The United Kingdom remains a monarchical state. At first sight the 'Crown' appears to be purely ceremonial and of little consequence to the realities of government, politics and power. As with so much of the British system, however, outward appearances disguise underlying factors. The readily visible structure of government – Prime Minister and Cabinet – renders the Crown, its role and its legal powers hidden and invisible to the naked eye. To ignore the Crown, however, would paint a false picture of the constitutional arrangements in place and the fact that the Crown still holds real and significant powers – albeit conventionally not exercised – which underpin government.

Succession to the throne is dictated by Act of Parliament. The Act of Settlement 1701 decreed that there be a Protestant line of succession to the exclusion of Roman Catholics on the doctrine of primogeniture: succession through the male line. The cost of monarchy is financed through the Civil List, established in the reign of George III (1760–1820), which provides moneys for expenditure on official business and expenses of the Queen and the Duke of Edinburgh. Since 1992 finance for other members of the royal family undertaking official duties has been financed by the Queen, although the Prince of Wales receives financial support from revenues from the Duchy of Cornwall. In exchange for Civil List provision, revenues from the Crown's substantial hereditary holdings are paid direct to the Exchequer. Civil List money is drawn from the Consolidated Fund – a fund voted on by Parliament without debate and which finances not only the monarchy but also other politically sensitive matters such as judicial salaries. Since 1992 the Queen has paid tax on her personal income, although she remains exempt from some forms of taxation. Monarchy is expensive.[1] The Queen personally owns two palaces – Balmoral and Sandringham – but it is the state which maintains seven other palaces for royal use, and provides £7.9 million towards annual office and staffing costs; in 1994–5 it also provided a total of £11.5 million for the Royal Train and Queen's Flight. While the need to finance a head of state – whether hereditary or republican – inevitably means high costs to a nation, what is objected to in relation to the British arrangement is that state funding is enjoyed not only by the Queen, the Duke of Edinburgh and their children, but also by lesser relatives, on the basis that they undertake public duties. A 'slimming down' of monarchy has been called for and responded to.

That the monarch should remain above politics, and never be seen to involve him- or herself in politics, is essential to the continued

---

[1] The cost of maintaining the monarchy in the year 2000 was £35 million.

acceptance of the monarchy in Britain. The former American colonies overthrew monarchical rule back in 1776 and established a republican government headed by a President. In the former Soviet Union, republicanism was established with the overthrow and bloody murder of Tsar Nicholas II and his family. More recently, there is a strong republican movement in Australia.[2] But the idea of republicanism has never taken deep root in the United Kingdom. The only period of republican government in Britain followed the Civil War in the seventeenth century which resulted in the execution of Charles I in 1649.[3] That experiment was to be short-lived, and the monarchy was restored in 1660, since which time there has been continuity.

While pure democracy – rule by the people as opposed to an autocratic ruler – was a political fact in ancient Greece, rule by personal authority – by a monarch – had become the accepted norm in most societies by the Middle Ages. Nowadays, however, where monarchies continue to exist, the monarch is for the most part best understood as the formal figurehead of state, rather than as a ruler with personal power. In the case of the United Kingdom, it is an interesting question as to why this should remain the case. What are the advantages of monarchy? How can it be, in a society so firmly committed to the ideal of democracy, that the monarch continues to hold fundamentally important legal powers, even though these are restricted in practice by conventional rules?

Aside from political apathy of the people – the British are rarely accused of being revolutionary – and 'popular sentiment', which continues to view the monarchy with affection, there are other factors which explain the continuation of this arrangement. Looking at the reign of Elizabeth II, the Queen has been head of state for half a century. During that period there have been ten Prime Ministers, seven heading Conservative governments, three Labour governments. It has been remarked by more than one former Prime Minister that the Queen has a deep understanding of British political affairs. In the nineteenth century Walter Bagehot[4] commented that the Crown had the right to

---

[2] By a referendum in 1999 the Australian people narrowly voted to retain the Queen as head of state. The decision surprised many and is explained more by the unattractive alternatives than approval of the *status quo*.   [3] See Chapter 12.

[4] In *The English Constitution*, 1867 (London: Fontana, 1993).

advise, the right to encourage and the right to warn the government. This remains the essence of the royal position today. The Crown cannot dictate to government, and no government would tolerate interference in its affairs by the Queen. However, the position of the Queen enables Prime Ministers to draw on her long experience of government. The Prime Minister has a weekly audience (meeting) with the Queen, and the Queen is entitled to, and does, receive copies of Cabinet papers. The Queen's advice is perhaps particularly valuable in matters relating to foreign affairs, especially where this involves relations with other Commonwealth countries, each of which accepts the Queen as the Head of the Commonwealth.

The Queen is also the head of the established church: the Church of England.[5] The Crown's role as head of the Church – and status as a monarch ordained by God – is a legacy of the medieval period. Nor is this of little relevance today. The line of succession to the Crown still excludes Roman Catholics or those married to Roman Catholics.[6] The Queen also appoints bishops, on the recommendation of the Prime Minister. Through the Crown, Church and State are inextricably linked.

The honours systems – another medieval relic – also operates in the Crown's name. Now under the scrutiny of the Political Honours Scrutiny Committee, to which political party leaders make recommendations, the Crown as the 'fountain of honour' has little discretion in the award of honours, save for the few awards which remain in the personal gift of the Queen. Twice a year, on the Queen's official birthday and at New Year, hundreds of honours, ranging from the prestigious Order of the Garter which dates from the fourteenth century to the now common Order of the British Empire introduced in 1917, are awarded to those deemed to have made a significant contribution to society. Whether the Queen has the right to refuse an honour is unclear. The honours system remains controversial. While overt political abuse of the system is rare, too often the award of knighthoods and life peerages can be seen as a reward for contributions to political parties – generally in the form of money. In 1996 a Yorkshire businessman gave £4 million to

[5] See Chapter 12.
[6] Act of Settlement 1701. 12 and 13 Will 3 c 2.

the Conservative Party: he received a knighthood. More recently still, the Conservative Party Treasurer, whose contributions of funds from overseas caused a political furore, was knighted. If the honours system is to remain, there is a need to remove it from the political control of the Prime Minister and place it in the hands of a body independent of government. Only then will the discredited system be rescued from the criticism that honours are bought and paid for, rather than given on true merit for contributions to public life.

The monarch represents a state figurehead over and above the cut and thrust of party politics. While the Queen opens Parliament each year and delivers the Queen's Speech outlining her government's proposals for the forthcoming parliamentary year, she herself does not dictate the contents of the speech. Irrespective of her personal views about proposed legislation, the Queen faithfully follows the government line. Playing such a formal and symbolic role would be impossible if the Queen were to become publicly embroiled in government policies and proposals. It is most likely that at the weekly meeting with the Prime Minister, the Queen voices her opinion about the wisdom of this or that proposal (such meetings remain absolutely confidential), but that is the limit of the Crown's involvement in government and politics. And the future of the monarchy depends on such political anonymity.

The requirement of political anonymity explains why occasional concern is expressed about the heir to the throne's expression of personal views on such matters as architecture and agriculture – most recently in relation to genetically modified products. While not apparently overtly political (compared, say, to his expressing a view about the wisdom of the NATO operation in Kosovo), such expressions of opinion lead the Prince of Wales dangerously close to involvement in the political arena. Such involvement, even if perceived but not real, damages the political and constitutional requirement of political neutrality and could suggest that, as King, Charles's views would be too well known for him to have harmonious dealings with Prime Ministers of different political persuasions. The Crown's role – at the heart of the constitution but above its politics – can only function if political anonymity is preserved.

As head of state, the monarch also plays a role in promoting British interests overseas. Whereas in the practical conduct of trade and other international negotiations it will be the relevant Minister of State who presides over negotiations, through established links with overseas heads of state, again most particularly with Commonwealth countries (of which there are currently fifty-four, comprising some 1.7 billion people), the Crown is able to promote harmonious relations and favourable conditions under which substantive agreements can be reached by the government. The stability and continuity of monarchy, compared with the transience of governments, contributes to the smooth running of international relations.

From the point of view of democracy there are conflicting views about the desirability or otherwise of a continuing constitutional monarchy. Despite the actual limitations of power imposed on the Crown since 1689 and the conventional rules which restrict the exercise of that power, it has been seen above that the Crown, in legal terms, still holds great power. In constitutional terms these reserved powers provide a guarantee against extreme government. The life of a Parliament is fixed by law at a maximum of five years. Twice this century that period has been extended with the approval of the House of Lords and the Crown, but both these occasions were in times of war. Should a government with a large majority in the Commons (and, with the reformed House of Lords, possibly also in the Lords) choose to pass a Bill to extend its own life in order to avoid calling a general election, it would be the constitutional right and duty of the Crown, in the interests of the people, to refuse to assent to the Bill. Moreover, if a government decided to call a general election midway through a Parliament, purely for the purposes of increasing its own mandate and perhaps offering inducements to the electorate such as tax reductions, it would again be the constitutional right of the Crown to refuse to dissolve Parliament, if that dissolution was requested for improper purposes and against the interests of the people. Faced with government intransigence the Queen would also be entitled to call on the police and the army to support her right.

On the other hand, notwithstanding the constitutional guarantees which the monarchy represents, it is argued by some that the monarchy should either be abolished or that its legal powers should be removed, leaving the royal family with purely ceremonial functions, or removing even these and essentially 'privatizing' the royal family, as has occurred in Denmark and Sweden. The strongest argument against continued monarchy lies with the hereditary principle. Heredity offers no guarantee of the suitability of the person who inherits the throne, and the suitability or otherwise of the office-holder is an accident of birth. In the past there have been both kings mad and kings bad. The argument extends further than the personality and qualifications of the office-holder, however. Monarchy underpins an outdated class system, as exemplified by the hereditary peerages, and gives the impression that Britain is a traditionalist nation reliant on the pomp and ceremony of the past. From this perspective, modernization of the country's image requires the abandonment of those elements of the constitution that derive from the medieval structure of government. As all would-be reformers discover, however, there is no simple solution to the issue of constitutional reform, and so it is with monarchy. When the current government took office with its substantial constitutional reform package, the Prime Minister offered an assurance that the government had no current plans for reform of the monarchy. That does not preclude future reform, although the idea of republicanism in Britain currently harnesses little popular support.

Any suggestions for radical reform have difficult constitutional implications. Removing the legal powers of the Crown would require first and foremost a constitutional document that would define and reallocate powers. Defining the existence and scope of the prerogative is by no means a simple task. Reallocating such powers would also prove controversial: to leave them both legally and in practical terms in the hands of the Prime Minister would for many be vesting a potentially dangerous amount of power in a political figure, especially where that Prime Minister has a large majority in Parliament. The alternative, the election of a President, would seem to offer little practical advantage over the *status quo*.

THE PRIVY COUNCIL

The Privy Council is one of the oldest institutions of government. Historically, it was through the Privy Council that monarchs exercised powers without consulting Parliament. Today the Council has over four hundred members, approximately half of whom are peers, the rest commoners. In practice, it is a few ministers meeting with the Queen who reach decisions. Appointments are made by the Crown on the advice of the Prime Minister. All present and past Cabinet members are appointed to the Council. Also included in its membership are members of the Royal Family, senior judges, two archbishops, British ambassadors, the Speaker of the House of Commons, present and former leaders of the opposition and leading Commonwealth spokespersons and judges. On appointment, a new member of the Council takes the oath of allegiance or affirms loyalty, and the oath binds the member to secrecy in relation to any matters discussed in Council. The Leader of the House of Commons acts as President of the Council. Privy Council functions may be divided into two: its executive and political functions and its role as the Judicial Committee of the Privy Council.

When decisions are reached under the royal prerogative, Orders in Council issued by the Privy Council give effect to them. The majority of Privy Council functions are undertaken in committees. Privy Council meetings take place approximately once a month, meeting wherever the Queen is at the time. Four is the usual number of those attending the meetings. Emergency meetings may be held when required, as occurred in 1998 when approval was needed for the United Nations Security Council order to allow the Lockerbie trial to be held in the Netherlands. The meeting was held in the VIP lounge at Heathrow Airport. More recently, the possibility arose that the Queen would be asked to approve emergency orders to deal with the fuel crisis in September 2000 which threatened to paralyse the country. A Privy Council meeting was urgently arranged at Balmoral Castle, attended by the Queen, the Trade and Industry Secretary and two senior departmental colleagues who were also Privy Council members. The Queen's private secretary also attended.

The Privy Council also has a number of functions relating to those bodies which are incorporated under Royal Charter, and in relation to regulatory bodies which govern a number of professions and the world of higher education, such as the General Medical Council, General Dental Council and Royal College of Veterinary Surgeons.[7] Its role includes the approval of the appointment of lay members to such bodies and the approval of governing regulations. The Judicial Committee also has a role in hearing appeals against disciplinary procedures in the professions, and hears appeals from the few Commonwealth countries which retain the right to appeal to the Privy Council.

PRIME MINISTER, CABINET AND MINISTERS

With the Crown's powers curtailed by the Bill of Rights 1689, and the rise in the supremacy of Parliament over the Crown from that date, the nature of government changed. Although not resulting from any formal document such as an Act of Parliament, the practice grew for there to be a first, or prime, minister within the House of Commons.[8] It is generally agreed that the first Prime Minister was Sir Robert Walpole, appointed in 1721. At the time, although political parties in the Commons existed, they did not have nation-wide organizational structures or distinctive political policies. Also, in the eighteenth century, and for much of the nineteenth, there was no system of democratic elections for Members of Parliament in the form that is recognizable today. The right to vote was limited and tied to property; landowners and gentry often had more than one vote.[9] The property-less working class did not have a vote, and women were excluded from any right to vote until the early twentieth century. There was no secret ballot, and a great deal of corruption existed in such system as there was. The absence of any real democracy in the country meant that until the right to vote was totally

---

[7] Also the General Osteopathic Council, General Optical Council, General Chiropractic Council, Council on Professions Supplementary to Medicine and the Architects Registration Board.   [8] See Appendix II.

[9] On the franchise and voting systems see Chapter 6.

reformed,[10] the House of Commons was a non-representative debating and law-making body.

With a Prime Minister in place, acting as a communications link between the Commons and the Crown, there also developed the idea of Cabinet – the inner circle of the government machine. Formally, the Cabinet is the government's central decision-making body in which the most senior ministers in government sit and which endorses proposals for policy, finance and law. However, the idea of Cabinet government disguises a complex matrix of power relations and decision-making processes, the net effect of which is that Prime Ministers can and do control the extent to which the full Cabinet is involved in decision-making.

The office of Prime Minister

As with so much of the British system, the office of Prime Minister is not one created by law but one which has evolved through history. The Prime Minister has no legal powers as such, and the office has little recognition in Acts of Parliament.[11] Originally there was no theoretical distinction between the Prime Minister and other Cabinet ministers – all were equal, the Prime Minister being the 'first among equals': *primus inter pares*, being the principal source of advice to the Crown on behalf of the government as a whole. This view has long lost credence: the Prime Minister in reality holds and exercises great, but not unlimited, powers. As leader of the governing party, head of the Cabinet, representative of the government to the Crown and representative of Britain in international affairs, the office of Prime Minister is the repository of unparalleled powers: 'All the power lines lead to Number 10.'[12] The Cabinet Secretary, Sir Richard Wilson, has stated of the office of Prime Minister that it is 'if not impossible . . . only just on the right side of possible'.[13]

---

[10] Which took several Acts of Parliament stretching over the period 1832–48.
[11] The first statutory reference to the office was in the Treaty of Berlin 1878. Subsequent recognition is given in the Ministers of the Crown Act 1975 and Ministerial and Other Salaries Act 1975.
[12] P. Hennessy, *Whitehall* (London: Fontana, 1990), p. 383. 'Number 10' refers to the Prime Minister's official residence, 10 Downing Street.
[13] *Blair's Thousand Days*, BBC2, 30 January 2000.

In terms of appointment to office, under modern political arrangements, once a political party wins power at a general election the leader of that party will be appointed Prime Minister by the Queen and the office in reality combines a cluster of substantial powers. The job of Prime Minister is one which is in a sense isolated: the Prime Minister has no 'department' of his own, but relies on a web of support provided by the Cabinet Office and secretariat, his or her Private Office, ministers and specialist policy and political advisers.[14]

As noted above, in addition to heading the government and being its principal spokesperson to Parliament and the people, the Prime Minister is also the leader of his or her political party in Parliament: the role is thus both governmental and party political. The Prime Minister must so juggle his or her role as to ensure that he or she leads a strong and united government maintaining popular electoral support in the country, and also the support of the party in Parliament. No Prime Minister can afford to ignore the parliamentary party and sufficient time and energy must be found to keep a finger on the pulse of the parliamentary party, through personal contacts and through the Whips – the 'eyes and ears' of the party in the Commons – and to a lesser extent the House of Lords. The Prime Minister also holds the post of First Lord of the Treasury. This ancient title signifies the formal head of the nation's financial affairs, although in practice it is the Chancellor of the Exchequer who is in charge of the Treasury and who formulates policies for government revenues and expenditure. In addition, since 1968 the Prime Minister has also been formally in charge of the civil service as Minister for the Civil Service. On occasion, the Prime Minister may hold an additional post, as for example did Winston Churchill in the Second World War when he assumed the office of Minister of Defence.

The Prime Minister also has duties to fulfil outside the United Kingdom. In terms of time commitment, the most demanding is usually the European Union, whose summit meetings and intergovernmental conferences[15] the Prime Minister attends with the Foreign Secretary. On occasion, international incidents such as the Gulf War, and most recently the international effort to eliminate terrorism, require prime ministerial input through negotiations with allies, NATO and the United Nations.

---

[14] On which see page 82 below.   [15] See Chapter 4.

On taking office the Prime Minister has overall responsibility for all areas of government policy and the maintenance of parliamentary and public support. His or her first task is to decide the size of Cabinet (which is nowhere fixed in law) and who will hold what ministerial post and which posts will be represented in Cabinet. Prime Ministers vary in the number of Cabinet members who are appointed, although the number usually rests between sixteen and twenty-four members. Significant variations occur, however, particularly in wartime. For example, during the First World War Lloyd George formed a Cabinet in 1916 of only five ministers; in 1939 with the outbreak of the Second World War, Chamberlain appointed nine ministers, and in 1940 Churchill appointed a Cabinet of only five ministers. In peacetime, certain offices of state are always represented in Cabinet, including the Lord Chancellor, the Chancellor of the Exchequer, Home Secretary, Foreign Secretary, Secretaries of State for Defence, Trade and Industry, Education and Employment, Social Security, Environment, Health, Scotland, Wales and Northern Ireland. All ministers – whether inside Cabinet or not – are appointed by the Crown on the advice of the Prime Minister. The power to dismiss a minister also lies with the Prime Minister. One stark example of the exercise of this power came in 1962 when Prime Minister Harold Macmillan dismissed seven Cabinet members overnight. Perhaps the most ruthless display of prime ministerial power was seen following the 2001 general election when the Prime Minister sacked eighteen ministers and accepted the resignation of one further minister.

The choice of Cabinet members is not without its constraints, aside from the conventional practices dictating the inclusion of certain offices. When a change in government occurs, as in 1979 and 1997, leading party figures who have held positions in the former Shadow Cabinet will expect a Cabinet post. Different Prime Ministers experience different constraints. Some may find themselves obliged by political forces to include in Cabinet those who do not share the new Prime Minister's views. In Mrs Thatcher's first administration from 1979 to 1983 this was clearly the case. Margaret Thatcher had successfully challenged Edward Heath in 1975 for leadership of the Conservative Party. She had relatively little experience of high government office, having been in Heath's Cabinet for three and a half years as Education Secretary, and not part of the 'inner circle' of government policy formation. By contrast, many members of the Shadow Cabinet before the Conservative election victory of 1979 had held senior Cabinet posts, and moreover most had been loyal supporters of her predecessor Edward Heath.

Mrs Thatcher made it clear that she wanted in Cabinet only those who would follow her determined and radical modernizing objectives and policies: in September 1981 she dismissed four unsupportive ministers – the 'wets' – Norman St John Stevas, Christopher Soames, Ian Gilmour and Mark Carlisle, and sidelined James Prior from the Department of Employment to Northern Ireland. Resignations were to follow. In 1982, following the Argentinian invasion of the (British) Falkland Islands, Thatcher's Foreign Secretary Lord Carrington resigned. In 1983 Cecil Parkinson resigned over an extra-marital affair. In 1986 Michael Heseltine, Secretary of State for Defence, and Leon Brittan, Trade and Industry Secretary, resigned over the Westland affair.[16] Keith Joseph also resigned in 1986, while in 1987 Mrs Thatcher suffered the loss of one of her staunchest and most loyal supporters through ill-health, Lord Whitelaw. Norman Tebbit also resigned following the IRA's attempt to destroy the Cabinet during the Conservative Party's annual conference in a Brighton hotel bombing in 1984. In 1989, close to the end of her tenure, the Chancellor of the Exchequer, Nigel Lawson, resigned over monetary policy and Lawson's perception that Alan Walters, Mrs Thatcher's economic adviser, undermined his authority. Her Foreign Secretary, Geoffrey Howe, also abandoned the Prime Minister, resigning in 1990, in part in protest against her overbearing style of leadership. By 1990, the final year of her premiership and leadership of the party, no Cabinet member remained from her first Cabinet, and Mrs Thatcher had lost the support of the Conservative Party. When challenged for the leadership in November 1990, Mrs Thatcher declared her intention to fight the challenge. Having failed to secure the requisite proportion of votes on the first round, and despite the warnings of numerous senior Party figures, she obstinately refused to resign, only to suffer ignominious defeat.

Margaret Thatcher had been Conservative Party Leader since 1975 and Prime Minister since 1979 – the longest term of prime ministerial

---

[16] On which see Chapter 1.

office last century. Under her leadership, the Conservatives had won an unprecedented three general elections: a clear endorsement from the electorate (although the principal opposition party, the Labour Party, had been perceived throughout the 1980s as 'unelectable'). Her loss of power and the manner in which it was executed represents an unprecedented political *coup d'état*, illustrating not only the dangers inherent in the long tenure she enjoyed but more than anything the need for a premier to maintain the confidence and support of his or her political party. Margaret Thatcher was a radical and reforming Prime Minister pursuing a political ideology with a zeal unprecedented in modern times – promoting free market forces over state dependence, privatizing former state-controlled industries such as electricity, gas, nuclear power, telecommunications, the railways and water industry, modernizing and streamlining the civil service, curbing the power of trade unions and promoting individualism over collectivism. No other Prime Minister has yet promulgated a personal political creed as she did with 'Thatcherism', a legacy which continues to haunt the post-Thatcher Conservative Party. But Thatcher's ideology and zeal blinded her to the need for ministerial and parliamentary party support. By the end of her term of office, she had alienated those willing to support her and those on whom her continued premiership and party leadership depended; seemingly oblivious to her own growing isolation from her political power base, Mrs Thatcher dug for herself her own parliamentary and political grave.

Her successor John Major presented a very different style of leadership. A natural conciliator and lacking in ideological rigidity, Major, briefly formerly Thatcher's Foreign Secretary (succeeding Geoffrey Howe), later Chief Secretary to the Treasury and Chancellor of the Exchequer, had limited experience of high government office, having had like Thatcher only three and a half years in Cabinet. Far from dominating Cabinet, as Thatcher had done, Major returned to a more collegiate style of Cabinet meetings: his former Chancellor labelled Major's Cabinet, the 'Cabinet of chums'.[17] But Major inherited the problems left behind by his predecessor, and gathered many of his own. It was left to him to unravel the unpopular system of local taxation –

[17] See J. Barnes, 'Clarke on Cabinet Government', *LSE Magazine* (Winter 1999), p. 8.

the 'poll tax' – which Thatcher had introduced and which had rapidly become unenforceable. In relation to Europe, Thatcher had developed a 'euro-sceptic' style which exasperated European leaders: Major adopted a more balanced approach, seeking to ensure that Britain was at the heart of Europe while remaining cautious about monetary and closer political union. His Cabinet, however, became increasingly divided. Political storms brewed over the signing of the Maastricht Treaty in 1992 which committed Britain to the newly established Union and to ever closer co-operation across a range of new areas such as foreign affairs, defence and security, and justice and home affairs. With a much reduced parliamentary majority and splits in the Conservative Party, Major resorted to threats to use the royal prerogative should Parliament fail to approve the Treaty. Europe was to split the Party and herald the downfall of the Conservative government. By 1994 other storms were brewing, this time in the form of allegations in the press that ministers had been accepting cash in return for asking questions in Parliament.[18] So serious did the allegations of 'sleaze' become that the government seemed to be riddled with corruption, despite the fact that only a few real offenders existed. The arms to Iraq affair, discussed in Chapter 1, further reduced the government's standing. The Scott Inquiry into the matter confirmed the worst suspicions about government secrecy and lack of candour before Parliament. With a parliamentary majority that had dwindled away and allegations of wrongdoing, the government faced a general election certain that loss of office was to follow. The 1997 election returned the Labour Party to power under Tony Blair with the largest majority in Parliament in recent times, and a second term of office, again with a substantial majority, was won in 2001.

Tony Blair, having modernized the Labour Party – getting rid of Clause IV which committed the Party to socialism and moving New Labour to the centre-ground of politics in unprecedented fashion – made the Party 'electable' once more.[19] With the radical and fresh approach of a revitalized party headed by a relatively young and radical leader, the Labour government made modernizing the system of government a priority, with a raft of constitutional reforms to be introduced at an early date. As they had taken the reins after eighteen years of

---

[18] See further Chapter 3.   [19] See Chapter 6.

Conservative rule, all aspects of government fell under scrutiny, with task forces established to conduct investigations into existing policies and practices.

With the exception of Dr John Cunningham, none of Blair's Cabinet had experience of government office, although many had participated in Labour's Shadow Cabinet in the Thatcher years. Tony Blair made it clear that his style of leadership was to be radical and authoritative. He entered Downing Street, not only on a wave of popular and electoral support, but with a team of political supporters in the form of his Press Secretary, Chief of Staff and political advisers which soon gave rise to allegations that Blair was intent on conducting a government centred on his personal power base at Number 10, at the expense of the parliamentary party. In order to achieve his programme of reform according to his timetable, Blair introduced a system of annual agreements with not only Cabinet ministers but also Permanent Secretaries (heads of government departments), by which aims and objectives for achievement would be set. Of this innovation, Peter Hennessy commented that 'We've never seen such a tangible instrument of prime ministerial power, an extension of prime ministerial power, as this before'.[20]

The Labour government was also indirectly aided in the early days of government by an official opposition which had fallen from grace through dissent and allegations of impropriety. The Conservative Party's leader, John Major, announced his resignation from the leadership once the election results were known, and was succeeded by William Hague, a strong parliamentarian but lacking, in the eyes of the public, personal charisma.[21]

The Cabinet

Under the unwritten rules and practices of the constitution, the Cabinet meets regularly to make major policy decisions. The reality, as seen below, is however rather different. When the Cabinet takes a decision,

[20] Speaking on *Blair's Thousand Days*.
[21] For the Conservative Party the general election in 2001 proved a disaster, and William Hague resigned from its leadership.

that decision is binding on all members of Cabinet and also on all non-Cabinet ministers and their Parliamentary Private Secretaries. This is the concept of collective Cabinet responsibility, discussed in Chapter 1, which is of prime importance in British government. Two rules underpin the responsibility of ministers. The first is the confidentiality of Cabinet discussions and Cabinet papers: the contents of discussions may never be disclosed save on the authority of the Prime Minister – a rule in part deriving from the constitutional theory that the Cabinet (through the Prime Minister) offers confidential advice to the Crown. To leak the content of discussions is a matter requiring the resignation of a minister.[22] The second rule is that once a decision has been reached, no minister – whether inside or outside the Cabinet – may speak against the decision. If a minister cannot abide by the decision, and speaks out publicly against it, he or she must resign. Underlying the idea of collective responsibility is the need for secure government and for the government to continue to have the support of Parliament and the people. Quite simply, if the government is not seen to be united it will be a weak government, and one likely to lose Parliament's and the electorate's support. If Parliament loses confidence in the government over a matter of central importance to the government's programme, it can pass a 'motion of no confidence' and force the government to resign, resulting in a general election being called in order that the people can express their views, either endorsing the government or electing another. In addition to collective responsibility, every minister is individually responsible to Parliament (and the electorate) for the management of his or her government department, and for complying with high standards of personal conduct.

Four members of Cabinet are drawn from the House of Lords. The most controversial of these is the Lord Chancellor. The office of Lord Chancellor predates that of Prime Minister by centuries: the first was appointed in 1066. A political appointee, the Lord Chancellor sits in the House of Lords in which he is both the Speaker who presides over matters and controls debates, and the representative of the Cabinet in

---

[22] This rule disguises the political fact of unofficial 'leaks' from government and 'unattributable briefings' through the Lobby system, on which see further pages 91 ff. below.

the Lords.[23] Apart from the Lord Chancellor who always has a Cabinet seat, the Chancellor of the Exchequer, Foreign Secretary, Home Secretary, Education and Employment Secretary, Trade and Industry Secretary, Defence Secretary, Health Secretary, Social Security Secretary and Leaders of the House of Commons and House of Lords will traditionally have Cabinet seats, as will the Chief Secretary to the Treasury and the Chief Whip. As with so much of the constitution, however, none of this is set in stone, and while conventionally these offices are represented in Cabinet there is no legal requirement that they should be, although political difficulties would inevitably arise if a Prime Minister suddenly and without good reason decided to depart from past practice.

Organization of Cabinet, June 2001

Prime Minister, First Lord of the Treasury and Minister for Civil Service
Deputy Prime Minister and First Secretary of State
Chancellor of the Exchequer, Chief Secretary to the Treasury
Lord Chancellor
Secretary of State for Foreign and Commonwealth Affairs
Secretary of State for the Home Department
Secretary of State for Education and Skills
Secretary of State for the Environment, Food and Rural Affairs
Secretary of State for International Development
Secretary of State for Work and Pensions
Secretary of State for Transport, Local Government and the Regions
Secretary of State for Health
Secretary of State for Northern Ireland
Secretary of State for Wales
Secretary of State for Scotland
Secretary of State for Defence
Chief Secretary to the Treasury
Lord Privy Seal and Leader of the House of Lords
Secretary of State for Trade and Industry

---

[23] In addition, the Lord Chancellor is also head of the judiciary with significant powers of appointment of judges and magistrates and responsibilities in relation to the courts and administration of justice. The post accordingly straddles all aspects of government – the executive, the legislature and the judiciary. See further Chapters 1 and 9.

Secretary of State for Culture, Media and Sport
Chief Whip and Parliamentary Secretary to the Treasury
Minister without Portfolio and Party Chairman.[24]

Ministers outside Cabinet

The Ministerial and Other Salaries Act 1975 effectively controls the
number of ministers who may be appointed by limiting the number of
salaried ministers sitting in the House of Commons to ninety-five.
The complete list of government departments, ministers and Special
Advisers in June 2001 was as follows:

Cabinet members:	Ministers and advisers:
Downing Street: Prime Minister and First Lord of the Treasury and Minister for Civil Service	
Cabinet Office and Office of Deputy Prime Minister: Deputy Prime Minister and First Secretary of State	Minister for the Cabinet Office and Chancellor of the Duchy of Lancaster; two Ministers of State, one Parliamentary Secretary
Treasury: Chancellor of the Exchequer	Chief Secretary to the Treasury, Paymaster General, Financial Secretary, Economic Secretary, four special advisers
Foreign and Commonwealth Office: Secretary of State for Foreign and Commonwealth Affairs	Minister of State for Trade, Minister of State for Europe, three Ministers of State and two special advisers

[24] Three Ministers outside Cabinet also attend Cabinet: the Minister of State for Work,
the Chief Whip of the House of Lords and the Minister for Transport.

Cabinet members:	Ministers and advisers:
Lord Chancellor's Department: Lord Chancellor	Three Parliamentary Under-Secretaries of State, one special adviser
Home Office: Secretary of State for the Home Department	Minister of State for Criminal Justice, Minister of State for Crime and Policing, Minister of State for Citizenship and Immigration, three Parliamentary Under-Secretaries of State, three special advisers
Department of Education and Skills: Secretary of State for Education and Skills	Minister of State for School Standards, Minister of State for Lifelong Learning and Higher Education, three Parliamentary Under-Secretaries of State
Privy Council Office: President of the Council and Leader of the Commons	One Parliamentary Secretary; Lord Privy Seal and Leader of the House of Lords
Defence: Secretary of State for Defence	Minister of State for the Armed Forces, Minister for Defence Procurement, Minister for Veterans, two special advisers
Health: Secretary of State for Health	Minister of State for Health, Minister of State for Mental Health and Social Care, three Parliamentary Under-Secretaries of State, two special advisers
Culture, Media and Sport: Secretary of State for Culture, Media and Sport	Minister of State for the Arts, one Parliamentary Under-Secretary of State, one special adviser

Cabinet members:	**Ministers and advisers:**
Northern Ireland Office: Secretary of State for Northern Ireland	Minister of State for Security, Prisons and Policing, one Under-Secretary of State, one special adviser
Wales Office: Secretary of State for Wales	One Parliamentary Under-Secretary of State, two special advisers
Scotland Office: Secretary of State for Scotland	One Minister of State, one special adviser
Environment, Food and Rural Affairs: Secretary of State	Minister of State for the Environment, Minister of State for Rural Affairs, two Parliamentary Under-Secretaries, two special advisers
Trade and Industry: Secretary of State	Minister of State for E-Commerce and Competitiveness, Minister of State for Trade, Minister of State for Industry and Energy, Minister of State for Employment Relations and the Regions, three Parliamentary Under-Secretaries, one special adviser
Work and Pensions: Secretary of State	Minister of State for Work, Minister of State for Pensions, three Parliamentary Under-Secretaries of State
Transport, Local Government and the Regions: Secretary of State	Minister of State for Local Government, Minister of State for Housing and Planning, three Parliamentary Under-Secretaries of State, one special adviser

Cabinet members:	Ministers and advisers:
Whips Office:	House of Commons: Deputy
House of Commons:	Chief Whip, Comptroller of Her
Government Chief Whip	Majesty's Household,
	Vice-Chamberlain of Her
	Majesty's Household, five Whips
	and seven Assistant Whips
House of Lords: Government	House of Lords: Deputy Chief
Chief Whip	Whip, five Whips

In addition to the above ministries are the Law Officers of the Crown, the Attorney-General, his deputy the Solicitor-General, Lord Advocate (Scotland) and Solicitor-General for Scotland. While the legal profession is represented in Cabinet by the Lord Chancellor, the other law officers do not hold Cabinet rank. The Attorney-General, like the Lord Chancellor, is a political appointee and acts as legal adviser to the government. He or she has a number of important functions: for a number of criminal offences the Attorney-General alone has the power to decide whether to prosecute. He or she also appears for the Crown in important cases. There also exist a number of government posts which are not tied to any particular department. On occasion, Prime Ministers may also appoint 'Ministers without Portfolio': ministers having no particular departmental responsibility but being appointed to fulfil a particular task in government. Margaret Thatcher had one Minister without Portfolio, Lord Young, who acted as her economic adviser;[25] John Major appointed none and on entering office Tony Blair appointed Peter Mandelson with responsibility for co-ordinating government policy and presentation, based in the Cabinet Office.

Prime Ministers may also choose to streamline Cabinet and improve government co-ordination through the amalgamation of departments. Former Prime Ministers have experimented with departmental organization in the attempt to produce greater co-ordination and efficiency in government. During his premiership (1951–5) Winston Churchill

[25] Between 1984 and 1985. In 1985 Lord Young was made Secretary of State for Employment and in 1987 Secretary of State for Trade and Industry.

introduced a system of 'Overlords', three in number, who had the responsibility for co-ordinating departments. Each of these was a member of the House of Lords and hence not accountable to the Commons. In assuming their co-ordinating role, they reduced the need for departmental ministers to sit in Cabinet, but thereby caused a certain confusion as to who precisely was responsible for the particular department – the minister or the overlord. Edward Heath, Prime Minister from 1970 to 1974, also experimented with 'super-ministries' in an attempt to streamline Cabinet, amalgamating Trade, Power and Aviation into a Department of Trade and Industry, and the Departments of Transport, Works and Housing and Local Government became the Department of the Environment.[26] In his first term of office, Tony Blair merged Transport with the Environment and the Regions into one department headed by the Deputy Prime Minister. Concerns over agriculture, however, led to the introduction of a Department of Environment, Food and Rural Affairs in 2001, and a separate Department for Transport, Local Government and the Regions.

The traditional picture of the working of Cabinet government has long given way to the realities of effective decision-making. The practice of government in a complex modern state is rather different from that of the nineteenth century when theories of Cabinet government developed. A weekly gathering lasting two hours and often less, of ministers who are hard-pressed by their own departmental, parliamentary and constituency business, is an unwieldy forum for discussion and decision-making on diverse matters of government. The Ministerial Code of Practice[27] states that Cabinet business consists in the main of questions which significantly engage the collective responsibility of the government, because they raise major issues of policy or because they are of critical importance to the public, and questions on which there is an unresolved argument between departments. Other matters should not be brought to Cabinet or to a Ministerial Committee unless the Minister wishes to have the advice of colleagues. The Code requires that issues involving more than one department should be examined

[26] Subsequently Heath removed Transport from the Environment, and Energy from Trade and Industry.
[27] *A Code of Conduct and Guidance on Procedures for Ministers*, Cabinet Office, 1997.

interdepartmentally, before submission to a Ministerial Committee, so that decisions required may be clearly defined.[28]

The practice of establishing Cabinet committees, some 'standing', many *ad hoc*, developed in the nineteenth century to ease the problem. The formation of Cabinet standing committees to reach decisions, while not a new phenomenon, has until recently been shrouded in secrecy, ostensibly justified by the constitutional doctrine of the confidentiality attending Cabinet decision-making. *Ad hoc* committees are the informal gathering of Prime Minister and one or two chosen ministers, formed to reach a decision on a particular matter.[29] In wartime it had proved essential to have decisions reached by a small tight-knit group. With the expansion of government machinery, particularly since 1945, the need for more efficient decision-making than full Cabinet could provide, increased. Decisions reached in Cabinet committees bind the whole Cabinet. For a Prime Minister, who dictates the existence and membership of Cabinet committees, committees offer a very significant advantage over full Cabinet: the careful choice of a committee's membership may ensure that a group of like-minded individuals, most importantly sharing the Prime Minister's view, can avoid full discussion in a potentially divisive environment. By this means, Prime Ministers can ensure efficient decision-making outside the formal Cabinet arena. This can be taken further by a Prime Minister operating a system of *ad hoc* committees outside even the recognized Cabinet committee system. Cabinet standing committees have formal rules of conduct: they have a set membership and are attended by a member of the Cabinet Office who takes minutes. By contrast, *ad hoc* committees may be an informal grouping of the Prime Minister and one or two chosen – and supportive – other ministers. The secrecy which attends full Cabinet also applies to Cabinet committees, and until John Major's administration the existence of Cabinet committees was not even formally recognized, a feature representing the British preference for secret government which makes the whole practice of government extremely difficult for outsiders to understand.

[28] Ibid., paragraph 3.
[29] See J. P. Mackintosh, *The British Cabinet* (London: Stevens, 3rd edn., 1977), for discussion of the early development of Cabinet committees.

Given the inherent degree of flexibility in the system, it cannot be assumed that the practice of one Prime Minister will necessarily be followed by another. While normal practice at least from the 1960s suggests a weekly meeting of Cabinet, and that major decisions must be reached by all members of Cabinet, Prime Ministers can and do depart from these unwritten understandings. Mrs Thatcher held full meetings of Cabinet once a week, and followed the established practice of creating below Cabinet level a series of small Cabinet committees, staffed by three or four ministers and chaired by herself or another, to reach decisions over issues, following which the decision would be put to full Cabinet as a *fait accompli*, thereby enhancing her own power at the expense of Cabinet, although the number of committees – whether standing or *ad hoc* – was considerably reduced under her administration. Former Chancellor of the Exchequer Kenneth Clarke has recorded that Thatcher would resort to informal *ad hoc* groups of ministers to reach policy decisions, and that these tended to be randomly selected from those ministers who were likely to support her own view as to the policy to be pursued.[30]

There are of course good arguments in favour of a small group of ministers – an Inner Cabinet – assuming the role of directing government. Such an arrangement need not even be one which comprises ministers with departmental responsibility, but could be one comprising the Prime Minister and his chosen advisers, although there would be constitutional and political difficulties unless these members were democratically accountable to Parliament. In practice it is increasingly the case that many decisions will be reached by assorted *de facto* Inner Cabinets – whether standing committees or less formal *ad hoc* meetings between the Prime Minister and others, comprising the chairperson, who may or may not be the Prime Minister, and two or three ministerial colleagues directly involved in the subject-matter for decision.

As has been seen, the size and number of government departments, and hence the number of Cabinet ministers and ministers outside Cabinet, is a matter of style. On occasion, and especially in wartime, the Cabinet has been reduced to a small inner core of ministers. During the 1982 Falklands War the Prime Minister effectively managed the war

[30] Barnes, 'Clarke on Cabinet Government', p. 8.

through a small group of ministers who met daily and rarely reported their deliberations to the full Cabinet. The use of such Cabinet committees, while it undermines the nature of full and collective Cabinet responsibility, nevertheless promotes efficiency in decision-making. All Prime Ministers make use of Cabinet committees. Peter Hennessy calculates that in the Attlee government there were 148 standing and 313 *ad hoc* groups in just over six years; Churchill established 137 standing committees and 109 *ad hoc* committees in over three years; between 1974 and 1976, Harold Wilson had some 120 *ad hoc* groups, and between 1976 and 1979 James Callaghan had some 160 *ad hoc* groups. By contrast Mrs Thatcher had only 30 to 35 standing committees and over 120 *ad hoc* committees in six and a half years. Hennessy, writing on Thatcher's premiership, thought she ran 'the slimmest Cabinet machine since before the Second World War', in that the number of standing committees she established was considerably less than her predecessors.[31] Matters for discussion in Cabinet are for the Prime Minister to decide, although ministers may feel that they have a legitimate expectation that their own point of view of a particular matter will be heard on matters within their departmental responsibility. The alleged failure of Mrs Thatcher to allow Michael Heseltine, then President of the Board of Trade, in 1986, to put his views to Cabinet on whether the Westland Helicopter Company should receive backing from either an American firm or a consortium of European companies led to Heseltine's resignation.

John Major, Thatcher's successor, reverted to a more traditional style of Cabinet government. Kenneth Clarke states that Cabinet under Major 'became a genuine discussion group for policy on a large number of significant issues'.[32] Nevertheless, Clarke points to the inefficiency of such a policy: often decisions would not be reached; discussions would be protracted as Major, unlike Thatcher, sought unanimity in Cabinet rather than imposing his own will on the discussions. Tony Blair, however, has followed Thatcher's precedent, with meetings once a week at which Cabinet mostly endorses decisions already reached elsewhere, and he has reportedly reduced the length of Cabinet meetings from

[31] P. Hennessy, *Cabinet* (Oxford: Blackwells, 1986), pp. 100–101.
[32] Barnes, 'Clarke on Cabinet Government'.

over an hour to roughly forty minutes. This practice risks undermining the cohesiveness of Cabinet and the individual capacity of ministers to participate in and contribute to collective decision-making, and greatly increases the power of the Prime Minister. The notion of Cabinet government, so long the conventional model of governance, gives way to prime ministerial government, with the Prime Minister acting as chief executive and controlling lesser ministries. Disclosure of the existence of formal Cabinet committees does not of itself reveal the full picture of the working of Cabinet, the style of operation of which is a matter for the Prime Minister of the day and is cloaked in a high degree of secrecy. The existence of Cabinet committees masks the even more informal *ad hoc* decision-making process in which the Prime Minister may reach decisions with chosen ministers irrespective of committees.

Under the Labour government elected in 1997, the following ministerial Cabinet committees[33] were formed:

Economic Affairs
Environment
Local Government
Home and Social Affairs
Legislative Programme
Children and Young People's Services
Millennium Dome
Constitutional Reform Policy
Defence and Overseas Policy
Northern Ireland
Intelligence Services
Defence and Overseas Policy.

While the Prime Minister effectively controls Cabinet, excessive or heavy-handed ministerial control exercised at the expense of Cabinet cohesion can contribute to a Prime Minister's downfall if he or she fails to keep key ministers and the parliamentary party loyal in his or her support. Splits in Cabinet over policy issues and ministerial resignations damage the authority of the Prime Minister and government as a whole and undermine public confidence in the strength of government.

[33] In addition to committees there are sub-committees.

Nevertheless, the power of the Prime Minister, while not absolute, is considerable, leading to allegations that the British system of government has been transformed from one of Cabinet government to prime ministerial government. While there is some force in this, it is too simplistic an evaluation of the governmental machine. Cabinet government as traditionally portrayed has long since ceased to operate, if indeed it ever did. To understand 'Cabinet government' it is necessary to incorporate into the picture the several factors which affect its operation: the role of the Cabinet Secretary and senior civil service; Cabinet standing committees, *ad hoc* bilateral meetings between the Prime Minister and other ministers, the Prime Minister's Private Office, the Press Office, policy-formation groups such as the former Central Policy Review Staff (CPRS) set up as part of the Cabinet Office by Edward Heath in 1970, and its successor the Policy Unit established by Harold Wilson.

GOVERNMENT SUPPORT SYSTEMS

The Cabinet Office

Prior to 1916 Cabinet was conducted with remarkable informality and no member of the civil service attended. The Cabinet Secretariat was formed in 1916 under Lloyd George's premiership and has been a central and constant feature of government ever since. The Cabinet Office is the machinery which makes Cabinet work, providing the organization for Cabinet meetings and acting as a link between Cabinet and government departments, ensuring that non-Cabinet ministers are fully briefed of Cabinet decisions and that departments deliver the required measures to give effect to decisions. Since its inception, only eight people have filled the post of Cabinet Secretary, reflecting the continuity and permanence of office which facilitates the smooth change-over from one government to the next, particularly when there is a change of political party in power. Led by the Head of the Home Civil Service and Cabinet Secretary (currently Sir Richard Wilson, formerly deputy to Cabinet Secretary Robin Butler who served Thatcher, Major and, in his first year of office, Blair[34]), the Cabinet Office has a staff of some six hundred. Its principal role is the organization of Cabinet, preparing the agenda, minuting proceedings, following up on its decisions, advising non-Cabinet ministers of those decisions and ensuring that action is taken by the relevant departments.

The Cabinet Office serves the Prime Minister and Cabinet in an advisory and organizational capacity, but mostly represents the link between government and the civil service. Of fundamental constitutional importance is the fact that the Cabinet Secretary defends the independence of the civil service from the government of the day: symbolically the Cabinet Secretary's office is separate from Number 10 Downing Street. Since 1983 the Cabinet Secretary has also chaired the Senior Appointments Selection Committee. With his unique access to both permanent secretaries – heads of civil service departments – and to ministers inside and outside Cabinet, the Secretary enjoys unrivalled knowledge of the personnel and performance of both the civil service and politicians. Because of his (there has never been a woman Secretary) experience of government and civil service, the Cabinet Secretary is not only able to advise an incoming Prime Minister on the workings of office, but has also a wide-ranging knowledge of all aspects of government on which the Prime Minister can draw. Mackintosh records that Sir Norman Brook accompanied Harold Macmillan on a tour of India in 1958 and that 'his function was clearly to give advice rather than to act as a secretary'.[35] Robert Armstrong, Cabinet Secretary under Margaret Thatcher from 1979 to 1987, played an unusually prominent and public role in the dispute over membership of trade unions at the Government's Communications Headquarters (GCHQ), the Westland saga and the government's ultimately futile attempts to ban the circulation of *Spycatcher*, former MI5 officer Peter Wright's whistle-blowing book on the security services. Armstrong achieved public notoriety inconsistent with the anonymity of the civil service when in the High Court of Australia he now famously conceded the possibility of being 'economical

---

[34] The first Secretary, Maurice Hankey, 1916–38, served five Prime Ministers; Edward Bridges, 1938–47, served three; Norman Brook, 1947–62, served four; Burke Trend, 1963–73, served four; John Hunt, 1973–9, served four; Robert Armstrong, 1979–87, served one; and Robin Butler, 1987–97, served three.

[35] *British Cabinet*, p. 549.

with the truth'. However, there are dangers inherent in a Prime Minister appearing to be too closely influenced by the Cabinet Secretary at the expense of his or her Private Office, Cabinet colleagues and, to a lesser extent, the parliamentary party. Conversely, there are dangers to the impartiality of the civil service if the Cabinet Secretary becomes too closely identified with the Prime Minister, as did Robert Armstrong with Mrs Thatcher: he was at one point dubbed by commentators as 'Deputy Prime Minister'. Administratively, the Cabinet Office is divided into five secretariats, economic and home affairs, overseas and defence, Europe, central and constitutional and security and intelligence. The senior posts in the Office are held by civil servants on secondment from their departments, usually serving a three-year term. Variations exist: Robert Armstrong served Thatcher for eight years, giving rise to the perception that the Prime Minister was closer to her Cabinet Secretary than to her Cabinet colleagues.

The co-ordination between ministers and their departments in the presentation of the government line is central to promoting the ideal of a competent and successful administration. In ministerial terms, the Minister for the Cabinet Office – formally introduced by Tony Blair's administration – has responsibility for ensuring greater co-ordination between ministers and civil service departments in achieving the government's policies. The Cabinet 'enforcer' as the office has become known is supported by the Minister of State in the House of Lords and a Parliamentary Secretary.

The Prime Minister's Private Office

While often mooted, and its absence an apparent anomaly in a sophisticated system of government, there has never been a 'Prime Minister's Department' dedicated to the task of organizing, co-ordinating and liaising on behalf of the Prime Minister. Instead, a British Prime Minister's team comprises civil service support and non-civil service political support, in the form of a specially appointed team of advisers. Heading the Prime Minister's support system is his Principal Private Secretary who has close relations with both the Cabinet Secretary and the Queen's Private Secretary. A civil servant, usually seconded from the Treasury for a three-year period, the Private Secretary co-ordinates the work of the Prime Minister, controlling the flow of paper into Number 10, and prioritizing matters for prime ministerial attention. In addition to the Private Secretary, there are Private Secretaries for Overseas and Defence Affairs, Economic and Home Affairs, Europe, Central and Constitutional Affairs and Security and Intelligence. The Private Secretaries link the Prime Minister with Cabinet, other government ministers and civil servants, and attend prime ministerial meetings and Cabinet meetings. The Prime Minister's Diary Secretary – a political appointment since 1979 – also plays a key role in the inner corpus of prime ministerial support, controlling the Prime Minister's time and engagements. A Duty Clerk is responsible for maintaining links between Number 10 and the outside world, and manning the Prime Minister's office in the absence of the Private Secretary. The Prime Minister's secretariat, known as the 'Garden Room Girls' (*sic*) since Lloyd George's premiership, completes the support staff at Number 10.

These appointments represent the Prime Minister's staff in his role as head of government. In addition, the Prime Minister must, as discussed above, maintain close links with his parliamentary party and with the party in the country. Given the requirement of political neutrality in civil servants, this would be an inappropriate task for the Private Office and as a result this responsibility falls on his or her Political Secretary, a post funded by the party rather than the taxpayer. Harold Wilson was the first Prime Minister formally to appoint a Political Secretary, Marcia Williams, and all subsequent Prime Ministers have felt the need for this particular support mechanism. A Parliamentary Private Secretary (PPS), a Member of Parliament, assists in liaison with the party, meeting Members of Parliament, accompanying the Prime Minister for Prime Minister's Question Time and generally facilitating lines of communication between the party and its leader.

Chiefs of Staff

The political office of Chief of Staff within the Prime Minister's Private Office is one which some Prime Ministers introduce. The first Chief of Staff was Algernon West, a civil servant who became William Gladstone's Private Secretary and, on retirement from the civil service, his Chief of Staff from 1892 to 1894, assisting the Prime Minister with the formation of Cabinet and staff appointments. A Chief of Staff was mooted in Harold Macmillan's premiership, but not given effect. The idea was again considered but initially rejected under Margaret Thatcher's premiership, on the basis that this might interfere with the relationship of the Prime Minister and her Cabinet colleagues, and undermine the role of the Cabinet Secretary, although having had second thoughts she brought in David Wolfson, a businessman and manager of Great Universal Stores, who served from 1979 to 1985 as part of her Political Office. In the run-up to the 1997 election Tony Blair appointed as Chief of Staff Jonathan Powell, a former diplomat at the Foreign and Commonwealth Office who had worked at the British Embassy in Washington. Heavily involved in preparations for entering office, his subsequent role was to be one of ensuring that once in power decisions were implemented. Powell is one of the two appointees brought in by Blair to play a political role and authorized to give instructions to civil servants, a move which has heightened concern that the civil service is being 'politicized' by government, an issue discussed further below.

Policy groups and special advisers

In the absence of a 'Prime Minister's Department', and, given the breadth of responsibility the Prime Minister bears in relation to government as a whole, it is not surprising that Prime Ministers choose to import into Number 10 their own specialist and politically sympathetic advisers as a foil to the advice given by the politically impartial permanent civil service. The implementation of policy objectives relies on establishing and maintaining working relations with the politically neutral civil service, which alone in the web of government has the benefit of specialization, experience and longevity in government. But while civil servants – the 'permanent government of the country' – draw on expertise born of experience and can advise the elected government on the viability or otherwise of various political objectives, they cannot, without threatening perceptions of political neutrality (a key characteristic of Britain's civil service, on which see below) inject into government overtly political advice.

Prime Ministers feel the need for their own politically supportive advisers, a group sharing the same philosophy of government and political objectives who can speak freely and confidentially to the Prime Minister without the constraints imposed on civil servants who must appear to remain 'above politics'. However, the constitutional status of such advisers is unclear: they are neither democratically elected politicians (and hence not accountable to Parliament), nor are they civil servants in the traditional sense for whose actions ministers will be held responsible before Parliament and the electorate. To give constitutional formality to their role, the Prime Minister can use the prerogative to confer the special status of temporary civil servants on personally appointed advisers, as was the case in 1997 when Tony Blair announced, through Order in Council (the prerogative order), that Jonathan Powell (Chief of Staff) and Alastair Campbell (Chief Press Secretary, but see page 94 below for changes) could not only play a political role, but also give instructions to civil servants. The phenomenon of special advisers is not new, although interest in their role rose to new heights under the Labour government's first term in office.

When Edward Heath became Prime Minister in 1970 he established a Central Policy Review Staff (CPRS) headed by a non-civil servant, Lord Rothschild, to undertake research and formulate policy free of civil service influence. In 1973 Lord Rothschild resigned and the CPRS came under the control of a former Treasury official, and part of the civil service. Mackintosh describes the CPRS as 'more like a standing, all-purposes, fast-moving royal commission'.[36] Harold Wilson, becoming Prime Minister in 1974, formed his own non-civil service Policy Unit to advise the Prime Minister (as opposed to the

[36] See Mackintosh, *British Cabinet*, p. 518.

whole Cabinet) on all matters of policy. Mrs Thatcher abolished the CPRS, but the Policy Unit has survived to the present day. In addition to appointed advisers, all Prime Ministers have the need for their own private staff – since the Second World War this function has been fulfilled by the Number 10 Office. The Office comprises a high-class secretariat providing support for the Prime Minister.

The appointment of special advisers in government – whether at Number 10 or in government departments – arouses controversy. Their role *vis-à-vis* Cabinet ministers, ministers outside Cabinet, Parliament and the civil service is ill-defined, capable of arousing suspicions as to where real power lies at the heart of government. Harold Wilson brought into Number 10 his own Political Secretary, Marcia Williams, to deal with party political matters, in his Private Office. Before long, as it became apparent that Wilson had a group of close confidants at Number 10, there were allegations that he had a 'kitchen cabinet' which had the potential to isolate the Prime Minister from other ministers, the civil service and the parliamentary party. Margaret Thatcher appointed Alan Walters, an economist, as her adviser, which led to conflicts between the Prime Minister and her Chancellor of the Exchequer. Tony Blair has a veritable army of advisers. On assuming office in 1997 after eighteen years of Conservative rule, the Labour government pledged itself to review – with an eye on reform – all aspects of government. Whereas the Conservatives had thirty-six political advisers, the Labour government in 2000 had seventy-seven and the Prime Minister a force of twenty-eight at Number 10,[37] and in addition eighteen 'task forces' were established to examine government policies, and a further eighty review bodies were formed to advise on diverse issues, ironically including the question of whether there are too many 'quangos'.

Largely unknown to the public, these assorted bodies which review and formulate policy for government operate in private and avoid the normal democratic control of parliamentary scrutiny. The 'centralizing tendencies' of Blair's premiership, the close-knit group of advisers, the co-ordination of the dissemination of the government's message, has inevitably led to criticisms that Blair is conducting a more 'presidential'

[37] At an estimated cost to the taxpayer of £3.9 million, of which Downing Street advisers account for £1.5 million.

style of leadership than any of his predecessors. He is not the first Prime Minister to be so criticized: when those outside the inner circle feel that their position and influence is actually or potentially undermined, the 'presidential' allegation is frequently wheeled out, with its implications of isolation from the parliamentary party, the party outside Parliament, and potential 'politicization' of the civil service. Lord Neill QC's Committee on Standards in Public Life examined a whole range of issues in 1999, including the role of special advisers, lobbying, sponsorship and public appointments. On special advisers, the Committee recommended that there be introduced a code of conduct enshrined in a Civil Service Act and that there be a statutory limit to the number of ministerial aides appointed.[38] However, while accepting that there was no evidence that special advisers were 'politicizing the civil service', the Committee expressed the concern that '[T]he considerable increase in numbers, particularly at No. 10, where influential roles are played by special advisers, raises the question of whether their authority outweighs that of objective advisers' and that '[A]ny future growth in numbers would raise questions about a move towards the establishment of a "cabinet system" within departments'.[39]

Special advisers are servants of the Crown. As such there is no entitlement to a period of notice before the termination of employment. However, the *Model Contract for Special Advisers*[40] provides that, other than where employment is terminated by agreement or results from disciplinary proceedings, inefficiency or grounds justifying dismissal at common law, advisers will be given not less than three months' notice in writing. Otherwise employment automatically terminates at the end of the current government administration or when the relevant Cabinet minister leaves the government or moves to another appointment or in the event of a general election, on the day after polling day. Schedule I of the *Model Contract, The Role and Duties of Special Advisers*, states that special advisers 'must always be guided by the basic principle that they are employed to serve the objectives of the government and the department in which they work'. They are exempt from the general

[38] Such limits have already been imposed in relation to the Scottish Parliament and Welsh Assembly.
[39] See *Reinforcing Standards*, the *Report of the Committee on Standards in Public Life*, 2000.   [40] Published May 1997.

civil service requirement that appointments must be made on merit on the basis of fair and open competition, provided that they are appointed 'for the purpose only of providing advice to any Minister'.[41] Their constitutional position is ambivalent: they are 'servants of the Crown but not a formal part of the departmental hierarchy', do not work directly under a permanent civil servant or have permanent civil servants working for them. 'Special advisers are appointed to advise the Minister in the development of Government policy and its effective presentation.'[42] As Crown employees paid out of public funds, special advisers operate to support the interests of the government rather than the government's political party, although they act as a channel of communication between government and party.

Whereas a civil servant must be politically neutral in relation to government, special advisers are overtly political and must have a high degree of party political commitment. Their functions include advising ministers on issues having party political implications, researching, the preparation of speculative policy papers, contributing to policy planning within the government department, liaising with the party, briefing party MPs, liaising with outside interest groups, speech writing and 'adding party political content to material prepared by permanent civil servants' and providing expert advice as a specialist in a particular field. Towards these ends special advisers are entitled to attend party functions, but not to speak at the Party Conference, take part in policy reviews or advise ministers on any departmental business which may arise when the minister is taking part in party political activities. They are not, however, entitled to take part in the work of the political party's national organization, and in the course of elections while they may

[41] Article 3(2) of the Civil Service Order in Council 1995 as amended by the Civil Service (Amendment) Order in Council 1997. This position was affirmed by the Employment Appeal Tribunal which ruled in *Lord Chancellor and Another v. Coker and Another, The Times* 23 January 2001, that the Lord Chancellor did not discriminate against two women, one of whom was black, on the grounds of sex or race when he appointed as special adviser a white male who was well known to him, without advertising the post. The appointment process with regard to special advisers was not subject to the general rules that applied to the appointment of civil servants since special advisers were not civil servants. In appointing a special adviser a key quality in the applicant was a commitment to the political understanding of the particular minister. [42] *Model Contract*, Schedule I (iii).

not take active part in the campaign they may continue to give specialist and political advice to ministers. Special advisers may not speak publicly on matters of national political controversy, nor publish on such matters, nor may they stand as candidates for Parliament or the European Parliament without first resigning their appointment.

Communicating the government's message

The task of government, in terms of maintaining public confidence and an appearance of openness (on which more below), lies in the release of sufficient information through the media consistent with presenting information in its best light (from the government's point of view). Whereas in the United States of America the freedom of the press is a fundamental aspect of freedom of expression, legally protected under the Constitution and incapable of abridgement, the freedom of the press in the United Kingdom, while lip-service is paid to it, is constrained by a number of legal and political factors. British government – as epitomized by Cabinet and Whitehall – is cloaked in secrecy. The doctrine of collective responsibility of Cabinet and the attendant secrecy of Cabinet discussions are in part based on constitutional doctrine ('advice to the Crown': discussed above), and in part on law, most particularly the Official Secrets Act 1989.[43] Civil servants are equally rigidly regulated by the Official Secrets Act which makes any 'unauthorized disclosure' of official information that is 'damaging' to the categories of information covered a criminal offence.[44] The secrecy of Whitehall is an established feature of British government, described as 'a conspiracy of secrecy, to preserve the sanctity of Government behind the walls of Whitehall's forbidden city'.[45] John Major pledged greater

[43] On which see Chapter 8.
[44] The prohibition on disclosure of security and intelligence information is absolute; in other cases the offence is qualified by the concept of 'damage' and by definition of lawful disclosure as being 'in accordance with his official duty': there is no concept of disclosures being justified 'in the public interest'.
[45] James Margach, political correspondent of the *Sunday Times*, in *The Abuse of Power: The War Between Downing Street and the Media from Lloyd George to James Callaghan* (London: W. H. Allen, 1978), p. 1, cited in Hennessy, *Whitehall*, p. 363.

openness in government and the present government has introduced a Freedom of Information Act to further that objective, but that Act falls far short of justifying the release of certain forms of information, most particularly that relating to advice given to ministers by civil servants which is specifically excluded.

While successive governments seek to keep the press and public in ignorance of that which the government wishes to keep secret, the responsible press (as opposed to the irresponsible tabloid press) has a democratic duty to inform the public as to what its government and civil service machine is doing. With no guaranteed freedom of the press, however, this has long been a battle which the press could not win. British compromise kicked in in the nineteenth century with the intro-duction of the 'Lobby system'. Introduced in 1884, the Lobby consists of those reporters who are accredited by the Speaker of the House of Commons as authorized to attend Parliament, in the Members' Lobby, in order to receive non-attributable briefings from ministers or their spokesmen. By this means, the press receives and is able to impart to the public that information which the government wishes to reveal without that information being attributable to any one government spokesperson, a system described by Peter Hennessy as 'a cosy arrange-ment which suits, like all monopolies, the insider traders, the losers being the consumer, in this case the reader, the public, the electorate'.[46] There is no equality in the system: no right for accredited (let alone unaccredited) journalists to receive information which is in the public interest; rather it is information which the government spokesperson – representing government largesse – is authorized to disclose, which by definition is information which the government regards as in its interest to disclose, and interpreted in such a way as to present the government in its best light. The potential sanction employed against the press is that Lobby status can be denied to any journalist overstepping the bounds of propriety (as defined by the government), and Lobby briefings suspended totally.[47]

At the heart of government, in Number 10 Downing Street, is the all-important Press Office which plays an increasingly important role in

[46] Hennessy, *Whitehall*, p. 364.
[47] As occurred in Harold Wilson's final two years as Prime Minister.

disseminating to the public information which it is in the government's interests for the public to receive. The first official Press Officer was appointed under Neville Chamberlain, Prime Minister from 1937 to 1940, although the task was originally confined to handing out government statements. The Press Office is now an established part of the Number 10 machine. Press Secretaries may be drawn either from the civil service, usually but not invariably the Central Office of Information (COI), and generally seconded for a three-year term of office,[48] or from the pool of journalists known to the Prime Minister. The task of co-ordinating the information flowing from government to the public is sensitive, and requires the co-operation of civil service department press officers, ministers, the COI and the Press Office. As with all organization of Number 10, each Prime Minister has his or her own style, and this is reflected in the role of the Press Secretary. Bernard Ingham, Thatcher's Press Secretary, carried unusual influence in relation to the Prime Minister and government. Ingham was made acting head of the Central Office of Information in 1988, influenced the appointment of information officers in many government departments, chaired meetings of information officers to co-ordinate government communications, attended briefing sessions for Question Time, liaised with senior ministers over the co-ordination of government presentation, and briefed ministers on Cabinet decisions.[49] In Kavanagh and Seldon's view, '[P]robably no other single figure was so important to her [Mrs Thatcher] during her premiership.'

The Press Office works most closely with accredited Lobby journalists. While 'unattributable briefings' from government spokespersons had been the norm since the introduction of the Lobby system in 1884, Blair moved quickly to formalize matters and to ensure that there was adequate co-ordination of the government message. In large measure, the move was forced in 1998 by contrary messages being given by the Press Secretary and the Chancellor of the Exchequer's special adviser, Charlie Whelan, over the government's approach to entering the European single currency, and later over press allegations concerning

[48] The exception being Margaret Thatcher's Press Secretary, Bernard Ingham, who served for eleven years.
[49] See D. Kavanagh and A. Seldon, *The Powers Behind the Prime Minister: The Hidden Influence of Number Ten* (London: HarperCollins, 1999), p. 190.

financial dealings between Peter Mandelson and Treasury minister Geoffrey Robinson, the ultimate outcome of which was the resignation of both Mandelson and Robinson. Whelan also resigned over criticisms of his role. This 'rival spinning' undermined the government's authority and cohesiveness and Blair determined to ensure that government messages were centralized under the authority of his Press Secretary at Number 10. Following a review of the government's communications, conducted by Sir Robin Butler, former Cabinet Secretary, Peter Mandelson, Alastair Campbell and Mike Grannat, head of the Government Information Service, it was decided that, for the first time in over a hundred years, the Prime Minister's Press Secretary, Alastair Campbell, would 'go on the record'. In Labour's first term of office, Campbell held two briefings a day, at 11 a.m. in Downing Street and 4 p.m. at the House of Commons, thus centralizing the presentation of the government's message to the public. Not only did Campbell give on-the-record briefings, but he was also cited as the 'Prime Minister's official spokesman', and controlled all media access to the Prime Minister. Alastair Campbell was the first Press Secretary to attend Cabinet and he also attended *ad hoc* meetings between the Prime Minister and other ministers. Quite where the boundary lines lay between the transmission of government information and involvement in the formation of particular policies is difficult to discern, and perhaps for this reason the power and influence of the Prime Minister's Press Secretary gave rise to concerned speculation from parliamentarians.[50] In part because of such concerns, immediately following the 2001 general election it was announced that the post of Chief Press Secretary to the Prime Minister would be abolished. In place of Alastair Campbell the Prime Minister appointed two senior civil servants to act as his official spokespersons.

[50] The Government Information Service has been renamed the Government Information and Communications Service. In January 1998 a Strategic Communications Unit answerable to the Prime Minister through the Chief Press Secretary was established, staffed by both civil servants and journalists, and civil servant departments have established Strategic Planning Units to work alongside their press offices.

The Government Information Service (GIS)

A government's support network includes the Government Information Service, which has responsibility for presenting government policy and information to the media. The Government Information Service is publicly funded, and its Information Officers are charged with explaining government policies to the public and informing the public of government services available to them. *Guidance on the Work of the Government Information Service*[51] regulates the work of Press Officers, and states that 'A minister is entitled to use the Press Office to ensure that Government policy and actions are explained and presented in a positive light'. However, 'spinning' the message – accentuating the positive and eliminating the negative – must, according to the *Guidance*, however implausibly, be conducted in a manner so as to avoid the impression that taxpayers' money is being used for party political purposes. Press Officers 'are there to assist the media to understand the policies of the government of the day'.[52] A number of basic, general and specific conventions (obligatory non-legal rules) govern the workings of the GIS. Public funds may not be used to support publicity for party political purposes, and the *Guidance* makes clear that this rule includes not only decisions relating to what is published but also the 'content, style and distribution of what is published'.[53] It is improper for Press Officers to attack opposition parties and their policies: a rule underpinned by the requirement of impartiality of the civil service of which Press Officers are members. What is required, therefore, is a delicate balancing act between the positive presentation of government policies and the avoidance of the impression that Press Officers are politically allied to the government and its policies.

The sheer number of civil servants now working within government departments on media relations and publicity campaigns gives rise to controversy. By January 2001, there had been a 40 per cent increase in numbers since the 1997 general election, with 1,083 full-time staff. Within the Department of Health, for example, there had been an increase from 84 to 151, including 48 press officers, 9 staff in a

[51] Cabinet Office, 1997.   [52] *Guidance*, paragraph 11.   [53] Ibid., paragraph 4.

communications planning unit, a 27-strong campaigns division and 45 people working in corporate communications.[54]

THE CIVIL SERVICE

The constitutional and practical role of the Civil Service is, with integrity, honesty, impartiality and objectivity, to assist the duly constituted Government of the United Kingdom, the Scottish Executive or the National Assembly for Wales whatever their political complexion, in formulating their policies, carrying out decisions and in administering public services for which they are responsible.[55]

They do not control policy; they are not responsible for it. Belonging to no Party, they are for that very reason an invaluable element in Party Government. It is through them, especially through their higher branches, that the transference of responsibility from one Party or one Minister to another involves no destructive shock to the administrative machine.[56]

The civil service spans the administration of the state from local and regional departmental offices to central government, delivering services to the public in accordance with the policy of the government of the day: it represents the vast and complex machinery of the state. Over the past two decades the civil service has seen widespread changes. Its numbers have been slimmed down, financial management techniques and 'value for money' initiatives introduced. In addition, the formerly monolithic structure of the service has been fundamentally altered with the establishment of specialist agencies, headed by a chief executive, staffed largely by civil servants, and under the ultimate responsibility of the relevant departmental minister. The focus here is on Whitehall – the heart of the United Kingdom's administration – and the upper

[54] *Information and Press Officers Directory*, Central Office of Information, January 2001.
[55] *The Civil Service Code*, revised 13 May 1999.
[56] Lord Balfour, 'Introduction', in W. Bagehot, *The English Constitution*, 1867 (Oxford: Oxford University Press, 1928), pp. xxiv–xxv.

echelons of the civil service which administer central government. Numerically, while there are some five million people employed by public authorities in Britain (there are difficulties in statistical precision due both to the fluidity of the definition of a 'civil servant' and the exclusion of many public employees – for example local government employees – who are not technically civil servants), under half a million of them are in central administration in Whitehall. While the elected government is democratically accountable for the administration of the state, it is the higher civil service – the elite, commonly dubbed the mandarins of the state – which translates the political agenda of government into workable practices. Traditionally, the key character-istics of the civil service are its anonymity, political neutrality and permanence.

The concept of anonymity derives from the relationship between civil servants, ministers and Parliament: civil servants are responsible to ministers, ministers are accountable to Parliament and act as a screen of protection around their departments. Without political neutrality, civil servants could not effectively serve political masters of differing ideological persuasions; without permanence, there could be no smooth continuity in administration, which depends largely on the wealth of experience garnered throughout a career in public service. But while permanence and stability of senior personnel oils the machinery of state – the higher civil service is often described as a Rolls-Royce – it also brings with it its own ethos. Senior civil servants, as in earlier centuries, continue, notwithstanding structural changes to the service, to exude the aura of a largely middle- or upper-middle-class, public-school, Oxbridge-educated, male and middle-aged group, steeped in the tra-ditions and mind-set of generations past while serving very different governments with differing political agendas. Any incoming govern-ment following a general election which ushers a different party into power, must within days come to terms with the monolithic service on which it depends for its future success.

Almost uniquely among Western democracies, the British civil ser-vice is largely unregulated by statute. Civil servants are technically 'servants of the Crown' and appointed under the royal prerogative, and the regulation of the service is under Orders in Council (prerogative orders) rather than Act of Parliament, together with regulatory Codes:

Questions of Procedure for Ministers and the Civil Service Code, neither of which have the force of law.

Every new government comes to power with its own political agenda. Incoming Prime Ministers inevitably differ in style: some arrive with a radical agenda for change – Margaret Thatcher and Tony Blair being two prime examples. Others conduct a more moderate and conciliatory approach to government, as did John Major when he succeeded Thatcher, and James Callaghan on succeeding Harold Wilson. Irrespective of style, every government needs its programme translated into administration and it is the civil service which fulfils this function. Civil servants represent the 'doers' behind the policy-makers (government) and law-makers (Parliament). It is the civil service which must implement and administer the government's policies, translating the broad political objectives into workable arrangements.

In Britain the change-over of power following a general election is both swift and brutal. The leader of the former government which has lost power at a general election tenders his or her resignation to the Crown immediately the results are known.[57] The incumbent of Number 10 Downing Street will leave that same day, with the newly appointed Prime Minister arriving shortly thereafter. There is no transitional period in which either the old or new government can come to terms with election defeat or success, or for the civil service to adjust to a new set of political masters. This presents the first practical obstacle for any new government. Traditionally, any new government is prevented from access to a former government's papers – on the basis that the business of government is confidential to the Crown. Equally, no political party aspiring to success at a general election is entitled to access to government papers or civil servants.

When governments change, particularly after a long period in opposition (as with the Labour governments in 1964 and 1997), there are real difficulties in ensuring that the new administration will be 'up and running' from day one. Although since 1975 public money has been available to parliamentary parties in sums proportionate to their pre-

[57] There are rare exceptions to this rule, as in 1974 when the general election produced no clear result and Prime Minister Edward Heath sought, unsuccessfully, to form an alliance with the Liberal Party which would ensure the government's continuance in power.

vious electoral success (in terms of the number of seats won in Parliament), the research resources of political parties are paltry compared with the vast knowledge and experience of the permanent civil service. Yet a new minister, often with no prior experience of government or of the department he or she is to head, must make an immediate mark on his or her department. In an effort to smooth the transition of power between one government and another, in 1964 Prime Minister Alec Douglas-Home formulated the convention that shadow ministers should be granted limited access to permanent secretaries (civil service heads of government departments) in the period immediately before a general election in order to ease the transition. This cuts both ways; just as the opposition parties need access to the civil service to prepare the latter for a new administration, so too the civil service will be researching the best possible approach to the likely impact of a change in government, scrutinizing manifestos, considering the implications of election promises, and foreseeing advantages and disadvantages of various proposals, which, however attractive to the voters, may – in the view of the 'mandarins' – prove impossible to achieve. It is not surprising that the view has been expressed, most forcibly by left-wing Labour politicians in the past, that there is some kind of 'conspiracy' operating in Whitehall, which follows its own agenda, guided by its own ethos, irrespective of which political masters are in power, although this view is equally strongly contested by others. Following the Second World War, for example, the Labour government entered office with a radical reforming programme which included substantial nationalization of industry, seemingly ideological anathema to the 'conservatively minded' civil service, yet Clement Attlee was subsequently able to record that whereas there were 'certainly some people in the Labour Party who doubted whether the Civil Servants would give fair play to a Socialist Government . . . all doubts disappeared with experience'.

Pre-election meetings between shadow ministers and permanent secretaries can ease the transitional problem, but only to an extent, for with large departments of state and complex subject-matter, only experience of office can mitigate the vast gulf between political objectives and aspirations and inexperience of office on the one hand and the wealth of knowledge and expertise of the higher civil service on the other. Tony Blair's preparations for office made full use of the

Douglas-Home convention, with a hand-picked team preparing for the hand-over of power, including discussions with the Cabinet Secretary and the Prime Minister's Principal Private Secretary.

The evolution of the civil service

A 'civil service' in the sense of a body of men serving the Crown has existed since time immemorial, originally and primarily in the form of servants of the Crown who kept the royal accounts. The term civil service distinguishes those Crown servants who act in a civil rather than military capacity. Until the mid-nineteenth century the civil service was an essentially 'gentlemanly' and amateur profession entered into by the sons of upper-class establishment figures, an alternative to a career in the established Church, the Army, Parliament, law or medicine. Royal and aristocratic patronage featured large. Early on the Treasury, the department responsible for public expenditure, controlled the civil service. In 1853 a major inquiry into the civil service was undertaken by Charles Trevelyan and Stafford Northcote, two Treasury officials. The inquiry was to lead to the first major overhaul of an antiquated system. The Northcote–Trevelyan Report 1854[58] was to result in a civil service, the ethos of which has changed little and the organization of which survived largely intact until the 1980s, albeit with significant modifications introduced following the other major inquiry into the service: the 1968 Fulton Report,[59] and more fundamental reforms introduced by Margaret Thatcher, who was determined not only to cut down the size of government administration but also to inject a hitherto unknown degree of efficiency. The principal recommendations of the Northcote–Trevelyan Report included the ending of patronage, the division of the service into higher and inferior classes, the introduction of open competitive examination for entry to the service, the establishment of a central board to conduct examinations, the emphasis on recruiting young men straight from education as opposed to more mature candidates with experience 'in the real world', and promotion based on merit.

---

[58] *Report on the Organisation of the Permanent Civil Service*, C. 1713 (London, 1854).
[59] On which see below.

In 1855 the Civil Service Commission came into being, but it was not until 1870 that real open competition became the norm by which appointments were made, with the exception of posts in the Home Office and Foreign Office, both of which resisted the reforms. The emphasis of the British civil service, unlike France and the United States of America, has never been on the recruitment of specialists, but rather on the recruitment of gifted amateurs to be trained while in post.

But while the industrial revolution had transformed society by the nineteenth century, and the state grew ever more active in administration and regulation, the civil service remained as devised by Northcote–Trevelyan. Two World Wars and the growth of the welfare state changed the scale and scope of the civil service, but no fundamental reappraisal of its structure or role accompanied such developments. By the 1960s Britain was seen as in economic decline, unable to match the growth of her European neighbours: attention turned to the role of the civil service. In 1966 Prime Minister Harold Wilson appointed Lord Fulton to lead an inquiry and to make recommendations for the modernization of the service. The Fulton Report 1968[60] made twenty-two recommendations, few of which were implemented. The Report opened with the controversial view that the civil service remained the product of the philosophy of the Northcote–Trevelyan Report, and that it remained 'too much based on the philosophy of the amateur' (or 'generalist' or 'all-rounder'). It recommended the setting up of a Civil Service Department, separate from the Treasury, and under the control of the Prime Minister, with a Permanent Secretary designated Head of the Home Civil Service. Greater 'professionalism' among specialists and administrators was called for, with better training in management. It recommended that a Civil Service College should be established to provide training courses in administration and management for new recruits, to replace the traditional 'in-house' training via experience. The Report also called for greater mobility between the civil service and other employments, with temporary appointments, short-term interchanges of staff and freer movement out of the service. Principles of accountable management should be applied, with clear allocation of

---

[60] *Report of the Committee on the Civil Service, 1966–1968*, Cmnd. 3638 (London: HMSO, 1968).

responsibility and authority to accountable units with defined object-ives, and all departments should establish Planning Units.

Official opposition and intransigence largely undermined Fulton's impact. In 1968 a Civil Service Department was established to take over the control formerly exercised by the Treasury, with the mandate to implement reforms to the structure of the service recommended by Fulton, including revision of the rigid structure of classes within the service, which determine recruitment and career advancement. While some tinkering with the system resulted, no major revision took place, the head of the Department being 'unconvinced' by the merits of the reform. In 1969 the Civil Service College was established and placed under the control of the Civil Service Department. In its early years it provided only rudimentary post-selection training, concentrated into less than two years, and offering courses in administration, manage-ment, vocational subjects and economics (a course lasting only four weeks). The Civil Service Department was dismantled by Margaret Thatcher in 1981, and control over numbers, pay and conditions of service reverted to the Treasury, while the Cabinet Secretary became Head of the Civil Service (with the Prime Minister being the responsible Minister for the Civil Service).

When Edward Heath took over the premiership in 1970, he expanded the interaction – as Fulton had proposed – between civil servants and the 'outside world'. Heath brought in a team of businessmen, seconded from their companies for a two-year term to bolster management in government. Heath also set up the Central Policy Review Staff (CPRS), a 'think tank' of multi-disciplinary forward-looking policy strategists in the Cabinet Office, operating under the Prime Minister and headed by Lord Rothschild, with the remit of looking to the longer term than politicians with their heavy departmental responsibilities and often relatively short tenure of office were able to do. The head of the CPRS and his deputy established the right to attend Cabinet committees. Membership of the CPRS, varying between thirteen and twenty, was divided between civil servants and members drawn from industry, the professions and universities. The CPRS was designed

to work out the implications of . . . basic strategy in terms of policies in specific areas, to establish the relative priorities to be given to the different sectors of

[the] programme as a whole, to identify those areas of policy in which new choices can be exercised and to ensure that the underlying implications of alternative courses of action are fully analysed and considered.[61]

Edward Heath also set in motion a trend which was to be developed fully by his successor, Margaret Thatcher: the hiving-off from central government departments responsibility for specific areas of administration within specialized agencies, headed by a Chief Executive.[62] Heath's administration was beset by economic and industrial crises: in 1974 he called a general election on the issue of 'who rules Britain' – the trade unions (most particularly the National Union of Miners) or the government – to be narrowly defeated at the polls by the Labour Party under Harold Wilson. In 1975 Heath was successfully challenged for the Conservative Party leadership by Margaret Thatcher, whose impact on the civil service during her long leadership (1975–90) and premiership (1979–90) was to be profound.

Margaret Thatcher's government and civil service reform

When Margaret Thatcher entered Number 10 she did so with an unprecedented parliamentary majority of 144 and with reforming zeal. Mrs Thatcher intended to 'turn Britain round', employing free-market economics, and she was intent on cutting down the size of government. Unlike her three predecessors, Wilson, Callaghan and Heath, Mrs Thatcher had never been employed in the civil service, and by the time she became Prime Minister it was clear that she had little empathy with the cautious higher civil service ethos, regarding it as an impediment to achieving her radical agenda for change: indeed, she came to power with an already established reputation for being hostile to the government machine. On entering office Mrs Thatcher appointed Sir John Hoskyns as a government adviser, with the task of investigating the efficiency of the civil service.

[61] White Paper, *The Reorganisation of Central Government*, Cmnd. 4506 (London: HMSO, 1970).
[62] Initially the Procurement Executive, Property Services Agency and Manpower Services Commission. See further below.

It was obvious to the government that the civil service had remained immune from and untouched by modern accounting practices. In 1980, following an earlier study by Sir Derek Rayner, the Information System for Ministers (MINIS) was introduced first in the Department of the Environment, at that time under Michael Heseltine. Its objective was to set out clearly the organization of a department and the responsibility of individuals for each area of policy. It was claimed in 1986 that when MINIS was introduced in the Ministry of Defence it facilitated the discovery that 'the Department had three separate units each ordering false teeth for the three different armed services'.[63] A spin-off of the MINIS programme that was also aimed at greater efficiency and financial accountability was the Financial Management Initiative of 1982, supervised by the Financial Management Unit, designed to enable managers to assess performance in relation to objectives, assess value for money and to identify aspects of training or expert advice needed to ensure effectiveness in administration.

When Mrs Thatcher took office in 1979, civil service numbers were 732,300, the highest ever. By 1986 the number had fallen to 594,400, through a freeze on recruitment and retirement and resignations.[64] The Prime Minister also tackled the issue of civil service pay, introducing pay rates related to merit, a move which met with considerable resistance from the service.[65] In 1981 Mrs Thatcher abolished the Civil Service Department, bringing control over the service back into the hands of the Treasury and the Cabinet Secretary. Between 1979 and 1984 Mrs Thatcher cut the number of civil servants by 15 per cent. Mrs Thatcher was to play an unusually personal role in appointments at the level of Permanent Secretary and Deputy Secretary, to the extent that by 1987 she had personally appointed the majority of senior civil servants, leading – inevitably – to charges that she was 'politicizing the civil

---

[63] C. Hughes, 'Whitehall: The System Strikes Back', *The Times*, 24 March 1986, quoted in G. Drewry and T. Butcher, *The Civil Service Today* (Oxford: Basil Blackwell, 1988), p. 204.   [64] Civil Service Statistics, 1986. By 1999 the figure had fallen to 460,000.
[65] See M. Thatcher, *The Downing Street Years* (London: HarperCollins, 1993), chapter 2. When employees at Government Communications Headquarters (GCHQ) at Cheltenham threatened to step up industrial action and to distrupt the interception of signals intelligence, Mrs Thatcher peremptorily abandoned union–government negotiations and used the royal prerogative to ban future union membership at GCHQ, on the basis that further union action threatened the security of the state.

service' by appointing to high office those who shared her political convictions,[66] a charge refuted by the Royal Institute of Public Administration which investigated and reported in 1987, concluding that 'most of the recent rumours about "politicisation" are groundless ... We do not believe that appointments and promotions are based on the candidate's support for or commitment to particular political ideologies or objectives; style rather than political belief is important.'[67]

The establishing of the Efficiency Unit in 1979 led to fundamental structural changes. The Efficiency Unit was set up within the Cabinet Office, and initially headed by Sir Derek (later Lord) Rayner. Sir Derek, from Marks and Spencer, had earlier been brought in as an economic adviser to Edward Heath between 1970 and 1972.[68] His approach was to scrutinize government departments with a view to 'savings or increased effectiveness'; to 'propose solutions to any problems identified', and to 'implement agreed solutions, or begin their implementation, within twelve months of the start of the scrutiny'.[69] Departmental scrutinies were to be completed within ninety days, with officials focusing on why particular aspects of work were 'done at all', 'why is it done as it is', and 'how could it be done more efficiently and effectively at less cost?'[70] When Rayner left government following the 1983 general election, '130 scrutinies had produced £170 million savings and economies of 16,000 posts a year, plus £39 million more in once-and-for-all savings with another £104 million worth of possible economies identified'.[71]

In 1983 Derek Rayner was succeeded at the Efficiency Unit by Sir Robin Ibbs, formerly of ICI. Sir Robin Ibbs was to usher in the Next Steps Agencies, an initiative designed to produce greater efficiency and thereby 'value for money' by establishing specialist bodies, each with its own executive appointed through open competition. Executive agencies now cover diverse areas of administration. By way of example, the

[66] See, *inter alia*, C. Ponting, *The Right to Know: The Inside Story of the Belgrano Affair* (London: Sphere, 1985), pp. 7–8; or Ponting, *Whitehall: Tragedy and Farce* (London: Hamish Hamilton, 1986).

[67] Royal Institute of Public Administration, *Top Jobs in Whitehall: Appointments and Promotions in the Senior Civil Service* (London: RIPA, 1987).

[68] Rayner became head of the Defence Procurement Agency set up by Edward Heath.

[69] *The Scrutiny Programme: A Note of Guidance by Sir Derek Rayner*, cited in Hennessy, *Whitehall*, p. 596.

[70] Ibid.   [71] Ibid.

Benefits Agency, Child Support Agency, Employment Agency, Driver and Vehicle Licensing Agency, Stationery Office, Land Registry, Passport Agency, Ordnance Survey, Prison Service Agency and Patent Office all became autonomous executive bodies, with chief executives responsible for administration, while ministers remained, as before, responsible to Parliament for policy. By 1999 three-quarters of all civil servants were employed in agencies.

Next Steps Agencies fundamentally changed the structure of the civil service, leaving a small core of civil servants in the central departments, with the majority transferred to agencies, under a chief executive responsible for administration. The Ibbs Report, *Improving Management in Government: The Next Steps*, stated that:

The aim should be to establish a quite different way of conducting the business of government. The central Civil Service should consist of a relatively small core engaged in the function of servicing Ministers and managing departments, who will be the 'sponsors' of particular government policies and services. Responding to these departments will be a range of agencies employing their own staff, who may or may not have the status of Crown servants, and concentrating on the delivery of their particular service, with clearly defined responsibilities between the Secretary of State and the Permanent Secretary on the one hand, and the Chairmen or Chief Executives of the agencies on the other. Both departments and their agencies should have a more open and simplified structure.[72]

Whatever the merits of efficiency, however, the agencies raise important questions about the issues of accountability and responsibility. Two illustrations reveal the constitutional difficulty. The Child Support Agency was introduced in 1993, under the Child Support Act 1991, charged with the duty to trace absent parents, assess maintenance for their children, and to enforce the maintenance obligation of absent parents towards their children. The first Chief Executive was Mrs Ros Hepplewhite. The government had made great claims for the Agency, predicting that it would cut the cost of child maintenance previously borne by the taxpayer, speed up the process of ensuring child support, reduce the discretion which had previously lain with the courts in

[72] London: HMSO, 1988, paragraph 45.

the assessment of maintenance, achieve uniformity for children and improve the enforcement of parental obligations, which had proved notoriously difficult when the courts had made financial orders in children's favour. The first year of the Agency's operation proved disastrous, and led to widespread criticism in the media, allegations of wrongful identification of fathers, miscalculations of assessments and allegations by absent parents that Agency awards left them with inadequate resources even to travel to see the children they were supporting, or to maintain the children in their second families. In addition, the Agency failed to meet the savings target set by government. The Director, Mrs Hepplewhite, resigned, thereby taking responsibility for the Agency's initial failures. The minister responsible to Parliament was able to deflect responsibility onto the Agency head, on the basis that the Chief Executive was responsible for administration of the system, notwithstanding that the problems in administration were a direct consequence of the policy behind the Act and the formulation of the detailed rules for assessment which were provided in the Act. The government had set a performance target for the Agency, namely an annual saving to the Treasury of £530 million. In order to achieve the set target, the Agency focused on those absent parents (the vast majority of whom were fathers) who were identifiable through court records of divorce settlements or maintenance orders granted, rather than even-handedly seeking to identify all absent fathers, whether easily traceable or not. The Act itself, for which government and Parliament bore responsibility, caused the majority of the problems encountered by the Agency in attempting to carry out its work: the tacit if not overt acceptance that this was the case lay in the government's reform of the Act in 1995.

The other high-profile illustration is that of the Prison Service Agency, set up to administer the prisons and headed by Derek Lewis as Director-General. Lewis was appointed from outside the civil service. A prison break-out from the high-security Whitemoor prison operated as the catalyst for controversy over the issue of who was responsible for what, and the difficulties entailed in attempting to separate policy issues from administration. Following an official inquiry into the situation,[73] the

[73] Cm. 3020 (1995).

then Home Secretary, Michael Howard QC, sacked the Director-General, identifying the problems as 'operational' rather than matters of 'policy' for which the Home Secretary bore responsibility. In this, Howard was relying on a precedent set in 1984, when James Prior, then Secretary of State for Northern Ireland, made the same distinction between operational matters and policies, a distinction which for many fails to convince, but which enables ministers to evade their constitutional responsibility for the failure of a service under their control, while accepting that they alone remain 'accountable' to Parliament in the sense of being the only person able to address Parliament – through making ministerial statements and answering parliamentary questions.[74] In Derek Lewis's case, it was established that Michael Howard had intervened in operational matters, to the point of directing Lewis to dismiss the governor of Whitemoor prison. Following his departure, Lewis sued the Home Office for wrongful dismissal, and a settlement was reached which awarded him £12,500 compensation – yet the Home Secretary escaped unscathed.

Responsibility lies at the heart of democratic government, and where lines are drawn between policy and operation, responsibility and accountability, there is an inherent risk of a black hole appearing, in which neither the Chief Executive nor the minister is truly responsible for areas of administration – and their occasional failures. Chief Executives have an acknowledged role in policy formation: the 'framework documents' of agencies often refer to this policy function; the Chief Executive of the Employment Service, for example, may make proposals to the minister for 'changes in the policies and programmes operated by the agency', while the Benefits Agency is directed to 'contribute to the department's policy development', and the Chief Executive of the Prison Service is stated to be the 'government's principal adviser on prisons policy'. What matters to the citizen is a clear picture of responsibility, not arcane distinctions between administration and policy which leave him or her without redress. One of the principal functions of Members of Parliament has been to undertake inquiries on behalf of citizens *vis-à-vis* the administration: to be fobbed off with the excuse

---

[74] Heads of agencies may be called to give evidence before parliamentary Select Committees investigating a particular aspect of administration.

that this is a matter for the Chief Executive and not the relevant minister undermines confidence, and democratic accountability.

John Major's government and the civil service

When John Major succeeded Margaret Thatcher as Prime Minister in 1990 he continued the drive to greater efficiency in the provision of public services. Next Steps had had a relatively slow start in Mrs Thatcher's last two years in office, with only eight agencies being created in the first year of the programme. Under John Major, progress accelerated. In 1991 Major announced the Citizen's Charter, which set out the principles of public service that the public could expect from government, and was intended to provide an effective complaints system. The principles were listed as 'standards, information and openness, choice and consultation, courtesy and helpfulness, putting things right, and value for money'.[75] Public services, whether privatized utilities, such as gas, electricity and water, or government departments and Next Steps Agencies, were required to set targets and measure their own achievement against consumer satisfaction, thereby increasing their accountability to the consumer as well as their efficiency and effectiveness. Standards of excellence are awarded the Charter Mark, while failures are penalized by sanctions ranging from explanations and apologies to financial compensation. The Charter also presaged a further move towards the fragmentation of government services in pursuit of improved quality and lower costs. The Charter was followed later in 1991 by the government's White Paper, *Competing for Quality: Buying Better Public Services*.[76] Under Margaret Thatcher, local government reform had included the concept of 'contracting out' in order to improve standards and efficiency in the provision of local services. Whereas local authorities had formerly been the principal providers of services such as refuse-collection and so on, in future a local authority was under an obligation to put such services out to tender, and could continue to provide the service only if it could demonstrate that its provision was

---

[75] *The Citizen's Charter*, Cm. 1599 (London: HMSO, 1991).
[76] Cm. 1730 (1991).

more competitive than that of those outside companies who submitted tenders. Under John Major's government, this principle was extended to central government, leading to significant cuts in civil service numbers and a change in the character of public services. No longer would it be assumed that government departments would be the primary providers of services, rather their role would change substantially to being – where market-testing had established that a function could be provided more cost-effectively by the private sector – one responsible for contracting out services to the private sector and monitoring the economy, efficiency and effectiveness of service provision. In 1992 the government's stated objective was to have 25 per cent of departmental work carried out by outside bodies: within two years the contracting-out had led to the loss of some 27,000 civil service jobs.

Following the 1992 general election, the government established the Office of Public Services to take responsibility for Next Steps, the Citizen's Charter and market-testing (in considering contracting out), with representation in Cabinet, thereby emphasizing the government's commitment to further reform.[77] Next Steps and contracting-out did not represent the end of the government's quest for greater cost-effectiveness. In 1993 the government announced that in future all Next Steps agencies would review their work after a five-year period, with a view to evaluating whether the agency remained the most efficient vehicle for the delivery of services. Agencies were required to consider, first, whether their functions were still needed, or whether they could be abolished, secondly, if the work was still necessary, whether it should be provided by the agency, or whether market-testing and contracting-out was indicated, and finally whether, as an alternative, the agency's work would be more effective if the operation was privatized.

Complementing the Citizen's Charter, the last Conservative administration took tentative steps towards greater openness in the process of government. The 1993 White Paper, *Open Government*, declared that it was the government's intention to 'make government in the United Kingdom more open and accountable', and to restrict access to infor-

---

[77] In 1998 the Office of Public Service was merged with the Cabinet Office.

mation 'only where there are good reasons for so doing'.[78] The White Paper identified areas where the 'right to know' had to give way to secrecy: in relation to defence and national security; international relations; law enforcement and legal proceedings; internal opinion, discussion and advice; management of the economy and the collection of taxes; public authorities' commercial and negotiating interests; personal privacy; commercial confidentiality and information given in confidence. The accompanying *Code of Practice on Government Information*[79] came into force in 1994, and sought to extend access to official information, unless disclosure would be contrary to the public interest (i.e. relating to matters itemized above). Reasonable requests for information should be provided by government departments and other public bodies within a twenty-working-day period. If access to information is wrongly denied, complaints may be made to the Parliamentary Commissioner for Administration. However, laudable though the *Code* is, it did not confer on citizens a legal right to access to government files. Nevertheless, it was an attempt to balance the public interest – as defined by the government – of limiting openness with the public interest in access to government information, and the *Code* created a presumption in favour of disclosure to citizens, unless the harm likely to arise from disclosure would outweigh the public interest in making the information available.

The Blair government and the civil service

They really do say yes Prime Minister ... You have to learn a whole new language. You see they're not frankly in the habit of calling anything a good idea ... When they describe a proposal as 'ambitious', or even worse 'interesting', what they really mean is they think it's a stupid idea dreamed up at the last minute for your manifesto; when they describe it as 'challenging' they mean there's not a hope in hell of making it work; and most of all when they say a policy is 'really a very brave proposal Prime Minister' it sort of means they've got the doctors waiting outside to sign the certificate.[80]

[78] Cm. 2290 (1993), paragraph 1.7.
[79] Ibid., Annex A.   [80] Tony Blair, speaking on *Blair's Thousand Days*.

When the government entered into office in May 1997, it arrived not only with a radical mandate to reform the constitution, but also to improve efficiency in the civil service. In March 1999 the government published its White Paper on *Modernising Government*, described by Cabinet Secretary Sir Richard Wilson as 'a key document which signals a change of course for the Civil Service for the next ten years as important as Next Steps ten years ago'.[81] The aim, he said, was 'modernisation with a purpose: better policy making, better responsiveness to what people want, and more effective public services'. The White Paper proposed a range of reforms, including the commitment to make public services available on a twenty-four-hour, seven-days-a-week basis; removing unnecessary regulations and requiring departments that are preparing policies involving new regulations to submit Regulatory Impact Assessments, following consultation with the Cabinet Office; and creating greater incentives for civil servants, including considering financial rewards for staff who identify financial savings or service improvements. In Whitehall, all Permanent Secretaries were required to 'ensure that their Department has the capacity to drive through achievement of the key Government targets and to take a personal responsibility for ensuring that this happens'. To facilitate this the government called for the introduction of more people from outside the civil service. While the focus was on improved management and the delivery of service to the consumer, sight was not lost of the core civil service values. Selection and promotion were to remain based on merit, and political impartiality and the giving of best independent advice to government were to be maintained.

Five key commitments were presented in the White Paper. The first related to policy-making which was designed to 'deliver outcomes that matter' rather than simply reacting to short-term pressures. A new Centre for Management and Policy Studies was introduced to identify and spread best practice throughout the service. There was to be a refocus on the delivery of public services to ensure that services met the needs of citizens rather than of the service-providers: 'joined-up working' of departments to ensure that the citizen is not faced with

[81] Sir Richard Wilson, *The Civil Service in the New Millennium*, May 1999: see www.cabinet-office.gov.uk/1999/senior/rw_speech.htm

bureaucratic barriers to responsibility for services. To eliminate 'mediocrity' in government, all central and local government departments' services were to be reviewed over a five-year period to identify the best suppliers of services. All public bodies were set new targets for improving quality and effectiveness, and closer monitoring was to ensure the maintenance of quality. The government's information technology systems were to be geared to meeting the needs of citizens and business. A People's Panel, five thousand randomly selected individuals, was appointed to advise government on all aspects of the provision and delivery of services. Equality in the areas of gender, race and physical disability within the service has been highlighted. In 1999 only 18 per cent of senior civil servants were women, and 1.6 per cent from ethnic minority backgrounds. By 2004–5, the target is for 35 per cent women and 3.2 per cent from ethnic minorities, and targets are to be set for people with disabilities.

In January 2000 the Prime Minister's Performance and Innovation Unit's Report *Wiring It Up* reinforced the White Paper's aims on modernization while focusing on the need for departments to engage in closer co-operation over issues that cross departmental boundaries, and the introduction of bonuses and promotion for those who work on multi-faceted problems such as social deprivation, crime reduction, young people at risk and rural issues. In the Foreword to the Report, Tony Blair stated that '[M]any of the challenges facing government do not fit easily into traditional Whitehall structures', and that drug addiction, the criminal justice system and dealing with run-down areas all required a range of departments and agencies to work together.

As with previous programmes for reform of the civil service, Blair's modernizing agenda has come under criticism. Cost is one factor: the government wants to recruit more people from the private sector and to introduce early retirement schemes to encourage more civil servants to retire in their fifties rather than the usual retirement age of sixty, particularly those who are unlikely to reach the top of the service. Performance bonuses also cost money, and an estimated £100 million is needed to fund the changes. In order to improve management, experience outside the civil service has become a requirement, with the objective that by 2005 at least 65 per cent of civil servants will have experience in the private sector.

The recruitment from outside generated criticism from civil service unions that ministers could use the system to appoint their own supporters into the service, while the Conservative Party claimed that the reforms were mere 'window dressing' to avoid the issue of the increasing numbers of special advisers in Downing Street and Whitehall, which, in their view, suggested greater politicization of the service. This is an old jibe, a knee-jerk reaction, trundled out to gain political advantage via media space rather than an objective assessment. It is also one firmly denied by the architect of the new reforms, the Cabinet Secretary, Sir Richard Wilson, who insisted that it was 'a reform programme devised by the Civil Service, for the Civil Service and led by the Civil Service'.[82] The Labour government's second term of office began with a renewed commitment to achieving reforms in public services. Education and health were identified as the prime areas in need of reform and a vast injection of public money was promised. In large measure the immediate reorganization of government departments was geared to the delivery of improved public services.

[82] See *The Times*, 16 December 1999.

THE UNITED KINGDOM PARLIAMENT: WESTMINSTER

INTRODUCTION

In this chapter the role, functions and procedures of the United Kingdom Parliament are considered. In addition to the procedures which regulate Parliament, the relationship between the executive and Parliament as a whole is discussed in order to evaluate their respective powers and the balance of power between them. The role of ordinary Members of Parliament, having no ministerial or shadow ministerial role, is central to calling governments to account through the processes of scrutiny in the Commons. As will be seen, while numerous avenues for scrutiny exist, whether such measures are adequate is another question. The scrutiny of government proposals for legislation is carried out both by debate and through the Committee system in the House. Shortcomings in the process exist, and although repeated calls are made to improve the scrutiny mechanisms available to backbench members, these are generally resisted by governments intent on securing the passage of their proposals into law in the shortest possible time. The cumulative effect of parliamentary procedures and their weaknesses raises the question of whether it is the executive which controls Parliament, or Parliament which controls the executive.

Over the past twenty years, Parliament's role and the manner of its working has changed. Parliament's role is limited by membership of the European Community and Union which has law-making powers in relation to increasingly large areas. With devolution to regional assemblies, the administration of government is more diffused than hitherto, and the Westminster Parliament has relinquished law-making and administrative powers to the nations of Britain. As a result of these factors, Parliament's power and role have diminished, as has the public's interest in Parliament, a factor reflected in and exacerbated by decreased media coverage of Parliament's work.

THE STRUCTURE AND MEMBERSHIP OF PARLIAMENT

Parliament is bicameral: that is to say, there are two Houses of Parliament – the House of Commons and the House of Lords.

The House of Commons

The 'people's chamber' is the elected House of Commons, currently having 659 Members of Parliament each representing one of the 659 constituencies in the United Kingdom. There is no fixed term for the 'life' of a Parliament: but by law no Parliament may run longer than five years from the date of the last general election.[1] Members are elected to serve for the life of a Parliament, under the simple majority – or first past the post – voting system.[2] One consequence of this voting system is that a large number of Members are elected by a minority of those who vote, although once elected the Member is the representative of all his or her constituents regardless of how they voted.

The Commons is dominated by the two major political parties – Labour and Conservative – and a minority of Liberal Democrats, Ulster Unionists, Democratic Unionists and SDLP, Plaid Cymru, and Scottish Nationalists.[3] Proceedings are adversarial in character: the ruling party

[1] Parliament Act 1911.   [2] See Chapter 6.
[3] In the 1997 and 2001 general elections just one independent Member of Parliament was elected.

which makes up the government and its supporters in the House on the one side, all other parties making up the opposition on the other side, although only the second largest party, currently the Conservatives, forms Her Majesty's Loyal Opposition. Even in its seating arrangements the adversarial format is preserved. Unlike most other legislative bodies which sit in a semi-circle with blocks of party representatives sitting together, in the Commons the chamber is rectangular with government 'benches' facing opposition benches – the distance between them being that of two swords' length.

The House of Lords

The Second – or Upper – Chamber of Parliament is the House of Lords. The older of the two Houses of Parliament, the House of Lords until 1999 was comprised of a majority of unelected hereditary peers and a minority of unelected appointed life peers. As discussed further below, hereditary peers (until 1999) were entitled to sit in the House of Lords by the simple reason of birth into a titled family, and the title is automatically succeeded to by (usually) the eldest son of the deceased peer. Life peers, however, are appointed on the basis of having achieved some standing in society, and the peerage does not carry on beyond the death of the appointee. This unelected, undemocratic House – a remnant from medieval times – lies at the heart of government and, as will be discussed below, plays a vital role in the passage of law.

THE FUNCTIONS OF PARLIAMENT

In 1861 the liberal philosopher John Stuart Mill stated that Parliament was 'radically unfit' for the function of governing, and so it remains.[4] The task of governing is for the elected government of the day, not Parliament. Also writing in the nineteenth century, Walter Bagehot tells

---

[4] See J. S. Mill, *Representative Government*, 1865 (Indianapolis: Bobbs-Merrill, 1958), p. 99.

us that the Commons has firstly an *elective* function: 'it elects the people it likes. And it dismisses whom it likes too.'[5] The former part of this view certainly no longer holds true, but the second most certainly does. The Commons is 'elective' only in so far as the government of the day is drawn from Parliament – the personnel of government is thus provided from the membership of Parliament, both in the Commons (the majority) and the Lords. But control over the appointment of the Prime Minister and ministers is not for Parliament; that is down to the party in power which elects its leader who in turn, as Prime Minister, appoints ministers in the name of the Crown. In terms of the power of dismissal of governments, but not individual ministers, it is the Commons which dominates: any government losing the support of the House on a matter central to its political programme will be forced out of office, as was James Callaghan's Labour government in 1979. Second for Bagehot is the Commons' *expressive* function: 'its office [is] to express the mind of the English people on all matters which come before it.' Third comes the *teaching* function: '[i]t ought to teach the nation what it does not know.' Fourth, is the Commons' *informing* function, laying before the nation such 'grievances' and 'complaints' as come to light. And only then does Bagehot list the function of *legislating*, to be followed finally, and least significantly, by the *financial* function. More recently, Leo Amery advanced the view that 'The main task of Parliament is still what it was when first summoned, not to legislate or govern, but to secure full discussion and ventilation of all matters, legislative or administrative.'[6] To these functions must be added the *legitimating* function: every proposal for legislation must be endorsed by Parliament; government policy finds its expression and approval in Parliament and government administration is scrutinized in Parliament. The extent to which this is successful in controlling governments with a sound majority in Parliament is debatable and depends on the adequacy of procedural mechanisms and the zeal of Members.

It was once remarked that in the absence of a written constitution, the procedures in Parliament were the only guarantee of individual

---

[5] *The English Constitution*, 1867 (London: Fontana, 1993), p. 153.
[6] L. S. Amery, *Thoughts on the Constitution* (Oxford: Oxford University Press, 1947).

freedoms. There are three implications entailed in this assertion. First, that Parliament alone can create new law, and that, the House of Commons being both representative of the people and accountable to the people and also having the final say over the House of Lords in relation to the content of legislation, individual rights and freedoms will be guaranteed by Parliament. Secondly, and equally importantly, that Parliament as a whole is designed to scrutinize the workings of government and proposals for legislation, in other words to keep the executive branch of the state under the control of the representatives of the people. Thirdly, that Parliament as a whole, both Commons and Lords, is engaged in the process of interaction and communication with the people and interest groups outside Parliament who seek to bring matters to its attention. It is through the procedural mechanisms in place that these principal functions are served. How well they are served is a different question: numerous issues require consideration. The existence of the executive in Parliament raises the fundamental question of the nature of government in Britain.

Under most constitutions there is a clear separation of powers between the executive government and the legislature: the executive formulates policy, the legislature enacts or rejects those proposals.[7] In the United States of America, for example, the President and his Cabinet are strictly separated from Congress which enacts laws. A balance of power is secured by giving Congress and the President carefully defined powers in relation to legislation. One detrimental consequence of this separation can manifest itself in legislative deadlock when Congress is dominated by the party in opposition to the elected President. The American situation, however, does highlight the close fusion of powers between executive and legislature that exists in Britain, where the government is not only drawn from Parliament but also sits in Parliament. The natural question which flows from the close fusion, which Bagehot labelled the 'efficient secret of the English Constitution',[8] is whether the British system lends itself to governmental abuse through domination of the Commons, or whether there exist sufficient checks and balances in the system to ensure that government is 'under' rather than 'above' the law and the constitution. How is the British system of

---

[7] On separation of power see Chapter 1.   [8] Bagehot, *English Constitution*, p. 67.

government most accurately described? Is it a system of parliamentary government, Cabinet government or prime ministerial government?

THE LIFE OF A PARLIAMENT

Under the Parliament Act 1911 no Parliament may lawfully run for longer than five years, and a general election must be held to bring a new Parliament into being. Exceptionally, as during the First and Second World Wars, the life of a Parliament may be extended, but only with the agreement of both Houses and the Crown. While there is a legal limit to the length of a Parliament, there is, however, no fixed minimum term for which Parliament must sit. Control over the timing of general elections is in the hands of the Prime Minister who has the right to request the Crown to dissolve a Parliament for the purposes of calling an election. While the Crown retains, under the royal prerogative, the legal right to refuse a dissolution, by convention this does not happen, and as with so much of the British system doubts exist as to the real power of the Crown to do so.[9]

The flexibility of the life of Parliament in practice gives the Prime Minister a considerable political advantage over other parties, as he is able to get the governing party's election machinery and its electoral programme in good shape prior to seeking a dissolution. However, where a government has only a slim majority in Parliament, this flexibility can also have its disadvantages, and a government which loses the support of Parliament over a matter central to its policies may, through a vote of no confidence in the House, find itself forced to call a general election at a time when it least wishes to do so. There is a related problem in the event of a general election which results in no clear and outright winning party. The problem here relates to the power of the Crown to appoint the Prime Minister, and again the unwritten constitution offers no clear solutions, although precedents exist which suggest possible answers. While the usual scenario, one encouraged by the voting system for general elections, is that one party will win a

[9] See Chapter 1.

significant majority over all other parties, and therefore have the legitimate right to have its leader appointed Prime Minister by the Queen, occasionally there is no clear majority for any one party. Should the voting system be changed to one producing more proportionality between the votes cast and the number of seats won in Parliament, this problem could become a more regular feature in Britain, as it is in other countries employing a proportional voting system.[10]

THE MEETING OF PARLIAMENT

Parliament is required to meet each year. If it did not do so it would not be possible to legitimize the grant of money for government expenditure and costs relating to the maintenance of the armed forces which by law must be ratified by Parliament. The annual parliamentary session runs from approximately November to October, although most Members of Parliament enjoy long summer vacations and the House adjourns for three weeks at Christmas, a week at Easter and a further week for the spring bank holiday. Any uncompleted sessional business will be dealt with after the summer recess and before Parliament is formally prorogued and before the state opening of the next parliamentary session. Parliament is not a professional, full-time institution. The average session may have only 172 sitting days, although some sessions will be considerably longer and others rather shorter. Nor does Parliament operate a nine-to-five office day. On Mondays to Thursdays the main business of the House begins at 2.30 in the afternoon and often continues long into the night. The explanation for this seemingly haphazard state of affairs lies in history.

Being a Member of Parliament in the nineteenth century and earlier was very much a part-time, voluntary, unpaid occupation. It was also an upper- and middle-class institution: there were no working-class representatives in the Commons before the late nineteenth century,

[10] Forms of proportional representation have been introduced for the European parliamentary elections, elections to the Scottish Parliament, Welsh Assembly, Northern Ireland Assembly and Greater London Assembly elections.

and Members of Parliament (MPs) remained unsalaried until 1911. Those in employment elsewhere had to fulfil their duties in the mornings, or at times such as Christmas, Easter and the summer when Parliament was in recess. This arrangement also explains the low representation of women in the Commons. Having domestic and family duties and the care of children, as women still do despite the so-called age of equality, effectively makes it impossible for many women to stand for election. The highest number of women ever elected to Parliament was in the 1997 election which returned 120 women to Parliament – 18 per cent of all MPs.[11] Parliament remains very much 'one of the best male clubs in London': its working conditions and practices masculine, adversarial and biased in favour of male, white, middle-class MPs.

Proposals to regularize the working hours of the Commons have frequently been made and as frequently rejected. The Modernization Select Committee of the Commons proposed that the Commons move towards a more civilized timetable, but such suggestions are rejected as the majority of MPs cling to the discriminatory *status quo*. The perceived cost of making the Commons a full-time occupation would be the loss of those – and they are in an overwhelming majority – who have established careers outside the House. Far from being a detriment, the outside work of MPs, whether in the professions or other paid employment or on boards of directors of companies, is seen to be advantageous in keeping Members involved in the 'real world' outside Parliament. That this brings with it the problem of conflicts of interest between parliamentary duties and outside obligations is inevitable, but this is seen as a question of adequate regulation of Members' interests through registration of interests and appropriate declarations of interest when such actual or potential conflicts arise. As will be seen later, in the Major government of 1992–7 the difficulties and inadequacies of the system controlling outside interests led to serious allegations of 'sleaze' in Parliament and the consequent loss of esteem for Parliament among the general public.

[11] The Labour Party's attempt to force constituency parties to adopt women candidates in preference to men for the 1997 general election was declared unlawful by an industrial tribunal.

THE SPEAKER

In charge of proceedings in the Commons is the Speaker. Once elected (by the House itself) the Speaker abandons his or her party political allegiance to adopt a rigidly neutral stance in the regulation of the House, thereby enhancing the authority of the office. The Speaker controls parliamentary debates, choosing who will speak and monitoring the length of speeches. The Speaker can exercise disciplinary powers to control Members who are repetitious or obstructive or engage in any disorderly conduct. Any Member failing to comply with the Speaker's orders can be, first, formally 'named', and if the misconduct continues ordered to leave the House for the remainder of the day, and in the case of serious misconduct the House can order a Member to be suspended, without pay, for a period of days (usually five to ten), or ultimately for the remainder of the parliamentary session.

THE ORGANIZATION OF BUSINESS IN THE COMMONS

The government dictates the parliamentary timetable, with priority being given to the enactment of its policies into law, which in any session means that approximately 50 per cent of parliamentary time will be taken up with the scrutiny of legislation, and a further 25 per cent of time dictated by government business. However, much more besides goes on in the Commons on a daily basis, and the order of business for the following week is decided by the House at its Business Meeting on the preceding Thursday. The daily papers of the House announce the expected business of the day. The business of the day starts with prayers, at 2 p.m., other than on Wednesdays when business commences at 10 a.m.[12] There then follows ministerial (and on Wednesdays Prime Ministerial) Question Time, at which ministers, on a rota

---

[12] On Fridays during the session no normal business takes place, to enable Members to carry out their constituency work.

system, answer questions from Members about matters within their ministerial responsibility. These last no more than forty-five minutes. There are then opportunities for 'private notice questions' and emergency debates, both of which are rare and are granted only at the Speaker's discretion after an application is made by a Member.

On Tuesdays and Wednesdays there is also an opportunity for one Member to introduce a proposal for legislation.[13] The Member has ten minutes in which to propose the Bill, and opponents have equal time to speak against it. The matter is then voted on. Success for such proposals is rare, and depends on the acceptance of the government (which controls the legislative timetable) of the proposal being put forward. Nevertheless, the opportunity is popular and many Members will compete for the brief slot in which to raise their own, and their proposal's, public profile. If an issue of privilege or contempt of Parliament has arisen, this is debated at this stage. There then follows the major business of the day, one or more matters for debate, which may last until 10 p.m. Ten o'clock is the time at which the House should finish the business of the day, with the final proceeding being an 'adjournment debate'. However, this does not always occur. If a debate is still in progress at 10 p.m., the government may move a motion to suspend the rules preventing debate after 10 p.m. One day's notice is required to be given to the House for this to be effective. Where it happens, debate may run its natural course, often late into the night and occasionally through the night, which can cause the next day's business to be abandoned. If one sitting is still going on at the time at which the next day's sitting is due to start, the whole of that next day is lost. Examples of such sittings include a debate on the privatization of British Telecom in 1981 where debate lasted for twenty-five hours; in 1984 a debate on the Bill to abolish the Greater London Council lasted thirty-two hours.

[13] Under Standing Order No. 19, the Ten Minute rule Bill Motion.

PARTY ORGANIZATION IN THE COMMONS

Each of the major political parties in Parliament is organized for maximum effectiveness in either promoting or defending its policies (in the case of the governing party), or in opposing the government. The government is represented in the Commons by the Prime Minister, Cabinet ministers and other ministers outside Cabinet, government whips and the parliamentary private secretaries to ministers. Together this amounts to a hard core of government supporters in the Commons of about 120, although this may rise (as in 1994–5) to about 150. By law there are no more than 95 holders of ministerial office in the Commons.[14] The official opposition, the party with the second largest number of seats, is organized so as to present itself as an 'alternative' government. Accordingly the Leader of the Opposition will appoint a Shadow Cabinet and other shadow ministers who take responsibility for monitoring their opposite numbers in government with a view to ensuring full and open debate and scrutiny. The constitutional significance of the opposition is emphasized in its formal title Her Majesty's Loyal Opposition, and in the fact that public money is used to finance its duties in Parliament. In the Lords, although party organization is less rigorous, there is also representation on government and opposition lines. Some government ministers sit in the Lords, the Lord Chancellor being the most significant Cabinet member to do so. Equally, the opposition parties will have official spokesmen and -women in the Lords.

Central to disciplining Members, most notably in the Commons but to a lesser extent in the Lords, are the party 'whips'. The whips are appointed by the party to exercise disciplinary functions and to act as channels of communication between the party leadership and the backbench (i.e. non-ministerial) Members. On the government side, all whips are salaried. For the opposition there is a salaried Chief Whip and two salaried assistants, with up to a dozen non-salaried whips. The government Chief Whip, officially titled the Parliamentary Secretary to

[14] House of Commons Disqualification Act 1975; Ministerial and Other Salaries Act 1975.

the Treasury, is aided by around a dozen junior whips. The Chief Whip is responsible for organizing the daily business of the House and for nominating Members to sit on parliamentary committees (other than Select Committees, see below). The whips act as parliamentary sounding-boards: their work is crucial to ensuring that the government succeeds in its legislative programme by getting Members to vote, and also to picking up on dissent in the party and reporting this to the government. When the House 'divides' for a formal vote, the whips are responsible for ensuring that their Members are present in sufficient numbers to get a measure approved. Where attendance at a vote is mandatory, the parliamentary papers will be marked with a 'three line whip'; less vital votes will be marked with either a 'two line' or a 'one line' whip. Members who defy the whip system put their parliamentary careers in danger. To defy the party on a major issue, as eight Conservative MPs did in the last government over Europe, is to invite the leader of the party to remove the whip, thus leaving the Member without the support of the party. However, as Major found in his administration, removing the whip is a politically dangerous act, leaving a government with an already slim majority potentially without the support of a vital number of Members.

THE ROLE OF THE BACKBENCHER

The Member of Parliament without ministerial office, or without a portfolio in the Shadow Cabinet, is a 'backbencher'. He or she may be new to Parliament, or may have been in Parliament for many years without holding office. In 1999 MPs received an annual salary of £47,008, an annual office allowance of £50,264 and an 'additional costs allowance' of £12,984 per annum. In addition there are car (and bicycle) mileage allowances and expenses for travel on parliamentary business can be claimed. The House of Commons controls the salaries of its Members, voting for the level of increase.

The backbencher must balance his or her time between meeting the needs of the constituency and spending adequate time in Parliament on parliamentary duties, such as attending debates, Question Time, sitting on committees and voting. Friday is usually the day free of ordinary parliamentary duties, when most Members hold constituency surgeries. For many citizens the Member of Parliament is a first line of communication for complaints about government policies or the working of government departments. Where a complaint is made about a government department, the office of Parliamentary Commissioner for Administration is available to investigate and report. The Commissioner can act only *after* the matter had been raised with a Member of Parliament who then has discretion whether to attempt to resolve the issue him- or herself, or to pass the complaint to the Commissioner for formal inquiry and report. This 'filter' mechanism is subject to much criticism. Not only is the United Kingdom the only country to require complaints to go to the Commissioner through a Member of Parliament, but the requirement also diminishes public awareness of the role of the Commissioner. The Parliamentary Commissioner (Amendment) Bill 1999 would have removed the filter requirement but failed to pass in Parliament.

For the ambitious, or merely conscientious, backbench Member it is essential that he or she makes an impact in Parliament. For the government, depending on whether it has a safe majority and on the size of that majority, the support of the backbencher is needed to get its policies and legislative programme safely through the parliamentary session. Where, as currently, a government has a majority of some 170 in the Commons, the opportunities for the individual backbencher are naturally thin, whereas towards the end of Major's government when there was a bare majority of only two and all Members were thus crucial to the government's continued existence. From the point of view of the opposition, backbenchers are needed to add weight to the opposition's claims about government. From the perspective of the citizen, the Member of Parliament must be seen to be supporting the interests of the constituency, subject to the constraints of party policy. Where these interests conflict the Member of Parliament on the government side must be able to justify government policy to his constituents, thereby promoting interaction between government and the governed and consolidating government support in the constituency. Also important from the citizen's perspective is the manner in which Parliament as a whole – both Commons and Lords, but principally Commons –

exercises its functions of scrutiny and control of government, whether in terms of legislation or administration, to ensure that the government operates under the law and according to accepted conventional rules. How these competing demands can be met is best considered via the procedures in Parliament.

Backbench procedures in the Commons

Participation in debate on the floor (in the Chamber) of the Commons is much sought after. The Speaker controls debates, and will call Members to speak in a predetermined order, notice having been given to him or her of the wish to participate. The rights of members of the government, official opposition and minority parties are respected. It is axiomatic, however, that time is short and the number of potential participants in debate large.

As noted above, Question Time is a daily opportunity (except on Fridays) to question members of government directly. This event, the most publicized of all parliamentary proceedings, ensures that ministers, including the Prime Minister, face the Commons as a whole and defend the government against criticism. Aside from the Prime Minister, who faces questions on Wednesdays for thirty minutes, each minister in charge of a department appears according to a rota and in general addresses the Commons once a month. In any one parliamentary session, but depending on its length, some 40,000 questions may be raised. Each receives either an oral or written reply and the questions and answers become a matter of public record through the daily reporting of Parliament in its official journal Hansard.

Questions to ministers may only concern matters directly within his or her departmental responsibility. By convention only backbench Members put questions. Notice must be given in advance, to the Table Office of the Commons, which ensures both that the minister has adequate time to prepare an answer and that questions are not stale by the time they come up for answer. A number of restrictions limit the effectiveness of Question Time. The first relates to the question of direct responsibility. As noted in the previous chapter, one feature of government over the past two decades is the establishment of executive agencies to undertake the work formerly carried out by government departments. Where an agency has been established, it will be headed by an Executive Director who is responsible for administration. Accordingly, while a minister may face parliamentary questions concerning the policy underlying the system, he or she need not answer for any operational matters within the Executive's remit. Two examples of this fragmentation of responsibility are seen in relation to both the Metropolitan Police and the prison service. In relation to the Metropolitan Police, the Home Secretary has certain powers in appointments, funding and government policies with regard to policing, but has no power to control operational police matters which are the responsibility of the Police Commissioner. In relation to the Prison Service, the Home Secretary has responsibilities in the funding and provision of prisons, and more generally issuing sentencing guidelines which affect the prison population, but he or she has no control over operational aspects of the prison service. Accordingly, when as in the 1980s and 1990s it was discovered that there had been escapes by terrorists from prisons and that drugs and weapons had been found in prisons, the respective Home Secretary, faced with parliamentary questions, was able to avoid responsibility to Parliament by stating that these were 'operational matters' outside his control and the responsibility of the relevant prison governor.

Immunity from questioning is also provided by the conventional rules which dictate that certain matters are not for questioning in Parliament. These rules ensure that there is blanket protection for ministers. The list is long. Among the least controversial, perhaps, are matters relating to diplomacy and international relations, defence and arms sales, national security, advice given to ministers by officials and commercial confidences. Less convincing are those listed by *Erskine May*[15] as including 'defence contract prices, forecasts of future levels of unemployment, government borrowing, tax affairs of individuals or companies, forecasts of overseas aid, telephone tapping . . . and details of the arrangement of government business'. There is also an exempted category which relates to answers which could only be secured at

[15] The parliamentary 'bible', *Parliamentary Practice* (London: Butterworth, 22nd edn., 1997).

'disproportionate cost' to the department concerned. Other than these wide-ranging exclusions, a Member can expect an answer.

If a matter of public interest of an urgent nature is raised it is possible for a Member to ask a Private Notice Question (PNQ). These may only be asked via the Speaker who has a discretion to allow them. PNQs allow the notice requirement for ordinary questions to be avoided. Few requests are granted, mainly because the ordinary question procedure is adequate, or because the question is deemed not sufficiently important to disrupt the rest of the day's business. On the rare occasions, once or twice a year, that permission is granted, the question will be put directly after normal Question Time. Emergency debates may also be requested of the Speaker, enabling, if granted, an early debate about an urgent matter, and may last on average up to three hours (although this is extendable). One curious device available to Members is the Early Day Motion (EDM). Translated, this is a request for a debate at an early day. Devised in the nineteenth century, the EDM is a written form of request to the government to allow time for discussion of a particular matter. Unlike other procedures which have carefully controlled timing, the EDM is available to Members throughout a parliamentary session. A Member, with supporters for his or her request, will, in parliamentary language and in less than 250 words, make the request for a debate on any matter whatsoever. The request made, the EDM will remain to enable other Members to add their support. Success for EDMs is rare, but on occasion these generate such large numbers of supporters that they represent a very real pressure on government to allow parliamentary time for discussion. Occasionally, dramatic developments follow. In the 1978–9 session, for example, the then leader of the opposition, Margaret Thatcher, put down an EDM which resulted in the government's ultimate defeat in a confidence vote and its resignation. Less spectacular, but noteworthy, was an EDM put down in 1988 in relation to an Education Reform Bill. Two senior members of government opposed their own government's policy over the abolition of the Inner London Education Authority. The motion having attracted support from more than 120 Conservative backbenchers, the Secretary of State amended the Bill. In any one session the EDM provides a tangible weathervane of opinion in the House which conveys to the party whips and party leadership the concerns of Members.

SCRUTINIZING GOVERNMENT ADMINISTRATION

Scrutinizing the work of government departments is one method through which a backbencher can make a significant contribution to Parliament and the public. Select Committees are the most important mechanism for involvement in this process. Select Committees come in various forms. Some relate to the working of the Commons itself. Examples include the Procedure Committee which keeps procedures under review and recommends reforms to the Commons, and the Committee of Standards and Privileges which dates from the seventeenth century. Other *ad hoc* Select Committees may be set to investigate matters of current and particular concern. There is also the important Committee on Public Accounts which investigates expenditure in departments and evaluates whether departments are providing value for money.

Most important are the departmentally related Committees. These were reorganized in 1979 to provide a more rational and extensive system of scrutiny. Each major department of state has a related committee: Agriculture, Defence, Education, Employment and so on through to the Treasury and Civil Service Committee and Welsh Affairs Committee. A Liaison Committee, itself a Select Committee, exists to ensure a rational separation of work between the committees. The terms of reference of Select Committees are to 'examine the expenditure, administration and policy' of the departments and any public bodies associated with them. Most Committees have a membership of eleven, although the Northern Ireland Committee has thirteen. While membership reflects the party political strength in the Commons overall, thus giving a government with a healthy majority an advantage over other parties, the chairperson is not necessarily a government member: that is a matter for negotiation between the major parties. The proceedings in Select Committees also differ from the floor of the House in that they are not adversarial: members are there to carry out an impartial examination of the work of a department and to produce, wherever possible, a unanimous report for the consideration of the Commons as a whole.

Select Committees can appoint specialist advisers, and call for witnesses and for documentary evidence from the department concerned.

No one can dictate to the Committee which aspect of a department's work it will investigate. Governments have repeatedly undertaken to co-operate with Committees, although it is evident that on occasion this co-operation breaks down. Two factors come into play. The first is the occasional ministerial reluctance to provide the Committee with the information it seeks. Notoriously this happened in 1988 when the then junior Health Minister, Edwina Currie, refused to attend Committee to answer questions over the contamination in eggs by the salmonella virus. Her defence was that she had nothing further to add to what was already known. Earlier in the 1986 Westland Helicopter rescue saga, three Select Committees inquired into the matter. The government refused to allow civil servants from the Department of Trade and Industry to appear before the Defence Select Committee. In 1992 the arms to Iraq affair gave rise to similar concerns. When ministers were questioned by Committee, the answers given were found – retrospectively and by an inquiry headed by a senior judge – to have been less than full and frank. While Select Committees may summon ministers and other Members of Parliament to attend hearings, they cannot compel attendance: only an order of the Commons itself can do that.[16]

THE PASSAGE OF LEGISLATION

In an average parliamentary session some fifty Bills will be passed into law. Many but not all of these will have been announced in the Queen's Speech which details the government's intentions for the coming year. In order for a proposal to become law it must follow a number of stages through the Commons before going to the House of Lords for similar scrutiny and ultimately for the Royal Assent. Some Bills also start their life in the Lords where the procedure, with minor differences, reflects that of the Commons. In any one session, legislation will occupy about half the time of the Commons. Here an outline of the process is given to show how effectively Parliament monitors proposals for legislation.

[16] See the discussion on ministerial responsibility in Chapter 1.

The origins of Bills

While the majority of Bills before Parliament will arise from government proposals, and will have been listed in the Queen's Speech at the start of the session, many others have different sources. Members of Parliament themselves may introduce Private Members' Bills, although these have little chance of success unless the government is prepared to make parliamentary time available for their consideration. This is, however, a useful process, and occasionally a Member will introduce a Bill – an example is the Abortion Bill 1967 which became law – which the government is not opposed to as such, but which, because of its controversial nature, it is unwilling to be seen to be promoting. Also, a Member will occasionally introduce a Bill which captures the mood of the public and Parliament and results in unexpected success: an example of this is the Private Members' Bill to remove solicitors' monopoly over conveyancing. Proposals for legislation also come from the Law Commission, the standing body under a statutory duty to keep the law under review and recommend reforms. Most notably, the Law Commission has overhauled much of the law relating to the family over the past two decades, leading to reforms in relation to child law, divorce and domestic violence. Sometimes legislation is proposed and passed to deal with unforeseen circumstances which are perceived to demand immediate attention. Examples include the Official Secrets Act 1911, passed within twenty-four hours in order to deal with the perceived threat of German spies in the country before the First World War. The Prevention of Terrorism (Temporary Provisions) Act 1974 was passed to enhance police powers in relation to suspected terrorists, following the bombing of a pub in Birmingham that year. The Dangerous Dogs Act 1991 was rapidly passed to deal with the growing problem of certain types of dog savaging children and others. More recently, in response to the shootings at a primary school at Dunblane, Scotland, the Firearms Act was passed, making British law the most stringent in Europe in relation to gun control.[17]

---

[17] See also the Anti-Terrorism, Crime and Security Act 2001.

Getting a Bill through Parliament

The start of the process is the First Reading. This is entirely a formality, with notice being given to the Commons that a Bill is about to come before it. A date is then set for the all-important Second Reading. On the date set, the Bill will be considered by the Commons as a whole. The objective at this stage is not to examine every detail and aspect of the Bill but to discuss the principles and policies underlying it. This is the first formal occasion on which a proposal may be tested for support: the relevant minister must not only defend the Bill, but also demonstrate to the satisfaction of the House that the Bill deserves support. Of course, where (as currently) the government has a large majority, the prospect of successfully opposing a Bill is slight. Conversely any government with a slim majority knows that its Bills are vulnerable to attack. Any Bill which fails to pass this stage is lost for that parliamentary session and must start life afresh in the next, if the government thinks that it will have more success.

Once a Bill has survived its Second Reading it stands 'committed' to a Standing Committee. This is the stage at which the Bill is theoretically subjected to detailed scrutiny. In the process of scrutiny amendments may be suggested to improve a Bill. In theory the Committee will consider it from its first to its last clause in order to ensure that the Bill which emerges is in the best possible form. The reality, however, is very different and there are a number of defects in Standing Committee proceedings. The first difficulty lies in the nature and composition of the Committee. 'Standing Committee' is a misnomer: it suggests that the Committee is formed at the start of the Parliament and lasts until the next general election, thereby bringing continuity and expertise to the scrutiny of Bills. This is far from being the case: Standing Committees are *ad hoc*, in that they are formed to consider a particular Bill and then disbanded. The membership of the Committee is drawn from Members of Parliament in direct proportion to party political strengths in the Commons. Again, a government with a sound majority will be at an advantage. There is also a problem of expertise. Many Bills are long and complex and in addition may confer powers on ministers or local authorities to draw up detailed supplementary rules which will later become law. The Bill before the Committee is therefore not a full reflection of the law which will ultimately emerge. Members are appointed where possible on the basis of their expertise, but the number of members of a Committee varies between sixteen and fifty, so expertise cannot be the sole criterion for selection. Appointment to Standing Committees is in the hands of the party whips whose task it is to select Committee members best suited to scrutinize the Bill in question.

It is the minister in charge of the Bill who is responsible for steering it successfully through Committee. This raises the difficulty of an imbalance in expertise between the defending minister, backed by his civil servants, and members of the Committee, a problem which is exacerbated by the lack of power of Standing Committees (unlike Select Committees in this respect) to appoint specialists and call witnesses and for further documentation. Despite many calls from reformers, including the Procedure Committee of the House and the Study of Parliament Group, for Standing Committees to operate more like Select Committees in order to enhance the scrutiny of Bills, and despite the House itself ruling that Special Standing Committees should have preliminary sittings where evidence could be taken in a nonadversarial manner before reverting to the normal adversarial scrutiny process, in nearly twenty years only five Bills have been dealt with in this way. The basic problems are the tight control over the legislative timetable, and the shortness of many parliamentary sessions into which scrutiny of all Bills before the House must be squeezed.

Compounding the difficulties under which Standing Committees operate is the lack of automatic timetabling of Bills and the ability of the government to propose that scrutiny time be limited. Automatic timetabling, which has also been proposed many times, is the logical way to proceed: it ensures adequate time for inquiry without enabling a Committee to delay matters unduly. But governments and Members have consistently opposed such a reform, on the basis that it might unduly inhibit investigation. The sceptic might suggest that it might unduly disadvantage government by ensuring adequate scrutiny. Where the government considers that its programme for legislation is under pressure of time, it is possible to limit the amount of remaining time available for Committee stage. The most controversial manner in which this can be done is through the Allocation of Time Motion, colloquially called the guillotine motion. This is a device which government can use to propose to the Commons that the remaining consideration of a Bill be timetabled. The motion is put to the Commons, a debate follows, then a vote is taken. If the government has a sound majority, it is unlikely that it will lose such a vote. Thereafter the business managers of the House can impose strict deadlines on the remaining stages of consideration of the Bill. The guillotine can be applied for at any stage of a Bill and once agreed can limit time at any stage. Second Reading, Committee, Report and Third Reading (see below) can all be timetabled. The effect of this can be dramatic, with a Bill emerging from Standing Committee with much of it not considered at all. Given that the Third Reading and Report are both usually formal and brief proceedings, one consequence of the guillotine is that any further detailed scrutiny can only be carried out in the House of Lords.

Report stage and Third Reading

When the Bill emerges from Committee it is reported back to the House, having been reprinted with any amendments agreed to. Generally little or no debate takes place, although on occasion there may be a lengthy debate on a controversial Bill. Once through Report, the Bill is read a third time, only minor grammatical amendments being made, and is sent to the House of Lords for consideration.

NATIONAL FINANCE

The Crown demands, the Commons authorizes: this is the constitutional settlement which emerged from the seventeenth-century conflicts between Crown and Parliament over finance. No taxation may be levied on citizens without parliamentary approval, and any attempt by a public body to raise revenue without such approval is unlawful.[18]

[18] e.g. *Attorney General v. Wilts United Dairies Ltd.* (1921) 37 TLR 884; *Congreve v. Home Office* [1976] QB 629.

However, there are limits to Parliament's effectiveness in scrutinizing government programmes of taxation, borrowing and expenditure. The government's annual Budget is put to the Commons in the spring. This is the moment when rates of direct and indirect taxation are announced for the coming year. The Budget provision must be incorporated into the annual Finance Bill, although opportunities for its amendment are slim, given that it is the most carefully calculated of all government proposals. Between the presentation of the Budget, which may introduce almost immediate increases in taxation, and the passage of the Finance Bill, the raising of taxation is legitimized by 'ways and means resolutions' voted in the Commons. Revenue raised by government through borrowing follows protracted negotiations between government departments for their share, but largely escapes parliamentary scrutiny. Some government expenditure does not require parliamentary approval. Issues which could prove constitutionally contentious – such as the Civil List which finances the public work of the monarchy, judges' salaries and moneys needed for Europe – are not subject to debate but are merely set against the Consolidated Fund, which as a whole is approved annually by Parliament.

Opportunities to scrutinize the actual expenditure of government departments are rather better. The Public Accounts Committee of the Commons, formed in 1861, has considerable clout. Working on data provided by the inquiries of the Comptroller and Auditor General, head of the National Audit Office, the Public Accounts Committee issues reports to the House. The chair of the Committee, which has a membership of fifteen, is by convention a member of the opposition. One day per parliamentary session is set aside for debate on the Committee's reports. The Comptroller and Auditor General is independent of government, the office being established under the National Audit Act 1983. He is an officer of the House of Commons, appointed by the Crown. The Comptroller conducts investigations into the 'economy, efficiency and effectiveness' of government departments' spending and issues Value for Money Reports. Within the Commission's remit are local authorities and the National Health Service which between them spend around £100 billion a year, or 15 per cent of the nation's gross domestic product. Over 13,000 bodies fall for scrutiny by the Commission. The Audit Commission operates independently from government, and is self-financing with its income deriving largely from fees charged to local authority and National Health Service bodies for audit work.

THE HOUSE OF LORDS

One of the most extraordinary features of British government is the existence of a legislative chamber which is unelected. The House of Lords, older even than the House of Commons, plays a significant, if ultimately subordinate, role in the passing of Acts of Parliament. For centuries the Lords remained staffed by hereditary peers, who possessed no necessary qualification other than the right to succeed on the death of a father. Archbishops and bishops of the Church of England, twenty-six in all, also sit in the Lords, remnants of the power of the established Church. Judges also play their role, with up to twenty-eight senior judges entitled to exercise not only their judicial functions in the highest domestic court of appeal, but also legislative functions. The most senior of these judges is the Lord Chancellor – a member of the Cabinet and head of the judiciary – who presides over the House as its Speaker, and also represents the government of the day.[19]

The House has undergone significant reforms over the years, but until very recently none which went to the heart of the problem of its domination by hereditary peers. In 1958 the membership of the Lords was reinvigorated by the introduction of life peers under the Life Peerages Age 1958; life peers being appointed by the Crown on the advice of the Prime Minister. In total the membership of the Lords was almost more than double that of the Commons, although in practice daily attendance in the Lords rarely exceeds 400. In 1998 there were 759 hereditary peers, out of a total membership of 1,273, the balance comprising 462 life peers, 26 archbishops and bishops, and 26 judges. As seen below, in 1999 this composition changed, with all but ninety-two of the hereditaries being removed from the House. The composition of

---

[19] The office of Lord Chancellor straddles the three major institutions of the state: the executive, the judiciary and the legislature, contrary to the doctrine of separation of powers discussed in Chapter 1.

the House of Lords has been criticized for decades. How, it is asked, can it be acceptable that a democratic state has at the heart of its legislature people who are not elected to their seats and are accordingly unaccountable to the people? Inherited titles offend democratic principles, and offer no guarantee of the fitness of the title-holder to a role in making law and indirectly governing the country. Nor are life peers less objectionable in principle, with the system of appointment rigorously under the control of the Prime Minister of the day, thus giving him or her an immense power of patronage and the ability to alter the balance of party political power in the Lords to the government's advantage: a power which is subject to reform. The question of hereditary peers in the Lords is an issue which the Labour government elected in 1997 set about reforming, although, as will be seen later, the shape the reforms are finally to take is by no means clear or uncontroversial.

The House of Lords does not 'represent' the people, in the sense that it has a mandate from the people. The hereditary peers exist by virtue of their birth into the aristocracy; life peers by virtue of their contribution to various fields of public life (the great and the good); the archbishops and bishops represent the established Church of England; the judges the elite of the still male-dominated, white, public-school-educated legal profession. Before reform, of the hereditaries only sixteen women sat in the Lords, while of the life peers some eighty were women. The bishops and judges are all male. However, while from the perspective of democracy this composition is offensive, it is not determinative of the quality of the work done in the Lords. Paradoxically, it will be seen that in practice very real advantages flow from this anomalous body: the very lack of accountability to the electorate or to the government of the day lends the Lords an independence which no elected body could enjoy. This independence can lead and frequently has led to governments being forced to revise legislative proposals according to the House of Lords' demands in order to get its Bills through Parliament without delay, although under the relevant legislation the Commons has the ultimate right of veto over the Lords.

Membership of the Lords is unsalaried, a daily attendance allowance and expenses only being payable. This continues the British habit of amateurism at the heart of the system, depending on the willingness of members to attend and exercise their functions. While the House overall, until the 1999 reforms, had a membership of over 1,200 (the majority being hereditary peers), average attendance varies between 300 and 400 peers. Some peers have a high attendance record and are rightly regarded as 'working peers'. However, many attend only when summoned by government to vote. These are the 'backwoodsmen': largely Conservative Party supporters and landowners. The use by Conservative governments of the power to summon the backwoodsmen to ensure the passage of its legislative proposals is the most offensive aspect of the way the Lords has worked for centuries: peers with little or no interest in the working of Parliament turn up on demand to secure success for a Conservative government. It has been this political imbalance, the product of history, which is the greatest threat to a democratic system. For Labour governments, duly elected by the people, may find their programme of legislation delayed, amended and ultimately defeated by the unelected and mainly politically opposed Lords. Small wonder that the Labour Party viewed the Lords as hostile to its objectives.

This system has endured for 800 years. Attempts have long been made to reform this anomalous and undemocratic chamber, and back in 1911 the Parliament Act of that year envisaged, in its *Preamble*, that the House would be reformed to an elected House. As noted above, in 1958, in order to breathe new life into the near-moribund House, the Life Peerages Act enabled the Crown, on the advice of the Prime Minister, to appoint to the House individuals, often former members of government, who had played a significant role in public life. In 1968 reform proposals put forward by the then Labour government nearly succeeded, but ultimately failed over a quite unrelated matter. The 1968 reform would have produced a House with a two-tier membership of voting and non-voting peers, the right to vote being linked to attendance requirements. Over thirty years later, as will be seen below, reform has finally occurred. Not that this ends the controversy over the Lords: reform is to take place in two phases, the first to eliminate the right of the vast majority of hereditary peers to attend, the second still to be decided.[20] In the interim, the Lords is no more democratic than before. Its members are a minority of hereditary peers who survive until the second phase is reached, the remainder being political appointees.

[20] The government's White Paper of 2001, Cmd. 5291, sets out the options.

The functions of the House of Lords

Before looking at the advantages and disadvantages of the reformed House of Lords it is useful to consider its functions and powers. The major functions of the House lie in scrutinizing, amending and approving law-making proposals which have been passed by the Commons. Bills may also start their legislative passage in the Lords, a useful device for relieving the hard-pressed Commons. The powers of the Lords are limited by the Parliament Acts 1911 and 1949. These Acts provide that in relation to Money Bills (those Bills solely concerned with finance), the House of Lords must approve the Bills within one month. In relation to other Bills, which are the vast majority, the Lords may delay a Bill for up to twelve months over two parliamentary sessions, suggesting and negotiating amendments to the Bill. After this period, if the Lords has rejected a Bill twice, or amended it in a manner unsatisfactory to the Commons (which is the same thing), the government may employ the Parliament Acts to overcome House of Lords' opposition and go straight for the royal assent, which is the final requirement for making a Bill an Act of Parliament.

The Lords is also a debating chamber. Less controlled by the party whip system than the Commons, the Lords have greater individual freedom. This freedom is also enhanced by the fact that members of the Lords, whether hereditary or appointed, are unelected, and do not hold their seats at the mercy of government. Once appointed, a member's position is secure. Whereas, in the Commons, time on the floor of the House is largely controlled by the government of the day, and dominated by the government's need to get its legislative programme through Parliament within the annual session, the Lords' time, while still restricted by legislative scrutiny, is less dictated by government need than by the Lords' perception of matters of public interest which require debate. Government may find a particular issue morally sensitive or best avoided because of the political consequences. The Lords, politically unaccountable to an electorate, have no such qualms: issues that are 'unpopular' (with government) or controversial matters such as euthanasia, abortion, embryo experimentation, poverty and welfare, housing and employment may get a better airing in the

Lords than the Commons. The House of Lords also plays a role in the scrutiny of government, and in the scrutiny of European legislation and delegated legislation.

Irrespective of its membership, a second chamber is a vital institution. Not only does the Lords enable issues to be aired in a less partisan atmosphere than in the Commons, with the opportunity to delay proposals and to heighten public awareness of issues, but it also gives government a chance for second thoughts over proposals, and an opportunity to introduce amendments at the Lords stage which were not introduced in the Commons. The Commons is not, and has never been, a full-time professional body. The sheer weight of legislation and the pressure on parliamentary time dictates that a second chamber is essential. Only wholesale reform of the Commons and its procedures could eliminate the need for a second chamber, and even then a second chamber would remain desirable as a forum in which alternative views may be expressed and legislative proposals improved.

The balance of power between Lords and Commons

Until 1911 the relationship between the two Houses was regulated by conventions, the principal rule being that the Commons was sovereign over matters of finance. However, conflict arose in 1908 over the Liberal government's budget, which the Lords rejected. Two general elections later, and under threat from the King to create sufficient new peers sympathetic to the government, the Lords accepted the demands of the Commons. The government's reaction was swift. The Parliament Act 1911 was passed, with the consent of the Lords, to eliminate any further abuse of the convention by the Lords. Over money Bills – which must deal solely with financial matters – the Lords have one month in which to examine the Bill, but have no right to reject it. As for other Bills, these could originally be delayed by the Lords for up to three parliamentary sessions, with a minimum of two years passing in the interim. The Parliament Act 1949, itself passed under the Parliament Act procedure, cut this delay to two sessions, or just over a year in practice. Once the one-year period expires, the Commons may bypass the Lords and go straight for the royal assent (which itself is an automatic process, not involving the Queen personally), which brings the statute into force.

The Bills which have been passed under the Parliament Act procedures are exceptional rather than routine. The reason the Acts have not been used more widely lies in the rules regulating relations between the two Houses, neatly called the 'ping pong'. When disagreement arises between Lords and Commons, a Bill which has been amended by the Lords (as is their right) returns to the Commons for reconsideration. It may be that amendments have been proposed by the government itself when the Bill reaches the Lords, perhaps as a result of disquiet expressed in the Commons, or a reappraisal of the wisdom of a proposed measure. Lords' amendments may also be acceptable to the government as a compromise measure to ensure the safe passage of a Bill. Here the Lords may succeed on one or more issues, to which the government accedes rather than lose the Bill as a whole. While the Parliament Acts ended the potential abuse of convention and unconstitutional behaviour on the part of the Lords, in practice the Acts have been little used. In 1914 two Bills were passed under the Act, the first relating to Irish Home Rule which remained unimplemented, the second disestablishing the Church of Wales. To get the Parliament Act 1949 on to the statute book, the procedure was again invoked. It was not until 1991 that the Acts were used, in relation to the War Crimes Bill. This controversial legislation permitted the prosecution of persons suspected of committing war crimes during the Second World War. It was retrospective in nature, and, given the likely age of any defendants put on trial and that of any necessary witnesses, met with profound objections in the Lords. The Lords twice defeated the Bill at Second Reading stage, and the Parliament Act procedure came into play.

The Acts were again used in relation to the 1998 European Parliamentary Elections Bill. Here the Lords engaged in a defiant exercise of brinkmanship, knowing that their days were numbered. The constitutionality of their actions was questionable, although there is little doubt that there were genuine and real concerns over the proposed changes. The government intended to introduce a 'closed list', proportionally representative voting system for elections to the European Parliament, which were scheduled for June 1999. The Bill had been promised in the Labour Party's election manifesto, and accordingly was subject to the 'Salisbury convention', namely that the Lords could not defeat a measure which had formed part of the electoral manifesto and thus had democratic legitimacy. In order for the system to be in place in time, it was essential to get the Bill through Parliament, at the very latest by January 1999, although the government had expected to get it through by the end of the 1997–8 session.

The actual voting system employed for European elections is discussed in Chapter 6. The Lords' objections to the Bill centred on the fact that for the first time the government intended to use the 'closed list', a system which gives to the political parties, rather than the voters, the right to choose which successful candidates will be elected, and in which order. As a result, the voter could choose which party he or she supported, but not the actual candidate standing for the party he or she preferred. It was to this power of party patronage that the Lords took principled objection. Five times the Bill went back and forth between the Commons and Lords, with the Lords insisting on introducing amendments unacceptable to the government. Here the Conservative opposition used its majority of supporters in the Lords to its fullest effect, threatening the rejection of a Bill which had been mandated, and thus flouting the Salisbury convention. When it was clear that the Bill could not get through in the remaining one day of parliamentary time, it was withdrawn, to be immediately reintroduced in the new session. Again the Lords rejected the closed list, whereupon the government invoked the Parliament Acts and forced the Bill through without the Lords.

Since a Bill which fails to pass in one session is then 'lost' and has to be reintroduced in the next session, it is axiomatic that the power of the Lords to delay legislation in order to force concessions from the government is at its highest towards the end of a parliamentary session. The end of the 1998–9 session illustrates this clearly, although that session had the added ingredient of the House of Lords Reform Bill which removed the right of most hereditary peers to sit in the Lords, and this added piquancy to the situation. The date for Parliament's prorogation, which signals the end of a session, was set for Thursday, 11 November, extendable only to Friday the 12th. Still in the parliamentary machinery, and needing the royal assent by the end of the week, were the Immigration and Asylum Bill, the Greater London Authority Bill, the Food Standards Bill, the Welfare Reform Bill and the House of

Lords Bill. It was the Welfare Reform Bill which proved the most contentious, both in the Commons (where fifty-four Labour Members of Parliament defied the government) and the Lords. In the Lords amendments had been pressed and concessions made by the government. The government was determined not to make further concessions to the Lords, and warned the Lords that they had reached the limit of their constitutional legitimacy in defying the Commons. Given that the House of Lords Bill also remained in Parliament, the government made it clear, through Baroness Jay, the government Leader in the Lords, that the House of Lords Bill would be the last to be passed. Given that the Bill had been amended by the government to allow ninety-two hereditary peers to remain in the House in the interim reform period, the threat was clear: that amendment would be removed and all hereditaries ejected from the Lords unless the Lords backed down over welfare reform measures. This they did at the last minute, but not before forcing the Bill back a third time for consideration, after which they gave way, in line with the Salisbury convention.

Arguments for and against reform of the Lords

The very tenacity of the Lords, until the 1999 reforms, itself implies that reform has proved problematic. Few, other than die-hard, rose-tinted-spectacled traditionalists, would deny that a second legislative chamber comprising a majority of Conservative-supporting hereditary peers is an affront to democracy. The problem, however, has been less a principled debate over either the value of the Lords (however made up) or the hereditary principle, but more what form of chamber should replace the Lords, and the constitutional implications this would have *vis-à-vis* the relationship between the two Houses. At root, reform of the Lords has foundered on the question of the balance of power between Lords and Commons: a democratically elected Lords would pose a threat to the supremacy of the Commons; a continuance of the *status quo* would be democratically unacceptable. Traditionalists opposed to reform have naturally obfuscated the issue. It has been claimed that a threat to the hereditary peers in the Lords amounts to a threat to the monarchy. This argument cannot be sustained. True, the British monarchy is hereditary, but in practical terms the monarch is the politically neutral head of state whose role is largely ceremonial, who symbolizes some sort of continuous national identity and who represents Britain overseas, principally in Commonwealth countries and on formal state occasions. What the monarch does not do is participate in the law-making process, in a manner which has the capacity to defeat, albeit on relatively rare occasions, the mandated policy of the democratically elected government of the day. Heredity as such, and the role of the Crown, is not the issue. The issue is rather about the legitimacy of hereditary peers in a Parliament which is supposed to represent the people. Quite what proportion of the population, other than themselves and their families, the hereditaries can claim to represent is a moot point, but on any reading it is minuscule.

Writing in the nineteenth century, Walter Bagehot argued that the Crown and Lords represented the *dignified* rather than the *efficient* aspects of the constitution.[21] However, the political imbalance in the Lords which favours Conservative governments and opposes Labour governments ensures that the Lords is neither dignified nor efficient: there is no dignity in an unelected chamber defeating the legitimate right of an elected government to govern according to the principles on which it was voted into power. Any second chamber must be constituted (whether elected or appointed) in a manner which ensures a balance of power between the two chambers, with clear rules established to ensure that constitutional deadlock between the two does not defeat the expectations of the electorate. This the Lords signally failed to do, using their Conservative majority to shore up Conservative legislation and significantly disadvantage a Labour government. The record of the Lords under Labour governments too clearly supports the argument of political bias.

This is not to say that the Lords did not play a valuable role in relation to legislation. But for the political imbalance it is arguable that the Lords would have escaped far longer without root and branch reform, in spite of the principled objections to the hereditary membership of the Lords. The most challenging task in reforming it is to retain the merits of the second chamber while redressing the democratic deficit

[21] *English Constitution*, p. 123.

and political imbalance which it has hitherto shown. It is this difficulty which explains the Labour government's caution in relation to Lords reform.

Reform of the House of Lords was but one of the incoming Labour government's 1997 pledges of constitutional reform. The first stage was to get rid of the hereditary peers. The House of Lords Act 1999 gave effect to this. Even that proved controversial and the government was obliged to strike a deal with the Conservative leader in the Lords, Viscount Cranborne, enabling ninety-two hereditaries to remain during the interim first phase of reform, in order to ensure that the Lords did not procrastinate or attempt to defeat the Bill totally.[22] The Bill received the royal assent on the last day of the parliamentary session. The shape of the Lords when the new parliamentary session opened the following week looked both different and less different than the government had initially hoped. The effect of Cranborne's deal, put into the House of Lords Bill on an amendment by Lord Weatherill, is that the membership of the House overall is 640. Of those, about 230 are Conservative Party members, and 180 Labour members. Over a hundred hereditaries remain: ninety-two from the Weatherill amendment, a further ten former Leaders of the Lords and first-creation hereditaries, plus some Labour and Liberal Democrat hereditaries who became life peers. The remainder are independents, the 'crossbenchers' who do not take any party political whip but have their own form of organization. The remaining hereditaries now have greater claims to legitimacy, ninety-two of them having stood for 'election' by their fellow peers before the axe fell on the remainder. The government, however, could not rely on the House being more co-operative in relation to its policies, first because the hereditaries have become more 'democratic' in their own right, and secondly because the crossbenchers have always been unpredictable in their allegiances.

The 'new' House of Lords was not prepared to be more acquiescent towards government legislative proposals. Even before the new year started, the Lords were proclaiming their renewed 'legitimacy' as a

[22] Cranborne entered into negotiations with the Prime Minister, without consulting the Leader of the Opposition, William Hague, and was promptly sacked as Conservative Leader in the Lords.

revising chamber. The Conservative Leader in the Lords, Lord Strath-clyde, had in December 1999 called for a strengthening of the Lords' powers *vis-à-vis* the Commons, suggesting that the Lords abandon the convention whereby delegated legislation is not opposed in the Lords, and warning that the House would not give way easily when it came to disagreement over a Bill. The government Leader in the Lords also referred to the Lords, post-reform, as 'more legitimate'. With the second stage of reform of the Lords postponed by the government, the revised House of Lords soon made an impact on the government's legislative programme. The Criminal Justice (Mode of Trial) Bill, which in part removed the right of defendants charged with 'either way offences', such as theft and burglary, to choose their mode of trial, was introduced in the Lords. The effect of this is that the Parliament Act procedures do not apply, thus making it easier for the Lords to press home its objections to the Bill successfully. The Lords rejected the Bill, forcing the govern-ment to reintroduce the Bill in the Commons where at Second Reading the government secured a substantial majority. The government also suffered a defeat of its proposals to introduce a new executive structure for local government.[23] Most controversially, the Lords opposed the government's proposal to repeal 'Section 28', which prohibits the pro-motion of homosexuality in education, causing the government to delay enactment until the summer of 2000 when more Labour life peers had been appointed. Their appointment secured a majority for the government in the Lords that ensured the passage of the Local Govern-ment Bill. Difficulty was also caused by the Lords over the government's proposal to lower the age of consent for homosexual sex to sixteen years; in opposing the Sexual Offences (Amendment) Bill, they forced the government to employ the Parliament Act procedure. The Care Standards Bill, which would introduce regulation of private hospitals and establish two bodies to inspect and impose standards, one for National Health hospitals, one for private hospitals, was also opposed by the Lords which inflicted its tenth defeat on government legislative proposals since the removal of the hereditary peers in 1999.

[23] The Local Government Bill 2000.

The Royal Commission Report

The Royal Commission Report was published in January 2000. To the disappointment of those advocating radical reform, the Commission (chaired by the Conservative peer Lord Wakeham) recommended that the Upper House, having around 550 members, comprise a majority of nominated members and a minority of selected or elected members representing regional interests. However, despite widespread consultation the Commission reached no consensus on the most difficult issue: the number of selected or elected members and the method by which members would be selected.

The powers of the second chamber would remain broadly as they are at present, with the second chamber being able to delay but not ultimately to defeat primary legislation. The Salisbury convention would continue to be respected. The Report recommended that there be greater use of pre-legislative scrutiny of Bills. The second chamber should be given power to delay the implementation of secondary legislation and to voice its concerns. The power to defeat secondary legislation – in practice never used – would be removed.

In relation to composition, three options were put forward. Model A provided for 65 members selected by dividing up a regional allocation of seats according to each party's share of the vote in that region at general elections, with one third of the regions selecting regional members at each general election. Model B, supported by a majority of the Commission, proposed 87 members, directly elected at the same time as the European Parliament elections under a system of proportional representation. Model C provided for 195 regional members directly elected at the same time as the European Parliament elections.

On the system of nominations for the House, the Commission recommended that an independent Appointments Commission be established. The Commission would have eight members, three nominated by the main political parties, one nominated by crossbenchers (independents), and four independents one of whom should be chairman or -woman. Establishing the Commission would sever the link between the granting of honours and the political patronage of the Prime Minister and government. Members of the House of Lords – a new name for which the Commission did not decide – would not be known as 'peers'. The current system of granting of honours would remain, but would not result in membership of the House of Lords. The granting of a peerage is therefore no longer to be a precondition for membership of the second chamber. The remaining hereditary peers would cease to be entitled to sit and vote once the regional members join the second chamber. Hereditary peers would, however, be eligible to seek nomination as regional members or apply for appointment by the Appointments Commission. The Commission will be under a duty to maintain balance in the composition of the House of Lords. It will ensure that at least 20 per cent of the members are not affiliated to one of the major parties; it will be under a statutory duty to ensure that a minimum of 30 per cent of new members are women, with the aim of gradually achieving gender balance within the House. It will also be required to attempt to ensure a representative level of membership from ethnic minority groups, and appropriate representation for all religious faiths. Regional members would serve for the equivalent of 'three electoral cycles' and appointed members should serve for a fixed fifteen-year term. The earliest the new system for regional members would operate would be 2004.

The Commission recommended that existing life peers appointed before the publication of the Report who wish to remain in the second chamber should be deemed to have been appointed for life, whereas life peers appointed between the publication of the Report and the necessary legislation implementing the Report's recommendations should be deemed to be appointed for a fifteen-year term from the date of the award of the life peerage.

On remuneration, the Commission recommended that the financial arrangements be adequate to make regular attendance economically viable, and that remuneration should be linked to attendance in Parliament. Payments made, however, for time and lost income should be less than the basic salary of a Member of Parliament over an average session.

The Report's recommendations were far removed from the aspirations of those seeking a democratically elected second chamber. That radical option foundered on the problem of the constitutional balance of power between two elected chambers, and the fear – which has always dogged reform of the House of Lords – that the Commons might lose its supremacy. But the Wakeham Commission Report does foresee a second chamber with at least the same powers as the current House of Lords, and one which is broadly representative of British society. In breaking the link between peerages and membership of the second chamber, the Commission has removed one of the most contentious aspects of the political honours system in which membership of the second chamber is seen to be conferred for political services to the governing party. Instead, the Commission seeks a second chamber which 'should be authoritative, confident, and broadly representative of the whole of British society', and whose members should have a breadth of experience outside the world of politics, possessing skills and knowledge relevant to the careful assessment of constitutional matters. The Commission stated that its intention was to recommend proposals which were not only 'persuasive and intellectually coherent but also workable, durable and politically realistic'.

The government signalled its acceptance in principle of the Commission Report. As of January 2002 the future composition of the House of Lords was undecided, with different propositions for elected members under consideration.

THE PRIVILEGES OF PARLIAMENT

Parliament, as the supreme law-making body, claims for itself certain privileges in order to protect its working. These exist for Parliament as an institution and for individual members of both Houses, the Commons and the Lords, which enjoy similar if not identical privileges. The historical purpose of privilege was to protect the fledgling House of Commons from the power of the Crown to interfere in its workings. Given the early battles between Crown and Commons, which are discussed in Chapter 12, it was imperative that members of the Commons be protected from arrest by the Crown for speeches which were critical of the Crown. Equally important was the protection of freedom of movement to and from Parliament, again to protect Members from arbitrary arrest. While the position remained insecure and uncertain until the end of the Stuart era, the Bill of Rights 1689 – the settlement between Parliament and Crown – laid the matter to rest, Article 9 of the Bill proclaiming that Members' freedom of speech could not be impugned in any place outside Parliament, including the courts of law.

These privileges remain, although the location of threats to Parliament's integrity and authority is much changed. Nowadays, attacks on Members of Parliament, individual or collective, are more likely to come from the media and pressure or interest groups seeking to influence Parliament. In the last few years of the Conservative government that was ousted at the 1997 general election the matter came to the fore with allegations that individual Members had accepted inducements to ask questions in Parliament and otherwise to promote a particular cause. The consequence of such allegations was to bring contempt on the government and a general loss of Parliament's prestige as it became tainted by 'sleaze'.

The principal privileges

At the start of each parliamentary session the Speaker of the Commons proclaims Parliament's privileges in a 'Speaker's Petition to Her Majesty', which claims the exclusive right of Parliament to regulate its own composition and procedure, right of access to the Sovereign (via the Speaker) and the right to the 'favourable construction' by the Sovereign in regard to Parliament's work. The principal individual privileges remain freedom of speech and freedom from arrest for civil (but not criminal) matters which guarantees Members' attendance in Parliament.

Freedom from arrest is scarcely necessary or justifiable. The power of arrest has long been abandoned in relation to civil matters, save for the failure to pay maintenance awarded in matrimonial causes. Freedom of speech, however, remains of fundamental importance but also has serious implications for those outside Parliament who find themselves without a legal remedy if their reputation is falsely damaged by what is said in Parliament. Absolute freedom of speech ensures that no individual Member of Parliament can be coerced into silence by his or her political party, or by the threat of legal action by anyone who considers that they have been damaged by the exercise of free speech. Provided that the speech takes place during a 'proceeding in Parliament', that speech is absolutely protected from legal action, however slanderous it may be. On the other hand, the immunity from legal action is confined to 'a proceeding in Parliament' and no further, although this phrase, which comes from the Bill of Rights 1689, has never been authoritatively and conclusively defined and accordingly remains a flexible notion. Some matters are clear: speech during debates in the House and its Committees is absolutely privileged. 'Speech' relating to an imminent proceeding in Parliament is also protected. Speech falling outside the scope of parliamentary proceedings is not protected, one result of which is that if a defamatory remark is made in Parliament it is protected absolutely, but if it is then repeated outside Parliament the Member may face legal action. The position of the media is also relevant here. Any fair and accurate reporting of Parliament is protected from legal action under the Parliamentary Papers Act 1840. Also protected are 'parliamentary sketches' of proceedings, provided that they are made without malice: the boundaries here are unclear, some parliamentary sketches stretching the limits of what is malicious or not.

The privilege of free speech works both ways. Not only is a Member protected from legal action from outside Parliament, but until recently he or she was also prohibited from using debates and proceedings in Parliament in order to support a libel action against an outside person or body. This problem became apparent during the 'cash for questions' affair, discussed further below, during which the *Guardian* newspaper alleged that a Member of Parliament had accepted large amounts of cash (in brown envelopes) in payment for posing parliamentary questions to further an individual cause. The MP, Neil Hamilton, found himself unable to use in evidence what had been said in Parliament in support of his libel action. The libel action collapsed when the *Guardian* printed further evidence against the MP, but the saga nevertheless raised an important issue of principle. This was finally resolved by the Defamation Act 1996. The Act enables a Member of Parliament to 'waive' the protection of Article IX of the Bill of Rights 1689, allowing him or her to use what was said in Parliament in evidence in legal proceedings. This produces the anomaly that while the Member of Parliament may set aside the Bill of Rights protection, if she or she refuses to do so the other party to the legal proceedings cannot invoke this right, with the likely result that the legal proceedings will be stopped.

Freedom of speech in Parliament represents a paradox. On the one hand, it is crucial for democracy that Members of Parliament collectively and individually are free from the threat of outside interference, through legal proceedings or through intimidation, in order to conduct their business without fear of reprisals, either from outside Parliament or from the executive within it. On the other hand, absolutely protected free speech creates the potential for abuse. For this reason, Members are cautioned to exercise care in what they say, so as not to cause harm to individuals or organizations for whom there is no legal redress. The public interest is served where privilege is used to uncover wrongdoings outside Parliament, for example in the naming of Kim Philby in Parliament as a Soviet spy. However, where allegations prove false, as was the case when a Member of Parliament alleged that a director of Rolls-Royce was guilty of financial malpractice and the charge was not withdrawn for over six weeks, the position is more contentious.

Theoretically, any criticism of Parliament or its Members which harms Parliament's authority and integrity is a contempt of Parliament. Contempt is a wider concept than breach of privilege. Privileges are defined and their scope not extendable; contempt on the other hand is any conduct or words which 'reflect on the dignity of the House'. In the past this has been used to control the media, with action being taken against editors of newspapers who have criticized Parliament. In recent years this has had little force. There is no power to fine for a breach of privilege or contempt. The most that can happen is that the rights of journalists to attend the House can be removed, and the editor called to the House to apologize.

Members' outside interests

Until 1911 Members of the House of Commons were unsalaried, membership being regarded as a privilege and a part of public service. For the most part, Members were relatively affluent and could afford to serve Parliament without financial reward. With the extension of the franchise in the nineteenth century, which gave a voice to ordinary working men (not women), representation of the 'working class' emerged, initially under the wing of the Liberal Party, but by the turn of the twentieth century through the newly formed Labour Party. In order to stand for election, funds are necessary. For those of limited means funds came from sponsorship, most readily in relation to Labour candidates through funding by trade unions.

Members, irrespective of party, have always been free to engage in outside employment, and contracts of employment or the holding of remunerative consultancies and directorships has never been viewed, despite the inherent risks to independence, as a threat to Parliament or to the integrity of its Members. The proviso to this is that Members must register their outside interests in Parliament in order to make clear where any outside connections lie. Equally, when speaking in debate or in Committee, Members must take care to ensure that their outside interests are known. While there exist old resolutions, dating back to 1695, prohibiting Members from taking offers of money to promote matters in Parliament, no systematic procedure to ensure openness existed until the Register of Members' Interests was introduced in 1974. This is published annually, and Members are required to register any remunerative employment, financial sponsorships, visits or hospitality paid for by others, the names of any clients of lobbying companies for whom the Member plays a parliamentary role, and any other interests which may affect the independence of the Member. Paradoxically, failure to register, or refusal to register, does not carry any penalty. A failure to declare an interest in a relevant proceeding, however, will attract the attention of the Committee on Standards and Privileges, via the Speaker, if another Member suspects that there is something improperly undeclared. This was the fate of Michael Mates when, as chairman of the Defence Select Committee, he failed to alert the Committee to his interests in two defence equipment manufacturers to whom he acted as a consultant. Mates's defence was that members of the Committee knew full well of his links with the companies, and that his interests were duly entered on the Register. This did not suffice; the Committee of Privileges sanctioned Mates for falling below the high standards set by the House and warned other Members to take note.

Where a Member of Parliament has an interest which is duly registered, any outside influence which might impede his or her independence in the exercising of parliamentary duties is open and above board. The inadequacies of registration and the possibility of undue influence, however, remain a threat to Parliament's integrity. Nothing raised public awareness of the system's deficiencies so much as the 'cash for questions affair' which gave rise to serious allegations about 'sleaze' in Parliament, led to a reduction in public confidence in Parliament and its Members, and made a substantial but unquantifiable contribution to the electorate's decisive rejection of the Conservatives in 1997. The saga began in 1994 when allegations surfaced in the media concerning money passed to Members of Parliament in exchange for putting down parliamentary questions related to the interests of those paying the money. Further allegations were made that Members of Parliament had accepted hospitality, in the form of paid hotel bills, which had not been declared to Parliament.

Cash for questions resulted in a formal inquiry into Members' interests, under the chairmanship of Lord Nolan. The Committee on Standards in Public Life was established to monitor and make recommendations in relation to all aspects of Members' interests. In its First Report in 1995, the Committee found that in general there was no evidence of a growth in actual corruption in Parliament. On the other hand it was also clear that there was widespread loss of confidence among the public. A code of conduct for MPs was introduced, and the Commons voted formally to ban paid advocacy and to submit any agreements with outside bodies for the provision of services in their capacity as Members of Parliament to a newly established Parliamentary Commissioner for Standards. The Committee of Privileges was renamed the Committee on Standards and Privileges.

The first Report of the Commissioner for Standards, published in 1997, found, *inter alia*, that the rules regulating interests had been breached by several members. Against Neil Hamilton (who by then had lost his parliamentary seat) the Commissioner found the evidence in relation to cash for questions 'compelling'. That issue was not yet resolved. In 1999 Neil Hamilton sued Mohamed Al Fayed for libel. The trigger for the action was Al Fayed's accusation on television that Hamilton had taken cash to put down questions concerning Mr Fayed's citizenship application, which had been turned down by the Home Secretary. Hamilton lost the libel action.

A fresh issue arose in 1999 with the leak of Select Committee reports to ministers. In July 1999 a senior Labour Member of Parliament, Ernest Ross, was forced to resign from the Foreign Affairs Select Committee after he had been found responsible for leaking to the Foreign Secretary, Robin Cook, a report critical of the Foreign Office's role in allegedly breaching a United Nations arms embargo in Sierra Leone. The leak had the potential, if used by the Foreign Secretary, to interfere with the work of the Select Committee. After criticism by the Standards and Privileges Committee, Ross apologized to the House and was suspended for ten days. Subsequently two Labour Members, one who had leaked a Social Security Select Committee Report and one who had received the Report, were suspended from the Commons for three and five days respectively. The Prime Minister and the Cabinet Secretary then issued directions to ministers and senior civil servants that any leaked documents should be returned immediately, and without use being made of them, and that the Ministerial Code of Practice should be amended to cover the leaking of such reports which potentially undermine the authority of Select Committees.

Reform of parliamentary privilege

In 1999 a Joint Committee of both Houses of Parliament considered the problems posed by privilege. On the circumstances surrounding the Hamilton case, and Section 13 of the Defamation Act 1996 enacted to remedy the defect which flowed from Article IX (namely, a plaintiff being unable to pursue his action for defamation because the defendant newspaper was prevented, by Article IX, from justifying what it had written), the Committee was extremely critical and recommended reform of the law. Section 13, which allowed a Member of Parliament to waive Article IX, but did not allow non-members to do so (which made it impossible for newspapers and others to establish the truth of their allegations), had 'created indefensible anomalies of its own which should not be allowed to continue'.[24] Having reviewed alternatives for reform, the Committee recommended that the individual Member

---

[24] *Report of the Joint Committee*, paragraphs 68 and 69.

should no longer have the right to waive the protection of Article IX, and that this right should be given to the House as a whole, subject to the overriding consideration that such a waiver was in the interests of justice and would not result in a Member attracting legal liability in a court of law. In considering the mechanism for reaching such a decision, the Committee recommended that, since the Committee of Privileges of the House of Lords would always contain four law lords, it was therefore the appropriate forum for decision. In the Commons it would be appropriate for such decisions to be reached by the Speaker, assisted by advice from a small committee of Members to include the Leader and Shadow Leader of the House along with the Attorney-General and representatives of the political parties.

Defining 'proceedings in Parliament'

Rejecting earlier suggested definitions of parliamentary proceedings as too wide, the Committee proposed the following statutory definition:

(1) For the purposes of Article IX of the Bill of Rights 1689 'proceedings in Parliament' means all words spoken and acts done in the course of, or for the purposes of, or necessarily incidental to, transacting the business of either House of Parliament or of a committee.

(2) Without limiting (1), this includes:

    (*a*) the giving of evidence before a House or a committee or an officer appointed by a House to receive such evidence

    (*b*) the presentation or submission of a document to a House or a committee or an officer appointed by a House to receive it, once the document is accepted

    (*c*) the preparation of a document for the purposes of transacting the business of a House or a committee, provided any drafts, notes, advice or the like are not circulated more widely than is reasonable for the purposes of preparation

    (*d*) the formulation, making or publication of a document by a House or a committee

    (*e*) the maintenance of any register of the interests of the members of a House and any other register of interests prescribed by resolution of a House.

(3) A 'committee' means a committee appointed by either House or a

joint committee appointed by both Houses of Parliament and includes a sub-committee.

(4) A document includes any disc, tape or device in which data are embodied so as to be capable of being reproduced therefrom.

Other suggested reforms

The Committee recommended that 'contempt of Parliament' be statutorily defined. In relation to immunity from arrest in civil matters, the Committee recommended that this be abolished. On sanctions, it is recommended that the statute stipulate the power to fine offenders and that the power to imprison be abolished, other than for the temporary detention of persons misconducting themselves within the precincts of Parliament. On contempt of Parliament by non-members, the courts should be given concurrent jurisdiction. Failure to attend proceedings or to answer questions or produce required documents should constitute criminal offences, punishable with an unlimited fine or up to three months' imprisonment. In relation to the reporting of parliamentary proceedings, the Parliamentary Papers Act 1840 should be replaced by a modern statute.

To complement the statute, the Committee recommended that there should be a statutory Code. Notwithstanding the difficulties of codification, such as reduced flexibility for the future, the advantages of clarification for both Members and non-members of Parliament would outweigh such problems, particularly if the Code were to include definitive statements of principle followed by illustrative, but not exhaustive, examples.

The Committee on Standards in Public Life Report 2000

In 2000 the Committee on Standards in Public Life made recommendations designed to improve discipline over Members of Parliament. In *Reinforcing Standards* Lord Neill of Bladen recommended that legislation be introduced to bring Members of Parliament, and those who offer bribes to Members, within the reach of bribery laws. Serious allegations of misconduct would be heard by a new tribunal, chaired by an independent legal expert and senior backbenchers, rather than the Standards and Privileges Committee. Before a case is referred to the tribunal, it would be considered by the Committee on Standards and

Privileges and the accused Member would be able to make representations to the Committee. Financial assistance would be made available to fund legal representation before the tribunal. The tribunal's findings would be reported back to the Committee which would decide what penalty should be recommended to the House of Commons. The Neill Committee also recommended that an appeals procedure should be introduced to enable a Member to appeal against the decision to refer his or her case to the tribunal, and against the tribunal ruling. The appeal would be heard by a retired senior judge. Proceedings before the Committee should be held in public. The government is considering the Report, but is unlikely to propose early reform which would in any event require parliamentary support.

THE EUROPEAN COMMUNITY AND UNION

INTRODUCTION

The European Union formally came into being in 1992 under the Treaty on European Union, known as the Maastricht Treaty. The origins of the Union, however, lie in the years immediately following the Second World War. In 1945 much of Europe was economically and physically devastated. The need for reconstruction, and the desire for a permanent end to political divisions in Europe which had resulted in over a hundred years of sporadic wars, led to demands for a Europe which integrated various nation-states under a powerful central government: a 'United States of Europe'. However, this dream had to be tempered by the political reality that states were fearful of conceding their sovereign powers to centralized control. This divergent approach to Europe – which still endures – is best summed up in the terms 'federalist' and 'antifederalist' or 'intergovernmentalist'. The federalists remain true to the original dream of a United Europe, with a form of centralized government supreme over all subordinate member states; the antifederalists, or intergovernmentalists, prefer the idea of a working partnership within Europe, with each participating member state retaining its sovereignty and national identity while contributing to the advantageous features of greater economic co-operation.

THE EVOLUTION OF THE EUROPEAN COMMUNITY AND UNION

While the long-term objective of the founding fathers of modern-day Europe was a form of federalism, the origins of what is now the Union lay in the creation of three European Communities (now European Community) with rather more modest aims. The overarching desire to avoid another war led to the proposal to place the raw materials of war – coal, steel and atomic energy – under a form of centralized control on a 'supranational' level. The objectives were achieved with the formation, by treaty, of the European Coal and Steel Community (the ECSC) and the European Atomic Energy Community (Euratom) in 1951 and 1957. The treaties establishing these separate Communities were signed by Belgium, France, Germany, Italy, Luxembourg and the Netherlands. Meanwhile, plans had developed to introduce a European Economic Community (EEC) which would gradually remove all barriers to free trade within the territories of the member states, and establish common tariffs for imports into and exports from the Community. The European Economic Community – or Common Market – came into being in 1957 with the signing of the Treaty of Rome. The Common Market was founded on four principles: freedom of movement for persons, goods, capital and services.

Since 1957 and the original six member states, the European Union – of which the Community forms the major part – has grown to encompass fifteen member states,[1] and there are plans for future expansion to up to twenty-six members. Not only has the Union expanded physically, it has also broadened its aims and objectives far beyond the original objective of a Common Market based on the four freedoms of movement. States which are admitted into membership of the Union do so on the basis of accepting the *acquis communautaire*, or 'Community patrimony': meaning the 'whole range of principles, policies, laws, practices, obligations and objectives that have been agreed or that have

[1] The current membership of the Union, with dates of accession, is as follows: Belgium (1957), France (1957), Germany (1957), Italy (1957), Luxembourg (1957), Netherlands (1957), Denmark (1972), Ireland (1972), United Kingdom (1972), Greece (1981), Portugal (1985), Spain (1985), Austria (1995), Finland (1995), Sweden (1995).

developed within the European Union', including 'most notably the Treaties in their entirety, all legislation enacted to date, the judgments of the Court of Justice, and joint actions taken in the areas of the Common Foreign and Security Policy and Justice and Home Affairs'.[2] Joining member states thus become bound by all the previous and present developments, principles, policies and laws of the Union, even though such matters were determined before the date of the state's entry.

The driving force behind the establishment of the European Coal and Steel Community, which came into effect following the signing and ratification[3] in 1952 of the Treaty of Paris, was the perceived need to place the raw materials of war beyond the control of nation-states, and most particularly France and Germany. From the French perspective, Germany's post-war industrial recovery represented a potential threat; from Germany's perspective (still divided into four zones occupied by the victorious allies), there was a need for a national rehabilitation within a Europe which Hitler had almost destroyed. The French Foreign Minister, Robert Schuman, launched the ECSC initiative at a press conference in May 1950, and it came into being under the leadership of Jean Monnet, the chief architect of the Schuman Plan. The third protagonist for greater union was the German post-war leader, Konrad Adenauer. From this experiment in multi-national controls the British held back, fearful then, as for so long afterwards, of the 'federal' nature and implications of such a development. Rather than ally itself with 'Europe', as represented by the ECSC, Britain turned her attention towards the United States and to her traditional trading partners, the 'British' Commonwealth.[4] The next stage of development was the formation of the European Atomic Energy Community under the Treaty of Rome in 1957, motivated by the same forces as the ECSC. The ambitions of the founding fathers of modern Europe were not, however, confined to the supranational control of materials of war. The desire to see European nations united within a trading bloc, free of internal tariffs and other restraints against free trade, and having a common external border and tariff mechanism, led to the establishment of the European

[2] T. Bainbridge, *The Penguin Companion to European Union* (Harmondsworth: Penguin, 2nd edn, 1999), p. 4.
[3] Approval by signatory states according to individual constitutional requirements.
[4] On which see Chapter 11.

Economic Community – the Common Market – in 1958 under the Treaty of Rome. The broad objectives of the European Economic Community, the most ambitious of the three Communities, were stated in the Treaty as being

by establishing a common market and progressively approximating the economic policies of Member States to promote throughout the Community, a harmonious development of economic activities, a continuous and balanced expansion, an increase in stability, an accelerated raising of the standard of living and closer relations between the states belonging to it.[5]

The principal institutions of the three Communities which eventually would result in the European Union were established under these Treaties, although the names have changed in relation to two of them. Originally, there was established a High Authority for each of the three Communities which had the power to propose initiatives for European development and whose loyalty was to Europe, not any individual member state. Separate Councils of Ministers for each Community were also established, to represent the interests of individual member states and with executive and law-making powers. In addition, there was set up a supervisory and advisory Assembly (now the European Parliament) to be shared by each Community, and the European Court of Justice of the Communities, with power to rule on the legality of actions of Community institutions and to interpret the provisions of the Treaties. In 1965 a Merger Treaty was signed, establishing a single European Commission to replace the High Authorities, and a single Council of Ministers to serve all aspects of the Communities.

Fearful of the implications of a united Europe, and in particular of a loss of national sovereignty, Britain formed the European Free Trade Area (EFTA) together with Austria, Denmark, Norway, Portugal, Sweden and Switzerland. By 1961, the then Conservative government had come to the conclusion that the economic benefits of membership of the Communities outweighed the fears of loss of national autonomy and decided to apply for membership of the EEC, only to have its application rejected by the French. It was not until 1972 that another Conservative government, now under Edward Heath, successfully

---

[5]   Treaty of Rome (EC Treaty), Article 2.

applied for and was granted membership of the EEC.[6] In order for the law of the Community to become part of British law, the United Kingdom Parliament passed the European Communities Act 1972.

Major Treaty revisions are agreed by member state governments at periodic Intergovernmental Conferences (IGC). Any amendments to the Treaties require the national legislatures of member states to ratify the provisions before they can formally come into effect. In 1992 the Maastricht Treaty was signed, following a prolonged and controversial intergovernmental conference. The Maastricht Treaty brought about the European Union, of which the Community (comprising all three original Communities and renamed in the singular) is a part. The aims and objectives of the Union are far broader than the original aims of the Economic Community. European Monetary Union is provided for via the single European currency, the euro. Co-operation in Foreign and Security Policy is also an objective of the Union, as is co-operation between police and judicial authorities. The Treaty on European Union, the Amsterdam Treaty, signed in 1997, consolidated previous developments and reorganized the structural edifice of the Union, although it left unresolved key questions. The Intergovernmental Conference of 2000 resulted in the Treaty of Nice. Most of the agreements reached were aimed at adjusting mechanisms to cope with an expanded Union membership once the new-applicant states become members. These included adjustments to the size of the European Commission, the number of members of the European Parliament and adjustments to the voting system used in the Council of Ministers.

THE STRUCTURE OF THE EUROPEAN UNION

The Union in 1992 had a structure with three main 'pillars': the Economic Community, Foreign and Security Policy, and Justice and Home Affairs, each existing under the overall Union. The Justice and

---

[6] On Britain's relationship with the Community and Union see H. Young, *This Blessed Plot: Britain and Europe from Churchill to Blair* (London: Macmillan, 1998, revised 1999), and see further Chapter 11.

The European Union

The European Communities	Common Foreign and Security Policy	Co-operation in Justice and Home Affairs
European Economic Community: Customs union and single market Agricultural policy Structural policy Trade policy New or amended provisions on: EU citizenship Education and culture Trans-European networks Consumer protection Health Research and environment Social policy Asylum policy External borders Immigration policy **European Atomic Energy Community** **European Coal and Steel Community**	**Foreign policy:** Co-operation, common positions and measures on: Peace-keeping Human rights Democracy Aid to non-member countries **Security policy:** Drawing on the WEU: Questions concerning the security of the EU Disarmament Financial aspects of defence Long-term: Europe's security framework	Co-operation between judicial authorities in civil and criminal law Police co-operation Combating racism and xenophobia Fighting drugs and the arms trade Fighting organized crime Fighting terrorism Criminal acts against children Trafficking in human beings

Source: K.-D. Borchardt, *The ABC of Community Law* (Luxembourg: Office for Official Publications of the European Communities, 1999).

Home Affairs pillar, which originally contained asylum, visas, immigration and other policies relating to free movement of persons and police and judicial co-operation in relation to criminal matters, was radically overhauled under the 1997 Treaty, with all matters relating to 'free movement of persons' being transferred to the Community, leaving only provisions on police and criminal judicial co-operation in the third pillar. The third pillar facilitates Europe-wide police co-operation between police forces and through the European Police Unit (Europol), originally established under the 1992 Treaty on European Union, and promotes co-operation in relation to the criminal jurisdiction of courts throughout the Union.

Differences exist in the procedures employed in relation to the three pillars. The vast bulk of Union law is that of the Community, the law-making processes of which are discussed below. Decisions on Foreign and Security Policy and the third pillar, being essentially matters of high policy and politically sensitive, are reached through negotiation and agreement at head-of-state level. Furthermore, whereas the Court of Justice has a controlling role in relation to the European Community, it has no role to play in relation to Foreign and Security Policy, and only has a role to play in relation to the third pillar if member states agree to its having jurisdiction to rule on a particular matter. It was this weakness in judicial control over the third pillar, and the lack of democratic control via the Parliament, which led, in large measure, to the majority of its provisions, particularly those relating to the free movement of persons, being transferred into the European Community 'pillar'.

THE EUROPEAN COMMUNITY

The 'European Community' is the label which now attaches to all three of the original Communities – the EEC, ECSC and Euratom – although constitutionally these remain separate organizations sharing common institutions. The former European Economic Community is the largest and most ambitious organization. The principles of the Community are set out in Part One of the EC Treaty.[7] The general aims of the Community are now stated to be as follows:

The Community shall have as its task, by establishing a common market and an economic and monetary union and by implementing the common policies or activities referred to in Article 3, to promote throughout the Community a harmonious and balanced development of economic activities, sustainable and non-inflationary growth respecting the environment, a high degree of convergence of economic performance, a high level of employment and of social protection, the raising of the standard of living and quality of life, and economic and social cohesion and solidarity among Member States.[8]

Central to the achievement of its objectives are the four freedoms: freedom of persons, capital, goods and services. Between member states there must be no barriers to free trade, and all customs duties and quantitative restrictions on imports and exports must be eliminated and replaced by a common customs tariff and common commercial policy towards non-European Union states. Any obstacles to the freedom of movement of citizens of the Union and of services and capital must be abolished. Between member states common agricultural, fisheries and transport policies are established. In addition, the Treaty provides for the harmonization of laws of member states 'to the extent required to facilitate the proper functioning of the single market'.[9] Revision of Article 3 led to its extension, and it now includes such social matters as education, health, consumer protection and the environment and culture. Extension of the Community's role (technically 'Community competence', on which see below) into social matters proved controversial and the British Conservative government under Margaret Thatcher refused to sign up to a Charter of Fundamental Rights for Workers which the Community adopted in 1989. The Maastricht Treaty had included a Social Chapter, but again British objections led to its being binding on only eleven member states until 1997 when the incoming Labour government announced that Britain would agree to

---

[7] Which has been substantially amended by the Single European Act 1986, the Treaty on European Union 1992 (Maastricht) and the Treaty on European Union 1997 (Amsterdam), the latter of which, confusingly, renumbers the majority of EC Treaty articles.
[8] Article 2 EC Treaty.   [9] Article 3 EC Treaty.

the Chapter. It is now incorporated into the EC Treaty under the Treaty of Amsterdam 1997.

Non-discrimination, rights and fundamental freedoms

Fundamental to the Community is the principle of non-discrimination on the grounds of nationality in relation to economic equality of opportunity, which has been employed creatively by the European Community's Court of Justice to extend the protection of equal economic rights.[10] Where any matter falls within the scope of the Community, the non-discrimination principle will be applied to it. Equally important is Article 141 of the EC Treaty (formerly Article 119) which prohibits sexual discrimination in relation to access to employment, promotion, training, working conditions, social security, retirement and equal pay.

More generally, while not articulated in the original EC Treaty, the principle of respect for fundamental rights and freedoms has moved centre-stage in the Union. The Court of Justice had incorporated the principle of respect for rights and freedoms commonly recognized in the legal systems of member states in the 1970s, in an attempt to prevent member states resisting the application of Community law on the basis that Community measures conflicted with human rights protection under their constitutions.[11] The Treaty on European Union 1992 articulated the commitment to rights and freedoms, stating that

The Union is founded on the principles of liberty, democracy, respect for human rights and fundamental freedoms, and the rule of law, principles which are common to the Member States.

The Union shall respect fundamental rights, as guaranteed by the European Convention on . . . Human Rights . . . and as they result from the constitutional traditions common to the Member States, as general principles of Community law. . . .[12]

---

[10] Article 12 EC Treaty.
[11] See *Internationale Handelsgesellschaft GmbH v. EVST* [1970] ECR 1125, [1972] CMLR 255.
[12] Treaty on European Union 1992, Article F, now Treaty on European Union 1997, Article 6.

To the extent that the Court of Justice has jurisdiction in relation to Community law and in relation to the third pillar, the Court will apply the principles of non-discrimination and respect for rights and freedoms to the actions of state authorities. With enlargement of Union membership looming, which will extend the Union eastwards, concerns over human rights standards in applicant Eastern European countries has led to the introduction of a political sanction for states which commit serious and persistent breaches of Community principles relating to liberty, democracy, respect for human rights and freedoms or the rule of law. Where a serious and persistent breach of these principles is found, either the Commission or a group comprising at least a third of the member states may propose to the Council that the sanction be applied. The Council, acting unanimously (but without the vote of the offending state), may suspend certain membership rights, including voting rights. Where the Council makes such a decision, it must be endorsed by the European Parliament.

The proposed Charter of Fundamental Rights

In 2000 the European Council approved the setting up of a Convention consisting of representatives of the 15 national governments, 30 national parliamentarians, 16 Members of the European Parliament and the Commission, charged with drafting a Charter of Fundamental Rights for the European Union. The European Court of Justice and the Council of Europe have observer status at the Convention. The draft Charter covers fifty basic rights, including

The dignity of the human person and equality before the law; the right to life; right to respect for the integrity of the human person, which includes a ban on eugenic practices, informed consent, ban on financial gain from the human body and a ban on reproductive cloning; prohibition of torture and inhuman treatment and the right not to be expelled or extradited to a state where there would be a danger of the death penalty or torture; prohibition of slavery and forced labour; right to liberty and security; right to an effective remedy for violations of rights and freedoms; right to a fair trial; presumption of innocence; no retrospective criminal liability; the right not to be tried twice; respect for private life; the right to marry and found a family, and enjoy legal, economic and social protection of the family; freedom of thought, conscience and religion; freedom of expression; the right to education; freedom of assembly and association; the right of access to documents of the European Parliament, Council and Commission; data protection; the right to property; right to asylum in accordance with the Geneva Convention of 1951; the right to equality and nondiscrimination; children's rights; the principle of democracy; the right to form political parties; the right to vote and stand for elections; the right to fair administration; the right to refer to the European Ombudsman allegations of maladministration; the right to petition the European Parliament; freedom of movement; social rights; freedom to choose an occupation; workers' rights to information and consultation; rights of collective bargaining action; right to rest periods and annual leave; safe and healthy working conditions; protection of young people in employment; right to protection against unjustified or abusive termination of employment; right to reconcile family and professional life, including parental leave after the birth of a child; right of migrant workers to equal rights; social security and social assistance; health protection; social and vocational integration for the disabled; environmental protection; consumer protection; the prohibition against the destruction of Charter rights.

The draft Charter was submitted to heads of government at the December 2000 summit in Nice. Disagreement over the status of the Charter, and whether it will be enforceable by the European Court of Justice, caused any final decision to be postponed for future negotiation.

Facilitating Community goals

The obligations which member states assume in relation to giving effect to Community requirements are governed under the vague but all-embracing Article 10,[13] which requires

Member States to take all appropriate measures, whether general or particular, to ensure fulfilment of the obligations arising out of this Treaty or resulting from action taken by the Community. They shall facilitate the achievement of

[13] Formerly Article 5 EC Treaty.

the Community's tasks. They shall abstain from any measure which could jeopardise the attainment of the objectives of this Treaty.[14]

The duty imposed on member states – the duty of Community solidarity or fidelity – is therefore both positive and negative. Not only must the requirements of Community law be given effect within the national legal system, but no action which could impede achievement of the full effect of Community law may be taken. This reflects the supremacy of Community law within the legal systems of all member states and facilitates the harmonization of different legal systems in order that European citizens' rights are given full effect irrespective of the national laws of differing member states.

Two further Treaty articles – both broad and ill-defined – also facilitate Community goals. The first is Article 94 of the EC Treaty, and, since the Single European Act 1986, Article 95, which both relate to the harmonization of laws in the Single Market; the second is Article 308 which confers a 'general competence' on the Commission and Council. Each relates to 'Community competence', that is to say, the right and power of the Community institutions to act in pursuit of Community goals. Article 94 provides that

The Council shall, *acting unanimously* on a proposal from the Commission, issue directives for the approximation of such provisions laid down by law, regulation or administrative action in Member States as directly affect the establishment or functioning of the common market.

This gives to the Council of the EU a general power to act to harmonize laws between member states in relation to all matters governed by the Treaties. It does require, however, that the Council act unanimously, thereby enabling a single member state or minority group of member states to block a particular measure. However, that position was rectified by Article 95; introduced under the Single European Act 1986 to facilitate accelerated achievement of the single European market, this alters the voting rules in Council and provides that:

---

[14] It is this Treaty article which has been increasingly employed by the European Court of Justice to ensure that Community rights are given effect within member states, under the principle of 'indirect effect', on which see pages 205 ff. below.

The Council shall, *acting by a qualified majority* on a proposal from the Commission in co-operation with the European Parliament and after consulting the Economic and Social Committee, adopt the measure for the approximation of the provisions laid down by law, regulation or administration action in Member States which have as their object the establishment and functioning of the internal market.

Accordingly, harmonization measures can now be pursued by the Council, even where there is no unanimity – all that must be achieved is the 'qualified majority' of votes in Council (discussed further on page 192 below). The need to move to qualified majority voting arose in large measure from the difficulties of ensuring that fifteen representatives of member states reach agreement – with the result that stagnation would follow through the inability to agree on legislation. In order that individual member states would not have their national interests ignored or overridden, Article 95 introduces an escape route. All actions taken under Article 95 are subject to the right of a member state, or group of states, to claim that it, or they, should be allowed to apply *national* provisions in place of *Community harmonization provisions* where they have 'major needs' in relation to 'public morality, public policy or public security; the protection of health and life of humans, animals or plants',[15] or in relation to 'protection of the environment or the working environment'. Where this claim is made, it is for the Commission to confirm the measure – effectively an 'opt-out' – having satisfied itself that it does not represent 'arbitrary discrimination or a disguised restriction on trade between Member States'. By means of Article 95, total harmonization of laws is sacrificed in favour of lesser harmonization but greater member state compliance – without which the Community cannot function.

Article 308 is the broadest of the three expansionist articles, and makes provision for the Council, here acting unanimously, to take 'appropriate measures' to fulfil Community objectives in relation to the operation of the single market, subject to consultation with the Parliament, even where the EC Treaty has not otherwise provided the necessary powers. As can be seen from the above, the introduction of

[15] These terms are laid down in Article 36 of the EC Treaty in relation to imports and exports or goods in transit.

decision by 'qualified majority' in Council, under Article 100a, removes the threat of a particular measure being blocked by an individual member state on its own or in conjunction with another dissenting state. However, the very broad power conferred under Article 308 is conditional upon the Council acting *unanimously* – a requirement which enhances the power of a dissenting state to block Community action. Conversely, where all member states are agreed on a proposed action, this enables the Community to expand and move forward towards fulfilment of its objectives. In so far as it is compulsory to consult the European Parliament, an element of democratic legitimacy is introduced at the European level. The Parliament, however, having been consulted, is not in a position to veto a proposal, save where specific Treaty articles confer that right on it, so where the Treaty is silent as to the legislative procedure to be followed, as it is in relation to Article 308, the right is one of consultation alone, not a power to amend or reject a proposal. However, given that the use of Article 308 is confined to action which it is '*necessary* to attain in the course of the operation of the common market, one of the objectives of the Community', it is for the Court of Justice to rule on the 'necessity'. In fact the Court has never been called on to make such a ruling, perhaps best explained by the fact that Article 308 can only be used where all members of Council are agreed on a proposed measure.

These broad facilitating articles raise the whole question of Community competence – or Community power to act in relation to its objectives, with or without the unanimous support of its member states. In order to appreciate the scope of Community competence, it is essential to consider not only individual Treaty articles, but also the fundamental principles which underlie the Community and now Union. These may be termed *supremacy*, *competence* and *subsidiarity*, and more recently, increasing *flexibility* through the 'co-operation procedures' and the concept of 'minimum harmonization'.

Supremacy, competence, subsidiarity, 'closer co-operation' and flexibility

Supremacy

In any legal order, which may contain a variety of law-making institutions such as a national parliament, regional parliaments, local authorities and not least the judges, there must be an identifiable sovereign body whose actions are unimpeachable.[16] Under a written constitution, such as that of the United States of America, this will be the Supreme Court which acts as the guardian of the constitution. In Britain, with its unwritten constitution, in relation to internal matters unaffected by Community or international obligations it is the United Kingdom Parliament at Westminster. In relation to the European Community, although the Treaties are silent as to the issue of supremacy or sovereignty, it is clear from the case law of the European Court of Justice, discussed at page 203 below, that it is Community law which reigns supreme. As the Court stated in a seminal early case, *Van Gend en loos v. Nederlandse Tariefcommissie*,[17] by signing the Treaties member states had created a new legal order, in which individual states had limited their sovereign rights. This became more explicit in *Costa v. ENEL*[18] in which the Court stated that

The transfer by the States from their domestic legal system to the Community legal system of the rights and obligations arising under the Treaty carries with it a permanent limitation of their sovereign rights against which a subsequent unilateral act incompatible with the concept of Community law cannot prevail.

Hence, where the Community institutions make valid law according to the procedures laid down in the Treaties, that law becomes – subject to the form it takes, on which see pages 205 ff. – applicable and effective within the fifteen national legal systems. It creates enforceable rights for citizens of the Union, rights which can and must be given effect to in the domestic courts, subject only to guidance given by the European Court in relation to the correct interpretation of the law.

[16] On the concept of sovereignty see Chapter 1.   [17] [1963] CMLR 105.
[18] [1964] CMLR 425.

The supremacy of Community law is effective even against fundamentally guaranteed rights and freedoms of citizens of member states.[19] However, in order to preserve respect for rights and for the integrity of member states' constitutions, the Court ruled that the respect for fundamental rights formed an integral part of the 'general principles of law' protected by the Court, and that the protection of such rights, inspired by traditions common to member states, must be ensured within the framework of the structure and objectives of the Community.

The effect of Community supremacy, which is essential to ensuring uniformity and harmony throughout the Community, requires that the national courts in member states become Community courts. Without such judicial co-operation the European enterprise would founder. This creates particularly sensitive problems for judges in the United Kingdom, who, operating under the traditional doctrine of allegiance to Parliament's will as expressed in Acts of Parliament, must reconcile the conventional constitutional duty with the duty imposed by the European Communities Act 1972 to give effect to Community law. Nowhere was this more apparent than in the *Factortame cases*.[20] *Factortame* concerned the right of Spanish companies to fish in British waters. The United Kingdom government, in an attempt to prevent over-fishing and protect the domestic fishing industry, had passed legislation imposing stringent registration requirements for 'foreign' fishing companies that ran counter to the Community's fish conservation policy, which laid down quotas for each member state. Finding its boats unable to work, the Factortame company sought an injunction restraining the application of domestic law, which *inter alia* it alleged was contrary to Community law relating to fishing rights and discriminatory on the grounds of nationality. The House of Lords ruled that it had no jurisdiction to grant an injunction against the Crown, in order to set aside the domestic legislation. The matter went to the European Court of Justice which ruled that, despite the fact that the Spanish company was seeking to take advantage of the system by registering its

[19] See e.g. *Internationale Handelsgesellschaft GmbH v. EVST* Case 11/70 [1970] ECR 1125; [1972] CMLR 255.
[20] A total of seven cases ensued from the *Factortame* issue. See principally [1989] 2 CMLR 353 (No 1); [1991] AC 603 (No 2).

boats under the British quota allowance,[21] the British legislation was contrary to Community law, infringing the principle of freedom of establishment and the prohibition against discrimination. Not only did the British government lose the case, but it was also ordered to pay compensation for breach of Community law. The Court also ruled that it was for the national courts to adjust their laws relating to remedies (i.e. the injunction issue) in order to give full effect to Community obligations. The issue of legal hierarchy and supremacy is also inextricably linked to the question of competence to act.

Competence

The power to make valid law is dependent on the Treaties for there is no other legal base from which to act. Specific Treaty articles will also specify the procedure to be followed in making law in relation to specific matters, other than under the articles discussed above which confer a more general source of power. To act without a legal base or to act in disregard of the procedural requirements of the Treaties renders an act liable to annulment by the European Court of Justice, at the suit of a member state or one of the Community institutions.[22] Community competence is therefore to some extent defined in the Treaties, as elaborated through the employment of Community law principles by the Court of Justice. However, nowhere in the Treaties is there to be found a list of matters which fall within the exclusive competence of the Community or of matters which fall within the exclusive competence of member states. Accordingly, the setting of boundaries has fallen to the Court of Justice and as a result Community competence has been gradually extended over ever-wider areas of activity. This is well illustrated in relation to the power to enter treaties with non-EU states. Treaty-making power is an essential feature of sovereign states, a component of an independent state's foreign relations. However, where a matter – for example, transport regulation – falls within the

[21] Once a member state is allocated a quota allowance, these may be traded between fishing companies.
[22] Under Article 230 of the EC Treaty which refers to legality of acts of the Council and Commission, but interpreted by the Court of Justice to include also the European Parliament: *Parti Ecologiste Les Verts v. European Parliament* Case 294/83 [1986] ECR 1339.

Community's competence under the EC Treaty, there exists also an implied competence to enter into agreements on behalf of member states with non-EC countries, thereby removing that competence from the individual member states.[23]

Community competence can be exclusive, in which case member states have no independent power to act, or it can be shared between the Community institutions and member states. Where the Community has no competence at all, the matter remains within the exclusive competence of the member states. While this explanation appears straightforward, the position is in fact rather more complex, and the issue of competence goes to the heart of the constitutional organization of the Community and Union and the relationship between the Union and its component member states.

In some areas of activity, the Treaties provide that Community institutions may take 'all necessary measures' to achieve Community objectives. Examples of this very broad conferment of power include common transport policy,[24] agricultural policy[25] and freedom of movement of workers.[26] Elsewhere, the Treaties limit the power conferred on Community institutions, thereby retaining scope for member states to act, provided they do so in a manner compatible with Community objectives. Areas where powers are so shared include culture and education,[27] public health and consumer protection[28] and environment policy.[29]

Community law comprises principally the EC Treaty, as amended, Regulations and Directives (discussed at pages 203 ff. below). Each of these sources creates legal obligations and rights which enter the fifteen legal systems, with greater or lesser involvement on the part of national authorities. As the Community expanded, both in terms of its membership and in terms of the subject-matter it governed, the quest to achieve uniformity in the application of Community law within all member states proved problematic. Coinciding with the move towards less unanimity and greater qualified majority voting, came the demand, most particularly from member states such as the United Kingdom which has traditionally favoured more 'intergovernmentalism' and less

---

[23] See *Commission v. Council (ERTA case)* Case 22/70, [1971] ECR 263.
[24] Article 70 EC.   [25] Article 32 EC.   [26] Article 39 EC.
[27] Articles 149 and 151 EC.   [28] Articles 152 and 153 EC.   [29] Article 174 EC.

'federalism', that there be greater flexibility built into the European venture. This objective was achieved in the Treaty on European Union 1992 (Maastricht), through the incorporation of the principle of subsidiarity, and through the principle of closer co-operation introduced in the Treaty on European Union 1997 (Amsterdam).

Subsidiarity

The subsidiarity principle is designed to determine the appropriate allocation of powers between the Community and its member states and to control the exercise of Community powers. It has been described, variously, as 'the principle of necessity, or proportionality, or effectiveness, an elementary principle of good government, or simply a principle of good sense'. The Maastricht Treaty 1992 inserted Article 3b into the EC Treaty, which following the Treaty of Amsterdam became Article 5 of the EC Treaty: the subsidiarity rule. Article 5 provides, in part, that in areas where the Community does not have exclusive competence the Community will act in accordance with the subsidiarity principle and only take action 'if and so far as the objectives of the proposed action cannot be sufficiently achieved by the Member States . . .'. Moreover, any action taken by the Community 'shall not go beyond what is necessary to achieve the objectives of this Treaty' (the doctrine of proportionality). In essence, Article 5 lays down a positive duty on Community institutions to act where EC objectives can be better achieved at Community level, and a negative requirement that Community institutions must not act where the objectives can be achieved by member states acting individually. At a meeting of the European Council in October 1992, it was agreed that

Decisions must be taken as closely as possible to the citizen. Greater unity can be achieved without excessive centralisation. It is for each Member State to decide how its powers should be exercised domestically . . . Action at the Community level should happen only when proper and necessary.

What is, or is not, within the Community's exclusive competence is, in the absence of a definitive listing, a matter for argument and by no means clear-cut. Nevertheless, where it is agreed that there is no exclusive competence, member states enjoy the power to act provided that the Community has not already done so. The power is concurrent unless and until the Community has acted, whereupon the power is pre-empted by the Community institutions. Should either a Community institution or a member state misconstrue the right to act, a challenge can be lodged with the Court of Justice for a ruling on the legality of the action. Subsidiarity thus provides for member states' potentially greater control over substantial areas, and represents a further recognition that the monolith of rigid uniformity which was the original emphasis in the Community must give way to the greater goal of Community-wide compliance, albeit with variations. The official guidelines for assessing the need for action at Community rather than national level provide that Community action is to be preferred where

the issue under consideration has transnational aspects which cannot be satisfactorily regulated by action by Member States;

actions by Member States alone or lack of Community action would conflict with the requirements of the Treaty or would otherwise significantly damage Member States' interests;

action at Community level would produce clear benefits by reason of its scale or effects compared with action at the level of Member States.[30]

Where action at Community level is required, 'Community measures should leave as much scope for national decision as possible, consistent with securing the aim of the measure and observing the requirements of the Treaty', and further actions by the Community are not to go 'beyond what is necessary to achieve the objectives of the Treaty'.

Matters which involve EU-wide, cross-border issues may most appropriately be dealt with at Community level. However, this does not mean that all aspects of the issue must be decided at Community level. So, for example:

where the development of policies to combat global warming might be best undertaken at the international or supranational level . . . planning decisions as to the preservation of 'greenbelt' areas or on the zoning of land are more appropriately adopted at national or local levels.[31]

[30] The Protocol on Subsidiarity. See S. Weatherill and P. Beaumont, *EU Law* (Harmondsworth: Penguin, 3rd edn., 1999), pp. 27–32.

[31] G. De Burca, *Reappraising Subsidiarity's Significance after Amsterdam* [1999] Jean Monnet Working Papers, www.jeanmonnetprogram.org/papers/99

In relation to the second and third pillars of the EU (Foreign and Security Policy, and co-operation between police and judicial authorities in criminal matters), member states have not transferred their powers to EU institutions, but rather are encouraged to co-operate with each other, and to do so by pursuing joint courses of action.

'Closer co-operation'[32]
Moving even further from the priority of unanimity is the principle of 'closer co-operation'. Envisaging enlargement of membership of the Community and Union, and mindful of the difficulties in sustaining complete uniformity of policies and laws within the larger Union, the Treaty of Amsterdam 1997 introduced the principle of 'closer co-operation', itself a synonym for greater flexibility or 'variable geometry'. The provisions on closer co-operation[33] enable a group of member states, no fewer than eight in number, to agree to closer co-operation over a range of issues under the EC Treaty and the third pillar relating to freedom, security and justice and subject to certain criteria, without the participation of the remaining member states. The non-participating member states must be free to join in the future. The closer co-operation procedure may only be used where agreement over achieving Treaty objectives cannot be reached between all member states. The competence, rights, obligations and interests of non-participating member states must not be affected by the action. Applications relating to Community matters under the closer co-operation provisions must be scrutinized by the Commission, and if it approves the measure it must then be authorized by the Council of the EU[34] voting by a qualified majority. Non-participating states may block the proposal on the grounds of important reasons of national policy. Closer co-operation is excluded from matters which fall within the exclusive competence of the Community. Furthermore, the proposed action must not affect Community policies or programmes, nor concern citizenship of the Union or be discriminatory in relation to nationals of member states

[32] See Weatherill and Beaumont, *EU Law*; S. Langrish, 'The Treaty of Amsterdam: Selected Highlights' (1998) 23 EL Rev. Feb. 3.
[33] Set out in Articles K. 15 to K. 17 of the 1997 Treaty, and Articles 11 EC Treaty and K. 12 TEU 1997.
[34] The Council of the EU was formerly called the Council of Ministers.

or amount to a restriction of trade between member states. The measure must also be one within the ambit of Community powers. In relation to the third pillar, only two conditions apply: the measure must be compatible with the powers of the Community and the objectives relating to freedom, security and justice, and be facilitative of achieving Union objectives more rapidly. A non-participating member state may seek to block the measure on the ground of important reasons of national policy. Authorization for measures under the third pillar is given by the Council acting by a qualified majority. If a member state seeks to oppose the measure, the matter is to be referred to the European Council which must decide on the basis of unanimity. 'Closer co-operation' enables those member states who desire greater integration in relation to particular areas to move forward – subject to possible veto – without being held back by those member states (most notoriously at times the United Kingdom) who wish to conserve greater independence. Whether or not this represents a 'two-speed Europe', or 'Europe à la carte' as former Prime Minister John Major would have favoured, will possibly only be seen in the future, and most markedly when the Union and Community expands to its projected twenty-six members. An early example of closer co-operation is the move towards eliminating internal EU border controls, which resulted in the Schengen Agreement, discussed below.

Flexibility: minimum harmonization

Moving beyond the 'closer co-operation' process is the notion of minimum harmonization. This permits member states to set their own measures in relation to specific Community goals. The EC Treaty, as amended, provides (in respect of some matters) that the Community lays down minimum goals to be achieved, and leaves member states to set more stringent standards. For example, in relation to environmental protection, Article 176 provides that 'The protective measures adopted pursuant to Article 175 shall not prevent any Member State from maintaining or introducing more stringent protective measures. Such measures must be compatible with this Treaty. They shall be notified to the Commission.' As Professor Stephen Weatherill explains, 'The value of minimum harmonisation lies in its contribution to a modern Community which is more multi-functional than a mere free trade area. Total harmonization confers on the Community an exclusive competence which it is simply ill-equipped to discharge.'[35] However, while minimum harmonization represents a move away from exclusive Community competence in defined areas, and subject to the control of the Commission, it is also a pragmatic realization that total harmonization is an impractical goal, given the ever-broadening areas of Community activity across an ever-expanding membership of the Union. It is a far cry from the Court of Justice's early assertions concerning the need for clear-cut, absolute sovereignty of Community regulation.

THE TWO UNION 'PILLARS'

Common Foreign and Security Policy

The Maastricht Treaty 1992 introduced the Common Foreign and Security Policy pillar,[36] recognizing that the greater the economic integration of the Union, the greater the need to pursue common goals in relation to external affairs. Article 11 of the 1997 Treaty now provides that

The Union and its Member States shall define and implement a common foreign and security policy, governed by the provisions of this Title and covering all areas of foreign and security policy.

The objectives of the common foreign and security policy shall be:

– to safeguard the common values, fundamental interests and independence of the Union;

– to strengthen the security of the Union and its Member States in all ways;

– to preserve peace and strengthen international security, in accordance with the principles of the United Nations Charter as well as the principles of the Helsinki Final Act and the objectives of the Paris Charter;

– to promote international cooperation;

– to develop and consolidate democracy and the rule of law, and respect for human rights and fundamental freedoms.

[35] *Law and Integration in the European Union* (Oxford: Clarendon, 1995), p. 154.
[36] Under Article J.1 Treaty on European Union 1992. See further Chapter 11.

Central to the second pillar is the Western European Union (WEU). The WEU was established in 1955 with a view to furthering the collective defence of Western Europe.[37] Foreign and Defence Ministers of member countries meet in Council, twice yearly at ministerial level and approximately twice a month at ambassadorial level. A parliamentary body, the Assembly, debates security issues and issues reports. At the 1992 Lisbon Summit, the factors to be taken into account when deciding areas for joint action were stated to be the geographical proximity of a region or country to the Union and the importance of the political and economic stability of a region or country to Union interests, and the existence of threats to the security interests of the Union. At operational level, the WEU has no independent military force but is dependent upon the forces of member states. However, the number of forces 'answerable to the WEU' now include the Belgian, British, Dutch and German Multinational Division, Eurocorps, the British/Dutch and Italian amphibious force and a Dutch/German corps. It has been proposed that there should be established a 'European army', with its own insignia, and with the capability of mounting large-scale peace-keeping and humanitarian missions in and around Europe, that could operate independently of America, which currently has an effective veto on most international military actions in Europe because it provides the bulk of NATO's capability. The proposed force – a sixty-thousand-strong rapid reaction force – has, however, produced disagreement over the relationship between NATO and the force, with the fear that NATO's dominance in European defence might be weakened.

At the political level, the Union's record on common Foreign and Security Policy is patchy at best. In the Gulf War 1990–91, the Union's record over 'common positions' in relation to conflict was poor. In 1991 there was no common approach to the problem, save in the attempt to secure diplomatic action and to impose sanctions. Only British and French troops participated in the American-led assault to drive

[37] The current membership of the WEU comprises Belgium, France, Germany, Greece, Italy, Luxembourg, the Netherlands, Portugal, Spain and the United Kingdom. Austria, Denmark, Finland, Ireland and Sweden are observer members. Iceland, Norway and Turkey have associate status. Ten Central and Eastern European countries are 'associate partners'.

Iraqi forces out of Kuwait. In relation to the break-up of the former Yugoslavia, there was again a lack of consensus, and of Union members only Britain and France committed sizeable numbers of troops to the civil war, with smaller units from the Netherlands and Spain. In both cases the Union appeared weak and fragmented, especially when compared to the reactions from NATO and the United Nations.

The Treaty on European Union 1992 describes the WEU as 'an integral part of the development of the Union', and the 1997 Treaty describes the WEU as central to framing the defence aspects of the Common Foreign and Security Policy. The WEU is formally integrated into the Union as an executive body of the Common Foreign and Security Policy.

Justice and Home Affairs (since 1997 co-operation between police and judicial authorities in criminal matters)

Introduced by Article K.1 of the Treaty on European Union 1992, the Justice and Home Affairs pillar related to asylum policy, immigration, judicial co-operation in civil and criminal matters and police co-operation. However, under the Treaty on European Union 1997, this pillar was severely truncated by the transfer of provisions on visas, asylum, immigration and other policies relating to free movement of persons to the European Community, leaving only judicial co-operation on criminal matters and the police within the Union pillar. Police co-operation is facilitated by the European Police Drug Unit, established in 1993 to combat illegal drug trafficking and extended to cover trafficking in radioactive and nuclear materials, immigration networks and stolen vehicles. In 1996 the Unit's mandate was extended to cover trafficking in human beings. Europol, the European Police Unit, was established under the 1992 Treaty on European Union but only came into effect in 1998.

In relation to judicial co-operation in criminal matters, the objective, in part, is to develop common procedures: however, this may prove problematic given the fundamental differences between legal systems and even more difficult following the expansion of membership of the Union from fifteen to twenty-six or twenty-eight states.[38]

The significance of the distinction between the Union 'pillars' and the Community 'pillar' lies in the degree and mode of regulation. In relation to Foreign and Security Policy and Justice and Home Affairs, the Commission, European Parliament and Court of Justice are excluded. Decisions are to be reached by the European Council and the Council of the EU, generally on the basis of unanimity. Member states, mindful of the Court of Justice's dynamic interpretation of the Treaties, clearly wanted control over these matters kept at the intergovernmental, ministerial, level. In relation to the Parliament, the Treaty states that it is to be consulted and kept informed of decisions reached, but it has no power that it can exert over decisions.

The reordering of the Union pillars in 1997 brings all matters relating to free movement of persons, including immigration and asylum matters, within the normal Community decision-making processes and the guardianship of the Court of Justice. This at least has an aura of symmetry, since the creation of Union citizenship by the Maastricht Treaty falls under the Community pillar. The abolition of internal frontiers to facilitate free movement of persons is politically controversial, particularly in the United Kingdom and Ireland, whose geography presents particular policing difficulties given the numerous potential points of unlawful entry by sea. In 1985, at Schengen in Luxembourg, Belgium, France, Germany, Luxembourg and the Netherlands signed an agreement designed to further the abolition of frontier controls at common boundaries. The resultant Schengen Agreement, supplemented by a Convention on the application of the Agreement, essentially providing the detail absent from the Agreement itself, came into force in 1995 in the five original states, together with Portugal and Spain and, from 1997, Austria, Greece and Italy, and subsequently Denmark, Finland and Sweden. Thirteen of the fifteen Union member states accordingly subscribe to the Agreement. The Treaty of Amsterdam 1997 integrates the Schengen Agreement in the

---

[38] See the Mutual Legal Assistance Convention, adopted and signed by the Justice and Home Affairs Ministers at the Council Meeting of May 2000.

Treaty framework of the Union through a Protocol. However, Denmark, the Republic of Ireland and the United Kingdom were not prepared to submit to the Agreement and special measures were demanded to enable those states to maintain their own border controls, through an 'opt-out' expressed in the form of three separate Protocols to the 1997 Treaty. Those states are accordingly permitted to continue their own national regulation of border controls and are not bound by Community rules, although they may choose to 'opt-in' in the future. The Treaty on European Union 1997 effectively absorbs the Schengen Agreement.

THE INSTITUTIONS OF THE EUROPEAN UNION

All three Union pillars are served by a common set of institutions, although the role and powers of the institutions vary according to which pillar of the Union is in question. In relation to the European Community, the institutions – as opposed to the member states – have the most extensive powers.

The European Council

The European Council, confusingly, is a distinct body with a different role from that of the Council of the EU (on which see below). While other European institutions were created under the Treaty of Rome, and derive their powers and functions from the Treaty, the European Council came into being by political practice rather than any legal provision, and was first given formal recognition under the Single European Act 1986 and confirmed in the Treaties on European Union 1992 and 1997. The European Council is made up of heads of state and Foreign Ministers of each member state. Every year, two Summit Meetings are called, at which Prime Ministers and Foreign Ministers meet to discuss the future development of Europe.

The 1997 Treaty (Amsterdam) describes the role of the Council as being to 'provide the Union with the necessary impetus for its development and . . . define the general political guidelines thereof',[39] and to 'define the principles of and general guidelines for the Common Foreign and Security Policy'.[40] It is at these biannual meetings that the real and highest-level political decisions are reached. A primary purpose of the meetings is to review economic and social matters such as inflation, economic growth, unemployment, the European monetary system, international political issues and constitutional issues such as applications for membership of the Union and political integration. Also for decision will be those matters which have been left unresolved after discussions in the Council of the EU.

The Council of the EU (formerly the Council of Ministers)

Representing the interests of the individual nation-states are members of the Council of the EU. Unlike the identifiable and appointed Commissioners, however, the identity of the Council of Ministers changes with the subject-matter which the Council is considering. For example, if the Council is meeting to discuss agriculture, the relevant state representatives will be Ministers of Agriculture; if the issue is transport it will be Ministers of Transport from all member states which make up the Council. It is therefore more accurate to speak of differing 'Councils' rather than a single Council of the EU.

The Council of the EU is headed by a President, who holds office for a six-month term. The presidency rotates between the member states. For example, in 2001 both Sweden and Belgium held the presidency, while in 2002 it is Spain and Denmark and for the first half of 2003 it will be Greece. In order to ensure continuity and a smooth transition from one presidency to another, the current President and his or her immediate predecessor and successor comprise a 'troika'. Since 1996 each 'troika' has included one minister from one of the large member states. The head of state of the member state fulfils the role of President-in-Office. Presidents set their own agenda for achievement during the six-month period: some will be more ambitious than others. It is the

[39] Article D.   [40] Article 18. See now TEU 1997, Title V.

President who speaks for the Union in its relations with non-EU countries and represents the EU in meetings of the United Nations' General Assembly.[41]

Composition of the Council

One representative of each member state at ministerial level, with composition varying according to the subject discussed, for example:

General Affairs Council
Economic and Financial Affairs Council (Ecofin)
Transport Council
Agriculture Council
Permanent Representatives' Committee 'COREPER I and II'
Special Committee for Agriculture
Working groups
General Secretariat (approximately 2,200 officials)

Tasks

Drawing up legislation
Co-ordination of economic policy
Budgetary control
Appointments
External relations

It is in Council that the major decisions about the development of European law are reached. Whereas the Commission (for more on which see below) proposes legislation, it is the Council which for the most part makes law. The Treaties determine the law-making process. That is to say, the Treaties state by whom decisions can be made and what procedure is to be followed. The Commission and the Council of the EU interact to produce viable laws. The European Parliament, originally called the Assembly, has a role to play, and one which has been significantly expanded. However, as discussed further below, in spite of the increase in its role in approving legislation, it would be wrong to assume that the European Parliament is principally a

[41] On the United Nations see Chapter 11.

law-making body, or the principal law-maker. That power rests with the Commission and Council of the EU.

At first glance, this appears a strange constitutional arrangement. In Britain, as in most other countries, individual citizens have the right to vote for Members of Parliament, and following a general election the political party with the majority of seats in Parliament forms the government of the day. Government proposes legislation, and Parliament either accepts, amends or rejects the proposal, which when accepted becomes law. In the European Community, however, the dominant law-making power is the executive in the form of the Commission proposing and the Council of the EU enacting, with or without the Parliament's intervention. It is this feature of the Community machinery which attracts the accusation that there is a 'democratic deficit' in Europe, although the powers of the Parliament have been considerably enhanced under the 1992 and 1997 treaties. Furthermore, it is arguable – although the argument is weak – that democracy operates in relation to the Council through the accountability of its members to their national Parliaments and the electorate.

In order to understand the workings of the European institutions it is necessary to appreciate the complex forces at work in the European enterprise. In the development of the Community – now the Union of which the Community forms a major part – individual states have shown either greater or lesser enthusiasm for the European project. Some states, notably Germany, are more enthusiastically 'federalist' in their approach. On the other hand, as anyone in the United Kingdom well knows from the media, British governments have always appeared publicly wary of Europe, regarding it as at worst a threat to national sovereignty and at best a necessary, but not particularly welcome, interference in domestic affairs. Under Mrs Thatcher's Conservative government, hostility to Europe was particularly marked, with the Prime Minister, when in dispute over the level of British contributions to the Community budget, at one time bluntly demanding that Britain be given 'her money back'. Nevertheless, it was Margaret Thatcher who signed the Single European Act 1986, an Act which enhanced the supremacy of the Union at the expense of national sovereignty. While John Major's premiership revealed an ostensibly softer approach to Europe there was still a reluctance to commit absolutely to the European dream of a United States of Europe. Major appeared to favour an 'à la carte' Europe – a Europe in which member states could opt in and out of assorted measures – but he nevertheless signed the Maastricht Treaty which ushered in the Union and Monetary Union. So split was his government over Europe that Europe became a dominant factor in the government's defeat in 1997. Political argument and debate over the single European currency epitomize concerns over Europe. While the current Labour Prime Minister, Tony Blair, has adopted a more constructive and enthusiastic approach to Britain's participation in the European Union, doubts nevertheless remain over the single currency, the euro, and when Britain will actually accept it.

While the Treaties form the legal basis for action, and are subject to interpretation and enforcement by the European Court of Justice, ultimately success rests on the political will of member state governments and national administrations. Intransigence on the part of one member state and its impact was best demonstrated in 1965 when President Charles de Gaulle withdrew France from Community decisions for six months through operating an 'empty chair' policy. The conflict with France arose, in part, over the proposal to introduce majority voting over many new areas which had previously required a unanimous vote. De Gaulle claimed the right of a member state to insist on unanimity in voting in areas which it regarded as central to its own national interests. As a consequence, compromise was reached through the Luxembourg Accords, an agreement for which there was no Treaty provision, but which enabled the Community to resume its normal functioning. The Accords provided that where a member state considered that its own vital national interests were at stake, rather than proceed by ignoring that state's interests, negotiations would continue until unanimity could be achieved in Council. The Accords have assumed an importance far beyond the original conflict, and while devoid of legal status and agreed to resolve a particular conflict, echoes of the Accords continue to be heard in the ongoing debate about reconciling Union interests and the interests of individual states.

One of the key components in the Community–member states relationship lies in the voting system adopted in the Council of the EU, which remains, albeit subject to increased powers being given to the European Parliament, the principal policy-making and law-making forum.

The Treaty of Rome, as amended, lays down the voting procedure to be used for decisions to be reached. Each member state has a number of votes which are very roughly proportional to the size of its population. Following the Treaty of Nice 2000, the number of votes has been altered to ensure that when Union membership is enlarged, to twenty-six or possibly twenty-eight members, the larger states have greater power. Smaller states lost voting power, others remained the same, while Britain, France, Germany, Italy, Spain and the Netherlands secured increased voting power. Britain's vote increases from ten to twenty-nine in line with Germany, France and Italy. Spain's vote increases from eight to twenty-seven and the Netherlands from five to thirteen. The consequence of the realignment of voting power means that any three of the largest states in combination will be able to block decisions.

Differing Treaty articles will state whether a vote in Council must be made by a unanimous vote, a qualified majority vote, or a simple majority vote. A qualified majority vote is one where, to reach a binding decision, a certain number of votes must be achieved. The idea behind this somewhat complex process is that, in the interests of both harmony between member states and the development of the Community, there should be different levels of voting for decisions relating to matters of greater or lesser political significance.

The voting system is crucial to the development of the Community and Union. If one member state could always block a decision, through a veto, then the Community and Union would rarely make progress. On the other hand, if a simple majority vote was required for all matters, the vital interests of one or more member states could be overridden in the interests of the Community and Union. A balance is therefore attempted between the need for respecting member states' interests and the interests of the Community and Union. However, this balance cannot be achieved at the expense of Community development, especially with the Union now having fifteen members and prospectively twenty-six. The use, and extended use, of the qualified majority vote (QMV) has been the focus of much debate. However, the price of extending the qualified majority vote in Council has been the move towards lesser uniformity and greater flexibility in terms of regulation, through the devices of the subsidiarity principle and the measure relating to 'closer co-operation'.

The Council meets on average about ninety times a year, and in different years different topics will have greater importance and urgency and require more meetings. Backing up the Council is the Committee of Permanent Representatives (COREPER), itself comprising two Committees. The first deals with issues such as foreign affairs and economics and finance, the second deals with other matters. COREPER is made up of national delegates from member states, headed by a senior diplomat and staffed by some thirty to forty officials, principally drawn from the diplomatic service and government ministries. In addition, the Special Committee on Agriculture deals with all matters relating to the Community's agricultural policies. Also enabling the Council to function are an assortment of committees and working groups which carry out detailed studies on proposals coming from the Commission for consideration by the Council. The Council Secretariat, comprising a staff of over two thousand, is responsible for the day-to-day administration and co-ordination of Council matters.

The European Commission

Each member state is represented in the Commission. The largest states, France, Germany, Italy, Spain and the United Kingdom, currently have two Commissioners, while smaller states have one. From 2005 the largest states will give up their second Commissioner, and a rotation system may be used to keep the number to under twenty-seven as new member states join. Unreformed, there would be a Commission of over thirty members, which would be unworkable: there is already a problem with an insufficient number of portfolios of equal weight to distribute among the twenty existing Commissioners. Reducing the size of the Commission, however, is controversial since the smaller states are reluctant to give up their Commissioner, for having a distinctive voice in the Commission protects the interests of smaller states against the potential domination of the more powerful member states.

Commissioners are appointed by their national governments, for a renewable five-year term of office, but once appointed Commissioners must be entirely independent of their governments and act solely in the interests of the Community. Under the Treaty of Rome, which defines the powers of the institutions, Commissioners must neither seek nor take advice from their governments. The Commission is headed by a President who is appointed for a renewable two-year term of office. Each Commissioner has one or more areas of responsibility, or portfolios, and is supported by the European civil service which is divided into subject-specific Directorates General. Directorates General vary in size and organization. The general pattern of organization is for the Directorate General to be subdivided into directorates which in turn may be subdivided into divisions. The Directorates General may be imprecisely likened to government departments, the permanent nature of which ensures that ministers, irrespective of their own expertise, have access to specialist knowledge and advice.

Commission personnel, Europe's civil service, are drawn from member states, and it is Community policy to maintain a broadly proportionate number of staff from each member state. This not only facilitates confidence on the part of all member states, but also makes the processes of negotiation and interaction with the Commission easier. European Commissioners tend to be former politicians who have achieved prominence in public life. Britain's two current Commissioners are Neil Kinnock, former leader of the Labour Party, and Chris Patten, former Chairman of the Conservative Party and Governor of Hong Kong. Although they are nominees of member state governments, the President of the Commission and other members of the Commission are subject to a vote of approval by the European Parliament. Following the Parliament's approval, the President and Commissioners are appointed by the 'common accord' of member state governments.

The Commission has several roles to play. First, it is the Commission that has the principal power to make proposals for implementation, subject to restraints imposed by the European Council and Council of the EU. This power of initiative is exercised after wide consultations with interest and other representative groups throughout the countries of Europe. The Commission also has a 'watchdog' role. It is the Commission which has the duty to make sure that Community law is implemented, and enforced, throughout the Community. In this role, the Commission supervises the application of Community law; it has the power to require a defaulting member state to comply with Community requirements, and, at the end of the day, in the face of opposition, to take that member state to the European Court for a judicial ruling. The Court may impose a financial penalty on any obstructive member state. However, scrutinizing policy implementation is no easy task and in large measure the Commission is dependent upon member state co-operation through national agencies; the Commission has inadequate funding and staff to ensure detailed and effective scrutiny across fifteen nations.

The Commission also has responsibility in relation to European Union finances, subject to controls of the Council and subject to the Parliament's power to approve, amend or reject the annual proposed budget. In relation to revenues the Commission must ensure that proper rates are levied and that moneys are collected. In relation to expenditure, the Commission is responsible for administering funds for agricultural price support purposes, and for the disposal of product surpluses. The Commission also administers the 'structural funds' – the European Social Fund and the Regional Development Fund.

The European Parliament

According to the original Treaty, the Assembly was to have 'supervisory and advisory' powers. It was not conceived as a law-making body remotely similar to a national parliament. In the early days, and until 1979, the Assembly was made up of delegates from national parliaments, each of whom had a 'dual mandate': that is to say, a role in two parliaments. In 1979 the system of direct elections for the European Parliament, as it was now called, was introduced. Since then the majority of Members of the European Parliament (MEPs) have had a single mandate, and sit only in the European Parliament, although it is not prohibited for an MEP also to have a seat in his or her national parliament. The Parliament is headed by a President, elected by a majority of votes cast, and serving a two-and-a-half-year term, and there are fourteen Vice-Presidents, also elected by the Parliament.

Each member state has a number of seats proportional to its

Political Parties in the European Parliament (as at September 1999)

Group of the European People's Party, EPP (Christian Democrats) and European Democrats	233
Group of the Party of European Socialists, PES	180
Group of the European Liberal, Democrat and Reform Party, ELDR	50
The Green Group in the European Parliament/European Free Alliance, GREEN/EFA	48
Confederal Group of the European United Left/Nordic Green Left, GUE/NGL	42
Union for a Europe of Nations, UEN	30
Group for a Europe of Democracies and Diversities, EDD	16
Non-attached	27

population size. Members of Parliament are elected for a term of five years. Members do not sit in Parliament according to their nationality, but according to their party political allegiance, although this does not correspond exactly to the major political parties in Britain.

The Committee structure of the Parliament comprises:

Committee on foreign affairs, human rights, common security and defence policy
Budgets
Budgetary control
Citizens' freedoms and rights, justice and home affairs
Economic and monetary affairs
Legal affairs and the internal market
Industry, external trade, research and energy
Employment and social affairs
Environment, public health and consumer policy
Agriculture and rural development
Fisheries
Regional policy, transport and tourism
Culture, youth, education, the media and sport

Development and co-operation
Constitutional affairs
Women's rights and equal opportunities
Petitions.

Under the European Parliamentary Elections Act 1999, the United Kingdom is divided into electoral regions. England is divided into nine, and Scotland, Wales and Northern Ireland each constitute a single electoral region. The number of MEPs elected in the United Kingdom is 87, of whom 71 are elected for England, eight for Scotland, five for Wales and three for Northern Ireland.[42] The voting system employed in England, Wales and Scotland is the regional list system,[43] and in relation to Northern Ireland the single transferable vote.[44] The EC Treaty restricts the number of MEPs to 700.[45] The Parliament, which currently has 626 Members, will increase to 738 when the twelve applicant states join. To avoid an overlarge membership the number of MEPs from different states has been reduced. Britain will in future have 74 as opposed to 87 MEPs, in line with France and Italy. Germany, however, has negotiated to retain its number of MEPs at 99 to reflect its population enlargement since reunification.

The Parliament holds plenary sessions for one week each month except August. The plenary sessions take place in Strasbourg, France. However, other sessions can be held in Brussels, and over 70 per cent of committee meetings take place there. The position is further confused by the fact that much of Parliament's secretariat is based in Luxembourg. All attempts to rationalize the Parliament's location into one permanent place have failed as the relevant member states – keen to maintain the prestige associated with the Parliament – block any attempt at reform.

Demands that the European Parliament have more power in the decision-making process in Europe led to the development of its role from that of being merely supervisory and advisory. A European agreement, the Single European Act 1986, increased the Parliament's role and, in limited areas, gave it a power of co-decision with the Council of the EU and the Commission. The Act introduced what is known as

---

[42] European Parliamentary Elections Act 1999, section 1.   [43] Ibid., section 3.
[44] Ibid., section 3A.   [45] Article 189 of the EC Treaty (formerly Article 137).

the 'co-operation procedure'.[46] Here, in defined areas as laid down in the Treaties, where the Commission and Council are required to consult the Parliament, and no agreement is reached, it is required that within a strict time-period there is established a Conciliation Committee, made up of representatives of the Commission and Parliament, to reach agreement. If this fails, special rules apply which generally require the Council of the EU to be unanimous in its rejection of the Parliament's view. The Treaty of Amsterdam (the Treaty on European Union 1997) further extended Parliament's role, largely abandoning the co-operation procedure of Article 189c[47] and replacing it with the co-decision procedure.[48] The co-decision procedure has been extended across wide areas of Community policy. Where there is agreement between the Council of the EU and Parliament in relation to a proposal, the measure can be adopted. Where there is a disagreement, however, whereas formerly the Council could insist on a measure notwithstanding Parliament's rejection of it, the Parliament can now veto a decision.

The Parliament also has the right to question the Commission, and, in cases of severe mismanagement to dismiss the entire Commission. The parliamentary question time is very similar to that in the United Kingdom Parliament, and ensures that the Parliament plays a real supervisory role in the administration of the Community. The right to dismiss the Commission, however, is less useful. In order to be successful, a vote of two-thirds of all MEPs is required. In 1999, after growing concerns over the mismanagement of Community funds, for which the Commission is responsible, there were demands that the Parliament sack the Commission. Even in the light of clear evidence, Parliament failed to reach the required two-thirds majority. In the event, the scandal grew to such proportions that all members of the Commission, including the President, resigned. One power which is significant and which the Parliament has always had, is the power to approve, amend or reject the annual Community budget which is put forward by the Council after receiving proposals from the Commission.

[46] After entry into force of the Treaty on European Union 1992 this became Article 189c of the EC Treaty, subsequent to the Treaty on European Union 1997, Article 252 EC Treaty.

[47] But retaining it for the purposes of monetary policy provisions of the Treaty.

[48] Formerly Article 189b EC Treaty, now Article 252 EC.

The Court of Auditors

The Court of Auditors [49] comprises fifteen appointed members who serve a six-year term. A President, appointed for a renewable term of three years, heads the Court. The Court of Auditors controls the manner in which Community money is spent and audits Community accounts, and it has the formal status of a Community institution. The significance of the Court of Auditors being given this status under the Maastricht Treaty is that it makes available to the Court the full range of legal redress available to other institutions, thus reinforcing the safeguards which ensure that it is able to perform effectively. The Court of Auditors' task is to assist the European Parliament and the Council of the European Union in exercising their powers of control over the implementation of the budget. The Court may also submit observations on specific questions and deliver opinions at the request of one of the European institutions.

The Court of Auditors is required to provide the Council and Parliament with a Statement of Assurance relating to the reliability of accounts and the legality of the underlying transactions. In its auditing function, the Court of Auditors may examine records provided and if necessary may do so in the European institutions and the member states. The Court of Auditors examines the accounts of Community revenue and expenditure and considers whether these have been respectively received and incurred in a lawful manner and whether the financial management has been sound. The Court of Auditors is independent and has the power to carry out its audits at any level. In addition to monitoring the internal revenues and expenditure of the Union, the Court of Auditors also monitors co-operation agreements between the European Union and many developing countries, and the system of Community aid to Central and Eastern Europe.

[49] Articles 246–248 EC.

The Economic and Social Committee

The Economic and Social Committee [50] is an advisory and consultative body comprising representatives of employers, workers (usually trade union members) and assorted interests drawn from agriculture, business and the professions. Members are proposed by national governments and formally appointed by the Council of Ministers, and serve for a renewable four-year term. The main Committee works through nine subsidiary committees: agriculture and fisheries; industry, commerce, crafts and services; economic, financial and monetary issues; social, family, education and culture; transport and communications; external relations, trade and development; energy, nuclear issues and research; regional development and town and country planning; protection of the environment, public health and consumer affairs. Supported by a secretariat, the Committee considers Commission proposals and issues opinions, and liaises with other international bodies and Union institutions. In some instances the Treaties require the Committee to be consulted by the Commission or by the Council, in other cases the Committee may be consulted on an optional basis. While the Committee is a useful forum for deliberation, it has little real power. Even where the Committee's opinion is required, it is not mandatory for the Council or Commission to act on the Committee's view, nor can the Committee delay legislation.

The Committee of the Regions

Regionalism assumes greater importance as the Community and Union expand in membership. Community and Union policies and laws have to be capable of implementation within member states with very different economies, and within economies of differing regions with varying levels of poverty and prosperity. The European Regional Development Fund, established in 1975, is designed to ameliorate disparities in regional wealth through funding. To give an organized forum for the

[50] Articles 257–262 EC Treaty. ECOSOC is the representative of 'organized civilized society'.

consideration of regional issues the Committee of the Regions was established[51] under the Maastricht Treaty of 1992. Members of the Committee are appointed by the Council of the EU following nominations by member states. The functions of the Committee are advisory, and the Treaty provides that the Committee must be consulted by the Council or the Commission in relation to specified matters, on which it then gives its opinion.

The European Investment Bank

Originally established in 1958,[52] the Bank is charged with the task of promoting the 'balanced and steady development of the common market in the interest of the Community'. The Bank operates on a non-profit basis, and grants loans and gives guarantees which facilitate the financing of a number of projects, including regional development, modernization or conversion projects and projects of common interest to several member states.

The Court of Justice

Central to the enforcement of Community law is the Court of Justice.[53] Under the Treaty of Rome the Court of Justice (ECJ) was established with the power to rule on the legality of Community actions, and on the interpretation of the Treaty provisions and secondary legislation made under the Treaty. It is the Court of Justice which has led to a rapid extension of Community law within member states, and to the doctrine of the supremacy of the law of the Community over the domestic law of member states.

The Court is made up of fifteen senior judges, or lawyers with similar qualifications, drawn from the member states; and eight Advocates-General. In 1986 a Court of First Instance was introduced to relieve some of the pressure on the principal Court. To a great extent the

[51] Articles 263–265 EC Treaty.   [52] Articles 105–115 EC Treaty.
[53] Articles 220–245 EC Treaty.

Treaty provides for co-operation between national courts and the European Court. Under Article 234 of the Treaty national courts and tribunals may refer questions of Community law to the ECJ for decision. Courts and tribunals at any level may refer a question where it is necessary to have the ECJ's ruling in order to reach a decision. Where a question of Community law is raised in a 'court of last resort', that is, one from which there is no further right of appeal available or possible, that court or tribunal *must* refer the question. It is through this mechanism that harmony and uniformity between Community law and national law is achieved.

The structure of Community law

While in the United Kingdom law consists principally of judge-made law, or 'common law', and Acts of Parliament, or statutes, Community law takes very different forms. The Treaties themselves are the principal source of law. All powers possessed by the Union, of which the Community is the most significant part, are contained in the Treaties, as interpreted – where conflict arises – by the European Court of Justice. The Community and Union institutions have no legal powers save those arising from the Treaties. Treaty articles, if they are clear and unconditional, confer obligations on governments of member states and create rights for the citizens of both the member state and all other European Union citizens. For example, Article 141 provides for gender equality in the workplace in respect of pay. As a result, an employee may use the Treaty article in a local court to enforce his or her Community law rights against the employer, whether public or private.

In addition to articles of the Treaty, the Council of Ministers and the Parliament (to the extent that the Parliament has law-making powers) enact Regulations and Directives. The Treaty of Rome itself provides that Regulations are to be directly applicable and that they are 'binding in their entirety'. The meaning of these phrases, according to the European Court of Justice, is that once a Regulation is passed in Europe it automatically takes effect within the fifteen member states' legal systems, without any need for national legislation. Being 'binding in their entirety' means that no member state may avoid giving effect to the full scope of the Regulation: there is no discretion left to pick and choose how, when or the extent to which the Regulation should be given effect. Directives, on the other hand, do give some leeway to member states in terms of how they will achieve the result which is desired. For example, a Directive may be passed which requires member states to achieve the objective of lowering river water pollution to a prescribed level by a certain date. The measures to be used to achieve the desired result are left to member states to work out. However, this is the limit to the flexibility allowed, and if a member state fails either to achieve the result, or fails to meet the deadline for compliance, then financial penalties may be applied by the European Court. In addition, once the date for implementation has passed without compliance, an individual who is in some way harmed by the member state's failure may rely on the legal right which arises under the Directive on the date for its implementation and seek compensation for any loss incurred.

The laws of the Community derive from the original Treaties, as amended subsequently, and secondary legislation which is drafted by the Council, Commission and the European Parliament, and by the decisions of the Court of Justice. The Community is very much a unique legal system, the laws of which enter into the legal system of each member state and take priority over domestic, or national, law. As long ago as the early 1960s the Court of Justice was proclaiming the supremacy of Community law over domestic law. Any domestic law which conflicts with Community law must be repealed or set aside. Community law gives citizens of member states legal rights which the domestic courts must uphold and enforce.

Treaty articles, Regulations and Directives, then, represent major sources of Community law. However, of equal importance are the decisions of the European Court, which has the power to interpret Community law and to enforce compliance with the law. The case law or 'jurisprudence' of the European Court is therefore an important source of Community law. In addition to these four sources, the law-making institutions also make decisions, issue opinions and make recommendations. Decisions have less widespread effect: they are binding on those member states or organizations to which they are addressed. Recommendations and opinions, on the other hand, have no binding legal force, but are merely persuasive.

By signing the original Treaty, member states committed themselves to accepting the whole body of Community law, whether introduced before the individual state joined or later. The Treaties impose obligations on the member state to accept, implement and enforce the law of the Community, over and above domestic law. Because there are now fifteen member states, it is of crucial importance to all citizens that their Community law rights are equally respected throughout the European area. There could be no true meaning to Community law if it were to be interpreted differently by judges of differing member states. In the words of the ECJ, by signing the Treaty member states created a new and 'unique legal order', or system, which does not merely exist in parallel to domestic law but takes priority or precedence over it. Community law is supreme, or sovereign.

The Court has adopted imaginative techniques by which to further the applicability and superiority of Community law within the fifteen legal systems. A glance at a few seminal ECJ decisions will explain the way in which the Court works to develop Community law and to ensure its supremacy. The supremacy of Community law has the consequence that its requirements take precedence over all national legislation in relation to matters falling within the ambit of the Community. British Acts of Parliament, whether enacted before the entry of Britain into the Community or subsequently, must be amended or repealed if they conflict with Community law. Equally, even constitutionally guaranteed rights under a written constitution must give way to Community requirements. An early example of this latter phenomenon is provided by *Internationale Handelsgesellschaft GmbH v. EVST*.[54] In that case, under Community law, in order to export produce the company was required to obtain a licence, for which a 'permanent deposit' had to be paid. If the goods were not exported within the licence period, the deposit was to be forfeited. The company paid the deposit, failed to complete the export and forfeiture was made. The company sued the agency involved for return of the deposit, arguing that the forfeiture was contrary to the Constitution of the Federal Republic of Germany. The ECJ ruled that the validity of Community law could not be affected even by allegations that its measures ran counter to fundamental rights as formulated by the constitution of member states.

It is not merely on bare assertions of supremacy – based on the

[54] Case 11/70, [1970] ECR 1125; [1972] CMLR 255.

'transfer of sovereignty' through signing the Treaties – that the Court relies in order to further the integration of Community law throughout the fifteen legal systems. As noted above, the concepts of direct applicability and direct effect determine the application of Community law within national legal systems. In addition, the concept of indirect effect is central to the Court's expansion of the application and binding force of Community law. Direct applicability, which is unique to Regulations, is provided for in the EC Treaty,[55] which states that Regulations are directly applicable in all member states, meaning that once a measure is passed according to the requirements of the Treaty it automatically becomes law: there is no need for action on the part of the legislature of the member state. On the other hand, Directives do not automatically become law within the many legal systems. As discussed above, Directives set an objective to be achieved, and a date for its achievement, but leave a measure of discretion to the national legislatures as to how to achieve the required objective. To this extent the discretion may be regarded as a form of subsidiarity. There is no discretion as to whether or not to implement the Directive: the Article 10 (formerly Article 5) duty imposed on member states makes it clear that all measures that are required to be taken to give effect to Community law must be taken, and failure to act will render a member state liable to proceedings for enforcement of the duty.

The principle of direct effect is nowhere expressed in the EC Treaty: it is a creation of the Court of Justice. Direct effect means that individual citizens may rely on a provision of Community law before their own national courts. If a Community law measure has direct effect, it creates legally enforceable rights. In order for a measure to have direct effect, certain conditions must be fulfilled, namely, the provision must be sufficiently precise, unambiguous and unconditional. For example, Article 6 of the EC Treaty (now Article 14) prohibits discrimination on grounds of nationality in relation to matters governed by the Treaty. That is clear, unambiguous and unconditional: it is therefore directly effective. The original Article 2 of the EC Treaty on the other hand, set out on page 168 above, which states the broad objectives of the Community, is not capable of direct effect because it does not set

[55] Article 249 (formerly Article 189) EC Treaty.

clear, unambiguous standards which the court could enforce: it is not 'justiciable'.[56]

Treaty articles, Regulations and Directives are capable of having direct effect if they meet the required standards. However, the scope of direct effect differs between Treaty articles and Regulations on the one hand and Directives on the other. Treaty articles and Regulations having direct effect can be invoked against the state – this is *vertical direct effect*. However, they may also have direct effect in relation to private parties – known as *horizontal direct effect*. For example, in *Defrenne and Sabena* [57] the Court of Justice ruled that Article 119 of the EC Treaty (now Article 141) had direct effect. Article 141 provides for equal pay for men and women. The article is clear, unambiguous and unconditional: it therefore has direct effect which not only binds the member state but also extends horizontally to bind private employers. By way of contrast, the rights which arise under Directives may only be invoked against the member state's administrative bodies, and, by a subsequent extension developed by the Court, to bodies which, while not formally 'state' bodies, are nevertheless fulfilling functions of the state and are therefore deemed to be 'emanations of the state'.[58]

However, the refusal of the Court of Justice to give directives horizontal direct effect has been compensated for by a further judicial invention – the concept of indirect effect. Article 10 of the EC Treaty (formerly Article 5) imposes a duty on member states to do all in their power to give effect to Community obligations and objectives, and to abstain from taking any measures which could impede the Community. It is this article which the Court of Justice has used imaginatively to further the application of Community law. The Court of Justice has interpreted Article 10 to mean that the obligation it imposes falls not only on the member states but also on all their public authorities, including courts of law.[59] The

---

[56] On direct effect and justiciability see Weatherill, *Law and Integration in the European Union*, chapter 4.   [57] [1974] ECR 1405.

[58] See e.g. *Marshall v. Southampton and South West Hampshire Area Health Authority* [1986] CMLR 688; ECR 723, in which the Health Authority was held liable in relation to sex discrimination as an 'emanation of the state'. See also *Foster v. British Gas* [1991] 2 AC 306.

[59] See *Von Colson v. Land Nordrhein-Westfalen* Case 14/83 [1984] ECR 1891; [1986] 2 CMLR 430.

significance of including national courts within the duty imposed by Article 10 lies in ensuring that courts interpret national law in such a way as to ensure that the obligations imposed by Community law are achieved. Accordingly, where a Directive is made stipulating a time limit for its implementation, as is the usual case, member states are under the obligation to comply with both the content of the Directive and its time limit. Once the date for implementation has passed without implementation an enforceable right arises under the Directive, either directly or indirectly. In addition, national authorities are liable for loss sustained by the state's failure to implement a Directive. Accordingly, should a member state fail to comply with its duty of implementation, it cannot rely on that failure to escape liability under Community law and compensation becomes payable.[60]

One recent clear example of the Court's control is seen in the case of *Commission of the European Communities v. United Kingdom of Great Britain and Northern Ireland*[61] in which the ECJ ruled that the United Kingdom had failed to meet its obligations under a Community clean water Directive. The Commission acted under Article 169 (now Article 226 EC), seeking a declaration that the United Kingdom had failed fully to comply with a Council Directive[62] concerning the protection of waters against pollution caused by nitrates from agricultural sources. The United Kingdom authorities had identified only surface waters intended for extraction of drinking water, whereas the Directive also required the identification of surface freshwaters not intended for the abstraction of drinking water which contained excessive nitrate concentrations or could do so. In addition no 'vulnerable zones' had been identified in Northern Ireland, and those areas which had been designated had been designated on the incorrect criteria as in the rest of the United Kingdom. The fact that the authorities were now taking action to remedy the failure did not remove the state's liability for breach of its obligations under the Directive.

---

[60] See *Marleasing SA v. La Comercial Internacional de Alimentacion SA* Case 106/89 [1992] 1 CMLR 305; *Francovich and Bonifaci v. Italy* Cases C-6, C-990 [1993] 2 CMLR 66; *Dillenkofer and Others v. Federal Republic of Germany* Cases C-178–179, C 188, C-190/94 [1996] ECR I-4845, [1996] 3 CMLR 469.

[61] Case 69/99, *The Times* 19 December 2000.

[62] Directive 91/676/EEC of 12 December 1991.

EUROPEAN MONETARY UNION

The introduction of a single currency was the most ambitious, and controversial, aim of the European Union. European Monetary Union (EMU) facilitates the free movement of capital, one of the four freedoms on which the original Economic Community was founded, and is designed to cut transaction costs throughout the Union, thereby making it more competitive, and to ease the free movement of persons between the countries of the Union. The objective of introducing a single European-wide currency was first mooted in 1969, although in the face of adverse economic circumstances nothing was to come of it. In 1977 the then President of the European Commission, Roy Jenkins, resurrected the plan, which resulted in the introduction of the European Monetary System (EMS) in 1979, intended to create greater stability among European currencies. Central to the EMS were the European Currency Unit – the ecu – and the Exchange Rate Mechanism (ERM). The Exchange Rate Mechanism established an agreed margin within which individual currencies were allowed to fluctuate, thereby helping to stabilize currencies. Initially eight countries participated: Belgium, Denmark, France, Germany, Ireland, Italy, Luxembourg and the Netherlands. Spain joined in 1989, the United Kingdom in 1990 and Portugal in 1992. The currencies were permitted to fluctuate within 2.25 per cent, but the escudo, lira, peseta and pound sterling allowed a broader band of 6 per cent. In 1992, following 'Black Wednesday', the lira and pound sterling left the ERM. In 1993 the ERM suffered another blow from currency speculation, forcing the band of permissible fluctuation to be increased to 15 per cent. In 1996 Finland joined the ERM, followed by Italy rejoining in 1996, Greece entering in 1998.

No mention of the single currency was made in the Treaties until the 1986 Single European Act.[63] Substantial progress came with the presidency of Jacques Delors, a former French Foreign Minister. The *Delors Report* of 1989[64] led to the 1990 Intergovernmental Conference on EMU, which in turn led to the Treaty on European Union 1992,

---

[63] Which amended the EC Treaty to include provisions for Co-operation in Economic and Monetary Policy.   [64] *Report on Economic and Monetary Union.*

the Maastricht Treaty. The Maastricht Treaty laid down a three-stage timetable for achievement of the single currency, now renamed the euro,[65] and provided strict 'convergence criteria' which currencies had to meet before being eligible to join. The first stage, beginning in 1990, focused on achieving greater convergence between the economies of member states. The second stage commenced in January 1994, during which member states were to work together to avoid substantial budget deficits and were to move towards ensuring the independence of their national banks from government. The European Monetary Institute was established as a forerunner to the European Central Bank. The third stage involved the introduction of the single currency by January 1999, and the withdrawal of national currencies.

Under the Maastricht Treaty, member states could only join the single currency once their economies satisfied the convergence criteria, which involved four separate requirements.[66] First, the average rate of inflation in a one-year period must not exceed by more than 1.5 per cent the average of the three best performing member states. Secondly, there was to be an annual budget deficit of no more than 3 per cent of Gross Domestic Product and an overall public debt ratio not exceeding 60 per cent of Gross Domestic Product. Thirdly, the member state's currency must have been within the bands of the Exchange Rate Mechanism for two years prior to the assessment. Fourthly, the member state's average long-term interest rate, measured over a year, must not exceed by more than 2 per cent the average interest rates in the three best performing states in terms of inflation.

These stringent requirements proved difficult to meet. Indeed, in 1995 neither France nor Germany – the principal architects of the rules – could meet the criteria and a survey in 1996 showed that America, Canada and Japan could not meet them and of developed nations only Singapore could satisfy the requirements.[67] When in 1998 the European Council met to assess which states had matched the convergence criteria

---

[65] Following agreement in the Council of Ministers, an agreement which should technically have been incorporated by means of a formal Treaty amendment, but was not.

[66] *The Protocol on the Convergence Criteria*, relating to Article 121(1), formerly Article 109j(I) EC Treaty.

[67] See *Sunday Times*, 14 January 1996.

and thereby qualified for entry into the single currency from 1 January 1999, Greece could not achieve the first and fourth criteria and only four states had achieved the debt ratio target (Finland, France, Luxembourg and the United Kingdom). Despite that, the Commission recommended that all states apart from Greece qualified because the ratio was by then diminishing and moving towards the required position, an assessment which was at odds with the reality of the position, emphasizing, in Weatherill and Beaumont's analysis, the discretion or 'interpretative latitude' accorded to the Commission under the Treaty provisions.[68]

The British government's position on monetary union has moved from John Major's cautious 'wait and see' policy to the Labour government's more constructive commitment to join the euro when economic conditions are right – subject always to the right of the British electorate to decide via a referendum. European monetary union poses particularly acute problems for the present British government, some of which must be laid at the door of its predecessors. With the former Conservative government ambivalent and the current government still formally unprepared to commit itself wholeheartedly to joining, and with disagreements among those most qualified to judge the arguments for and against, such as the Institute of Directors and Confederation of British Industry, it is small wonder that the people are wary.

The problem is compounded by two other factors which have a more general relevance to the European enterprise than monetary union. First, successive governments have expressed public unease, if not aversion, to a deepening of European integration that could undermine national sovereignty. The signing and ratification of the Maastricht Treaty almost tore the last Conservative government apart. But at the same time as ministers are seemingly empathizing with the anti-European sentiments fuelled by a largely jingoistic press,[69] they are also collectively furthering European integration. It was Margaret Thatcher (she of the 'we want our money back' in 1984 over the dispute about British financial contributions to the Community budget) who, notwithstanding her overt displeasure over Europe, nevertheless signed the

---

[68] See Weatherill and Beaumont, *EU Law*, pp. 769–75.

[69] Generally the tabloid and Conservative-minded press – most memorably summarized in the *Sun*'s headline in 1986 'Up Yours Delors'.

Single European Act 1986 which significantly furthered integration by setting the timetable for achieving the single market and setting the scene for European Monetary Union which would follow at Maastricht. Secondly, successive governments have failed to provide citizens with the raw material for decision-making over Europe: information. Whereas in France, for example, in the run-up to the signing and ratification of the Maastricht Treaty, the government ensured that all citizens had access to copious information about the aims, objectives and implications of the Union that was coming into being, in order that a rational decision could be reached at the referendum, in Britain the government issued no official publications which reached into the homes of its citizens. It was largely left to the mainly hostile press to 'inform' the public. The third problem in relation to public perceptions of the Community and Union is the lack of transparency in European government and the perceived 'democratic deficit' which has always afflicted Community and Union decisions. Simply expressed, too few citizens understand Europe, particularly in Britain, where turn-outs for European parliamentary elections remain the lowest among member states. There exist uninformed but nevertheless damaging and not totally unfounded suspicions concerning the European institutions – no more convincingly illustrated than by the corruption scandal in the Commission which led to its block resignation in 1999. And there remains the largely historically determined feeling – notwithstanding nearly thirty years of membership of the Community – that Europe is 'over there' – a 'foreign' and not understood form of 'government', of which, quite wrongly, Britain is seen not to be a part. Such intangible but perceptible forces are manifest in repeated opinion polls which record dissatisfaction at least, and aversion at worst, to all that is 'European'.

EXTENDING THE UNION AND FURTHER INTEGRATION: 'WIDTH AND DEPTH'

The expansion of membership of the Union is the most obvious form of 'widening' the Union. The Union does not encourage applications, particularly from states which are not economically, politically or socially comparable to existing member states. However, for the applicants, the prospect of joining the Union offers clear economic advantages, through the opening up of access to the single market and the availability of Union financial aid for their economies. The current applicant states include Cyprus, Malta and Turkey, the remainder are from Eastern and Central Europe: Bulgaria, the Czech Republic, Estonia, Hungary, Latvia, Lithuania, Poland, Romania, Slovakia and Slovenia. This is not without its difficulties, and many matters remain to be resolved before those states which have applied for membership can be admitted. The negotiations for accession span a two-year period, and before being admitted applicant countries are required to implement social and economic reforms, and to show stable democratic government and a reasonable record in the protection of individual rights and freedoms. Several applicant states may fail for lack of a stable democratic government and for a poor human rights record. However, the timetable is not rigid: Hungary, for example, applied for membership in 1994. It was originally believed that it would be admitted by 2000, but the decision has been delayed and could remain so until 2005.

The decision on membership must be reached by unanimity, and admission approved by the European Parliament. Both political and financial factors affect the decision. Cyprus's application is bedevilled by the island's division into Turkish-Cypriot and Greek-Cypriot territories and the long-standing hostility of Greece towards occupying Turkey. Turkey's application dates from 1987, and, even without the complicating factor of Cyprus, Turkey's record on human rights is too poor for admission – even if Greece's hostility could be overcome. All the applicant nations are poorer economically than current member states, which presents the intractable problem of adjusting Union finances, both to provide financial aid to bring the weak economies more in line with the rest of Europe and to avoid pouring a disproportionate amount of Union finances into aid. The Commission estimated that the cost of pre-accession aid would amount to £2 billion annually between 2000 and 2006. The problem is exacerbated by the disparity in the populations and economies of applicant states. At the one end is Cyprus with a population of 0.7 million and a Gross Domestic Product (GDP) of 60 per cent of the European Union average, to Poland with a population of 38.6 million and a GDP per head of 31 per cent of the European

Union average. The problems facing applicant states also concern the requirement to accept, on membership, the complete *acquis communautaire* – the laws, policies and principles on which the Community and Union are founded – which in practical terms means adjusting to some 12,000 pages of rules and regulations.

As an interim measure, special agreements have been made with applicant states which offer advantages without full membership. The European Economic Area (EEA) is an example of such arrangements. The EEA was established by a treaty signed in 1992 to accommodate the European Free Trade Area (EFTA) states within the Community's single market, thereby facilitating the free movement of capital, goods, persons and services. It came into being in 1994.[70] Austria, Finland and Sweden moved from the EEA to full membership of the Union within a year, leaving only Iceland, Liechtenstein and Norway (which voted against membership of the Union) in the EEA together with the fifteen member states of the Union. With the break-up of the Soviet Union, Central and Eastern European states entered into Association Agreements with the Union, as a forerunner to possible full membership once the necessary conditions are achieved. The EEA does not extend to the European Monetary System or Economic and Monetary Union, nor do the Common Agricultural Policy or Common Fisheries Policy apply in the EEA. The common Foreign and Security Policy and Justice and Home Affairs pillars of the Union do not apply to the EEA. The expanding membership raises institutional issues which were due to be tackled at the 1996 Intergovernmental Conference leading to the Treaty of Amsterdam 1997, but which remained unresolved.[71]

Related to the Commission size is the question of voting in the Council of Ministers. Unanimous voting is required over major constitutional issues, such as admission to the Union, the appointment of members of the Commission and revision of the Treaties. With enlargement, the question for resolution is whether it can remain the case that the smallest state has the power to block Union progress through the use of the veto. For a state with a population of 0.7 million

[70] The EEA Treaty was signed under Article 238 of the EC Treaty and is formally an Association Agreement.
[71] One of these issues related to the size of the Commission, agreement on which was reached at the Nice 2000 summit meeting, as discussed above.

(Cyprus) to be able to block the will of the Union would represent a disproportionate amount of power. On the other hand, the Union is founded on the equal respect for all member states, which suggests that there could be no compromising on the unanimity principle. As has been seen above, under qualified majority voting – which is increasingly the norm – the weighting of votes in Council greatly favours smaller states. This is a consciously designed formula which protects smaller states against the dominance of the largest members. However, with enlargement an adjustment of qualified majority voting was an inevitable consequence. The argument centres less on the number of votes a member state should have, and rather more on the percentage of votes needed to block a proposal. From 1995 the qualified majority was fixed at 62 votes with a blocking minority of 25 votes. Any increase in the size of the blocking minority is resisted by the larger states as weakening their relative position. At the Nice 2000 summit, this proved to be the most contentious area for negotiation. Britain gave up the right of veto over a further thirty-nine areas of decision-making. However, unanimous voting has been retained for taxation, social security, most immigration policies and trade in audiovisual products.

The other aspect of 'widening' of the Union and Community relates to the scope of matters which fall within Union competence. As has been seen, the original aims of the three founding Treaties, the European Coal and Steel Community, European Atomic Energy Community and European Economic Community, involved relatively modest goals. The dominant Community, itself aimed at establishing a Common Market regulated by 'supranational' institutions. Notwithstanding the federalist objectives of modern Europe's founding fathers, the Common Market with its four freedoms was a far cry from the Union which has emerged over the past ten years. Citizenship of the Union, increasing competence of the Community at the expense of member state competence, European Monetary Union, the Common Foreign and Security Policy with the emerging common defence policy and co-operation in policing and criminal law matters, all represent an increasingly broad-ranging governmental experiment which looks far closer to a 'United States of Europe' than at any time hitherto.

CONCLUSION

The widening of the Union's membership has been accompanied by the realization that ever-closer integration – the 'depth factor' – is increasingly elusive. The principle of subsidiarity, discussed above, witnesses this realization as do the 'minimum harmonization' principles, whereby the Community sets the minimum standards to be achieved but leaves member states free – within the confines of the aims and objectives of the Community – to adopt more stringent standards. It is this fundamental conundrum which remains unresolved at the political level. At the 2000 summit, greater flexibility was provided for in decisions, allowing for member states to opt out of certain areas and to opt in at a later stage if they choose to do so.[72] The widening membership, encompassing economically disparate states, many of which have a legacy of former Soviet rule, raises acutely the difficulties entailed in harmonization across the Union. The price of 'width' may be the lessening of 'depth'. The dangers in less depth – weaker integration and harmonization – threaten the whole Union endeavour as it was originally conceived. On the other hand, given the cultural, economic and political diversity of its current and potential members, less depth may yet save the Union from either (or both?) fragmentation or stagnation.

[72] An Intergovernmental Conference is to take place in 2004 to discuss future development of the Union.

5

REGIONAL AND LOCAL GOVERNMENT

INTRODUCTION

For centuries the United Kingdom has been a highly centralized state, with law-making and administration concentrated in Westminster and Whitehall – the square-mile hub of government in London. However, no institution, or complex of institutions as represented by the centralized executive, Prime Minister, Cabinet and other ministers, government departments and Parliament, could realistically be responsible for the administration of the four nations of the United Kingdom – England, Northern Ireland, Scotland and Wales – and the different regions. While the United Kingdom Parliament is legally supreme or sovereign in its law-making power, and the elected government represents all areas of Britain, powers have been devolved to subordinate bodies within the state. Historically, the oldest form of devolved power has been to local government: the several hundred local authorities, directly elected by voters in the counties and boroughs, and responsible for providing local services, ranging from education, housing, library services, leisure amenities and social services to waste disposal.

In recent years there have been growing demands for greater autonomy for the nations of Britain, most particularly from Scotland. While devolution from Westminster has long been on the political agenda, it was not until 1998 that it was effected in relation to Scotland and Wales. Northern Ireland had enjoyed some fifty years of near self-rule until the 1970s when civil strife caused power to be returned to Westminster. As seen below, power was redevolved in 1998, but subject to the condition that the terms of the Peace Agreement were complied with. In addition to its pledge to devolve power, the Labour government also set in train the process of having an elected Mayor and Assembly for London, a measure which could extend to other major cities in the future. The issue of the representation of and for England and its regions lies in the future.

The making of the United Kingdom was an evolutionary process rather than a self-consciously and formally designed plan. The union of the four countries, England, Ireland, Scotland and Wales, was complete by 1800, although by 1921 Ireland had been partitioned, with the south becoming the independent and sovereign Republic of Ireland and six counties of the nine-county province of Ulster remaining in the United Kingdom, but (until 1972) with its own Parliament and a high degree of legislative and administrative autonomy.

NORTHERN IRELAND

Ireland first came under English control in the twelfth century, although by the fifteenth century English rule extended only to the Pale, a stretch of coastal land running some fifty miles north of Dublin and twenty miles inland. The province of Ulster remained largely unaffected by English rule until the sixteenth century when Elizabeth I decided that government in Ireland should, as far as possible, be approximated to that of England. The Irish people, however, with their own language and culture and adhering to the Roman Catholic Church with which Henry VIII had broken in 1536, did not submit willingly to English imperialism. Two centuries of intermittent rebellion and suppression followed before a political union was formed by Treaty in 1800. The province of Ulster always posed particular problems for England, the seeds of intractable and enduring difficulties sown early. Settlers from England and Ireland gravitated towards Ulster, and under James I (1603–25) a comprehensive scheme of 'plantation' began: by 1622 some 21,000 English, Scottish and Welsh immigrants had settled, bringing with them a foreign language and a different religion. In the period of Commonwealth government, from 1649 to 1660 when the monarchy was restored in England, continuing opposition to English rule led to suppression. With conquest achieved in 1652, the terms of settlement were set out in the Act of Settlement for Ireland, which included the provision that every Irish landowner would have his estate forfeited unless he could prove that he had shown 'constant good affection to the interests of the Commonwealth of England'. By 1660, the share of land owned by native Catholics had declined from 60 per cent to 20 per cent of the total, the native population having been displaced by immigrants who had either fought for the English and accepted land in lieu of pay, or by those who had lent money to the government to suppress the rebellion. When James II fled from England to France in 1688, he attempted to use Ireland as a means to regain his throne. At the Battle of the Boyne in 1690 James was defeated by the army under William III. Protestantism was again in the ascendant and some 12,000 Catholics went into exile.

A century later, two organizations were formed to represent conflicting interests: in 1791 the Society of United Irishmen was established in Belfast, with republicanism – full independence from England for an Irish State – as its political platform. In 1794, in the north, the Protestant and staunchly pro-English Orange Order was established. The year 1800 brought political union, the Act of Union 1800 providing for union between England and Ireland on the basis of theoretical equality, with equal independence and guarantees of Catholic emancipation. The Kingdom of Ireland and the Kingdom of Great Britain were united under the United Kingdom of Great Britain and Ireland. Irish interests were to be represented in the United Kingdom's House of Lords by twenty-eight Irish peers and four bishops; representation in the House of Commons was by one hundred Irish members.

By the late nineteenth century Catholic demands for Irish Home Rule were becoming insistent. Two Home Rule Bills were introduced into Parliament in 1886 and 1893, both of which were defeated, largely on the issue of 'taxation and representation': if Ireland was to have its own legislative body, albeit subordinate to the Westminster Parliament, the question arose as to the appropriate level of representation of Irish interests at Westminster. The British Parliament was to retain the right to legislate for Irish taxation. It followed therefore that it was necessary to have continued representation of Ireland at Westminster. On the other hand, continued Irish representation would, unless a workable solution could be found, mean that Irish representatives would be voting on matters relating solely to English and Scottish affairs. With no solutions forthcoming, relations between England and Ireland deteriorated.

In 1905 Sinn Fein was established, pursuing strongly nationalist objectives. By the outbreak of the First World War in 1914, Ireland was close to civil war. In 1916 nationalists in Dublin initiated an uprising. On Easter Monday rebellion broke out in support of Home Rule and the end of English imperialism. It was brutally suppressed, and fifteen men were executed. Although it was unsuccessful, the uprising consolidated the nationalist cause. In the 1918 general election, Sinn Fein candidates won in all but the staunchly Unionist north, securing 73 seats with 48 per cent of the votes cast: the Unionists secured only 29 per cent of the vote. The government proceeded to ban Sinn Fein, and its leader Éamon de Valera was arrested. In response, Sinn Fein Members of Parliament refused to take their seats at Westminster,[1] and instead issued a Declaration of Independence and established the first Irish Parliament – the Dáil Éireann. Civil unrest, terrorist campaigns against the authorities and brutal repression followed. The pressure of public opinion in Ireland, England and from overseas demanded a settlement.

It came with the partition of Ireland under the Government of Ireland Act 1920. In the south, the Parliament of Southern Ireland rejected the Act, and the struggle for independence continued. In the new Ulster, now six of the original nine counties,[2] however, a Parliament – subordinate to Westminster but enjoying considerable autonomy over Northern Irish affairs – was established. In each of these six counties, Protestants were in the majority. In the excluded counties, Cavan, Donegal and Monaghan, Catholics were in the majority, and the Unionists, who in any case did not want Home Rule, were not prepared to accept Home Rule via a Parliament in which they could not be assured

---

[1] A situation which currently exists, with both Martin McGuinness and Gerry Adams of Sinn Fein refusing to take their seats in Parliament.

[2] Antrim, Armagh, Down, Fermanagh, Londonderry and Tyrone.

of a majority and thus control. The solution of Home Rule for the north carried with it the irony that it was only in the north that British rule was both acceptable and wanted. The Unionists alone wanted continued rule from Westminster, and yet had a Parliament thrust upon them.

In 1921 agreement was finally reached over the south, and the Irish Free State, with Dominion status under the Crown, represented by a Governor General, was established. The Anglo-Irish Treaty establishing the Irish Free State gave to the Parliament of Northern Ireland the choice as to whether or not it should be part of it: the north opted out, turning its face inwards. The 1920 Act had provided for a Council of Ireland, a cross-border organization, represented by equal numbers of members of the Parliaments of the north and south. Not only would this have provided a forum for discussion and resolution of cross-border issues, but it was also to have the power to reach politically binding decisions as to the future of the whole of Ireland, without reference to Westminster. This could have provided the mechanism for either maintaining what was now the *status quo*, or for the eventual resolution of nationalist and religious conflicts and the reunification of all Ireland, without the involvement of the British government. As the south rejected the 1920 Act and the north opted out of membership of the Irish Free State, the Council never came into being.

The position of the south remained uncertain until 1937 when the Constitution of the Irish Free State was drafted by de Valera, proclaiming the 'inalienable, indefeasible and sovereign right' of the Irish nation to choose its own form of government, 'to determine its relations with other nations, and to develop its life, political, economic and cultural, in accordance with its own genius and traditions'. It was not until 1949 that the United Kingdom Parliament accepted this separation and passed the Ireland Act of that year.

In Northern Ireland, the failure to introduce the cross-border Council of Ireland isolated the north from the south, cutting off what could have been a forum for the representation of Catholics living in the north. But Northern Ireland was also now cut off from Westminster. The powers devolved from Westminster to Stormont, while based on the principle of the supremacy of Westminster and subordination of Stormont, were considerable. Moreover, the Government of Ireland Act, the juridical foundation of self-government in the north, made it clear that matters which had been devolved could no longer be debated in Westminster: a rule enforced by the Speaker of the House of Commons. In 1922 the Civil Authorities (Special Powers) Act had been passed which provided – among other measures – for detention and internment, a measure which inflamed anti-Unionist opinion among Catholics who feared that the Act would be used against them. The Act remained in force until 1972, when the Northern Ireland Parliament was suspended by Westminster. Since representation at Stormont was always dominated by Unionist representatives, and the executive equally dominated by the Unionists, the considerable Catholic minority in the north was under-represented, and had no right of appeal to the United Kingdom Parliament about its grievances. And they were many. Protestants dominated the police force, with Catholic officers never being more than 20 per cent of the force. The part-time police force, the 'B Specials', was entirely Protestant, and gained a reputation for discrimination and violence. Housing and education were both segregated – Catholics being allocated the poorest quality services. The electoral system further inflamed Catholic discontent. Initially, a system of proportional representation was used, a system which ensured a proportional representation of Catholics within the legislature. That electoral system was subsequently abandoned in favour of the simple majority – the 'first past the post' system – the consequence of which was to reduce Catholic representation and ensure the hegemony of Unionists. Mutual distrust and antagonism between the two communities in the north intensified.

By 1968 Northern Ireland was a community about to ignite. A campaign of civil disobedience and unrest began. For Catholic protesters the targets were the systematic discrimination in education and housing and the continued union with mainland Britain. By 1969 British troops were deployed to Northern Ireland to support the police whose operational control over security matters became subject to military control. In 1972 the Democratic Unionist Party was formed by the ultra-right wing Unionist, the Reverend Ian Paisley, a passionate opponent of republicanism and staunch supporter of Northern Ireland's continued link with the rest of the United Kingdom. By the end of 1972, 474 deaths had occurred in the escalation of sectarian killing by Protestant murderers and the Irish Republican Army (IRA). No longer could

Westminster afford to ignore the 'Irish problem': the Northern Ireland Parliament was prorogued indefinitely and the powers of the Northern Ireland government were transferred to a Secretary of State for Northern Ireland.

An attempt to resurrect government in Northern Ireland was made in 1973 through power sharing. An Assembly was to be established, having 78 members elected under the single transferable vote system, and an executive drawn from the three major parties. The refusal of the Ulster Unionist Party caused the collapse of the initiative and direct rule was imposed from 1974. As the virtual civil war continued, the government sought the co-operation of the Republic of Ireland to reach a settlement. In 1985 an Anglo-Irish Agreement was concluded, signed by the Prime Ministers of the United Kingdom and the Republic. The Agreement held out the hope of greater co-operation in relation to security, economic, social and cultural matters and the promotion of reconciliation between the north and south. An Intergovernmental Conference was convened to consider further developments. Once again, the Ulster Unionists opposed the Agreement, claiming that it involved an unwarranted interference by the Republic of Ireland in Northern Ireland affairs.

The year 1993 saw the start of the current round of the search for a lasting peace and the reinstatement of self-rule for Northern Ireland. In that year a Joint Declaration was signed between the British and Irish governments, recognizing the preservation of the union of Northern Ireland within the United Kingdom for as long as the majority wished, but also indicating that the government was neutral as to the long-term future of the province. In 1994 the IRA announced a ceasefire of hostilities. The prospects for peace were now higher than they had been since direct rule was imposed. However, the British government, while prepared to enter negotiations with Sinn Fein – the political wing of the IRA – made this conditional on the IRA agreeing to decommission its weapons. Stalemate followed. Then in 1996 the IRA bombed Canary Wharf in London, killing two people, and Manchester city centre, together causing millions of pounds' worth of damage to property. The ceasefire was over.

The general election of 1997 brought renewed hopes of reviving the peace process. The IRA announced a further ceasefire in September, and all-party talks began, only to be frustrated by renewed IRA violence which led to Sinn Fein's expulsion from the talks. An olive branch was extended, however, Sinn Fein being told that it could return to the talks if the violence ceased. On 10 April 1998, Good Friday, agreement was finally reached. The Good Friday Agreement focused on five principal points. First, Northern Ireland would remain a part of the United Kingdom, and the Republic of Ireland agreed formally to amend its constitution to remove its claim to Northern Ireland. Secondly, a Northern Ireland Assembly of 108 members was to be elected, to be run by an executive of 12 members drawn from all political parties. Thirdly, a North–South Ministerial Council was to be established to co-ordinate relations between Ireland and Ulster. Fourthly, a British–Irish Council was to be set up, its membership drawn from the Parliaments at Westminster, Dublin and Edinburgh and the Welsh Assembly, with representatives of the Isle of Man and the Channel Isles, to consider matters of mutual interest. The Agreement required ratification by the people and in May 1998 was approved by a referendum. In Northern Ireland, on a turn-out of 81.1 per cent, 71.1 per cent voted for peace, while in the Republic, on a turn-out of 56 per cent, 94 per cent voted for peace. Parliament passed the Northern Ireland (Elections) Act 1998 to establish elections for the new Assembly which were held in June 1998, and the Good Friday Agreement was formalized in the Northern Ireland Act 1998.

The Agreement, however, provided one important caveat. The power-sharing executive came into being in 1998, led by David Trimble, Leader of the Unionist Party, and his deputy, Seamus Mallon, Deputy Leader of the Social Democratic Labour Party. The offices are jointly held, and if one resigns so too must the other. This power-sharing formula is a unique experiment in the United Kingdom, for the First Minister and his Deputy were elected on the basis of cross-community support which required that they each secured a majority of the votes of designated Unionists and nationalists. The First Minister, however, unlike a Prime Minister, does not have the power to appoint ministers to the executive. Appointment to the executive is on the basis of the proportion of party strengths in the Assembly, thus ensuring that the executive reflects cross-community interests. The executive was to start functioning once the IRA had satisfied the terms of the Good Friday

Agreement and commenced decommissioning arms. When the IRA dragged its feet over this, and devolution looked doomed, David Trimble persuaded his Ulster Unionist Party to compromise – agreeing to work in government with the other parties. As a result, for the first time in history the opposing forces of the unionists and nationalists came together for the greater good of Northern Ireland. Martin McGuinness, reputedly a former chief of staff in the IRA and member of the Westminster Parliament, became Northern Ireland's Minister of Education. The ten-person executive is made up of three Ulster Unionists, three Social Democratic and Labour Party members, two Democratic Unionist Party members and two members of Sinn Fein, Gerry Adams and Martin McGuinness.

Legislative power, however, as defined in the 1998 Act, would not be devolved to the Assembly unless and until the IRA began its programme for decommissioning arms. This, as in previous attempts at peace, was to prove a sticking-point, which further delayed the devolution of power. The system adopted was that of a decommissioning body, headed by General John de Chastelain, who would deal in confidence with a chosen representative of the IRA. By late 1999, however, little progress had been made and the prospects for devolution were becoming increasingly uncertain. In two reports issued in February 2000, General de Chastelain's Commission revealed that the IRA had given no information as to when it would start decommissioning, but that the IRA had indicated that ways could be found to put weapons 'beyond use' – that is to say, in sealed and inaccessible sites rather than being handed over to the government. Ulster's unique attempt at power sharing came to an end that month, the executive being suspended after just seventy-two days in office, and the threat of permanent direct rule returned, only to be averted by the IRA's commitment to put its arms 'beyond use' and the Ulster Unionist Party accepting an extension of time for the IRA to give effect to its promise. Power was restored to Northern Ireland in May 2000.

The Assembly has full legislative and executive power over agriculture, education, economic development, health and social services, environment and finance. Powers over the police, security, prisons and criminal justice system are, however, reserved to Westminster, and the Assembly has no tax-raising powers.

The Northern Ireland Act 1998 reiterates earlier pledges in relation to the status of Northern Ireland, confirming that the province remains part of the United Kingdom and that it 'shall not cease to be so without the consent of the majority of the people of Northern Ireland voting in a poll' held specifically to determine that question. In addition to defining the roles and powers of the executive and Assembly, the Act builds in several features which reflect the aspects of past troubles in the province. The Act makes clear that neither ministers nor Northern Ireland Departments have the power to make subordinate legislation or to do any act which is incompatible with rights protected under the European Convention on Human Rights or Community law, provisions which are common to other parliaments. The Act also, however, protects against discrimination against individuals, or classes of individuals, on the grounds of religious belief or political opinion. Furthermore, the Act gives to the Assembly the power to exclude a minister or junior minister or a political party from the Assembly if they no longer enjoy the 'confidence of the Assembly' – a concept defined as being that the person or party is not committed to non-violence and exclusively peaceful and democratic means. If the Assembly passes a resolution to exclude a person or party, the exclusion is to last for twelve months, which may be extended for a further twelve-month period. If the Secretary of State for Northern Ireland considers that the Assembly ought to pass such a resolution, he or she may require the Presiding Officer (the equivalent to the Speaker of the House of Commons) to put such a motion to the Assembly. The considerations which the Secretary of State must take into account in requiring such a motion to be put to the Assembly include whether a person or party is committed to peaceful means, whether that person or party has ceased to be involved in acts of violence, whether that person is directing or promoting acts of violence by other persons and whether they are co-operating with the decommissioning Commission.[3] The Act also establishes a Human Rights Commission, an institution which has no equivalent in the rest of the United Kingdom despite many demands that such a body be introduced. The functions of the Commission include overseeing the adequacy and effectiveness of law and practice in relation to

---

[3] Northern Ireland Act 1998, section 30.

the protection of human rights, and reporting to the Secretary of State such recommendations as are considered necessary to improve law and practice. The Commission has a duty to advise the Assembly on the compatibility of Bills with human rights. The Commission is also under a duty to promote understanding and awareness of the importance of human rights in Northern Ireland. The Commission may undertake any investigations which it considers necessary. The Commission may also give assistance to individuals and bring proceedings in relation to human rights law and practice.[4] Where a person applies for assistance, the Commission may grant the application on the grounds that the case raises a question of principle; that it would be unreasonable to expect the person to deal with the case without assistance; or that there are other special circumstances warranting assistance. Assistance includes the provision of legal advice, arrangements for legal representation and any other assistance the Commission thinks appropriate.[5]

The Act also establishes an Equality Commission for Northern Ireland, consisting of between fourteen and twenty Commissioners appointed by the Secretary of State who, so far as practicable, must ensure that the Commissioners as a group are representative of the community in Northern Ireland.[6] The Equality Commission replaces bodies formerly promoting equal opportunities.[7] A statutory duty is imposed on all public authorities to

have due regard to the need to promote equality of opportunity between persons of different religious belief, political opinion, racial group, age, marital status or sexual orientation; between men and women generally; between persons with a disability and those without and between those with dependants and those without. It is unlawful for a public authority to discriminate, or aid or incite another to discriminate, against a person or class of persons on the ground of religious belief or political opinion.[8]

These measures are designed to reassure the Catholic minority that their rights will be protected and that they will be treated equally in relation to all civil liberties and human rights, and that no public bodies

---

[4] Ibid., section 69.
[5] Ibid., section 70. No person may bring an action unless he or she is a 'victim' of the alleged unlawful act.   [6] See also ibid., Schedules 8 and 9.
[7] Ibid., section 74.   [8] Ibid., section 76.

will be able to act in a discriminatory fashion, or if they do, there will be a remedy in law. An issue remaining for resolution following devolution is that of the position of the police in Northern Ireland. The Catholic minority in the province has never been adequately represented in the Royal Ulster Constabulary which has been and remains an essentially Protestant force. As part of the Good Friday Agreement, the government agreed to appoint an independent commission on policing for Northern Ireland, and that the commission would be 'broadly representative with expert and international representation among its membership'. In 1998 the Prime Minister appointed Chris Patten, former governor of Hong Kong, to chair an independent inquiry into policing in the province. The terms of reference of the Commission required that the Commission's proposals were designed to ensure that

The police service is structured, managed and resourced so that it can be effective in discharging its full range of functions (including proposals on any necessary arrangements for the transition to policing in a normal peaceful society);

The police service is delivered in constructive and inclusive partnerships with the community at all levels with the maximum of delegation of authority and responsibility;

The legislative and constitutional framework requires the impartial discharge of policing functions and conforms with internationally accepted norms in relation to policing standards;

The police operate within a clear framework of accountability to the law and the community they serve . . .

The Commission reported in 1999. In response, the government introduced legislation to give effect to the Commission's proposals. The Police (Northern Ireland) Act 2000 includes arrangements for the equal recruitment of Catholics and non-Catholics to the service and introduces a new Policing Board to hold the police to account. The Board is to include representatives from all the major political parties. The Board supplements the office of Police Ombudsman which is already established. The Act also provided for the Royal Ulster Constabulary to be renamed the Police Service for Northern Ireland.[9]

---

[9] With effect from November 2001.

SCOTLAND

Scotland has a total area of some 30,000 square miles representing an area three-fifths the size of England, with a population of some 10 per cent of the United Kingdom total. Following centuries of armed conflict, the two formerly sovereign nations of England and Scotland were united in 1707 under the Treaty of Union, ratified by the respective independent Parliaments in the Acts of Union. In 1885 the office of Secretary for Scotland was established, which in 1892 became a Cabinet post. A degree of administrative autonomy for Scotland has long been in place, with Boards created to administer agriculture, fisheries, local government, prisons, health and education, each operating under the supervision of the Scottish Secretary of State. When Scotland joined the Union it had an established legal system which had developed along different lines from that of England and Wales. This system was specifically protected under the Treaty of Union, and remains a distinctive body of law with its own court system.

In 1968 the government set up the Royal Commission on the Constitution to consider the question of devolution to both Scotland and Wales. The Report[10] was divided on the issue of devolution, a powerful minority setting out the objections to devolution, which included the fragmentation of 'sovereignty' within the United Kingdom. Concern was also expressed over the fact that devolution would confer on Scottish and Welsh citizens greater political rights than English citizens. There were also principled objections to giving Scottish and Welsh Members of Parliament law-making powers in which English Members of Parliament could not participate, while Scottish and Welsh Members of Parliament could vote on purely English affairs (a problem which had bedevilled the Home Rule debate in relation to Ireland in the nineteenth and early twentieth centuries).

Nevertheless, the demands from Scotland for greater self-rule remained. The Labour government's attempts at devolution in the 1970s

---

[10] *Report of the Royal Commission on the Constitution 1969–1973*, Cmnd. 5460 (London: HMSO, 1973).

failed through lack of local popular support. That did not end the debate however, which was revitalized in the 1980s under Margaret Thatcher's premiership. The Conservative Party had long lacked substantial support north of the border. In 1955 Conservative candidates took over 50 per cent of the vote, but by 1987 this had declined to 24 per cent, with only ten Conservative Members of Parliament in Scotland, in contrast to Labour's fifty Members elected with 42.4 per cent of the vote. Mrs Thatcher's reform of the rating system, through the introduction of the 'poll tax' which came into force in 1989, a year before being applied in England and Wales, provided a focus for Scottish discontent, leading to widespread avoidance and the inability of the authorities to collect the tax. Mrs Thatcher's 'experiment' with the Scots was to fuel the fires of devolution as the only means of securing national self-determination and escaping the 'tyranny' of government centred in London. The Labour Party, meanwhile, having far greater electoral support than the Conservatives, continued while in opposition to support devolution, a commitment which by the 1997 general election had become an unequivocal election manifesto pledge.

The campaign for devolution in Scotland was spearheaded by an all-party Campaign for a Scottish Assembly, which in 1988, through its Constitutional Steering Committee, issued a Claim of Right for Scotland. In 1989 a Constitutional Convention was established to explore the issue further, publishing two major reports, *Towards Scotland's Parliament* in 1990 and *Scotland's Parliament, Scotland's Right* in 1995. Once in office, the Labour government set in train the devolution process, first through referendums in both Scotland and Wales to ensure popular support. In relation to Scotland, two questions were asked of the electorate. First, whether there was support for a Scottish Parliament and secondly whether the Parliament should have tax-varying powers. The referendum, held in September 1997, which had a 60.2 per cent turn-out, resulted in 74.3 per cent in favour of the Parliament and 63.5 per cent in favour of tax-varying powers.

Previous attempts at devolution of power, the most recent in 1968, had failed, either through the failure to reach agreement over constitutional matters or through loss of popular support. Most significant of the constitutional problems was the issue of Scottish representation at

Westminster: the 'West Lothian question'.[11] At root, the issue concerns over- or under-representation in the Westminster Parliament once legislative power is devolved to a regional Parliament. This gives rise to two-way concerns. The first problem is that of regional representation at Westminster, and the right of Members of the Scottish Parliament to vote on legislative proposals which relate solely to English affairs. Secondly, whilst Scottish Members of Parliament may influence or indeed affect the outcome of English legislation, English Members of Parliament have no corresponding influence in the Scottish Parliament over devolved matters. When a government has a large majority in Parliament, this gives rise to few problems in practical terms, although the issue of principle remains. However, in a situation where a government has no clear and workable majority, the difficulty is more pronounced. In this situation, it may well be that the government of the day becomes dependent on Scottish representatives at Westminster in order to enact legislation. The question of legitimacy becomes more acute when the proposed legislation relates exclusively to English matters.

Three possible solutions to the West Lothian question have been considered over the years. The first is that Scottish representation at Westminster could be completely excluded. This, however, is not constitutionally possible, since in matters not devolved to the Scottish Parliament, Westminster still has law-making power. The maxim 'no taxation without representation' certainly precludes this option, unless all matters of taxation had been devolved to Scotland, which they have not. The second solution could be to reduce the amount of representation at Westminster for Scotland, in order to reduce the impact which Scottish Members could have on legislation. This, however, would appear to reduce the standing of the union between Scotland and England in Scottish eyes and would as a result be politically unacceptable. The third possibility is the 'in and out' solution which was considered in relation to Irish Home Rule but rejected by Gladstone as unworkable. The 'in and out' solution requires a process whereby

---

[11] So named since the Member of Parliament for the West Lothian constituency, Tam Dalyell, raised the issue in the 1960s. The same issue caused difficulties earlier in the twentieth century over the question of Home Rule for southern Ireland.

legislation is classified as applying to either the United Kingdom as a whole, or to Scotland in matters reserved to the Westminster Parliament, or solely to England. Where a matter relates solely to England, Scottish Members would be prevented from voting, but they would be allowed to vote on matters relating to both Scotland and England, or on Scottish matters reserved to Westminster. The objection remains, however, that a government with a weak majority might find itself defeated by Scottish representation, or alternatively, where a government (as with the last Conservative administration) finds itself devoid of electoral support in Scotland, it might to be forced to compromise its policies in order to guarantee Scottish support.

There is no single or simple solution to this particular problem, which is inherent in any system of devolution of power. Tony Blair's government made it clear that the issue was to be avoided, and – on the basis of supporting rather than undermining Scottish and English union – that Scottish representation was to remain the same for the immediate short term. However, since the current position results in Scotland having an over-representation at Westminster, with effect from the date of the next elections to the European Parliament, Scottish representation will be reduced.

Devolved and reserved powers

Rather than stipulating those powers which are devolved to the Scottish Parliament, the Scotland Act 1998 identifies the legislative competence of the Parliament from a negative perspective, specifying those Acts, including the Acts of Union, the European Communities Act 1972 and other assorted legislation, which may not be amended or modified by Parliament.[12] The Act then specifies five general categories of matters which are reserved to the United Kingdom Parliament, namely the constitution, the registration of political parties, foreign affairs, the civil service, and defence and treason. Specific reservations are made under eleven headings relating to financial and economic matters, home affairs, trade and industry, energy, transport, social security, regulation

[12] Scotland Act 1998, Schedule 4.

of the professions, employment, health and medicines, media and culture and miscellaneous.[13] Specific exceptions are detailed in the Act which apply to the specific reservations. Matters reserved facilitate United Kingdom-wide uniformity, while power is devolved to the Scottish Parliament to regulate non-reserved matters according to national requirements. Where a dispute arises, as inevitably it will in the course of interpreting the detailed statutory provisions, the Act makes detailed provision for the resolution of such disputes by the courts, with the Judicial Committee of the Privy Council having the ultimate jurisdiction to rule on a devolution dispute.[14] Challenges over legislative competence may arise in judicial review proceedings, or in the course of civil or criminal proceedings where the court in question may make a reference to the Judicial Committee. The Act also provides for the Law Officers to institute proceedings to determine whether or not an Act of the Parliament is within its competence.

WALES

Wales, an area of some 8,000 square miles and a population of approximately five million, was initially conquered by the English in 1282, and from 1284 English law extended to Wales. The enduring union was to be achieved by Act of Parliament in 1536. Whereas Scotland became united with England through a Treaty which effectively dissolved Scotland's own Parliament, Wales had never established its own institutions of government which could give focus to national identity. The legal system of England became that of Wales from the thirteenth century, again unlike Scotland, which by the time of the union with England had an established legal system that continued to operate after union. Wales, unlike Scotland, was institutionally assimilated into England. Wales also had none of the grievances of the Irish which fuelled nationalism and the demand for Home Rule. No invasions of settlers displaced the local population from their land, and no alien religion intruded.

The Welsh nationalist party, Plaid Cymru, was established in 1925.

---

[13] Ibid., Schedule 5.   [14] Ibid., Schedule 6.

Its principal aim was to encourage the use of the Welsh language, which had declined over the years. By the start of the 1990s only 18 per cent of the Welsh population spoke Welsh. Plaid Cymru never enjoyed great electoral support or success, nor was it stridently seeking (as was the Scottish Nationalist Party) devolution within the United Kingdom. In 1973 the Royal Commission on the Constitution issued its report, recommending that there should be a Welsh legislature, a Senate, with power to make law on specifically defined matters. The Senate was envisaged as having one hundred members, elected on the basis of proportional representation and serving a four-year term. When the Labour government came to power in 1974, it revised the proposals, envisaging an elected assembly with executive rather than legislative powers. While the Wales Act 1978 was passed by Parliament, for it to take effect it had to be accepted by the people of Wales in a referendum, with a majority of votes cast and representing not less than 40 per cent of those eligible to vote. In the event, only 11.9 per cent voted in favour, with 46.6 per cent against and 41.7 per cent abstaining.

The result was very different when the Labour government held a referendum on devolution to Wales in 1998, although the majority in favour was not convincing. On a turn-out of only 50 per cent, 50.3 per cent voted in favour. The Government of Wales Act 1998 differs markedly from the Scotland Act 1998. Whereas Scotland has considerable autonomy in law-making, the Welsh Assembly has executive and administrative rather than law-making powers. The Assembly sits for a fixed four-year term of office and has sixty members. An Executive Committee, which sits in private, provides the overall direction for the Assembly and comprises members of the majority party alone. The Leader of the Assembly is elected by the Assembly itself, rather than by direct election by the people.

The form of devolution to Wales is markedly different from that to Scotland. Scotland has secured the right to pass its own Acts: it has real legislative power in relation to all matters stipulated by the Scotland Act. Wales, on the other hand, has been given not autonomous law-making powers but devolution in the form of executive and administrative powers. The only power to make law is confined to secondary legislation, the detailed rule-making required to implement Acts of Parliament passed at Westminster. The Welsh system appears to be far closer to the conventional form of local government, albeit at a different, unifying, country-wide level, than to 'true devolution' of power such as has been given to Scotland.

The Assembly is elected under the additional member electoral system. Forty constituency members are elected on the simple majority system, and twenty additional members elected from the party list. The overall political direction of the Assembly is provided by the Leader of the Assembly, elected by the Assembly, and the Executive Committee. While the Assembly has no power to enact primary legislation (Acts), it does have power to prepare secondary legislation for submission to the Assembly for debate and approval. A subordinate legislation scrutiny committee is established to consider draft subordinate legislation and report. The Assembly takes over many of the responsibilities formerly held by the Secretary of State for Wales. A number of Assembly commit- tees are established, known as subject committees, covering agriculture, forestry, fisheries and food, ancient monuments, culture, economic development, education and training, the environment, health and health services, highways, housing, industry, local government, social services, sport and tourism, town and country planning, transport, water and flood defence and the Welsh language. As with Scotland, the Government of Wales Act makes detailed provision for the resolution of disputes over matters devolved with ultimate jurisdiction lying with the Judicial Committee of the Privy Council.

The Assembly elections produced a membership in which only twenty-eight were Labour members. The Labour government's auth- ority suffered harm when Alun Michael, its preferred First Secretary of Wales, was perceived to be imposed on the Assembly by London, in preference to Rhodri Morgan who was the Labour Party's first choice in Wales, and was further damaged when Alun Michael faced a vote of no confidence in the Assembly in February 2000. Rather than await the verdict of the Assembly, Michael resigned, leaving Rhodri Morgan to fill the shoes of the First Secretary.

THE GREATER LONDON ASSEMBLY AND MAYOR

Until 1985, London had enjoyed a measure of self-government under the Greater London Council (GLC). However, conflict between the Labour-controlled GLC and other high-spending Metropolitan County Councils and the Conservative government led to Mrs Thatcher's insistence that they be abolished and their functions redistributed to London and other boroughs. Ironically, as later events were to prove, the GLC had been led by the left-wing Labour politician, Ken Livingstone.

When Labour came to power in 1997 it was with the intention of establishing a new body for London, through a directly elected Mayor and Assembly, with possible extension of the system to other major cities. A Board of Transport for London, a new London Development Agency, Metropolitan Police Authority and London Fire and Emergency Planning Authority have been established to co-ordinate strategies and services on a London-wide basis. The Mayor appoints all board members and the chief executive of the London Development Agency, twelve of the twenty-three members of the new Metropolitan Police Authority and nine of the seventeen members of the Fire and Emergency Planning Authority. A Cultural Strategy Group has been established, with responsibilities for tourism, sport and the arts, headed by a chairperson and board appointed by the Mayor. The Mayor is supported by a mayoral policy unit of ten members appointed by the Mayor, and two political advisers.

The major political parties each adopted their own form of selection process for mayoral candidates. The Liberal candidate, Susan Kramer, generally unknown to the public, was selected without trauma. The experience for Labour and the Conservatives was far from simple, and in the event both parties provided a fair amount of humour at their own expense as the process descended into farce. On the Conservative side, members of the Party in London had the choice of candidate. Steven Norris, a former Cabinet minister with transport experience, stood for selection as did Lord Archer, former Conservative Party chairman, better known as novelist Jeffrey Archer. In the selection process, Steven Norris lost to Lord Archer. It was later revealed that

Lord Archer faced allegations of lying in court in libel proceedings some years earlier. The Conservative Party abandoned him, and subsequently expelled him from the Party for a five-year period. Steven Norris was then approached once more and, despite allegations about his personal life, was selected.

On the Labour side, the selection process was something of a novelty. Whereas Neil Kinnock, John Smith and Tony Blair, as leaders of the Party, had struggled to free the Party from the dominance of trade union power by introducing the 'one man (*sic*), one vote' rule (OMOV) into the Party's decision-making process, the Party now resurrected a tripartite process of selection via an electoral college which gave votes to the unions, Members of Parliament and Members of the European Parliament, and individual Party members. The Party's preferred candidate was former Health Secretary, Frank Dobson, who resigned from Cabinet in order to stand as a mayoral candidate. Also standing for selection was Glenda Jackson, Member of Parliament for Hampstead, and a well-known former film and stage actress. But Labour also faced the prospect of Ken Livingstone, former Leader of the long-defunct GLC, standing as a candidate for selection. Livingstone, Member of Parliament for Brent East, represented everything about 'old Labour' from which the government sought to disassociate itself. This raised the spectre of a maverick left-wing politician, who paradoxically enjoys great personal support in London, being elected as Mayor of London with a constituency of over five million people, and possibly on the road to conflict with the Labour government. The Labour Party's opposition to Livingstone forced him to choose between his Party and the chance of becoming Mayor of London, standing as an independent candidate. When he finally declared his intention to stand for election, the Labour Party disowned him, and public opinion and support – as people sensed the hand of the Prime Minister controlling events from behind the scenes – swung behind Livingstone, who was duly elected in May 2000.

Further troubles faced the government over the election in May 2000. For elections to the Westminster Parliament, Scottish Parliament and Welsh Assembly, but not local government elections, candidates are entitled to send one piece of campaign literature to every constituency voter free of charge. Aside from disseminating information to the voters, the free post service ensures that smaller, less well financed parties are able to get their message across. For the mayoral election, however, the government decided that it would be 'too expensive' to permit the use of free postage – estimated at a cost of around £15 million.[15] The challenge to the government's refusal to allow free postage in London came from the newly reformed and reinvigorated House of Lords. Here a technicality of law-making procedure came into play. While a principal function of the Lords is to scrutinize, and, if it deems necessary, attempt to amend primary legislation (Bills which will become Acts of Parliament), it has long been the convention that the Lords will not amend secondary legislation – the detailed rules which supplement primary legislation. These are normally accepted without demur, the Lords having no power to suggest amendments, but only the power to accept or reject the secondary legislation as a whole. This rule has held firm, and was last breached only in 1968, when the Lords rejected the then Labour government's Southern Rhodesian Sanctions Order. If the detailed rules for the election were not accepted and passed into law, it is theoretically possible that the Lords could have forced the government to delay the mayoral election. A neat irony existed: the prospect of the undemocratic unelected House of Lords defying the elected government over an electoral issue on the basis that the government's stance on the free post issue was against the principles of democracy. The government finally gave way: a composite election package was delivered to all constituents and the Representation of the People Act 2000 legitimated free postage for the election.

The mayoral and Assembly elections in May 2000 elected a Mayor and Assembly for a four-year term of office.[16] Every eligible elector has one vote for the mayoral candidate, one vote for an Assembly member and one vote – a 'London vote' – for a registered political party, elected under the Party List system, and once elected representing the interests of the whole of London. The simple-majority voting system is used for

[15] The Electoral Reform Society stated that the cost would be between £2 and £4 million, if the literature of all candidates was posted together, either separately or attached to the polling cards which the government in any event must distribute.

[16] Greater London Authority Act 1999, section 3.

the mayoral election unless there are three or more candidates. Where three or more candidates stand, the Mayor is elected under the supplementary-vote system, a vote which indicates the voter's first and second preferences, which may then be redistributed.[17] The Assembly members are elected under the simple-majority system.[18]

To qualify for election as Mayor or an Assembly member the person must be a Commonwealth citizen; citizen of the Republic of Ireland or citizen of the European Union and be twenty-one years of age.[19] In addition, the candidate must have demonstrable links with Greater London, either by being a local government elector for Greater London, or by virtue of residency or having had their principal employment in Greater London throughout the preceding twelve months.

Finance and the London Authority and Mayor

The central system of government in London is financed through a mixture of government funding and contributions from local councils. The amount contributed by the City of London and other London boroughs varies according to property values. In turn, contributions vary according to the differing valuation bands of property within local areas.[20] In 2001–2 the Assembly's spending plans amounted to £310,500 million. After deducting income, other than general funding from the government and the council tax, the GLA had a budget requirement of £2,345.3 million for the year.

---

[17] Ibid., section 4(2), (3) and Schedule 2 Part I.   [18] Ibid., section 4(4).

[19] Ibid., section 20.

[20] For example, the contributions made by council tax payers in valuation band A in 2001–2 is £21.35 for City of London taxpayers and £100.59 for London Borough taxpayers, while at the upper end of the scale, taxpayers in valuation band H will contribute £64.06 if City of London taxpayers and £301.76 if London Borough taxpayers. The wide disparity between City of London and London Borough contributions is explained by the fact that three-quarters of council tax goes to fund the Metropolitan Police; this does not cover the City of London area which has its own police force.

The Greater London Authority

The general power of the Assembly, as defined by the Greater London Authority Act 1999, is to 'do anything which it considers will further any one or more of its principal purposes', which are defined as including the promotion of economic development and wealth creation, promoting social development and promoting the improvement of the environment in Greater London. In exercising these powers the Authority must also consider the effect on the health of persons in Greater London and, more broadly, the achievement of sustainable development in the United Kingdom. The Secretary of State can issue guidance to the Authority in relation to the above general power.[21] The Act lays down requirements of consultation with London councils and representative voluntary bodies and interest groups.[22] All the functions of the Authority are carried out on the basis stipulated in the Act. In some cases the Mayor may act on behalf of the Authority, other functions are for the Authority alone and some functions are exercised by the Mayor and the Authority acting jointly.

The Authority is regulated by Standing Orders defining its procedures, which are made in consultation with the Mayor. A Chair and Deputy Chair are elected by the Assembly from members of the Assembly.[23] The Assembly is required to meet initially within ten days of an election for the purpose of electing the Chair and Deputy Chair and thereafter on ten occasions in each calendar year, the first meeting being held within twenty-five days of the election.[24]

The Assembly has a duty to keep under review the Mayor's exercise of statutory functions, and has the power to investigate and report on any actions and decisions of the Mayor and members of staff of the Authority. It may also investigate and report on matters relating to its principal purposes and any other matters which the Assembly considers to be of importance to Greater London.[25]

---

[21] Greater London Authority Act 1999, section 30.   [22] Ibid., section 32.
[23] Ibid., section 51.   [24] Ibid., section 52.   [25] Ibid., section 59.

The London Mayor

The post of Mayor is full-time.[26] The Mayor has a duty to prepare, keep under review and revise strategies relating to transport, the London Development Agency, spatial development,[27] the London Biodiversity Action Plan, municipal waste management, air quality, ambient noise and culture.[28] When preparing or revising any strategy the Mayor must consider the effect which the strategy would have on the health of London inhabitants and, more broadly, the wider implications of sustainable development in the United Kingdom. In addition, strategies must be consistent with national policies and international obligations, available resources and the desirability of promoting and encouraging the safe use of the River Thames, in particular for the provision of passenger transport services and freight.[29]

In preparing or revising strategies, the Mayor must consult the Assembly, the functional bodies, each London borough council, the Common Council of the City of London and any other 'appropriate person or body'.[30] Strategies are published and copies provided to the Common Council and each London borough council.[31] The Secretary of State can require the Mayor to prepare and publish any strategy which he or she has not undertaken and set time limits for its preparation.[32]

Accountability

The Mayor must report to the Assembly, not less than three clear working days before each meeting of the Assembly, on major decisions taken by him, the reasons for them, and his response to proposals

[26] And salaried. In 2000 he was paid £84,385 plus an increase based on senior civil service grades.
[27] Separate provision is made for revision of spatial development strategy under section 340.
[28] Greater London Authority Act 1999, section 41: section 142, Regional Development Agencies Act 1998, section 7A(2), Greater London Authority Act 1999 Part VIII, GLA 1999 section 352, sections 353, 362, 370 and 376 respectively.
[29] Ibid., section 41(4), (5).   [30] Ibid., section 42.   [31] Ibid., section 43.
[32] Ibid., section 44.

submitted to him by the Assembly.[33] The Mayor must attend all meetings of the Assembly and answer questions put to him about matters relating to his statutory functions.[34] Questions are answered orally 'so far as practicable to do so', or in writing before the end of the third working day following the day on which the question was asked at the meeting.[35] An Annual Report is prepared by the Mayor as soon as practicable after the end of each financial year, reporting on his activities during the year.[36] In practice, the Mayor's Report to the Assembly is published two weeks in advance of its meeting.

In his Ninth Report covering the period of 9 January to 12 February 2001, the Mayor reported on developments in relation to the future funding and management of the London Underground (see further below), on planning matters referred to him, on his Draft Transport Strategy, on his Draft Air Quality Strategy, his Draft Biodiversity Strategy and a Drug and Alcohol Strategy, on international issues which impinge on London and cultural matters. The sheer range of mayoral activities can be gleaned from these brief reports. In relation to air quality, the Mayor reported that London has the worst pollution levels in the United Kingdom and among the worst in Europe. Since road traffic is the primary cause of air pollution, the air quality strategy ties in closely with the transport strategy, including such matters as traffic reduction, promoting less-polluting engine technology, reducing emissions of vehicles and promoting alternative fuels. On biodiversity, the Mayor reported that a key concern is to conserve London's plants, animals and their habitats, to promote access to nature and to increase environmental education. The Mayor aims to work with the GLA to reduce the harmful effects of alcohol and drugs. On international issues, the Mayor reported on the need for a GLA building in Brussels, to facilitate better representation of London within the European Union. He also visited New York and Washington, examining policing issues and transport systems. Cultural concerns include developing strategies and facilities for expanding black culture working with the community through the GLA Cultural Projects Unit.

---

[33] Under section 60 of the Greater London Authority Act 1999.

[34] Should the Mayor be absent from six consecutive monthly Assembly meetings, he or she is disqualified from office: section 13.

[35] Greater London Authority Act 1999, section 45.   [36] Ibid., section 46.

In each financial year the Mayor must hold and attend a 'State of London debate', open to all members of the public.[37] In addition, twice yearly, a 'People's Question Time' is to be held, open to all members of the public, for the purpose of putting questions to the Mayor and Assembly members. People's Question Time is held within one month of the State of London debate.[38]

Transport functions of the Authority: Transport for London (TfL)

The Mayor is required to develop and implement policies for the 'promotion and encouragement of safe, integrated, efficient and economic transport facilities and services to, from and within Greater London'.[39] The Act stipulates the respective powers and duties of the Secretary of State, the Mayor and London borough councils. 'Transport for London' (TfL) is the functional body established to implement the Mayor's transport strategy, and takes over the functions previously exercised by a number of differing bodies. TfL has wide-ranging responsibilities, including traffic management, maintenance of roads, the London Underground, the management and regulation of bus and rail services, road safety and parking, including the fixing of parking and other charges for London. The making of public-private partnership agreements is provided for, enabling contracts between the London Authority bodies and private companies for the provision, construction, improvement or maintenance of railways.[40] Once agreement has been reached on the Public-Private Partnership for London Underground, TfL will assume responsibility for it. TfL also manages the GLA road network, regulates taxis and minicabs, runs London River Services, helps to co-ordinate 'Dial-a-Ride' and 'Taxicard' schemes for door-to-door services for the disabled, and is responsible for London's traffic lights. TfL comprises a Board of between eight and fifteen members, appointed by the Mayor. The Mayor may be a member, and if he chooses to do

---

[37] Ibid., section 47.   [38] Ibid., section 48.   [39] Ibid., section 141.
[40] Ibid., section 210.

so, may be its chairman.[41] The Mayor may issue guidance, general directions and specific directions as to the exercise of its functions.[42]

The future of the London Underground has been politically controversial, involving as it does the proposed inclusion of private sector funding under the Tube Public-Private Partnerships (PPP). The government is committed to injecting £4.5 billion to the network for the period 2001–8. The Mayor appointed Bob Kiley, an American transport expert with previous experience of reorganizing underground rail services in Boston and New York, as London's Transport Commissioner, working with the Secretary of State for the Environment, Transport and the Regions, to develop the PPP agreement. The Draft Transport Strategy also covers extensions of the rail network in an attempt to reduce traffic congestion in London. The London Underground carries more passengers on working days than does the entire overland rail network: over three million passengers. The system is unreliable and, transport unions argue, unsafe. The PPP entails central government funding, via the Treasury, with private consortiums running the rail lines and the train services being managed by the public sector. The three private companies would be paid more than £20 billion over thirty years. After numerous discussions with the Secretary of State, John Prescott, negotiations between TfL and the government broke down in March 2001, with no agreement over Kiley's demands that the Tube be managed in a unified manner, rather than splitting off responsibility for the tracks from that for the rail services. The Transport Commissioner sought judicial review of the PPP agreement.

The London Development Agency

The Act establishes the London Development Agency and amends the Regional Development Agencies Act 1998 in relation to London. The Mayor is responsible for appointing the fifteen members of the London Development Agency, and must ensure that at least four members are elected members of the Assembly, a London borough council or the

---

[41] Ibid., Schedule 10, paragraphs 2 and 3.
[42] Ibid., section 155. See also Schedules 10–24.

Common Council of the City of London. The Mayor must consult the London Assembly before making appointments. The Chairman is chosen by the Mayor, and must be a 'person who has experience of running a business'.[43] The functions of the London Development Agency are to further economic development, promote business efficiency, investment and competitiveness, promote employment and enhance the development and application of skills relevant to employment, and to contribute to sustainable development. The Mayor is responsible for preparing and publishing the London Development Agency (LDA) strategy, assisted by the Agency. The LDA was established in July 2000.

The London Plan: the 'Spatial Development Strategy'

The London Plan sets out the initial proposals for consultation on the future development of London, as required by the 1999 Act and its 'Spatial Development Strategy'.[44] Envisaging a population growth for London of some 10 per cent over the fifteen years to 2016, the strategic plan proposes an increase in the building of new homes to more than 33,000 a year. The plan envisages co-operation between the GLA and property companies for the production of housing developments. Many developments will be focused on the East End of London which is the site of the Channel Tunnel rail link. Other areas will include the corridors leading to Stansted, Gatwick and Heathrow airports. Public transport will be improved in order to cater for the population growth without the need to increase traffic levels in the capital.

The Metropolitan Police

Whereas all other police forces in Britain have a Police Authority,[45] comprising of local councillors and magistrates, the Metropolitan Police was earlier under the direct authority of the Home Secretary; this meant

[43] Ibid., section 304.
[44] See www.london.gov.uk/mayor/strategies and *Guardian*, 8 May 2001 (www.guardian.co.uk/livingstone).   [45] On which see further Chapter 10.

that London lacked the degree of local accountability existing outside London. The introduction of the Metropolitan Police Authority redresses this lack of accountability, and also ensures that the Mayor and Assembly have a role to play in the combatting of crime in the capital. The Metropolitan Police Authority consists of twenty-three members. Twelve members are members of the London Assembly appointed by the Mayor (one of whom must be the Deputy Mayor), one is appointed by the Secretary of State, six are appointed by members of the Metropolitan Police Authority itself from persons on a short-list prepared by the Secretary of State, and four are magistrates for commission areas which are wholly or partly within the Metropolitan Police district. Members generally serve a four-year renewable term. The Authority appoints a chairman from among its members.[46]

The Authority is responsible for ensuring the maintenance of an efficient and effective police force.[47] The Metropolitan Police Force is under the direction and control of the Commissioner of Police of the Metropolis,[48] appointed by Her Majesty on the recommendation of the Secretary of State following any recommendations made to him by the Metropolitan Police Authority and representations made by the Mayor.

London Fire and Emergency Planning Authority

The Fire and Emergency Planning Authority replaces the London Fire and Civil Defence Authority.[49] The reconstituted Authority is responsible to the Mayor. The Fire and Emergency Planning Authority consists of seventeen members, of whom nine are Assembly members appointed by the Mayor and the remainder members of London borough councils appointed by the Mayor on the nomination of the London borough councils acting jointly. The Mayor is under a duty to ensure, so far as practicable, that members for whose appointment he is responsible

---

[46] Greater London Authority Act 1999, Schedule 26.

[47] Ibid., section 311, inserting new subsection 5 to section 6 of the Police Act 1996.

[48] Ibid., section 314.

[49] Ibid., section 328. The Fire and Civil Defence Authority was established under the Local Government Act 1985.

reflect the balance of political parties within London borough councils.[50] Members are appointed for a renewable one-year term of office. The Mayor is also responsible for appointing a chairman from among the members of the Authority.

Planning

The Greater London Authority Act gives to the Mayor a role in planning, although the local planning authorities for the Greater London area remain. The Mayor has a duty to prepare and publish a 'Spatial Development Strategy' (SDS) document for Greater London,[51] which includes his general policies in respect of the development and use of land in Greater London. The Secretary of State may direct the Mayor to prepare and publish either such alterations of the SDS as he directs, or a new SDS to replace the existing one.[52] When preparing the SDS, the Mayor must consult the Assembly and the functional bodies.[53] Copies of the SDS must be sent to the Secretary of State and local councils and others to whom the Mayor considers it appropriate to send a copy. The Mayor is under a duty to keep the SDS under review, and if the Secretary of State so directs, the Mayor shall review the strategy as specified in directions from the Secretary of State.[54]

Environmental functions

Within three years of the first election, and within four years from the date of the previous report, the Mayor must produce and publish a Report on the environment in Greater London, known as the 'state of the environment report'.[55] The Report must contain information about: air quality and emissions to air, including in particular emissions from

---

[50] Ibid., Schedule 28, paragraph 1.   [51] Ibid., section 334.
[52] Ibid., section 341.
[53] Defined as Transport for London, the London Development Agency, the Metropolitan Police Agency and the London Fire and Emergency Planning Authority: section 424.
[54] Greater London Authority Act 1999, sections 339 and 340.
[55] Ibid., section 351.

road traffic; road traffic levels; water quality and emissions to water; ground water levels; energy consumption and the emission of substances which contribute to climate changes; land quality; biodiversity; the production, minimization, recycling and disposal of waste; noise; national resources, and litter.[56] The Mayor is also to prepare and publish a 'London Biodiversity Action Plan', containing information concerning the ecology of Greater London, wildlife, conservation proposals and commitments made as to conservation and promotion of biodiversity within Greater London.[57]

The Mayor also prepares and publishes a 'municipal waste management strategy', containing proposals and policies for the recovery, treatment and disposal of municipal waste,[58] and a 'London air quality strategy' detailing implementation of policies on national air quality strategy and the achievement of air quality standards provided for under the Environment Act 1995. In addition, the Mayor must prepare and publish a 'London ambient noise strategy', detailing information about noise and the impact of noise and proposals to counteract the effect of noise, including aircraft noise.[59]

Culture, Media and Sport

A Cultural Strategy Group for London (CSGL) is established under the Act, which has the function of advising the Mayor on the implementation of culture strategy.[60] The CSGL formulates a draft strategy containing proposed policies relating to culture, media and sport. The policies may relate to arts, tourism and sport; ancient monuments and sites; buildings of historical or architectural interest; museums and galleries; library services; archives; treasure and movable antiquities; broadcasting, film production and other media of communication.[61] The Authority can provide financial or other assistance for the purposes of any museum, gallery, library, archive or other cultural institution in Greater London.[62] The functions of the Authority include the duty to promote

---

[56] Ibid., section 351(3)(a)–(k). [57] Ibid., section 352. [58] Ibid., section 353.
[59] Ibid., sections 370 and 371. [60] Ibid., section 375. [61] Ibid., section 376.
[62] Ibid., section 377.

tourism to Greater London.[63] The CSGL consists of between ten and twenty-five members appointed by the Mayor, following consultation with relevant bodies, and for a term of office decided by the Mayor.[64]

LOCAL GOVERNMENT[65]

Central government is ill-equipped to deal with many matters which require special local knowledge and regulation on the basis of local needs, ensuring that decisions affecting the locality are made by those representing that area. Local government allows a measure of local democracy and self-regulation while being controlled by government policy, Acts of Parliament and the courts. The system is of great antiquity, traceable to Saxon times. Historically, the basic units of local democracy were the shires (the rough equivalent in modern times being the counties), and the hundreds, or townships. Some towns were granted royal charters, becoming royal boroughs – a designation which still holds. The 'system' underwent major reform in the nineteenth century.[66]

The merits of local government have been summarized as being:

(a) pluralism, through which it contributes to the national political system;

(b) participation, through which it contributes to local democracy; and

(c) responsiveness, through which it contributes to the provision of local needs, through the delivery of services.[67]

Local government in Britain varies. England and Wales have one system, Scotland and Northern Ireland each have their own systems. The

---

[63] Ibid., section 378.   [64] Ibid., Schedule 30, paragraph 2.

[65] See S. Bailey, *Cross on Principles of Local Government Law* (London: Sweet & Maxwell, 2nd edn., 1997); A. Byrne, *Local Government in Britain* (Harmondsworth: Penguin, 7th edn., 2000): G. Jones (ed.), *The New Government Agenda* (Hemel Hempstead: ICSA, 1997).

[66] With the Municipal Corporations Act 1835, the Local Government Act 1888 and the Local Government Act 1894.

[67] The Widdicombe Report, *The Conduct of Local Authority Business*, Cmnd. 9797 (London: HMSO, 1986).

emphasis in this chapter is on the system in England and Wales. The law governing the rationalized structure was consolidated under the Local Government Act 1933 and endured until a reformed structure was put in place in 1974. Local government, and the law relating to it, is a complex subject requiring specialist study.[68] Not only is the entire system closely regulated by law, all local government powers deriving from Acts of Parliament, but there is little uniformity in its organization and there is an absence of any philosophical or political consensus as to the constitutional role and status of local government, save that it is subordinate to Parliament.

Local government areas are determined by the Local Government Boundary Commissions, of which there is one each for England, Scotland and Wales. In 1992 a Local Government Commission was appointed by the Secretary of State to review the structure, boundaries and electoral arrangements of all areas except London and the metropolitan areas.[69] The government's intention was to increase efficiency and reduce overlapping functions and bureaucracy. It was thought that that would best be achieved through the introduction of unitary – as opposed to two-tier – authorities. The result, however, was not the achievement of uniformity throughout the country, and while thirty-two unitary councils were introduced in Scotland and twenty-two in Wales, in England no uniformity was achieved and the system remains a mix of unitary and two-tier authorities. Overall, the total number of councils in Britain was reduced from 515 to 442 between 1994 and 1998. The number of authorities in Scotland was reduced from 62 to 32 unitary councils, and in Wales, 45 councils were reduced to 22 unitary councils. In England in 1998 there were 238 District Councils, 34 County Councils, 33 London Borough Councils and the Greater London Authority, 36 Metropolitan Borough Councils, and 46 new unitary authorities. As has been seen above, the Mayor of London and Assembly established in 1999 represents a return to a London-wide system of government. The City of London has always enjoyed autonomy, having

---

[68] In light of this, this section does not presume to be more than an introductory note to the subject, detailed treatment of which is beyond the scope of this work.

[69] i.e. the Metropolitan Counties governing urban areas surrounding Birmingham, Leeds, Liverpool, Manchester, Newcastle-upon-Tyne and Sheffield.

a Mayor and its own distinctive council, the City of London Corporation.

In Northern Ireland local government is organized into 26 District Councils and 9 Area Boards. The councils are responsible for local environmental services, gas undertakings, entertainments and recreation, licensing and consumer protection, and for markets. The area boards are responsible for health and social services, education and libraries. There is also a Housing Executive and single Fire Authority.

However, a description of the structure of local authorities, untidy though that structure is, does not comprehensively portray the system of local administration. While local authorities were traditionally regarded as service providers, even before the Thatcher era (when market forces entered the picture, pitting local authorities against commercial operators in the quest for value for money), there were other factors in the delivery of services. The interference of central government in local regulation, initially in the nineteenth century and continuing to the present, was felt not only in central government organization and reorganization of the structure of local authorities. The Public Health Acts of 1848 and 1878 gave local authorities powers and responsibilities in relation to health and sanitation. The Education Act of 1870 provided for local regulation of the building and management of schools. In the first half of the twentieth century local government responsibilities in relation to health and sanitation increased. With the introduction of the welfare state in 1945 local authorities acquired responsibilities in relation to social welfare and health services. In addition, town and country planning functions were devolved to local government. But as powers and responsibilities increased, these were always subject to the overriding control of central government departments. While local authorities represent the best form of local democracy and give local residents a voice in the management of their area, local democracy can only exist to the extent that its substance is considered to be consistent with the national interest in both the setting and maintenance of standards and within the financial controls which place limits on what local councils can achieve. Service provision is also complicated by the existence of specialist providers. Responsibilities in relation to health services have largely been transferred away from local authorities to local and regional organizations of the National

Health Service. Services such as water and sewage were transferred to nationalized Regional Water Boards in 1974; in 1990 the Water Boards were privatized. National government departments with regional and local offices, such as the Inland Revenue and Department of Social Security, also restrict local government administration.

The functions of local authorities

Local government has no powers other than those conferred by Parliament. Local government income (on which see further below) is made up of a system of local rates – the Council Tax – and grants from government. Local authorities are not free, however, to raise and spend money as they think fit, whatever the views of local constituents. The traditional role of local government as the major provider of services for the area, in relation to housing, education, highways, social services, fire, police, child care facilities, provision for the elderly, libraries and leisure facilities and waste management, has become increasingly controlled by central government.

Local authorities also play an important role in relation to the police and to the administration of justice in the local Magistrates' Courts. In addition to the Metropolitan Police in London and the City of London Police, there are forty-one local police forces.[70] For each force there is a police authority[71] with responsibility for setting policy objectives for the force, subject to the Home Secretary's general power to determine the objectives of authorities.[72] Chief Constables have responsibility for operational matters,[73] and report annually to the police authority. In relation to the Magistrates' Courts, local authorities are responsible for providing the accommodation and paying the expenses of the

[70] On the organization of the police, see further Chapter 10.
[71] Comprising seventeen members, of which nine are local authority councillors. See the Police and Magistrates' Courts Act 1994, Schedule 2.
[72] Police Act 1996, section 37. Note that until 2000 the Home Secretary was the police authority for the Metropolitan Police. Under the Greater London Authority Act 1999, the police authority is established for London.
[73] In London, operational control of the police is under the Metropolitan Commissioner of Police.

Magistrates' Courts Committee, the ninety-six bodies in England and Wales responsible for the administration of the Magistrates' Court service.[74]

The management of local government

Local government differs from central government in having no executive, or Cabinet, which formulates policy.[75] Local authorities appoint a salaried chief officer or executive and employ senior administrators, clerical officers and secretarial and other office staff. Local authorities have some discretion as to their management arrangements. For the most part, decision-making is undertaken by committees, their decisions being ratified by meetings of the full council. Meetings of the council must be publicized, and are open to the public unless in exceptional cases confidentiality requires a meeting to be held in private.[76] Local councillors are elected for a four-year term of office and represent 'wards' within the local government area. In metropolitan districts, a third of councillors retire each year, other than in a year in which there are to be County Council elections. In other, non-metropolitan districts, councillors retire every four years. The voting system reflects that used for general elections, being the simple majority or 'first past the post' system.[77] A candidate for election must be able to demonstrate a close connection with the locality. He or she must either be on the local register of electors, or have been resident or occupied property or have his or her place of employment within the local authority area for a twelve-month period preceding nomination day.[78] Bankruptcy, conviction for corrupt or illegal practices, a conviction and sentence of three months' imprisonment within five years of the election, or the imposition of a surcharge by the Audit Commission for unlawful government expenditure, all disqualify a person from standing for election. Councillors are not salaried, although Chief Executives are,

[74] See the Justices of the Peace Act 1997, and see further Chapter 9.
[75] See however the Local Government Act 2000, discussed below.
[76] Local Government (Access to Information) Act 1985; Public Bodies (Admission to Meetings) Act 1960.   [77] On which see Chapter 6.
[78] Local Government Act 1972, section 79.

and chairpersons and vice-chairpersons of County and District Councils receive expense allowances. Other councillors receive travelling and subsistence allowances, attendance allowances and reimbursement for loss of earnings.

Standards of conduct

The Prevention of Corruption Acts 1906 and 1916 made it a criminal offence for a member of a council to accept payments, in money or kind, for services. Under the Local Government Act 1972 councillors must disclose the existence of any direct or indirect financial interest in council business. The control over ethical standards in local government is problematic: local councils wield considerable power in relation to planning permissions and the licensing of leisure facilities, including gambling facilities. In 1974, following a scandal involving councillors in the North of England concerning contracts for a private architect (John Poulson), official inquiries were launched into the standards of conduct in public life.[79] While it was found that, in general, local government members' conduct was 'honest', a number of reforms were introduced. A statutory Register of Members' Interests[80] was set up and a Code of Conduct introduced relating to non-financial interests. A further inquiry has been undertaken by the Committee on Standards in Public Life,[81] which examined local government in relation to the seven principles of public life – selflessness, integrity, objectivity, accountability, openness, honesty and leadership. The Local Government Act 2000, discussed below, implements recommendations relating to standards of conduct.

[79] *Conduct in Local Government*, Cmnd 5636 (London: HMSO, 1974); *Report of the Royal Commission on Standards in Public Life 1974–76*, Cmnd 6524 (London: HMSO, 1976). See also *The Conduct of Local Authority Business*, Cmnd 9797 (London: HMSO, 1986).   [80] Local Government and Housing Act 1989, section 18.
[81] On which see Chapter 3.

Local government finance

Some 60 per cent of local government revenue comes from central government grants. These are either specific grants – for example, for particular services such as fire or police (50 per cent) – or general grants: a central government contribution to local authority funds. In addition, local authorities may borrow money, subject to strict control by the Treasury, and raise money from the imposition of charges, for example, for services such as swimming-pools and recreational facilities and the sale of council houses and for transport services. The major element in locally raised local authority income comes in the form of the Council Tax, levied on all properties within the area at a price determined according to the market value of the property. The local revenue system is of some antiquity. In relation to domestic properties, from around 1600 and until 1988 local domestic rates were in existence. The rates, calculated according to the value of property, were cheap and easy to collect and generally regarded as fair by the public. By 1974, however, the Conservative Party had committed itself to abolishing local rates and at that time favoured replacing the property tax with a local income tax. By 1979, following further analysis of the effect of a local income tax, that view had changed. The Party was committed to reducing all forms of direct taxation, and it therefore became undesirable to continue to entrust to local authorities the ultimate power to raise local direct taxation. A local sales tax was favoured for a short period but the realization of the anomalies that would arise from differing rates of sales tax within different parts of the country and different authorities caused its demise.

What ultimately found favour with the then Prime Minister, Margaret Thatcher, was a system which in large measure contributed to her political downfall: the Community Charge, or poll tax as it quickly became dubbed. The tax entailed a flat-rate charge to be imposed on every adult – as opposed to the property owner – within a local authority area. The perceived advantages of such a tax were those of fairness and accountability: fairness in that all adults would contribute to local authority income, accountability in that taxpayers would demand that their local authority account for the expenditure of their money. Introduced in 1988,[82] and operating first in Scotland, the tax rapidly became regarded as iniquitous, and as a result, uncollectable. Its imminent implementation in England led to riots and conflict over its introduction led to reform and the introduction of the Council Tax, revenue once again being based on property values.[83]

Controlling local government spending in recent years has been a priority with central government. A number of devices have been employed in order to contain local government within the boundaries of reasonable expenditure as determined by the government. The perception that local government was 'profligate, wasteful and out of control' was one which led to the introduction[84] of a new Block Grant, distributed according to 'grant-related expenditure assessments', to be determined by central and not local government. Overspending councils were penalized by a 'grant taper', a device which reduced the central government grant to a local authority where the Secretary of State considered that a local authority was spending too much. When this failed to check local spending, a 'grant holdback' was introduced.[85] Again, the restraint was to prove ineffective, with local authorities simply increasing the annual sum due from ratepayers to make up the shortfall in revenue. 'Rate capping' was introduced,[86] preventing rate increases above a target set by central government and conferring wide powers on the Secretary of State for the Environment to impose sanctions. Further changes were introduced in 1993[87] following the introduction of the Council Tax. Grant-related expenditure assessments gave way to Standard Spending Assessments, by which the Department of the Environment calculates the level of resources which each local authority needs to achieve the 'standard level of service' across a range of services that a local authority is required to provide under statute. The calculation involves a complex formula, which results in an estimation of the resource needs in relation to specific services such as education and social services. The Assessment is combined with the amount which the Department considers appropriate for a local

[82] Under the Local Government Finance Act 1988.
[83] Under the Local Government Finance Act 1992.
[84] Under the Local Government Planning and Land Act 1980.
[85] Under the Local Government Finance Act 1982.   [86] Under the Rates Act 1984.
[87] Local Government (Finance) Act 1993.

authority to raise through the Council Tax and business rates, resulting in the Revenue Support Grant for a particular authority. Over and above that, government sets for each authority the percentage level at which the authority is 'capped' – that is to say, the absolute maximum budget which that authority is permitted to spend in the financial year. If a local authority decides that it needs to spend more than the cap figure, the revenue needed can only come from an increase in local Council Tax: the government will not provide any moneys over the cap, and local authorities exceeding the cap are liable to the full range of penalties available under the statute. Further changes to the financial management of local government are made under the Local Government Act 1999, which is discussed below.

To illustrate the income position, in the year 2001–2 the London Borough of Richmond upon Thames received a Revenue Support Grant of £25.726 million, or 16 per cent of all income. A further £52.114 million, or 32 per cent, came from business rates, while £82.618 million, or 52 per cent, came from Council Tax payments. The Revenue Support Grant amounted to £134 per person. Business rate allocations are decided by central government on the basis of a council's population. In 2001–2 Richmond collected £271 per person from the business rate pool. A further £430 per person was collected via Council Tax.

The Local Government Act 1999

The Labour government came to power in 1997 with a pledge to reform local government. The Local Government Act 1999 represented a first stage in reform, removing the requirement of compulsory competitive tendering imposed by the 1988 Local Government Act, and introducing the concept of Best Value. The Act also amended the scheme of rate capping that had been put in place under the 1992 Local Government Finance Act, introducing greater flexibility into the rate-capping mechanisms. Under the 1992 Act, local authorities were classified according to type, and the same principles applied to all local authorities within a particular class, which prevented the particular circumstances of individual authorities from being taken into consideration when decisions were made in relation to capping. The 1999 Act enables the

Secretary of State to apply different capping principles to individual authorities. The Act also introduces the power of the Secretary of State to warn a local authority that its spending is becoming excessive.[88] The Secretary of State has the power to notify the authority of the maximum amount he proposes should be calculated by the authority as its budget requirement for the year.[89]

The abolition of compulsory competitive tendering and the 'Best Value' concept

The 1999 Local Government Act gave effect to the government's intention to abolish compulsory competitive tendering.[90] Tendering, however, while no longer compulsory, continues to form one part of the government's quest for value and efficiency in the provision of local authority services. The Act defines the local authorities to which the 'Best Value duty' will apply, which extends beyond local authorities proper and includes such bodies as the police authorities, Transport for London and other metropolitan transport authorities, waste disposal authorities, fire authorities and the London Development Agency.

The general duty imposed on Best Value authorities is to 'make arrangements to secure continuous improvement in the way in which its functions are exercised, having regard to a combination of economy, efficiency and effectiveness'.[91] In deciding how to fulfil its duty, authorities must consult local taxpayers, service users and representatives of persons appearing to have an interest in any area in which the authority carries out functions. The Secretary of State may lay down 'performance indicators', by reference to which an authority's performance can be measured and 'performance standards' met. Differing performance indicators or standards may be set for different functions and different

---

[88] Local Government Act 1999, Schedule 1, paragraph 52B, 52D. Schedule 1 inserts a new Chapter IVA into Part I of the Local Government Finance Act 1992.

[89] Ibid., paragraph 52E.

[90] Ibid., section 21. This repeals the compulsory competitive tendering requirements in the Local Government, Planning and Land Act 1980, the Local Government Act 1988 and the Local Government Act 1992 with effect from January 2000.

[91] Local Government Act 1999, section 3.

functions may apply at different times.[92] A Best Value authority must conduct reviews of its functions with the aim of improving the way its functions are exercised. The Secretary of State may require an authority to consider whether it should carry out a particular function, and the level at which it should be exercising that function. It should also assess its performance, and the competitiveness of its performance, by reference to other Best Value authorities and to commercial or other businesses, and consult other authorities and commercial operations about the exercise of the function. It must also assess its progress towards meeting performance standards which have been specified.[93]

Each authority prepares a Best Value Performance Plan for the financial year and is required to review and examine all its services every five years to ensure they meet the needs of residents. The Best Value Performance Plan lists those reviews which have been completed in that financial year, and those which will be completed in the following year. For example, Richmond upon Thames Council had concluded reviews of street cleaning, construction and property services and access to services by 2001. For completion within 2001 are parks, open spaces and cemeteries; sports provision and development; financial support; IT services; financial services; and early years services for children and families (in part). Services to be reviewed during 2001–2 include support for primary and secondary education; transport; services for people with learning difficulties; services for children and families (in part); housing needs and procurement arrangements.

The performance plan published for a financial year is audited by the authority's auditor (on audit see further below).[94] The authority must respond to the auditor's report, and where recommendations have been made, state what action it intends to take and its proposed timetable for action. The Audit Commission can carry out inspections of an authority's compliance with the requirements, and inspectors have a right of access and may require individuals to provide such information, explanation or documentation as is required.[95] Where the Commission issues a report stating failure to comply with its requirements, the

---

[92] Ibid., section 4.   [93] Ibid., section 5.   [94] Ibid., section 7.
[95] Ibid., section 11.

authority must, in its next performance plan, record that fact and any action taken by the authority as a result of the report.[96]

The government controls local authorities by way of audit.[97] The Audit Commission[98] of Local Authorities and the National Health Service in England and Wales is the principal body responsible for supervising local government and health service audits. The Commission consists of not less than fifteen and not more than twenty members appointed by the Secretary of State.[99] Auditors have a right of access to every document relating to a body which appears to them necessary for the purposes of their functions under the Act.[100] It is an offence to fail to comply, without reasonable excuse, with any requirement of the auditor.[101]

If in the course of an audit of a local government body, other than a health service body, the auditor considers that an item of account is contrary to law and has not been approved by the Secretary of State, an application may be made to the High Court for a declaration that the expenditure is unlawful.[102] If the High Court makes such a declaration, it may require the responsible person to repay any unlawful expenditure in whole or in part. If the unlawful expenditure exceeds £2,000, and at the time the person responsible was a member of a local authority, the Court may order him or her to be disqualified from being a member of a local authority for a specified period and may order rectification of the accounts. The High Court must not make an order if it is satisfied that the responsible person 'acted reasonably or in the belief that the expenditure was authorised by law', and in any other case shall 'have regard to all the circumstances, including that person's means and ability to repay the expenditure or any part of it'.[103] If a person has failed to bring into account a sum, and that failure has not been sanctioned by the Secretary of State and a 'loss has been incurred or deficiency

---

[96] Ibid., section 13.

[97] See the Audit Commission Act 1998.

[98] The Audit Commission was established in 1982 to supervise local government audit. Its role was extended to the National Health Service in 1990.

[99] Audit Commission Act 1998, section 1, and see Schedule 1.

[100] Ibid., section 6.   [101] Ibid.

[102] As in *Hazell v. Hammersmith LBC* [1992] 2 AC 1.

[103] Audit Commission Act 1998, section 17.

caused by the wilful misconduct of any person' the auditor must certify that the sum, or the amount of the loss or deficiency, is due from that person.[104] Wilful misconduct has been held to include the failure to collect fees which were due,[105] and a delay in setting the rate resulting in the authority losing interest on money which would otherwise have been collected.[106] A person aggrieved by the auditor's decision to certify a sum or amount due may appeal to the High Court.[107]

In relation to authorities, other than a health service body, the auditor may issue a 'prohibition notice', if he has reason to believe that the body is about to make or has made a decision which involves incurring unlawful expenditure, or has taken, or is about to take, action which is unlawful and likely to cause a loss or deficiency, or is about to enter in the accounts an item of unlawful expenditure.[108] No prohibition order may be made in relation to the period covered by the report. Where a prohibition order is issued, it is not lawful for the body concerned to make or implement the relevant decision or undertake the course of action to which the prohibition order relates. The body concerned may appeal against the prohibition order to the High Court.[109] The auditor has power to apply for judicial review of a local authority's (but not a health service body's) decision or failure to act.[110] The Commission has the power to direct an auditor to undertake an extraordinary audit, and the Secretary of State may require the Commission to direct such an audit.[111]

The Commission has responsibility for undertaking or promoting comparative or other studies for improving the economy, efficiency and effectiveness of local authority services, and of other bodies, and for improving the financial or other management of bodies subject to audit.[112] Bodies subject to the Act may require the Commission to

---

[104]   Ibid., section 18(1).   [105]   *R v. Roberts* [1901] 2 KB 117.
[106]   *Lloyd v. McMahon* [1987] 2 WLR 821.
[107]   Audit Commission Act 1998, section 18(10). In relation to health service bodies, section 19 provides that if the auditor has reason to believe that the body, or an officer of the body, has made or is about to make a decision which involves incurring unlawful expenditure, or to undertake a course of action which would be unlawful and likely to cause a loss or deficiency, the auditor must refer the matter to the Secretary of State.
[108]   Ibid., section 20.   [109]   Audit Commission Act 1998, section 22.
[110]   Ibid., section 24.   [111]   Ibid., section 25.   [112]   Ibid., section 33.

undertake such studies.[113] The right to make studies and receive requests for studies extends to higher education funding councils, the governing bodies of institutions within the higher education sector and further education sector, the Funding Agency for Schools and the governing body of a grant-maintained school.[114] The Secretary of State may request the Commission's assistance in studies designed to improve the economy, efficiency, effectiveness and quality of performance in relation to social services functions of local authorities.[115]

The Act also gives the Secretary of State the power to direct an authority to take any action which he considers necessary or expedient to secure compliance with Best Value requirements. The Secretary of State may also remove a function from an authority and place it in the hands of a person nominated by him.[116] In this situation, and if, for example, where planning functions have been taken over, the Secretary of State is also the final arbiter of an appeal against that planning decision, regulations may be made to avoid this.[117]

The Local Government Act 2000

The Local Government Act 2000[118] provided for new executive arrangements to be introduced into local government, and empowered local authorities to decide whether to introduce the arrangements,[119] consisting of an elected mayor and two or more councillors of the authority appointed by the elected mayor to the executive. The Act introduces a further layer of management to local government, and is subject to the approval of electors expressed in a referendum.[120] Where a local authority, with referendum approval, introduces an executive, the Secretary of State may order that any functions of a local authority become the responsibility of the executive.[121] Every local authority must draw up proposals for the operation of executive arrangements and

---

[113] Ibid., section 35.   [114] Ibid., section 36.   [115] Ibid., section 37.
[116] Ibid., section 15(6).   [117] Ibid., section 15(7), (8).
[118] Introducing the Bill, the Secretary of State declared that he was unable to declare that the Bill was compatible with the Human Rights Act 1998.
[119] Local Government Act 2000, section 10.   [120] Ibid., section 26.
[121] Ibid., section 13.

send a copy of the proposals to the Secretary of State. The proposals must indicate the form the executive is to take, following local consultation, and where the executive arrangement includes a Mayor and Cabinet executive a referendum is required. In other cases, where a referendum is not required, the authority must implement the proposals in accordance with a timetable included in the proposals.[122]

The Act also regulates standards of conduct in local government, and empowers the Secretary of State to specify the principles which are to govern the conduct of members of relevant authorities in England in a model code.[123] In relation to Wales, the National Assembly may specify standards. Local authorities are under a duty to adopt a code of conduct. Every local authority, other than a parish council or community council, must establish a standards committee[124] to promote and maintain high standards of conduct and assist members of the authority to observe the code of conduct. The standards committee also has power to advise the authority on the adoption or revision of a code, monitoring the operation of the code, and advising, training or arranging to train members of the authority in relation to the code of conduct.[125] Adjudication tribunals are established to consider allegations of non-compliance with the code, and to report to the standards committee. Every local authority must establish and maintain a register of members' interests.[126]

The Act regulates the duty of local authorities to promote the economic, social or environmental well-being of the relevant area. Every local authority is given power to prepare a strategy for promoting such well-being. The authority must consult or seek the participation of appropriate persons and must have regard to any guidance issued by the Secretary of State.[127] The Secretary of State has the power to amend, repeal or revoke enactments relating to the strategy.[128]

---

[122] Ibid., section 25.   [123] Ibid., section 49.   [124] Ibid., section 53.

[125] Ibid., section 54.   [126] Ibid., section 81.   [127] Ibid., section 4.

[128] Ibid., sections 6–8.

CONCLUSION

The recent devolution of power to national assemblies, with broad legislative powers being devolved to Northern Ireland and Scotland, and the introduction of a London-wide authority as a prototype for adoption in other cities in the future, has changed the face of government in Britain. Aside from local government which enjoys limited autonomy, Britain was formerly a highly centralized state; devolution has now moved the decision-making processes away from Westminster and Whitehall to bring them closer to the people of the nations which make up the United Kingdom. Whether the additional layers of representation and democratic accountability result in increased efficiency and consumer satisfaction with government is an issue which can only be addressed at some point in the future. What seems certain, however, is that these shifts in power downwards from the centre to the local, together with the dispersal of power outwards to the European Community and Union, mark an ever-increasing limitation on the *de facto* powers of the United Kingdom Parliament.

6

THE DEMOCRATIC PROCESS

INTRODUCTION

Britain is characterized as a Western liberal democracy. While the concept of democracy is easily understood in the abstract, problems arise when it comes to providing a clear-cut, substantive interpretation which can be translated into the reality of modern government. The 'idea' of democracy has troubled political philosophers and political scientists for centuries. The problem of defining democracy in any meaningful way lies in finding a definition which corresponds to the reality of a working democracy. As Giovanni Sartori writes:

When we use the term, it clearly *stands for* something. The question is not only: What does the word mean? but also: What is the thing? And when we try to answer this latter query, we discover that there is little resemblance between the facts and the label, between our findings and the name. So although 'democracy' has a precise literal meaning this does not really help us to understand what an actual democracy is.[1]

In the oft-quoted definition of Abraham Lincoln, democracy represents the 'rule of the people, by the people, for the people'. This, however,

[1] G. Sartori, *Democratic Theory* (New York: Frederick A. Praeger, 1965), p. 4. The word democracy derives from the Greek *demos* (people) and *kratia* (government): government by the people.

cannot be taken at face value. In any state, the democratic process involves the election by qualified citizens of people representing different interests. The system is therefore *indirect* rather than *direct*.

Direct democracy entails the involvement of all qualified citizens, not only in appointing a government to represent their interests, but also playing a central role in making decisions affecting the manner in which they are governed. While this was a viable system in ancient Greek city-states,[2] and remains viable in small self-governing communities (such as Swiss cantons), and in part remains relevant to local government in the United Kingdom, direct democracy has limited application in a complex state with a sizeable population comprising citizens with differing cultural, racial, regional, occupational, economic and industrial interests. The British system is one of *indirect democracy*. In relation to the United Kingdom (Westminster) Parliament, eligible voters exercise their right to elect a local representative periodically and at least once every five years. Through this process an elite class of the people's representatives is placed in Parliament from which the political party winning a majority of seats at a general election forms a government. There is accordingly a three-tier level of involvement: the voter registers his or her preference through the ballot box, the winning party assumes the majority of seats in Parliament, from which the leader of the winning party, then appointed by the Crown as Prime Minister, selects his or her principal ministers of state and junior ministers, allocating portfolios at his or her discretion, subject always to the (now

[2] Ancient Greece was not a 'state' in the modern sense of the word, rather it was a collection of geographically limited city-states with relatively small populations. However, even in ancient Greece – that most 'democratic' of early forms of government characterized by decisions being made by qualified representatives – democracy did not literally mean rule by *all* the people. Then, as now, certain categories of persons were excluded from participation. Children, women, slaves and non-native citizens of the city were excluded from the people's Assembly. Moreover, even with these exclusions (and the exclusion of women meant the exclusion of half of the population) it was not realistic to expect thousands of people to have a direct say in decisions. In order for efficient administration to exist it was necessary for the Assembly as a whole to choose an electoral college which elected officials to carry out the day-to-day administration of the state. It is clear even from this cursory glance at ancient Greece, from which most of our modern ideas of government still derive, that 'government by the people' did not bear its literal meaning.

automatic) endorsement of the Crown in whose name all ministerial appointments are made. The United Kingdom is divided into constituency areas, each of which elects a single Member of the United Kingdom Parliament. In addition, Scottish electors vote for Members of the Scottish Parliament, the Welsh for Members of the Welsh Assembly and the people of Northern Ireland for Members of the Assembly. Elections also take place for the European Parliament. Below the primary level (elections to Westminster) and the secondary level (elections to the European Parliament and regional assemblies), the voters elect local councillors in local government elections.

While the system is indirect there are nevertheless mechanisms which facilitate (to an extent) individual involvement in significant constitutional issues. First and foremost among these is the role of referendums to establish the views and wishes of the people, although the extent to which these are binding on government, or more accurately viewed by governments as binding on them, is another matter. In 1975, for example, the result of the referendum held to enable the people to decide whether Britain should continue to be a member of the European Community was regarded by the government as morally, but not legally, binding, and the government retained its ultimate right to decide for the people. More recently the Labour government consulted the people in relation to the devolution of power to regional assemblies in Northern Ireland, Scotland and Wales and in relation to the establishment of a Greater London Assembly and Mayor.[3] In the future, referendums will be held within local government areas in order to enable voters to choose the style of government for their area.[4]

The essential feature of elections in the United Kingdom is that voters are not voting for a representative who will be bound to support their individual interests, but rather voting for a representative for their geographical area. Historically this has been the dominant idea: in the era of non-democratic monarchical rule, monarchs considered that they 'represented' their subjects' interest. Accordingly, no direct representation was necessary. At the same time, however, it was established by the fourteenth century that the monarch should be 'informed' by elite local representatives in order to assist his judgment. Reflecting

---

[3] On devolution see Chapter 5. [4] Under the Local Government Act 2000.

this approach, while a Member of Parliament 'represents' his or her constituents, he or she is not bound by their views. Having been elected, the member is free to make his or her own judgment and to vote independently of the wishes of the electors, albeit at the risk of being rejected by them at a subsequent election.

The electoral process determines the terms and conditions under which political representation of citizens is given effect. The system comprises three main elements: political parties, election campaigns and the voting system used for elections. The outcome of elections will decide which political party holds power in the representative assembly, whether that is the United Kingdom Parliament, the European Parliament, regional assemblies or local councils. If voters are to enjoy true equality in democratic participation, it is essential that the system embodies four principles:

(i)   that there is a full franchise, subject to limited restrictions;
(ii) that the value of each vote cast is equal to that of every other vote;
(iii) that the conduct of election campaigns is regulated to ensure legality and fairness;
(iv) that the voting system is such as to produce both a parliament (or assembly or local council) which is representative of the electorate and a government with sufficient democratic support to be able to govern effectively.

It is the fourth requirement which in practice entails the most difficulties: ensuring that there is both a representative body and an effective government. Depending upon the voting system used, the elected body may be more – or less – representative. Equally, the voting system will determine whether the elected government is effective. By effectiveness is meant the ability to carry through the policies on which the electorate has cast its vote, which can only be achieved if the elected government has a sufficient majority in Parliament to get its proposals through the legislative process without making major changes to them.[5] Some voting systems ensure that the number of popular votes cast in an election result in an allocation of parliamentary seats which are proportionate to the popular vote. This is proportional representation, which takes

---

[5] On the legislative process in Parliament see Chapter 3.

several forms, and maximizes the representative criteria. Proportional representation systems, however, may not result in effective government as defined above. On the other hand, non-proportional systems – such as the simple majority system employed for elections to the United Kingdom Parliament – may result in the membership of the law-making body, expressed through the number of seats won at the election, being at odds with the proportion of the popular vote. This system accordingly reduces the level of representativeness. The system does, though, generally result in a Parliament in which one political party has a strong majority of seats. Since the government of the day is elected through this system, it usually ensures a government which will be effective.

POLITICAL PARTIES

The evolution of political parties[6]

For over three hundred years the British system has been characterized as primarily a 'two-party system' or, more accurately, a system dominated by two parties. A political party is a grouping of people with shared political outlook and interests seeking to represent its supporters in government, or at least to gain a foothold in the legislature where it can exert influence on government. With the extension of the right to vote in the nineteenth century, the organization of political parties outside Parliament became all-important: parties had to campaign in the constituencies for the votes of those previously not entitled to vote, and whose support or otherwise would significantly affect a party's fortunes. The introduction of the secret ballot in 1872[7] and the elimination of corrupt practices by candidates and parties in 1883[8] laid the foundations for the modern conduct of elections.

Until the early twentieth century, the Whigs (Liberals) and Tories (Conservatives) dominated the political landscape. The factor which broke the mould of this system was the birth of the Labour Party, which

---

[6] See also Chapter 12. [7] The Parliamentary and Municipal Elections Act 1872.
[8] The Parliamentary Elections (Corrupt and Illegal Practices) Act 1883.

by the 1920s had taken over from the Liberals as one of the two leading parties. Historically, the Liberals stood for democracy against hereditary monarchical power, for a supreme Parliament which would protect individual liberties and rights, and for constitutional and social reform. The Conservatives on the other hand (originally the Court party) stood for the hereditary monarchy, the House of Lords, the established Church and for conservative (traditional) social values. Before the franchise was broadened in the nineteenth century, political parties were essentially parliamentary groupings, with little organization and structure outside Parliament. Ideologically, although the emphasis of the parties was different – the Liberals favouring change, the Conservatives favouring the stability of existing political institutions – there was little to separate them in terms of policies. While the Conservative Party might be characterized as middle-class, and adhering to traditional values and social structures, it nevertheless did much to improve the lot of the working class. Under Disraeli, Conservative Prime Minister from 1874 to 1880, the Public Health Act, Artisans Dwelling Act, Merchant Shipping Act and trade union legislation were all directed to social reform.

With the Reform Acts 1832, 1867 and 1884, much of the 'working class' became enfranchised, but the right to vote was tied to property qualifications until 1918 and, until the Reform Act of that year, up to 50 per cent of adult males (and all women) were excluded. In 1911 it was estimated that the total number of registered voters amounted to less than 30 per cent of the adult population. Notwithstanding the increase in the franchise, the working class had no specific political party representing their interests. Until the Labour Party came into being, the Liberal Party acted as the agent of working-class interests and provided support for Labour candidates standing for Parliament.

The extension of the franchise by the Reform Acts required party organization for the registration of voters and electoral campaigns throughout the country. In 1874 the Liberal Central Association was formed for the organization of elections, and in 1877 the National Liberal Federation was formed. Candidate selection, despite attempts to control it from the centre, remained with the local constituency association, which generally resisted any attempts to restrict its independence of choice. The Liberal Party needed more working-class support, and unsuccessfully tried to persuade local associations to adopt working-class candidates. When these efforts failed the Labour Party emerged as the champion of the working class. The Conservative Party also reacted to the wider franchise and the greater need to organize at local level. In 1832 only the Carlton Club in London represented a focus for the Party outside Parliament. In 1867 the National Union of Conservative Associations was born to co-ordinate the work of local working men's clubs and associations which had taken on the role of providing electoral support for the Party. In 1870 the Conservative Central Office was established, with responsibility to the Party leader but no control over policy.

The failure of the Liberal Party to work for social reform for the working class and its failure to adopt working-class candidates for elections contributed to the emergence of the Labour Party, and in some measure to the demise of the Liberal Party as a major political force in the twentieth century, despite a resounding electoral victory in 1906. The fortunes of political parties are determined by complex and multifarious factors and no simple explanation can be given for the changes. One factor which had a profound effect on the Liberal Party was the emergence of the Irish Home Rule Party to give political representation to the demands for greater self-government for Ireland. Within the Home Rule movement itself there were divisions of view, the radicals wanting complete independence for Ireland, the majority wanting self-government within the United Kingdom. The issue of Home Rule was to split the Liberal Party in 1886. Between 1885 and 1910 the Home Rule Party had a substantial block of Members of Parliament, and in times of weak government – particularly between 1892 and 1895 when the Liberals had only 274 seats compared with the Conservatives' 268 – it held the balance of parliamentary power. Chronologically, the First World War marked the watershed for both the Liberal Party and the Irish Home Rule Party: by 1918 their support had dwindled and the Liberal Party returned only twenty-eight Members of Parliament, while only seven were returned for Home Rule.

Disaffection with the Liberal Party's failure to promote working-class candidates for election, to sponsor the payment of Members of Parliament[9] or to seek legislation for better working conditions provoked

---

[9] Members of Parliament remained unpaid until the introduction of salaries in 1911.

reactions which manifested themselves in several forms. In 1881 the Marxist Social Democratic Federation came into being; in 1884 the middle-class intellectual Fabian Society was established, and in 1893 the Independent Labour Party was born. The role and support of trade unions was vital to the Labour Party. Dissatisfied with the Liberals whom they had previously supported, the unions redirected their support to a new party dedicated to working-class interests. In 1899 the Trades Union Congress voted in favour of working with all socialist organizations for the formation of the new party. In 1900 the Labour Representation Committee – later renamed the Labour Party – emerged, and in the 1900 election won two parliamentary seats. By 1922 the Labour Party had overtaken the Liberals, which was by now in permanent decline.

Whereas the Liberal and Conservative Parties were created inside Parliament and only later, reacting to electoral change, organized systematically outside Parliament, the Labour Party's foundations were laid outside Parliament. The structure of the Party outside Parliament consisted of local organizations, while the central structure consisted of the Annual Conference and the National Executive Council, elected by Conference. In 1918 the Party revised its constitution, with Clause IV stating the Party's commitment to socialism:

To secure for the producers by hand or by brain the full fruits of their industry, and the most equitable distribution thereof that may be possible, upon the basis of the common ownership of production, and the best obtainable system of popular administration and control of each industry or service.

The power of the unions within the Party and Clause IV of the constitution were features of the Party until the 1990s. Nevertheless, the Labour Party had established itself by the 1920s as one of the two main political parties. It was to hold office from 1924 to 1929 and from 1929 to 1931, to participate in coalition government from 1931 to 1945, to resume office from 1945 to 1951, from 1964 to 1970, and from 1974 to 1979, and then after eighteen years in the wilderness, suffering defections from its membership to form the Social Democratic Party, and having reformed its structure, was returned to power with an outstanding parliamentary majority in 1997.

The decline of the Liberal Party as a party of government did not lead to its extinction, although in terms of the number of seats in

Parliament, its representation is weak. The Party nevertheless maintained a nationwide appeal and has a strong local base. In 1974 the Party polled 19 per cent of the total vote. In 1981 in an electoral alliance with the Social Democratic Party, the Party secured 25 per cent of the vote, but because the voting system penalizes smaller parties (see further below), this significant proportion of the vote translated only into 3.5 per cent of seats in the House of Commons. In 1992 the Liberal Democrats secured twenty seats, polling 17.8 per cent of votes, in 1997 forty-six seats, polling 17.2 per cent of votes and in 2001 fifty-two seats, polling 18.8 per cent of the votes.

In 1981 the Social Democratic Party (SDP) was formed and represented a brief but remarkable and significant political aberration. Formed by four leading Labour politicians[10] dissatisfied with the Labour Party's management, and in particular the changed rules for the election of the Party leader and the reselection of MPs, the SDP quickly attracted and grew in popular support. By 1982 it had thirty-two MPs and some 70,000 members. Having no distinctive programme, the SDP was forced to co-operate with the Liberal Party at election time. When the Liberal Party suggested a formal merger in 1987, the SDP split. Within three years, and having lost most of its MPs at the 1987 election, the SDP abandoned its quest. Nevertheless, a new leader and a new name – respectively Paddy Ashdown and the Liberal Democrat Party – emerged out of the attempt to secure a stronghold for the middle ground of politics.[11]

Nationalist parties also exist to promote their interests, the Scottish Nationalist Party being the most radical in its demands for independence from the rest of the United Kingdom. Since the devolution of power to the Scottish Parliament in 1998, the Nationalists have become the major force of opposition to the majority Labour Party. In Wales, Plaid Cymru plays a similar role to the Scottish Nationalist Party, although its aims are more modest and more related to sustaining the Welsh language and culture. In Northern Ireland two principal opposing political forces exist: the Ulster Unionist Party and Sinn Fein. Both parties have a long history and diametrically opposed objectives, the

---

[10] Roy Jenkins, Shirley Williams, William Rodgers and David Owen.
[11] The current leader of the Liberal Democrat Party is Charles Kennedy.

Protestant Unionists seeking to preserve the union with the United Kingdom, Catholic Sinn Fein seeking a united Ireland and freedom from British rule. The less-strident Social and Democratic Labour Party also shares power and enjoys intra-religious support in its campaign for a peaceful Northern Ireland. With power being devolved to the Northern Ireland Parliament the political parties are forced to work in co-operation rather than in opposition to one another.[12]

The significance of political parties

Political parties are the vehicles through which alternative and competing approaches and policies for government are articulated and communicated to the voters. Political parties, with their national and local organizations, also play a practical role in the election process, promoting policies, canvassing for support and ensuring that supporters actually vote. While election campaigns at the constituency level are far overshadowed in terms of expenditure and effectiveness by the national party campaign, the local party organization and candidate for election is the first and often only point of contact for the individual voter.

Since the emergence of the Labour Party as one of the two major parties, power has oscillated between Labour and Conservative governments. The first Labour government took office in 1924,[13] the second was in power from 1945, and in 1950 Labour was returned to power but governed for only eight months before its defeat led to Conservative rule from 1951 to 1964, when Labour was returned and governed until 1970. Labour was in power again from 1974 to 1979, after which time the Conservatives governed for eighteen years until their dramatic and crushing defeat in the 1997 election. This pattern of changing fortunes of the two parties suggests that the party system is adversarial, with each ideologically opposed to the other's approach on major issues, thus offering the electorate a clear-cut choice of alternative policies. Undeniably the parties seek to maximize the appeal of their unique approach,

---

[12] See further Chapter 5.
[13] The economic and political crises of the late 1920s saw a national (or coalition) government in power, while during the Second World War, 1939–45, a second coalition government was formed.

and use the media and the services of image consultants and the advertising industry to full effect. The organization of Parliament itself enhances the idea of adversarial politics, with the two major parties ranked on benches facing each other, separated only by the 'despatch box' and controlled by the politically neutral Speaker of the Commons.

The popular image of adversarial politics with irreconcilable party ideologies and policies, however, is easily exaggerated. While in the run-up to elections the parties emphasize their distinctive approach and offer a 'real alternative' to the electorate, once a party gains power and forms a government the situation changes. Constitutionally, Her Majesty's Loyal Opposition, as the second major party in Parliament is formally labelled, has a duty to oppose the government and to act as an alternative 'government in waiting' should the government be forced out of office. This does not mean, however, that every policy of government or every proposal for new laws is opposed as a matter of routine. In any parliamentary year the House of Commons as a whole, with varying degrees of dissent, will approve legislative proposals, and this suggests a higher degree of consensus between the parties than the term 'adversarial politics' suggests. However radical a political party seeks to appear to the electorate at election time, the radicalism is tempered once in government by a number of restraints both internal and external to Parliament. First, there is the practical matter of forming an administration, allocating ministries and getting to grips with the civil service which has the detailed knowledge and experience of practical government. Secondly, there is the need to gain the support of Parliament as a whole in order to ensure that promises in manifestos are translated into reality. Where a government has a strong majority in Parliament, as does the current Labour government with a majority of 164, the government's control over the Commons is generally secure, although it may face more trouble from the House of Lords. Nevertheless, as Conservative Prime Minister Margaret Thatcher found in 1986, even with a majority of 188 over Labour and a majority overall in relation to the other parties, including Labour, of 144, the Commons as a whole can defeat a controversial proposal. In Mrs Thatcher's case it was the Shops Bill 1986 which sought to deregulate Sunday trading. This emphasized the need for any Prime Minister, however dominant, not only to have the support of the opposition parties but also to retain that of his or her own party in Parliament.

Governments are also constrained by the laws which they inherit: no government has the energy or ability to dismantle in any wholesale fashion the system which already exists. Too great a degree of attempted radicalism on the part of any party in government or opposition can lead to alienation not only from the party but from the public at large, as the Labour Party found to its cost in the 1980s under the leadership of Michael Foot when, *inter alia*, it promised to renationalize those formerly state-owned and -controlled industries which the Conservatives had been privatizing. At times, all political parties are in agreement over a particular issue, and the role of the opposition then is less to oppose than to ensure scrutiny of proposals with a view to producing effective laws. An example of this is the Child Support Bill which became the Child Support Act 1991, designed to ensure that children of single parents are supported by the absent parent rather than the state. Not only did the Labour Party support the measure, but the Conservatives had actually adopted the idea from Labour. Then there are single-issue matters which arise through some event which demands an immediate response: the shootings of schoolchildren in Dunblane resulted in unopposed, swift and effective legislation giving Britain the most stringent gun control laws in Europe.[14] The greatest external constraint on government is membership of the European Community and Union. The European Community which Britain joined in 1973 has its own legal system and an extensive body of law which governs areas covered in the Treaties. The British government is bound by those laws, and Parliament, while theoretically still 'sovereign', has no power – as long as Britain remains in Europe – to legislate contrary to the requirements of the Community. With the introduction of the European Union in 1992 and the extension of its aims and objectives into areas such as European monetary union (the single currency) and home affairs and common defence and security policies, no governing party – and no opposition party hoping to have a realistic chance of success at a future election – has autonomy in relation to Europe but can at best seek to influence the development of Europe in a manner favouring British

[14] Firearms Act 1998.

interests. The splits which developed in the last Conservative government over Europe represent a significant explanatory and contributory factor to its massive defeat in 1997.

Political parties are essential to a healthy democracy. The interactive process between parties both inside and outside Parliament ensure full and open debate about contemporary issues, and facilitate the choices to be made by voters at election time. Without diversity in political views there would be a danger of political stultification and rule by an oligarchy which, unopposed, could abuse its power. In Parliament the role of the government is to govern in accordance with the programme it has been elected to pursue, and for the opposition parties not automatically to oppose – for that would defeat the wishes of the electorate – but constantly to scrutinize and question government, to suggest alternatives, to raise issues which a government might otherwise choose not to promote for debate, in order to ensure as far as possible that government is conducted with openness and integrity and subject to law.

Changes in the Conservative and Labour Parties

Both the Conservative Party and Labour Party have undergone key changes in the last two decades. The Conservative Party, under the leadership of Margaret Thatcher from 1975 to 1990, became overtly ideological and radical. Market-forces and competition were the two dominant creeds of Thatcherism. Mrs Thatcher encouraged individualism and the entrepreneurial spirit. While splits occurred during her premiership, and in 1990 she was rejected by the Party as its leader, Mrs Thatcher changed the tone of British Conservatism. Frustrated by the over-burdening state, she streamlined the civil service, introducing executive agencies, with executive directors, to manage vast areas formerly under the centralized civil service. Towards the same end, formerly nationalized industries and services were privatized. To monitor quality and efficiency, a range of new regulatory bodies was introduced: for example Ofwat (water), Oftel (telecommunications) and Oflot (the national lottery). Mrs Thatcher was also determined to curb the power of trade unions, in order to free industry from the constant threat of industrial unrest and strikes epitomized by the miners' strikes of 1984 and 1985 which could have brought the economy to a halt. Policing the strike cost over £140 million; the strikes involved violence, causing injuries to 1,392 police officers and an untold number of injuries to strike-supporters.

Universities and other higher education institutions were also targeted in the name of greater efficiency. The funding of universities was cut, encouraging funding sourced from the Higher Education Funding Council. This was staffed not by academics but by businessmen who set their funding criteria according to research output and quality assessment exercises. Student grants were cut, to be replaced by student loans, repayable once in employment. Seeking to reform the system of funding local government, the Conservative government set about reforming the rating system. Unwisely, almost fatally, they opted for a system which was operated elsewhere only in Papua New Guinea: the Community Charge, or poll tax. The tax was deeply unpopular and, more importantly, unworkable and uncollectable.

One issue which dogged the premierships of both Margaret Thatcher and her successor John Major was Europe.[15] In 1986 Mrs Thatcher signed the Single European Act, which had two principal long-term consequences that now appear obvious but were unforeseen at the time. The first related to the voting system employed in the Council of Ministers which represents the interests of member states. While previously this had been mainly by unanimous voting, weighted qualified majority voting was now extended, thus curtailing the power of any one member state to block European development. The second consequence was an expansion of the power of the European Parliament in the legislative process. In 1990 the government reluctantly entered the European Exchange Rate Mechanism (ERM): following splits in Cabinet Britain withdrew in 1992. The political fall-out weakened public confidence in government further. Under the premiership of John Major from 1990 to 1997, the Maastricht Treaty of 1992 split the Conservative Party further, with 'euro-sceptics' becoming an increasingly vociferous force in the Party. As its parliamentary majority dwindled in the face of public opposition across a number of fronts, the government was

---

[15] See further Chapter 4.

then hit by allegations of corruption and sleaze in public life. It was the last straw in the electoral fortunes of the Party: in the 1997 general election Labour swept to power. John Major resigned as Party leader, to be replaced by William Hague whose public popularity remained at a low ebb, especially when compared with the popularity of the Labour Prime Minister. By 1999 the Conservative Party looked unelectable and destined for the political wilderness for the foreseeable future, a view confirmed by the results of the 2001 election.[16]

It was not, however, only the misfortunes of the Conservative administration which resulted in the landslide election of the Labour Party to government. The Labour Party itself had undergone transformation. While the Labour administrations of Harold Wilson[17] and James Callaghan[18] were regarded as politically moderate and conciliatory, in the 1980s radicalism in the Party rose to new heights. When left-winger Michael Foot became leader of the Party in 1981 the Party redeclared itself in favour of nationalizing privatized industries, seeking unilateral nuclear disarmament and withdrawing from the European Community. At the 1983 election, Labour won its smallest number of seats since it first became a political force, and Foot resigned. Contributing to Labour's failure to win power was the impact of the Falklands War. When the Argentinians invaded the Falklands, Prime Minister Thatcher's response was swift and decisive. Without prior parliamentary approval, and using the royal prerogative, she despatched British troops to the Falklands and repelled the Argentinians. While the Prime Minister's popularity ratings were at a low ebb before the war, at its successful conclusion they soared. It was both a military and political triumph for her.

The more moderate and conciliatory Neil Kinnock replaced Michael Foot, successfully abandoning the latter's radical policies and moving the Party towards the centre of the political spectrum, and tackling the 'loony-left' faction of the Party which had a stranglehold on several local councils. But while Kinnock rescued the Party, enabling it to increase its share of the vote and the number of seats won in Parliament at the 1992 election, it was not enough: the Conservatives were once again returned to power, albeit with a smaller majority. Kinnock resigned the leadership

---

[16] Following which William Hague was replaced as leader by Iain Duncan Smith.
[17] 1964–6.   [18] 1976–9.

and was replaced by John Smith, a Scottish lawyer. If the Labour Party was to become capable of election, the Party needed further and radical modernizing. Two factors, both deriving from the Party's origins and constitution, required attention. The first was the power of the trade unions, the second, Clause IV of the constitution (see page 271). Traditionally, unions have sponsored election candidates, contributing to their campaign costs and providing financial support for their parliamentary work. Of the 269 Labour Members of Parliament elected in 1979, for example, 134 were sponsored by the unions. Equally important is the traditional reliance of the Party on union contributions to party funds (on political funding see further pages 291–5 below).

Under the constitution of the Party, there are four principal actors: the Annual Conference, the National Executive Committee, the Parliamentary Labour Party and the membership of the Party. In theory, Conference has the ultimate say over policy. In reality, especially when in office, the leader of the Parliamentary Labour Party has the final say and can persuade but ultimately – although this is politically dangerous – ignore Conference. Conference elects the membership of the National Executive Committee (NEC), of which the Party leader is a member. The NEC is responsible, in theory, for policy decisions between Annual Conferences. The Parliamentary Labour Party consists of all elected Labour Members of Parliament. The membership of the Party has two aspects. Individual members who join local Party associations and pay a modest subscription to the Party, and the unions whose members were affiliated to the Party through a political levy which goes to Party funds. At Conference, decisions are reached by majority vote.

Before reform of the system in 1993, union representatives had a card indicating the number of affiliated members he or she represented, and that number was the number of votes the union wielded. One problem with this was that the number of affiliated members claimed by a union did not, so an investigation in 1984 concluded, match up with the actual number of affiliated members. More seriously still, the votes of the unions dominated the vote at Conference and accordingly disempowered the vote of local constituency branches. When John Smith replaced Neil Kinnock as leader, he successfully campaigned for the principle of 'one man, one vote', which had the effect of limiting the power of the unions' vote to 50 per cent of the total and equalizing it with that of constituency branches. John Smith died prematurely in 1994, and was replaced by Tony Blair. It was Blair who carried on the reform programme and achieved the greatest success of all by persuading the Party – against all predictions – to abandon Clause IV of the constitution. Rather than radicalizing the Party back towards the left, Blair adopted many centrist policies – support for low public expenditure, lowering rates of income tax and continuing the Conservative-led policy of privatization.

With a general election looming in 1997, the Labour Party manifesto pledged significant constitutional reform with a view to modernizing Britain: reform of the House of Lords, devolution of power to the nations, incorporation of the European Convention on Human Rights into domestic law, reform of political party funding, a re-examination of the voting system and the adoption of a more pro-European approach than in earlier years. Not only had Tony Blair made Labour a party of moderation and modernization, he had made it appear electable once more. In many respects, he was following the lead of Margaret Thatcher, a politician whom he personally admired: he entered office as a strong leader, brooking no dissent from waverers in the Party, adopting policies which in many respects might well have come either from the liberal wing of the Conservative Party or from the centrist Liberal Democrat Party.

Blair's first term of office was dominated largely by the government's constitutional reform programme. Despite the problems encountered in the agriculture industry (BSE and Foot and Mouth Disease in cattle), transport problems and concerns over entry into the single European currency, the government's popularity remained high. Its success in the 2001 general election heralded a term of office during which the government is committed to reforming public services.

INTEREST GROUPS AND PRESSURE GROUPS

Assisting the process of interaction between government and the people are those mechanisms that facilitate communication between government and the people, either directly or through the medium of interest and pressure groups, which back in 1958 were described by Professor

S. E. Finer as the 'anonymous empire' existing outside Parliament and government but which government cannot afford to ignore.[19] Whereas the atomized individual may be powerless against the state, the coming together of many individuals with common concerns into organized groups with defined purposes amounts to a more significant force. Interest groups come in many forms. The most obvious are trade unions which developed to protect the rights of workers against the power of the bosses, and which came to dominate the Labour Party until recent reform both of the power of the unions under the Thatcher government and in the constitution of the Labour Party. Powerful groups also exist on the management side of business and industry, the Institute of Directors and the Confederation of British Industry being the largest. Other groups both represent the interests of their members and also have a regulatory function within their own sphere. Examples of these are the General Medical Council and the Law Society and Bar Council.

Other groups are purely policy related, as with Greenpeace, Friends of the Earth and the Environmental Protection League, promoting environmental protection both at home and abroad. Others have a more limited mandate organized around specific objectives. The National Society for the Prevention of Cruelty to Children, the Howard League for Penal Reform, the Royal Society for the Protection of Birds, the Worldwide Fund for Nature, the Royal Society for the Prevention of Cruelty to Animals and the Cat Protection League are all examples. Others may be formed to exert pressure on government in relation to a single issue, such as the Campaign for Nuclear Disarmament and the Rose Theatre Trust which was formed in the 1980s to campaign for the protection of the remains of Shakespeare's theatre against property developers.

Interest and pressure groups representing the views of their members vary not only in size and objectives, but also in their influence on government, both at the domestic level and within the European Community and Union. Consultation in the policy-formation process is vital to the success or otherwise of policy implementation. To ignore the views of the legal profession, for example, when considering the reform of the legal system would be to ignore an important dimension of expertise and opinion. Equally, in the formation and implementation

[19] S. E. Finer, *Anonymous Empire* (London: Pall Mall, 1958).

of agricultural policy, now a matter largely for the European Community, consultation with the National Farmers' Union in Britain and its equivalent in other member countries is essential to ensuring the acceptance of policy and compliance with its consequences.

Group representation is a means of empowering individuals *vis-à-vis* government and the democratic process. Unlike political parties, interest and pressure groups are not concerned with the contesting and winning of parliamentary seats to promote their interests, but rather in securing avenues into the processes of government, exerting pressure on government departments and on Members of Parliament to further their objectives. In relation to law-making, interest groups have a central role to play in making representations to bodies charged with keeping the law under review. To take one example, the Law Commission was established in 1965 with the task of keeping the law under review and making recommendations for reform.[20] In reviewing areas of law, the Commission typically sets out its views in a Working Paper which invites comments by a stipulated date. Individuals and groups give evidence to the Commission which is considered before the Commission issues its Report containing detailed recommendations for reform of the law. These are then submitted to the Lord Chancellor and Parliament for consideration. While the Law Commission's role is advisory and therefore not binding on governments, significant law reform is often the outcome of the Commission's considerations, although too often (in the Commission's view) governments with a heavy legislative programme may fail to implement its proposals.

THE ELECTORAL SYSTEM

The right to vote

The right to vote is a hallmark of citizenship. Entitlement to vote is dependent upon being entered on the electoral register. Until the year 2000, residency and registration on the electoral register were the only

[20] Under the Law Commission Act 1965.

prerequisites for voting, unless a person was legally disqualified on the grounds of mental incapacity or detention following conviction for a criminal offence.[21] The register was updated annually, but under the Representation of the People Act 2000 it is now updated monthly. The 2000 Act also extended the right to vote in parliamentary or local elections (other than for those disenfranchised) to those who have no fixed residence, through 'declarations of local connection', as well as extending the right to postal votes. A declaration of local connection must state the name of the declarant and either an address to which election correspondence can be delivered or a statement that he or she is willing to collect such correspondence periodically from the registration officer's office. The declaration must be dated, and on the date of declaration the voter must also be otherwise qualified to vote by virtue of relevant citizenship and age. A declaration of local connection may be cancelled at any time by the person concerned. The declaration has no effect unless it is received by the relevant registration officer within a period of three months beginning at the date of the declaration.

In the United Kingdom the age at which the individual is entitled to vote is the age of majority: eighteen years.[22] While minors may join the army or get married below the age of majority, the right to vote is withheld until the eighteenth birthday. Citizenship and residence form the basis of entitlement to vote. Only citizens, either British or Commonwealth, or citizens of the Republic of Ireland, may exercise the vote: 'aliens' resident in the country prior to obtaining citizenship (which lies in the Home Secretary's discretion) are excluded. Citizens subject to legal incapacities, that is, those detained under the Mental Health Act, are disentitled. More contentiously, a person convicted of an offence and detained in prison is disfranchised for the duration of that sentence. Entitlement to vote includes the right to vote in local government elections, general elections, elections for the Scottish, Welsh and Northern Ireland assemblies and elections to the European Parliament.

---

[21] Representation of the People Act 1983.
[22] Reduced from twenty-one by the Family Law Reform Act 1969.

General elections

By law, the life of a Parliament may not last more than five years, although no minimum term is set down.[23] It is within the discretion of the Prime Minister to fix the date for an election, and on reaching the decision the Prime Minister formally requests a dissolution of Parliament by the Crown. The campaigning period in Britain is short compared with other countries: generally three to four weeks is the maximum time before polling day. In practice, campaigning for election starts unofficially long before the date of the election is fixed, and both government and opposition will be vying for the voters' approval through their policies.

Parliamentary constituencies

The principle of 'one person, one vote, one value' is of fundamental importance to political equality. The extent to which it is possible to respect this principle depends in part on the size of constituencies. Historically there were vast anomalies between constituencies. Before the great Reform Act 1832 the representation of constituencies depended on landowners who controlled who should sit in Parliament, and this choice in turn was related to the aristocracy sitting in the House of Lords which could nominate their children or relatives to sit in the Commons. The boroughs, urban areas so designated by the Crown, had disproportionate representation compared with the larger rural county areas. Old Sarum for example, now long abandoned, returned two Members of Parliament representing seven constituents. University graduates had special entitlements, being able to vote for Members representing their own residential constituency in addition to a Member to represent the university, an anomaly which endured until 1948. The 1832 Act removed most of the most offensively corrupt constituencies, some areas with less than 2,000 voters losing a representative, and those with between 2,000 and 4,000 having their representation reduced from

[23] Parliament Act 1911.

two members to one. The borough seats abolished were redistributed to the previously unrepresented towns, and to the counties. This reform, while modest in comparison with the present distribution of seats, was a move towards a more representative democracy as now understood. It was not until 1944 that the determination of constituency boundaries was taken out of political control and placed in the hands of independent Boundary Commissions, nominally headed by the politically neutral Speaker of the Commons, and in practice headed by a High Court judge.[24]

There are currently 659 parliamentary constituencies in the United Kingdom, each of which returns just one Member to Parliament, representing an average of 65,000 voters. In charge of keeping boundaries between constituencies under review is the Electoral Commission.[25] There are four Boundary Committees (known as Commissions until 2000), one each for England, Wales, Scotland and Northern Ireland. If equality in voting power is to be both established and preserved, it is important that reviews be conducted regularly to recommend changes necessitated by population shifts. A number of difficulties have hitherto been entailed in this operation, not least the legal rules which regulate the work of the Boundary Committees. First, there is the problem that each Committee works in isolation from the others. Secondly, reviews are only required to be carried out every eight to twelve years, which hardly enables boundary sizes to be kept constantly under review. Thirdly, the rules laid down in the Parliamentary Constituencies Act 1986[26] stipulated that parliamentary constituencies should be the same as local government areas. Finally, the rules provide that where there are special geographical features, the rule favouring equality in voting numbers may be displaced. As a consequence of these differing requirements, the Commissions aimed not at absolute equality but rather at achieving as small a percentage of deviance as possible from the arithmetical mean size of eligible voters overall when divided by 659.

Prior to 2000, the Boundary Commissions reported to the Home

---

[24] The system was reformed in 2000. See below.
[25] Established under the Political Parties, Elections and Referendums Act 2000.
[26] Which continues in force subject to changes made by the Electoral Commissioner.

Secretary, who in turn was required by law to present its recommendations to Parliament with a view to introducing the recommended changes. On occasion this gave rise to both political and legal disputes, when either a Home Secretary considered that laying the report before Parliament would result in constituency changes which would disadvantage the ruling party at the next election, or when the opposition parties made the same objection. Few challenges succeeded, however, since by law the Commissions enjoyed considerable discretion as to how their powers were to be exercised, and short of any blatant disregard for the rules enshrined in law there was little prospect for a successful challenge.

Under new arrangements[27] the Electoral Commissioner reports to a newly established Speaker's Committee, comprising the Speaker of the House of Commons, the Home Secretary, Chairman of the Home Affairs Select Committee, the minister responsible for local government and five other Members of Parliament who do not hold ministerial rank. The Commissioner is under a duty to submit a five-year plan to the Speaker's Committee, setting out the aims and objectives of the Commission and the estimated financial resources required for the five-year period.[28]

Candidates and legal controls

The selection and reselection of candidates is for the local constituency political parties: no formal controls over the process lie with the parliamentary party or the party leader. Any person, whether a member of a political party or not, may stand for Parliament. However, in order to avoid frivolous attempts, a candidate must have the support of ten nominees and put down a deposit of £500, which will be forfeited if less than one-twentieth of the vote is secured. To ensure fairness, each candidate is entitled to send one piece of campaign literature to voters in the area free of postal charges and to use a public hall for an election meeting without paying rental.

---

[27] Introduced under the Political Parties, Elections and Referendums Act 2000.
[28] The Electoral Commissioner also has responsibility for ensuring compliance with the income and expenditure rules regulating political parties. See further below.

Expenditure on the campaign is in theory strictly controlled by law, although the difficulty in checking the accuracy of returns gives rise to the suspicion that 'creative accounting' is used. Until the electoral system was reformed in the nineteenth century, in relation to the right to vote, the secret ballot and to controlling the manner in which elections were conducted, wealthy individuals were able to 'buy' votes for their chosen candidates, either through direct payments or through the inherent coercion that came with a system of voting which was not secret and which enabled a land-owning employer to check on the votes of those who were dependent on him in some way. In 1883 Parliament passed the Corrupt Practices Act designed to stamp out the corruption. Nowadays, the Representation of the People Act 1983 governs the matter and provides for a number of criminal offences associated with election practices: exceeding allowable expenditure, bribery, 'treating' (which includes providing gifts or hospitality with a view to influencing a voter), 'undue influence' (which includes threats or attempts to intimidate voters). Any candidate found guilty of such practices by an Election Court may be disqualified from membership of the Commons, or if the offence comes to light subsequently, the Member can be excluded from Parliament.[29]

All candidates are entitled to spend a defined amount, which differs in urban and rural areas. For the 1997 election, the amount permitted was approximately £8,000. The actual total amount is made up of a flat sum – dependent upon whether it is an urban or rural constituency – plus a fixed sum multiplied by the number of voters in the area. All expenditure must be through a named election agent, who may be the candidate him- or herself. The third-party restriction gave rise to an application under the European Convention on Human Rights, alleging that the law represented an unjustified restriction on freedom of expression, a complaint upheld by the European Court of Human Rights.[30] The agent is responsible for making returns of expenditure within three weeks of the date of the election. In relation to advertising, it is an offence for anyone to distribute literature or take out

[29] In 1999 a Labour Member was disqualified for making a false return, but her conviction was overturned on appeal.
[30] *Bowman v. United Kingdom* (1998) 26 EHRR 1.

advertisements in the media with the specific intention of dissuading voters from voting for another identified candidate, as opposed to promoting the candidate's own campaign. General advertisements in support of a political party, rather than a specific candidate, escape this restriction.[31]

The media and elections

When it comes to the role of the media, a distinction must be drawn between radio and television and newspapers. In relation to broadcasting, the law attempts to ensure fairness and equality between candidates. Only broadcasts by the BBC or IBA are lawful, and no broadcasting is permitted from overseas. Advertisements 'directed towards any political end' are unlawful,[32] and political parties may not buy advertising time. Both the BBC and the IBA are under a duty to act impartially and to provide equal time for pre-election party political broadcasts by the major parties and also to provide adequate time for smaller parties, which is allocated according to the number of seats won at the last election.[33] This works unfairly against the Liberal Democrat Party which in recent elections has polled between 17 and 25 per cent of the popular vote, but because of the voting system has won only a few parliamentary seats.[34] In addition, no broadcast may be made without the consent of the candidate, and where one candidate participates in a broadcast to promote his or her own election, all other candidates in the constituency must consent to the broadcast.[35] Originally intended to prevent unscrupulous candidates from seeking unfair advantage by gaining greater coverage than other candidates, the restriction has resulted in

[31] See e.g. *R v. Tronoh Mines Ltd.* [1952] 1 All ER 697; *DPP v. Luft* [1977] AC 962; *Walker v. Unison* 1995 SLT 1225.

[32] Broadcasting Act 1990, sections 8, 60, 92.

[33] Broadcasting Act 1990, sections 6, 90; BBC Charter (Cm 3248).

[34] For unsuccessful challenges to the rules see *R v. Broadcasting Complaints Commission ex parte Owen* [1985] QB 1153; *R v. British Broadcasting Corporation ex parte Referendum Party* (1997) *The Times* 29 April.

[35] Representation of the People Act 1983, section 93; see *Marshall v. BBC* [1979] 3 All ER 80.

any candidate – even a candidate standing as an independent or one representing an unelectable party – being able to veto any broadcast about the constituency.

While broadcasters are under a legal duty to act impartially and are subject to legal sanctions, the position is very different in relation to newspapers. In the eighteenth century, William Blackstone wrote of the fundamental importance of a free press:

The liberty of the press is indeed essential to the nature of a free state . . . Every free man has an undoubted right to lay what sentiments he pleases before the public; to forbid this, is to destroy the freedom of the press: but if he publishes what is improper, mischievous or illegal, he must take the consequences of his own temerity.[36]

The British press is politically partisan, with the majority of newspapers traditionally supporting the Conservative Party. In 1997, for the first time, the Labour Party enjoyed the majority of press support. Unlike broadcasters, newspapers are under no duty to provide unbiased and objective reporting or comment, and newspaper proprietors use their freedom of speech to promote their subjective preferences. In the tabloid press this can be reduced to hyperbole. In 1992, for example, the *Sun* headline read: 'If Kinnock wins today will the last person to leave Britain please turn out the lights'; and subsequently the *Sun* made the crass claims that it was the *Sun* 'wot won it' in 1992, and 'It's the *Sun* wot swung it' in 1997. Such blatant attempts to manipulate the vote and to exaggerate the influence of the press, however, seem incapable of empirical verification, not least because the data is ambivalent concerning the impact of the press on public opinion and the mix of other factors which enter the picture. Some voters remain loyal to one party for their entire voting lives, others remain politically independent of all parties and thus represent the important sector of 'floating voters' who may be more influenced by the media than those committed to one party irrespective of the subjective views of the press.

---

[36] *Commentaries on the Laws of England*, vol. 4 (1769), pp. 151–2.

Disputed elections

If an allegation is made about wrongful practices at an election the matter is resolved by an Election Court, which has the power to order a new election in that constituency, disqualify the winning candidate or impose fines. In the case of corrupt practices, imprisonment is an available penalty. While the law regulates election campaigns and expenditure at local constituency level, at the national party level legal regulation, until recently, has been scant. Although the law relating to broadcasting applies equally to political parties as to individual candidates,[37] when it comes to transparency about the source of donations the law has been silent.

Funding of political parties

At the 1997 general election the Conservative Party spent approximately £28 million and the Labour Party £26 million.[38] Political parties have never been funded by the state in Britain, but rely on individual party subscriptions or donations from supporters. The essential problem, from the standpoint of democracy, is the right to know who or what corporate body or institution is contributing to party funds and the basis on which this is done. Pure altruism is a rare feature of politics. Traditionally, political parties refused to disclose the source of their funds, regarding it as a private matter and quite simply no one else's business. The furore over the outside interests of Members of Parliament,[39] however, returned the issue of party funding to the political agenda.

While the original committee (the Nolan Committee) established to inquire into Members' interests had no remit to examine party funding, in 1997 the Prime Minister extended the committee's terms of reference to include party finances. In 1998 the Committee on Standards in Public

[37] See *Grieve v. Douglas-Home* 1965 SLT 186.
[38] Fifth Report of the Committee on Standards in Public Life (the Neill Committee), *The Funding of Political Parties in the United Kingdom*, Cm. 4057–I.
[39] Discussed in Chapter 3.

Life, chaired by Lord Neill of Bladen QC, published its Report. The Nolan Committee had identified 'seven principles of public life' which relate to holders of public office: selflessness, integrity, objectivity, accountability, openness, honesty and leadership. It was on three of these principles that the Neill Committee focused in its evaluation of party political funding: integrity, accountability and openness. Accepting the view that political parties are essential to democracy, the Committee's task was to examine the present system and to make recommendations for any necessary reforms to ensure that the public perception of political parties was that they operated honestly and openly and that donations to political parties did not undermine their integrity.

The Committee looked to where the money to finance parties originated, both in relation to funding election campaigns and for their parliamentary work between elections. In 1997 the Labour Party's estimated income totalled £24.1 million, as against the Conservative Party's £42.5 million. The Liberal Democrat Party's estimated income for that year was £3.8 million. Breaking down these overall figures for the two main parties into sources, and comparing the most significant of these with earlier years, some interesting trends appear. In relation to Labour, in 1992 £7.1 million came from trade union affiliation fees; by 1997 this had declined to £6.4 million. By contrast, in 1992 donations to the Labour Party amounted to only £3.5 million, but in 1997 this had increased to £14.5 million, with each year showing a steady increase. On the other hand donations to the Conservative Party in 1992 and 1997 remained more constant, with £20.0 million in 1992 and £38.2 million in 1997 (both election years), the figures for intervening years showing a marked decrease. During the period 1992–7, the Labour Party received nearly 300 donations of more than £5,000, compared with over 1,300 donations over £5,000 for the Conservatives. During the same period, Labour received no donations from overseas, compared with the Conservative Party's 47 overseas donations worth a total of £16.2 million.

General elections are expensive, and the significance of the national election campaign has changed out of all recognition over a century. When the Corrupt Practices Act 1883 was enacted the issue was the fairness of the campaign in the local constituency and the need to avoid those practices which meant that votes were in effect being bought. In the nineteenth century there was no national campaign to speak of. Nowadays, a general election is very much a party-led, nation-wide campaign. As noted above, while the legal controls on individual expenditure in the constituencies are tight, until very recently the paradox remained that at the national level minimal controls exist and there were no limits on expenditure. Nor were there any checks on where funds come from to meet campaign expenditure or any criteria laid down to ensure fairness between various political parties in relation to their ability to launch and sustain an effective campaign. Furthermore, there was no independent body to keep the system under control and review.

The Registration of Political Parties Act 1998 introduced a register of political parties. A political party is entitled to be entered on the Register of Political Parties if it intends to have one or more candidates at parliamentary elections, elections to the European Parliament, Scottish Parliament, National Assembly for Wales, the Northern Ireland Assembly or local government elections. Registration is intended to clarify the identity of bona fide political parties and thereby make regulation more certain. No party political broadcast may be made by broadcasters other than on behalf of a registered political party.[40]

The expenditure on general election campaigns of the two main parties doubled in the years between the 1992 and 1997 campaigns. In 1992 the Conservatives spent some £12.7 million; in 1997, £28.3 million, an increase of 123 per cent. As for Labour, its expenditure in 1992 was £11.2 million and in 1997, £26 million, an increase of 132 per cent. There has been an 'arms race' between the two parties for funds. Where those funds come from, and the basis on which they are made, is critical to the democratic process. Where donors are unidentified suspicions are inevitably raised as to their motives. Was the donation linked to a pledge to pursue a particular policy which would favour the donor? As the Neill Report expresses it, 'where both the names of the givers and the amounts given are unknown – as has been customary – there is room for unlimited speculation and rumour as to the identity of those who may be "bank-rolling" this or that political party'.[41] The dangers,

---

40 Registration of Political Parties Act 1998, section 14.
41 Fifth Report, paragraph 4.6.

real or imagined, were manifested in 1997 when shortly after having a meeting with the Prime Minister to discuss exempting Formula 1 racing from the ban on tobacco advertising, it was revealed that Bernie Ecclestone, the leading figure in Formula 1, had donated £1 million to the Labour Party to help finance its 1997 election campaign.[42]

In 1999 further concerns were raised over the propriety of donations, amounting to £1 million a year, to the Conservative Party by its Party Treasurer, Michael Ashcroft, through a trust in Belize, Central America. The revelation contradicted William Hague's statement in 1997 that the Party would 'no longer accept foreign donations', and raised important questions about how a 'foreign donation' is defined. In November 1999 the Conservative Party published its guidelines concerning funding from overseas. The relevant part of this document states that donations will be accepted from individuals who are entitled to vote in parliamentary and other elections and/or holders of British passports who may live abroad. This definition is broader than both the Neill Committee's definition (see below) and the definition adopted in the government's draft Bill published in July 1999 which required not only an entitlement to vote but that the individual be actually registered to vote. The affair also raised the question of how a party treasurer, with responsibility for overseeing the rules relating to donations and for reporting to the proposed Electoral Commission, could undertake his role ethically and responsibly when he himself was making donations from an overseas source. The response of the Conservative Party, through its deputy chairman, Tim Collins, was that Ashcroft was not a foreign donor, and that it was irrelevant whether the donation came from 'a branch of Barclays in Birmingham or a bank in Belize or a bank on the far side of the moon'.[43] The draft legislation, however, included a prohibition of donations via a foreign-based trust. Although Mr Ashcroft is registered, according to the Conservative spokesman, as an overseas voter in the constituency of Maidenhead, and would therefore be entitled to make donations in his own name, the fact that the name on the donation was the Belize Bank Trust Company meant that it fell outside the proposed restrictions on foreign donations.

The Neill Committee proposals aimed to ensure transparency in

---

[42] The money was subsequently returned.   [43] *The Times*, 25 November 1999.

relation to donations, backed up by a system of reporting and the appointment of an independent Electoral Commission to call for information and to investigate the financial affairs of political parties. Deliberate failure to report disclosable donations is now a criminal offence. Donations include sponsorship and donations in kind.[44] All donations to political parties from one source of £5,000 or more must be disclosed, and any donations to party constituency organizations or to regional organizations of political parties which total £1,000 or more in one year must also be recorded. Anonymous donations of £50 or more must be refused. Donations from foreign sources are banned. No upper limit is imposed on the amount which may be donated: the individual remains free to do with his or her money what he or she wishes, and political parties remain free to raise funds from domestic sources as best they can, provided they are openly disclosed.

State funding of political parties was also considered by the Committee, but rejected. The Committee recognized that the arguments for and against state funding were finely balanced. In favour are the arguments that state funding which would reduce dependence on large donors would 'purify' the political process. In addition it would free the parties from the 'arms race' to acquire funds for election purposes and enable them to focus better on policy issues. On the other hand, state funding involves compelling taxpayers to contribute to political parties whose policies are objectionable to them. State funding might also encourage lethargy among the established parties secure in the knowledge that their coffers would be replenished automatically by the state, whereas small or emerging parties would be discriminated against until they could demonstrate a level of support justifying state funding.

While rejecting the arguments in favour of state funding, the Committee did recommend that a state-funded Policy Development Fund be set up to enable political parties to focus on policy development. In terms of financial support for opposition parties in relation to their parliamentary duties, Neill recommended a review by the political parties in the House of Commons, the Scottish Parliament and National Assemblies of Northern Ireland and Wales, and by the parties in the House of Lords. The financial support system in the Commons, known

---

[44] See Political Parties and Referendums Act 2000.

as 'Short money', was introduced in 1975 by the Right Honourable Edward Short, then Leader of the House of Commons.[45] In 1996 a similar system, 'Cranborne money', was adopted in the House of Lords by Viscount Cranborne, then Leader of the House. In the parliamentary session 1 May 1997–March 1998, Short money was allocated as follows:

Conservative	£986,762
Liberal Democrat	371,997
Scottish National	46,167
Plaid Cymru	21,210
Ulster Unionist	47,580
Democratic Unionist	11,618
SDLP [46]	18,553

The voting system

As with so much of the constitution, the voting system used in Britain has been subject to review and to change. Traditionally the simple majority system – 'first past the post' – has been used for general elections to the House of Commons and for local government elections. With membership of the European Union and the devolution of power to Northern Ireland, Scotland and Wales and the introduction of an elected mayor for London, different systems have been introduced. The simple majority system is also under attack, and subject to recommendations for change. The diversity in the system requires separate consideration of the differing systems.

Elections to Westminster

The current voting system is based on the simple premise of one person, one vote, and the equally straightforward notion that the candidate who polls the highest number of votes in a constituency is elected as Member of Parliament. A one-vote majority over the next highest candidate suffices: this is the simple majority, or 'first past the post' system. There are a number of advantages with this system, which

---

[45] Subsequently Lord Glenamara.
[46] Social Democratic Labour Party (Northern Ireland).

explains the traditional resistance of governments – despite the system's democratic shortcomings – to the introduction of a more representative system. First, the system is simple for voters to understand: they are presented with a list of candidates, and the name of the political party each represents: a cross is placed beside the chosen candidate and the vote is cast. At the end of polling, usually 10 p.m., the votes are counted and the highest candidate declared duly elected. The system ensures that each constituency has a single, identifiable representative in Parliament. The system also results, though not invariably, in the election of a political party which then forms a government with a clear majority in Parliament with the legitimate right to expect, and to get, its election promises through Parliament in the form of legislation.

With all ministers bound by the convention of collective responsibility,[47] the government is able to present itself to the public as united, effective and strong. Deviations from the clear majority outcome occasionally occur, as in the February 1974 election when the Conservative government failed to gain a majority of seats, but attempted to stay in office rather than resign immediately, by trying to establish a pact with the Liberal Party. Where a government has a weak majority and cannot rely on the support of smaller parties in Parliament, it becomes particularly vulnerable to defeat, especially where the main opposition party is able to enter an alliance with other minority parties. Loss of office occurs during the life of a Parliament (as opposed to ending at a general election, the timing of which lies with the Prime Minister), by convention, where a vote of confidence on a matter central to the government's policy is lost. Generally, however, a strong government is more likely to emerge from the British voting system than from alternative systems.

Notwithstanding the advantages of simplicity, close links between a constituency and a single Member, and strong government, there are a number of significant and fundamental objections which can be made against the system. First and foremost is the fact that it does not result in a House of Commons made up of elected members whose electoral support, in terms of the share of the popular vote, is *proportionate*. There is a mismatch between votes cast and seats won. A simple example

---

[47] On which see Chapter 1.

suffices. If A, B and C stand for election in a constituency and A gains 5,000 votes, B 4,500 votes and C 4,000 votes, A is duly elected in spite of the fact that he or she polled fewer votes than were polled for B and C taken together. Only about 37 per cent of the constituency electorate voted for A, whereas the remainder voted for B and C. When this anomaly is extrapolated on to the national scene, the problem is considerable: in the 1997 election 53 per cent of all candidates were elected on a minority of the popular vote. No government in recent decades has been elected with a majority of the popular vote, and there has been no proportionality between votes cast and seats won; all recent governments have in effect been 'minority governments'. A glance at the last three general elections reveals the extent of the problem. In 1992 the Conservative government was returned to power with 336 seats (or 51.6 per cent of total seats), a majority of 21 seats, with 41.9 per cent of the popular vote. In 1997, the Labour government was elected with 418 seats (or 63.4 per cent), a majority of 179 seats, with a popular vote of 43.2 per cent. The 2001 general election reflected little change. The Labour Party won 413 seats with 42 per cent of the vote, the Conservative Party 166 seats with 32.7 per cent of the vote and the Liberal Democrats 52 seats with 18.8 per cent of the vote.[48]

The problem of a lack of proportionality between votes cast and seats won is exacerbated by other factors. While generalizations are dangerous, and the 1997 election may have changed the position, traditionally support for the two main parties, Conservative and Labour, tends to be concentrated in particular areas, with the Conservatives being strongest in the south of England and in rural areas, and Labour being strongest in industrial and urban areas. There is a north–south divide, complicated by urban versus rural areas. Gender, race and religion are also factors which have an impact on voting. Further complicating any analysis of voting behaviour and party support is the number of 'floating voters' and those who do not vote at all. Voting is optional: there is no legal requirement, as in Australia for example, for a voter to exercise his or her right.

The position, however, is complicated by the so-called class issue.

[48] The turn-out for the 2001 general election was exceptionally low, with only some 59 per cent of eligible voters voting.

Traditionally, Labour Party support was concentrated in urban industrialized areas on the basis that its traditional rationale was representation of the less well-off in society and the betterment of conditions for them. Conservative support was predominantly upper or middle class, on the basis that the Conservatives represent stability in traditional institutions and the protection of wealth and property. However, in the 1992 election, 41 per cent of working-class votes in the south were for the Conservative Party, 36 per cent in the Midlands, 30 per cent in the north of England, 27 per cent in Wales and just 18 per cent in Scotland: an average of 34 per cent of the vote across Great Britain. Conversely, the Labour Party won 36 per cent of the working-class vote in the south, 46 per cent in the Midlands, 54 per cent in the north, 53 per cent in Wales and 47 per cent in Scotland, an average of 45 per cent across Great Britain. When it comes to the third largest party, the Liberal Democrats, a similar pattern is found to that of the Conservatives: declining proportions from south to north. The working-class vote in the south was 22 per cent, in the Midlands 16 per cent, in the north of England 14 per cent, in Wales 15 per cent and in Scotland a mere 9 per cent, an average across Great Britain of 17 per cent.[49] However, between the 1992 and 1997 elections, party fortunes across the country changed significantly. In 1997 in Scotland, Wales and Northern Ireland no Conservative candidates were elected, while in the Midlands 28 Conservatives were elected compared with 74 Labour Members, and in the north a mere 17 were elected, as against Labour's 138. In the south, 120 Conservatives were elected, as against 116 Labour Members, thus showing a wide-scale swing to Labour in the heartland of former Conservative support. The 2001 election appeared to confirm this pattern. The Labour Party lost eight seats and gained two, the Conservatives gained nine but lost eight, and the Liberal Democrats gained eight and lost only two seats.

While strong government may be viewed as a 'good thing' in so far as it is likely to prove stable and have the ability to enact its mandated programme into legislation without major compromises being reached with other parties, it carries with it inherent dangers, not least the impression that it is oligarchic and responsible to no one during

[49] Source: MORI.

the life of its first parliament. However, this may be countered by the argument that any government, even or maybe particularly one with a strong majority to defend, is keenly aware of its standing in the opinion polls and of the inevitable need to submit itself for re-election within five years. On the other hand, it is a first principle of democratic government that a government be, and be seen to be, challenged by opposition in Parliament both as to its policies and its administration. Where, as was the case with Tony Blair's first administration, the official opposition, the Conservative Party, had seen its popular support crumble in an unprecedented fashion and had lost senior party figures through their either not standing for re-election or failing to be returned to Parliament, and the leader was now an untried and untested politician, the result was an ineffective and weak official opposition. A strong government and a weak opposition is constitutionally undesirable.

If a different voting system had been in place for the 1997 election, a greater balance in parliamentary power would have resulted. The Electoral Reform Society analysed the alternative outcome of the election had a system of proportional representation been adopted. Rather than Labour winning 418 seats, it would have won 286. The Conservatives instead of 165 would have won 199 and the third-largest party, the Liberal Democrats, who always suffer most under 'first past the post', would have won 109 as opposed to 46 seats. While the Labour Party before the 1997 election committed itself to a review of the electoral system, and indeed appointed a commission of inquiry, the government did not act to introduce any electoral reform in its programme of legislation for the 1999–2000 session of Parliament.

Europe, London, Northern Ireland, Scotland and Wales

Elections for the London Mayor, first held in 2000, employ the supplementary vote system. Here the voter marks his or her first and second preferences on a ballot paper. To win, a candidate must have an overall majority of first preferences. If no candidate reaches a majority, all but the top two candidates are eliminated from the list, and the vote of a voter whose first choice candidate has been eliminated will be transferred to his or her second preference candidate, if the latter is one of the two still in the contest. The system is not one ensuring proportionality, nor does it necessarily produce a winner with an overall majority of votes, since the votes for unsuccessful candidates will not count unless one of those votes is for the eventual winner.

For elections to the European Parliament the closed regional list system is used. Here there are multi-member constituencies. The list comprises names chosen by the political parties, and ranked in the order of preference of the party, plus any individuals who choose to stand as independents. It is this feature – the closed list – which caused great opposition in the House of Lords when the European Elections Bill was in Parliament, with the Lords rejecting the Bill and forcing the government to use the Parliament Act procedure to get the Bill into law in time for the European elections. The objections of the Lords – which were eventually rejected by the government – lay in party political control over the list, which is (in this view) undemocratic in so far as it effectively curtails the voter's choice. Each voter has one vote, and the seats are allocated to the parties in accordance with the proportion of the votes received. The winning candidates are those highest on the list of the party.

While the turn-out for general elections for Westminster averages about 75 per cent, for Europe in the June 1999 election the turn-out was close to a mere 23 per cent. Contrary to all predictions, voters in Europe as a whole and Britain in particular swung to the right of the political spectrum, and while the Labour government elected under 'first past the post' in Britain in 1997 won a massive majority, in the 1999 European elections it was the Conservatives who emerged as the victors. An immediate calculation of how the Westminster Parliament would look had this been a British general election in June 1999 showed that there would have been a Conservative government elected, with 352 Conservative Members of Parliament, 261 Labour and a mere 3 Liberal Democrats, with 43 MPs from minor parties: a clear disincentive to reform of the existing system for the current government.

In relation to the Scottish Parliament and the Welsh and London Assemblies the additional member system is used. This is a combination of the 'first past the post' system and the regional list system. Here the single-member constituencies are retained but grouped together into regions. Votes in the single-member constituency are counted on the 'first past the post' basis. Seats from the regional list are allocated between parties, taking account of the constituency members, on the basis of achieving proportionality between votes cast and seats on the regional list. The voter has two votes, one for the constituency candidate of his or her choice, and one for their preferred political party.

Northern Ireland uses the single transferable vote system for elections to the new Assembly and for the European Parliament and local government elections. Under the single transferable vote system there are multi-member constituencies and voters number candidates in their order of preference. The winning candidate must achieve a quota of first-preference votes. The quota is the total number of votes cast, divided by a number which is one greater than the number of members to be elected, plus one vote: so if 300,000 voters vote and there are five members to be elected, the quota will be 300,000 divided by six plus one, or 50,001. Any votes for the winning candidate surplus to the quota requirement are transferred to the voters' next-preference candidates. Candidates polling least votes are gradually eliminated as their votes are transferred to the voter's next highest preference candidate who has not already reached the quota. Casting the vote is a simple matter, the voter simply numbers the candidates in order of preference. Counting the vote, however, is complex. The single transferable vote has the merit of a high degree of proportionality between the actual votes cast and party representation, and minimizing the problem of 'wasted' votes as occurs most significantly under the 'first past the post' system. It also enables voters to choose between candidates standing for election from the same political party. This can be controversial, for while it enables the voter to express his or her preference for the personal politics of different members of the same political party, it also enables the party to select the candidates who are going to be put forward and to 'block' any potential candidate of whose policies the party does not approve.

One of the manifesto pledges of the Labour Party before the 1997 election was a review of the electoral system for the Westminster Parliament, and once in office the government appointed the Liberal Democrat peer Lord Jenkins of Hillhead to review the system. The Jenkins Commission reported in October 1998, and came up with a novel, if complex, solution. The Commission, wanting to retain single-member constituencies but also to inject a greater degree of proportionality into the system, opted for a 'mixed system' made up of the alternative vote and regional list systems. Constituency Members would be elected on the alternative vote system, and comprise 80 to 85 per cent of Members, with additional Members, 15 to 20 per cent, elected on the regional list basis. Greater proportionality would be achieved, while the traditional strong link between a Member and his or her constituency would be retained. The system would also, the Commission claimed, avoid coalition governments and in its estimation would have produced single-party majority government in three out of the four last general elections.[50]

The experience of the European elections and doubts about the Jenkins formula, its complexity and the risk of coalition government, have put further electoral reform on the political backburner. Whatever the 'unfairness' of the 'first past the post' system, its usual result is a party returned to power with not only a clear majority of seats in the Commons but also the ability to put into effect its manifesto pledges, without reliance on the support of minority parties. Democracy may be better served by a proportional representation system in the sense that the number of seats won in Parliament correlates closely to the number of votes cast in the country and the elected government – irrespective of its number of seats – is the real choice of the people. In another sense, however, democracy is best served by a government with a clear majority – irrespective of the fact that that majority may have been secured by less than 45 per cent of the popular vote – able to carry through its policies without compromise being forced upon it by other parties in Parliament. This is the fundamental dilemma of electoral reform. Given the self-interest of any existing or prospective government in being returned to power for a further term of office with the strong working majority which usually results from the simple majority system, it is unlikely that radical reform will take place in the near future.

---

[50] Cm. 4090–I, paragraph 161. This claim has been disputed by M. Pinto-Duschinsky who calculates that coalition would have been the outcome in nine of the last fourteen elections: *The Times*, 29 October 1998.

CONCLUSION

The question of further electoral reform remains firmly on the constitutional agenda. While different voting systems are employed in the
United Kingdom for different elections – each having its own strengths
and weaknesses – the two main political parties remain resistant to
radical change for elections to Westminster. As has been seen above, the
simple majority system (or first past the post) is flagrantly undemocratic
when viewed as a representation of the views of voters in terms of the
popular vote cast and its translation into membership of the House of
Commons. If the essential constitutional principle of 'one person, one
vote, one value' – endorsed by the Supreme Court of the United States
of America in *Baker v. Carr*[51] as a prerequisite for democracy – is to
have true meaning in the United Kingdom, then the case for reform is
unchallengeable. The simple majority system serves to perpetuate the
dominance of the two main political parties at the expense of smaller
parties, the largest of which – the Liberal Democrats – consistently polls
between 15 and 20 per cent of the popular vote but remains excluded
from real power. From any principled perspective this is an unconstitutional state of affairs. And yet, as with so much of the British system,
arguments of principle have little persuasive force when set against
pragmatism. In the case of electoral reform there has recently been
much experimentation with different voting systems. But where principle matters most, at the very heart of the democratic process – elections
to the House of Commons – tradition and the political power it has
given to the two principal political parties combine to ensure resistance
to change.

[51] 369 US 186 (1962).

7

THE PROTECTION OF HUMAN RIGHTS

INTRODUCTION

The story of individual freedoms and rights, and demands that they be protected against arbitrary power, is as old as human society. In modern democracies, individual freedoms and rights, public order and government power jostle against one another in a tripartite search for an appropriate balance. In the nineteenth and early twentieth centuries imperialism and colonialism – the legacy of Britain's Empire – led to the collective demands of subjected nations for self-determination: the right to determine the terms and conditions of their own society without outside interference. From the mid-twentieth century extensive immigration caused urban British society to become multi-cultural and multi-racial, and minorities had to face either assimilation into the mainstream culture with the accompanying loss of identity, or struggle for the recognition of their distinctive identities and individuality within the dominant group. For countless individual citizens throughout history, irrespective of the nature of their government, there have been personalized campaigns for justice under law. From individual protest and peaceful civil disobedience, through to bloody revolution, people have struggled, suffered and died for human rights, whether individual or collective.

'Man is born free; and everywhere he is in chains,' wrote Jean-Jacques

Rousseau in 1762.[1] The oppression of the people led, *inter alia*, to the American and French Revolutions; to the Civil War in the United States (1861–5) over the question of race and slavery; to the campaign of Mahatma Gandhi in India for freedom from British rule. Racism led, most starkly, to the Holocaust: the extermination and concentration camps of Hitler's Nazi regime, and to the struggle against apartheid in South Africa. Within the United Kingdom, the continued bloodshed in Northern Ireland and the intractable problem of reaching a settlement acceptable to all warring parties remains a constant reminder of a past which laid the foundations for inter-religious strife, discrimination and the partition of Ireland.

The names of champions of rights fill the history books and illuminate the power of the individual against state injustice. John Locke, Thomas Paine, Thomas Jefferson, Mahatma Gandhi, Martin Luther King, Nelson Mandela: giants in the story of social and political rights. And at the less obvious and often less public level are countless men and women who strive, on their own behalf and on behalf of those they represent, to create a world less unequal, less discriminatory and more free. In contemporary Western societies, characterized by democracy and freedom, true equality nevertheless remains elusive. Nowhere is this more apparent than in the campaign for racial and sexual equality.

The struggle for women's rights is too often overlooked in the story of human rights. It is an old grammatical truism that the word 'man' includes 'woman': in reality this is far from the case, at least until recent years. Women have largely been left to fight alone for their own individuality, their identity and rights in society and in law.[2] The struggle, historically and throughout most of the Western world, was initially for the right to participate in public affairs, to have access to education on an equal basis with men and to enter the public domain of employment on equal terms. The right to vote is the hall-mark of citizenship, and yet in Britain this right was only finally won on equal terms in 1928. More recently the struggle has been one for

---

[1] *The Social Contract*, 1762 (London: Dent, 1977), chapter 1.
[2] But see J. S. Mill, *The Subjection of Women*, 1869 (Cambridge: Cambridge University Press, 1989).

equal economic rights – the right to equal employment, the right to equal pay and conditions of work, the right not to be subjected to the demands of motherhood and family.

As these battles are slowly won, in Parliament, in the domestic courts and in the European Court of Justice (of the European Community) and the European Court of Human Rights (which adjudicates on conflicts between pan-European standards of individual rights and the domestic law of those states which make up the Council of Europe), so other more subtle claims emerge: the claim to recognition of gender identity, rather than the more straightforward demands for purely sexual equality. Suddenly the issue of male and female identity becomes less distinct: transsexuals, and gay men and women, all seek equal recognition alongside 'men' and 'women' as conventionally and culturally interpreted and traditionally understood. In contemporary British society, as elsewhere, the parallel campaign for rights for disabled people is increasingly heard: the right to conditions, facilities and services which will enable the disabled to play a full and active part in public life. Children's rights also press for recognition: the claims of children, at least at the age of 'maturity and understanding', are being heard: the right to autonomy, to make their own decisions, to decide on their own lifestyle and future.

The twentieth century was the century of struggle for rights. But rights talk – the discourse of rights – so prevalent throughout the developed world presupposes an understanding of the nature of rights and freedoms. How are rights correctly understood? How do and should rights stand in relation to governmental power in a democratic society? What are the advantages and disadvantages of the traditional British approach which hitherto has centred on freedoms rather than rights?[3] How, specifically, does the idea of rights and freedoms become translated into reality within the context of British government?

The enduring history of rights from time immemorial is beyond the scope of this book. In British terms, a useful starting-point is still, however, some way back in time.[4] The Civil War, the execution of Charles I and the era of republican rule between 1649 and 1660,

---

[3] A position which has recently changed: see pages 337 ff. for discussion of the Human Rights Act 1998.   [4] See Chapter 12.

prompted Thomas Hobbes to write *Leviathan*.[5] This powerful and influential work of political philosophy stated the case for strong government in order to secure the freedoms of the people. Not that it was a plea for individual rights, as now understood: rather it was a defence of power, with the added ingredient of the perception that power must be limited by the requirement that government act for the common good of the people. Hobbes's work marked a significant departure from medieval thought. First, he denied the notion that kings had a 'divine right' to rule: the link between God and King was broken, the King deriving his authority not from God but from the consent of the people governed. Secondly, this secularization of monarchical power paved the way for the future development of the idea of a contract between government and people, and ultimately for the idea of rights that transcend government power and stipulate clear limits on what government can and cannot do.

In 1690 John Locke published the altogether more radical and revolutionary text *Two Treatises on Government*.[6] Writing against the background of the 'Glorious Revolution' of 1688, the flight of James II and the constitutional settlement which brought William and Mary to the English throne, Locke advocated enforceable rights against government, rights which limited government power. So revolutionary were Locke's ideas that he was forced to flee into exile under the threat of charges for sedition. Essentially, Locke's thesis centred on the notion of contract between government and governed, the terms of which are not final and conclusive, but subject to constant renewal by the people, who are politically sovereign and have the power to withdraw their consent if government abuses its power. All government power henceforth was to be viewed as conditional.

These ideas, and those of Thomas Paine writing almost a century later, set the scene for the future rights debate. For Paine, a former customs and excise officer who emigrated to America under the patronage of Benjamin Johnson, rights trumped state power. Rights entitled citizens to overthrow a government which abused the rights of those for whom they held power on trust. Involved in both the American Revolution of 1765–88, and the French Revolution of 1789, Paine

---

[5] 1651 (London: Dent, 1973).   [6] London: J. M. Dent, 1977.

expressed his idealism and philosophy of rights in *Common Sense*, 1776, in which he argued for independence from British rule, and most importantly in *The Rights of Man* published in 1791 and 1792,[7] written in England in support of the French Revolution. While in America Paine assisted Thomas Jefferson in drafting the American Constitution: his philosophy shines through in Jefferson's ringing declaration that

> We hold these truths to be self-evident, that all men are created equal; that they are endowed by their Creator with certain inalienable rights; that amongst these are life, liberty, and the pursuit of happiness. That, to secure these rights, governments are instituted among men, deriving their just powers from the consent of the governed; that, whenever any form of Government becomes destructive of these ends, it is the right of the people to alter or abolish it, and to institute a new government, laying its foundations on such principles, and organizing its powers in such form, as to them shall seem most likely to effect their safety and happiness.

THE TRADITIONAL BRITISH APPROACH TO RIGHTS AND FREEDOMS

Although the 'Glorious Revolution' of 1688 finally brought royal power under the control of Parliament, albeit at the time an undemocratic Parliament, individual rights have seldom been at the forefront of political debate in Britain, nor has there been a 'people's revolution' fought against governmental power in the name of rights for all. As with so much of the historical development of the system of government, it has been by gradual evolution rather than revolution that freedoms and rights have been secured, to a degree. Instead of a constitutionally guaranteed set of rights which could override the power of the legislature, the incremental approach has left rights vulnerable to government power and the 'tyranny of the majority'. Nevertheless, successive governments have encouraged the view that liberty of the citizen is the fundamental hallmark of British society, and that there is no need for a written constitutional settlement defining the rights and freedoms of individuals. But the rhetoric of the liberal state, however appealing,

[7]   ed. H. Collins (New York: Penguin, 1984, repr. 1998).

rings hollow in the light of the evidence of infringements of liberty by agencies of the state: most particularly the police and the security forces, the former operating under statute and non-legal, unenforceable Codes of Practice, the latter only belatedly brought within a statutory framework but still unaccountable in any democratic sense.

Three essential factors explain the British approach which endured until the Human Rights Act 1998 was enacted (see further below, pages 337 ff.). The first is the generally peaceful continuity of the system of government, at least since 1660 and the restoration of the monarchy. The second is the dominant political philosophy of liberalism, with its insistence that citizens are entitled to a sphere of privacy into which government and law must not intrude, other than for the protection against harm to others. The third factor is the nature of the British legal system. For centuries, the judges developed the common law through their decisions: Parliament as the principal law-maker did not assert its supreme law-making power to the fullest until well into the nineteenth century, when state regulation was necessitated by the explosion of industry and the need for intervention in the economy and the provision of assistance and services in such areas as housing, health and welfare. At no time along the evolutionary continuum has there been a time when a code of citizens' rights was deemed essential for the protection of rights and freedoms. Rather, the underlying premise of government and law has been that the individual is free to do whatever he or she pleases, provided that it does not violate any law.

With a written constitution and a Bill of Rights – as in the United States of America – citizens are able to identify those rights with which no government or public body may interfere, and to seek the assistance of the courts to uphold their rights. The positive statement of rights, and their interpretation and reiteration by judges, gives rise to a cultural awareness of rights, and, as a corollary, the limits of government power. By contrast, in the United Kingdom, with its largely unwritten constitution and the doctrine of parliamentary supremacy, Parliament can at any time legislate to protect rights, or to limit rights. From one perspective this makes rights fragile and inadequately protected against Parliament's law-making power. On the other hand, it is argued by those who oppose formal guarantees of rights in Britain (and there remain many) that it enables the democratically elected Parliament to make laws which accord with the needs of the times and the wishes of the people, without being limited as to their content.

Two examples illustrate the positive and negative effects of this law-making power on people's rights. On the one hand, when in the 1950s and 1960s Britain, through its immigration policies, gradually became a multi-racial and multi-cultural society, the resulting tensions were dealt with by an ordinary Act of Parliament – initially the Race Relations Act 1965, the defects of which led to the Race Relations Act 1976 and other legislation protecting minority groups from racial discrimination. On the other hand, when civil unrest and violence erupted once again in Northern Ireland in the 1960s, Parliament speedily passed the Prevention of Terrorism (Temporary Provisions) Act 1974. This Act, and its successors,[8] introduced swingeing powers of extended detention of terrorist suspects and a system of exclusion orders, both of which violated the principles that citizens are entitled to access to a court of law with minimal delay and the right to freedom of movement.

In some instances where Parliament has acted to protect rights, the standard set – consciously or inadvertently – by the legislation falls below that set at a European level. In relation to sexual equality, for example, although Parliament passed the Equal Pay Act 1970 and the Sex Discrimination Act 1975, those Acts – as interpreted by the judges – failed to protect women in employment from discriminatory practices. It has been the European Court of Justice of the European Community which, using the broadly phrased text of Article 119 of the EC Treaty[9] and Directives passed under that article, has provided greater equality for women in terms of pay, conditions of work and entitlement to maternity leave and pensions.

With the judiciary subordinate to Parliament, Parliament has the right to overturn any judicial decision.[10] Being subordinate, the judges have not proved themselves unambiguously to be the champions of individual rights and freedoms. Under the rules relating to the interpret-

---

[8] See now the Terrorism Act 2000 and the Anti-Terrorism, Crime and Security Act 2001, discussed in Chapter 8.

[9] Following the Treaty on European Union 1997, the EC Treaty article numbers have changed: Article 119 is now Article 141. See further Chapter 4.

[10] See the discussion of *Burmah Oil v. Lord Advocate* and the case of *Shaw v. Director of Public Prosecutions* in Chapter 1.

ation of Acts of Parliament and the rules relating to the development of the common law,[11] the judges work within certain parameters which, while not rigid, impose limits on the capacity for judicial creativity. The law reports and texts on civil liberties abound with illustrations of the courts' record. In large measure the doctrine of parliamentary supremacy ensures that judges cannot step beyond the legitimate boundaries of action which Parliament sets down. This is not to say that there are not seminal cases in which the judges have proven themselves bold in the face of executive and parliamentary power. There are, however, many cases in which either self-imposed restraints or judicial timidity suggest a less than impressive record in relation to rights and freedoms.

When it comes to protecting rights, the royal prerogative gives rise to particular difficulties.[12] The royal prerogative is a legal source of power, a remnant from the days of powerful monarchy, which legitimizes executive action outside an Act of Parliament and without Parliament's prior approval. The prerogative spans wide areas of action, ranging from treaty-making powers, declarations of war and peace, control of the armed forces through to the dissolution of Parliament, the appointment of the Prime Minister and, most significant in terms of rights, matters relating to national or state security. Because the prerogative relates primarily, but not exclusively, to matters of high government policy, the judges – mindful of their unelected and subordinate status (to Parliament) – exercise self-imposed limits on their jurisdiction to rule on the legality of actions taken under the prerogative. A classic example of the consequences of a claim to prerogative power came in the *GCHQ case*.[13] Workers at the Government's Communications Headquarters (GCHQ), the signals intelligence gathering organization, had been entitled to belong to trade unions since 1946. In the course of an industrial dispute, the government decided that the threat to increase industrial action threatened the flow of signals intelligence, and thereby national security. The then Prime Minister, Margaret Thatcher – who was also Minister for the Civil Service – used the prerogative to remove the rights of workers to belong to unions. The

[11] The doctrine of precedent, discussed in Chapter 9.
[12] See the discussion in Chapter 1.
[13] *Council of Civil Service Unions v. Minister for the Civil Service* [1984] 3 All ER 935; [1985] AC 374.

unions challenged the ban under judicial review proceedings. In the High Court they were successful, the Court ruling that the government had not conducted itself according to the required standard of consultation. In the Court of Appeal and House of Lords, however, the government won – the government now having introduced in its defence the national security trump card.

Malone's case also reveals the weakness of legal protection of 'rights'.[14] Malone was prosecuted for handling stolen goods. In the course of trial, it became apparent that his telephone had been bugged by the police in order to obtain evidence. No warrant had been issued under an Act of Parliament authorizing the interception. Malone claimed, unsuccessfully, that the interception amounted to a breach of his right to privacy. The Court ruled that English law did not recognize a right to privacy, and that as a result there was no available remedy for the intrusion into his home.[15] Malone then trod the long road to Strasbourg for a ruling under the European Convention. Here he was more successful. The Court of Human Rights ruled that the absence of clear statutory rules regulating the issue of warrants for intercepts fell short of the standards required by law. However, Malone's victory was hollow. Accepting the judgment of the Court, the government proceeded to pass the Interception of Communications Act 1985, not only giving statutory authority for the issue of warrants, but also prohibiting any disclosure to any court as to the existence or otherwise of such a warrant. The Act did, however, also set up a complaints machinery for those who are aggrieved by such interceptions, although, as will be seen in Chapter 10, this protection falls below any adequate standard for a number of reasons.

In times of national emergency judges may be unable to protect individual rights against state power. In *Liversidge v. Anderson*, decided in 1942,[16] for example, the House of Lords ruled that the Home Secretary's decision to detain an individual, without warrant, could not be challenged in times of emergency. By contrast, as early as 1765 in *Entick v. Carrington* the court had ruled that without a specific warrant the Home Secretary had no power to enter and search a person's property

---

[14] *Malone v. Metropolitan Police Commissioner* [1979] Ch 344.
[15] The court also declined to accept that intercepting a telephone line amounted to a trespass by the police.   [16] [1942] AC 206.

and to seize personal possessions in order to establish whether a case was made for a charge of sedition against the state.[17] However, if Parliament passes an Act giving power to the authorities to enter without a warrant and on broad terms, the judges are powerless to protect the individual, as evidenced in the *Rossminster case*.[18] There, the homes of those suspected of revenue offences were raided at dawn by the police, with children's bedrooms being searched for evidence – but no illegality occurred since the officers were acting under lawful authority.

Other people vulnerable to state power exercised in the name of 'national security' or even more vaguely 'in the public interest' are non-citizens caught up in the immigration system. Two cases suffice to illustrate the problem. In *M v. Home Office*[19] an asylum-seeker was deported on the orders of the Home Secretary, who acted in defiance of a court order designed to protect the refugee from torture in Zaire. Both the Court of Appeal and the House of Lords were critical of the arrogance shown by the Home Office, and the then Secretary of State, Kenneth Baker. The House of Lords ruled, for the first time, that the courts had the power to hold ministers and their officials guilty of contempt of court if court orders were disobeyed. While the court ruled that Baker was not personally liable, it was made clear that where officials acting on his behalf flouted the law, the minister would be found liable in his official capacity and that if he were personally liable a contempt ruling would be made against him personally. Although this was of no help to the refugee in that case, the ruling on contempt in relation to ministers at least provides some protection for others in the same situation.

The second illustrative case is that of *Cheblak*.[20] Abbas Cheblak, a respected writer and teacher, had been resident in the United Kingdom for sixteen years at the time of the outbreak of the Gulf War in 1990, when some 160 Iraqi and Palestinian residents were detained with a view to deportation on the grounds of 'the public good'. Cheblak, who had protested against Saddam Hussein's invasion of Kuwait, was arrested in January 1991 and imprisoned with a view to deportation. Cheblak brought habeas corpus proceedings, to test the legality of his

[17] (1765) 19 St Tr 1029.
[18] *R v. Inland Revenue Commissioners ex parte Rossminster* [1980] AC 135.
[19] [1992] 4 All ER 97; [1993] 3 All ER 537.
[20] *R v. Home Secretary ex parte Cheblak* [1991] 2 All ER 319.

detention. The Home Secretary, in justifying the arrest of Cheblak, stated that the basis for the arrest was Cheblak's 'known links' with unspecified terrorist organizations, and that to reveal further details would itself be 'an unacceptable risk to national security'. This the court accepted without demur, relying on the Home Secretary's 'account-ability to Parliament' – itself a myth, since national security is an established exception to the rules of ministerial accountability. Cheblak was released at the end of the Gulf War, having appeared before the Home Secretary's panel of advisers – the 'three wise men' – whose only powers were to consider the evidence and 'advise the Home Secretary'. No legal representation was allowed before the panel of 'three wise men', nor were detainees told of the case against them. The blanket acceptance of a Home Secretary's assertion of national security without revealing any evidence runs contrary to the rule of law and the judicial protection of individuals, who are left at the mercy of the executive, which remains unaccountable to anyone.[21]

Civil liberties and police powers[22]

Whereas the courts have scope to protect rights and freedoms in the absence of an Act of Parliament regulating a particular matter, if Parliament gives wide-ranging powers to the police and other enforce-ment agencies, the courts are restricted as to what they can achieve.[23] In

[21] National security is an area on which governments may refuse to answer questions in Parliament. See also the discussion of ministerial responsibility in relation to the arms to Iraq affair, discussed in Chapter 1.

[22] The organization of the police and the criminal justice system is discussed in Chapter 10.

[23] With the Human Rights Act 1998 now in force, however, which incorporates into law the rights guaranteed under the European Convention, discussed below, there now exists another avenue through which rights and freedoms can be protected against the power of public authorities, including the police, by the domestic courts. It is to be expected that Convention rights, particularly those relating to the right to liberty and the right to fair trial – the former of which impinges on police powers in relation to arrest and detention, the latter of which includes actions of the police prior to trial – will produce a wealth of case law as individuals and the legal profession get to grips with Convention rights before the domestic courts.

relation to police powers judges insist that the police act within the limits of their powers as defined by Parliament. As will be seen below, however, there are defects in judicial protection. One problem in protection is that much of the regulation of police powers, especially in terms of the treatment of suspects at police stations, including the conditions of detention and interviewing, is not defined in an Act of Parliament, but in 'Codes of Practice'.[24] These Codes of Practice – a device widely used in relation to public authorities – do not have the force of law, and therefore cannot be enforced by the judges, which leaves the citizen dependent upon the working of police complaints procedures and civil actions against the police. A further difficulty lies in ensuring that in the operation of their powers the police conduct themselves according to law, particularly in the gathering of evidence to be used against the accused.

Prior to 1984, when the controversial Police and Criminal Evidence Act (PACE) was passed, many of the powers of the police were ill-defined and contained in disparate statutes or had their source in the common law. It was accordingly the judges who had developed much of the law, and here again divergent attitudes to individual freedoms can be found. On the positive side of the balance sheet are to be found such early seminal cases as *Entick v. Carrington*, discussed on page 312, and more recently *Rice v. Connolly*.[25] In *Rice v. Connolly* the question related to the right of a citizen to refuse to answer police questions. Rice was seen lurking in an area with a high rate of burglaries. The police asked him to accompany them to the police station to check on information he gave to them. When he refused, the police arrested him for obstructing a police officer in the execution of his duty. That, the court ruled, they could not do: there may be a moral or social duty to assist the police, but there was no legal duty to do so. Short of arrest, the police cannot insist that individuals answer their questions, or accompany them to the police station. 'Helping the police with their inquiries' is a notion unknown to law. As Lord Justice Lawton said in *R v. Lemsatef*,[26] 'It must be clearly understood that neither customs officers nor police officers have any right to detain somebody for the

---

[24] Drafted under the Police and Criminal Evidence Act 1984.
[25] [1966] 2 QB 414.   [26] [1977] 1 WLR 812.

purposes of getting them to help with their inquiries.' In *Christie v. Leachinsky*,[27] it was established that the police could not arrest someone without disclosing the grounds for arrest. As the House of Lords expressed it, '[a police officer] is not entitled to keep the reason to himself or to give a reason which is not the true reason. In other words a citizen is entitled to know on what charge or suspicion of what crime he is seized.'

On the other hand, in *Thomas v. Sawkins*[28] respect for private property did not extend to ruling unlawful a police officer's entry into private premises for the purpose of satisfying himself whether seditious speeches might be made, nor was his remaining after being told to leave ruled unlawful. *Duncan v. Jones*[29] also falls on the negative side of the balance sheet, and marked a serious restriction on the 'right' to freedom of expression. A speaker was ordered to get off her soap-box. When she refused, she was arrested for wilful obstruction of a police officer. The police claimed, relying on a disturbance the previous year involving the defendant, that they reasonably apprehended a breach of the peace: the court agreed and ruled that their conduct was lawful. An altogether more liberal attitude was apparent in *Redmond-Bate v. Director of Public Prosecutions*,[30] in which it was held that a police officer acted unlawfully in arresting a preacher on the grounds that he feared a breach of the peace. There was no imminent breach of the peace, and if there had been, the threat came from hostile people in the crowd rather than the preacher.

Freedom of expression, the right to which is guaranteed under the European Convention subject to certain limits, is the hallmark of a civilized society and democracy. Without freedom of expression, including freedom of the press, there can be no debate. Without freedom of expression there can be no political dissent and protest against the perceived wrongs of law and government. Freedom of expression, however, cannot be absolute, either in its content or in the form of its expression. It can clash, among other things, with the right to nondiscrimination on the grounds of race, and right to freedom from speech inciting racial hatred. When it is in the form of explicit sexual

---

[27] [1947] AC 573.   [28] [1935] 2 KB 249.   [29] [1936] 1 KB 218.
[30] *Times LR* 28 July 1999.

imagery which amounts to pornography as defined by law, it also conflicts with the right of (mostly) women to respect on the grounds of gender. In the form of political protest, freedom of expression can conflict with the rights of other nonprotesting citizens to freedom of movement; it can clash also with the rights of all to public order and freedom from violence. There is thus a complex matrix of factors encompassed in this superficially straightforward concept. The manner in which the law achieves a balance between complex competing rights is crucially important to a healthy society.

Freedom of expression has had a mixed fortune before the British courts. Where a breach of the peace has been committed and there are reasonable grounds for believing that it will be continued or renewed, or where a breach of the peace is 'reasonably apprehended', there is a common law (as opposed to statutory) power of arrest.[31] Under statute, the Public Order Act 1986 and the Criminal Justice and Public Order Act 1994 provide a welter of controls on freedom of expression. Under English law there is no 'right' of peaceful assembly or processions or to hold meetings in public places.[32] Meetings and processions are regulated by the police, who have the power to regulate the routes of processions, and in exceptional circumstances to ban a procession altogether with the consent of the Home Secretary. In addition to statutory powers of control, marchers may also be caught by the law relating to 'obstruction of the highway', which in essence precludes any use of the highway other than the right to move along it in a 'reasonable' manner. Increasing use is also being made of the law of trespass – the infringement of the property owner's right to enjoyment of land free from the presence of others who have entered without permission. The Criminal Justice and Public Order Act 1994 controversially extended the law of trespass to catch New Age travellers and gypsies, by creating an offence of criminal trespass, thereby crossing the boundaries of enforcement from the civil to the criminal sphere. The 1994 Act also restricted access to land by conferring on the police the power to prohibit convoys from descending

[31] This is the only remaining common law power of arrest; all other powers of arrest are granted under Acts of Parliament.

[32] With the exception of meetings held during election campaigns, when public halls may be used for the holding of meetings.

on monuments such as Stonehenge, the site for annual gatherings at the time of the summer solstice.[33]

The case of *Hubbard v. Pitt*[34] illustrates a restrictive attitude of the judges towards protesters. In that case, there was a peaceful demonstration by a group of social workers who were complaining about a local estate agent. The estate agent claimed that leaflets which were being distributed were libellous, and that the demonstrators were causing a nuisance outside his premises. The Court of Appeal, Lord Denning dissenting, ruled that there was no right to demonstrate known to English law, and that the owners of the highway (the owners of adjacent premises or the local authority) can sue in trespass for conduct other than the lawful movement along the highway. On the other hand, in a significant advance for civil liberties, in *Director of Public Prosecutions v. Jones*[35] the House of Lords ruled, albeit by a majority of three to two, that the defendant should not have been convicted for taking part in an assembly which she knew was prohibited by an order under the Public Order Act 1986. The central issue was the extent of the rights of members of the public to use the highway, and whether that right included peaceful assembly. Whether the use of the highway was reasonable was a matter of fact, and in this instance it was reasonable.

THE EUROPEAN CONVENTION ON HUMAN RIGHTS AND THE HUMAN RIGHTS ACT 1998

The European Convention

Following the Second World War, European nations came together in the attempt to provide for the better protection of human rights. The Council of Ministers was established in 1949, under which authority the European Convention was drafted and came into force in 1953. The Convention is an international treaty. While the British government

---

[33] Criminal Justice and Public Order Act 1994, section 70 inserting section 14A into the Public Order Act 1986.   [34] [1976] 1 QB 142.   [35] [1999] 2 WLR 625.

played a key role in drafting the Convention, it was not prepared at that time to allow individual citizens to use the Convention machinery. In large part this was due to the perception that to allow a citizen to appeal to a court outside the United Kingdom was a radical move which could undermine the authority of Parliament, especially since the Convention required that decisions of the Court of Human Rights were binding on all signatory states. It was not until 1966 that such access was allowed. With the Human Rights Act 1998 now in force, citizens no longer need to go to Strasbourg to enforce Convention rights. However, if the domestic courts fail to match the protection given under the Convention by the European Court of Human Rights, applications may still be lodged before the European Court.

Applications under the Convention may be lodged by individual citizens or by other member states of the Council of Europe. An example of an application by a state – an inter-state application – is *Ireland v. United Kingdom* (see below) on an issue alleging torture. The issue of torture was also raised in the earlier inter-state case of *Denmark v. Greece*.[36] Here it was found that the Athens security police had used a system of torture against political detainees, and torture was defined as including not only physical torture but also 'the infliction of mental suffering by creating a state of anguish and stress by means other than bodily assault'.

The Convention covers civil and political rights, but not social and economic rights. Guaranteeing social and economic rights – such as a decent standard of living, housing and guaranteed employment – requires positive action on the part of the state. Civil and political rights, on the other hand, require only that the state refrain from acting in a manner inconsistent with the identified rights, and therefore do not require a course of positive action involving substantial public expenditure. The Convention protects such areas as the right to life; the right to freedom from torture; to freedom from slavery; to freedom from unlawful detention; in the case of civil actions and criminal proceedings, the right to a fair and impartial tribunal and the protection of suspects, including the right to legal representation; a prohibition against 'retrospective' law, which takes effect on a date prior to the passing of

[36] (1969) 12 YB Eur Conv HR special vol.

the legislation and thereby makes previously lawful conduct unlawful; the right to privacy in relation to family life and correspondence; the right to freedom of conscience and religion; the right to freedom of expression; the right to freedom of assembly and association; the right to marry; the right to an effective remedy in the case of a breach of any of the foregoing and the right to enjoy Convention rights without discrimination.

In order to facilitate maximum compliance with the Convention by all the member countries of the Council of Europe who would adopt the Convention, the drafters of the Convention incorporated wide areas of discretion. This is justified in so far as it recognizes the diversity in political and cultural traditions. This discretion – known as the margin of appreciation – provides for flexibility in the application of Convention rights but also limits their effectiveness in relation to an aggrieved citizen.[37] The margin of appreciation allowed in relation to individual Convention rights varies, although in relation to the prohibition against torture or inhuman or degrading treatment or punishment[38] there is none at all: the right is absolute. Elsewhere, however, the margin of appreciation manifests itself in different ways. One frequent formulation is that the exercise of rights may be subject 'only to such limitations as are prescribed by law and are necessary in a democratic society in the interests of public safety, for the protection of public order, health or morals, or for the protection of the rights and freedoms of others'.[39] The exercise of rights may also be subject to the requirements of national law. For example, the right to marry and found a family under Article 12 is subject to national legal regulation. By this means, states can control the form of marriage which is recognized in law: in the United Kingdom for example, only men and women may marry, a limitation which precludes same-sex or transsexual marriage.[40] Further, marriage is monogamous: no man or woman may marry a second spouse while lawfully married to another. In the Republic of Ireland, the law prohibits

[37] See N. Lavender, *The Problem of the Margin of Appreciation* [1997] EHRLR 380.
[38] Article 3.
[39] This formula is adopted, with slight variations in wording, in relation to the right to respect for private and family life (Article 8); freedom of thought, conscience and religion (Article 9); and freedom of assembly and association (Article 11).
[40] On transsexualism see further page 335.

a divorced person from marrying, and this was upheld as a legitimate restriction in *Johnston v. Ireland*.[41]

The margin of appreciation is not, however, unrestricted. The phrasing of restrictions in terms of their necessity gives to the Court of Human Rights power to rule on whether such necessity is actually proven. As the Court observed in relation to permissible restrictions on freedom of expression under Article 10:

Nevertheless, Article 10(2) does not give the contracting states an unlimited power of appreciation. The Court . . . is responsible for ensuring the observance of those states' engagements, is empowered to give the final ruling on whether a 'restriction' or 'penalty' is reconcilable with freedom of expression . . . The domestic margin of appreciation thus goes hand in hand with a European supervision.

In order to strike a balance between the rights of citizens to a remedy against the violation of their rights, and the legitimate demand on the part of the state to provide its own remedies for legal wrongs, the Convention places a number of hurdles in the way of those seeking its protection. Most importantly, an aggrieved citizen must first exhaust any legal remedies which are available within the domestic legal system before applying under the Convention. Secondly, the action must be brought promptly and within six months of the date on which he or she failed to get a remedy in the local courts, or, in the absence of any remedy, within six months of the date on which he or she knew that an application could be taken under the Convention. Next, the application must relate, rather obviously, to a right actually protected under the Convention, and must not be frivolous or blatantly without any substance. If a similar case has been decided, and the application raises no new issues, the application may be refused, because the citizen may then rely on that recent judgment in defence of his or her rights.

The process has three stages. First the application must be ruled – according to the above requirements – to be 'admissible'. If that hurdle is overcome, there is next an attempt to secure a 'friendly settlement' with the state complained about, in order that full legal proceedings against the state may be avoided and the state given an opportunity to

[41] (1986) 9 EHRR 203.

remedy the situation voluntarily. The negotiations are confidential. Should that process fail, the application will be referred for a hearing of its merits before a Chamber of the Court.[42] Following the Chamber's judgment, either party to the case may apply within three months for the case to be referred to the Grand Chamber. The ruling of the Grand Chamber is final, and is binding upon the state, which undertakes, in signing up to the Convention, to respect the decisions of the Court. One exception exists: that is where the state in question regards a particular issue as of such domestic importance that a change in the law, as required by the Court, would damage the interest of the state.

This power of 'derogation' is a manifestation of the attempt to make the Convention acceptable to the many differing conditions in member states (or High Contracting Parties as they are officially known). States may also enter 'reservations' about individual articles of the Convention when they join. The power both to derogate and enter reservations is exercised with caution, for it undermines the protection of the Convention for citizens. In the case of Britain, terrorism in relation to Northern Ireland has provided the situation which led to a derogation being entered. In the case of *Brogan v. United Kingdom*,[43] the applicants petitioned on the basis that their Convention rights had been violated through the power to detain terrorist suspects under the Prevention of Terrorism Act, without access to a court of law, for up to seven days, on the authorization of the Home Secretary. Article 5 of the Convention requires that suspects shall be 'brought promptly before a judge or other officer authorized by law to exercise judicial power and shall be entitled to trial within a reasonable time or to release pending trial'. The Court upheld the complaint. Rather than reform the terrorist legislation, however, the government chose to enter a 'derogation' suspending the application of Article 5 in relation to terrorist suspects. In the vast majority of cases, however, the government's response is positive and a change in the law, to bring it into line with the Convention requirements, takes place.

---

[42] Under the rules of Procedure of the European Court of Human Rights, a Chamber consists of seven judges, and includes a judge from the Contracting Party involved (member states). Exceptionally, it may be decided that the case should go directly to the Grand Chamber and not to a Chamber.   [43] (1988) 11 EHRR 117.

Convention case law

Article 2: the right to life

Few cases have succeeded under this article. Where a state permits abortion, for example, this does not violate Article 2. In *R (Pretty) v. DPP*,[44] *inter alia*, the applicant claimed that the refusal of the Director of Public Prosecutions to grant immunity to her husband should he assist her in ending her life amounted to a violation of this article. The House of Lords disagreed. Discontinuing the use of life-support equipment, without which a patient in a vegetative state would die, with the sanction of a court, does not violate Article 2 in that it does not entail a positive action in terminating a life.[45] Where the police or security forces kill suspects during operations, the state may be liable under Article 2 if the operation is not sufficiently controlled by the authorities.[46]

Article 3: freedom from torture, inhuman or degrading treatment

Article 3, which prohibits 'torture, or inhuman or degrading treatment or punishment', has given rise to a number of applications. The first was an application brought by the Republic of Ireland against the British government, alleging that interrogation procedures applied to detainees suspected of terrorist offences in Northern Ireland violated Article 3. The police and security forces had detained a large number of suspects. While the majority of these were released without further action, a number were detained with a view to further interrogation. The suspects were subjected to hooding, sleep deprivation and being leaned against walls for prolonged periods. Subsequently, it was found that the techniques led to physical and psychological harm. The Court ruled that while the actions did not amount to torture, they did amount to inhuman or degrading treatment. No justifications – such as that the techniques could, if successful, lead to the saving of other lives or reveal information which could lead to the apprehension of terrorists – could

---

[44] *Times LR* 5 December 2001.   [45] *Airdale NHS Trust v. Bland* [1993] AC 789.
[46] See *McGann, Farrell and Savage v. UK* (1995) 21 EHRR 97; *Jordan and others v. UK*, *Times LR* 18 May 2001.

take away from the liability of the state.[47] Article 3 has also been invoked successfully to ban corporal punishment in state schools, on the basis that it is degrading treatment.

Article 3 has been the basis of challenges to immigration laws and practices. The rights of non-citizens to enter a country, claim asylum and remain there, raise particular difficulties for any nation. The rise in the number of refugees seeking asylum in the United Kingdom over recent years has placed the whole system under strain. An early case on rights of entry was seen in *East African Asians v. United Kingdom*.[48] Here, the applicants were citizens of the United Kingdom and colonies who had been refused permission to enter and remain with their wives who were already in the United Kingdom. They alleged that such treatment was racially discriminatory and amounted to degrading treatment contrary to Article 3. Article 3 has also been used to challenge decisions to deport a person to a country where he or she will suffer persecution by the state authorities, as in *Chahal v. United Kingdom*[49] where the Court ruled that to return the applicant, a Sikh separatist leader, to India would place him at serious risk. Article 3 was also considered in *D v. United Kingdom*.[50] The applicant had come to the United Kingdom, and was found on his arrival to be in the possession of cannabis. He was charged with unlawful possession and sentenced to six years' imprisonment. In 1996 the immigration authorities decided to deport D to his home country, St Kitts. In 1994, however, he had been diagnosed as HIV positive and suffering from AIDS: his life expectancy was estimated to be between eight and twelve months. His argument was that to be forced to return home where there was no one to care for him and no guaranteed medical treatment violated Article 3: the Court agreed, stating that Article 3 did not relate just to treatment suffered as a direct result of state action, but also covered the consequences that would follow from his being deported.

Article 4: freedom from slavery

Article 4 prohibits slavery, and no cases have been successful. Prisoners have attempted to use the Article to challenge the length or terms of their detention, and a barrister has attempted to use it to argue that

---

[47] *Ireland v. United Kingdom* (1978) 2 EHRR 25.   [48] (1973) 3 EHRR 76.
[49] (1996) 23 EHRR 413.   [50] *Times LR* 12 May 1997.

the requirement of the Belgian legal profession that a lawyer give a proportion of his time to *pro bono* work (working for no reward in the public interest) violated Article 4.[51]

Article 5: the right to liberty

Articles 5 and 6 which relate to the right to freedom and security and the right to fair trial have generated a number of cases from many countries. The United Kingdom is no exception. In *Hussain v. United Kingdom*,[52] the applicant had been detained 'during Her Majesty's pleasure' (an indeterminate sentence), and had been unable to have the lawfulness of his continued detention reviewed by a court, thereby violating Article 5.4. Where detention is for a long period of time, the lawfulness of that detention must be reviewed from time to time. For example, exceptionally a person may be detained on a life sentence, with the period to be served meaning that person's natural life.

This is the position in relation to Myra Hindley, the child murderer, who was convicted in 1965 and sentenced to life imprisonment. Successive Home Secretaries have reviewed Hindley's sentence. In 1990 the Home Secretary decided that the applicant's sentence should be for her whole life, a decision upheld by the Home Secretary in office in 1997. In a challenge to the Home Secretary's power[53] it was held that the decision in 1990 was unlawful, as excluding any consideration of exceptional circumstances, whereas the incoming Home Secretary had issued a statement committing him to take into account the progress made by Hindley as part of his determination of the appropriate length of time she should serve in prison.[54]

The Home Secretary's powers were found to violate Article 5 of the Convention in respect of two minors convicted of murdering a two-year-old child in *T and V v. United Kingdom*.[55] The Court of Human Rights ruled that there were violations of Article 5.4 and a violation of

---

[51] See respectively *Van Droogenbroeck v. Belgium* (1982) 4 EHRR 443 and *Van der Messele v. Belgium* (1983) 6 EHRR 163.   [52] *Times LR* 26 February 1996.

[53] The power derives from the Criminal Justice Act 1991 which confers discretion as to the length of the penal element in a sentence.

[54] *R v. Secretary of State for the Home Department ex parte Hindley*, *Times LR* 19 December 1997. The decision was upheld by the House of Lords.

[55] *Times LR* 17 December 1999.

Article 6.1. Following their conviction, the Home Secretary had set the tariff period to be served for retribution and deterrence. Accordingly, there was no opportunity for the lawfulness of their detention to be assessed by a judicial body, and that violated Article 5. The Home Secretary's response to the decision was to announce that legislation would be introduced to regulate the matter which would place such decisions in the hands of judges, and that in the interim his decisions would be made in consultation with senior members of the judiciary.

Article 5.1 was violated in the case of *Johnson v. United Kingdom*.[56] In this case, the applicant had been convicted of a number of assaults, and having been found to be suffering from mental illness within the Mental Health Act 1983, in 1994 was ordered to be detained indefinitely. In 1989 the Mental Health Review Tribunal decided that the applicant was no longer suffering from mental illness. However, since no suitable accommodation for the applicant could be found, he was detained until 1993. That detention violated the requirements of lawful detention.

Article 6: the right to fair trial

Article 6 has also been used to great effect to test the terms and conditions of convicted prisoners. In 1975, *Golder's case*[57] resulted in reforms being introduced to allow prisoners access to legal advice while in prison. In *Campbell and Fell v. United Kingdom*[58] the issue related to the powers of the Board of Prison Visitors to impose punishment on prisoners for breach of the prison rules, in this case participating in a riot. That was held to breach Article 6, even though the proceedings were in name disciplinary rather than judicial.

Article 6 was violated by the authorities in the case of *Saunders v. United Kingdom*.[59] Ernest Saunders was prosecuted for corporate fraud. By law, Saunders was compelled to answer questions put by the investigators, under the threat of contempt of court and possible imprisonment.[60] The evidence obtained from the inquiries was passed to the Crown Prosecution Service which in turn made it available to the police who then began their own investigation. The Court of Human Rights

---

[56] Case 119/1996/738/937.   [57] (1975) 1 EHRR 524.   [58] (1984) 7 EHRR 165.
[59] (1997) 23 EHRR 313.
[60] Powers contained in the Companies Act 1985, sections 532(2) and 436(3).

ruled that there had been a violation of the right not to incriminate oneself, as guaranteed by Article 6.

The right to legal advice during detention by the police is also protected under Article 6. In *Magee v. United Kingdom* [61] the applicant had been arrested under terrorist legislation on suspicion of involvement in an attack on military personnel. He had requested to see his solicitor, but was held for forty-eight hours before he was allowed access to legal advice. During that period he signed a confession. Magee alleged that he had been coerced into incriminating himself. The Court of Human Rights agreed: 'to deny access to a lawyer for such a long period and in a situation where the rights of the defence were irretrievably prejudiced is – whatever the justification for such denial – incompatible with the rights of the accused.'

Benham v. United Kingdom [62] related to Benham's sentence of imprisonment for failing to pay the Community Charge (the system of local taxation then in force). The Court ruled that while the sentence of imprisonment was not of itself unlawful, the fact that Benham had not had legal representation in the proceedings, which involved complex issues, violated Article 6.

Articles 5 and 6 have also provided the basis for recent challenges in relation to military proceedings in *Hood v. United Kingdom* [63] and *Jordan v. United Kingdom*.[64] In *Hood's case*, the applicant had been tried and convicted of criminal charges under the Army Act 1955. The applicant's commanding officer had decided on pre-trial detention, and had subsequently played a role in hearing the case against the applicant. Accordingly he could not be impartial, and the proceedings did not meet the requirements of independence and impartiality required by Article 6.1. In *Jordan's case*, the applicant had completed a sentence of imprisonment, but continued to be detained, under close arrest, on the basis of further suspected offences under investigation by military police. Jordan had been released following habeas corpus proceedings and had brought proceedings against the Ministry of Defence claiming unlawful detention. The commanding officer, who had been involved in Jordan's case

---

[61] *Times LR* 20 June 2000.   [62] *Times LR* 24 June 1996.
[63] *Times LR* 11 March 1999.
[64] *Times LR* 17 March 2000. See also *Findlay v. United Kingdom, Times LR* 27 February 1997.

since 1995, could not be considered impartial, and there was a violation of Article 5(3) and 5(5).[65]

In *McGonnell v. United Kingdom*,[66] a case relating to the position of the Deputy Bailiff of Guernsey as President of the States of Deliberation, Guernsey's legislative body, and subsequently as the sole judge of law in proceedings relating to the applicant's planning application which had been refused, the Court of Human Rights held that the Deputy Bailiff's position was 'capable of casting doubt' as to his 'impartiality' and as a result was in violation of Article 6.1 of the European Convention of Human Rights, which guarantees 'a fair and public hearing . . . by an independent and impartial tribunal established by law'. The Bailiff in Guernsey occupies a number of positions. He is a senior judge of the Royal Court and is *ex officio* President of the Guernsey Court of Appeal. In his non-judicial capacity, the Bailiff is President of the States of Election, of the States of Deliberation, and of four States committees (the Appointments Board, the Emergency Council, the Legislation Committee and the Rules of Procedure Committee). He also has a role in communications between the Guernsey authorities and the United Kingdom government and the Privy Council. Referring to its earlier decision in *Findlay v. United Kingdom*,[67] the Court restated the requirements of 'independence' and 'impartiality'. On independence the Court declared that in establishing whether the court or tribunal was independent, regard had to be had, *inter alia*, to the 'manner of appointment of its members and their term of office, the existence of guarantees against outside pressures and the question whether the body presents an appearance of independence'. On impartiality, the Court restated the proposition that the tribunal 'must be subjectively free of personal prejudice or bias. Second, it must also be impartial from an objective viewpoint, that is, it must offer sufficient guarantees to exclude any legitimate doubt in this respect . . .' In the instant case, there was no question of actual bias on the part of the Bailiff; nevertheless the Court considered that 'any direct involvement in the passage of legislation, or of executive rules, was likely to be sufficient to cast doubt on the judicial

---

[65] See also *Coyne v. United Kingdom* (Case No 124/1996/743/942) in which a court martial conducted before the Armed Forces Act 1996 came into force was held to be not an independent and impartial tribunal.

[66] *Times LR* 22 February 2000.   [67] *Times LR* 27 February 1997.

impartiality of a person subsequently called on to determine a dispute over whether reasons exist to permit a variation from the wording of the legislation or rules at issue'. Accordingly, 'the mere fact that the Deputy Bailiff presided over the Court ... was capable of casting doubt on his impartiality . . .' There was accordingly a violation of the requirements of fair trial before an independent and impartial tribunal.

Article 7: non-retrospective law

The rule in Article 7 against retrospective legislation – law which makes conduct which was lawful when done, subsequently unlawful – has led to several challenges. Of these, the most surprising recent case in relation to the United Kingdom was the decision in *SW v. United Kingdom*.[68] For centuries, under English law a husband could not be held liable under criminal law for raping his wife. This ludicrous exemption from criminal law was based on the fiction that when a man and woman marry, they become 'one flesh', and since one cannot rape oneself, it therefore follows that one cannot rape one's 'other self'. For all the equality achieved by women during the twentieth century, this rule continued to apply until 1991. Then came the breakthrough. The House of Lords ruled that the exemption was anachronistic and incompatible with any notions of real sexual equality. An application was lodged under the Convention, claiming that the House of Lords' decision offended against the rule against retrospective liability. That argument was clearly correct: when the applicant raped his wife there was no such offence: it only became an offence when the House of Lords declared it to be so, long after the actual act. However, strict logic and legal analysis was not going to deter the Court of Human Rights from outlawing marital rape and supporting the House of Lords' decision. The Court ruled that the House of Lords' decision was – given the general trend towards equality – foreseeable, and no more than a recognition of the correct legal position.

---

[68] (1995) 21 EHRR 404. See also *R v. R* [1992] 1 AC 599, the decision which led to the challenge under the Convention.

Article 8: the right to respect for private and family life, home and correspondence

In *Halford v. United Kingdom*, the applicant was a former Assistant Chief Constable of Police who had unsuccessfully sought promotion. There were allegations of sexual discrimination made against the police. It was suspected by the applicant that the police had 'bugged' her telephone at work: she alleged a violation of Article 8, which the Court of Human Rights upheld, thus extending to individuals, as employees as well as in their private lives, the right to privacy.[69] In *Buckley v. United Kingdom*[70] the issue related to whether Article 8 could provide a remedy to a family of gypsies who had purchased land and then been refused planning permission to build a home by the local authority. It was alleged that this violated the right to family life, and the right to enjoy the protection of the Convention without discrimination. The Court, by a majority of judges, ruled that the right to respect for family life and a home could be, and in this case was, restricted by the discretion given to the state.

In *Dudgeon v. United Kingdom*[71] the issue raised was the criminalization of all homosexual behaviour in Northern Ireland. The Court ruled that a person's sexual life was a 'most intimate aspect' of his or her private life: the legislation violated Article 8. The prosecution and conviction of a man, for engaging in non-violent homosexual acts in private with up to four other men, was likewise a violation of Article 8. The Court of Human Rights so held in *ADT v. United Kingdom*.[72] The applicant had been arrested and charged with gross indecency between men, contrary to section 13 of the Sexual Offences Act 1956. The government had argued that the sexual activity concerned fell outside the scope of 'private life' within the meaning of Article 8.1. The activities had been recorded on videotapes which were seized by the police when conducting a search under warrant. The Court ruled that there was no likelihood of the contents of the tapes being rendered public, deliberately or inadvertently, nor had the applicant been prosecuted in relation to offences involved in the making or distribution of the tapes. The

---

[69] See also *Malone v. United Kingdom* (1984) 7 EHRR 14, and the case discussed at page 312 above.   [70] (1997) 23 EHRR 101.   [71] (1981) 4 EHRR 149.
[72] Application No 35765/97, Judgment 31 July 2000. *Times LR* 8 August 2000.

Court ruled that the applicant was a victim of an interference with the right to respect for his private life, both as to the existence of legislation prohibiting consensual sexual acts between more than two men in private, and as to the conviction for gross indecency. The interference was not justified as being 'necessary in a democratic society' for the protection of morals and the rights and freedoms of others.[73]

Covert surveillance by the police, prior to the enactment of the Police Act 1997 which provided for statutory authority for such surveillance, violated the right to respect for private and family life as guaranteed by Article 8. The Court of Human Rights so held in *Khan v. United Kingdom*.[74] The applicant had been convicted for drug dealing on the basis of evidence improperly obtained by a secret listening device installed by the police. The evidence so gained was the sole evidence against the accused. The applicant had appealed to the Court of Appeal and to the House of Lords, both of which had dismissed his appeal, the House of Lords ruling that although the evidence had been obtained in circumstances which amounted to a breach of Article 8, that was not determinative of a judge's discretion to admit or exclude such evidence under section 78 of the Police and Criminal Evidence Act 1984. The applicant alleged that his trial was unfair and in breach of Article 6, that his right to respect for private life under Article 8 had been breached and that his right to an effective remedy under Article 13 had also been breached. On Article 6, the Court of Human Rights ruled that the applicant had had ample opportunity to challenge the use of the evidence and had done so before the trial court, the Court of Appeal and the House of Lords, and that the domestic courts had considered the question of admissibility. Accordingly there was no violation of Article 6. There was, however, a violation of Article 8. The principal issue was whether the action of the police was justified under Article 8.2, as being 'in accordance with the law' and 'necessary in a democratic society'. The law had to be sufficiently clear and certain to give individuals adequate indication as to the circumstances and conditions in which public authorities were entitled to resort to such measures. In the

---

[73] Contrast *Laskey v. United Kingdom* (1997) 24 EHRR 39, in which the Court ruled that Article 8 was not violated where the applicants were imprisoned as a result of sadomasochistic activities with 44 other homosexual men, involving offences including assault and wounding recorded on videotape.   [74] *Times LR* 23 May 2000.

absence of statutory authority, the interference could not be considered to be in accordance with law and accordingly violated Article 8. On Article 13, the Court considered the avenues open to the applicant, principally the police complaints mechanism. Having considered the respective roles of Chief Constables, the Police Complaints Authority and that of the Home Secretary in relation to the appointment, remuneration and dismissal of members of the Police Complaints Authority, the Court ruled that the system of investigation of complaints did not meet the requisite standards of independence needed 'to constitute sufficient protection against the abuse of authority and thus provide an effective remedy'. Accordingly there was a violation of Article 13.[75]

Article 9: freedom of thought, conscience and religion
Few cases are brought under this Article. Furthermore, the Article's protection is weakened by Article 9(2) which permits limitations in terms of the *manifestation of beliefs* which may be prescribed by law. While the freedom of religious belief is absolute, the manner in which it is expressed is not. Accordingly, challenges under Article 9 have failed where the applicants allege that their rights of religious freedom have been restricted by contractual employment rights. For example, in *X v. United Kingdom*[76] the decision of the London Education Authority not to release a Muslim schoolteacher to attend mosque on Friday was not a breach of the Convention, since he had not disclosed this need either at interview or during the first few years of his employment. Also in *Stedman v. United Kingdom*[77] there was no violation of Article 9 in the requirement of a private company that a Christian employee should be required to work on Sundays.

Article 10: freedom of expression
Article 10, which protects freedom of expression, has been the source of a number of cases involving the United Kingdom, one of the most significant early cases being *The Sunday Times v. United Kingdom*.[78] This case involved the suppression of information, by an injunction, in

---

[75] On the admissibility of evidence gained through foreign intercepts and consideration of *Khan v. United Kingdom*, see *R v. X, Y and Z*, Times LR 23 May 2000 (Court of Appeal, Criminal Division).   [76] (1981) 22 DR 27.   [77] [1997] EHRLE 545.
[78] (1979) 2 EHRR 245.

relation to Distillers Ltd., the manufacturers of the thalidomide drug, which it was alleged caused birth defects. At the time the injunction was granted, Distillers argued that newspaper articles would prejudice the negotiations it was undertaking with the parents of the affected children. In its defence, the government argued that the injunction was necessary in order to protect the impartiality of the judiciary. The Court of Human Rights disagreed: the courts were unlikely to be affected by newspaper articles, and the injunction – which had remained in force for over three years – represented a wrongful interference with freedom of expression. As a result, the government introduced the Contempt of Court Act 1981, amending the law.

The rights of protesters to freedom of expression was considered by the Court in *Steel and Others v. United Kingdom*[79] and *Hashman and Harrup v. United Kingdom*.[80] In the first of these, Ms Steel had been arrested during a protest, detained by the police, cautioned and charged with breach of the peace, and later with an offence under the Public Order Act 1986.[81] In total she was detained for approximately forty-four hours. She was later convicted on both charges. On appeal, she was fined for the public order offence and ordered to agree to be bound over to keep the peace for twelve months. She refused to be bound over and was committed to prison for twenty-eight days. The protest was regarded by the Court as a legitimate expression of opinion within Article 10. By refusing to be bound over, however, the applicant challenged the authority of the court. The committal to prison was intended to deter future breaches of the peace but also pursued the aim under Article 10(2) of maintaining the authority of the judiciary. Although the measures taken amounted to serious interference with freedom of expression, regard had to be had to the dangers inherent in such protest activity and the risk of disorder arising from it: the actions of the police in arresting Steel were not disproportionate, nor was it disproportionate for the applicant to be committed to prison for refusing to comply with the order of the court. However, in relation to the three remaining applicants, the interference with the exercise of their right to freedom

[79] (1998) Crim LR 893; (1999) 28 EHRR 603. This case is also relevant to Articles 5 and 6, discussed above.   [80] *Times LR* 1 December 1999; (2000) Crim LR 185.
[81] Under section 5 which regulates threatening, abusive or insulting behaviour likely to cause harassment, alarm or distress.

of expression was disproportionate to the aims of preventing disorder and protecting the rights of others and was not necessary in a democratic society. Their protest had been entirely peaceful. In the absence of obstruction or provocation of others to violence, their arrest and detention was unlawful within Article 5 and also amounted to a violation of Article 10.

In *Hashman and Harrup v. United Kingdom* the issue concerned freedom of expression relating to hunt saboteurs who disturbed the hunt by blowing a hunting horn and shouting at hounds. The Crown Court, to which they appealed, found that as there had been no violence or threat of violence, there had been no breach of the peace. Nevertheless, their actions had been unlawful and exposed hounds to danger, and were *contra bona mores*. *Contra bona mores* is an antiquated legalism, defined as meaning 'behaviour which was "wrong rather than right in the judgment of the majority of contemporary fellow citizens"'. The applicants were bound over 'to be of good behaviour' for one year. The applicants claimed that the concept of behaviour *contra bona mores* was so broadly defined that it did not comply with Article 10(2) of the Convention, that any interference with freedom of expression must be 'prescribed by law'. The Court of Human Rights ruled that the definition of *contra bona mores* was particularly imprecise and failed to give the applicants sufficiently clear guidance as to how they should behave in future. Accordingly, the interference with the freedom of expression was not 'prescribed by law' and there had been a violation of Article 10.[82]

Article 11: freedom of peaceful assembly and association

Freedom of peaceful assembly and of association include the right to form and to join trade unions. That right also includes the right not to join a trade union.[83] The ban on trade union membership at Government Communications Headquarters (GCHQ), however, did not violate Article 11, the restriction being justified under Article 11(2) on the basis of national security.[84]

---

[82] See also *Alison Redmond-Bate v. DPP* TLR 28 July 1999; (1999) Crim LR 998, in which free expression under Article 10 was considered in relation to obstruction of a police officer in the execution of his duty.

[83] *Young, James and Webster v. United Kingdom* (1981) 4 EHRR 38.

[84] *Council of Civil Service Unions v. United Kingdom* (1988) 10 EHRR 269.

Article 12: the right to marry and found a family

The 'right to marry and found a family' is the subject of Article 12, which also provides that this right is in accordance with the national law governing its exercise. Under English law, the right to marry is restricted to 'one man and one woman': transsexuals and same-sex partners are not entitled to marry. The original rationale of this rule lay in Christian doctrine; more recently it is seen to lie in the interest of the state to promote the conventional family unit, in ways which both privilege the married unit and exclude others who do not fall within the accepted definition of male and female. Under English law the latter is a matter of biological sex at birth, rather than any psychological or social meaning. With advances in medical science and technology it has become possible for individuals to undergo sex-change operations where there is a mismatch between physical sexual identity and psychological gender and identity. Two cases illustrate the difficulties. In both *Rees v. United Kingdom* [85] and *Cossey v. United Kingdom* [86] transsexuals challenged British law under Article 12. The Court, however, in both cases upheld British law: it was for the national authorities to determine the qualifications for marriage. In *Cossey's case*, however, there were some expressions of sympathy for those finding themselves in the position of being unable to marry, despite having undergone the long and traumatic experience of a sex change. On the other hand, what weighed heavily with the Court of Human Rights was the fact that, in its view, public opinion had not yet reached a level of sympathy for transsexuals which would justify a different result.

Article 13: the right to an effective remedy

Article 13 imposes on states the duty to provide effective remedies for any violation of the substantive rights protected by the Convention. Under the Human Rights Act 1998, discussed below, Article 13 has not been introduced into domestic law. Instead, the domestic courts are given the power to grant remedies which they regard as 'appropriate and just' and which fall within their ordinary power to grant remedies. In some cases damages will be the appropriate remedy. In others, where a public authority has violated a Convention right, the court may nullify

[85] [1987] CLY 1914.   [86] [1992] 2 FLR 249.

the authority's decision. In all cases the domestic courts must take into account the principles which the European Court of Human Rights applies to decisions on remedies. One example of the interpretation given to effective remedies by the European Court is provided by *Chahal v. United Kingdom*, discussed above.[87] In that case, a Sikh separatist leader had been detained with a view to deportation, the Home Secretary taking the view that his presence posed a threat to national security. The Court of Human Rights ruled that his deportation would violate Article 3 (the right to freedom from torture and inhuman and degrading punishment). However, there was (at that time) no mechanism in place by which the Home Secretary's decision could be reviewed, and accordingly there was no effective remedy. The Court of Human Rights has discretion over the award of remedies. In the case of *McCann, Farrell and Savage v. United Kingdom*[88] for example, although finding that there was a violation of the right to life, Article 2, the Court declined to award damages in view of the terrorist activities of the deceased.

Article 14: the right to nondiscrimination

Article 14 does not represent a free-standing right to non-discrimination. Rather, it provides the right to nondiscrimination in relation to the enjoyment of the other Convention rights. The grounds on which discrimination is prohibited include sex, marital status, sexual orientation, legitimacy or illegitimacy, membership of a particular group (whether trade union, military, prisons or other organizations).

Convention Protocols

In addition to the Convention Articles, there are a number of Protocols which supplement the provisions, ranging from the right to enjoy one's personal property, parental choice in education, free elections, freedom of movement, abolition of the death penalty, rights of aliens and sexual equality and minority rights.

---

[87] (1996) 23 EHRR 413.   [88] (1995) 21 EHRR 97.

The Human Rights Act 1998

The British government having for so long refused to incorporate the Convention, in order that citizens could seek to enforce their rights in the local courts rather than in Strasbourg, the Labour Party pledged in its 1997 election manifesto to 'bring rights home'. On their return to power this commitment was honoured in the Human Rights Act 1998. There had long been a demand for the 'localization' of the Convention, but doubts existed as to how this could be achieved without altering the fundamental structure of the constitution. Two principal difficulties were perceived. The first was how to incorporate Convention rights without undermining parliamentary supremacy. The second related to the position of the judges, and the perceived danger that if domestic judges rule on Convention rights this would undermine their impartiality by drawing them into the political arena. Rather than accept defeat on the basis of these doubts, the government found and has adopted a formula which has a peculiarly British flavour.

The Human Rights Act was hailed by the Home Secretary as being the most significant Act since the Bill of Rights 1689, but until the full scope of the Act becomes clear through case-law, that judgment must remain speculative. In force in Scotland and Wales in 1998, the Act was not fully implemented in England until 2000, following a substantial programme of research and training for judges and officials. Under a written constitution, it is the normal arrangement for human rights to be given priority over any legislation or acts of government and public bodies. If a challenge is launched as to the legality of legislation or acts of government bodies, the ultimate forum for resolving the issue is the Supreme Court which has the power to invalidate legislation as being inconsistent with the constitution, and to declare unlawful the acts of government. Under the British arrangement, however, the position is rather different. One problem with the rights debate has always been the status of Parliament and, to a lesser but important extent, the position of the judges. As has been discussed before, in Britain Parliament has long been regarded as 'supreme' or 'sovereign', and the judges in a subordinate position to Parliament, careful to preserve their independence and integrity by operating only within well-defined limits which exclude any suggestion that they are not politically impartial or neutral.

The result of these concerns is a carefully balanced, but from a rights perspective potentially unsatisfactory, statutory formula. Rather than give priority to rights over the legislature, the Human Rights Act 1998 preserves parliamentary supremacy and control over the substance of law. Judges in the High Court and above in England and Wales, and judges in the superior courts in Scotland are not given the power to invalidate primary legislation (Acts of Parliament) on the basis that it is incompatible with Convention rights. In relation to delegated, or secondary, legislation (laws drafted under the authority of an Act of Parliament), this may be invalidated by the courts. However, a public authority will not act unlawfully if that authority could not have acted differently because of the provisions of an Act of Parliament or legislation made under that Act. The following example illustrates this arrangement.

An Act of Parliament stipulates that the ultimate decision-maker is X. Delegated (or secondary or subordinate) legislation sets out the procedures to be followed by X and provides that X cannot delegate his or her power to any other decision-maker. An individual is aggrieved by X's decision and alleges that X's power to make the decision contravenes his or her right to fair trial (under Article 6). If the court hearing the complaint agrees that X was – by the nature of his or her position – likely to be biased, a *declaration of incompatibility* may be made. X, however, had not acted unlawfully under Article 6 since he or she could not have acted any other way, because the legislation *required* him or her to decide and made it *impossible* for X to pass the decision-making to any other person or body.[89]

The declaration of incompatibility is then referred to the government, and the relevant minister may, but need not, propose an amendment to the law, or in some circumstances may take immediate action to remedy the position, subject to subsequent parliamentary approval. For a challenge to be successful under the Act, the aggrieved citizen must therefore pursue his or her case to the appropriate level of court which

---

[89] This sort of problem was revealed in *R v. Secretary of State for the Environment, Transport and the Regions ex parte Holding and Barnes plc and Others*, discussed below.

may make a declaration, and if that is successful (in relation to primary legislation) rely on the political process to have the law amended. The manner in which the Act operates will become clearer as the detailed rules are considered.

Convention rights and the working of the Act

All the Convention rights enter into domestic law, save for Article 13 of the Convention which requires that anyone whose rights are violated 'shall have an effective remedy before a national authority' (on which see further below). The rights are incorporated as Schedule 1 of the Act. All domestic courts are under a duty to take into account any prior judgment of the Court of Human Rights and opinions and decisions reached by the Commission and Council of Ministers. The second duty of the courts is to interpret all legislation in such a way as to make it compatible with Convention rights. However, where this cannot be done any incompatible primary legislation remains valid and in force until a minister makes a 'remedial order' amending the offending legislation. Until that happens, the legal position of the applicant remains the same: a declaration of incompatibility does not affect his or her legal rights.

The Act makes it unlawful for a 'public authority' to act in a way which is incompatible with Convention rights.[90] Public authorities include courts and tribunals, but specifically exclude Parliament. The meaning of 'public authorities' is wide: it extends beyond purely governmental bodies, and includes 'any person certain of whose functions are functions of a public nature'. This is sufficiently broad to encompass privatized services and utilities which, while not directly governmental bodies, fulfil functions which would otherwise be undertaken by the state. It is also likely to include purely private organizations which undertake activities under contract with an individual, which otherwise would have been performed by the state: one example might be a private nursing home caring for the elderly. However, where a 'public authority' is bound by primary legislation which makes it impossible to act in

[90] Human Rights Act 1998, section 6(1).

conformity with Convention rights, that action is not unlawful: it is up to Parliament to ensure that such incompatible legislation is reformed in order to prevent public authorities from being caught between two conflicting pieces of law.

The Act works in two directions. On the one hand, an aggrieved citizen may take action against a public authority if he or she considers its actions unlawful. On the other hand, should a citizen find him- or herself involved in litigation started by a public authority, he or she may rely on a Convention right to defend the action. An example may clarify this: if a local authority takes action to recover possession of property from a tenant who has breached the terms of his tenancy, or from a squatter who has no legal rights in the property, the tenant or squatter may plead a Convention right, such as the right to privacy and respect for family life under Article 8, to defend the action for possession. Using a Convention right as a defence has the advantage that the cost of instigating proceedings is borne by the public body.

One limitation built into the Act relates to who may bring proceedings. Whereas in applications for judicial review of administrative action, an individual may apply, or a representative body (such as a trade union or group representing the interests of its members) may apply on behalf of its members, under the Human Rights Act only a 'victim' of an unlawful act, or prospective unlawful act, may apply. This restriction also applies to applications for judicial review brought under the Act. The applicant must also bring his or her complaint to the courts within defined time limits: one year is the maximum time between the action complained of and the application to the court, unless other legislation (such as the Supreme Court Act 1981 which regulates judicial review proceedings) stipulates a shorter time period. The court or tribunal may, however, extend the time limit if it considers that it would be 'equitable' to do so. The restriction to direct victims of the alleged unlawful act is contentious: it places the whole burden of commencing proceedings, and the potential cost of proceedings, on the shoulders of the individual, and excludes the possibility of actions being brought by an organization representing the interests of a defined section of the population equally affected by the act in question. Coupled with the cost of litigation, the limitations on legal aid, and the need to pursue the action to the level of High Court or above for a declaration of incompatibility to be granted, this exclusion places the individual in a disproportionately disadvantageous position *vis-à-vis* the public authority in question.

In order to avoid unforeseen clashes between new legislation and Convention rights, the Act requires that ministers introducing legislation to Parliament are required to declare in advance whether or not the proposed Act will conform to Convention rights. If the government proposes legislation – for example, in relation to terrorism – which will breach Convention rights, the relevant minister must, in writing, either declare that the proposal complies with Convention rights, or that it does not but that the government nevertheless wishes to proceed with the Bill. Whether that incompatible piece of legislation is passed or not will depend on Parliament as a whole, although where the government has a substantial majority in the Commons any principled objections to the proposals are more likely to come from the House of Lords.

It was noted above that Article 13, requiring an effective remedy, has been omitted from the Act. In its place are the power to grant declarations of incompatibility and section 8 which provides that courts may grant 'such relief, or remedy, or make such order, within its powers as it considers just and appropriate'. The meaning of this is expanded in section 8 to include damages or compensation by a court which has the power to make such orders in civil proceedings. In considering whether to make an order for compensation, the court must take into account the principles used by the European Court of Human Rights in making such orders. The exclusion of Article 13 is regrettable, but understandable from a constitutional point of view: the inclusion of Article 13 would have empowered judges to invalidate primary legislation and would have overturned the balance of power between Parliament and the judiciary. However, the exclusion itself is likely to be the basis of applications, and ultimately of appeal to the Court of Human Rights for a ruling on its legality.

Where a declaration of incompatibility is made, the matter goes back to the executive for a decision as to how to proceed. The same procedure also applies if the Court of Human Rights has decided a case against the United Kingdom after the coming into effect of the Act. Where a minister 'considers' that there are 'compelling reasons' he may make amendments to legislation to remove the incompatibility under the primary Act or to remove the incompatibility which has been found in subordinate legislation which compels a public body to act inconsistently with the Convention as a result of the wording of an Act. Schedule 2 of the Act amplifies the procedure. While the power given to ministers enables swift action to be taken to comply with the Convention, the manner in which this power may be exercised raises some difficult questions. It has long been a principle of English law that parliamentary legislation cannot be amended without the approval of Parliament: it is Parliament alone which is supreme, not ministers of the Crown. A power to amend primary legislation, without Parliament's advance approval, is reminiscent of the prerogative right of kings of old, its antiquity being highlighted by the relevant phrase, 'Henry VIII clauses'. Here the Henry VIII power is reactivated, but with restrictions. The 'remedial order', as it is called, may contain any measures which the minister considers 'appropriate'; it may take effect earlier than the date on which it is made, although no criminal liability will arise out of this backdating power. The normal procedure is for the minister to present to Parliament a draft of the proposed order, and for that order to be approved by each House of Parliament after a sixty-day period dating from when the order was laid before Parliament. If no approval is forthcoming at the end of 120 days, the order lapses. If the matter is 'urgent' (and that is for the minister to decide) a remedial order may be made without prior approval of Parliament, but the minister must then lay it before Parliament for subsequent approval, again within time limits. In this situation, while Parliament has the final say over whether or not an order is approved, it gives to ministers an extra-parliamentary law-making power before approval is given.

Early case law under the Human Rights Act 1998

The impact of the Act was first felt in Scotland where Convention rights became enforceable on devolution under the Scotland Act 1998, whereas in England the Act came into force in 2000. The first challenge came in a manner which raises important questions about the legal system. It is a first principle of justice that justice is 'not only done, but seen to be done'. Any bias, whether in terms of financial interests or otherwise, on the part of a judge – real or perceived – goes against that principle. In 1999 a legal challenge was launched in relation to the appointment of part-time judges in Scotland which indicates the seriousness with which judicial independence and impartiality is viewed. Under the Sheriff Courts (Scotland) Act 1971, the Secretary of State has the power to appoint temporary sheriffs in order, among other things, to avoid delays in the administration of justice. The appointments are temporary: they exist until the Secretary of State so decides and are renewable annually. The High Court of Justiciary noted that temporary sheriffs performed 25 per cent of the total work of the sheriff courts. Qualification for appointment as a temporary sheriff is lower than that for a full-time permanent appointment, thus making it an attractive starting-point which could lead to a permanent appointment, depending on the sheriff's tested suitability during a period of 'apprenticeship'. Article 6 of the Convention requires that any person involved in civil litigation or facing criminal charges is entitled to 'a fair and public hearing within a reasonable time by an independent and impartial tribunal established by law'. In *Starrs v. Procurator Fiscal, Linlithgow*,[91] the question which arose was whether the involvement of temporary sheriffs in criminal proceedings offended Article 6. The Court ruled that it did. Whether the temporary sheriffs in question had acted impartially or not was not at issue: it was the absence of security of tenure and the renewable aspect of their appointment which offended against Article 6. In the judgment of the Court, any temporary sheriff, while not actually influenced by these factors, could potentially be influenced, especially where his or her term of office approached the date of renewal by the executive. The Court noted that 'in almost all other European countries . . . the appointment of a temporary judge by the Executive for a period of one year, renewable at the discretion of the Executive, would be regarded as unconstitutional'.

In the *Locabail (and others) cases*,[92] the question of the independence of the judiciary and the issue of judicial bias was again tested, and Article 6 of the Convention cited by the Court of Appeal as amounting to a 'fundamental right'. The Court of Appeal refused applications for permission to appeal by three applicants alleging bias, but granted

[91] *Times LR* 17 November 1999.   [92] *Times LR* 19 November 1999.

permission to appeal to one applicant, Mr Timothy Gormley, on the grounds of bias. In *Timmins v. Gormley* the claimant, Mrs Gormley, had been awarded substantial damages in relation to a car accident involving Mr Timmins. The case was decided by a recorder (a part-time judge) who was also in private practice dealing with personal injury cases, 'primarily but not exclusively' acting for claimants. In addition the recorder acted as a consultant editor to a leading publication concerning personal injury claims, was a member of the Association of Personal Injury Lawyers and wrote 'prolifically' in relation to personal injury law. The Court referred to the recorder's academic writings and noted that he was 'extremely sympathetic' to claimants and 'strongly disapproved' of insurers who 'in his eyes adopted unacceptable tactics'. In the view of the Court of Appeal, the writing of academic articles did not as such disqualify a judge from hearing cases relating to that subject-matter. What concerned the Court was that his opinions were expressed in such a tone as to suggest a preconceived view on the subject, which raised the question as to whether he could try a case 'with an open mind'. There was no question of actual bias in relation to the parties, and the judge had disclosed to the court his interest in personal injury litigation. On the other hand, his strongly held views were such that the Court was concerned that they might have led the judge to 'unconsciously have leant in favour of the claimant and against the defendant in resolving the factual issues between them'. As a result, there was a real danger of bias, which justified the order for the issue to be retried before another court.[93]

The Lord Chancellor – head of the judiciary in England and Wales – fully aware of the implications of the *Starrs case*, has a number of issues to ponder. The first relates to recorders and assistant recorders and to paid magistrates whom he appoints. In Scotland, the Lord Chancellor's counterpart, the Procurator Fiscal, is in charge of criminal prosecutions, a factor which weighed heavily on the court. While the Lord Chancellor is not responsible for prosecutions in England and Wales, he is nevertheless a Cabinet minister and a member of the legislature, and might therefore be felt to have an interest in the law being enforced. Since recorders are appointed for a three-year renewable term, they might

[93] See also the *Pinochet case* discussed in Chapter 9.

be perceived to be influenced by the Lord Chancellor's powers of reappointment.

The first declaration of incompatibility made under the Human Rights Act related to the powers of the Secretary of State for Transport, the Environment and the Regions in relation to planning matters and again raised the question of impartiality in decision-making. In *R v. Secretary of State for the Environment, Transport and the Regions ex parte Holding and Barnes plc and Others*,[94] the High Court ruled that the processes by which the Secretary of State made decisions relating to planning matters[95] were incompatible with Article 6.1 of the Convention.[96] The Secretary of State was not impartial in relation to planning decisions since his own policy was at issue. He could not be 'both policy maker and decision taker'. However, on appeal the matter went to the House of Lords which allowed the Secretary of State's appeal and declared his powers to be compatible with Article 6. The key to whether a decision-maker's powers were compatible lay with the courts' power of judicial review of administrative decisions. Provided there was sufficient judicial control which enabled the High Court to scrutinize the procedures through which a decision was reached – and the power to set aside any decisions which were made without regard to the correct procedures – there was no incompatibility.

When a court made a declaration that medical treatment could be withdrawn in a case where the patient was in a permanent vegetative state, there was no infringement of the right to life, according to the High Court in *NHS Trust A v. M; NHS Trust B v. H*.[97] For a medical

[94] *Times LR* 24 January 2001.

[95] Under the Town and Country Planning Act 1990, the Transport and Works Act 1992, the Highways Act 1980 and the Acquisition of Land Act 1981.

[96] The Court made a declaration of incompatibility under section 4 of the Human Rights Act 1998, but held that the Secretary of State had not acted unlawfully under section 6(1) of the Act (which makes it unlawful for a public authority to act incompatibly with Convention rights) because of section 6(2) which provides that section 6(1) does not apply to an act where the public authority could not have acted otherwise because of primary legislation, or where such legislation could not be interpreted to make it compatible with Convention rights. The requirements of independence and impartiality required by Article 6 could only be met if the decision-maker was independent from the executive and from the parties.

[97] *Times LR* 29 November 2000, [2001] UKHL/23 (HL).

team not to provide treatment would only be incompatible with Article 2 where the circumstances were such as to 'impose a positive obligation on the state to take steps to prolong a person's life'. In circumstances where a person was in a permanent vegetative state there was no such continuing obligation.

Article 5 of the Convention was considered in *In re K (a Child) (Secure accommodation order: Right to liberty)*.[98] A secure accommodation order had been made by a circuit judge in order to ensure that a teenager was under educational supervision. The Court of Appeal ruled that while such an order resulted in a loss of liberty, there was no incompatibility with Article 5 of the Convention. Article 5 provided for lawful restrictions of liberty and this situation fell within the restriction.

In *Venables and Another v. News Group Newspapers and Others*,[99] the High Court had to consider Article 2, the right to life, in relation to Article 10, freedom of expression. Jon Venables and Robert Thompson, convicted as children of murdering the toddler James Bulger, and whose release from detention was expected shortly, sought injunctions to protect their identity from future disclosure. The Court ruled that in exceptional circumstances, taking into account the Human Rights Act 1998 and in particular the right to life under Article 2 of the Convention, the Court had the power to curb freedom of expression, where 'not to do so would be likely to lead to serious physical injury, or the death of the person seeking that confidentiality, and there was no other way to protect the applicants'.

A declaration of incompatibility was granted by the Court of Appeal in *R (H) v. Mental Health Review Tribunal, North and East London Region and Another*.[100] At issue was Article 5 of the Convention which guarantees the right to liberty and the right to take proceedings to determine the lawfulness of detention. The applicant, H, was detained under the Mental Health Act 1983. Section 73 of the Act provides *inter alia* that in order to satisfy a mental health review tribunal that he was entitled to discharge, the burden of proof fell on the restricted person to show that he was no longer suffering from a mental disorder warranting detention. This reversal of the burden of proof was contrary to Article

[98] *Times LR* 29 November 2000.   [99] *Times LR* 16 January 2001.
[100] *Times LR* 2 April 2001.

5: if they were to continue to detain the applicant it should have been for the authorities to prove that he was unfit for release.

The right to fair trial (Article 6) was considered in *Stott (Procurator Fiscal, Dunfermline) and Another v. Brown*.[101] The Court ruled that it was not a breach of a defendant's right to fair trial under Article 6 of the Convention for a prosecutor to rely at the trial on the defendant's admission, obtained compulsorily under the Road Traffic Act 1988. The High Court of Justiciary had ruled that such an admission could not be relied on at trial. On appeal, the Privy Council overturned that decision. Lord Bingham stated that the Convention 'contained no express guarantee of a privilege against self-incrimination. While it could not be doubted that such a right had to be implied, there was no treaty provision which expressly governed the effect or extent of what was to be implied.' Provided that the overall fairness of a trial was not compromised, the constituent rights 'whether expressly or implicitly, within Article 6 were not themselves absolute'.

In *R v. Smith (Joe)*,[102] the Court of Appeal ruled that Article 6 of the European Convention was not breached by the use of material not disclosed to the defence in an *ex parte* hearing considering public interest immunity evidence.[103] The police had reasonable grounds for suspicion and for the arrest of the appellant on charges of burglary for which he was sentenced to four years' imprisonment. The only evidence for the finding of reasonable suspicion was contained in material excluded from trial following the *ex parte* hearing. There was a balancing exercise to be carried out when assessing the competing interests of public interest immunity and the requirement that there should be no prejudice to a defendant's right to have a fair trial.

Article 6 also came into play in *In re M (a Child: Secure accommodation order)*.[104] Here a fifteen-year-old girl appealed against a secure accommodation order made by a Family Proceedings Court. She was a young mother with a history of drug problems and suspected of involvement in prostitution. When she discharged herself from hospital and went to her parents' home in possession of cocaine her father called in social

---

[101] *Times LR* 6 December 2000.   [102] *Times LR* 20 December 2000.
[103] Evidence which is protected from disclosure in open court, in order, for example, to protect the identity of police informants.   [104] *Times LR* 5 April 2001.

services who admitted her to a secure unit. The local authority then applied for a secure accommodation order. The girl alleged that she had been denied a fair trial in the hearing for the interim care order and secure accommodation order. She had obtained separate legal representation but only met her solicitor on the day of the hearing. The Court of Appeal ruled that although proceedings for a secure accommodation order were not criminal proceedings within the meaning of Article 6, where such an order was sought the child should be accorded the minimum rights to a fair trial. The appeal was nevertheless dismissed.

The House of Lords upheld the right of prisoners to freedom of expression in *R v. Secretary of State for the Home Department ex parte Simms; Same v. Same, ex parte O'Brien*.[105] The Court ruled that an indiscriminate ban on all visits to prisoners by journalists or authors in their professional capacity was unlawful. A prisoner had a right to seek to persuade a journalist, through oral interviews, to investigate his allegations of miscarriage of justice in the hope that his case might be reopened. The Court of Appeal had allowed an appeal by the Secretary of State from the decision of the High Court granting judicial review of the Home Secretary's decision that the applicant could receive visits in prison from journalists only if the journalists signed written undertakings not to publish any part of the interviews as laid down in Prison Rules issued by the Home Secretary.[106] The applicants were serving life sentences for murder, and having had their renewed applications for leave to appeal against conviction turned down, continued to protest their innocence. The Home Office had adopted a blanket policy that no prisoners had a right to oral interviews with journalists. Lord Steyn stated that the applicants wished to challenge the safety of their convictions, and that 'in principle it was not easy to conceive of a more important function which free speech might fulfil'. His Lordship was satisfied that it was administratively workable, and consistent with prison order and discipline, to allow prisoners to be interviewed for the purpose here at stake. The Home Secretary's policy and the governor's administrative decisions pursuant to that policy were unlawful.

Although the courts have previously been reluctant to review execu-

---

[105] *Times LR* 9 July 1999.   [106] [1999] QB 349.

tive decisions, since the Human Rights Act 1998 the court has had a positive duty to give effect to Convention rights and to ensure that there was an effective remedy in cases of suspected breach of Convention rights. In *R v. Secretary of State for the Home Department ex parte Javed; R v. Same ex parte Zulfqar Ali; R v. Same ex parte Abid Ali*,[107] the High Court granted an application for judicial review of the Home Secretary's decision to include and retain Pakistan in the list of designated countries in which it appeared to him that there was in general no serious risk of persecution, on the grounds that that was not justified by that country's human rights record; and of the decision to certify the three applicants,[108] and of the decision of the special adjudicator who rejected the applicants' claims to asylum. The Home Secretary had argued that the Court was not competent to challenge his decision, unless it could be shown that he had acted in bad faith. The Court rejected that contention. Since the Human Rights Act 1998 the courts have had to give effect to Convention rights, in particular here Article 3, the prohibition against torture, inhuman or degrading treatment. The decision to include Pakistan was, on the evidence, plainly wrong. There was the clearest evidence that two of the applicants had been tortured in Pakistan in the past and if returned to Pakistan would be likely again to be the subject of torture amounting to persecution. In the case of the third applicant it was clear that the state had been unable or unwilling to protect him from persecution by non-state agents. The Home Secretary had erred in law in the designation decision. The order of the special adjudicator in each case would be quashed.

CONCLUSION

The position of rights and freedoms in the United Kingdom is a product of the unwritten constitution and its evolutionary nature of development. Rarely proactive, successive governments have been

---

[107] *Times LR* 9 February 2001.
[108] Under the Asylum and Immigration Appeal Act 1993, as amended by the Asylum and Immigration Act 1996.

forced – through public protest, changing standards of morality, and more recently the decisions of the European Court of Human Rights – to react and reform the law to bring it more into line with pan-European standards of protection. That the rights guaranteed under the European Convention have hitherto remained unenforceable in the domestic courts reflects the traditional suspicion of governments towards the real and effective protection of rights and freedoms which challenge governmental power. The Human Rights Act 1998 is therefore a milestone, albeit a peculiarly British compromise between protecting Parliament's power from the judges while improving judicial protection of rights. The success of the Act will depend on the willingness of individuals to pursue their rights, which in turn is dependent upon raising public consciousness about rights. It will depend also on the vigour with which judges are prepared to uphold the rights protected under the Act, and the willingness of ministers to take remedial action and reform the law where the protection of rights is held to have fallen below the required standard.

DEFENCE OF THE REALM: NATIONAL SECURITY

INTRODUCTION

Defending the nation against threats – military, terrorist, economic or ideological – has throughout history been a principal concern of any government. Engaged in the many-faceted task of protecting national security is a matrix of institutions, each surrounded by a high degree of secrecy. Before the demise of Communism and the end of the Cold War, even the existence of the external Secret Intelligence Service, SIS or MI6, was not officially acknowledged. No Act of Parliament defined the role of the services nor regulated their work in any form. Parliament exercised no scrutiny over them, leaving them outside the democratic mechanisms of supervision and control. Official secrecy law ensured that no person outside this hidden world of agencies preserving national security could glean information as to its organization, role, functions and modes of operation.

The secret and shadowy world of state security is far removed from the public eye yet lies at the heart of government. In the Cabinet Office in Downing Street sits the Joint Intelligence Committee, the controlling and co-ordinating body of the British security forces. It is here that intelligence data is sifted and analysed, assessments made as to security risks and plans laid to counteract any actual or perceived threats to national security. Next door at Number 10 Downing Street is the Prime Minister, with overall responsibility for security and the right of access to all security intelligence. Just round the corner in Queen Anne's Gate is the Home Office, whose Secretary of State is formally in charge of the internal Security Service, MI5. At the Ministry of Defence, again in Whitehall, is the Defence Intelligence Staff, the Ministry's intelligence wing. Also under the Ministry of Defence is the army's Special Air Service, or SAS, based at Hereford, a specialist rapid-reaction military unit employed at home and abroad to defeat terrorism and, increasingly, to train the forces of Britain's allies. Its naval equivalent, the Special Boat Service, carries out specialist tasks in war and peace, most recently assisting in the fight against international smuggling and trafficking. Close by is the Foreign and Commonwealth Office, with responsibilities for the external security service, the Secret Intelligence Service, SIS or MI6, and for preventing drug trafficking into the United Kingdom, operationally controlled by Customs and Excise and its criminal investigation arm the National Investigation Service. Custom House, on the Thames, is the headquarters of Customs and Excise. Assisting the police services, the National Crime Squad and Customs is the National Criminal Intelligence Service, NCIS, with its headquarters in London and five regional offices. The NCIS is also home to the National Central Bureau, NCB, through which all Interpol inquiries pass. In addition the NCIS plays an important role in the exchange of intelligence on organized crime through Europol, the Europe-wide organization for the policing of criminal activity. Special Branch of the police forces[1] assists the security forces in the carrying out of operations.

Within half a mile of Parliament – the Palace of Westminster – is Thames House, the restored neo-gothic home of the Security Service. Across the Thames, at Vauxhall Cross, is the state-of-the-art green and glass home of the Secret Intelligence Service, the external wing of the security forces. At Cheltenham in Gloucestershire is the Government's Communications Headquarters, GCHQ, which, in co-operation with the United States National Security Agency, NSA, is responsible for the gathering of international signals intelligence – 'sigint' – and which has intelligence-gathering bases around the world. This is the map of the secret world governing British national security.

---

[1] There is no national police force in the United Kingdom. The structure of police forces is discussed in Chapter 10.

State security, however, cannot be seen as a purely domestic matter. Increasingly, the threats to the security of Britain, continental Europe and the West are on an international scale requiring co-operation between the respective forces of Britain's allies. With the break-up of the Soviet Union and Warsaw Pact and the demise of Communism, these threats have moved far beyond intelligence and counter-intelligence operations designed to combat that of the Cold War. With human and fiscal intelligence resources freed from conventional concerns, the focus has moved to countering international terrorism, international criminal activity whether relating to conventional arms or drugs trafficking or the trafficking in people, and the need to monitor and control the risks emanating from weapons proliferation which now includes biological and chemical weaponry. Such challenges require international co-operation and the establishment of international agencies.

Aside from the Official Secrets Acts,[2] there existed no statutory regulation of security matters, until 1985, when in response to a decision by the European Court of Human Rights which was highly critical of the absence of clear legal criteria and safeguards, the Interception of Communications Act was passed.[3] In 1989 for the first time an Act of Parliament, the Security Services Act, was passed to regulate the Security Service (MI5).[4] The Act, however, made no mention of either the Government Communications Headquarters (GCHQ) nor the Secret Intelligence Service which remained outside statutory control until 1994. Some opening up of the security services came under John Major's premiership, with its commitment to greater openness about government, when for the first time the existence of SIS was publicly acknowledged and the identities of the directors of MI5 and SIS were made public. In 1992 the government announced that a quasi-parliamentary

[2] 1911, 1920 and 1989.
[3] Following *Malone v. United Kingdom* (1984) 7 EHRR 14. The 1985 Act is now superseded by the Regulation of Investigatory Powers Act 2000, on which see page 393 below.
[4] Once again motivated by the European Court of Human Rights, before which a challenge had been lodged by officers of the Campaign for Nuclear Disarmament (CND) and the National Council for Civil Liberties alleging violations to rights of privacy: see *Harman and Hewitt v. United Kingdom* (1992) 14 EHRR 657. A further application by CND was withdrawn after the announcement of the Security Services Bill: Application Nos 11745/85 and 13595/88.

committee, the Intelligence Services Committee, was to be established with the task of keeping under review policy on the security and intelligence services. In 1994 the Intelligence Services Act brought both SIS and GCHQ under statutory authority. For the most part, however, such knowledge as exists about the role of the services and their satellite organizations is gleaned not from official government sources but through journalists, state security researchers and disaffected 'whistle-blowers' within the services. Revelations about the work of the security services are strictly guarded by the law, with injunctions being sought by the government and granted by the courts to restrain unauthorized disclosures. Under the Public Records Act 1958, official records of all government departments are protected from disclosure, generally being withheld from public gaze for a thirty-year period, but subject to extensions, which in the case of the work of the security services, may increase to a one-hundred-year ban. The Official Secrets Acts 1911 and 1989 provide penalties for espionage and the 1989 Act imposes a lifelong ban on members and former members of the security forces revealing any details of their work or indeed any information gained in the course of their employment.

THE DILEMMA OF NATIONAL SECURITY

The concept of national security itself is far from clear and unambiguous, and is subject to changing interpretations over time and under changing circumstances. A democracy, characterized by individual liberties and rights and a government limited by law, presupposes a state secure from threats which undermine the stability of the nation, and adequate mechanisms to detect and counter external or internal threats. Here a distinction has to be drawn between threats – economic, ideological, military or terrorist – which come from outside the United Kingdom and threaten state security, and the perceived internal threats which give rise to security service operations affecting British citizens. Whether the threat is from a foreign power with imperial ambitions, such as Hitler's Germany, or from ideological hegemony as pursued by the Communist Soviet Union in the post-war Cold War era, or from religious fundamentalists targeting Britain, or organized international crime syndicates and drug traffickers, covert intelligence and counter-intelligence operations are justified in the name of state security.

When it comes to operations relating to its own citizens, however, the position is rather different. Eliminating terrorist threats and organized crime requires special measures. On the other hand, if individuals and groups find themselves under surveillance by the security agencies, there needs to be clear justification for invasions of privacy and the rule of law insists that those who hold power must operate under the law and be accountable to the democratically elected government. For the state to infringe civil liberties there need to be clear criteria and clear sources of power to act under the law. In a democratic state a balance therefore must be struck between the legitimate objectives pursued in defence of the realm, or national security, and the means used which may threaten individual rights and freedoms without justifica-tion. In the scales of justice lie on one side the rights and freedoms of individuals, on the other side defence of the realm. Citizens have – among other things – a moral right to privacy (but not a strict legal right, see further pages 330–2 above), and to freedom of association and movement. Freedom of expression, both individual and for the media, is an indispensable tool in the exchange of ideas and political debate. Individual citizens also have the right to nondiscrimination on the basis of nationality, race, class and gender, and the right to access to the law and fair trial. If these rights and freedoms are to remain protected, the security forces must act in a manner which respects these rights to the extent possible in the pursuit of the public interest in state security.

The smattering of isolated incidents and cumulative disclosures since the mid-1980s, principally from disaffected former security agents, have unifying themes: state security, secrecy and the problem for civil liberties. The individual rights and freedoms of citizens – civil, eco-nomic, personal and political – can only be safeguarded if the nation as a whole is free from threats of or actual subversion, internal and external, whether these come from espionage, terrorism or serious crime. National security is therefore fundamental to the well-being of the people, and government is under an obligation to ensure that mechanisms are in place which will provide for the protection of society in its broadest sense. State, or national, security, however, cannot be pursued by any means or at any cost. Defence of the realm, while a justifiable goal, must not of itself undermine, through its methods, the freedoms and rights of the people, except where any limitations on individual rights and freedoms are absolutely justified for the greater good of a peaceful state. Here lies the fundamental dilemma for the protection of civil liberties and rights against the power of the state. Vague definitions of functions, official secrecy and the lack of democratic accountability render it impossible for the individual citizen to know whether he or she has been targeted by the security forces as a 'security risk', whether the security services have a 'file' on him or her, the uses to which this may be put, the classification accorded to it and the length of time for which that file will be maintained. That 'national security' is a term defined by the agencies themselves, albeit vaguely defined in statute, is small comfort to the citizen who may find him- or herself the subject of investigation, with little prospect of lodging a successful complaint against the security services.

When the issue of national security is pitted against rights and freedoms, neither the normal democratic process nor adequate judicial scrutiny exists to protect the individual against the forces of the state. As discussed below, the work of the multifarious agencies employed to protect security is inherently, and necessarily, secret and is not subject to democratic scrutiny. As a result, a cloak of protection is thrown around security agencies and their work which makes any judgment about the legitimacy of their operations extremely difficult. This is not to say that the security services are not regulated by law. While this was the case until 1985 (in relation to interception of communications), 1989 (in relation to MI5) and 1994 (in relation to the SIS and GCHQ), when Acts of Parliament were passed defining the role of the services and providing for authorization for interference with mail and communications and property, the services now operate, on the face of it, within well-structured parameters. The Acts also introduced complaints procedures for aggrieved citizens and Commissioners to oversee the operation of the Acts. The Regulation of Investigatory Powers Act 2000 (RIPA) supersedes much of the foregoing statutory framework and is discussed at pages 393 ff. below.

An inherent problem relating to regulation of the security forces lies in the difficulty of definition, in part due to the vagueness of the language used and the desire to build sufficient flexibility into definitions so as not to disable the services from responding to novel and unforeseen threats to security. In the House of Commons in 1952 the Home Secretary, Maxwell Fyfe, stated in relation to the Security Service, MI5, that 'Its task is the defence of the Realm as a whole, from external and internal dangers arising from attempts at espionage and sabotage, or from actions of persons and organisations, whether directed from within or without the country, which *may be judged to be subversive of the state*'.[5] In the Home Secretary's Directive to the Director-General of MI5 issued in 1952, of which the above statement is a part, Maxwell Fyfe went on to state that

You will take special care to see that the work of the Security Service is strictly limited to what is necessary for the purposes of their task.

It is essential that the Security Service should be kept absolutely free from any political bias or influence and nothing should be done that might lend colour to any suggestion that it is concerned with the interests of any particular section of the community, or with any other matter than the Defence of the Realm as a whole.

The 1989 Act, the first Act of Parliament to regulate the internal Security Service, MI5, reflects these sentiments in defining the functions of the Service as being

the protection of national security and, in particular, its protection against threats from espionage, terrorism and sabotage, from the activities of agents of foreign powers and from actions intended to overthrow or undermine parliamentary democracy by political, industrial or violent means.

It shall also be the function of the Service to safeguard the economic well-being of the United Kingdom against threats posed by the actions or intentions of persons outside the British Islands.

It shall also be the function of the Service to act in support of the activities of police forces and other law enforcement agencies in the prevention and detection of serious crime.[6]

---

[5] Emphasis added.
[6] Security Service Act 1989, section 1(2), as amended by the Security Service Act 1996, section 1.

The Security Service is prohibited from furthering 'the interests of any political party'.[7]

The 1994 Intelligence Services Act defines the role of the Secret Intelligence Service, SIS or MI6, as being

to obtain and provide information relating to the actions or intentions of persons outside the British Islands, and perform other tasks relating to these in the interests of national security, with particular reference to defence and foreign policies . . . the interests of the economic well-being of the United Kingdom . . . or in support of the prevention or detection of serious crime.

In the 1989 Act the word *subversion* has disappeared, but the concept nevertheless remains, lying silently in the phrase 'actions intended to overthrow or undermine parliamentary democracy by political, industrial or violent means'. In debate on the Bill before Parliament in 1988, the then Home Secretary, Douglas Hurd, stated that

It does not matter if . . . people have views on the structure or organization of Parliament or if they are involved in seeking to change industrial practices in this country or to negotiate a better deal if they are members of trade unions, or if they seek to challenge or change the Government's policies relating to defence, employment, foreign policy or anything else . . . Its [the Service's] *sole criterion in relation to a subversive threat is whether there is a deliberate intention to undermine parliamentary democracy and whether that presents a real threat to the security of the nation.*[8]

However, there is sufficient evidence from the past to suggest that the security services have in fact targeted trade unions and pressure groups under the vague label of 'subversion'. MI5's stated position is that

The Service has never investigated people simply because they were members or office-holders of trade unions or campaigning organizations. But subversive groups have in the past sought to infiltrate and manipulate such organizations as a way of exerting political influence. To fulfil its function of protecting national security, the Service therefore investigated individual members of *bona fide* organizations when there were grounds to believe that their actions were 'intended to overthrow or undermine parliamentary democracy by political,

---

[7] Security Service Act 1989, section 2(2)(b).   [8] Emphasis added.

industrial or violent means'. The Service investigated the activities of the subversive groups, but not the organizations they sought to penetrate.

MI5 also states that 'the subversive threat to parliamentary democracy in the United Kingdom is now negligible and the Service accordingly has no current investigations in this area'.[9] This official explanation, however, begs a number of important questions: namely, just what is a subversive organization, when can organizations legitimately be regarded as a threat to the security of the state, and on what criteria is an organization labelled subversive?

The Campaign for Nuclear Disarmament (CND), for example, pursued (as its name makes obvious) the political objective of ridding the world of nuclear weapons. It pursued its objectives through peaceful means, holding annual marches, demonstrating at military sites, disseminating its message through whatever publicity it could. In 1984, the then Home Secretary, Leon Brittan, endorsed the legitimacy of CND, when he told the Commons that 'There is no doubt that peaceful political campaigning to change the mind of the government and people generally about nuclear disarmament is an entirely legitimate activity'.[10]

Nevertheless, in 1964 CND's Committee of 100 faced prosecution under the Official Secrets Act 1911 following a peaceful protest at an operational airfield.[11] The defendants were charged under section 1 of the Act with the offence of approaching, entering or inspecting a prohibited place. Evidence was given as to the importance of the base for national security. In defence, it was put to the court that the defendants were trying to bring about an end to nuclear armaments, which would itself be in the interests of the state. The court ruled that CND's claim to be acting in the interest of the state was irrelevant.

Furthermore, a member of CND, who was also a member of the Communist Party, Dr John Cox, was subjected to telephone tapping with a view to collecting data on him and other prominent members of CND. When in 1984 Cathy Massiter, a disillusioned former MI5 officer, revealed on television that she had been requested to identify a

[9] *Myths and Misunderstandings*, http://www.mi5.gov.uk/myth6.htm
[10] '20/20 Vision', cited in M. Hollingsworth and N. Fielding, *Defending the Realm: MI5 and the Shayler Affair* (London: André Deutsch, 1999), p. 78.
[11] *Chandler v. Director of Public Prosecutions* [1964] AC 763.

suitable member of CND for 'bugging', Joan Ruddock, later a minister in Tony Blair's government, sought judicial review of the legality of the intercept. The Home Secretary, who had signed the intercept warrant, argued that the court ought not to entertain the application for review 'because to do so would be detrimental to national security', and relied, according to Mr Justice Taylor, 'on the long established policy that a Secretary of State does not disclose or discuss the existence of a warrant'.[12] Mr Justice Taylor rejected the Home Secretary's submission, distinguishing between the situation where national security is used as a justification for action, and the instant case where national security was being employed to preclude the court from considering an action at all. Mr Justice Taylor went on to state that 'totally to oust the court's supervisory jurisdiction in a field where *ex hypothesi* the citizen can have no right to be consulted is a draconian and dangerous step indeed'.[13] However, the application failed. The court ruled that the warrant had been issued by the Home Secretary within the relevant criteria (which at the time were non-statutory) and that there was no evidence that the Home Secretary had flouted the guidelines for an improper purpose, namely for party political purposes.[14]

THE NATURE OF THREATS TO NATIONAL SECURITY

England's first known spy was probably Sir Francis Walsingham, Elizabeth I's chief secretary of state from 1573 to 1590, who recruited informers for money with a view to detecting plots against the Queen. In 1660 Parliament voted money to fund the secret service, without – and the precedent remains – demanding any accounting for its work or the destiny of its moneys. The secret services have always been a force owing their allegiance not to Parliament but to the monarch: a factor which explains the enduring role of the royal prerogative under which

---

[12] *R v. Secretary of State for the Home Department ex parte Ruddock* [1987] 2 All ER 518, at 524–5.   [13] Ibid., at p. 527.
[14] On allegations of the Service's surveillance of trade unions, see Hollingsworth and Fielding, *Defending the Realm*, chapter 3; see also L. Lustgarten and I. Leigh, *In From the Cold: National Security and Parliamentary Democracy* (Oxford: Clarendon, 1994).

the intelligence services functioned until late in the twentieth century when Acts of Parliament finally came to regulate – but not control – the work of the internal and external security forces.

Organized intelligence gathering was the child born of the 'Fenian threat' to security on the mainland of the United Kingdom during the campaign for Irish Home Rule. In the first decade of the twentieth century came the German threat, and public concern over enemy agent activity in Britain,[15] leading to the establishment of MI5 in 1909, the SIS in 1911 and the first Official Secrets Act in 1911. In 1917, with the Russian Revolution, a different theatre of threat came into being for Britain and the West: Communism. With its commitment to true socialism and the redistribution of wealth came the ideological objective to over-throw the forces of capitalism, without which, from a Communist perspective, true equality and freedom could not be achieved. For seventy-five years the spectre of Communism hung over the West, with the Cold War lasting from around the end of the Second World War until the demise of Communism in the early 1990s. Within the Soviet Union, the suppression of dissidents was crucial to upholding the power of the state against 'subversive forces', a factor largely hidden from Western eyes through the powerful apparatus of the state and its oppression of those who dared to question the Soviet regime. The security forces of the Soviet Union, originally Cheka (the Extraordinary Commission for Combatting Counter-revolution and Sabotage), its successor the KGB (Soviet security and intelligence service) from 1954 to 1991, and the GRU (Soviet military intelligence) and Spetsnaz (Soviet special forces), were an essential tool not only in suppressing dissent from within, but in the recruitment of foreign intelligence agents. By the 1920s Communism had travelled west. Among the young and ideological, Communism won many friends – the idealism of its object-ives blinding those attracted to it to the means employed to pursue the goal, and the potential threat posed to Western democracy by a subversive ideology backed by an increasingly menacing military force and ultimately a nuclear capability and the proliferation of weapons

---

[15] See C. Andrew, *Secret Service: The Making of the British Intelligence Community* (London: Heinemann, 1985); D. French, 'Spy Fever in Britain 1900–1915' (1978) 21 *Historical Journal* 355; W. Le Queux, *German Spies in England* (London: S. Paul, 1915).

capable of mass destruction, including biological weaponry. As late as 1990, when President Gorbachov had been pursuing an open dialogue with the West, official doubts existed as to the commitment to peace and the abandonment of the goal of global Communist hegemony. Mrs Thatcher, who had viewed Mikhail Gorbachov as 'a man she could do business with' in 1983, admitted that he 'remained a Communist to the end', unable to escape 'the Communist mindset and language'.[16]

In the 1930s the KGB targeted the universities of Oxford and Cambridge as a fertile recruiting ground. Not only were undergraduates at Oxbridge the cream of the British academic elite, but they were, of all British university graduates, the most likely to enter into government service and rise to the top of the Civil Service. The KGB agent and academic Arnold Deutsch arrived in England with the express task of recruiting spies. His success was considerable. Christopher Andrew states that KGB files reveal that Deutsch recruited twenty agents and had contact with a total of twenty-nine. Of these, however, by far the most important were Anthony Blunt, Guy Burgess, John Cairncross, Donald Maclean and Kim Philby, all of whom were recruited from Cambridge University in the 1930s.[17] Philby rose to the top of the Secret Intelligence Service (SIS), serving as Head of Station in Turkey from 1947 and as head of SIS in Washington from 1949. Maclean entered the Diplomatic Service and also ended up in Washington. Burgess entered the Foreign Office in 1944, while Cairncross moved from the Foreign Office to the Treasury. Blunt, who joined MI5 but worked as a recruiting agent for the KGB at Cambridge, and was from 1945 the Surveyor of the King's Pictures, was the last to be unmasked. Burgess and Maclean defected to the Soviet Union in 1951, Cairncross was interrogated by the security service, resigned and went abroad, Philby defected in 1963 while Blunt was caught in 1964 but granted immunity from prosecution and was not publicly unmasked until 1979. Christopher Andrew and Vasili Mitrokhin state that Philby, Burgess and Maclean were responsible for 20,000 pages of valuable documents and agent reports being passed to the KGB.

[16] M. Thatcher, *The Downing Street Years* (London: HarperCollins, 1993), pp. 463, 804, 805.

[17] C. Andrew and V. Mitrokhin, *The Mitrokhin Archive: The KGB in Europe and the West* (Harmondsworth: Penguin, 1999), p. 75.

A second major preoccupation of the security services in recent decades has been to counteract the threat of terrorism relating to Northern Ireland. While the Irish Republican Army (IRA) had lost much of its former virulence by the 1960s, the 'troubles' – civil unrest, violence and terrorism – which ignited in the late 1960s and continued through to the peace settlement of 1998, resulted in a reinvigorated military campaign by the IRA in pursuit of its republican goals. Civil disobedience by the Catholic community in Northern Ireland, against discrimination in housing, education and employment and exclusion from proportional representation in the police and legislature – Stormont – descended into a virtual civil war between the IRA and paramilitary Protestant groups. The police lost control and in August 1969 the Prime Minister, Harold Wilson, ordered the British army to the province. An official inquiry, the Cameron Commission, reported in 1969 a 'widespread sense of political and social grievances [on the part of the Catholic community] for long unaudited and therefore ignored by successive governments of Northern Ireland'.[18] The protests of the Catholic community were highlighted by the Northern Ireland Civil Rights Association. Protest demonstrations, however, were met with violence by the Royal Ulster Constabulary and the 'B Specials', a special constabulary, many of whose members were former loyalist paramilitaries. The arrival of British troops was initially welcomed by the Catholic community as a source of protection. The welcome was not to last. In January 1972 thirteen Catholic civilians were shot dead and thirteen wounded by British paratroopers in the course of a banned civil rights march in Derry: Bloody Sunday.[19] Heavy-handed operations by the army led to further hostility. Against this background, the IRA re-emerged to continue its quest to get the British out of Northern Ireland and reunify

[18] *Report of the Cameron Commission: Disturbances in Northern Ireland*, Cmnd. 532 (London: HMSO, 1969).

[19] A tribunal of inquiry was set up in 1972, the findings of which never satisfied those affected, and the matter was reopened in 1998 in light of fresh evidence and as part of the peace and reconciliation process. The Bloody Sunday Inquiry was established under the Tribunals of Inquiry (Evidence) Act 1921 and chaired by Lord Saville of Newdigate. See the Prime Minister's Statement to the House of Commons, Hansard 29 January 1998, cols. 501–3. See also *R v. Lord Saville of Newdigate and Others ex parte A and Others* [2001] *The Times* 21 December on the question of ensuring safety for security officers giving evidence before the Tribunal.

Ireland. In 1970 the Provisional Sinn Fein Party was formed and in 1971 the staunchly unionist Democratic Unionist Party was formed by the Reverend Ian Paisley. The Civil Authorities Special Powers Act (Northern Ireland) 1922 was unearthed by the authorities and used to intern suspected IRA terrorists without trial, a factor which increased rather than decreased sympathy for the nationalist cause. Disquiet about the handling of the troubles arose over the internment of suspects, and allegations of ill-treatment of detainees led to legal proceedings being initiated against the United Kingdom by the Republic of Ireland government under the European Convention on Human Rights. The Crompton Report of 1971[20] outlined the interrogation methods used as including continuous noise, deprivation of food, water and sleep and wall standing.

Three Privy Counsellors were appointed to examine the procedures. The majority report concluded that the techniques employed would be acceptable provided adequate safeguards were introduced in relation to their use. In a powerful minority report, however, Lord Gardiner, a former Labour Lord Chancellor, ruled that the procedures were unlawful, and the government accepted his view. The European Court of Human Rights ruled that the procedures amounted to inhuman and degrading treatment contrary to Article 3 of the Convention, but that they did not amount to torture.[21] As support for the protective British forces fell away, so the IRA campaign against the British intensified and unionist Protestant paramilitaries escalated their campaign against the Catholic community and IRA. By the end of 1972, 474 deaths had occurred in the escalation of sectarian killings by Protestant murderers and the IRA. In 1972, with the civilian death toll mounting, the United Kingdom government once again assumed responsibility for the province.[22] The devolution of power and self-rule of the province which had existed from 1920 to 1972 was at an end. A review of the Special Powers Act and internment was undertaken in 1972,[23] which confirmed the need for detention without trial as a short-term measure for certain alleged

[20] Cmnd. 4823 (London: HMSO, 1971).

[21] *Republic of Ireland v. United Kingdom* (1978) 2 EHRR 25.

[22] Under the Northern Ireland (Temporary Provisions) Act 1972.

[23] *Report of the Commission to Consider Legal Procedures to deal with Terrorist Activities in Northern Ireland*, Cmnd. 5185 (London: HMSO, 1972) (the Diplock Inquiry).

offences, and recommended the introduction of special courts which would sit without a jury, known as the Diplock Courts.[24]

Throughout the 1970s and 1980s a virtual civil war existed in Northern Ireland. Conor Gearty records that from 1971 to 1977 an average of 252 persons were killed and 3,269 shootings occurred each year, and that in the years 1977 to 1981 the averages fell, respectively to 82 and 1,574.[25] The terrorist campaign was not confined to Northern Ireland: increasingly the IRA carried out 'successful' operations on mainland Britain, targeting innocent civilians, politicians and the army. Among IRA atrocities were the explosions at the Aldershot army base which killed seven civilian employees. In 1974 a bomb blew up a bus full of British service personnel, killing eleven and injuring fourteen. In November of that year came the Birmingham pub bombings, killing twenty-one and injuring 162. In 1983 a car bomb attack on Harrods Knightsbridge store left five dead. The IRA claimed responsibility for murdering Airey Neave and Ian Gow, both Members of Parliament and the then Prime Minister's advisers on Northern Ireland. In 1984 came the IRA's most audacious attack when a massive bomb exploded at the Grand Hotel in Brighton, which was accommodating the Prime Minister and Cabinet members during the Conservative Party conference: five died and the Prime Minister and many of her Cabinet colleagues were lucky to escape alive. In 1989 an attack on the Royal Marine School of Music at Deal in Kent left eleven dead. In 1992 the IRA exploded a bomb in Soho and a few days later a bomb exploded in the City of London killing three people, injuring ninety-one and causing over £1 billion of damage: a reminder to the British that even the heart of the capital was vulnerable. In 1993 the British and Irish governments issued a Joint Declaration which, while it recognized the preservation of the union between Northern Ireland and the mainland United Kingdom for as long as a majority of the people of Northern Ireland so wished, also indicated for the first time that the British government was neutral over the long-term future of the province.

In 1994 came the announcement of a ceasefire by the IRA. In 1996, however, the IRA exploded a bomb at Canary Wharf in London, killing

---

[24] Northern Ireland (Emergency Provisions) Act 1973.
[25] C. Gearty, *Terror* (London: Faber & Faber, 1991), chapter 8.

two people, and bombed Manchester city centre, again causing massive damage. The Good Friday Agreement of Easter 1998 signalled the initiation of peace, with the return of legislative power to a Northern Ireland Assembly.

Arms and drugs trafficking, and the trafficking in people, has also become a major preoccupation of the security forces in recent times. The United Nations International Drug Control Programme (UNDCP) and the United Nations Centre for International Crime Prevention are the international umbrella organizations seeking to combat organized world-wide drug trafficking and crime.[26] In January 2000 the Foreign and Commonwealth Office announced funding totalling £2,286,000 for a range of projects under the UNDCP. According to the Foreign and Commonwealth Minister, John Battle, an estimated 95 per cent of the heroin on the streets of Britain comes from South-west Asia, principally Afghanistan, and Peru, Bolivia and Colombia are the world's largest producers of cocaine. About 30 per cent of the cocaine entering Britain comes via the Caribbean. Overall, 60–80 per cent of the cannabis resin entering the United Kingdom comes from Morocco; the single largest source of Ecstasy is the Netherlands. The government's objective, according to the Anti-Drugs Co-ordinator, Keith Hellawell, is to reduce the availability of drugs by 50 per cent by 2008 and by 25 per cent by 2005.[27] The international drugs industry is estimated to have annual proceeds as high as $500 billion. In a speech by Dick Kellaway, Chief Investigation Officer of the National Investigation Service (NIS), the criminal investigation arm of Customs and Excise, it was reported that in 1997 Customs seized a total of over 82 tonnes of drugs, with a street value in the United Kingdom of around £656 million. Heroin seizures were 135 per cent up on the 1996 total. In addition, Customs prevented a further £2.3 billion worth of drugs from being imported.

The international escalation in racketeering, illegal immigration and multi-million-pound fraud are perceived by government to represent a major threat to national security. At a meeting in Downing Street in 1999 between the Prime Minister and the heads of MI5, SIS and

26 United Nations Document ST/SGB/1998/17.
27 See also *Tackling Drugs: The United Kingdom's International Strategy* (Foreign and Commonwealth Office), and the White Paper *Tackling Drugs to Build a Better Britain*.

Government Communications Headquarters (GCHQ),[28] the Prime Minister is reported to have authorized a diversion of resources from counter-espionage and counter-terrorism to enable the security forces to expand operations against drug traffickers.[29] GCHQ is to step up the interception of computerized transactions involving money-laundering and fraud. Among the recently perceived threats are those of the 'red mafia', Russian and Eastern European criminal gangs involved in fraud, extortion and smuggling, and Albanian gangs involved in human trafficking, prostitution, arms dealing and drug smuggling.

The instability generated in the former Soviet Union has added new threats to security including the proliferation of chemical, biological and nuclear weapons of mass destruction, and the spread of organized crime.[30] However, the problem of the proliferation of weaponry, particularly weapons of mass destruction such as nuclear, biological and chemical weapons, is an international affair, with developing countries seeking to increase their security and standing, and others enhancing their economies through the development of weapons manufacture for export. Intelligence on the scale and location of weapons has become a central task of the Western intelligence community. The Iran–Iraq War, 1980–88, and Iraq's invasion of Kuwait in 1990 focused attention on the dangerous build-up of arms in the Middle East. Immediately following the Gulf War, both Iran and Iraq started rebuilding their weaponry, Iraq doing so despite the United Nations sanctions. Attention also focused on Syria and Libya, known to support international terrorism. In 1993, for example, SIS and CIA intelligence alerted the West to Libya's build-up of nerve gas, chemical weapons and ballistic missiles. Without intelligence it is impossible to know where emerging and changing threats are coming from.[31]

[28] Dr Stephen Lander, Richard Dearlove and Francis Richards respectively.

[29] *Sunday Times*, 5 December 1999.

[30] In June 2000 the discovery by Dover Customs and Excise officers of fifty-eight dead bodies locked in an articulated lorry container highlighted in a gruesome manner the tragedy of human trafficking. Two survived and were placed in protective custody. The fifty-four men and four women who died were believed to be Chinese, their illegal entry organized, at a cost of some $15,000, by Chinese triad gangs, and effected through a company set up in Rotterdam just four days before the fatal trip.

[31] On intelligence and trade in international weaponry see J. Adams, *The New Spies* (London: Pimlico, 1995). On the events of 11 September 2001, see pp. 408–9.

THE FORCES OF NATIONAL SECURITY

Police intelligence

At the level most visible to the general public are the police forces: maintaining public order, detecting and reporting crime to the prosecuting authority. While individual criminality and law enforcement processes do not impinge on the security of the state, organized crime, in the form of drug trafficking, arms dealing and terrorism, may. Here the police play a vital role in detection and prosecution. However, the police forces – of which there are fifty-five in the United Kingdom – cannot, in isolation, hope to combat terrorism or international crime. Special Branch was originally formed in 1883 as a section of the Criminal Investigation Department of the Metropolitan Police, to combat Irish terrorism on the mainland. Its responsibilities are stated to be the gathering, collation, analysis and exploitation of intelligence on extremist political and terrorist activity; initiation, development and conduct of intelligence operations against terrorists and political extremists; dissemination of intelligence for operational use to law enforcement agencies at local, national and international levels; the provision of armed personal protection for Ministers of State, foreign VIPs and others at threat from terrorist or extremist attack; policing the ports within the London area to detect terrorist or criminal suspects travelling into or out of the country; assisting other government agencies to counter threats to the security of the United Kingdom from: public disorder, the proliferation of weapons of mass destruction (whether nuclear, biological or chemical); espionage by foreign powers; subversion of the democratic process; terrorism by Irish or international groups; or sabotage of the infrastructure of the United Kingdom.[32]

In 1992 the National Criminal Intelligence Service (NCIS) was established to co-ordinate the fight against national and international organized crime. Its functions are now defined under the Police Act 1997. The Service became independent of central government in 1998 and is

---

[32] www.met.police.uk/police/mps/mps/specop/spec.htm

accountable to a service authority of nineteen members representing the public, law enforcement agencies and the government. Its role is to gather 'strategic intelligence to assess the scale and nature of threats from serious and organized crime, identifying potential areas for new legislation, recommending prevention techniques and forecasting future threats'. NCIS has an internal and external division. The United Kingdom Division has five regional offices and an office in Scotland. As a member of Interpol, the United Kingdom, in common with 177 other member countries, has a National Central Bureau which is part of the NCIS, based in London. The NCIS lists its functions as being to provide a secure flagging service to avoid duplication of effort by law enforcement agencies; providing a twenty-four-hour facility to search NCIS intelligence databases; acting as the interface between police forces and other intelligence agencies; providing advice/support for applications under the Interception of Communications Act 1985.[33] Also within the NCIS is Strategic and Specialist Intelligence Branch which gathers information on serious criminals, ranging from 'synthetic drug producers, organized criminal groups to paedophiles and football hooligans'. The intelligence database is available to operational law enforcement agencies.

European-wide investigations into serious and organized crime are aided by crime and drug liaison officers based in United Kingdom embassies and missions in Europe. Europol, established under the Treaty on European Union 1992, was launched in 1998, to facilitate the exchange of intelligence among European Union member countries; it has two NCIS liaison officers. Within its remit are arms and drug trafficking, organized illegal immigration networks, trafficking in human beings for sexual purposes, tracing paedophiles who travel outside the United Kingdom to gain access to minors, trafficking in stolen vehicles, nuclear and radioactive material and money-laundering related to the above, and, from 1999, terrorism.

[33] www.ncis.co.uk/web/

Customs and Excise

Customs and Excise has a staff of some 24,000, with the responsibility for the collection of VAT receipts and excise duties. Central to the fight against international organized crime is the National Investigation Service (NIS) of Customs and Excise, which in the 1997–8 financial year seized more than £3.3 billion worth of drugs and 200 illicit importations of firearms and explosives.[34] One hundred and thirty-one 'well established and highly organized criminal groups' were dismantled or disrupted. Approximately 80 per cent of the heroin seized in 1997 was consigned from Turkey, travelling the Balkan route from Istanbul through Bulgaria, Romania, Austria and Germany, through the Benelux countries and into Britain. In relation to cocaine, over two tonnes was seized. The principal sources are South America and the Caribbean countries, but the Service reports the opening up of new routes originating in South Africa. The main source of synthetic drugs, many of which are manufactured in Eastern and Central Europe, is the Netherlands and Belgium. Cannabis seizures amounted to nearly 77 tonnes, the principal sources being Colombia and Morocco, Afghanistan, Pakistan and Cambodia, and increasingly the Netherlands.

Headed by a senior civil servant, the Chief Investigation Officer, the NIS is based in London and has regional offices around the country. The aims of the NIS are stated to be the investigation of 'irregularities, fraud and smuggling to the highest professional standards to bring offenders before the courts and thereby defeat and destroy major criminal organisations'. The Service works with domestic and overseas customs, the police and intelligence agencies. It is a partner in the National Criminal Intelligence Service, occupying key management posts in the NCIS and providing officers for overseas drugs liaison posts in member states in Europol and Interpol.

---

[34] In addition to almost 3,000 endangered live animals and birds.

Military intelligence

The Ministry of Defence has its own Defence Intelligence Staff (DIS) which is the main provider of strategic defence intelligence to the Ministry of Defence and the Armed Forces. The Chief of DIS, a serving three-star officer drawn from any of the three services, reports to the Chief of the Defence Staff and the Permanent Secretary of the Ministry of Defence, and is a member of the Joint Intelligence Committee (on which see further below). The DIS has a total staff of 4,600, both military and civilian. About 700 are located in the London headquarters, the remainder in DIS Defence Agencies and other units in the United Kingdom and overseas. Approximately 60 per cent of personnel are serving members of the armed forces. DIS is divided into two main parts, the Defence Intelligence Analysis Staff (DIAS) and the Intelligence and Geographic Resources Staff (IGRS). DIAS is responsible for providing global defence intelligence assessments and strategic warning, and draws on classified information provided by the Government Communications Headquarters (GCHQ, on which see below). IGRS has six discrete policy branches, including the Joint Air Reconnaissance Intelligence Centre, the Defence and Security Centre and Military Survey.

DIS analyses GCHQ's signals intelligence with a view to assessing the strength of foreign armies and weaponry, including chemical weapons. Defence attachés at foreign embassies act as information-gatherers in the field. During the Cold War the role of DIS was principally intelligence analysis. In times of war, however, that function changes from intelligence-gathering and analysis to the provision of information for use of troops on the ground, as during the Gulf War.

The Special Air Service: SAS

The Special Air Service was the brainchild of Scots Guards officer David Sterling. Perceiving that the employment of large numbers of troops in wartime made operations vulnerable to detection and attack, Sterling presented his case for an elite core of highly trained and well-equipped soldiers who would operate in small units of four or five, capable of infiltrating an area and taking the enemy by surprise. In Sterling's own words, they would cover

Firstly raids in depth behind the enemy lines, attacking HQ nerve centres, landing grounds, supply lines, etc.; and, secondly, the mounting of sustained strategic offensive activity from several bases within hostile territory and, if the opportunity existed, recruiting, training, arming and coordinating local guerrilla elements.[35]

The original SAS Brigade, formed in 1941, consisted of just seven officers and sixty men. The Regiment is distinctive in several respects. Officers are recruited from other regiments for a three-year term, following which they return to their own units. Leadership is by merit, not rank, and those who do not perform to required standards are dismissed from the Regiment and returned to their units. Training is intensive and operations highly secret. What is known to the outside world comes from histories of the Regiment written by military historians, and from books written by former SAS soldiers.[36] Ken Connor, a former SAS soldier who served with the Regiment for twenty-three years, states that official faith in the SAS was vindicated by 'a series of outstandingly successful raids in the Western Desert; the SAS actually destroyed more enemy aircraft than the Royal Air Force. As the war moved on, it operated with equal distinction, if less dramatic impact, behind enemy lines in the Mediterranean, Italy and northern Europe.'[37] In 1945 the Regiment was disbanded – but not for long. As hot war turned to Cold War and Communism spread its tentacles in different directions around the globe, and the threat of nuclear weapons developed, so too the nations which had comprised the British Empire made their claims, one

[35] Quoted in K. Connor, *Ghost Force: The Secret History of the SAS* (London: Orion Books, 1998), p. 11.
[36] The literature is now extensive. See *inter alia*, J. Adams, *Secret Armies* (London: Hutchinson, 1987); P. de la Billiere, *Storm Command* (London: Collins, 1992) and *Looking for Trouble* (London: HarperCollins, 1994); A. McNab, *Bravo Two Zero* (London: Bantam Press, 1993), and *Immediate Action* (London: Bantam Press, 1995); J. Strawson, *A History of the SAS Regiment* (London: Secker and Warburg, 1984).
[37] Connor, *Ghost Force*, p 12.

by one, peacefully or violently, for self-determination via independence.

In Malaya rebellion broke out in 1948, and in 1950 the SAS was re-formed to operate as counter-terrorists in the peninsula. Its future role included deployment in the Gulf from 1958 to 1959, in Borneo and Brunei from 1962 to 1966, in Aden from 1964 to 1967, the United Arab Emirates from 1970 to 1977, the Falklands War 1982, Afghanistan from 1982 to 1989, the Gulf War from 1990 to 1991, and the former Yugoslavia as it disintegrated into warring factions. The SAS operated in Northern Ireland from 1968 to 1997, its role now heavily focused on countering terrorism. In the 1980 hostage siege at the Iranian Embassy in London, it was the SAS which successfully stormed the building in the full glare of the world's press and television. A further high-profile operation which again focused public attention was the tracking and ultimate killing of three suspected IRA terrorists, intelligence on whom led to the belief that they were about to bomb the British barracks on Gibraltar. Sixteen SAS men were deployed to avert the anticipated terrorist operation. Inaccurate intelligence concerning whether the terrorists were armed and as to whether the bomb was on Gibraltar and about to be activated led to the shooting of the suspects during their attempted arrest.[38]

The Security Service: MI5[39]

In Britain the internal security service is MI5, and operating principally outside the UK is its counterpart MI6, or Secret Intelligence Service (SIS). MI5 officers have no special legal powers in relation to investigation and in practice are assisted by Special Branch of the police in carrying out their functions. Alongside these security forces is the

---

[38] The issue came before the European Court of Human Rights in *McCann, Farrell and Savage v. United Kingdom* (1995) 21 EHRR 97. The Court ruled by a majority that the killings did not violate Article 2 (the right to life), but that the operation lacked appropriate care in the control and organization of the arrest operation. See also H. Kitchin, *Gibraltar Report: An Independent Observer's Report of the Inquest into the Deaths of Mairead Farrell, Daniel McCann and Sean Savage, Gibraltar, September 1988* (London: NCCL, 1989).   [39] The MI prefix stands for military intelligence.

Government Communications Headquarters (GCHQ) which gathers intelligence data from external sources for government eyes only.

In 1909 the internal security service was formed as part of the defence forces of the realm, created not under statute but under the royal prerogative.[40] No Act of Parliament regulated it until 1989. Its origins lie in the threat of German espionage before the First World War. Under Prime Minister Herbert Asquith, the Secret Service Bureau was formed to obtain intelligence about Germany's navy. The service was divided into internal and external operations, Captain Vernon Kell, 'K', of the South Staffordshire Regiment becoming responsible for counter-espionage within Britain, Captain Mansfield Cumming, 'C', responsible for gathering intelligence from outside Britain. The Service became known as MI5 in 1916, and the Security Service in 1931.

The organization of MI5

MI5 states that its role involves the collecting and dissemination of intelligence; the investigation and assessment of threat, and working with others to counter them; advising on protection; and providing effective support for those tasks. In carrying out its functions MI5 states that it is guided by a 'commitment to: legality, integrity, objectivity, a sense of proportion about its work and respect and consideration for each other and for those with whom they work outside the Service'.[41] The Service is headed by a Director General, currently Dr Stephen Lander CBE, and has its headquarters in Westminster. The Service employs some 1,900 staff, 55 per cent of whom are under the age of forty and 47 per cent of whom are women. The Service operates on a budget of some £200 million. In terms of the allocation of funds, in the financial year 1998–9, 30 per cent of funds went to combatting terrorism related to Northern Ireland, 22 per cent to international terrorism, 20 per cent to espionage, 11 per cent on protective security and 7 per cent on serious crime.

The recruitment of civil servants is through the Civil Service Selection Board which subjects candidates to rigorous tests and psychological screening. Traditionally, however, recruitment was informal – characterized by approaches to university students on behalf of the Service,

---

[40] On which see Chapter 1.   [41] See http://www.mi5.gov.uk/state.htm

described by former director of MI5, Stella Rimington, as the 'touch on the shoulder technique'.[42] Heavy reliance was typically placed on university tutors, particularly at Oxford and Cambridge, who would identify a 'suitable' candidate. In addition, joining the Service was an attractive option for former policemen and retired army officers. The result was a Service characterized by white, upper-class, probably Oxbridge-educated, males.[43] Reform was attempted in the 1970s, in an effort to widen the social background of recruits, with vague advertisements appearing in the media. In the 1980s the Service turned to recruiting from universities outside Oxford and Cambridge, and candidates undertook Civil Service Commission examinations and vetting. In their book, Hollingsworth and Fielding describe David Shayler's recruitment: an advertisement in the *Independent on Sunday*, entitled 'Godot Isn't Coming', led to an interview at a recruitment consultancy where psychometric tests and an interview took place. Subsequently Shayler, then a journalist, received a telephone call saying that there was interest in his application. At this point Shayler did not know what the job for which he had applied entailed. When he asked specifically, he was told it was in the Ministry of Defence, but a secret position. In a subsequent interview with an unidentified retired MI5 officer, Shayler finally learned that the job was with MI5, at which point he was required to sign the Official Secrets Act. Further interviews took place at the Civil Service Selection Board office. Security vetting, and eventually a job offer, followed.[44]

Organizationally, MI5 is divided into a number of Branches, A Branch dealing with operational support for officers and agents, B Branch dealing with protective security for MI5, personnel, training and recruitment. D Branch deals with non-terrorist organizations, the vetting of people outside MI5, counter-espionage particularly in relation to Russia and China, and organized crime. G Branch is devoted to international terrorism, while H Branch is concerned with corporate affairs, liaising

---

[42] 'Investors in People Annual Lecture', 1998. See also Hollingsworth and Fielding, *Defending the Realm*, chapter 2.

[43] An official pamphlet issued in 1993 stated that approximately a quarter of General Intelligence officers in MI5 were Oxbridge graduates.

[44] On David Shayler see further below.

with police, customs, ports and immigration. T Branch is concerned with Irish terrorism.

Security Service files

The absence of any right to official information makes it impossible for citizens to know whether the Security Service has a file on them, or to gain access to the information contained in it. Whereas in the United States, citizens are entitled to information gathered by the security agencies about themselves and access to their security file, in Britain this data is carefully guarded. The first citizen to discover that he had a file was Timothy Garton Ash, an Oxford historian who had been approached by SIS (MI6) in 1978, but declined. In *The File: A Personal History*,[45] the author reveals his astonishment at the admission by a security service officer, in an interview at Thames House, that it had a file on him, which he was not allowed to see, but which was classified as a 'white card file', meaning its subject was 'non-adversarial'.

Not even the Home Secretary, constitutionally the minister responsible for the Security Service, has access to his security file or the information contained within it. Former MI5 officer David Shayler revealed that MI5 had files on Home Secretary Jack Straw and the Secretary of State for Northern Ireland, Peter Mandelson. In Jack Straw's case, MI5's file had been opened because Straw was President of the National Union of Students between 1969 and 1971 at a time when the Communist Party was active in student politics, even though Straw himself was not a Party member. The file came to light in 1974 when Straw was in line for appointment by Barbara Castle, then Social Services Secretary, as her political adviser and security vetting of appointees was the norm. When he subsequently became Home Secretary, he declined to view the file, regarding it as an abuse of his official position to do so.[46] In the case of Peter Mandelson, his file was apparently opened in 1972 on the basis that he was a member of the Communist Party, an assumption made as a result of his joining the Young Communist League at the age of seventeen when a grammar school pupil. David Shayler, who reviewed Mandelson's file in 1992, was surprised to find

[45] London: HarperCollins, 1997.
[46] *How to be Home Secretary*, BBC2, 24 January 1999.

an active file on someone who had merely engaged in youthful left-wing politics at school. The Director General of MI5 denied that Mandelson's telephone had been 'bugged' by the Service, although David Shayler's record seems to confirm that it had been.[47]

In February 2000 it was alleged that the former Beatle John Lennon had been the subject of MI5 and Federal Bureau of Investigation (FBI) scrutiny in the 1970s. Evidence before a Los Angeles court revealed that Lennon, murdered in New York City in 1980, and his wife Yoko Ono had been spied on by the FBI for a period of fifteen months on the orders of its director, Edgar J. Hoover, at President Richard Nixon's request. It was thought by the American government that Lennon, who was seeking American citizenship, was an influence on American youth at the time of the Vietnam War and the civil unrest provoked by its opponents. David Shayler faxed an affidavit to the court, stating that he had read an MI5 file on John Lennon. The file contained results of a surveillance operation carried out in the 1960s as well as allegations that Lennon had made substantial donations to the Workers' Revolutionary Party (WRP) and contributions to the Irish Republican Army. It appears from the evidence thus far released that the FBI had received details of security information obtained through MI5's operation. The judge has ordered the FBI to release its data, something which the FBI is resisting on the basis that much of its evidence is data 'belonging to a foreign power'.[48]

According to MI5, there exist detailed criteria governing the opening of files on individuals and organizations, and files are kept under 'continual review and are formally checked for currency, relevance and propriety on an annual basis': a claim which runs contrary to the allegations discussed above. A total of 410,000 files have been opened since MI5 was established in 1909. Of these, some 40,000 concern 'subjects and organizations studied by the Service'. A further 75,000 concern people or groups who have not been the subject of investigation by the Service, but who have had contact with the Service, for example through receiving protective security advice. About 260,000 files relate to individuals or organizations who may have been subject to inquiry

---

[47] See Hollingsworth and Fielding, *Defending the Realm*, chapter 4.
[48] See *Sunday Times* and *Observer*, 20 February 2000.

or investigation by MI5. The number of files relating to individuals who may be under current investigation is around 20,000, of which about a third relate to foreign nationals, and the remaining 13,000 are active files on United Kingdom citizens.

The Secret Intelligence Service: SIS or MI6

The SIS was founded to undertake security activities overseas. Like its domestic counterpart, the Security Service, it was originally unregulated by Parliament, and remained so until 1994 when Parliament passed the Intelligence Services Act. Headed by a Director General, David Spedding, the SIS has a staff of less than 2,000 and an estimated annual budget of £140 million. The SIS deals with information-gathering and operations outside the United Kingdom. Whereas a degree of openness has been established concerning the work of MI5, the work of SIS remains closely guarded. It was only in 1992 that the then Prime Minister, John Major, acknowledged publicly for the first time that the Service existed. It is SIS which – together with military intelligence and the work of GCHQ – gathers intelligence from around the world through espionage and covert action. The SIS is formally under the control of the Foreign and Commonwealth Office, and requires its approval before launching operations. Politically sensitive matters require the personal approval of the Foreign Secretary. While in theory the SIS is confined to operations outside the United Kingdom, and hands responsibility over to MI5 once a matter becomes 'internal', there have been doubts expressed as to whether the boundaries are, or indeed can be, so clearly drawn.

The SIS is divided into General Service and Intelligence Branch. Within the latter are the high-flyers who traditionally served in the Soviet Bloc area. With the KGB having an estimated 100,000 counter-intelligence operatives in the Soviet Union, the work of the SIS in recruiting and running agents during the Cold War was both difficult and dangerous.

The KGB secured a number of significant recruits from within the British security forces (Blunt, Burgess, Cairncross, Maclean and Philby, and later Michael Bettany and Geoffrey Prime) and elsewhere (Melita

Norwood and Michael Smith[49]). One of the SIS's most notable successes was Oleg Gordievsky. Gordievsky had become disenchanted with the Communist regime in 1968 following the Soviet Union's invasion of Czechoslovakia. A KGB officer, he was twice posted to Copenhagen charged with the task of 'acquiring intelligence' and 'subverting Western policy and institutions',[50] and it was here in 1972 that he cautiously made contact with British SIS agents. He was formally recruited by the SIS in 1974, and in 1982 was posted to London. From this position, he was able to inform MI5 of the KGB's activities in Britain:[51] the KGB's objectives being 'to recruit agents who would be able to steal classified information of military or political value'.[52] Among the British targets of the KGB identified by Gordievsky (cautious in light of the law of libel) were left-wing politicians and trade union leaders who could be expected to be sympathetic to the Communist cause.

In the 1980s, with the Conservative government in power, the Labour Party was targeted in the hope that it would re-enter power. The Labour Party under its then leader Michael Foot – codenamed Boot by the KGB – was at that time advocating policies of unilateral nuclear disarmament, the removal of American nuclear bases from Britain and the refusal to deploy American Cruise missiles. Bruce Kent and Joan Ruddock, then respectively general secretary and chairman of the Campaign for Nuclear Disarmament (CND), were natural targets for the KGB, as were the leaders of trade unions among which Gordievsky mentions TASS the white collar union, the Seamen's Union, ASLEF the rail drivers' union, NATSOPA the print union, and Jack Jones head of the Trades Union Congress.[53] Tam Dalyell, Labour Member of Parliament for Linlithgow and a constant thorn in the Conservative government's side over his stand on the Argentinian cruiser the *General Belgrano* (torpedoed by the British in the Falklands War), was courted by the

---

[49] An electronics engineer arrested in 1992 on charges of espionage for the Russians. Smith had worked on classified defence projects. He was sentenced to twenty-five years, reduced to twenty years on appeal.

[50] See O. Gordievsky, *Next Stop Execution* (London: Macmillan, 1995), p. 191.

[51] See Andrew and Mitrokhin, *Mitrokhin Archive*, pp. 563–9.

[52] Ibid., p. 275.

[53] Gordievsky suggests that there were twenty-three KGB and fifteen GRU (military intelligence) agents working at the London embassy.

KGB, although Gordievsky doubted whether Dalyell 'realized that he had been dealing with a secret intelligence officer'. So extensive were the KGB's contacts with senior politicians and union leaders that, in Gordievsky's assessment, had the Labour Party won the 1983 general election, the 'KGB would have been in a strong position'. Small wonder that MI5's counter-intelligence gathering included those suspected of being targets of the KGB. In 1985 Gordievsky was betrayed by Aldrich Ames, an American intelligence officer arrested for spying for the Russians in 1994 and sentenced to life imprisonment. Gordievsky was returned to Moscow, interrogated and under the threat of death when an escape plan designed by the SIS was activated and he was rescued by agents and brought to Britain where he was to complete MI5's and MI6's knowledge of KGB methods and operations.[54]

Of major significance also was the achievement of the SIS in exfiltrating Vasili Mitrokhin, his family and six cases of notes on top secret KGB files, in 1992 from Russia. His presence in Britain remained a secret until the publication of *The Mitrokhin Archive: The KGB in Europe and the West* in 1999. Mitrokhin had worked for nearly thirty years in the foreign intelligence archives of the KGB. Over twelve years until his retirement in 1984, he laboriously compiled copious notes, smuggling them out of KGB premises and hiding them in a milk-churn beneath his dacha. In 1992 he left Moscow for the capital of an unnamed independent Baltic republic, and there presented himself to the British Embassy. A month later he met representatives from the SIS, and in September arrived in England. For three years he worked on his archive and in 1995 met Christopher Andrew[55] with whom he worked on *The Mitrokhin Archive*.

Among an unprecedented compendium of previously unpublished KGB data, it was revealed that from 1937 Melita Norwood, then a secretary at the British Non-Ferrous Metals Research Association, had been passing secrets to the KGB. Mrs Norwood was, 'on present evi-

---

[54] The KGB was reorganized in 1991 on the break-up of the Soviet Union. The overseas espionage service became the SVR, the signals intelligence arm became independent and the internal role of the KGB was transferred to a new Ministry for Security, MBR. Military intelligence remained unchanged.

[55] Professor of Modern and Contemporary History at the University of Cambridge and an authority on intelligence matters.

dence, both the most important British female agent in KGB history and the longest-serving of all Soviet spies in Britain'.[56] In December 1999 it was announced that Mrs Norwood, by then an eighty-seven-year-old great-grandmother, who had spied for the Russians for forty years, would escape prosecution for betraying nuclear secrets.[57] According to the Director General of MI5, Stephen Lander, Mrs Norwood – dubbed by *The Times* 'the spy who came in from the Co-op' – came to the attention of the security service in 1966, but was subsequently regarded as of relative unimportance, a view sharply conflicting with that of Christopher Andrew, who described her as 'an important, determined and very valuable spy'.[58]

When the threat of Communism lifted around 1990, one of the security forces' most important functions changed. No longer were the majority of its resources, financial and human, devoted to intelligence-gathering and counter-intelligence in relation to the threat presented to democracy by Communist ambitions. The security service had to redefine its goals, and find for itself a meaningful role for the future. With the ending of the Cold War, the break-up of the Soviet Union and the demise of Communism, economic espionage, in the form of scientific and technical intelligence, appears to have assumed new prominence for Russian intelligence, as has countering the threats of international criminal gangs, particularly the Russian mafia.[59]

Government Communications Headquarters: GCHQ

GCHQ's origins lie back in 1919, when the Government Code and Cipher School was established. In 1922 the School came under the control of the Foreign Office. It played a crucial role in the Second World War, deciphering the German Enigma code which enabled

---

[56] *Mitrokhin Archive*, p. 152.
[57] The Solicitor-General also announced that four other spies would escape prosecution.
[58] C. Andrew, 'Extraordinary secrets of the KGB that took my breath away', *The Times*, 14 June 2000.
[59] See M. Urban, *UK Eyes Alpha: The Inside Story of British Intelligence* (London: Faber & Faber, 1996), chapter 17.

Britain to 'foil Luftwaffe bombing raids, minimize U-Boat attacks and secure sea-based supply routes'. In 1946 the service became GCHQ, moving to Cheltenham, Gloucestershire, from London in 1952. GCHQ is the largest of the security agencies in terms of personnel, having some 4,500 staff at bases in Cheltenham, Cornwall and Scarborough, and an estimated budget in 2000 of £460 million. The focus of GCHQ's work changed significantly with the ending of the Cold War and the break-up of the Soviet Union in 1991. Its new emphasis, in place of the Soviet Bloc, is national security, economic well-being and the prevention and detection of serious crime.

The Intelligence Services Act 1994 placed GCHQ on a statutory basis, and defined its remit as acting 'in the interests of national security, with particular reference to the defence and foreign policies of Her Majesty's government in the United Kingdom'. The Director of GCHQ is responsible for the 'efficiency of the agency' and has a right of access to the Prime Minister and Secretary of State for Foreign and Commonwealth Affairs. The Act authorized the monitoring of communications with 'electromagnetic, acoustic and other emissions and any equipment'. As with the Interception of Communications Act 1985 and the Security Services Act 1989, a Commissioner and Tribunal were established to deal with complaints arising from GCHQ operations.

The Act is silent on the issue of international co-operation. However, such co-operation is a vital component of GCHQ's work. During the Gulf War, co-operation between the United States National Security Agency (NSA) and GCHQ enabled the government to keep abreast of Saddam Hussein's movements and intentions. Mark Urban records that the NSA intercepted calls between the Iraqi ambassador to the United Nations, which were then relayed from the NSA to the United Kingdom.

Co-ordination of intelligence: the Joint Intelligence Committee

In the Cabinet Office is the Joint Intelligence Committee (JIC) which co-ordinates the work of the SIS and GCHQ, and agrees intelligence requirements. The head of the JIC reports to the Cabinet Secretary and through him to the Prime Minister. The JIC has around thirty members, drawn on secondment from the Foreign Office and Ministry of Defence. Membership of the JIC includes the Director of GCHQ, the Chief of the Secret Intelligence Service, Chief of Defence Intelligence Staff and the Director General of the Security Service. Divided into geographic areas and by functions, the JIC meets weekly to review assessments. MI5 contributes intelligence to the JIC on national matters and particularly on Northern Ireland. The JIC also makes international assessments, drawing on intelligence from other agencies such as the United States Central Intelligence Agency (CIA). The intelligence requirements are reviewed annually by the Intelligence Co-ordinator. James Adams and Mark Urban, both of whom have researched the work of the JIC, differ in their evaluation of the Committee's worth. In Adams's view, compared with the unwieldy American intelligence system of analysis which involves thousands of analysts, the small JIC team produces analysis which is 'as good and frequently better than anything produced by the CIA'. The JIC produces a single unanimous report which goes to ministers and which 'represents the distillation of all the available intelligence as well as a recommendation for action or a firm conclusion . . . The finished product is therefore not the lowest common denominator but a fairly forthright view from independent analysts.'[60] Although Mark Urban supports the view that the JIC method 'has clear advantages over the US approach', he is more critical of the value of JIC reports, the effect of which is that '[I]ntelligence becomes sanitized to the point of blandness, and the views expressed represent an interdepartmental lowest common denominator'.[61] Whichever evaluation is correct, clearly there are limitations to what the JIC can achieve. It failed, for example, to predict the Argentinian invasion of the Falkland Islands in 1982, perhaps not surprisingly given that the SIS had only one officer in Latin America at the time. It also failed to assess accurately Saddam Hussein's intention to invade Kuwait, despite intelligence on Iraq's weapons build-up following the Iran–Iraq War. Nor was the Committee able to inform Prime Minister Margaret Thatcher about developments within Gorbachov's government. During her 1987 visit to the Soviet Union Mrs Thatcher told Gorbachov that the view from the West revealed

---

[60] Adams, *New Spies*, p. 43.   [61] Urban, *UK Eyes Alpha*, p. 296.

'Soviet subversion in South Yemen, in Ethiopia, in Mozambique, in Angola and Nicaragua. We saw Vietnam being supported by the Soviet Union in its conquest of Cambodia. We saw Afghanistan occupied by Soviet troops. We naturally drew the conclusion that the goal of worldwide communism was still being pursued.'[62]

In relation to GCHQ, which co-operates with the signals intelligence agencies of the United States, Canada, Australia and New Zealand, dividing up geographical responsibilities and sharing data, the raw material leaves Cheltenham for analysis by the Assessments Staff of the JIC. The end product of this analysis is the Weekly Survey of Intelligence, generally called the Red Book which goes to all the main government ministries. In addition, GCHQ produces its own digest of signals intelligence reports, the Blue Book; the Ministry of Defence also has a Weekly Intelligence Summary; and the SIS produces its Weekly Summary of Intelligence, CX or CX Book. The extent to which Prime Ministers involve themselves routinely in intelligence matters varies: Margaret Thatcher was known to take not only the Red Book but also the Blue Book and the CX Book to Chequers[63] at weekends.

The JIC does not determine the priorities of MI5. These are approved by a separate Cabinet Office interdepartmental committee, called SO(SSPP). Close links, however, are maintained between the JIC and MI5, with its Director General being a member of JIC. MI5 and SIS also co-operate to avoid duplication, and their financial resources in some areas are shared. The Security Service also contributes intelligence to the JIC Assessments Staff, and is a major customer for intelligence produced by SIS and GCHQ, particularly in relation to terrorism.

Agency proliferation and the future organization of security forces

With MI5, SIS or MI6, GCHQ, Customs and Excise, the National Crime Squad and National Criminal Intelligence Service all playing a role in the intelligence business and undercover operations, particularly in

[62] Thatcher, *Downing Street Years*, p. 481.
[63] The British Prime Minister's official residence outside Downing Street.

relation to organized crime, the inevitable question which arises is whether there need be such a proliferation of organizations, each protecting its own turf and duplicating investigations at public expense and probably at the expense of efficiency and effectiveness. Rivalry between MI5 and SIS has always been apparent. The SIS regards itself as the superior agency, characterized by university graduates and disdaining the more mundane, desk-bound domestic agency, MI5: the 'swashbuckling adventurers' versus the 'plodding bureaucrats'.[64] In 2000 a Home Office working party, headed by Home Secretary Jack Straw was investigating just such issues. The changing nature of security threats following the break-up of the Soviet Union, and the diversion of financial and human resources to combatting terrorist threats, also brings into question the division of labour, especially between the two principal agencies, the SIS and MI5.

The problem of Irish terrorism highlights the overlapping of the agencies' functions, but also has much to say about the problems of managing a single problem through the use of a number of differing forces.[65] Theoretically, Northern Ireland, being part of the United Kingdom, is the territory of MI5, while the Republic of Ireland is within the SIS's domain. Civil unrest in Northern Ireland escalated in the 1960s, with protests by the Catholic minority population against discrimination in employment, education and housing, and the lack of democratic representation in the Northern Ireland Assembly, Stormont. British troops were despatched to the province to back up the Protestant-dominated Royal Ulster Constabulary (RUC), another source of disquiet among the Catholic population. In 1976, with over 15,000 British troops in the province, the government sent in the SAS. Intelligence-gathering about the increased activity of the Irish Republican Army (IRA) was the responsibility of MI5 working with the RUC's Special Branch, although the army had also established the 14th Intelligence and Security Group to gather intelligence on terrorist suspects. However, the RUC, keen to protect its territory from outsiders, introduced its own covert surveillance section, the Special Support Unit (SSU) trained by the SAS. In 1978, following the murder of Captain Robert Nairac and an ambush of the SAS by members of the IRA, a

---

[64] Adams, *New Spies*, p. 99.   [65] See ibid., especially chapters 14 and 15.

new system of co-ordinating intelligence was put in place. In 1991 MI5 was given overall responsibility for the running of agents and intelligence analysis against the IRA on a world-wide basis. As the IRA increased its terrorist activity on mainland Britain, the counter-terrorist branch of the Metropolitan Police, SO13, developed the capability to despatch a rapid-reaction force to any part of the country. However, as James Adams argues, their use was dependent upon the willingness – which was slight – of the fifty-plus regional police forces to call them in. Notwithstanding the counter-terrorist agencies' efforts, as noted above, the IRA still managed to cause havoc in London and Manchester. The need for a nation-wide force devoted to countering terrorist activity has long been recognized, but resisted by local police forces: the introduction of the National Criminal Intelligence Service, discussed on pages 368–9, goes some way towards the better co-ordination of criminal and terrorist activity.

Whistleblowing: in the public interest?

For most citizens, awareness of the work of the agencies engaged in British security has long been confined to John le Carré's novels. Nevertheless, occasionally the cast-iron protective ring designed to ensure that the secret services remain truly secret has over the years failed to prevent the light of publicity falling on those involved in national security. In 1984, a former Security Service officer, Cathy Massiter, revealed on television that MI5 had spied on trade union leaders, the Campaign for Nuclear Disarmament and other 'left-wing' activists. Harriet Harman MP and Patricia Hewitt were officials at the National Council for Civil Liberties when it, like CND and other organizations, had been targeted by MI5 as subversive organizations. Harman and Hewitt applied for remedy under the European Convention on Human Rights, alleging that the government had violated their right to privacy under Article 10 of the Convention, and won.

In 1987 Peter Wright, a former MI5 officer, published his whistleblowing account of the work of the Service, in *Spycatcher*, a book which the government immediately had suppressed by an injunction. Little had been known about the work of MI5 until public attention was grasped by the government's reaction to *Spycatcher*. In its attempt to suppress publication and circulation in Britain the government, without ultimate success, applied for injunctions to restrain the publishers.[66] Before long, the injunction of the House of Lords still in place, *Spycatcher* was available around the world but not in Britain. Most revealing among Wright's allegations, in an often otherwise uninteresting account, was that the Service 'bugged and burgled' its way across London and elsewhere. Equally compelling, if paranoid and subsequently refuted, was the claim that Harold Wilson, leader of the Labour Party and Prime Minister from 1964 to 1970 and 1974 to 1976, was 'planted' by the KGB. Wright claimed that MI5 viewed the Labour Party's electoral victory of 1974 as being against the national interest and instigated a plot to feed anti-Labour information from MI5 files to pro-Conservative newspapers. The *Spycatcher* saga was to result in the passing of the Security Services Act 1989, discussed below.

In 1995 an SIS agent, Richard Tomlinson, was dismissed from the Service and denied the right to appeal to an industrial tribunal for unfair dismissal. His subsequent attempt to publish his memoirs led to prosecution for breach of the Official Secrets Act 1989, and a twelve-month prison sentence. Following his release, Tomlinson left Britain, first for New Zealand, then France and Switzerland, where he remained under threat of extradition proceedings to force his return to Britain to face possible further charges. In 1997 David Shayler, an MI5 officer from 1991 to 1997, made public his criticism of the Service, through contacts with journalists at the *Mail on Sunday*, in breach of the Official Secrets Act 1989. Shayler left the country immediately prior to the *Mail's* first article. Among Shayler's allegations was the claim that SIS was involved in a plot to assassinate the Libyan leader, Muammar Qaddafi, an allegation dismissed by Foreign Secretary Robin Cook as 'pure fantasy', but which appeared to be confirmed by the appearance on the Internet of an SIS document. Shayler also claimed that MI5 had information which could have prevented the bombing of the Israeli Embassy in London in 1994, and that the Service had files on politicians Jack Straw and Peter Mandelson and rock star John Lennon.

When in Paris, Shayler was arrested by the French Security Police at

---

[66] See M. Turnbull, *The Spycatcher Trial* (London: Heinemann, 1988).

the request of the British government with a view to extraditing him to Britain to face charges. After Shayler had spent nearly four months in prison, the French court denied the extradition request, on the basis that extradition for political offences was contrary to French law. Shayler remained in exile, hoping to negotiate with the government in order to return to the United Kingdom free of the threat of further prosecution. His defence against allegations of breach of confidentiality in respect of MI5 was that the absence of any adequate democratic control meant that wrongdoing and malpractice within the Service remained hidden from public view unless and until an insider 'blew the whistle'. He claimed not to have endangered security operations nor the identity of MI5 and SIS officers through his allegations, a view not shared by the government.

What David Shayler sought from the government was an inquiry into the Security Service in relation to his allegations. For its part the government was clearly intent on suppressing any further data stemming from the 'renegade spy'. To do so, the government resorted to law, issuing a writ for breaches of confidence and of contract and infringing Crown copyright through public disclosure. The government also sued the publishers of the *Mail on Sunday*, claiming damages from Associated Newspapers for causing 'injury to the national interest', and sought the return of all MI5 documents which Shayler had passed to the newspaper. Shayler's lawyer, John Wadham, director of the civil rights group Liberty, responded by stating that the case would be fought on 'the basis of freedom of expression and the public's right to know about malpractice in MI5'.[67] David Shayler ended his exile from Britain in August 2000 and was arrested on his arrival and charged under the Official Secrets Act 1989.

The government's obsession with secrecy and the suppression of information about the security forces seemingly borders on paranoia. In 1999 a former RAF squadron leader who served with General Sir Peter de la Billiere's staff in the Gulf War, Tony Geraghty, faced prosecution under the Official Secrets Act 1989 for publishing his book, *The Irish War*, on the troubles in Northern Ireland. Rather than resorting to the courts to obtain an injunction, the Ministry of Defence

[67] See *Guardian*, 26 February 2000.

issued an advisory notice to the publishers HarperCollins, instructing them not to publish. That threat was dropped when the Attorney General decided there was insufficient evidence of proof against the author. Nevertheless, Colonel Nigel Wylde, a decorated bomb-disposal officer who allegedly helped Tony Geraghty, remained targeted by the authorities, under threat of prosecution under section 2 of the Official Secrets Act 1989, notwithstanding the fact that the government had never attempted to take out an injunction to stop publication, and that the information revealed in *The Irish War*, including the security forces' surveillance of the civilian population, was already in the public domain and therefore incapable of damaging the national interest. Following hard on the heels of the attempted suppression of Tony Geraghty's book came the attempted suppression of *She Who Dared*, a book co-authored by an ex-Service woman under the pen-name Jackie George, revealing the work of the undercover, armed, plainclothes operation in Northern Ireland between 1983 and 1988, and thus hardly likely to damage current operations. The manuscript had been sent for clearance to the Ministry of Defence and given that clearance, subject to requested changes. Some two months *after* publication, and notwithstanding its earlier clearance, the Ministry of Defence obtained an injunction requiring the surrender of the book. Tony Geraghty questioned the Ministry of Defence's motives over *She Who Dared*: were the change of heart and now attempted suppression a political reaction due to the sensitivity of the forthcoming report by Chris Patten[68] recommending sweeping changes to the Royal Ulster Constabulary[69] (the unionist-dominated police force reviled by the Catholic community), of which the author was particularly scathing?

From the perspective of the disaffected security service employee, the lifelong duty of confidentiality imposed and the threat of prosecution under the Official Secrets Act 1989, allied to the lack of democratic accountability of the Services to Parliament, means that the only way in which allegations about mismanagement or wrongdoing on the part of the Services can be brought before the public – which, after all,

[68] Former Governor of Hong Kong, 1992–7; appointed by the Labour government to inquire into the much-criticized Royal Ulster Constabulary.
[69] See T. Geraghty, 'She Said Too Much', *Guardian*, 26 February 2000.

finances the Services – is by whistleblowing. Moreover, where a dispute arises between the Services and the employee there is no industrial tribunal to which the case can be taken for hearing. The attempt by Richard Tomlinson to take his grievances to an industrial tribunal led to the Foreign Secretary serving a 'gagging order' on him.[70] Whistleblowing, as seen in relation to Wright, Shayler and Tomlinson, has the inevitable consequence of forcing the renegade officer to flee abroad to avoid prosecution. The lack of democratic oversight of the Services is not something which has found favour elsewhere. In the United States, for example, both the Senate and House of Representatives have select committees on intelligence. The committees have the right to call for witnesses and documents and it is an offence for a security agency not to disclose the details of operations, however sensitive. In Canada, the Security Intelligence Review Committee (SIRC), comprised of Privy Councillors rather than Members of Parliament, has the right of access to any information held by the Canadian Security Intelligence Service (CSIS). Among other functions, the SIRC is required to satisfy itself that the activities of the CSIS 'do not involve any unreasonable or unnecessary exercise by the service of any of its powers'.[71] One of the major strengths of the SIRC is that it has a proactive capability: it need not wait for a request for investigation into CSIS activities.

In Britain, following a security scare in 1964 involving the Minister for War, John Profumo, a prostitute and a naval attaché, the Prime Minister announced the creation of a Security Commission. The Commission investigates and reports upon the circumstances in which a breach of security is known to have occurred in the public service, and upon any related failure of departmental security arrangements or neglect of duty, and advises whether any change in security arrangements is desirable.[72] However, the Commission meets at the request of the Prime Minister who consults the Leader of the Opposition and the Chairman of the Commission before making a reference to it. The Commission accordingly has no power of initiative in relation to the

[70] The chairman of the Intelligence and Security Committee, Tom King, called for the establishment of a special industrial tribunal to handle potentially highly sensitive cases: *The Times*, 22 October 1998.

[71] Canadian Security Intelligence Services Act 1984, section 40.

[72] See Hansard, HC Deb. cols. 1271–5, 23 January 1964.

matters it investigates. The Commission has undertaken inquiries, *inter alia*, into the conduct of former ministers,[73] into allegations that the head of MI5, Roger Hollis, was a KGB spy,[74] into investigations relating to GCHQ, and into the circumstances surrounding the conviction of Geoffrey Prime for spying for the KGB and passing on valuable information to the Russians which enabled them to protect their intelligence network. The position of witnesses before the Commission is weak: no legal representation is allowed. The Commission reports to the Prime Minister. But while the Commission is useful in investigating specific aspects of security at the behest of the Prime Minister, it has no role to play in hearing the grievances of disaffected service officers. Its jurisdiction arises when and only when the executive so determines.[75]

THE LEGAL FRAMEWORK

By 1989, as seen from the definitions of national security at pages 357–8 above, subversion had been eliminated from the 1952 catalogue of functions and by 1996 the prevention and detection of serious crime added to the Service's functions. A close reading of the statutory definition of the Service's functions, however, masks a number of significant questions concerning what the various phrases mean in practical terms, and the manner in which the Service works and the extent to which MI5's operations intrude on the lives and privacy of ordinary law-abiding citizens.

Prior to 1989 the Home Secretary had the responsibility for issuing warrants for surveillance operations, not under statute but under the prerogative. No one had authority to review the exercise of this power. That the power was legitimately exercised rested with the integrity of the Home Secretary operating under the rather vague definition of

---

[73] *Earl Jellicoe and Lord Lambton*, Cmnd. 5367 (London: HMSO, 1973).

[74] The Report remained unpublished.

[75] The Joint Intelligence Committee (JIC) also has no role to play in defusing conflicts between the Service and its employees. Its role is confined to the analysis and co-ordination of intelligence data and agreeing intelligence requirements, and making recommendations to ministers for approval.

national security. The courts of law exercise a self-restraining principle when it comes to pleas of national or state security – namely that such matters are for the executive to determine, not the courts.

It was the European Court of Human Rights which first forced the British government to move towards statutory regulation of the agencies and functions relating to national security. The catalyst for the first Act of Parliament was the case of *Malone v. Metropolitan Police Commissioner*,[76] the outcome of which resulted in an application under the European Convention on Human Rights alleging violation of the right to privacy guaranteed under Article 8. The defendant in criminal proceedings, Malone, had had his telephone tapped at the request of the police and on the authority of the Home Secretary. At the time, there was no statutory basis for the Home Secretary's power to authorize such interference. The evidence acquired as a result of the tap was presented to the court, a hapless policeman revealing that the evidence had come to light through a telephone intercept. The court was obliged to rule that there had been no illegality on the part of the authorities: the defendant had no recognized right to privacy under domestic law and the authorities had not, so the court ruled, trespassed on Malone's property. The judge declared that the issue was one which 'cried out for legislation'. In *Malone v. United Kingdom*[77] the Court of Human Rights ruled that Article 8 (the right to respect for private and family life, home and correspondence) had been violated. The Court ruled that the law was unclear and that accordingly 'the minimum degree of legal protection to which citizens are entitled under the rule of law in a democratic society is lacking'. In response the government introduced the Interception of Communications Act 1985.[78] The Act gave statutory authority to the Home Secretary to issue warrants, and introduced a Commissioner to investigate complaints relating to interceptions and a Tribunal to adjudicate on complaints. Ironically, however, the Act also made it clear that the existence or non-existence of warrants for intercepts could not be revealed to a court of law – thereby removing the possibility of further inadvertent and embarrassing public revelations.

[76] [1979] Ch 344.   [77] (1982) 5 EHRR 385.
[78] The Act is repealed by the Regulation of Investigatory Powers Act 2000.

Next in line for parliamentary attention was MI5. As described above, in 1987 a former MI5 officer, Peter Wright, in his autobiography *Spycatcher: The Candid Autobiography of a Senior Intelligence Officer*,[79] caused the government acute anxiety: not (perhaps) so much for what *Spycatcher* revealed – much of which was already known or suspected – but rather for the fact that the book was published at all. In the government's view, not only did such a work contravene the Official Secrets Act 1911 (as it then was), but it also violated the lifelong duty of confidentiality which security service personnel owed to the government. Prompted by Wright, the government introduced the Security Services Act 1989 which not only gave a statutory definition of the functions of MI5, but also introduced a complaints procedure for individuals aggrieved by actions of the Security Service and a Commissioner charged with the task of reviewing the procedure by which the Home Secretary issues warrants. However, the 1989 Act did not regulate either SIS, or Special Branch which carries out many of the functions of MI5, or GCHQ.

Statutory recognition of SIS and GCHQ came in 1994 with the Intelligence Services Act. As with the 1989 Act, the 1994 Act provides for procedures for the authorization of warrants for interference with property, and establishes a Commissioner and Tribunal. To the statutory framework regulating the services must now be added the Regulation of Investigatory Powers Act 2000 (RIPA), introduced to ensure that the security services' investigatory powers are used in accordance with the requirements of the Human Rights Act 1998.

The Regulation of Investigatory Powers Act 2000 provides a statutory basis for the authorization and use by the security and intelligence agencies, law enforcement and other public authorities, of covert surveillance, agents, informants and undercover officers. It is intended to regulate the use of such techniques and 'safeguard the public from unnecessary invasions of their privacy'.[80] Surveillance may be 'directed' or 'intrusive'. Surveillance is 'directed' if it is covert but not intrusive and is undertaken for the purpose of specific investigations. It is 'intrusive' if

---

[79] New York: Viking, 1987.

[80] Explanatory Note to the Regulation of Investigatory Powers Bill 2000, issued by the Home Office, paragraph 10.

it is covert surveillance that either involves the presence of an individual, or of any surveillance device, on any residential premises or in any private vehicle; or is carried out in relation to anything taking place on residential premises or in a private vehicle by means of any surveillance device that is not present on the premises or in the vehicle. Surveillance is not intrusive if it is carried out by means of a device designed or adapted principally for the purposes of providing information about the location of a vehicle, or if it is surveillance consisting in any such interception of a communication. Surveillance which is carried out by means of a device in relation to a residential premises or private vehicle, but is carried out without the device being present on the premises or in the vehicle, is not intrusive 'unless the device is such that it consistently provides information of the same quality and detail as might be expected to be obtained from a device actually present on the premises or in the vehicle'.

In relation to agents, a person is a 'covert human intelligence source' if he or she establishes or maintains a personal or other relationship with a person for the covert purpose of obtaining information or providing access to any information to another person, or the covert disclosure of information obtained by the use of such a relationship. The surveillance is covert if, and only if, it is carried out in a manner that is calculated to ensure that persons who are subject to the surveillance are unaware that it is or may be taking place. A purpose is covert if the relationship established or maintained is conducted in a manner calculated to ensure that one of the parties to the relationship is unaware of the purpose, and a relationship is used covertly, and information disclosed covertly, if it is used or disclosed in a manner calculated to ensure that one of the parties to the relationship is unaware of the use or disclosure.

Where authorization has been given for an operation, the conduct of the operation is lawful for all purposes provided that the conduct is in accordance with the authorization. The conduct authorized includes conduct outside the United Kingdom. Those designated to have power to grant authorizations must not grant an authorization for the conduct or use of covert human intelligence sources unless he or she believes that the authorization is necessary in the interests of national security; for the purpose of preventing or detecting crime or of preventing disorder; in the interests of the economic well-being of the United Kingdom; in the interests of public safety; for the purpose of protecting public health; for the purpose of assessing or collecting taxes or charges due to a government department or for any purpose which is specified by an order made by the Secretary of State. Furthermore, an authorization must not be granted unless the designated person believes that the authorized conduct is proportionate to what is sought to be achieved by that conduct or use. Finally, an authorization must not be granted unless there are arrangements in place which satisfy the statutory requirements relating both to the control of and the safety of agents. The measures are intended to ensure that agents and undercover officers act only within the strict scope of the authorization given, in order to protect the public from unnecessary intrusions on their privacy.

The Secretary of State is a designated person for the purposes of authorization for directed surveillance and the use of covert human intelligence sources combined with intrusive surveillance.[81] Otherwise the persons designated are senior officers of relevant public authorities – being the police, National Criminal Intelligence Service, National Crime Squad, the intelligence services, Ministry of Defence, Her Majesty's forces, Commissioners of Customs and Excise and any other such public authority granted power by order of the Secretary of State.[82] In relation to Northern Ireland, the grant of authorization is also exercisable by the First Minister and deputy First Minister acting jointly.[83] Neither the Secretary of State nor any senior authorizing officer shall grant an authorization for the carrying out of intrusive surveillance unless he or she believes that the authorization is necessary in the interests of national security, for the purpose of preventing or detecting serious crime, or in the interests of the economic well-being of the United Kingdom, and that the authorized surveillance is proportionate to what is sought to be achieved by carrying it out.[84]

---

[81] Ibid., section 29(2). [82] Ibid., section 29(4). [83] Ibid., section 29(6).
[84] Ibid., section 30.

Commissioners and the Tribunal

The 2000 Act repeals and replaces former provisions relating to Tribunals.[85] The Act imposes additional functions on the Security Services Act Commissioner and the Intelligence Services Act Commissioner, requiring them to keep under review, respectively – so far as they are not required to be kept under review by the Interception of Communications Commissioner (on which office see below) – the performance by the Secretary of State in relation to activities of the Security Service and activities of the Secret Intelligence Service and of GCHQ, and the activities in places other than Northern Ireland of officials of the Ministry of Defence and members of Her Majesty's forces.[86]

The Interception of Communications Commissioner is appointed by the Prime Minister.[87] A person may only be appointed as Interception of Communications Commissioner if he or she holds or has held a high judicial office.[88] The Commissioner is under a duty to assist the Tribunal in connection with the investigation of any matter by the Tribunal, or otherwise for the purposes of the Tribunal's consideration or determination of any matter. It is not the Commissioner's function to keep under review the exercise of any power of the Secretary of State to make, amend or revoke any subordinate legislation. It is the duty of all persons employed by the security and intelligence services and police to disclose or provide to the Commissioner all such documents and information as he or she may require for the purposes of enabling him or her to carry out his or her functions. If it appears to the Commissioner that there has been a contravention of the provisions of the Act in relation to matters with which he is concerned, and that the contravention has not been the subject of a report made to the Prime Minister

[85] The Act repeals section 5 and Schedule 1 of the Security Services Act 1989 which provided for a Tribunal to investigate complaints. Section 9 and Schedules 1 and 2 of the Intelligence Services Act 1994 which also provided for a Tribunal are repealed and replaced by the Regulation of Supervisory Powers Act 2000, Part IV.

[86] Additional functions are also conferred on the Chief Surveillance Commissioner whose powers derive from the Police Act 1997.

[87] The current Commissioner is Lord Nolan.

[88] Regulation of Investigatory Powers Act 2000, section 53.

by the Tribunal, the Commissioner must report to the Prime Minister. The Commissioner makes an annual report to the Prime Minister. The annual report is to be laid before each House of Parliament. If it appears to the Prime Minister, after consultation with the Interception of Communications Commissioner, that the publication of any matter in an annual report would be contrary to the public interest or prejudicial to national security, the prevention or detection of serious crime, the economic well-being of the United Kingdom or the continued discharge of the functions of any public authority whose activities include activities that are subject to review by the Commissioner, the Prime Minister may exclude that matter from the report laid before each House.[89]

The Interception of Communications Commissioner's Report for 1998[90] revealed that the number of warrants in force on 31 December 1998 and issued during the course of 1998 totalled 2,196 issued by the Home Secretary and 322 issued by the Secretary of State for Scotland. Of the former, 2,031 related to telecommunications, and 165 to letters.[91] The Commissioner reported that he had 'found no case in which the information supplied to the Secretary of State has been materially incomplete or inaccurate'. Nor had he found any 'case where the Secretary of State had issued or renewed a warrant without adequate justification'.[92] However, the Commissioner reported that the police and Customs and Excise had previously made extensive use of their capability to intercept radio pagers used by suspects engaged in serious crime. Until 1992, intercept powers were considered to fall within the provisions of the 1985 Act. The interception of radio pagers was then stopped on legal advice, following which Customs and Excise continued to conduct pager intercepts relying on the Wireless and Telegraphy Act 1949,[93] while the police relied on production orders granted by the Crown Court.[94] The latter practice was challenged by a judge at Worcester Crown Court who refused to grant a production order on two

---

[89] Ibid., section 54.

[90] *The Fifth Annual Report*, Cm. 4364 (London: HMSO, 1999).

[91] In 1999, the Home Secretary issued 1,645 telephone intercept warrants, and 89 postal intercept warrants. The First Secretary of Scotland authorized 288 telephone intercepts but no postal intercepts: *Sunday Times*, 9 July 2000.

[92] *Fifth Annual Report*, paragraph 10.   [93] Section 9.

[94] Under section 9 of the Police and Criminal Evidence Act 1984.

bases. First, that there could be no production order in relation to material which was not yet in existence (namely, a pager message). Secondly, the judge stated that the police had no power to intercept the messages, on the basis that the Act on which the police then relied covered only 'servants of the Crown', and as a matter of law police officers are not servants of the Crown. On the other hand, Customs and Excise were unaffected by that ruling, since they are servants of the Crown. The Association of Chief Police Officers advised all Chief Constables to suspend pager intercepts until a firm legal base was identified.[95]

The Tribunal is the only tribunal to which proceedings may be brought alleging that the security services have violated an individual's human rights.[96] The conduct complained of must have been conduct by or on behalf of a person acting for any of the intelligence services, any of Her Majesty's forces, any police force, the National Criminal Intelligence Service, National Crime Squad or Commissioners of Customs and Excise.[97] It is the duty of the Tribunal to hear and determine any proceedings brought, to consider and determine any complaint or reference made to them and to investigate any alleged conduct, the authority for any conduct which they find has been engaged in, and to determine the complaint by applying the same principles as would be applied by a court on an application for judicial review. The Tribunal is not under a duty to hear or determine any complaint which is frivolous or vexatious. Complaints must be brought within one year after the conduct to which they relate took place, but the Tribunal may, if it is equitable to do so, extend the time. The Tribunal has the power to make an award of compensation. In addition, the Tribunal may order the quashing or cancelling of any warrant or authorization and/or the destruction of any records or information.[98]

---

[95] Under new arrangements, the intercept of pagers is under the authority of the Home Secretary and Secretaries of State for Scotland and Northern Ireland who nominate officials to carry out the task.
[96] Under the Human Rights Act 1998, section 7.   [97] Ibid., section 57(6).
[98] Ibid., section 59.

The democratic deficit

Despite the relatively recent legislation relating to state security, there remains limited democratic control of the security services. The issuing of warrants, as seen, is a matter for the executive and not the courts of law. While legislation requires that reports on the work of the services are submitted to the Prime Minister, who in turn is required to place these before Parliament, there is the notable limitation that the Prime Minister may exclude from the report any issue which is regarded as too sensitive to reveal to Parliament. Moreover, while the Intelligence Services Act 1994 established the Intelligence and Security Committee (ISC), that Committee is not a parliamentary committee, but rather a committee which meets in the security of the Cabinet Office. The Intelligence and Security Committee itself reports to Parliament, but it was only in 1998 that Parliament had the opportunity to debate its content. The ISC's remit is to examine the expenditure, administration and policies (but not operations) of the Security Service, SIS and GCHQ. The Committee comprises nine parliamentarians, appointed by the Prime Minister following consultation with the opposition, drawn from the House of Commons and House of Lords, and is chaired by a former Conservative Defence Minister, Tom King. The Committee meets in secret and has secure premises. In 1999 the government, at the request of the ISC, appointed an investigator to assist the Committee. The investigator has access to the agencies' staff and papers, subject to requirements of confidentiality.

The ISC produces an Annual Report which goes to the Prime Minister, who, having edited out any sensitive material, lays it before Parliament. Parliament, however, has a minimal role to play in the oversight of the intelligence agencies. In 1992 the Select Committee on Home Affairs requested the then Home Secretary, Kenneth Clarke, to allow it to take evidence from the then Director-General of the Security Service, Stella Rimington. The request was refused. In 1993 the Home Affairs Committee published a report concluding that the Security Service should be made subject to the normal departmental select committee structure. This request also met with a negative response.[99] Then came the introduction of the ISC under the 1994 Act. However, as the ISC was a statutory committee and not a parliamentary committee, it lacked the normal powers of a parliamentary committee. Moreover, its members were appointed and could be dismissed by the Prime Minister, who also had the power to edit the Committee's Annual Report. With the election of the Labour government in 1997 came the commitment to greater openness and the introduction of an annual debate in the Commons on the work of the intelligence and security agencies.

While an improvement on the previous position, in its working the ISC is less than satisfactory. Its Chairman, Tom King, complained in the Commons that the 1998–9 Report, which was sent to the Prime Minister in August 1999, was only responded to by the government in January 2000, and that the debate on the Report only took place in June, five months later.[100] The Chairman stated that '[I]t is unacceptable that there should be such a time lag'.

OFFICIAL SECRECY

British government has always been conducted under a veil of secrecy considerably greater than that in many other democratic states, and nowhere is this more apparent than in relation to the work of the security services. Protecting the national interest through secrecy laws is also a feature of state security. Even democratic states need some measure of secrecy about matters fundamental to their economic, financial, defence and security interests. In Britain since 1911 there has existed an Official Secrets Act which regulates this area. In addition there exists a curious, if not bizarre, system of semi-official yet voluntary suppression of information in the media through Defence Notices.

Personnel of the security services are under a lifelong duty of confidentiality and may not disclose aspects of their work. The first Official Secrets Act was passed in 1911. That Act, passed through Parliament

[99] See Third Report of the Select Committee on Home Affairs: *Accountability of the Security Service.*   [100] *Official Report,* 22 June 2000, col. 487.

within an afternoon, was prompted by the fear of German spies in Britain. Section 1 of the Act, which remains in force, provides penalties for espionage. It is an offence to enter top-secret establishments or to collect, publish or communicate any official document or information which might be useful to a potential enemy, if the actions are carried out 'for any purpose prejudicial to the safety or interest of the state'. The accused has no 'right to silence' and a trial may be held in secret, or partly in secret. It is not necessary for the prosecution to prove that the accused is guilty: guilt may be established if 'from the circumstances of the case, or his conduct, or his known character as proved', it appears that his purpose was prejudicial to the safety or interest of the state. The normal burden of proof is therefore reversed in relation to espionage from the prosecution to the defence. It is also unlawful to hand over to another person, without lawful authority, any information or document. Section 1 of the 1911 Act was used as the basis of a prosecution against members of the Campaign for Nuclear Disarmament, discussed above.

Penalties for spying are harsh. George Blake, a former MI6 officer convicted of espionage, was sentenced to forty-two years' imprisonment.[101] In 1985 Michael Bettany, a former MI5 officer, was convicted of attempting to pass official information to the Russians and sentenced to twenty-three years' imprisonment. Geoffrey Prime, an employee at GCHQ, was sentenced to thirty-five years for disclosing material which assisted Russian intelligence in protecting their own signals intelligence system from eavesdropping by the West.

Section 2 of the 1911 Act, now reformed, was a catch-all device prohibiting the unauthorized disclosure of any official information. As an official inquiry into the Act revealed, section 2 was capable of generating 2,000 different criminal offences, including the disclosure of the number of cups of tea consumed in the MI5 canteen.[102] All civil servants must sign the Official Secrets Act, and it has been used in the past with powerful effect, although it fell into disrepute when a jury acquitted Clive Ponting OBE in the 1980s for passing information,

---

[101] Blake escaped from prison after twenty-five years. In 1989 he published his autobiography. In *Attorney General v. Blake* [1996] *The Times*, 23 April, Sir Richard Scott VC ruled that the Crown was not entitled to the profits gained by Blake through publication.
[102] *Departmental Committee on Section 2 of the Official Secrets Act 1911*, Cmnd. 5104 (London: HMSO, 1972), paragraph 16.

without authority, to a Member of Parliament. The background to the case was the sinking of the Argentinian cruiser the *General Belgrano* in 1982 in the Falklands War.[103] The ship was torpedoed, without prior warning, by a British submarine, with a loss of 323 lives. At the time the *Belgrano* was outside the 200-mile exclusion zone set by the British and had been steaming away from the Falklands for some eleven hours.[104] In Parliament, the government was evasive about the matter. At the time Ponting was head of a Ministry of Defence secretariat and adviser on naval operations. His investigation into the events surrounding the sinking resulted in a high security classified document. When Tam Dalyell unsuccessfully sought clarification in Parliament, Ponting sent him a note encouraging him to persevere. Meanwhile a Committee of the Commons was investigating the matter. Ponting considered that a Ministry of Defence response to Committee questions was misleading; as a result he sent a copy of a confidential memorandum and draft answers to the questions which Dalyell had been pressing in Parliament. Ponting was prosecuted for communicating information to someone other than an authorized person, or someone to whom it would not be in the interests of the state to disclose the information.[105] In his defence, Ponting pleaded public interest in the disclosure of truthful information to Parliament. The judge ruled that a civil servant's duty was his official duty, and that the only relevant interpretation of the 'interest of the state' was the interpretation of the government.

The *Spycatcher* saga and the Ponting trial made reform of the 1911 Act inevitable. In place of the catch-all section 2 of the 1911 Act, the 1989 Act creates offences directed to specific groups of people and information.[106] In relation to most areas, the prosecution must prove both that the information has been unlawfully transmitted and that the disclosure of the information is 'damaging'. The concept of 'damaging

---

[103] See D. Rice and A. Gavshon, *The Sinking of the Belgrano* (London: Secker & Warburg, 1984).

[104] In June 2000 it was reported that relatives of those who died intend to sue the British government under the European Convention on Human Rights.

[105] *R v. Ponting* (1987) 14 JLS 366. See R. Norton-Taylor, *The Ponting Affair* (London: Woolf, 1985).

[106] Security and intelligence, defence, international relations, and crime and special investigation powers.

disclosure', however, has not been incorporated into the Act as it relates to security and intelligence matters. Rather, under section 1 of the Act any person who is, or has been, a member of the security and intelligence services is guilty of an offence if 'without lawful authority' he or she discloses any information, document or other article related to security or intelligence. The ban on disclosures in relation to security matters accordingly imposes a life-long restraint on existing or former members of the services on freedom of expression in relation to security matters.

THE TERRORISM ACT 2000

The Terrorism Act 2000 reforms and extends existing terrorist legislation.[107] It repeals the Prevention of Terrorism (Temporary Provisions) Act 1989, the Prevention of Terrorism (Additional Powers) Act 1996, the Northern Ireland (Emergency Provisions) Act 1996 and the Northern Ireland (Emergency Provisions) Act 1998, and makes minor amendments to other relevant Acts. Whereas the Prevention of Terrorism Act 1989 required annual renewal, the Terrorism Act has permanent status. In relation to Northern Ireland, it had been hoped that special provision would no longer be required for Northern Ireland following the peace settlement. However, in light of the problems in implementing full devolution to Northern Ireland, special provisions are included in Part VII of the Terrorism Act which are time-limited to five years.

Defining terrorism

Whereas under the Prevention of Terrorism Act 1989, terrorism was defined as the 'use of violence for political ends, and includes the use of violence for the purpose of putting the public or any section of the public in fear',[108] the Terrorism Act 2000 adopts a wider definition, which

[107] See *Inquiry into Legislation Against Terrorism*, Cm. 3420 (London: HMSO, 1996); *Legislation Against Terrorism*, Cm. 4178 (London: HMSO, 1998).
[108] Prevention of Terrorism (Temporary Provisions) Act 1989, section 20.

encompasses the use or threat of violence for the purpose 'of advancing a political, religious or ideological cause which involves serious violence against a person or property, endangering the life of any person or creating a serious risk to the health or safety of the public or a section of it'.[109]

'Action' includes action outside the United Kingdom, references to 'person or property' refer to any person or property wherever situated, and a reference to 'the public' includes a reference to the public of a country other than the United Kingdom.[110] This definition is intended to cover not just terrorism for political ends, as in the case of Northern Ireland, but terrorism undertaken for religious or ideological motives which, while not necessarily violent in themselves, are capable of having widespread adverse affects. Examples cited are of disruption of key computer systems or interference with the supply of water or power where life, health or safety may be put at risk.

Proscribed organizations

Part II of the Act relates to proscribed organizations, listed under Schedule 2.[111] The Secretary of State may add or remove an organization from Schedule 2 or otherwise amend it, but may do so only if he believes that the organization is concerned in terrorism.[112] An organization is concerned in terrorism if it commits or participates in acts of terrorism, prepares for terrorism, promotes or encourages terrorism, or is otherwise concerned in terrorism.[113] The Act introduces a Proscribed Organisations Appeal Commission (POAC),[114] to which individuals or organizations may appeal, having first applied to the Secretary of State for de-proscription and been refused.[115]

---

[109] Terrorism Act 2000, section 1.   [110] Ibid., section 1(2).

[111] The Irish Republican Army, *Cumann na mBan*, *Fianna na hEireann*, the Red Hand Commando, *Saor Eire*, the Ulster Freedom Fighters, the Ulster Volunteer Force, the Irish National Liberation Army, the Irish People's Liberation Organisation, the Ulster Defence Association, the Loyalist Volunteer Force, the Continuity Army Council, the Orange Volunteers, the Red Hand Defenders. In 2001 a number of fundamentalist religious groups were proscribed.

[112] Terrorism Act 2000, section 3.   [113] Ibid., section 3(5).

[114] Ibid., section 5.   [115] Ibid., section 4.

The Commission must allow an appeal if it considers that the Secretary of State's decision was flawed when considered in the light of the principles valid for an application for judicial review. If the appeal is allowed, the Commission makes an order to that effect. Where an order is made the Secretary of State must lay a draft order before Parliament, or in urgent cases make an order removing the organization from the list in Schedule 2.[116] Appeals from the POAC, on a question of law, lie to the Court of Appeal, Court of Session or Court of Appeal in Northern Ireland. An appeal may only be brought with the consent of the Commission or, where the Commission refuses permission, the permission of the relevant court.[117] If an appeal to the POAC is successful, and an order made de-proscribing the organization, any individual convicted of an offence in relation to the organization, provided the offence was committed after the date of the Secretary of State's refusal to de-proscribe, may appeal against his conviction to the Court of Appeal or Crown Court and the Court shall allow the appeal.[118] Section 8 makes equivalent provision for Scotland and Northern Ireland. Section 9 makes provision for the Human Rights Act 1998, section 7, to apply to appeal proceedings brought before the POAC, in relation to section 5(4) and (5), sections 6 and 7 (appeals to a court of law from a decision of the POAC), and paragraphs 4–8 of Schedule 3 (relating to procedure before the POAC). In relation to the above, reference to the Commission allowing an appeal shall be taken as a reference to the Commission determining that an action of the Secretary of State is incompatible with a Convention right, and reference to the refusal to de-proscribe against which an appeal was brought shall be taken as a reference to the action of the Secretary of State which is found to be incompatible with a Convention right.[119] In order that individuals seeking de-proscription should not be deterred from pursuing an appeal or from instituting proceedings under section 7 of the Human Rights Act, through a risk of prosecution for offences in relation to a proscribed organization, section 10 provides that evidence relating to anything done, and any documents submitted for these proceedings, cannot be relied on in criminal proceedings for such an offence except as part of the defence case.

---

[116] Ibid., section 5.   [117] Ibid., section 6.   [118] Ibid., section 7.
[119] Ibid., section 94.

THE COURTS AND NATIONAL SECURITY

The *GCHQ case, Council of Civil Service Union v. Minister of State for the Civil Service*,[120] illustrates the power which the claim to state security has over the judges. Following industrial unrest at GCHQ, the government's communications headquarters, the Prime Minister, wearing her hat as the Minister for the Civil Service, used the royal prerogative to remove from workers at GCHQ the right to belong to trade unions. The Civil Service Union sought judicial review of this decision, alleging that the Prime Minister had abused her powers through failing to negotiate fully with the union. At first instance, in the High Court, the Union won. At that first hearing, however, the government had not argued the state security aspect of the case. On appeal to the Court of Appeal, the government used the national security weapon, and won. The Union took the case on appeal to the House of Lords which upheld the government.[121]

Individuals or groups who are perceived as hostile to the state may be detained and/or deported from Britain. For these purposes the Home Secretary (more formally known as the Secretary of State for the Home Department) has wide powers. The extent to which these powers are, or should be, controlled by the courts of law is a matter of controversy. In 1962, Dr Soblen, an American citizen who had been convicted of espionage in the United States, fled from that country before being sentenced. Whilst on an aircraft he cut his wrists and was landed in London for hospital treatment. The Home Secretary issued a deportation order on the basis that his continued presence was 'not conducive to the public good'. When Soblen applied for habeas corpus the Court of Appeal ruled that he had no right to make representations, and that deportation was an administrative matter for the Home Secretary.[122]

In *R v. Home Secretary ex parte Hosenball*,[123] two American journalists, Philip Agee and Mark Hosenball, were detained with a view to deportation on the basis that their work involved obtaining and publishing

---

[120] [1985] AC 374.   [121] The government reinstated union rights in 1998.
[122] *R v. Home Secretary ex parte Soblen* [1963] 2 QB 243.
[123] [1977] 3 All ER 452.

information prejudicial to national security. Where national security is pleaded, there is no appeal against the Home Secretary's decision. Instead, there is a right of a hearing before a panel of three advisers to the Home Secretary. When Hosenball tried to challenge the Home Secretary's decision in the courts, the Court of Appeal upheld the deportation order. While recognizing that the rules of 'natural justice' had not been complied with in the decision to deport, the Court of Appeal nevertheless ruled that the requirements of national security prevailed and that, in matters of national security, the Home Secretary was responsible to Parliament and not to the courts. The case of *R v. Home Secretary ex parte Cheblak*[124] also reveals the extensive powers of the Home Secretary to detain persons 'in the interests of national security'. During the Gulf War, 160 Iraqi and Palestinian citizens were detained with a view to deportation, on the basis that their continued presence was not 'conducive to the public good'. Abbas Cheblak and his family had been resident in the United Kingdom for sixteen years. In an application for habeas corpus the Court of Appeal accepted the Home Secretary's explanation that Cheblak had associations with an unspecified organization which supported the Iraqi government, and refused to press the Home Secretary for further information. Following a hearing before the Home Secretary's panel of three wise men, Cheblak was released.

CONCLUSION

In every state there is a need to protect vital interests, whether they be economic, defence-related or for the protection of the state against subversion of its political system from within or attacks from without, and from terrorist threats. What is remarkable about the British system relating to national security is the extent to which the security and intelligence agencies remained for so long hidden from the public eye and unregulated by Acts of Parliament. The need for legislation arose, not from any desire of the government to regulate security matters, but

124 [1991] 2 All ER 319.

from the pressure imposed, originally, by decisions at the European Court of Human Rights which criticized the lack of legal regulation, a deficiency which undermined the protection of individual rights and freedoms. Despite the stringent controls over the disclosure of information relating to national security, in the form of the Official Secrets Acts 1911 and now 1989, the public has learned more about security operations through the whistleblowing of security officers and the work of investigative journalists than through any openness on the part of government. The government's obsession with secrecy – despite commitments to greater freedom of information – continues undiminished. But as disaffected former security officers, though few in number, continue to reveal information about the services, even where this does not threaten the identity of agents in the field or operational matters, the public appetite for knowledge increases in direct proportion to the government's attempts to silence critics of the services. And so the situation will continue, until Parliament is given a greater role in the scrutiny of security matters – a role which the United States Congress has long exercised – and the public gains confidence that the wide powers given to the security agencies are directed at genuine threats to state security, and not against the individual rights of citizens.

POSTSCRIPT

With the bombing of the World Trade Center in New York on 11 September 2001 with the loss of over three thousand lives, the world awoke to the potential for terrorism on a hitherto unimagined scale. The uncovering of the international network of the fundamentalist militant al-Qaeda organization, spearheaded by Osama bin Laden and protected by the Taliban regime in poverty-stricken Afghanistan, served to underline the complexity and fragility of the capitalist world's security systems and defences. The aftermath saw a period of unprecedented co-operation and diplomatic effort to eliminate international terrorism. In Britain the government reacted swiftly to introduce tighter anti-terrorism laws. The Anti-Terrorism, Crime and Security Act 2001 which became law in December 2001 *inter alia* increased the powers of enforcement agencies to investigate personal data held by public authorities, introduced detention without access to a court of law, suspending Article 5 of the Convention on Human Rights, and removed the right to judicial review of detention decisions in relation to terrorist suspects.

THE ADMINISTRATION OF JUSTICE 1: THE CIVIL JUSTICE SYSTEM IN ENGLAND AND WALES

INTRODUCTION

Although a 'united kingdom', Britain has three separate legal systems. Northern Ireland and Scotland each have their own court system and laws. In this chapter, the focus is predominantly on the English legal system. It was in the reign of Henry II (1154–89) that the foundations of the system which survives today were laid. Henry established local courts throughout the kingdom, and judges would travel the country at 'assizes' on a regular basis to ensure that a uniform system of justice was being administered.

While most of continental Europe and to a lesser extent Scotland were much influenced by Roman law – a legacy of the Roman Empire – with its focus on broad comprehensive 'codes' setting out basic principles, English law developed as a distinctive system. In place of written authoritative legislative codes on various aspects of legal rights and obligations which required the interpretation of the judges, English law emerged early as a common law system – a corpus of law developed by the judges in the courts. The system was highly centralized by the thirteenth century. Over time, the processes of law became stultified, with causes of action having to fit into rigid and formalized procedures. The courts, divided into the courts of Exchequer, Common Pleas and King's Bench, insisted that cases had to fit within the established form of action, and the inability to fit one's complaint within an established procedure meant that for many there was no access to justice. To mitigate the injustices caused by aggrieved citizens not having access to law, a system of equity developed. Plaintiffs would petition the king for a remedy, the petitions being dealt with by the Lord Chancellor. These two systems – common law and equity – coexisted side by side but operated in mutually exclusive spheres, until late into the nineteenth century when the Judicature Acts 1873–5 fused the two jurisdictions. From then on all courts had the power to decide cases based on either common law or equity, although in the event of a clash equity would prevail.

Although Parliament had become the supreme law-maker in the seventeenth century, it was not until the nineteenth century that the state intervened in society and increased regulation by way of Acts of Parliament (statutes). In large part, the need for regulation was driven by the increasing complexity of society. The commercial and industrial revolutions, fuelled by scientific invention, and the resulting concentration of industry in urban areas and the related population movements, changed the face of Britain. As will be discussed in Chapter 12, society was no longer characterized by the aristocratic few and the agricultural masses coping as best they could in relatively small isolated economic units; instead, a new entrepreneurial commercial-managerial class developed. As education became more widespread, with compulsory education to the age of twelve years introduced in 1870 and in 1902 state-funded secondary education made available to all, so literacy and numeracy for the 'working class' became commonplace.

In 1832 came the extension of the right to vote, but on limited terms, and the great Reform Act of 1867 resulted in the majority of adult men in society being able to vote. Education and enfranchisement gave to ordinary people a voice in government, which before had been theright of the privileged propertied classes only. The nineteenth century was also the age of government investigations into the conditions of the people in this changing world: official report after report into health, conditions of work, sanitation, housing and poverty provided for government the statistical data on the country as a whole, and laid the foundations for unprecedented state regulation. In terms of law, whereas in previous centuries the judges had to interpret statutes, these were a minimal source of law compared with the body of judge-made common law. By the start of the twentieth century, Acts of Parliament had become the major source of law for citizens and judges alike.

The nineteenth century also saw an overhaul of the system of courts. Nevertheless, although much reformed, the legal system still exhibits many of its early origins and features: the system is old and it shows. It is not possible in a short chapter to outline all features of the contemporary legal system: any attempt would be unsatisfactory. Accordingly, after a brief outline of the courts and their respective areas of power (jurisdiction), and the tribunal network which exists alongside the courts and alternative mechanisms for dispute resolution, the focus will turn to key aspects of the system.

CATEGORIES OF LAW

Understanding 'law' and its role in society is the task of legal philosophers and theorists, and defining law is no simple task. For present purposes, law as a concept is taken to mean a formal system of social control, through which order is imposed on society and rules and procedures established for the authoritative resolution of disputes between individuals, and between the individual and the apparatus of the state. The courts of law, at differing levels in the hierarchical structure and having differing degrees of specialism, are the principal institutions which adjudicate on rights and duties where disputes arise. In order to break down the monolith of law, differing categories of law have developed. Common law and equity, mentioned above, are two examples of this categorization, as are, confusingly, civil law systems and common law systems referred to above. However, while categories of law may be helpful indicators, there are many overlaps, as will be seen below.

Civil law and criminal law

Civil and criminal law represent two major divisions in law. Civil law relates to disputes between citizens and between citizen and government over all matters not deemed to be criminal. Civil law is that body of law which regulates the relationships between individuals. Its focus is on the adjudication of rights and duties, and on rectifying distortions in legal positions. Prime examples of civil law are matters of contract, property and torts (wrongs such as defamation and negligence). The courts dealing with civil law matters are not concerned primarily with punishment, as are the criminal courts, but rather with restoring the correct balance between individuals and stating their legal rights. Civil law is a form of private law in that whether or not to pursue a legal action is a matter for the aggrieved individual to decide, not the state. This otherwise clear-cut division, however, appears to become blurred by the question of compensation for the victims of wrongdoing. An action in defamation (libel or slander) or negligence, for example, may lead to the award of compensation or damages for the victim. However, the payment of compensation or damages for injury caused in fact remains within the civil, non-criminal sphere, in so far as the award is to rectify a wrong rather than to impose a criminal sanction on the 'offender'. Conceptually this distinction appears unsatisfactory in some respects, particularly where, for example, punitive damages are awarded against the losing party.

Criminal law, on the other hand, is that body of law which deals with offences against the law, which Parliament deems to be so serious as to require trial and punishment by the state.[1] As Émile Durkheim expressed it, an action is criminal because it is deemed to be so according to the prevailing standards in society: it offends against the collective morality of society.[2] While this early view has some credence, in a multi-ultural and multi-racial society the theory has less application. Notwithstanding the weakening of shared values in contemporary society, there remain in all societies some basic taboos which the law will stigmatize as criminal – laws against murder, theft of property and incest are common to most legal systems. Nowadays, however, many offences dealt with by the criminal courts are more to do with social regulation than social morality. Many traffic offences, and offences relating to tax-ation, hygiene standards and other environmental matters, do not fit

[1] On the criminal justice system see Chapter 10.
[2] É. Durkheim, *The Division of Labour in Society*, 1933, tr. G. Simpson (New York: Free Press, 1964).

comfortably in the same company as murder, manslaughter, violence or theft but are nevertheless categorized as criminal by the state.

Public and private law

A further division in law relates to the distinction between public and private law. In essence, public law refers to those areas of law which concern the state and its institutions. While civil law is essentially private law, criminal law is categorized as a matter of public law. Most significantly, administrative law – a vital and fast-moving facet of public law – ensures (through proceedings for judicial review of administrative decisions) that public bodies to whom powers are delegated by Parliament are kept within the confines of the power which is delegated to them. Public law also encompasses aspects of law which are enforceable by the state, in the public interest, such as criminal behaviour which is prosecuted by the state. Private law, on the other hand, refers to aspects of law regulating relationships between individual citizens – the law of contract, disputes over property and the law relating to the family are major illustrations of private law.

Here again, however, the matter is not as clear-cut as these explanations suggest. 'Private law' suggests that the interests in question are a matter purely for the individual, and of no concern to the state. In many areas of law this is far too simple a view. One area illustrating the problem is that of the law relating to domestic violence. Violence within the home is an inherently private phenomenon: it occurs for the most part behind closed doors in the domestic sphere. Because of its private nature, the phenomenon of domestic violence went for long undetected and unrecognized by law. This is a problem relevant not just to the legal systems in the United Kingdom, but to all societies. Any precise measurement of the incidence of violence within the home is especially problematic. Domestic violence and sexual offences more generally are areas in which there is not only significant under-reporting of offences but also a failure on the part of the state to prosecute offenders – for complex reasons which generally focus on the problem of securing convictions because of the victim's unwillingness to give evidence. The protection of the state is also defective in so far as the police traditionally have been unwilling to intervene in 'domestic incidents'. By categorizing domestic violence as being a matter of private law, the impression is given – to both perpetrators and victims of violence and to society at large – that violence within the home is less worthy of intervention by the state than are incidents of violence which occur in public. The idea of privacy and the private sphere contribute to the plight of victims, most generally but not exclusively, women, and send a message to society that violence within the domestic sphere is 'not the state's business'.

In terms of law, domestic violence attracts the same criminal penalties as does violence outside the home. The law, ranging from assault to manslaughter and murder, applies to all irrespective of the location in which the offence occurred. But enforcement failures lead to a lesser standard of protection for victims of violence, depending upon the relationship between the parties (for example, husband and wife) and the location of the violence within the private sphere, the family home.

The law also provides remedies within the civil sphere for victims of violence. For example, the victim may seek a 'non-molestation order' from the Magistrates' Courts or from the County Courts. Where evidence of serious violence exists, these orders may include a power-of-arrest order which, in the event of a breach of the order, entitles the police to arrest the offender without first obtaining a further warrant from the courts.[3] In terms of classification of laws, this confuses matters by attaching a potential criminal sanction to the breach of a civil order. Where more serious or repeated violence occurs there is also the available remedy of a court order excluding the violent party from the family home. However, because these orders interfere with rights in property they are only granted sparingly, and will have time limits imposed on them. These remedies are only available if the victim is willing to pursue them: there is no power given to the police or members of social services, for example, to pursue a remedy on the part of the victim. When the Family Law Bill was before Parliament, provision was made for the police to apply on behalf of victims, but Parliament rejected

---

[3] For instance, the problem of stalking by strangers, which is dealt with under the Protection from Harassment Act 1997, an Act passed by Parliament in two days which makes harassment – not defined in the Act – a serious criminal offence.

the measure on the basis that this involved crime detection and enforcement officers applying for remedies which are essentially civil in nature.

THE CONTEMPORARY COURT STRUCTURE IN ENGLAND AND WALES

The court structure comprises courts having both criminal and civil jurisdiction. The principal focus in this chapter is on the civil courts. On aspects of the criminal courts, including the organization and role of the police and trial by jury, see Chapter 10.

The Magistrates' Courts

While the legal system is divided into two principal areas, criminal law and civil law, there are overlaps in the business of some courts. At the lowest level of the structure are the Magistrates' Courts, staffed mainly by lay persons with some, but little, training and no necessary knowledge of law, guided by a legally qualified clerk of the court, but in urban areas also staffed by 'stipendiary magistrates', full-time, legally qualified adjudicators.

Since the fourteenth century lay magistrates – Justices of the Peace – have been a feature of the legal system, representing the most localized and accessible forum for justice. Before the system of local government became established in the nineteenth century, magistrates performed a mixture of administrative and judicial functions. Drawn from the educated 'upper classes', magistrates served the community without financial reward, and this latter feature remains true today. Magistrates still fulfil limited administrative functions in relation to the licensing of premises such as clubs, pubs and bars. Although they deal principally with criminal matters – 98 per cent of all prosecutions start and end in the Magistrates' Court – a number of important civil matters may also be dealt with by magistrates.

The most significant aspect of this jurisdiction (which overlaps with the County Courts) relates to children, domestic violence and financial orders for separated spouses. Care and supervision proceedings under-taken by local authorities for the protection of children are dealt with in the Magistrates' Court, as are adoption proceedings. Disputes between parents about the upbringing of their children, or disputes between the child and its parents, may also be dealt with by the magistrates, although more commonly these cases will go to the County Court. As seen above, in relation to domestic violence, the Magistrates' Court has the power to grant 'non-molestation orders' and 'exclusion orders' against perpetrators of domestic violence.[4] The former is an order not to molest the applicant, while the latter – the exclusion order – requires the respondent (the other party to the proceedings) to leave the home or part of it, or the area in which the home is situated, in order to protect the applicant. For non-family members, the Protection from Harassment Act 1997 enables the magistrates to order a person not to harass an applicant further. Where the conduct is sufficient to warrant prosecution by the police, the magistrates will also hear the case. Relative to the County Court, however, the Magistrates' Courts family law jurisdiction is under-used: in the public perception the Magistrates' Court is primarily a criminal court, with all the associated overtones of criminality, wrongdoing and punishment, and most people prefer to have such cases heard in the lowest level, purely civil, County Court.

The advantage of Magistrates' Courts is claimed to be that they are the most localized forum for justice in a community, and that they are staffed by lay representatives of that community. In theory, as the magistrates are representative of the community their decisions are decisions by one's peers. However, it has long been recognized that the reality does not match the theory. Despite efforts to broaden the social background of magistrates, local benches remain characterized by white, middle-class, middle-aged men and women whose background and outlook has little in common with the clientele of the court. This disparity between 'judge' and 'client' – most often a defendant in criminal proceedings – creates not only general dissatisfaction with the quality of justice dispensed in the Magistrates' Courts but also a loss of confidence on the part of defendants in criminal proceedings who,

[4] Under the Family Law Act 1996, Part IV.

when given the choice between trial before the magistrates and trial by jury in the Crown Court will almost invariably opt for the latter.[5]

The County Courts

Introduced in 1846, there are now some 240 County Courts dealing with civil matters, and staffed by circuit judges and district judges. As seen above, part of their jurisdiction relating to family matters overlaps with that of the Magistrates' Courts, but there is also overlapping jurisdiction between the County Courts and the next rung in the hierarchy of courts, the High Court. Generally speaking, straightforward small claims which can be disposed of expeditiously are dealt with in the County Court, whereas high value complex claims go to the High Court, which also has a wider range of remedies available to it. In 1996 the financial limit for small claims cases in the County Courts was raised to £3,000 except in relation to personal injury claims, and in 1998 over 95,000 such cases were heard. In 1999 the limit was again raised, this time to £5,000. The procedure in the small claims court is such that cases can be dealt with quickly, within twenty-one weeks on average, through an informal process of arbitration and at a limited cost (compared with the High Court). The arbitration process injects greater flexibility into the settling of disputes. The County Court Rules give a wide degree of discretion to arbitrators to choose the procedures they consider most appropriate to the issue, and the normal strict rules of evidence do not apply. Formal legal representation is not encouraged, the preference being for the parties to handle their own cases, although legal representation is not prohibited and can be insisted on by either party to the case.[6]

---

[5] The choice of venue relates to offences which are 'triable either way'. The government has decided to remove the choice of venue from the defendant and to place it in the hands of the court. The Criminal Justice (Mode of Trial) Bill 1999 was, however, rejected by the House of Lords.

[6] See *Chilton v. Saga Holidays* [1986] 1 All ER 841, in which the Court of Appeal ruled that an arbitrator (a registrar) had been wrong to refuse to allow the defendant to be represented by a solicitor for the purpose of cross-examining the plaintiff on the grounds that the plaintiff was not legally represented.

The County Court also has jurisdiction relating to contract, property, tort, probate, bankruptcy and insolvency. In relation to family law, it is the County Court which deals with petitions for divorce and separation orders, and for resolving disputes about the upbringing of children, including their place of residence following a family breakdown. Adoption proceedings can also be dealt with in the County Court, as are applications for orders relating to domestic violence and occupation of the family home.

The High Court of Justice

Part of the Supreme Court of Judicature (the highest stratum of courts), the High Court was established in 1873 and is now divided into three divisions: the Queen's Bench Division, the Court of Chancery and the Family Division. While mainly sitting in London, the High Court can sit in any of twenty-seven cities and towns designated by the Lord Chancellor. The Lord Chancellor is nominally head of the Chancery Division, although usually it is the Vice-Chancellor who presides. In the Queen's Bench Division (QBD) the Lord Chief Justice presides, while the Family Division is headed by the President. In addition, up to ninety-six High Court judges sit in the High Court. In terms of jurisdiction, contract and tort are the most numerous actions. There is also a specialist Commercial Court which is part of the Queen's Bench Division, dealing with commercial disputes, banking and insurance. The QBD also has limited criminal jurisdiction. Appeals purely on matters of law from the Magistrates' Courts, and allegations that the Magistrates' Court has exceeded its jurisdiction, are heard by the Divisional Court of the QBD. The Divisional Court will also consider applications for judicial review and applications for writs of habeas corpus: the ancient action to test the legality of a person's detention.

The Chancery Division

Chancery deals primarily with property matters: mortgages, trusts, administration of estates, disputed probate, bankruptcy, company law and revenue law. Within Chancery there are two specialist courts dealing with patents and companies. The Chancery Court hears cases in London and in eight designated provincial High Court centres. The most specialized of all divisions, the Court is served by the Chancery Bar, and judges appointed to the Court are generally drawn from the Chancery Bar.

The Family Division

As its name implies, the Family Division deals with matrimonial matters. Contested divorces, which are now rare, go to the Family Division and appeals from decisions of the County Courts are heard here. Applications concerning domestic violence and difficult cases concerning children may also go to the Family Division. Most importantly, any disputes over the medical treatment of children are dealt with here, so that where, for example, the parents and medical profession disagree over treatment, or a child attempts to refuse treatment or to consent to treatment without its parents' approval, the issue is considered at a high level. Questions about the legitimacy of children, surrogacy and adoption may also be heard in the Family Division.

The Court of Appeal

The Court of Appeal is staffed by thirty-five Lords Justices of Appeal. The Lord Chancellor, President of the Family Division, Vice-Chancellor of Chancery and High Court judges may also sit. The Court has two divisions, civil and criminal. Appeals from the High Court will go to the Civil Division, unless and in exceptional circumstances permission is given to the appellant to 'leap-frog' over the Court of Appeal straight to the House of Lords.[7] This can only occur where the original judge hearing the case issues a certificate stating that the case concerns a point of law of general public importance in relation to which there is a binding precedent of either the Court of Appeal or House of Lords (from which, under the doctrine of precedent, the judge cannot depart)[8] and the House of Lords gives permission. The parties must also agree. In relation to criminal matters, appeals from the Crown Court will be

---

[7] Under the Administration of Justice Act 1969, sections 12–15.
[8] On the rules of precedent see pages 451 ff. below.

heard by the Criminal Division of the Court of Appeal and, ultimately, may go to the House of Lords.

The Court of Appeal is hard-pressed, with approximately 1,000 cases a year being heard, compared with a mere fifty in the House of Lords in an average year. Inevitably this leads to delay, and while 70 per cent of cases in 1996 were disposed of in fourteen months, 30 per cent took longer, and exceptionally appeals may remain outstanding for over five years. 'Justice delayed is justice denied' is a fundamental legal principle and reforms have been recommended: these are discussed further below.

The House of Lords

At the apex of the domestic legal structure is the House of Lords. This has both legislative[9] and judicial functions, although it is important to be clear that only qualified senior judges exercise its judicial functions. It is the final Court of Appeal in both civil and criminal matters in relation to England, Wales and Northern Ireland (Scotland having its own legal system and final court, although some aspects of Scottish law may be dealt with by the House of Lords). The Court is staffed by twelve Lords of Appeal in Ordinary, the 'Law Lords' (all of whom are men), but cases are normally heard by five judges, although exceptionally seven may sit on a particularly important case. Decisions are reached by a majority.

The Privy Council

The Privy Council is the modern-day successor to the historic King's Council: advisers to the monarch summoned to give opinions on matters of state. In terms of the legal system, it is the Judicial Committee of the Privy Council which has a number of roles. It was created in 1883 and is staffed by five Law Lords. History lingers: judicial decisions are not 'judgments' of the court but 'advice to the monarch'. First, appeals may be heard from British colonies or dependent territories, or from

[9] See Chapter 3.

former colonies where the right to appeal to the Privy Council has been retained. Secondly, the Privy Council has jurisdiction to hear appeals from the General Medical Council and the General Dental Council. Since 1998 issues relating to devolution have also been dealt with by the Privy Council.

REFORMING THE CIVIL JUSTICE SYSTEM

The civil justice system has long been regarded as costly and inefficient, and ripe for reform. In 1994, in an attempt to identify and seek to remedy the criticisms of the legal system, the government set up an inquiry, chaired by Lord Woolf MR.[10] In his Interim Report,[11] Lord Woolf noted that 'the key problems facing civil justice today are cost, delay and complexity' and that 'there is no clear judicial responsibility for managing individual cases or for the overall administration of the civil courts'. In order to increase efficiency and reduce costs a number of procedural reforms have been introduced.[12] While detailed discussion is beyond the scope of this book, an outline of the three main themes of the reforms is necessary.[13] The first objective has been to ensure that the judge is the 'manager' of cases, which are allocated to differing 'tracks' – small claims, fast-track and multi-track – which emphasizes flexibility. The judge, rather than the parties to litigation, is in charge of the timetabling of cases, and a number of sanctions are built in where parties refuse to comply with the rules. Secondly, in order to prevent lawyers from delaying matters before the case reaches court, and thereby running up extra costs, protocols have been drafted to apply to clinical negligence and personal injury claims, two of the largest areas of litigation, to encourage greater contact between the parties, promote co-operation and facilitate an early settlement of the case. Thirdly,

[10] Master of the Rolls, senior judge of the Court of Appeal.
[11] *Access to Justice*, 1995.
[12] See the Civil Procedure Act 1997 and Civil Procedure Rules 1998.
[13] For more detail see G. Slapper and D. Kelly, *The English Legal System* (London: Cavendish Publishing, 4th edn., 1999), chapter 7.

parties are encouraged to make use of alternative dispute resolution (on which see below) instead of the more formal court process.

Concern over the workload of the Court of Appeal led to a review being undertaken under the chairmanship of Sir Jeffrey Bowman. The Report of the review, published in 1998, recommended, *inter alia*, that all appeals to the Court of Appeal should be granted formal leave to appeal to that court,[14] and that there should be better management of cases with improved preparation for hearings and timetables being set and adhered to. Furthermore, there should be time limits imposed on oral arguments before the Court, and greater use made of information technology by the Court. More radically, the Report recommended that, in appropriate cases, academic or practitioner lawyers should be allowed to sit in the Court of Appeal,[15] and that on occasion cases should be listed for hearing before a single judge of the Court rather than the normal panel of three judges.[16] The Access to Justice Act 1999[17] gave effect to some of these proposals, including the requirement of permissions, facilitating the hearing of appeals at a lower level of court but ensuring that important cases continue to reach the Court of Appeal, and providing for single judges to hear appeals.

THE EUROPEAN COURTS

The European Court of Justice

The European Court of Justice (ECJ) sits over and above the highest domestic courts in matters relating to the European Community and Union. As discussed in Chapter 4, it has had a profound impact on domestic law as it extends the application, scope and supremacy of

---

[14] Other than adoption cases, child abduction cases and appeals against committal orders (resulting in imprisonment) and refusals to grant orders of habeas corpus.

[15] A practice common in Europe, but not in the United Kingdom.

[16] The Report to the Lord Chancellor was subject to consultation, and resulted in the Report, *Reform of the Court of Appeal (Civil Division): Proposals for Change to Constitution and Jurisdiction* (London: Lord Chancellor's Department, 1998).

[17] Part IV.

Community law over the national laws of member states. The jurisdiction of the ECJ comes from the Treaties governing Europe. The Court is staffed by judges drawn from all member states, and since 1986 there has been a 'Court of First Instance' established to relieve the Court of part of its workload. The ECJ has jurisdiction over disputes between member states, between the European institutions, and between the institutions and the member states. If, for example, the European Commission considers that the United Kingdom government is in breach of its treaty obligations, it will first try to resolve the matter itself, but failing that it may refer the matter to the ECJ for a decision which binds the member state. Not only can the Court order compliance with Community law, but it can also issue substantial fines to be paid by the defaulting state. The ECJ's most important jurisdiction lies in the interpretation of Community law, whether treaty provisions or secondary laws passed by the European institutions.[18] For this purpose, the Treaty of Rome built in a notion of partnership between the national courts and the ECJ.[19] In relation to the lower domestic courts from which there is an appeal available domestically, that court *may*, if it is necessary to do so in order to reach a decision and it is uncertain as to the correct interpretation of Community law, refer the matter to the ECJ for decision. When a matter reaches the highest available level of appeal court domestically, and that court is uncertain as to the correct meaning of Community law, that court *must* refer the matter to the ECJ for decision, and the ECJ's decision is binding on the national courts.

The European Court of Human Rights

Quite separate from the ECJ, the Court of Human Rights was established under the aegis of the Council of Europe to hear applications from citizens of member states under the European Convention on Human Rights. It is staffed by judges from all member states and sits in Strasbourg. The United Kingdom government first allowed its citizens

---

[18] Article 200 of the Treaty of Rome (formerly Article 164).
[19] Article 234 of the Treaty of Rome (formerly Article 177).

to apply under the Convention in 1965, since which time over fifty cases have been decided against the British government. With the incorporation of the Convention into domestic law in 2000 under the Human Rights Act 1998 (in Scotland it took effect in 1998), the majority of cases under the Convention are dealt with by the British courts. The Court of Human Rights will, however, remain available as an appeal court, and as a judicial forum for hearing applications relating to alleged deficiencies in the Human Rights Act 1998. For example, and as discussed in Chapter 7, the Human Rights Act does not incorporate Article 13 of the Convention which requires that the law should provide an 'effective remedy' in relation to breaches of Convention rights, but rather provides that the judges may issue 'declarations of incompatibility' whereupon the matter is remedied, if it is to be remedied, through the political and legislative process. This format was adopted, in part, in order to preserve the traditional division of responsibility between the judiciary and Parliament, and to prevent the judiciary invalidating Acts of Parliament, which have always been regarded as supreme and incapable of being invalidated by the courts. The issue of what is, or is not, an effective remedy, could well lie with the Court of Human Rights.

THE ADMINISTRATIVE TRIBUNAL NETWORK

Increasingly, dissatisfaction with the working of the formal legal system has led to a search for alternatives which offer less formality, greater speed and lower costs: arbitration and mediation have come to be settled features of the system. As a result, alongside the criminal and civil court structure there exists a network of tribunals designed, for the most part, to provide a less formal forum for the adjudication of disputes with correspondingly greater speed and lower costs.

Operating alongside the court structure is an extensive network of tribunals designed to resolve disputes with the minimum of delay, expense and formality and with a particular specialization in the matter in question. The existence of tribunals – as opposed to courts – lies in the expansion of state intervention over a wide range of areas. The welfare state in particular has generated the need for an efficient means of administering the system and adjudicating claims and disputes in accessible, specialist forums. Tribunals deal with over a quarter of a million cases a year, many times the volume of civil cases heard by the courts.

Many tribunals are established under statute, others not, but all are subordinate to the courts in the sense that their procedures may be examined by the courts if there are allegations of a breach of the procedural rules or the rules of natural justice developed by the courts of law. Currently, over sixty types of tribunals exist, and each of these may have multiple 'branches' hearing cases in different areas. They range in specialism from employment tribunals, social security tribunals, and mental health review tribunals, to rent assessment committees and the Land Tribunal. In addition there are tribunals established to deal with disputes in particular professions and trade unions: the Bar, the Law Society, British Medical Association, trade unions and universities all have disciplinary tribunals. Tribunals created by statute are regulated by the Council on Tribunals, its membership determined by the Lord Chancellor. Tribunals are staffed, generally, by three members two of whom will be lay persons, usually specialists in the relevant subject-matter, one of whom will be a legally qualified chairperson.

Given the differing modes of operation and degrees of formality, it would be inaccurate to label the tribunal network a 'system'. It is also difficult to characterize tribunals as purely administrative bodies or judicial/adjudicative bodies. Whereas speed and informality are the hallmarks of many tribunals, this is not a uniform feature: for example, the Land Tribunal, which deals with claims relating to compulsory purchase orders, operates with a high degree of formality that brings it closer to the formal courts than to the more informal tribunals. Flexibility and informality are features of most tribunals, procedures being adopted and adapted as appropriate, and the strict rules of evidence which apply in a court of law are not followed. Although legal representation is allowed, it is not required, and legal aid – state funding for legal representation – is not available other than in the more formalized tribunals. While legal aid is not available, thus reducing the cost to the state of cases heard before tribunals, limited free legal advice and assistance under the Green Form scheme is available to assist with the preparation of a case. However, the absence of legal representation (state funded or otherwise), while encouraging informality and lower costs, places the individual at a disadvantage both where the 'other side' is legally represented and where the individual is unfamiliar with any form of adjudicative procedure. It is well documented by empirical research that legal representation enhances an individual's chances of success.

ALTERNATIVE DISPUTE MECHANISMS: ARBITRATION AND MEDIATION

The traditional reliance on courts of law as the only appropriate forum for the resolution of disputes in society was weakened not only by the introduction of specialist administrative tribunals but by the introduction of alternative methods of dispute resolution. Consumer dissatisfaction with the delay, cost, formality and lack of specialization in some courts led to a search for better solutions. Western societies, with conventional perceptions about the rule of law and the centrality of law, for long ignored alternative solutions. Whereas in traditional oriental society recourse to law represents a breakdown in human and social communication and is seen as an unwelcome aberration, in the West it has long been assumed that such recourse is the most appropriate manner by which to solve conflict. Yet empirical research has also revealed that where there was mutuality and common understanding between parties, they were reluctant to go to law. 'Going to law' represented the final destination, not the first. For example, studies in the United States about the practices of the commercial community found that where a dispute arose every effort was made by the parties not to go to law: law and legal regulation undermined reciprocity within the business community and represented a breakdown in normal business relations.

With the courts overburdened, however, and the defects of court-based adjudication apparent, the focus has shifted towards a less court-centred process of solving conflict. The Arbitration Act 1996 regulates arbitration, and states that the objectives of arbitration are 'to obtain the fair resolution of disputes by an impartial tribunal without unnecessary delay or expense'. The parties may nominate a single arbitrator or a panel, the arbitrator(s) being specialists in the relevant subject-matter. The advantages of arbitration over courts are speed, informality, specialism and lower costs. While arbitration is widely used to settle disputes in the commercial sector, it is also available to settle small claims in the County Courts. This process is automatic in relation to cases involving up to £5,000 and may be used for greater sums where the parties agree. For personal injury cases the upper limit is £1,000. A district judge controls the process and may refuse to allow arbitration, as opposed to a trial in court, if there are difficult issues of law involved, where fraud is alleged, or where one of the parties needs legal representation (if eligible for legal aid this would be available in court proceedings and state funded; legal aid is not available for arbitration) and both parties agree to the matter being dealt with in court.

Mediation has come to play an increasingly important role in family matters. Whereas arbitration focuses on reaching a solution through adjudication by the arbitrator, mediation facilitates agreements made between the parties with the assistance of an impartial third party: the mediator does not reach or impose a decision. Under the Family Law Act 1996 mediation was placed centre-stage in relation to divorce. Previously, divorce was largely an adversarial, conflictual process involving allegations of guilt to establish the basis for divorce. This was not the intention of the law, which was based on the sole ground that the marriage had broken down irretrievably.[20] However, in order to establish the breakdown one or more of a number of 'facts' had to be proved, some fault-based, others not. The objectives of the legislation had been to make divorce less adversarial and acrimonious, but for many who wanted to get a divorce quickly, the only way to achieve this was to allege one of the fault-based facts of divorce: adultery, unreasonable behaviour or desertion. The non-fault separation facts required separation of the parties for either two or five years. Matters relating to the consequences of divorce were regarded as ancillary to the petition for divorce and where there was no agreement between the parties about children, property and finance, the matter would be resolved in court

[20] Originally the Divorce Reform Act 1969, now consolidated under the Matrimonial Causes Act 1973.

proceedings after the divorce itself had been granted. While many parties could and did reach an amicable settlement on their own, or through their solicitors, and that agreement could be translated into an order of the court, too many did not. The result was court-based resolution, the whole process of which inevitably intensified any already existing hostility between the parties and affected, in particular, any children of the marriage.

The Family Law Act 1996 retained the 'irretrievable breakdown' grounds and removed all subsidiary 'facts', and required the parties to deal with all ancillary matters during a transitional period between the initial 'statement of breakdown' and the granting of a divorce order. Consistent with the objective of making divorce less acrimonious, mediation was introduced into the process as a mechanism for encouraging the parties to reach their own decisions about children, property and finance, in a neutral setting with a mediator. A related objective of the Act was to minimize the role of lawyers in relation to divorce and thereby to reduce the cost of divorce to the state. While some mediators might be legally trained, it was envisaged that the majority would not be. However, in 1999 the government announced first that it would not, for the time being, implement the new process for divorce which had been due to come into force in 2000, and then that the reform would never be implemented. Underlying the government's change of heart was whether mediation – which had been subject to numerous pilot studies – was actually working, and the misgivings of many academics and legal practitioners about mediated settlements which, provided they were reached without coercion or fraud, would be binding on the parties. Too few people accepted mediation when encouraged to do so, and while research found that where mediation was adopted a high proportion of cases were settled through this means, for many people independent legal advice was what was wanted. It was perceived as a danger, rightly or wrongly, that reaching such important decisions for the future without legal advice would result in legal rights being sacrificed, especially in relation to property and finance. In addition, by the time many people reached mediation they were clear that they wanted a divorce, and did not want to be involved in processes which they regarded as unhelpful.

Closely related to mediation is conciliation. Rather than the parties being in the 'driving seat', as in mediation, conciliation involves an active third party negotiating with the parties to reach a satisfactory resolution of the dispute. Conciliation is widely used in industrial relations where the Advisory Conciliation and Arbitration Service (which is government funded) works to settle industrial disputes.

From this necessarily brief overview of the court structure and its alternatives, it can be seen that the administration of justice is far from a monolithic uniform structure, but one which has evolved to provide suitable means of dispute resolution tailored to meet differing needs in society.

THE LORD CHANCELLOR AND JUDGES

Heading the hierarchy of judges is the Lord Chancellor, who occupies a multi-faceted and controversial role in the constitution. Not only is the Lord Chancellor the head of the judiciary with responsibilities for the appointment of magistrates and judges, the promotion of judges and the administration of the courts, but he is also a political appointee with a seat in Cabinet, and acts as both the impartial Speaker in the House of Lords and the government's spokesman there. It is unsurprising that questions have for long been asked about the constitutionality of this office, on the basis that it represents a flagrant breach of separation of powers, and there have been calls for reform. As was seen in Chapter 1, the only checks against abuse of power lie in constitutional conventions which loosely define the limits between the three roles. It was also seen that successive Lord Chancellors have defended their role as bringing an invaluable injection of the views of the judiciary into the highest political arena, the Cabinet, and facilitating interaction between the executive, legislature and judiciary. As the current Lord Chancellor, Lord Irvine of Lairg, expressed it, his office is on 'a critical cusp of the constitution' and the natural 'conduit' between the judges and the executive. Nevertheless, there remain a number of serious concerns.

The system of appointment of judges has long been criticized and is to undergo reform. Far from being an open exercise, subject to independent scrutiny, the process has been steeped in secrecy. The Lord

Chancellor is responsible for two sets of judicial appointments. The first relates to the judges, from the most junior to the most senior, in relation to which the Lord Chancellor makes recommendations to the Prime Minister who in turn makes recommendations to the Queen who formally makes the appointments. The second relates to promotions within the Bar to the rank of Queen's Counsel, the coveted and privileged position from which judicial appointments are generally made. The system, which the current Lord Chancellor insists is merit-based and not driven by requirements of 'gender balance' or 'political balance', entails the process of taking 'soundings' among other judges and senior barristers about a candidate's suitability. The files on candidates are confidential, and hitherto there has been no independent scrutiny of this process, and no means of appealing against the Lord Chancellor's decisions. In 1999 he announced that the system was to be reviewed, and he did not preclude the possibility of a Judicial Appointments Commission being established with some lay membership to advise on the appointment of judges.

Several factors, of differing levels of significance, combined to bring the present system under renewed attack. The first is the personal relationship between the Prime Minister and Lord Irvine. Lord Irvine's career has been at the commercial Bar, and it was he who took both Tony Blair and his future wife into his chambers in the 1970s; Lord Irvine has been Blair's friend and mentor ever since. The second is Lord Irvine's enthusiasm for continuing the reforms of the legal profession and the administration of justice begun by his predecessor, Lord Mackay of Clashfern. Widely regarded as radical, Lord Mackay sought to reform both the legal profession and the cost of justice, and it was hoped by many in the profession that Lord Irvine would be more conservative and tone down what was perceived to be an attack on the profession in relation to restrictive practices, particularly in relation to rights of audience in court and the high cost of fees, many of which fell to be paid out of the public purse through the legal aid fund. Far from softening the tone, Lord Irvine soon demonstrated a determination to continue the process begun by Lord Mackay, insisting on cutting delays and expense in civil justice so long as these were cost-effective.[21]

---

[21] Press briefing to journalists, 6 June 1997. See *The Times*, 7 June 1997.

A further factor was concern over the impartiality of judges – a question which was renewed in the Pinochet case. General Augusto Pinochet Ugarte, former president of Chile, who in 1973 overthrew the democratically elected government and seized power in a violent army coup, was suspected of being, if not personally involved, then at least aware of torture, murder and the disappearance of individuals in Chile, and of having conspired to have these carried out. While he was on a private visit to Britain for medical treatment in 1998, Spain issued an extradition warrant and he was arrested and detained under house arrest in England. The question of his extradition went to the House of Lords. At the first hearing, the Law Lords ruled by three to two that he did not enjoy sovereign immunity from prosecution and could be extradited to Spain to stand trial.[22] One of the five judges hearing the case was Lord Hoffmann, who, it transpired, held a directorship with Amnesty International Charity Ltd., a company controlled by Amnesty International which had given evidence to the court, and who had not openly declared his interest in court.

Pinochet's lawyers immediately appealed to the House of Lords to overturn the decision on the basis that Lord Hoffmann was biased. In an unprecedented move, a panel of seven different Law Lords convened to consider the matter.[23] In the event, the decision was upheld, but on narrower grounds than decided by the first panel of judges. The criticism of Lord Hoffmann, an experienced and well-regarded judge, was sharp. Lord Hutton said that Hoffmann's links with Amnesty 'were so strong that public confidence in the integrity of the administration of justice would be shaken', while in Lord Hope of Craighead's opinion, although 'there has been no suggestion that he [Hoffmann] was actually biased' he had not been seen to be impartial, and that while 'he had no financial or pecuniary interest in the outcome . . . his relationship with Amnesty International was such that he was, in effect, acting as a judge in his own cause'.[24]

It has long been a principle of justice that justice must not only be

---

[22] See *R v. Evans and Another ex parte Pinochet Ugarte*; *R v. Bartle ex parte Pinochet Ugarte*; *In re Pinochet Ugarte*, *Times LR* 3 November 1998.

[23] *In re Pinochet Ugarte*, *Times LR* 18 January 1999.

[24] *The Times*, 16 January 1999.

done but 'must manifestly and undoubtedly be seen to be done'.[25] This requires that a judge disqualify him- or herself where there is not only some actual risk of bias through a financial interest, but also any perception that a judge could be biased. The problem with the current appointments system is that there is no mechanism for scrutinizing what political views or class-, race- or gender-bias a prospective judge might have. While no one in Britain has favoured the intensive and public interrogation of candidates as is done in the United States, some mechanism is required to ensure that judges are capable of acting with the integrity, independence and impartiality in office on which the legal system depends for its existence. The Pinochet case risked undermining public confidence, and rather predictably led to lawyers delving to find issues of bias which could disqualify a judge from adjudicating. In relation to four such challenges, the three most senior judges of the Court of Appeal, while dismissing three but allowing four of the appeals, took the opportunity to set guidelines on the issue of bias, stating that 'we cannot conceive of circumstances in which an objection could be soundly based on the religion, ethnic or national origin, gender, age, class, means or sexual orientation of the judge', nor could any objection ordinarily be taken to a judge's 'social, educational or employment background, or that of his family'.

Nevertheless, and notwithstanding the Court of Appeal's strong stand on challenges for bias, there exists disquieting evidence about incipient judicial bias. The judiciary is not representative of society. In 1996 four-fifths of judges went to both public schools and Oxbridge colleges; only seven out of 96 High Court judges were women, and only five of 517 circuit judges were black or Asian.[26] There has never been a female Law Lord or Lord Chancellor. It has been alleged that there is accordingly a homogeneity of background and political ideology among the senior judges. In *The Politics of the Judiciary*[27] Professor John Griffith argued that judges were predisposed to find against particular groups in society, most notably trade unions and students, to rule in favour of their opponents, and to give illiberal opinions in relation to civil

---

[25] Per Lord Hewart in *R v. Sussex Justices ex parte McCarthy* [1924] 1 KB 256.
[26] House of Commons Home Affairs Committee Report on Judicial Appointments, 1996.   [27] London: Fontana, 5th edn., 1997.

liberties, state security and terrorism, police powers and religion. However, as Griffith conceded, given the similarity in background between judges and members of the executive and Parliament, and given the often complementary nature of judicial work in upholding Parliament's will (and being subordinate to Parliament), it is hardly surprising that judges are not 'radical' in outlook.

Griffith's thesis remains influential but controversial and is not without its critics. One such critic is Simon Lee who argues cogently that a similarity in background – educational and social – does not necessarily and inevitably lead to similarity in political ideology, let alone to a coherent dominant philosophy shared by all judges. As he points out, many of the seminal cases which go to the House of Lords are decided by a majority of judges rather than a unanimous bench.[28] Disagreements between the judges at the highest level and in relation to the hardest cases of all belie the notion of judicial unanimity. In difficult cases different judges will be persuaded by different considerations within a case. To regard the outcome of judicial reasoning as somehow predetermined by social background and common professional experience is both naive and simplistic, and, in so far as it damages the reputation of the judiciary in the mind of the public, it is misleading and harmful.

Beyond Griffith's analysis is that of feminist scholars who argue that judges are inherently sexist. In Helena Kennedy's *Eve was Framed*,[29] much evidence is offered of discrimination against women in court proceedings, and, significantly, in judicial attitudes in rape trials. Kennedy cites Sir Melford Stevenson, who was lenient in sentencing a rapist on the basis that the victim, a sixteen-year-old, had been hitchhiking. In 1990 Mr Justice Jupp passed a suspended sentence on a husband who had twice raped his wife, on the basis of a distinction between rape by a husband and rape by a stranger. Mr Justice Leonard passed a reduced sentence on the perpetrators of a violent multiple rape, on the basis that the victim had made a 'remarkable recovery'. Perhaps most extraordinary are the words quoted by Kennedy of a judge in 1982 who said, in relation to the issue of consent, that

Women who say no do not always mean no. It is not just a question of how she says it, how she shows and makes it clear. If she doesn't want it she only has to

[28] *Judging Judges* (London: Faber & Faber, 1988).   [29] London: Vintage, 1992.

keep her legs shut and she would not get it without force and then there would be the marks of force being used.

Perhaps the sensitivity of judges has improved in cases such as rape for which, periodically, they have been much criticized. For the female victim, however, the perception of judicial bias is clear and a further deterrent to reporting sexual violence and pursuing justice through the courts. Unless and until there is a greater gender and racial balance in the courts, women and members of ethnic minorities will remain reluctant to seek access to a justice system which is so dominated by white, privileged male judges. The issue of a representative judiciary is capable of no short-term solution, being the inevitable outcome of selection from, principally, the Bar which has traditionally been a male bastion, and the insistence on merit-driven selection as opposed to aiming for gender and political balance. Recent years in particular have seen both the Bar and the Law Society (the solicitors' governing and representative body) working to eradicate racial and gender discrimination within the profession. Nevertheless, progress has been slow. While 50 per cent of law graduates are women, and a significant proportion of all graduates are from ethnic minorities, when it comes to entering the profession and advancement in the profession, the figures remain discouraging.

Judges

Once appointed, judges must act with impartiality and fairness towards litigants and defendants and, as importantly, in relation to the government of the day: the case law discussed below highlights the constitutional importance of this. In exercising judicial duties judges must set aside personal prejudices and any party political allegiances or preferences. Justice cannot be done without this essential element of impartiality and lack of bias. For current purposes two related matters are relevant. The first relates to the qualifications for judicial office, the second to the socio-economic characteristics of judges. In terms of qualifications, a successful career in the legal profession, still predominantly at the Bar, is a prerequisite. Judicial appointments are made from the profession itself, which enhances the cohesiveness of the legal profession and ensures continuity in the ethics of that profession. Of itself, this is perhaps unobjectionable, save for the race, class and gender bias which continues to characterize the profession. While the Law Society and the Bar strive to eliminate discriminatory practices in the profession, and membership is based on merit rather than on 'social standing', race or gender, it nevertheless remains the case that the legal profession is elitist and exclusionary. While 50 per cent of law and non-law graduates seeking entry to the profession are women, few women rise through the ranks of the profession to reach the point of consideration for judicial appointment. The same applies to members of ethnic minorities. In terms of class, a changing, outmoded but nevertheless still apparent feature of society, it is not class *per se* which excludes many from the profession, but rather the access to quality education which will lead to university and to the financial funding which is required to survive the courses for admission to the profession and training contracts (on the solicitors' side), or pupillage at the Bar.

The net effect of these factors results in a profession which is predominantly white, male and middle-class. It is from the most successful of these that judges are appointed, and the most successful of these will reach the higher echelons of the Court of Appeal and the House of Lords. The senior judiciary is comprised, as the inadvertent but direct consequence of the socio-economic profile of the profession, of a social elite which broadly corresponds with other establishment institutions: the armed forces, civil service, Church of England, House of Lords and, but to a lesser extent, members of the House of Commons. It is unsurprising to note that no woman has ever held judicial office in the House of Lords, nor been appointed Lord Chancellor, and that in 2001 of thirty-five judges of the Court of Appeal, merely two are women. This is not to suggest, necessarily, that the judiciary is not independent and independent-minded when it comes to controlling governmental abuse of power. What it does suggest, however, is that in its composition the senior judiciary reflects the background and training of the elite, and corresponds in that respect with other elite groups in society and remains in no sense representative of ordinary citizens.

In part this was Professor Griffith's thesis. Whether Griffith is right or not is important, but in the context of separation of powers, less important than the implications of this on the impartiality of the judges *vis-à-vis* government. It is Griffith's argument that there is an understandable empathy between government and judiciary. This should be viewed not as a sinister fact but as a natural consequence of shared backgrounds and of shared perceptions as to their respective areas of power. It is also a natural consequence of the British constitutional arrangement, which results in judges being subordinate to Parliament yet independent of Parliament and the executive, and yet having the constitutional duty to uphold Parliament's will as expressed in legislation. Judges complement the process of government, while keeping government under the law as expressed by Parliament.

THE LEGAL PROFESSION

The legal profession is divided into two branches, solicitors and barristers, each having its own training requirements, practices and areas of specialism. Those intending to enter the profession must therefore make a decision early in their careers as to which branch is the more suitable, although there is provision for transfer between the two branches, subject to additional training requirements. In the vast majority of jurisdictions around the world the legal profession is unitary, with lawyers performing all the many tasks required. The divided profession is therefore unusual and is a product of history. When reform is mooted, as is often the case, professional defence mechanisms are activated and reform resisted by both sides. Nevertheless, while the profession has been traditionally characterized by clear demarcation lines in terms of monopolies over certain activities and rights of audience in the higher courts, in recent years there have been substantial reforms aimed at making the profession more accessible, more efficient and less expensive.

Solicitors

The majority of entrants have a qualifying law degree, following which a one-year Legal Practice Course (LPC) is undertaken, followed by a training contract with a firm of solicitors. Those who have read a subject other than law at university may qualify to sit the LPC by the successful completion of a one-year conversion course, the Common Professional Examination. Following completion of the training contract, application is made to the Law Society to be admitted to the profession.

The solicitor is the first point of contact with the legal system for many citizens. Solicitors, until recently, had a monopoly over conveyancing (the transfer of title to property) and this still forms a major part of their income. If disputes arise over compensation for injury, employment or family matters, whether divorce or inheritance, it is to the local solicitor that people turn. The local solicitor is the general practitioner of the legal profession, although the growth in large city firms which focus on commercial work is an exception to this. When litigation becomes inevitable or necessary – and specialist advocacy is required – the first port of call is the solicitor's office. Individuals have no direct right of access to barristers, and if specialist advocacy is considered necessary the case is referred to counsel by the solicitor.

The conveyancing monopoly was broken in 1985,[30] when licensed conveyancers were permitted to practise. In the same year the Law Society permitted solicitors to sell property, in order to encourage 'one-stop' conveyancing. The Courts and Legal Services Act 1990 extended the right to provide conveyancing services to any person or body not already authorized to provide such services, subject to a successful application to the newly established Authorised Conveyancing Practitioners Board which now controls standards. The same Act permitted solicitors to go into business with non-solicitors, and to form multi-national partnerships. By 1999, of 8,524 firms of solicitors, only 420 had ten or more partners.

Solicitors have always enjoyed rights of audience before the lower courts – the Magistrates' and County Courts. However, the right to

[30] Administration of Justice Act 1985.

appear as an advocate before the higher courts (House of Lords, Court of Appeal, High Court and Crown Court) has been jealously guarded by the Bar, with the rights of solicitors only extended under the Access to Justice Act 1999, and then subject to additional training in the form of a higher courts advocacy qualification.[31]

Barristers

The barrister is by training a specialist advocate. The majority of entrants are law graduates, although a law degree is not a formal prerequisite. In 1998 there were 9,698 barristers in independent practice in England and Wales, of whom 7,288 were men and 2,410 women. There were 1,006 Queen's Counsel, the highest level of barristers, of whom only 72 were women.[32] The Bar Council is the profession's governing body, and barristers are organized through Inns of Court, run by Benchers, the senior members of the Inns.

Candidates for the Bar must register with one of the four Inns of Court and 'eat dinners' as required in order to become familiar with the Inn and its practices. On graduation a one-year professional training course is undertaken leading to the Bar Examinations. Non-law graduates must take the Common Professional Examination before taking the Bar Examinations. When they are successfully past that hurdle, pupillage is undertaken before they become qualified to practise.

Barristers work in 'chambers', run by barrister's clerks who organize the distribution of business for the barristers. Barristers enjoy immunity from claims of negligence in relation to their advocacy work,[33] an immunity now extended to solicitor advocates.[34] The exemption does not extend to negligent advice to a client, and only covers pre-trial work which is intimately connected with the conduct of the case in court. The justification for this privilege is that an advocate must be free from

[31] On the background to reform see the White Paper, *Legal Services: A Framework for the Future* (London: HMSO, 1989); *Rights of Audience and Rights to Conduct Litigation in England and Wales: The Way Ahead* (London: Lord Chancellor's Department, 1998).
[32] The General Council of the Bar, *Annual Report 1998* (1999).
[33] *Rondel v. Worsley* [1967] 3 WLR 1666.
[34] *Saif Ali v. Sidney Mitchell* [1980] AC 198.

threats in relation to his or her work, and that the barrister owes a duty to the court as well as to his or her client which could not be fulfilled if the barrister is constantly looking over his or her shoulder. A further justification lies in the 'cab rank' rule which requires barristers to take an available case, irrespective of whether he or she wishes to take the case, or approves of the issue involved. The cab rank rule is designed to ensure that even the least meritorious client – especially in criminal proceedings – has access to professional representation before a court.

Complaints about the profession

In relation to solicitors, the Law Society is the governing body. Complaints are lodged with the Office for the Supervision of Solicitors. In relation to fees, a Remuneration Certificate Department carries out reviews to ensure that they are fair and reasonable. The Bar Council is responsible for the Bar's Code of Conduct and for disciplinary matters. In relation to complaints, there are the Professional Conduct and Complaints Committee and a Complaints Commissioner. Compensation is payable to clients in cases involving inadequate service. The disciplinary tribunals of the Inns of Court have the power to disbar or suspend a barrister.

The Courts and Legal Services Act 1990 introduced a Legal Services Ombudsman. The Ombudsman has the power to 'investigate any allegation which is properly made to him [or her] and relates to the manner in which a complaint made to a professional body with respect to an authorised advocate, authorised litigator, licensed conveyancer, recognised body or notary who is a member of that professional body, or any employee of such a person, has been dealt with by that professional body'.[35] The Ombudsman cannot deal with complaints which are the subject of investigation by a court, or by the solicitors' professional body or the disciplinary tribunal of the Bar Council.

[35] Section 22.

THE FUNDING OF LEGAL SERVICES

Whereas in relation to health a national health service was established after the Second World War, in relation to access to law, rather than make state provision for the organization and delivery of legal services, the government introduced the legal aid system.[36] The provision of legal services remained in the private sector with legal aid introduced to give financial assistance to those involved in the civil and criminal system who met the eligibility requirements. The term 'legal aid' covers a variety of forms of assistance. Strictly speaking, legal aid refers to representation in court. However, before a case gets to court, individuals need legal advice and this is available through the Green Form scheme, which, again subject to the eligibility criteria, enables solicitors to provide up to two hours' worth of free legal advice and assistance. There is also provision of Assistance by Way of Representation (ABWOR), under which solicitors may attend court and represent a client in most civil proceedings in Magistrates' Courts.

The legal aid system expanded until in the 1950s some 80 per cent of the population were eligible to receive state aid. The burden on the taxpayer increased over the decades, and, since the 1980s at least, it has been the objective of Lord Chancellors to reduce the cost of legal aid. The criteria for aid were amended time and again to take more people out of the system, the overall effect being that only the poorest in society qualified for state aid, and with litigation costs high only the very rich could afford access to justice.

The civil legal aid system is run by the Legal Aid Board which administers two tests in relation to applications: the means test and the merits test. In relation to criminal proceedings, the decision to grant legal aid is made by the clerk to the court, again utilizing the means and merits tests, interpreted to mean 'in the interests of justice'. Where aid is refused the applicant is entitled to appeal to the Law Society's criminal legal aid committee. In 1993, in an effort to reduce expenditure and increase efficiency, the government introduced a franchising system whereby firms of solicitors were given the power to administer

---

[36] Under the Legal Aid and Advice Act 1949. See now the Legal Aid Act 1988.

certain aspects of legal aid. By mid-1999 over 2,500 firms were franchised.

Radical change was introduced by the Labour government, which stated that it wanted to see a 'clearer, fairer, better system, that will make justice available to all the people'.[37] The Access to Justice Act 1999 implemented reform. The principal features of the reform are that a Community Legal Service is introduced to co-ordinate the provision of legal services in every region. A Legal Services Commission replaces the Legal Aid Board. Civil legal aid is to be replaced by a system under which approved lawyers and service-providers work under contract with the Commission, thereby enabling tighter budgetary control. Legal aid is no longer to be available to those seeking personal injury compensation, except where clinical negligence is involved, nor in inheritance disputes, company and business matters, or cases between landowners over disputed boundaries. Instead, the government is encouraging the use of 'conditional fees' – the no win no fee arrangement – and the extension of legal insurance to meet the costs of claims. In relation to criminal legal aid, it is replaced by a new Criminal Defence Service run by the Community Legal Service. Criminal defence services will be provided under contract, with providers having to satisfy quality-assurance standards.

DEVELOPING THE LAW: STATUTORY INTERPRETATION AND THE DOCTRINE OF PRECEDENT

The interpretation of statutes

By the end of the nineteenth century, Acts of Parliament were fast overtaking the common law and regulating increasingly wide areas of life. While the judges are free – subject to certain restraints – to develop the law in the absence of an Act of Parliament, once Parliament has legislated, the Act of Parliament has supreme force and the judges are under a constitutional duty to give effect to its requirements. In

---

[37] The White Paper, *Modernising Justice: The Government's Plans for Reforming Legal Services and the Courts* (London: HMSO, 1998).

conventional theory, which has long been discredited, the judges merely state what the law is and to apply it: they do not make law, for that is the function of the sovereign legislature. Judges are neither elected nor accountable to citizens: Parliament – or at least the dominant House of Commons – is.

The interpretation of Acts of Parliament is, however, not always a simple task. Despite the best endeavour of legislative draftsmen and -women, on occasion the language used is obscure, or words and phrases occur that are capable of different interpretations. The inherent fluidity of language is also capable of suggesting different meanings for words when placed in different contexts. The interpretation the judges are seeking is that which best fits with the intentions of Parliament. However, even this simple, straightforward statement masks complexity. For example, some Acts of Parliament are of great antiquity and the question arises as to whether judges are to interpret Parliament's 'will' at the time Parliament passed the Act, or to interpret that 'will' as if Parliament had passed the Act under prevailing economic and social conditions. An additional factor arises in relation to European Community law. The legal systems of continental Europe are characterized by civil law, deriving from Roman law, the law being set out in broad statements of principle, rather than detailed technical language which is the norm in United Kingdom legislation. The European approach to the interpretation of law is consequently different, with judges seeking the interpretation which best fits with the purpose that the legislation was trying to achieve (the purposive or teleological approach) rather than the detailed word-bound interpretative technique traditionally employed in the English legal system. As Community law regulates an increasingly wide area, the domestic judges must adapt to the continental system of interpretation in order to ensure that Community law is interpreted in the United Kingdom in a manner consistent with that of the legal systems of other member states.

The judges themselves have developed a number of approaches or guidelines – rather misleadingly referred to as the 'rules' of statutory interpretation – in order to ensure the maximum degree of consistency in the law while remaining true to what Parliament intended the law to mean. In addition, certain principles, known as 'presumptions', are employed in the interpretative process. Furthermore the judges have had to decide whether they are entitled, in order to find the 'true meaning' of the Act, to look beyond the confines of the statute itself and consider other materials which may throw light on the correct meaning of words used, for example Law Commission reports recommending reform of an area of the law or Hansard, the official record of parliamentary proceedings. With the implementation of the Human Rights Act 1998, in Scotland in 1998 and England and Wales and Northern Ireland in 2000, an additional requirement comes into play, namely that the judges are under a statutory duty to interpret legislation in such a manner as to make it consistent – so far as possible – with the Convention rights which the Act incorporates into domestic law.

Approaches, guidelines and presumptions: the 'rules' of statutory interpretation

The dominant conventional approach in the English legal system is the literal approach. This presupposes that the true meaning of the Act is to be found from a literal interpretation of the words used, by giving to the words their ordinary commonplace meaning, and nothing more. This literal approach may only be departed from if the meaning derived from an analysis of the words used produces an absurd result, or a result which, while not absurd, is such that Parliament cannot have intended it. However, even the departure from the plain meaning to avoid absurdity is an extension of the classic rule, and was certainly not accepted at the end of the nineteenth century. In *R v. Judge of the City of London Court*, for example, Lord Esher stated that: 'If the words of an Act are clear, you must follow them, even though they lead to a manifest absurdity. The Court has nothing to do with the question whether the Legislature has committed an absurdity.'[38] The constitutional advantage of the literal approach is that it best reflects the traditional view that judges are subordinate to Parliament and merely declare what Parliament intended, rather than making new law by attributing new meanings to the words used. The literal approach, where operable, also lends itself to a high degree of consistency in the

[38] [1892] 1 QB 273 at 290.

law. If judges stick to the literal approach, there should be no room for subjective opinions to creep in and alter the meaning which Parliament intended. On the other hand, judges can and do disagree as to what the 'plain meaning' of a word is, or if agreeing that the meaning of the word is 'plain' they may still differ as to its precise interpretation. This is unsurprising given the inherent fluidity of language. Professor Herbert Hart in *The Concept of Law*[39] addresses this linguistic feature when he speaks of words having a 'core meaning' and a 'penumbra of doubt'. For Hart, in order to attribute the appropriate meaning to a word, it is necessary to place that word within its context. For example, if a local authority by-law prohibits 'vehicles' in a park, in order to understand the meaning of the word vehicle it is necessary to step outside the word and consider it in relation to the objective and scope of the by-law. While the word 'vehicle' may have a plain meaning for some purposes it may not for others. If the by-law is intended to provide a safe play area for small children, the word vehicle may be broad enough to cover the prohibition of rollerblades. On the other hand, if the purpose of the by-law is to provide a recreation ground for teenagers, rollerblades may not be interpreted as prohibited vehicles. Or yet again, if the purpose of the by-law is to provide a peaceful relaxation area for elderly people, rollerblades would again fall within the confines of prohibited 'vehicles'.

The Law Commission criticized the literal approach in the following manner:

To place undue emphasis on the literal meaning of the words of a provision is to assume an unattainable perfection in draftsmanship; it presupposes that the draftsmen can always choose words to describe the situations intended to be covered by the provision which will leave no room for a difference of opinion as to their meaning. Such an approach ignores the limitations of language, which is not infrequently demonstrated even at the level of the House of Lords when Law Lords differ as to the so-called 'plain meaning' of words.[40]

A further problem arises where Parliament has not expressed itself clearly, or has left a particular situation uncovered. On the strict view,

---

[39] Oxford: Oxford University Press, 1961.
[40] Law Commission Report, *The Interpretation of Statutes*, 1969, paragraph 30.

judges are not free – as Lord Denning occasionally decided to do – to put words into an Act which Parliament did not enact, for this is to 'usurp the legislative function' of Parliament. A classic illustration of Lord Denning's predilection for 'gap-filling' is seen in *Magor and St Mellons v. Newport Corporation*.[41] Newport Corporation had expanded its boundaries by absorbing two other smaller local authorities which in financial terms were relatively more affluent than Newport, thereby increasing Newport's local revenue. The Local Government Act of 1933 made provision for compensation to be paid to the councils that had been absorbed by the council which benefited from the takeover. However, the minister had made an order which subsumed the two councils into one, and this factor, Newport claimed, meant that it did not have to pay compensation, since the two old councils had now been abolished. In the Court of Appeal, the majority supported Newport Corporation. Lord Denning, however, was of a different view, ruling that Parliament and the minister had not intended to deprive the ratepayers of the amalgamated councils of the benefit which would accrue from their takeover, and that notwithstanding the amalgamation, compensation was due. On interpretation, Lord Denning stated that

I have no patience with an ultra-legalistic interpretation which would deprive them [the ratepayers] of their rights altogether ... We do not sit here to pull the language of Parliament and of Ministers to pieces and make nonsense of it. That is an easy thing to do, and it is a thing to which lawyers are too often prone. We sit here to find out the intention of Parliament and of Ministers and carry it out, and we do this better by filling in the gaps and making sense of the enactment than by opening it up to destructive analysis.[42]

The matter went to the House of Lords, which upheld the majority judgment of the Court of Appeal. On Lord Denning's approach, Lord Simonds was particularly scathing:

It appears to me to be a naked usurpation of the legislative function under the thin disguise of interpretation and it is the less justifiable when it is guesswork with what material the legislature would, if it had discovered the gap, have filled it in. If a gap is disclosed the remedy lies in an amending Act.

[41] [1950] 2 All ER 1226; [1951] 2 All ER 839 (HL).
[42] [1950] 2 All ER, at p. 1236.

The literal approach has been described by Professor Michael Zander as 'defeatist and lazy', and 'always wrong because it amounts to an abdication of responsibility by the judge'.[43]

To remedy some of the worst defects of the literal approach, the judges developed the golden rule. This is intended to enable judges to avoid the worst excesses of absurdity by finding a meaning which makes sense of the legislation without departing from its intentions. This is not to say that judges are free to decide that Parliament has created an absurdity and that accordingly they can depart from the clear meaning of the words used. There must be some genuine reasons justifying the departure from the literal approach. On occasion, the literal rule is no more than a choice exercised between two conflicting meanings, one of which would result in absurdity, the other of which would give effect to Parliament's intention. In other instances, the golden rule may be adopted to avoid an absurdity which would result from the literal rule being applied in circumstances which Parliament had not envisaged. For example, in *Re Sigsworth*[44] the court interpreted legislation relating to inheritance in such a manner as to exclude from the beneficiaries the person who had murdered the testator by employing the maxim 'no one shall profit from his own wrong'.

Where neither the literal rule nor the golden rule is capable of achieving a result in line with Parliament's overall intention, the judges may adopt the mischief rule, otherwise known as the 'purposive approach'. This 'rule' can be traced to *Heydon's Case* of 1584.[45] The mischief rule entails the court asking itself a series of questions in relation to the legislation, namely: (*a*) what the common law was before the statute was passed; (*b*) what the 'mischief' was which the common law did not cover, and (*c*) what remedy Parliament attempted to provide. And finally, what the reason was for adopting that particular remedy. As can be seen from the questions, this approach requires the court to go beyond the strict words of the statute and address the context in which the Act was passed. Judges, then, are required to understand the reasons for the legislation, both in terms of the former defect in the common law and in terms of the remedy

---

[43] M. Zander, *The Law-Making Process* (London: Butterworth, 1999), p. 125.
[44] [1935] Ch 89.
[45] (1584) 3 Co Rep 7a.

Parliament chose to redress the defect. This entitles judges to use both *intrinsic* and *extrinsic* aids to interpretation.

Intrinsic aids are those within the Act itself. For example, Acts of Parliament have both long titles and short titles, there are marginal notes printed at the side of sections which act as a guide to the meaning of the section, and there are headings which precede a number of related sections and which reflect the overall topic to which the sections relate. All Acts also have schedules, which are designed to amplify the sections of the Act. For example, the Greater London Authority Act 1999, which devolves power to a London Mayor and Assembly,[46] has 425 sections, supplemented by 34 schedules which fill in the details of the sections. Typically, an individual section will make reference to the appropriate schedule, as in section 5 of the Food Standards Act 1999 (which relates to the establishment of advisory committees in relation to the newly formed Food Standards Agency), subsection (4) of which reads: Schedule 2 (which contains supplementary provisions about advisory committees) has effect. In addition, Acts contain interpretative sections designed to clarify the intended meaning of words and phrases. All these aids may be used by the judges.

More contentious is the question of using extrinsic aids to interpretation: aids not within the Act itself but comprising former legislation and judicial decisions relating to the subject in question, international conventions and treaties on which the legislation is based, background materials relating to the Act and the record of parliamentary proceedings relating to the passage of the Act. However, while reference to such extrinsic aids may be legitimate in guiding the court towards a correct interpretation of the Act in question, the court may not rely on such materials to such an extent that the meaning of the Act is distorted. For example, the Law Commission is charged with keeping the law under review and making recommendations for legislation.[47] The Commission's reports are accordingly an authoritative source of what has preceded the particular Act, and where ambiguity is detected by the court, may be a fertile source for resolving the issue. However, even

---

[46] On the Act, see Chapter 5.
[47] Other relevant publications include reports of Royal Commissions and reports issued by departmental committees of inquiry.

where the court refers to Commission reports, it cannot be assumed that Parliament intended – without further evidence – to enact legislation exactly replicating the Commission's recommendations. Until relatively recently, there was an absolute prohibition on judicial recourse to official reports. The case which reopened the debate was *Black-Clawson International Ltd. v. Papierwerke Waldhof-Aschaffenburg AG*[48] in which the Law Lords were divided on the issue. However, all the judges in the House of Lords were united on the fact that it was permissible to consult the reports for the limited purpose of understanding the 'mischief' which Parliament was seeking to remedy.

More difficult is the weight to be put on the official record of parliamentary proceedings: Hansard. Although it is formally inadmissible, Lord Denning openly admitted that he referred to it as an aid.[49] The seminal case is that of *Pepper v. Hart*.[50] At issue was the level at which benefits in kind – in this case the right of schoolmasters to have their sons educated at a public school for 20 per cent of the normal fees – should be assessed by the Inland Revenue. In the House of Lords, reference was made to a parliamentary statement in which the purpose of the relevant provision was explained. The case for and against relaxing the prohibition on referring to Hansard was put, including the constitutional argument that judges were to interpret the statute alone, and that nothing said in Parliament during the passage of a Bill should distort that interpretation. The fact that access to parliamentary materials might also prove difficult for citizens and lawyers was also put. It was also argued that reference to Hansard infringed the privileges of Parliament and amounted to a judicial inquiry into proceedings in Parliament, contrary to Article 9 of the Bill of Rights 1689.[51]

However, in the leading judgment, Lord Browne-Wilkinson stated that the

exclusionary rule should be relaxed so as to permit reference to parliamentary materials where (*a*) legislation is ambiguous or obscure, or leads to an absurdity;

---

[48] [1975] AC 591.

[49] See *Davis v. Johnson* [1979] AC 264. See also *Pickstone v. Freeman* [1988] 2 All ER 803, [1989] AC 66, in which ministerial statements were admissible to aid interpretation of subordinate legislation.

[50] [1993] AC 593, [1993] 1 All ER 42.   [51] On which see Chapter 13.

(*b*) the material relied on consists of one or more statements by a minister or other promoter of the Bill together if necessary with such other parliamentary material as is necessary to understand such statements and their effects; (*c*) the statements relied on are clear.

Although the House of Lords was clear that it intended the relaxation of the rule to be limited to instances in which legislation is ambiguous, obscure or leads to absurdity, the courts appear to have further relaxed the rule. In *Three Rivers District Council v. Bank of England (No. 2)*[52] the rule was extended to cover unambiguous legislation in a situation in which it might nevertheless be ineffective in its intention to give effect to a European Community directive.

Judges also employ a number of presumptions in interpretation, presumptions which may be rebutted in the course of proceedings. These include the presumption that criminal statutes should be strictly construed in favour of the citizen, and that a person's liberty and right to property should not be restricted save where clear words are used in a statute to that effect. It is also presumed that *mens rea* – intention to commit an offence – is required before criminal liability arises. The classic case is *Sweet v. Parsley*[53] in which a schoolteacher had been convicted of allowing premises to be used for drug taking, contrary to the Misuse of Drugs Act 1971. The House of Lords ruled that her conviction could not stand: she had no idea of the use to which her tenants were putting the property, and the lack of knowledge meant that she could not have the necessary intention (*mens rea*) to commit the offence. On the other hand, Parliament may choose to make an offence one for which there is strict liability – that is to say, a person may be convicted of an offence without the necessary intention. There is also the presumption that statutes do not have retrospective effect, although again, Parliament may choose expressly to impose retrospective liability as it did in the War Crimes Act 1990, which enabled the prosecution and conviction of persons accused of war crimes in the Second World War. Retrospective liability is contrary to the European Convention on Human Rights, subject to the exception that a person may be tried and punished for acts or omissions which at the time when they were committed were 'criminal according to the general principles

[52] [1996] 2 All ER 363.　　　[53] [1969] 2 WLR 470.

of law recognised by civilised nations'. In *Waddington v. Miah*[54] Lord Reid commented that it was 'hardly credible' that Parliament would pass retrospective criminal legislation.

A further presumption is that Parliament did not intend to oust (exclude) the jurisdiction of the courts. Again, this is rebuttable. However, attempts to exclude the jurisdiction of the courts are most carefully scrutinized by the judges. Parliament frequently imposes time limits on challenges to administrative decisions, particularly in relation to planning matters where certainty and finality are important, and these the courts will respect.[55] However, if a statute attempts to exclude any form of challenge at all, the court may rule that even the words 'the decision ... by a tribunal ... is final' is incapable of excluding the court's jurisdiction.[56]

It is also a presumption that Parliament did not intend to change the common law, save where that intention is expressly stated. Furthermore, if a statute is intended to apply to the Crown, that intention must be expressly stated, otherwise the presumption will apply that it does not apply to the Crown. A number of presumptions apply to the interpretative process. Among these is the rule that 'words take their meaning from their context': *noscitur a sociis*. So, for example, if a statute prohibits betting in a number of outdoor places, it is unlikely to prohibit betting indoors.[57] Where a statute gives examples of persons or objects covered by a particular provision, the rule operates that a general class added to the end of specified examples must be interpreted in line with those examples: *ejusdem generis*. The *expressio unius exclusio alterius* rule provides that where a statute lists those matters covered by it, anything not included in that list is excluded – for example, a reference to coal mines will exclude limestone mines.[58]

Lastly, there is the presumption that Parliament does not intend to legislate contrary to international obligations, and the courts will

---

[54] [1974] 2 All ER 377.
[55] See e.g. *Smith v. East Elloe Rural District Council* [1956] AC 736; *R v. Secretary of State for the Environment ex parte Ostler* [1976] 3 All ER 90.
[56] See *R v. Medical Appeal Tribunal ex parte Gilmore* [1957] 1 QB 574; *Anisminic v. Foreign Compensation Commission* [1969] 2 AC 147.
[57] *Powell v. Kempton Park Racecourse* [1899] AC 143.
[58] *R v. Inhabitants of Sedgley* (1831) 2 B & Ad 65.

attempt to interpret domestic law in such a way as to make it consistent with international law. This presumption assumes particular significance in relation to the European Convention on Human Rights and the Human Rights Act 1998 which makes Convention rights enforceable before the domestic courts. As seen in Chapter 7, under the Human Rights Act judges are empowered to set aside subordinate legislation which does not conform to Convention requirements, unless that nonconformity is the effect of primary legislation. In relation to primary legislation (Acts of Parliament), the judges may not declare it invalid, but may – where an incompatibility with Convention rights is detected – issue a 'declaration of incompatibility'.

The doctrine of precedent

Justice requires that like cases are treated alike and that different cases are treated differently. It also requires that there is certainty in the law, in order that citizens may conduct themselves in the confidence that their actions are lawful. These principles underpin the rules which the judges have developed in their interpretation and evolution of the common law (judge-made law as opposed to statute) through the doctrine of precedent. Under common law, precedents are binding, according to the level of court in which proceedings are taking place. The doctrine of binding precedent is that of *stare decisis* – keeping to the decisions of previous cases. However, if precedent was always and invariably binding there would be no evolution of the law. Accordingly, a number of rules have been developed to achieve both certainty and a degree of flexibility in the law to accommodate new circumstances or changes in society.[59]

Exactly what constitutes a 'precedent' is the subject of much debate. Not all aspects of a previous case and the judgment of the court will 'bind' a future decision. What is binding is the *ratio decidendi* of a precedent case: the 'central core of meaning', 'its sharpest cutting edge', or 'a proposition of law which decides the case, in the light or in the context of the material facts'.[60] This is to be distinguished from other principles,

---

[59] This is a complex topic which can only be dealt with briefly within the confines of this book.   [60] Zander, *Law-Making Process*, pp. 262–3.

propositions and statements which are made in the course of a judgment, known as *obiter dicta* which, while persuasive in the future and sometimes determining the manner in which the law later develops, are not binding on the future court – even if that *obiter* is made by the House of Lords. Where there is more than one *ratio*, both are binding.

The system operates on the basis of the hierarchy of courts, the general rule being the higher the court the more binding its precedents, with the precedents of the House of Lords binding all lower courts. Accordingly, the decisions of Magistrates' Courts and County Courts, being the lowest in the hierarchy, are binding on no other court, but the Magistrates' Court and County Court are bound by decisions of the higher courts (High Court, Court of Appeal and House of Lords). The Crown Courts – the principal venue for the trial by jury of criminal cases – do not create precedent. The High Court is bound by decisions of the Court of Appeal and House of Lords. The High Court – comprising the Chancery Division, Family Division and Queen's Bench Division – is generally bound by its own previous decisions, with two exceptions. In relation to civil cases, it may depart from its previous decisions under rules developed by the Court of Appeal and discussed below; in criminal cases, the Queen's Bench Divisional Court may refuse to follow its own previous decisions on the ground that the previous case was wrongly decided, or decided *per incuriam*, meaning decided 'in ignorance or forgetfulness of some inconsistent statutory provision or of some authority binding on the court concerned'.[61]

The Court of Appeal is bound by decisions of the House of Lords, and bound by its own decisions save where the accepted exceptions apply. These exceptions were formulated in *Young v. Bristol Aeroplane Co. Ltd.*,[62] and were set out by Lord Greene MR:

(1) The court is entitled and bound to decide which of two conflicting decisions of its own it will follow.
(2) The court is bound to refuse to follow a decision of its own which, though not expressly overruled, cannot, in its opinion, stand with a decision of the House of Lords.

---

[61] *Per* Lord Evershed, *Morelle v. Wakeling* [1955] 2 QB 379. See also *Miliangos v. George Frank (Textiles) Ltd.* [1976] AC 443.
[62] [1944] 2 All ER 293; [1946] AC 163, [1946] 1 All ER 98 (HL).

(3) The court is not bound to follow a decision of its own if it is satisfied that the decision was given *per incuriam*.

When it comes to the House of Lords, the court is generally bound by its own decisions, and until 1966 was absolutely obliged to apply its own previous decisions, even where the Court felt that to do so was wrong. In 1966, however, greater flexibility was injected into the process with a Practice Direction which stated that the House of Lords could depart from its previous decisions, in exceptional cases, where it is right to do so. This power is, however, exercised cautiously because of its unsettling effect on the law that is applied in the lower courts. However, in some areas of the law where it is the judges rather than Parliament who have developed the law, the ability to depart from precedents is crucial to keeping the law in tune with current – rather than past – economic, social and moral standards.

One area which is characterized by judge-made rather than parliamentary law is that of negligence. The tort (civil wrong) of negligence concerns the liability of a person or body towards others in respect of injury caused to that other person through his or her failure to foresee the reasonable likelihood of injury to that other party. Examples of seminal cases in the law of negligence include *Donoghue v. Stevenson*,[63] *British Railways Board v. Herrington*,[64] *McLoughlin v. O'Brian*[65] and *Hedley Byrne v. Heller*.[66] In *Donoghue v. Stevenson*, the issue was the liability of a manufacturer to a consumer with whom he did not have a contractual relationship. Under contract law, only those parties to the contract may pursue remedies for defective manufacture. In *Donoghue*, the consumer was a woman who had been made ill through consumption of ginger beer which contained the remains of a decomposed snail. The victim had not purchased the ginger beer, which was bought for her by a friend in a café. Accordingly, the victim herself was not a party to any contract on which she could sue to recover damages. The matter went to the House of Lords, the highest domestic court. The House of Lords ruled that the manufacturer was under a 'duty of care' to the ultimate consumer, irrespective of the law of contract. The manufacturer had a duty of care to those who he could reasonably foresee

---

[63] [1932] AC 562.   [64] [1972] 1 All ER 749.   [65] [1983] 1 AC 410.
[66] [1964] AC 465.

would consume the product. This was the expression of the 'neighbour principle', forcefully expounded by Lord Acton.

The later case of *Herrington* revealed a further weakness in the law. Under the common law, there was generally no 'duty of care' towards a person who trespasses on property. A positive duty of care arose only in respect of persons lawfully on premises. At best, there was a negative duty not deliberately to attempt to harm trespassers, for example by placing man-traps. As a result there was no liability for injury caused to trespassers while on the property. In *Herrington*, a young child wandered on to a railway line, gaining access through an unrepaired fence. The child was injured. The House of Lords departed from an earlier decision[67] which would have denied the child a remedy and ruled that British Rail – being a public body having vast resources – had a responsibility, and hence a duty of care, towards child trespassers who were injured as a result of British Rail's failure to keep the fence under good repair. This was the doctrine of 'common humanity': occupiers with the knowledge, skill and resources to take steps to avoid accidents, owed a duty to do so.[68]

The issue which arose in *Hedley Byrne v. Heller* was the liability of a financial adviser towards his or her client who had acted in reliance on his or her advice and as a direct result suffered financial loss. While it had long been established that physical injury through another's negligence made the negligent person liable in law for damages, the position of financial loss through negligent advice had never been considered. In *Hedley Byrne* the House of Lords adopted the neighbour principle expounded in *Donoghue v. Stevenson*. The plaintiffs were advertising agents concerned about the financial status of one of their clients. Their bankers requested information from the client's bankers. The client's bank replied giving a favourable impression, but at the top of their letter placed a disclaimer of liability. The plaintiff relied on this information but then lost substantial sums of money when the client went into liquidation. The House of Lords ruled that, if it had not been for the disclaimer, the bank would have been liable for economic loss. However, the liability was not exhaustive. In order for a duty of care to

---

[67] *Robert Addie & Sons (Collieries) Ltd. v. Dumbreck* [1929] All ER 1.
[68] The Occupiers' Liability Act 1984 extended protection to adult trespassers, although this is less extensive than for visitors lawfully on premises.

arise, there must have been a reliance on information given within what the Court described as a 'special relationship' between the giver and receiver of information. That special relationship precludes merely social relationships, but subsequent interpretations illustrate that in any business or professional relationship there is the potential for a special relationship to exist.

McLoughlin's case illustrates a quite different aspect of negligence: that of psychological injury, in this case 'nervous shock'. Nervous shock, and a modern manifestation of it, 'post traumatic stress disorder', for long went unrecognized by the courts. The judges not only doubted its existence as a category of harm, but also feared the possibility of faked evidence. They were also wary on the grounds that any recognition of nervous shock would cause the 'flood gates' to open, with the courts being swamped by cases. In *McLoughlin* a wife and mother, who was at her home at the time, was told that her husband and children had been seriously injured in a car accident. The law at the time provided that a person who suffered psychological harm through another's failure in the duty of care, could only recover damages if he or she was at the scene of the injury.[69] What then was the position of a person who suffered emotional harm because of an event which he or she had not witnessed? When she reached the hospital to which her family had been taken, one of her four children had died and none of the survivors had been cleaned up and they were in shock. The House of Lords ruled that Mrs McLoughlin could recover damages for her injury.[70]

A further seminal case in which the House of Lords declared that the former interpretation of the law was wrong and therefore ceased to be

---

[69] Clearly rescuers at the scene of an accident were covered. In 1992 a fireman who had been involved in the rescue of victims of fire at King's Cross Underground station was awarded £147,683 for nervous shock: *Hale v. London Underground* (1992) 11 BMLR 81.

[70] The *McLoughlin case* left open many questions for future decisions, and later cases narrowed the liability for nervous shock. In *Alcock v. Chief Constable of South Yorkshire* [1991] 4 All ER 907, for example, the House of Lords rejected claims for nervous shock by relatives of the victims of the Hillsborough football stadium disaster in which 95 people died and 400 required medical treatment in hospital. The accident was broadcast live on television. The police admitted liability for allowing too many people into the stadium. The House of Lords ruled that three factors governed the issue of liability: the proximity of the plaintiff in time and space to the scene of the accident; the relationship between the accident victim and the sufferer; the means by which the shock had been caused.

relevant was *R v. R*.[71] This case concerned the immunity which husbands had enjoyed from the law of rape *vis-à-vis* their wives. Traditionally, the view expressed was that 'It is clear and well settled ancient law that a man cannot be guilty of rape upon his wife'.[72] Or, as the eighteenth-century jurist Sir Matthew Hale put it: 'The husband cannot be guilty of a rape committed by himself upon his lawful wife, for by their mutual matrimonial consent and contract the wife hath given up herself in this kind to her husband, which she cannot retract.' This remarkable doctrine which enabled husbands to rape their wives with impunity, safe from the reaches of the criminal law, survived for centuries. In *R v. R*, however, the House of Lords finally laid the rule to rest. When the defendant challenged the ruling by an application under the European Convention on Human Rights, arguing that the decision was retrospective and therefore contrary to Article 7 of the Convention, the European Court of Human Rights declared that the former exemption from the law of rape was inconsistent with current moral standards, and that the House of Lords had merely given a modern restatement of what the law should be. Accordingly, notwithstanding the retrospective effect of the decision, it did not violate the Convention. Finally, in terms of hierarchy, all courts are bound to follow the decisions of the European Court of Justice, and to apply Community law in a manner consistent with the interpretations given by the ECJ.

While courts are bound by precedents in the manner discussed above, there are means by which courts may 'escape' from a precedent. The interests of justice require certainty in the law and that cases which present the same facts be treated in the same manner. Conversely, where cases differ, it is of paramount importance that the relevant differences be considered. Aside from the power of the House of Lords to overrule an earlier decision, discussed above, the principal means by which a precedent may be ruled not to bind a court is through the process of distinguishing. It was seen above that the element of a judgment which binds a court in the future (subject to hierarchy) is the *ratio*, all other statements of law and principle being regarded as non-binding, but influential, *obiter*. To distinguish a case is to hold that there are material

---

[71] [1991] 4 All ER 481, [1992] 1 AC 599.
[72] See N. Naffine, *Law and the Sexes* (Sydney: Allen and Unwin, 1990).

differences between the present case and the otherwise binding case which enable the court to avoid the precedent. The process of judicial reasoning, however, is not purely a matter of the logical application of previous cases. Given the multiplicity of facts and circumstances, it will be a rare occurrence for two cases to be identical: indeed, if they were, it is unlikely that litigation would be undertaken, since it would be known to the lawyers that there is an authoritative case on that precise and identical question. Given the cost and time involved, parties only resort to law and to the appeal courts where important points are unclear or uncertain. Cases which proceed on appeal are inherently uncertain. In order to reach a decision, the first task is to select appropriate precedent cases, and to determine the relevant likenesses or differences between those cases and the present case. In doing so, the Appeal Court is in essence applying its own interpretation to the precedent cases, teasing out of the text of the judgments the 'true meaning' of the case and then testing its relevance to the current case.

A number of complications unsettle the certainty of precedent, not least of which are the circumstances under which the Court of Appeal is entitled to depart from its own previous decisions.[73] There may on occasion be two prior decisions of the Court of Appeal which are in conflict with one another. This situation arose in *Davis v. Johnston*.[74] The question in issue was an interpretation of the Domestic Violence and Matrimonial Proceedings Act 1976, which two recent and previous decisions of the Court of Appeal had interpreted to mean that a person with a proprietary interest in property could not be excluded from that property by an injunction in order to protect the applicant from domestic violence. A panel of five judges heard the case.[75] Of these, three ruled that the Court of Appeal could depart from its own previous decisions where the judges were satisfied that the previous decisions were plainly wrong. According to Lord Denning MR, the Court of Appeal should have the same freedom as the House of Lords in this situation. Two of the judges, Goff LJ and Cumming-Bruce LJ, disagreed with the majority. Lord Goff dissented on the basis that the preservation of certainty in the law dictated consistency. Lord Cumming-Bruce

---

[73] As formulated in *Young v. Bristol Aeroplane*, see above.
[74] [1979] AC 264.   [75] The normal number of judges is three.

agreed. The only court which should have the power argued for by Lord Denning was the House of Lords. When the matter went to the House of Lords, the view of the majority in the Court of Appeal was rejected: the need for certainty in the law dictated that only the highest court could have the flexibility for which Lord Denning argued.

The second exception identified in *Young's case* is less problematic. The Court of Appeal may depart from its own previous decision, if that decision is inconsistent with a decision of the House of Lords. Where the decision of the House of Lords is subsequent to that of the Court of Appeal, it may be taken to overrule, by implication, the inconsistent decision. However, where the decision of the House of Lords is prior to that of the Court of Appeal, the problem is more delicate, for the Court of Appeal must then decide whether to follow the House of Lords and reject its own previous decision, or remain true to its earlier pronouncement of the law and thereby implicitly reject that of the House of Lords. This situation arose in *Miliangos v. George Frank (Textiles) Ltd.*[76] In that case before the House of Lords, two of the Law Lords disagreed as to how the Court of Appeal should proceed.

The third exception relates to decisions reached *per incuriam*, meaning that the decision was made in ignorance of some significant fact. This exception is treated with caution, and will not apply simply because an argument was not fully formulated, or because there was faulty judicial reasoning, or because only one party to the case appeared. Rather, *per incuriam* is confined to those decisions which are 'given in ignorance or forgetfulness of some inconsistent statutory provision or of some authority binding on the court concerned: so that in such cases some part of the decision or some step in the reasoning on which it was based is found, on that account, to be demonstrably wrong.'[77]

As can be seen from the above brief discussion, the doctrine of precedent strains between the two goals of consistency in law and flexibility. To err too far in either direction risks either undermining the ability of citizens to plan their affairs according to settled law, or creating injustice through the failure to bring the law up to date and in line with prevailing conditions in society.

---

[76] [1976] AC 443.
[77] Per Lord Evershed MR in *Morell v. Wakeling* [1955] 2 QB 379 (Court of Appeal).

THE ADMINISTRATION OF JUSTICE 2: THE CRIMINAL JUSTICE SYSTEM IN ENGLAND AND WALES

INTRODUCTION

In this chapter, the organization and role of the police and aspects of the criminal justice system are discussed. At issue is the balance to be struck between the rights of all citizens to live in a society in which crime is effectively dealt with (which includes not only the detection and prosecution of offenders but also strategies which reduce the incidence of crime) and the requirements of justice for those accused of crime.

The criminal justice system is one which has been under challenge as successive governments try to curb crime in society, in part through improved crime-prevention measures and in part through an effective system of punishment for offenders. The Labour Party pledged before the 1997 general election that it would be 'tough on crime and tough on the causes of crime'. Much improvement has been achieved: the Home Secretary stated in 2001 that while demographic projections suggested that crime would rise between 1997 and 1999, the British crime survey showed an overall fall in crime by 10 per cent in that period. However, in his statement to the House of Commons in 2001, the then Home Secretary, Jack Straw, also commented that

Over the past twenty years, the performance of the criminal justice system has kept pace neither with long-term trends in crime nor with new types of crime.

Too few offences are detected and prosecuted successfully. Between 1980 and 1995 the number of recorded offences doubled, but the number of convictions in respect of those offences fell by a third. To put it mildly, the system has not been as successful as it should have been in catching, prosecuting and punishing criminals.[1]

The Labour government elected in 1997 embarked on an ambitious, and controversial, programme of reform. Among other matters, the government determined to limit the right to trial by jury, to cut the cost to the state of defence lawyers and to introduce a state defender system to replace the use of privately employed barristers. The government also advocated extending the disclosure of a person's previous convictions to a jury – previously not permitted on the basis that such information could prejudice a fair decision. In addition, powers were introduced to enable the police to stop supporters suspected of previous involvement in violence at football matches from going abroad to curb the hooliganism associated with overseas matches. Powers to detain innocent mentally ill persons were also on the agenda, in response to rising fears about the danger posed to society. The overriding objective, however, was to modernize the system of criminal justice. In this the government identified four key areas: crime prevention; detection and conviction of more offenders; ensuring that punishments fit the criminal as well as the crime, thereby reducing reoffending; and fourthly, radical improvement in the treatment of victims of crime.[2]

THE POLICE

The investigation of crime

Organizationally, there has never been a national police force in the United Kingdom. Instead, policing has always been a matter for local administration, coupled with centralized control – outside operational matters – by the Home Secretary who is democratically accountable to

[1] Hansard, HC Deb. col. 584, 26 February 2001.
[2] Ibid., col. 584, 26 February 2001.

Parliament for the police. Successive Acts of Parliament now regulate police powers, powers which formerly were developed largely by the judges under the common law. In England and Wales there are forty-three forces, in 1999 employing more than 127,000 officers. In Scotland there are six forces, in Northern Ireland one force. The Home Office has responsibility for financing and for setting target figures for police personnel. Fifty-one per cent of the cost of policing is met out of central government grants, the rest being raised locally. In 2000 the government set aside £667 million for an extra 4,000 police officers by 2003, but subject to improved recruitment from ethnic minorities.[3] A target of recruiting 8,000 officers from ethnic minorities has been set for 2009, including an additional 5,662 in the Metropolitan Police. Targets were also set to cut burglary by 25 per cent by 2005 and vehicle crime by 30 per cent by 2004. As crime figures rise and clear-up rates fall, there is an inbuilt temptation for police officers to abuse their powers to improve the statistics.

Each police force is under the operational control of a Chief Constable – in London titled the Metropolitan Commissioner. The power wielded by the forty-one Chief Constables, the Commissioner of Metropolitan Police and the head of the City of London Police is considerable. While the Home Secretary effectively controls police funding and can issue Circulars outlining government policies in relation to policing, there is no real form of control over how Chief Constables operate their forces. However, to strengthen central control, the Police and Magistrates' Courts Act 1994 empowered the Home Secretary to 'determine objectives for the policing of all areas of all police authorities'.

The local pattern of policing is challenged by such trends towards centralization. The National Crime Squad and National Criminal Intelligence Service (NCIS) both contribute to combatting nation-wide criminal activity. The NCIS, established in 1992, provides intelligence and information to national and international law enforcement agencies about large-scale crimes such as drug trafficking and money-laundering. The NCIS also contains the Central Bureau for Interpol

[3] The target figure for police numbers in the forty-three forces in England and Wales was set at 128,290 by 2004. However, Chief Constables have the final say on recruiting. Any targets set are also vulnerable to the number of officers leaving the service.

which targets organized crime. Europol represents the European Union-wide arm of Interpol, and includes the Europol Drugs Unit.[4] The Police National Computer contains details of 42.5 million registered vehicles and their owners, persons with criminal records and details of missing persons. The Computer gives twenty-four-hour access to 200,000 inquiries from police forces each day. A National Automated Fingerprint Identification System (NAFIS), available by the year 2001, enables the fingerprints of arrested persons to be processed locally and entered into the national database, which is linked to the Police National Computer. The National Reporting Centre (NRC) acts as a clearing-house for information relating to policing that covers several geographical areas. The NRC, which is operated by the Association of Chief Police Officers (ACPO), reports directly to the Home Secretary. National standard setting by the Home Office also impinges on operational autonomy.

A police authority for each force exists, comprising people nominated by the local authority and by local magistrates. The Chief Constable is appointed by the police authority, and the authority approves the annual budget and provides buildings and equipment for the force. The authority may require a Chief Constable to resign on the grounds of inefficiency, subject to the agreement of the Home Secretary, and may call on the Chief Constable for reports on local policing. The police authority represents an element of local democratic control, albeit weak, over the police, the major limitation being the Chief Constable's absolute control over operational matters.

Police forces guard their independence from government and politics fiercely: their constitutional role is to serve the local community and reflect community concerns – not to be subject to the will of any party political policy. That rose-tinted view, however, masks the problems inherent in modern policing, particularly in urban areas. It also hides the problems of racism and sexism and, too frequently, the abuse of power and downright criminality of a small number of police officers.[5] If rights and freedoms are to be enjoyed by all, citizens require protection

[4] Established under the Treaty on European Union 1992.
[5] Alarmingly, the Commissioner for the Metropolitan Police admitted in 1998 that he probably had 250 corrupt officers on his force.

from crime. The role of the police is therefore important in securing a relatively crime-free society. However, individuals also need the assurance that the police, who hold numerous broad powers, exercise their powers according to law. The government claims that 'The police in Britain have always been able to build up a trust with the general public because, as servants of the law, they are responsible to the public not the state'.[6] In recent years, however, there have been high-profile cases identifying miscarriages of justice which have resulted from wrongdoing by the police.

A racist murder in 1993 drew public attention to a more subtle and insidious problem within the police: 'institutionalized racism'. The Inquiry, chaired by Sir William Macpherson of Cluny, into the Metropolitan Police's investigation of the murder of black teenager Stephen Lawrence, having considered numerous definitions of institutional racism given in evidence, concluded that it amounted to

The collective failure of an organisation to provide an appropriate and professional service to people because of their colour, culture or ethnic origin. It [institutional racism] can be seen or detected in processes, attitudes and behaviour which amount to discrimination through unwitting prejudice, ignorance, thoughtlessness and racist stereotyping which disadvantage minority ethnic people.

It persists because of the failure of the organisation openly and adequately to recognise and address its existence and causes by policy, example and leadership. Without recognition and action to eliminate such racism it can prevail as part of the ethos or culture of the organisation. It is a corrosive disease.[7]

This 'disease', the Inquiry concluded, operates both within the largest police force, the Metropolitan Police, and in police services and other institutions countrywide.[8] The *Report* proceeded to elucidate manifestations of institutional racism. In the investigation into Stephen Lawrence's death, racism was apparent in the treatment of his family at the hospital to which he was taken, in the failure to recognize his murder as purely racially motivated, and in the lack of urgency and commitment

---

[6] *Police: Serving the Community* (London: Home Office, 1999).
[7] *The Stephen Lawrence Inquiry: Report of an Inquiry*, Cm. 4262–I (London: HMSO, 1999), paragraph 6.34.   [8] Ibid., paragraph 6.39.

in some areas of the investigation. The Inquiry also ranged more widely. Institutional racism manifests itself nation-wide in the disparity in 'stop and search figures' as between members of ethnic minorities and the majority white population.[9] In the Inquiry's view, notwithstanding the complexities of the issue, there exists a 'clear core conclusion of racist stereotyping'. Nation-wide also is the under-reporting of racist incidents, attributed to the 'inadequate response of the Police Service which generates a lack of confidence in victims to report incidents'. Police training also came in for criticism, with the Inquiry stating that 'not a single officer questioned before us in 1998 had received any training of significance in racism awareness and race relations throughout the course of his or her career'.[10]

The Macpherson Inquiry came eighteen years after the inquiry by Lord Scarman into the Brixton Riots.[11] While the backgrounds to the two inquiries differed, great similarities existed in the identification of the underlying causes of policing failures. Depressingly, while the Scarman Report was authoritative and widely welcomed, little progress was made to remedy the deficiencies identified by it in the political climate of the 1980s – with a government committed to spending cuts, economic recession, the Falklands War and then industrial unrest in the form of a miners' strike. In 2000, officers from ethnic minority backgrounds represented just 3.4 per cent of the Metropolitan Police Services' staff.[12] The government's setting of targets for percentages of officers from ethnic minorities goes some way towards remedying a serious under-representation of the ethnic minority community. However, the achievement of targets is conditional upon additional funding, and that funding needs to be set at a higher level than the inflationary cost of policing – which has not been the case. Furthermore,

[9] The major statutes conferring stop and search powers are the Police and Criminal Evidence Act 1984, the use of which is regulated by Code of Practice A; the Criminal Justice Act 1988 and Criminal Justice and Public Order Act 1994 extended the powers; the Terrorism Act 2000 also confers stop and search powers.

[10] *Stephen Lawrence Inquiry*, paragraph 6.45.

[11] Lord J Scarman, *The Brixton Disorders, 10–12 April 1981* (London: HMSO, 1981). Scarman refused, however, to accept that there was institutionalized racism.

[12] Her Majesty's Inspectorate of Constabulary (HMIC), *Policing London, Winning Consent* (London: Home Office, 2000), paragraph 5.1.

whether Chief Constables will succeed in eliminating the 'institutional racism' which pervades the police force, in the light of its insidious and deeply ingrained nature within police culture, will depend on better training in community relations – something advocated by the Scarman Report but not implemented. Whatever the future of police/ethnic minority relations, the Macpherson Report has given the police a sharp warning that something must change.

Enforcing rights against the police

Actions for false imprisonment and malicious prosecution may be taken against the police. False imprisonment is a civil wrong, or tort, which involves the wrongful deprivation of personal liberty and carries strict liability: that is to say, legal liability arises irrespective of the fault of the person complained about. If a person is detained by the police without being arrested and prevented from leaving the police station, that will amount to false imprisonment for which damages, including exemplary damages, may be awarded. Malicious prosecution involves the fabrication of evidence against innocent people. In one particularly serious case, *Taylor v. Metropolitan Police Commissioner*,[13] the police had planted cannabis on the plaintiff and then detained and maliciously prosecuted him. He was awarded £10,000 for false imprisonment, £20,000 for malicious prosecution and exemplary damages of £70,000.

A major restriction on making the police liable for their conduct lay until recently in the police's immunity from the law relating to negligence, which made it impossible to sue the police for incompetence.[14] That position changed with *Osman v. United Kingdom*.[15] In *Osman* the applicant's son had become the object of a fixation by a schoolmaster. The police had been called to disturbances, including an attack on the family home, and were aware that the teacher posed a risk to the family. Subsequently, the teacher went to the school and shot the headmaster

---

[13] (1989) *Independent* 6 December.
[14] See *Hill v. Chief Constable of West Yorkshire* [1988] 2 All ER 238.
[15] *Times LR* 5 November 1999.

and his son, and the son of the applicant. When the applicant sought to sue the police for negligence in relation to their failure to protect her son, she was barred by the decision in *Hill v. Chief Constable of West Yorkshire Police*.[16] The Court of Human Rights ruled that this represented an unjustified restriction on the applicant's right to access to a court, guaranteed by Article 6.

In *R v. Commissioner of Police of the Metropolis*[17] the House of Lords considered the liability of the police. In 1990 Martin Lynch, who had been remanded in custody on criminal charges, hanged himself in his cell in Kentish Town police station. He had made previous attempts at suicide and the police had noted that he was a suicide risk. The House of Lords ruled that authorities, such as the police or prison service, who were entrusted with holding prisoners in custody, had a duty to take reasonable care to prevent them from harming themselves or committing suicide. Where there was a breach of that duty and a suicide occurred the authorities were not entitled to rely on the defences of *volenti non fit injuria* (the deceased's actions) or *novus actus interveniens* (intervening causes) in an action for negligence brought by the estate of the deceased.

Complaints against the police

The alternative, and less satisfactory, avenue for ensuring that the police act lawfully is through the complaints machinery. Prior to 1984 there was no independent element in the complaints procedure. The introduction of the Police Complaints Authority remedied that to an extent, but although the Authority is under a duty to supervise the investigation of serious complaints, it has no investigatory powers of its own and relies on the investigation being carried out by the police themselves. Minor complaints, rudeness or insensitivity, are dealt with through conciliation, during which explanations and apologies where due are given. More serious complaints are dealt with through the disciplinary process under the Chief Constable. Penalties range from reprimands to dismissal from the force. In relation to complaints involving a loss of

[16] [1989] AC 53.   [17] *Times LR* 16 July 1999.

life or serious injury caused by the police, a report may be made to the Director of Public Prosecutions for consideration of criminal charges. The complaints machinery remains unsatisfactory: of those who do complain, a high proportion of their complaints are dropped. Those who persevere have a slim chance of any real satisfaction. There is an air of complacency – admittedly rocked by the Stephen Lawrence murder and its aftermath – and of closed ranks which protect officers from real scrutiny and accountability.

Questioning by the police

In general, there is no obligation to answer questions: 'helping the police with inquiries' is not legally required. Unless a person is arrested, he or she is free to refuse to answer questions.[18] In *Rice v. Connolly*[19] the Court of Appeal endorsed this right. In that case, the police had arrested a person who had refused to answer their questions, on the basis that he had committed the offence of obstructing a police officer in the exercise of his duties.[20] A similar issue arose in *Kenlin v. Gardiner*.[21] There, police officers attempted to question two boys. One of them attempted to run away, whereupon a police constable tried to stop him and a scuffle broke out. The boys were then charged with assaulting a police officer in the execution of his duties. There was no doubt that an assault had taken place, but what was in issue was whether the police constable was acting 'in the execution of his duties', or not. Since the police had no right to detain the boy for questioning, the constable was acting *outside* his duties, the attempt to restrain the boy amounted to an assault *on him*, and the boy's actions were not unlawful.

However, there are circumstances when police questions must be answered. Under road traffic law, for example, there is a duty to provide one's name and address, and a refusal to do so and to give up one's driving licence and other motoring documents when required to do so is an offence.[22] Further powers exist under the Official Secrets Act

---

[18] On the 'right to silence' and its implications, see page 475 below.
[19] [1966] 3 WLR 17.   [20] Contrary to section 51(3) of the Police Act 1964.
[21] [1967] 2 QB 510.   [22] Under the Road Traffic Act 1988, section 163.

1989[23] and under the Companies Act 1985 and Criminal Justice Act 1967 in relation to fraud investigations. Under the Terrorism Act 2000 and Drug Trafficking Offences Act 1984 similar duties are imposed.

Stop and search powers

Wide-ranging powers are given to the police to stop and search people and property. However, there must always be a legal basis for such conduct, otherwise the actions of the police are unlawful. Stop and search powers are inherently controversial: they confer on the police the power to interfere with the liberties of citizens. There have been numerous allegations that the police target certain groups in society – particularly young black males – a belief which further contributes to suspicions that the police are racist.[24] The Code of Practice (A) which regulates the use of stop and search powers, however, states among other things that 'a person's colour, age, hairstyle or manner of dress', or the fact that he or she is known to have a previous conviction for possession of an unlawful article, cannot be used 'alone or in combination with each other as the sole basis on which to search that person'.

The Police and Criminal Evidence Act 1984 gives the police power to search any person or vehicle, and to detain the person or vehicle if officers have reasonable grounds for suspecting that they will find stolen or prohibited articles.[25] However, the safeguards contained in the Act do not apply to searches which are made with the person's consent, a weakness capable of being manipulated by the police to avoid the strictures of the Act. Searches of the person which involve the removal of more than an outer coat, jacket, gloves, headgear or footwear may only be made by an officer of the same sex as the person searched.

After arrest a person may be searched away from the police station when there are reasonable grounds to believe that he or she might either harm him- or herself, or escape or dispose of evidence.[26] Where a person

---

[23] On which see Chapter 8.
[24] See above on the findings of the Macpherson Commission inquiring into the handling of the Stephen Lawrence murder investigation.
[25] Police and Criminal Evidence Act 1984, section 1.   [26] Ibid., section 32.

is detained at a police station, he or she may be searched, and property seized, although clothing and personal effects may only be kept if the custody officer (who is in charge of detainees) believes that such items may be used to cause injury to him- or herself or others, or to escape or to interfere with evidence.[27]

Powers to search and seize property

Before the Police and Criminal Evidence Act 1984 was enacted, there was considerable doubt about the power to enter and search property without a warrant obtained from a court of law. Two very early cases indicated the limited nature of a right to interfere with a citizen's property. In *Semayne's case*,[28] for example, it was declared that an 'Englishman's home is his castle'. In *Entick v. Carrington*[29] the Secretary of State had authorized entry to property and seizure of any goods that were evidence of publishing literature which would undermine the security of the state. In an action for trespass against the Home Secretary, the Chief Justice, Lord Camden, stated that 'by the laws of England, every invasion of private property, be it ever so minute, is a trespass'. Accordingly, any entry into property must be authorized by the law. The European Convention on Human Rights also provides protection from invasions of privacy in the form of Article 8 which guarantees the protection of a person's privacy in relation to his home, correspondence and family life.[30]

The Police and Criminal Evidence Act 1984 now regulates powers of entry and search. For the most part, entry is authorized under a warrant granted by a magistrate. Over and above entry under warrant, however, there are cases in which the police may enter without a warrant; for example, if a person has committed a serious 'arrestable' offence, and the police enter with a view to arrest. Entry without warrant is also lawful if it is done to save life or prevent serious damage to property, and where it is necessary to regain the custody of a court, prison or

---

[27] Ibid., section 54 and Code of Practice C.
[28] (1605) 5 Co Rep 91a.   [29] (1765) 19 St Tr 1030.
[30] See *McLeod v. United Kingdom* [1998] 2 FLR 1048; [1999] 27 EHRR 493.

mental hospital detainee.[31] Vehicles may also be seized and retained under the Act.[32]

Powers of arrest

There are two principal types of arrest power: arrest with a warrant and arrest without a warrant. Within the second category there are also limited powers of arrest which arise not from an Act of Parliament but from the common law (decisions of the judges). If an arrest is wrongly made in violation of the law, the person concerned has a right to damages. Where the police have reasonable grounds to believe that a person has committed an offence, they apply to a Magistrates' Court for a warrant to arrest that person.[33] Where an offence has been committed which carries a sentence fixed by law, or which may lead to a term of imprisonment of five years or more, that offence is 'arrestable' without a warrant from the court. In the case of a serious offence, it would be unreasonable to expect the police to wait until a warrant could be acquired before they arrest the suspect. Arrestable offences are all serious offences. Some offences are classified specifically as 'serious arrestable offences'.[34] Among these are such crimes as treason, murder, manslaughter, rape, kidnapping and serious sexual offences, particularly those against children. Other examples include sexual offences,[35] offences relating to drug trafficking,[36] causing death by dangerous driving,[37] possession and use of firearms,[38] and hostage-taking and hijacking of an aircraft.[39] The police also have the power to arrest without a warrant in relation to less serious crimes where the suspect refuses to give a name and address, or the police doubt the truth of the name and address, or where the police have reasonable grounds to believe that, without an

[31] Police and Criminal Evidence Act 1984, section 17.
[32] Ibid., sections 18 and 19.   [33] Magistrates' Courts Act 1980, section 1.
[34] Under section 116 and Schedule 5 of the Police and Criminal Evidence Act 1984.
[35] Under the Sexual Offences Act 1956 as amended by the Criminal Justice and Public Order Act 1994.
[36] Under the Drug Trafficking Offences Act 1986.
[37] Road Traffic Act 1972, section 1.   [38] Firearms Act 1968, sections 16–18.
[39] Taking of Hostages Act 1982, section 1; Aviation Security Act 1982, section 1.

arrest, the suspect will cause himself or herself, or others, or property, physical injury or damage. The police must give reasons for making the arrest, unless this is impossible (for example because the person is reacting violently). Failure to give reasons will make an arrest unlawful.[40]

Following a lawful arrest, a suspect may be detained by the police for questioning before a criminal charge is actually made. This enables the police not only to question the suspect, but also to try to obtain further evidence relating to the offence. Because detention amounts to deprivation of a person's liberty, the law provides that no one may be detained for more than twenty-four hours without being charged. The time runs from the time of the arrest, or if the arrest is made outside a police station from the time at which he or she is brought to the station.[41] The twenty-four-hour period is, however, extendable. A senior officer may extend the time period on the grounds that the offence is a serious arrestable offence and that further detention is necessary to find or preserve evidence or obtain evidence by further questioning. After twenty-four hours the detention is reviewed, and if necessary may be extended to up to thirty-six hours.[42] After thirty-six hours the detained person must be brought before the Magistrates' Court for a hearing. The Magistrates may extend the period of detention, but for no longer than a further thirty-six hours, although exceptionally the Magistrates' Court may extend the period of detention up to a maximum of ninety-six hours.

Conditions of detention

A detained person must be held in a cell on his or her own, with access to toilet and washing facilities, and is entitled to adequate food and daily exercise. These rules, however, are not laid down in an Act of Parliament, but contained within the Codes of Practice which regulate so much of the work of the police. The Codes do not have the force of

---

[40] *Christie v. Leachinsky* [1947] AC 573; Police and Criminal Evidence Act 1984, section 28.

[41] Police and Criminal Evidence Act 1984, section 41.

[42] Ibid., section 41.

law, but the courts will be astute to ensure that they are complied with. Non-compliance will not, however, cause a case to fail. The police also have a duty to ensure that detainees do not harm themselves or commit suicide while in custody, and the police may be held liable if they are in breach of that duty.[43]

The right to legal advice following arrest

A person arrested, other than those arrested under suspicion of terrorist offences, is entitled, if he or she so requests, to consult a solicitor privately at any time.[44] The arrested person is also entitled to contact a friend or relative or other person and tell them that he or she has been arrested, and where he or she is. Where the case is a serious one, there may be a delay in granting this right, but only if authorized by an officer of at least the rank of superintendent. The basis on which such a delay may occur is that there are reasonable grounds for believing that telling the named person of the arrest will lead to interference with, or harm to, evidence of witnesses or the alerting of others involved in the offence, or that it will hinder the recovery of property obtained as a result of the offence.[45] There are, however, loopholes in the right to legal advice. Persons 'helping the police with their inquiries', and by definition not under arrest, will be co-operating with the police without the benefit of a lawyer. At this stage, where the police are fishing for information which might culminate in an arrest, the individual is vulnerable to self-incrimination. The effect of entitling the police to delay access to a lawyer following arrest is potentially to hold the accused for up to thirty-six hours without access to any outside person. From the perspective of the police, this is advantageous in so far as it removes the opportunity for the accused to pass messages out of the station and the possibility of evidence being destroyed or witnesses intimidated. Where the accused does not have a solicitor, duty solicitors are available at the police station to assist. Here again, however, there may be a significant

---

[43] *R v. Commissioner of Police of the Metropolis* (1999) *The Times*, 16 July.
[44] The Police and Criminal Evidence Act 1984, section 58(1).
[45] Police and Criminal Evidence Act 1984, section 56 and Code of Practice C.

delay between the time the detainee arrives at the police station and the time that the duty solicitor is summoned and arrives. The temptation to agree to being interviewed in advance of a solicitor's arrival, in exchange for being allowed to leave, must for many prove insurmountable, possibly with disastrous consequences.

The right to legal advice following arrest was considered by the Court of Human Rights in *Magee v. United Kingdom*.[46] The applicant had been arrested in 1988 under the Prevention of Terrorism Act 1984 in connection with an attempted bomb attack on military personnel. He had been held for more than forty-eight hours without access to legal advice, despite his specific request to see a solicitor on arrival at the police station. He signed a confession statement at his seventh interview, and was only subsequently allowed to consult his solicitor. The Court of Human Rights considered that the central issue raised by the applicant's complaint was that 'he had been prevailed upon in a coercive environment to incriminate himself without the benefit of legal advice'. Although the right to legal advice is not expressly stated in Article 6 and may be subject to restriction for 'good cause', Article 6 normally requires that the accused be allowed access to a lawyer at the initial stages of police interrogation. The Court ruled that there had been a violation of Article 6, stating that 'to deny access to a lawyer for such a long period and in a situation where the rights of the defence were irretrievably prejudiced is – whatever the justification for such denial – incompatible with the rights of the accused under Article 6'.

The 'right to silence'

The right of the accused to remain silent in the face of police questioning was established in the eighteenth century. The right protects the suspect from self-incrimination, and in the case of the innocent is fundamentally important in protecting him or her from making statements in the panic of the moment while disorientated in the unfamiliar and oppressive surroundings of a police station. The principle bolsters the essential

---

[46] Application no 28135/95, Judgment 6 June 2000, *Times LR* 20 June 2000.

constitutional safeguard of the citizen, namely that the accused is innocent until proved guilty by the prosecution. However, the right to silence fell under attack – by the police and right-wing politicians – on the ground that it protected the guilty and unduly hampered the prosecution. As a result, the caution which is administered on arrest and prior to official questioning was changed. The caution used to read: 'You do not have to say anything unless you wish to do so, but what you say may be given in evidence.' The caution was changed to read: 'You do not have to say anything. But it may harm your defence if you do not mention when questioned something which you later rely on in court. Anything you do say may be given in evidence.'[47]

Designed to prevent the defence from ambushing the prosecution with fresh evidence at trial, the caution now makes it plain that material evidence relating to the defence must be disclosed to the police and, if withheld, that withholding may lead to adverse inferences being drawn at trial. However, where an adverse inference could be drawn from an accused's failure to give an explanation in interview which he later relies on in court, the jury cannot convict on the inference alone, and any conviction so made can be set aside.[48] Equally, if the accused – having pleaded not guilty and being fit to answer questions – fails to answer questions at trial 'without good cause', the court or jury may draw 'such inferences as appear proper from his failure to give evidence or his refusal, without good cause, to answer any question'.[49]

The right to silence has always been controversial, with the police and Home Secretaries[50] arguing that it is abused by knowledgeable criminals, and civil liberties organizations and the legal profession arguing that it is an essential constitutional right. It is argued by those who oppose the right to silence that if a person is innocent of any crime, then he or she will not hesitate to co-operate in answering police questions. On the other hand, it is also argued that criminals will refuse to answer police questions then fabricate evidence when a matter goes to trial (at which point it is too late for the police to investigate), or

---

[47] Code of Practice C, paragraph 10.4.
[48] *R v. Doldur, Times LR* 7 December 1999.
[49] Criminal Justice and Public Order Act 1994, section 35, but see also the Criminal Procedure and Investigations Act 1996.
[50] Who are constitutionally responsible for the police.

alternatively attempt to prevent witnesses or victims from giving evidence against them. On the day on which the convictions of the Birmingham Six were quashed by the Court of Appeal, a Royal Commission[51] was established to consider various aspects of the criminal justice system. The right to silence was one such matter. By a majority, the Commission recommended that the right to silence be maintained. The then Home Secretary, Michael Howard QC, however, disagreed, arguing that the right to silence was exploited and that it was to be limited.

The Criminal Justice and Public Order Act 1994 gave effect to the Home Secretary's intention. The trial court may invite the jury to draw 'adverse inferences' from an accused's silence, where he or she has been cautioned and has been questioned by the police about the crime.[52] However, maintaining silence alone is not enough for adverse inferences to be drawn – there must also be a *prima facie* case against the accused.[53]

Exceptions to the 'right to silence' exist: for example, under the Criminal Justice Act 1987, the Serious Fraud Office has the right to insist on questions being answered, and failure to do so may result in six months' imprisonment, and under the Companies Act 1985 Department of Trade and Industry inspectors have the power to compel answers and force information to be provided.[54] It was this latter power which was challenged successfully by Ernest Saunders, former director of Guinness plc, in *Saunders v. United Kingdom*,[55] under Article 6 of the European Convention on Human Rights which guarantees the right of fair trial. Article 6, in part, provides that 'everyone is entitled to a fair and public hearing within a reasonable time by an independent and impartial tribunal established by law' and that 'Everyone charged with a criminal offence shall be presumed innocent until proved guilty according to law'. The requirement to give incriminating evidence through questioning under threat of loss of liberty undermines the right to fair trial and the presumption of innocence and the requirement that the prosecution prove its case beyond all reasonable doubt.

---

[51] The Runciman Royal Commission on Criminal Justice. The Commission's Report (Cm. 2263) was published in 1993.
[52] Criminal Justice and Public Order Act 1994, section 34.   [53] Ibid., section 38.
[54] Analogous powers also exist under the Financial Services Act 1986, sections 177 and 178; the Insolvency Act 1986, sections 236 and 433.
[55] [1996] 23 EHRR 313.

The Convention has also come to the rescue of others whose right to silence was infringed by the authorities, most recently in the case of *Condron v. United Kingdom*.[56] In *Condron*, the applicants had been under police surveillance and were charged with drug offences. Following conviction, by a jury, by a majority of nine to one, the two applicants were sentenced to four and three years' imprisonment respectively. When interviewed by the police, the applicants, acting on the advice of their solicitor who was concerned that their state of withdrawal from drugs made them unfit to answer questions, had remained silent, only offering 'no comment' to questions. The applicants were cautioned that the jury could draw adverse inferences from their silence. At trial, the judge failed to give a proper direction to the jury on the correct approach to be taken to the drawing of inferences. Nevertheless, on appeal the Court of Appeal ruled that the convictions were safe. However, what the Court of Appeal did not consider – which was the essential consideration before the Court of Human Rights – was whether the trial of the defendants was fair in accordance with the requirements of Article 6 of the Convention.

The Court ruled that there was a violation of Article 6. The defendants had given evidence at their trial, and had explained that they had declined to answer questions at interview on the advice of their solicitor. It was the function of the jury, properly directed, to decide whether or not to draw an adverse inference from the applicants' silence.[57] They therefore have a discretion. However, the judge in his direction did not restrict that discretion, since he failed to advise the jury that it should only draw an adverse inference if it concluded that their silence was attributed to their having no answer to the charges or none that would stand up to cross-examination. The right to silence, according to the Court, 'lies at the heart of the notion of a fair procedure guaranteed by Article 6'. Accordingly, the applicants did not receive a fair trial.[58]

---

[56] Application no 35718/97, Judgment 2 May 2000, (2000) *The Times*, 9 May.

[57] Under section 34 of the Criminal Justice and Public Order Act 1994.

[58] In contrast, in the earlier case of *Murray v. United Kingdom* (1996) *The Times* 9 February, the Court of Human Rights ruled there was no violation of Article 6 where the defendant refused to give evidence at trial and the jury drew inferences from that refusal. In that case there was substantial other evidence against the accused.

The recording of interviews

Prior to the Police and Criminal Evidence Act 1984, the accused had no means whereby he or she could be confident that what was said at interview was accurately recorded by the police. Routinely, police officers would interview the suspect and subsequently agree on the substance of the interview in a written record. When questioned in court about their record of the interview, magistrates would ask when the record was made with the inevitable response – which was unverifiable – that it had been made immediately after the interview. The obvious solution,[59] the tape recording of all interviews of suspects accused on indictable offences,[60] was one initially opposed by the police. Fears were expressed that suspects would fabricate accusations about the police, and that defence lawyers would claim that tapes had been tampered with. These fears proved groundless. The tapes are time-coded, and far from attempting to manipulate the system to their own advantage, the number of suspects pleading guilty has increased.

The right to bail

Where a suspect has been charged with a criminal offence, there is an inevitable time-lag between the charge being laid and the decision whether to pursue a prosecution of the charge (see below), and a further period of delay before the actual trial takes place. Article 5 of the European Convention on Human Rights provides, in part, that no one shall be deprived of their liberty other than following a lawful arrest for the purpose of bringing that person before a court of law.[61] Article 5 also requires that everyone arrested or detained must be brought before a judge 'promptly' and is entitled to trial within a reasonable time or to

[59] Recommended by the Royal Commission on Criminal Procedure, and now regulated by section 60 of the Police and Criminal Evidence Act 1984 and Code of Practice E.
[60] Those triable by jury in the Crown Court.
[61] Article 5.1 (c) ECHR.

release on bail pending trial.[62] Article 6 of the Convention provides, in part, that everyone charged with a criminal offence shall be presumed innocent until proved guilty according to law.[63] Bail is the release of an accused person from custody pending trial. Since the accused is to be regarded as innocent until proved guilty at trial, there is a presumption in favour of an accused's release.

The decision to grant or refuse bail lies initially with the police, and subsequently with the Magistrates' Court before which the accused will initially appear. There is, however, no *right* to bail, and differing criteria apply to situations where a person has been arrested on a warrant, or without a warrant, and according to whether the person has been charged.[64] The decision whether or not to grant bail involves a weighing-up of several factors. Among these will be the likelihood of the accused committing further offences while on bail, and whether he or she is likely to abscond. Where a person has been arrested on a warrant, which will be granted by a Magistrates' Court to the police on the grounds that the police have reasonable suspicion to believe that that person is guilty of an offence, the warrant will specify whether bail should be granted or whether the accused should be detained in custody. Where the arrest is without a warrant, the decision as to bail is taken after he or she has been charged. Where a person has been charged, he or she must be released on bail unless his or her name and address are not known, or where his or her detention is necessary for his or her own safety, or there is a reasonable perceived risk that he or she will commit further offences, disappear or interfere with witnesses who will be called at the trial.[65]

Where bail is granted, conditions may be attached.[66] These may include a duty to report periodically (including daily) to a police station, or to surrender his or her passport to the police, or not to contact particular persons. The police cannot, however, require that a

---

[62] Ibid., Article 5.3.   [63] Ibid., Article 6.2.

[64] Bail is regulated under the Bail Act 1976, as amended by the Bail (Amendment) Act 1993, and the Police and Criminal Evidence Act 1984, section 47 and the Criminal Justice and Public Order Act 1994, sections 25–30.

[65] Police and Criminal Evidence Act 1984, section 38.

[66] Criminal Justice and Public Order Act 1994, section 27 amending the Police and Criminal Evidence Act 1984, sections 38 and 47.

person reside in a bail hostel. If a person has been required to report to a police station, and fails to do so, that person can be arrested without a warrant.

If bail is not granted by the police, then it will be considered by the Magistrates' Court. If the offence is one for which a term of imprisonment can be imposed, bail must be granted, unless the court is satisfied that if he or she were released on bail, he or she would fail to turn up for trial, or commit a further offence or interfere with witnesses or evidence. Bail can also be refused on the basis of the need to protect the accused, or refused on the basis that he or she has previously failed to comply with the requirement to attend. If the offence is one which does not carry a custodial sentence, the accused must be released unless there has been a previous refusal to surrender to bail and a risk that he or she would do so again.

Where a person is accused of a very serious offence, such as murder or attempted murder, manslaughter (causing death without the intention to kill), rape or attempted rape, then that person must not be granted bail.[67] The same applies to a person who has a previous conviction for these offences. Exceptionally, however, bail can be granted to those with convictions for rape or murder, if the court or police officer considering bail is 'satisfied that there are exceptional circumstances which justify it'.[68]

Challenging police detention

The ancient writ of habeas corpus is available to test the legality of detention whether by immigration officials, the police, prison authorities, hospitals or private institutions. The application can be made to a single judge, if necessary over the telephone, and, if there is a *prima facie* case to answer, the writ must be issued. The onus is therefore on the person detaining to justify the detention, rather than the detainee to prove that he or she is being unlawfully detained. However, the value

[67] Criminal Justice and Public Order Act 1994, section 25.
[68] Crime and Disorder Act 1998, section 56 amending section 25 of the Criminal Justice and Public Order Act 1994.

of habeas corpus has been severely undermined by the welter of statutes providing for lawful detention in differing circumstances for differing periods of time.[69] Of more use now may be Article 5 of the European Convention which regulates the circumstances in which the 'right to liberty and security of the person' may be limited, and provides that everyone arrested or detained is entitled to take proceedings 'by which the lawfulness of his detention shall be decided speedily by a court and his release ordered if the detention is not lawful'. In *Zamir v. United Kingdom*[70] there was a violation of Article 5 where the applicant had applied for habeas corpus and there was a delay of seven weeks between the application and a hearing.

THE PROSECUTION PROCESS[71]

Prior to 1984 the decision whether to prosecute an accused lay with the police themselves. Back in 1970, JUSTICE[72] published a report[73] in which it was argued, in part, that the police, having investigated an alleged crime and arrested a suspect, had a commitment to securing a conviction, even if the evidence was weak. This, and a number of other causes of dissatisfaction with the *status quo*, led JUSTICE to recommend that there be established a prosecuting authority independent of the police.[74] In 1985 the Crown Prosecution Act established the Crown Prosecution Service (CPS), a national prosecution service under the authority of the Director of Public Prosecutions. The decision whether or not to charge a suspect remains with the police, but thereafter the matter is handled by the CPS.

The early years of the CPS were beset by problems. Recruitment of

[69] Exceptionally, the original Prevention of Terrorism Act 1984 which provided for detention of up to seven days on the authority of the Home Secretary, a provision held to violate Article 5 of the Convention: see *Brogan v. United Kingdom* (1988) 11 EHRR 117.   [70] (1983) 40 DR 42.   [71] On the court structure see Chapter 9.

[72] The British section of the International Commission of Jurists.

[73] *The Prosecution Process in England and Wales.*

[74] The matter was referred to a Royal Commission on Criminal Procedure (the Philips Commission) which supported the proposal.

high-calibre lawyers to the Service proved difficult, and it was accused of inefficiency, having a low rate of success in prosecutions and being too willing to abandon prosecutions.[75] In 1998 a report issued by a review body was also highly critical, describing the Service as being 'bureaucratic and over-centralised', and calling for reform of the CPS. In 1999 the Service was further decentralized, the former thirteen CPS areas being expanded to forty-two to align with the police areas, and Chief Crown Prosecutors being appointed.

There is a discretion as to whether or not to prosecute an accused. Rather than passing a matter to the CPS to consider whether or not to pursue a prosecution, the police may choose to caution an offender. If a matter is referred to the CPS and the CPS considers that a caution would be more appropriate, the matter may be referred back to the police. In considering whether to caution an offender, the nature of the offence, the likely penalty, the offender's age and health, his or her criminal record and attitude to the offence in question are all considered. There is a presumption against prosecuting where the offender is a juvenile or young adult or elderly.

The decision whether to prosecute, where no caution has been administered, is governed by two basic considerations. The first is that there must be a 'realistic prospect of conviction', the second that prosecution is 'in the public interest'.[76] The Code for Crown Prosecutors lists a number of 'public interest factors' which will incline the CPS towards prosecution. These include such matters as whether a conviction is likely to result in a significant sentence (as opposed to a small or nominal penalty); whether the crime was one involving the use or threat of violence, and whether a weapon was used; whether the crime was one against a police officer or other public servant; whether there was a racial or other discriminatory motive involved. The CPS also has the power to discontinue a prosecution or, alternatively, where a prosecution proceeds, to withdraw evidence or offer no evidence in support of the prosecution.[77]

The Access to Justice Act 1999 extends the rights of the CPS to

---

[75] The former Director of the Service claimed that many of the problems lay with the poor preparation of cases by the police.

[76] The Code for Crown Prosecutors sets out the requirements.

[77] Prosecution of Offences Act 1985, section 23.

conduct prosecutions in the Crown Court, from which they were previously excluded and where accordingly they had to rely on independent barristers.[78] In order to avoid the possibility that the CPS has an inbuilt interest in securing as many convictions as possible, section 24 of the Access to Justice Act states that every advocate 'has a duty to the court to act with independence in the interests of justice'. Whether this duty will prove effective in deterring over-zealous prosecutions is a matter for argument. Professor Michael Zander, the leading authority on the legal system, for example, has argued that the CPS is 'under constant pressure in regard to the proportion of discontinuances, acquittals and conviction rates. These are factors in the day to day work of any CPS lawyer. It is disingenuous to imagine they will not have a powerful effect on decision making.'[79]

The classification of offences

Defendants are currently entitled to trial by jury for *indictable offences* and *offences triable either way*. The remaining category of offences are *summary offences* which are triable only before the Magistrates' Court, with the right of appeal to the Crown Court. Indictable offences represent the most serious category of offences, for example, murder, manslaughter, serious assault, rape and major theft. Offences currently triable either way include the intermediate range of crimes, such as theft and dishonesty. Offences triable summarily include a wide range of lesser offences, such as road traffic offences, minor assault and minor incidents of public disorder. Where an offence is triable either way, it is the defendant not the court who has the ultimate right to decide whether to opt for trial by jury or to be tried summarily by the Magistrates' Court. Before that decision is taken, the Magistrates' Court will assess whether, in its view, the case is sufficiently serious to warrant trial in the Crown Court, and whether if it decides to try the case summarily, it has sufficient sentencing powers for the offence if the defendant is found guilty. It then advises the defendant of that

---

[78] The Access to Justice Act 1999 amends the Courts and Legal Services Act 1990.
[79] Letter to *The Times*, 29 December 1998.

decision, and points out that if trial proceeds summarily and a conviction follows, the defendant may nevertheless be remitted to the Crown Court for sentencing if the Magistrates' Court's powers are too limited.[80]

The criminal courts

All criminal cases commence in the Magistrates' Court. Where an offence is triable only summarily (before the magistrates), or triable 'either way' and the defendant elects for trial by the magistrates, the matter will be disposed of in that court. Some 98 per cent of all criminal cases are dealt with by the courts summarily. Where the defendant elects for trial by jury, or the offence is only triable by a jury, the Magistrates' Court remits the case to the Crown Court.[81]

Appeals from the Magistrates' Court may take one of three forms. The defendant may appeal against conviction where the defendant has pleaded not guilty to the charge, or against the sentence imposed. These appeals go to the Crown Court. Additionally there may be an appeal made 'by way of case stated'. A 'case stated' appeal may be made either by the prosecution or defence and will be heard by the High Court.[82] The basis for such appeals is confined to appeals on a point of law or allegations that the magistrates acted outside their jurisdiction. Case stated appeals may also be made by the Crown Court to the High Court. Appeal from the Divisional Court is to the House of Lords. Either side may appeal, but the only ground on which an appeal is permissible is where there is a point of law of general public importance which requires clarification by the highest court.

---

[80] The maximum fine which can be imposed by a Magistrates' Court is £5,000, although for many summary offences the sum is much less. The maximum custodial sentence the court can impose is six months, except where the defendant is convicted of more than one offence, one or more of which is 'triable either way': Magistrates' Courts Act 1980. Under the Powers of the Criminal Courts Act 1973, as amended by the Criminal Justice Act 1988, the Magistrates' Court may make compensation orders.

[81] Crime and Disorder Act 1998, section 51.

[82] The Divisional Court of the Queen's Bench Division which consists of two or more judges, one of whom will be a Lord Justice of Appeal.

Appeals from the Crown Court go to the Court of Appeal (Criminal Division). Appeals may be against conviction or against sentence.[83] About 8,000 appeals a year will be heard by the Court of Appeal, the majority of which are against sentence. Where the appeal is against conviction, a large proportion of successful appeals are the result of an error having been made at the original trial. This issue is discussed further below after consideration of the role of the jury.

TRIAL BY JURY

'the lamp that shows that freedom lives . . .'[84]

The right to jury trial was settled in 1215 with Magna Carta, since which time it has been a central feature of criminal justice, and conventionally regarded as the hallmark of a civilized justice system. Constitutionally, trial by jury represents trial by one's peers, drawn from the local community. Jury trial is also available in a limited number of civil cases, but restricted to fraud, defamation, malicious prosecution and false imprisonment.[85] Not only do twelve randomly selected lay persons decide the guilt or innocence of the accused, but they also ensure that the application of the law is kept in touch with ordinary citizens. If the outcome of criminal prosecutions depended solely on the skill of opposing barristers and the legal wisdom of the presiding judge criminal justice could come to be seen as the exclusive preserve of professional lawyers and out of touch with the values of ordinary people. The jury injects a greater degree of plain common sense – as opposed to strict legal analysis – into criminal proceedings, and generates public confidence in the legal system by ensuring that the accused is judged by his or her peers, randomly selected and representative of the community. Jury trial also ensures that judges and barristers keep the law in touch with the public in so far as they are required to explain the law and unravel

---

[83] Criminal Appeal Act 1996.
[84] Per Lord Devlin, *Trial by Jury*, Hamlyn Lectures, 8th series (London: Sweet & Maxwell, 1956), p. 164.   [85] Supreme Court Act 1981, section 69.

complex facts in a manner which is comprehensible to the jury, rather than merely to themselves. That at least is the theory. Once empanelled, the jury reaches decisions on matters of fact. Advice on the law is for the trial judge.

The right to jury trial in relation to some offences is controversial and the current government is intent on reform. In 1993 the Runciman Commission on Criminal Justice recommended that defendants should no longer have the right to insist on trial by jury.[86] The reasons underlying this recommendation are several. First, it is felt that defendants prefer trial by jury rather than by magistrates on the basis that they feel that they are likely to get a fairer trial – or, more cynically, more likely to be acquitted – before the Crown Court. Secondly, trial by jury is relatively expensive compared with summary trial,[87] and is also a more lengthy process. Thirdly, many defendants are suspected of abusing the system. Research shows that whereas many defendants plead not guilty when they appear before the Magistrates' Court and the venue for trial is decided, when they finally get to the Crown Court some 70 per cent plead guilty to all charges and a further 13 per cent plead guilty to some of the charges. However, other research has shown that what underlay the decision of many defendants was the incorrect belief that even if found guilty by the jury in the Crown Court they would receive lesser sentences than if tried summarily. The Criminal Justice (Mode of Trial) Bill 1999 gave effect to the recommended changes. The Bill proved so contentious that the House of Lords rejected it, and the government was forced to withdraw the Bill. Before considering some of the perceived difficulties with trial by jury, a brief outline of the system is required.

The composition of the jury

Currently, all adults between the ages of eighteen and seventy on the electoral register who have lived in the United Kingdom for at least five years are eligible to serve on juries.[88] Some persons are deemed

[86] *Royal Commission Report on the Criminal Justice System*, Cm. 2263 (London: HMSO, 1993).
[87] The average cost of trial by jury is £13,500 compared with £2,500 for summary trial.
[88] Jury Act 1974, as amended by the Criminal Justice Act 1988.

ineligible to serve, including those with close links with the legal system such as judges, magistrates, police and probation officers and members of the clergy. Others are disqualified from serving, including those serving a term of imprisonment of five years or more, and those who have served a sentence in the past ten years, or been sentenced to a community service order or placed on probation. Yet others are excused from serving on the basis of their professions. Among these are members of the medical professions, Members of Parliament and members of the armed forces. Where a person can show a good reason why he or she should not serve, the court has a discretion to excuse him or her.

The underlying principle of selection of the jury is randomness. There is no attempt to ensure that a particular jury is composed of individuals who are representative of the community of the accused, in spite of the intention that a person accused should be tried by his or her peers. Women and members of racial minority groups are generally under-represented on juries, and challenges based on the lack of representativeness of the jury are not allowed.

Persons summoned to attend find themselves subject to challenges from the prosecution and defence, thereby reducing the 'randomness' of the system as defence and prosecution attempt to exclude those who are deemed to be potentially hostile to their case. Until 1988, the defence could use the *peremptory challenge* to exclude up to three jurors, without giving any reasons at all. This has now been abandoned, and challenges by the defence are limited to *challenges for cause*, that is, a challenge based on a specific stated reason. The reasons must be substantial, such as for example where a juror has had previous dealings with the defendant. Challenges based on a juror's race, religion, politics or occupation are not permitted, even though such factors may prejudice a juror against a particular defendant. For the prosecution there is greater leeway in the system. The prosecution may challenge for cause like the defence, but it may also ask particular jurors to 'stand by', which means that they will not be selected unless no other suitable jurors can be found. The possibility that this can lead to abuse by the prosecution led to a 1988 Practice Note which limited the right to stand by to preventing a 'manifestly unsuitable juror' from sitting, for example an illiterate person being selected to serve on a highly complex case involving documentary evidence, and to cases where a person had been 'vetted' and the finding showed that he or she might be a security risk.

Jury vetting is aimed at ensuring that jurors do not sit on cases where their personal background or characteristics might undermine the fairness of the trial. Vetting is not routine, and is confined to cases involving national security and terrorist cases and cases where, because of the sensitivity of the issue, part of the proceedings would have to be heard *in camera* (in private). In addition, checks may be run on criminal records to determine whether or not a juror has a criminal record and is therefore ineligible to serve.[89]

Occasionally, one or more jurors may be released from service, on grounds of health or otherwise. Provided that the number is not less than nine, the trial can proceed.[90]

The role of the jury

The jury decides the guilt or innocence of the accused according to the evidence before the court. Matters of law, and its interpretation, are for the judge: matters of fact for the jury. Sentencing is for the judge. Trial by jury is confined to the Crown Court and in fact is used for approximately only 1 per cent of all criminal trials. The vast majority, some 97 per cent, are decided in the Magistrates' Courts. Furthermore, approximately 75 per cent of all accused plead guilty, thereby eliminating the need for a finding of guilt and leaving the judge only to decide the sentence which should be imposed. However, the right to trial by jury for serious crimes is seen as a constitutionally fundamental right, albeit one which has declined in its usage. Once formally empanelled, the jury is under a legal duty to reach a decision on the case. It is a contempt of court (punishable by imprisonment) for a juror to refuse to come to a decision. The difficulty in evaluating the role of the jury is compounded by the law which prohibits any revelation of discussions in the jury room, and the fact that the jury need not give – indeed may not give – reasons for its decisions. If a jury decides to acquit a person, the decision

---

[89] *R v. Danvers* [1982] Crim LR 442.   [90] Juries Act 1974, section 16(1).

of the jury is unchallengeable, and there can be no appeal against an acquittal.[91] Where the jury cannot reach a unanimous decision, a majority verdict may be accepted where there are not less than eleven jurors and ten of them agree, or there are ten jurors and nine of them agree.[92]

Despite its long-standing emotional appeal, public confidence in the jury system can only be sustained if their decisions are seen to be untainted by any malpractice on the part of the police (the investigating body) in the gaining of evidence of guilt against the accused. Where miscarriages of justice occur – as from time to time they do in serious fashion – public confidence in the criminal justice system is damaged. Central to this issue is the admissibility of evidence, and the manner in which evidence has been gathered.

In addition to juries in criminal cases, juries have a role to play in civil (non-criminal) cases, albeit a limited one. There is a *right* to have the case tried by a jury in relation to allegations of fraud, false imprisonment, libel, slander and malicious prosecution. However, that right is qualified by the fact that the court can refuse jury trial if the trial is likely to require 'prolonged examination of documents or accounts or any scientific or local investigation which cannot conveniently be made with a jury'.[93] In other civil cases there is no right to trial by jury, but the court may in its discretion order it to be tried by jury.[94] In 1956 Lord Denning stated the rationale for trial by jury: 'Whenever a man is on trial for serious crime, or when in a civil case a man's honour or integrity is at stake, or when one or other party must be deliberately lying, then trial by jury has no equal.'[95] The right to trial by jury in defamation cases (libel and slander) has proven contentious, largely because juries are prone to award extraordinarily high levels of damages. In *Rantzen v. Mirror Group Newspapers*,[96] for example, the jury awarded £250,000, and in *John v. MGN Ltd.*[97] the award was for £350,000 for libel and £275,000 in 'exemplary' damages. In the former

---

[91] Although the Attorney-General may refer a case to the Court of Appeal for its advice on points of law raised at trial: section 36 of the Criminal Justice Act 1972. Such a reference does not affect the acquittal.

[92] Juries Act 1974, section 17.   [93] Supreme Court Act 1981, section 69(1).

[94] Ibid., section 69(3).   [95] *Ward v. James* [1966] 1 QB 273.

[96] [1993] 3 WLR 953.   [97] [1996] 3 WLR 593.

case the award was subsequently reduced by the court to £110,000 and in the latter reduced to £75,000 and £50,000.

The admissibility of evidence at trial

In the United States of America any evidence which has been obtained improperly is inadmissible at trial. In the United Kingdom, however, the position is far less certain. In relation to confessions made by the accused, the Police and Criminal Evidence Act 1984, section 76, provides, in part, that a confession made by an accused person may be given in evidence against him in so far as it is relevant to any matter in issue in the proceedings and is not excluded by the court. The grounds on which a confession must be excluded are that the confession was obtained by oppression of the persons who made it, or if the confession is likely to be unreliable as a result of anything said or done which influences the making of a confession. Where an allegation is made about these conditions, the court must not allow the confession to be used unless the prosecution can prove to the court, beyond reasonable doubt, that the confession was not obtained in the prohibited manner. Even where the defence does not raise the issue of the admissibility of a confession, the court may require the prosecution to prove that it did not obtain the confession in breach of the conditions. A confession is defined as including any statement 'wholly or partly adverse to the person who made it, whether made to a person in authority or not and whether made in words or otherwise'.[98]

The court may exclude the confession in whole or in part. Where a confession is excluded, evidence discovered as a result of the confession remains admissible, and where the confession is relevant to showing particular characteristics of the accused's speech, writing or manner of expression, that remains admissible. Oppression is defined as including torture, inhuman or degrading treatment, and the use or threat of violence, whether or not amounting to torture.[99] Special protection is given to mentally handicapped persons where the confession was not

[98] Police and Criminal Evidence Act 1984, section 82.
[99] Ibid., section 76(8).

made in the presence of an independent person, in the form of a warning to the jury to exercise caution before convicting a person in reliance on the confession. However, here there is a weakness in so far as the protection covers mentally handicapped persons, but not the mentally ill or otherwise disordered.

Notwithstanding these protective provisions, the manner in which the law has been interpreted indicates a preference for the admission of evidence, rather than its exclusion. In relation to confessions, the courts are slow to find that a confession has been obtained by oppression.[100] The second ground – confessions likely to be unreliable as a result of anything said or done to the suspect – covers such things as inducement by the police in order to encourage a confession, truthful or not. The discretion left to the trial judge as to whether to admit or exclude evidence on the basis of fairness, introduces the capacity for different results in different courts, disparities which can only be ironed out by appeals to the appeal courts.

In relation to other evidence, section 78 of the Police and Criminal Evidence Act 1984 provides that the court may refuse to allow evidence which the prosecution intends to rely on, if it appears to the court that 'the admission of the evidence would have such an adverse effect on the fairness of the proceedings that the court ought not to admit it'. The court has a discretion whether or not to admit such evidence. For example, if the accused made admissions to the police in the absence of a solicitor, not having been told of his or her right to legal advice, the court will be slow to admit the evidence. On the other hand, if the accused clearly knew his or her right to legal advice, but the presence of a solicitor would have made no difference to his or her response to questioning, the court may admit the evidence.[101] The court will look carefully to see if the police have followed the requirements of the Codes of Practice, and the greater the departure from the Codes, and the seriousness with which this affects the fairness of the trial, the more likely the court is to refuse to admit the evidence. In *R v. Absolam*,[102] for example, the Court of Appeal quashed a conviction for supplying cannabis where the defendant had not been told of his right to a solicitor

---

[100] See *R v. Miller* 1 WLR 1191; *R v. Fulling* [1987] 2 WLR 923.
[101] See *R v. Dunford* [1991] Crim LR 370.   [102] [1989] 88 Cr App R 332.

and the police had also broken the rules relating to the tape-recording of interviews.

The leading case on evidence and fairness of trial is *R v. Sang*,[103] in which the House of Lords ruled that in relation to a criminal charge there was no defence of entrapment, but that evidence could be excluded in favour of securing a fair trial for the defendant. Entrapment is the tricking of a suspect, by the police or through the use of *agents provocateurs*, into committing an offence which he or she would not otherwise commit.[104] In *Sang's case* the House of Lords ruled that evidence obtained through the use of an *agent provocateur* was not sufficient grounds for its exclusion at trial, and that other than in relation to confessions or issues of self-incrimination, no discretion existed to exclude evidence on the basis that it had been improperly or illegally obtained. The conduct of the police might lead to civil proceedings, but not to the exclusion of evidence. Only where the evidence in question has an effect which is more prejudicial to the defence when compared with its value as proof of crime will the evidence be excluded.[105]

This position compares unfavourably with that in the United States of America where the tricking of a person by an agent of the state into the commission of an offence automatically renders the evidence inadmissible. The Police and Criminal Evidence Act 1984 gives greater latitude to the courts to exclude evidence, but the discretion remains. Since this Act, however, the courts have been robust in calling the police to account for breaches of the law. Nevertheless, the very existence of discretion may act as an invitation to the police to abuse their powers: something which, in the light of miscarriages of justice in recent years, is an invitation too often accepted. The admissibility of evidence is likely to be the basis of challenges under the Human Rights Act 1998. Article 6 guarantees the right to fair trial and has spawned much case

[103] [1979] 3 WLR 263; [1980] AC 402 (HL).

[104] e.g. a case where undercover police ran a shop and offered large cash sums for stolen jewellery. Thirty 'customers' were caught in the operation, but the Court of Appeal refused to rule that their trials were unfair as a result of entrapment: *R v. Christou* [1992] 4 All ER 559.

[105] See also *R v. Spurthwaite and Gill* (1993) *Independent*, 12 August.

law. The Court of Human Rights in general leaves the issue of evidence to the domestic courts, and Article 6 does not require any particular rules of evidence provided that overall the trial is fair.[106] On the other hand, evidence obtained by ill-treatment (as opposed to torture) may be held to make a trial 'unfair', as might the use of evidence obtained by entrapment and the use of undercover agents.

MISCARRIAGES OF JUSTICE

In 1952 Derek Bentley was convicted of the murder of a police constable. The fatal shot was fired by Bentley's accomplice in a burglary attempt. Bentley was convicted on the basis that he was engaged in a 'joint enterprise', even though at the time of the shooting Bentley was under arrest and being restrained by a police officer. Bentley appealed against his conviction; his appeal failed and in January 1953 he was hanged. Numerous attempts were made to have his conviction posthumously set aside. However, it was not until 1998 that the Court of Appeal reconsidered Bentley's conviction. The Court of Appeal found that he had been deprived of a fair trial. The fact that he had a mental age of eleven had been withheld from the jury, and the judge's summing up of the case to the jury was biased in favour of the police. Bentley was cleared of murder, some forty-six years after he had been hanged.[107]

In recent years a small number of other cases have come to light in which it was ultimately established – after the accused had spent many years in prison – that the evidence was tainted. While these have been mercifully few in number, any case which is perceived to be a miscarriage of justice undermines public confidence and stands as an indictment of the criminal justice system. The cases of the Birmingham Six, the Guildford Four, Judith Ward and the Bridgewater Four are examples.[108]

---

[106] *Edward v. United Kingdom* (1992) 15 EHRR 417.
[107] The death penalty in Britain was abolished in 1965.
[108] See L. Blom-Cooper, *The Birmingham Six and Other Cases: Victims of Circumstance* (London: Duckworth, 1997).

The first three of these all involved terrorist activity related to Northern Ireland. In 1975 six men were convicted of the murder of twenty-one people in two public houses in Birmingham in 1974. In 1991 their convictions were quashed on the ground that their trial had been unfair, but it took three attempts before they had their freedom restored. Also in 1974, explosions at public houses in Guildford and Woolwich led to the prosecution of the Guildford Four for terrorist murder. Their convictions were quashed by the Court of Appeal in 1990 on the grounds that their conviction by the jury was 'unsafe and unsatisfactory'.[109] Confessions of the accused had been unlawfully obtained by the police. A bomb placed in a coach in 1974 killed twelve people. Judith Ward was charged and convicted of murder. Her conviction was quashed by the Court of Appeal in 1992, having been referred for review by the Home Secretary, although Judith Ward had not herself appealed. The Bridgewater Four case concerned the wrongful conviction of four men for the murder of Carl Bridgewater, a thirteen-year-old boy who was doing his newspaper round and was shot dead during a burglary in 1978. It was 1997 before the convictions were quashed.[110] A confession by one of the accused had been unlawfully obtained by the police through deception, and as a result their trial was unfair and the verdict unsafe.

On the day on which the Court of Appeal quashed the convictions of the Birmingham Six, the Home Secretary announced that a Royal Commission was to be established, chaired by Viscount Runciman, to investigate and report on the criminal justice system. The Runciman Commission reported in 1993. In the Report, the Commission recommended that a body should be set up, independent of the government, to take over the power to refer cases to the Court of Appeal for reconsideration of trial verdicts. The Criminal Cases Review Commission was established under the Criminal Appeals Act 1995.[111] The Commission takes over the former power of the Home Secretary to refer alleged cases of wrongful convictions and miscarriages of justice

[109] The relevant statutory language (in part) was that 'the conviction . . . is unsafe or unsatisfactory': Criminal Appeals Act 1968, section 2(1)(b). Under the Criminal Appeals Act 1995 the language adopted is that the Court of Appeal 'think that the conviction is unsafe'. For discussion see Blom-Cooper, *Birmingham Six and Other Cases*, chapter 5.
[110] One of the accused, Patrick Malloy, died in prison.
[111] The Commission started work in 1997.

to the Court of Appeal for reconsideration. The Commission has the power to investigate suspected miscarriages of justice. Its Chair is appointed by the Queen on the advice of the Prime Minister. It was the Criminal Cases Review Commission which successfully referred Derek Bentley's case back to the Court of Appeal.

THE CRIMINAL JUSTICE SYSTEM UNDER REVIEW

At the end of March 2000 there were 65,460 people in prison, and estimates indicate that if custody rates and sentence lengths remain at the same level the figure will rise to 70,400 by 2007.[112] The government is embarked on an ambitious programme to reform the criminal justice system, but also to tackle the causes of crime. In relation to the latter, much emphasis has been put on education of children, and on reducing dependence on welfare benefits through the government's welfare-to-work scheme. Tackling drug abuse is also a priority and a new national treatment agency has been introduced.[113] On the criminal justice front, reforms have been introduced to restructure the Crown Prosecution Service in order that local CPS boundaries coincide with local policing boundaries, and a local chief prosecutor has been introduced. From 2001, the principal agencies involved in the criminal justice system – the police, probation service, CPS and magistrates – all operate within the same boundaries. As noted above, the government is investing more in policing, intent on increased recruitment but also the setting of uniform targets for local forces to eliminate the widely divergent detection and clear-up rates in different areas. A national Youth Justice Board has been established and a nationwide system of youth offending teams introduced to ensure the co-ordination of effort in reducing youth crime.

[112] Home Office Publications: *A Guide to the Criminal Justice System*, www.homeoffice.gov.uk/rds/cjs
[113] Research conducted for the Home Office indicates that half of all crime is perpetrated by 'hard-core, highly persistent offenders' numbering around 100,000, and that 'many of the 100,000 most persistent offenders are hard drug users': the Home Secretary's Statement to the House of Commons, *Official Report*, 26 February 2001, col. 585.

In 1999 the Lord Chancellor appointed Lord Justice Auld to report on the working of the criminal court system. The terms of reference of the Auld Review are

A review into the practices and procedures of, and the rules of evidence applied by, the criminal courts at every level, with a view to ensuring that they deliver justice fairly, by streamlining all their processes, increasing their efficiency and strengthening the effectiveness of their relationships with others across the whole of the criminal justice system, and having regard to the interests of all parties including victims and witnesses, thereby promoting public confidence in the rule of law.

While the inquiry into the criminal justice system was being conducted by Lord Justice Auld, whose report was published in 2001, the government provided its own views on a modernized criminal justice system, while pledging not to pre-empt Lord Justice Auld's recommendations. In *Criminal Justice: The Way Ahead*[114] the government reviewed the whole criminal justice system, including crime prevention, youth justice, the role of the CPS, the police, the criminal law, criminal procedure and evidence, and sentencing philosophy and practice.[115] Much of this agenda overlaps with the Auld inquiry.[116] It remains to be seen how the independent Auld Report and the government's vision for the future will complement each other and together provide the foundation for a modern criminal justice system.

---

[114] Cm. 5074 (London: HMSO, 2001).

[115] On 19 February 2001 Lord Justice Auld issued a statement (in a press notice issued by the Criminal Courts Review) in which – with seemingly barely concealed anger – he said: '[W]hen it [the Report] is published, he trusts that it will be seen as an objective analysis unassociated with and uninfluenced by current Government political initiatives.'

[116] *Criminal Justice: The Way Ahead* revives a long-running debate about codification of the criminal law. The Paper proposes a 'reform and codification of criminal law providing a consolidated, modernised core criminal code to improve public confidence and make for shorter, simpler trials'. Britain is in a minority of countries without a Criminal Code, and the task of compiling one would be complex. See further *Reviving the Criminal Code*, [2001] Crim. LR 261.

BRITAIN AND
INTERNATIONAL RELATIONS

INTRODUCTION

Defending the realm and the conduct of international relations is a hallmark of the sovereignty of a state.[1] A nation's economic prosperity is dependent upon a secure state which engages on the basis of reciprocity in relations with other nations and groups of nations. The power to defend the realm from external or internal attack, and to promote the interests of the state through external relations, is of crucial importance. The foreign policy of any state is fashioned in part out of historical alliances and in part from reactions to international events. In most cases, it is underpinned by perceptions of self-regarding national interests, which may at the same time coincide with the interests of other individual or groups of nations. With globalization in finance, trade and the movement of workers, Britain's external relations are nowadays inextricably tied into a complex web of multi-national relationships. Globalization is also evident in the continued quest to secure peace between potentially and actually warring nations and better protection for human rights throughout the world. Environmental change – 'global warming' – also calls for co-operative action between nation-states, as does the threat from technological and other advances in weaponry which has resulted in the proliferation of weapons of mass destruction.

---

[1] State security is discussed in Chapter 8.

While historically nations conducted their foreign affairs through bilateral arrangements and alliances organized according to perceptions of national or mutual self-interest, the twentieth century – cut through by two World Wars – saw a movement towards greater regional and global co-operation. The League of Nations, established in 1916 and the precursor of the United Nations, the North Atlantic Treaty Organization, the Council of Europe, the European Communities (now Union), all illustrated the coming together of nations to reach solutions to problems of peace and the securing of human rights and better standards of living. Since that time the international relations of any nation have accordingly encompassed not only bilateral relations with other nations but also participation in regional and global organizations. National autonomy has been largely superseded by the need for interdependence. In the Preface to the 2000 *Departmental Report*, the British Foreign Secretary stressed the significance of globalization, stating that

Global communications, global markets, the increasingly global links between people are redefining old concepts of international relations. We live today in a world where nations are more interdependent than independent; where borders are becoming more bridges than barriers; where our opportunities and challenges are increasingly shared.[2]

In Britain, foreign affairs are conducted under the royal prerogative, and are therefore outside the immediate control of Parliament, but subject to parliamentary scrutiny.[3] Since 1991 the Foreign Office has issued Annual Reports to Parliament. The Secretary of State for Foreign and Commonwealth Affairs, less cumbersomely the Foreign Secretary, is a senior member of Cabinet and the Foreign and Commonwealth Office (FCO) is one of the most prestigious of all government departments. Other major departments of state have a profound effect on the conduct of external relations. The Ministry of Defence[4] has particular responsibility for all aspects of defence and security policy, while the

[2] Foreign and Commonwealth Office, *Annual Departmental Report, 2000*, www.fco.gov.uk/directory

[3] It was not until 1979 that a Foreign Affairs Select Committee in the House of Commons was established.

[4] Formed in 1946, co-ordinating formerly unconnected ministries each dealing with aspects of defence policy.

Treasury holds the purse strings of government and controls the funding of departments. Britain's economic prosperity in global markets is one of the key components of foreign policy and hence there is also a need for close co-operation between the FCO and the Department of Trade and Industry.

Many foreign relations matters are handled at the highest level of government, by the Prime Minister. Sir Anthony Eden took personal control over the renationalization of the Suez Canal in the 1950s (see below); Edward Heath took responsibility for the negotiations over Britain's entry into the European Community and Margaret Thatcher personally took control over the campaign to retake the Falkland Islands after the Argentinian invasion. It was also Prime Minister Margaret Thatcher who first bridged the gulf between the former USSR and the West through her meetings with President Mikhail Gorbachov. Similarly, Prime Minister Tony Blair seized an early initiative by visiting Russia's new President, Vladimir Putin, even before he formally took office, and following the terrorist attacks in New York in 2001 has played a leading role in international diplomacy.

THE FOREIGN AND COMMONWEALTH OFFICE (FCO)

Organizationally, the FCO is hierarchical.[5] Under the Foreign Secretary and junior ministers who are accountable to Parliament, the structure is headed by a Permanent Under Secretary who is also Head of the Diplomatic Service. It is the Permanent Under Secretary who is responsible for the flow of advice on all aspects of foreign policy to the Foreign Secretary, and also for the management of the FCO and Diplomatic Service. He is assisted by Deputy Under Secretaries, each supervising a particular area of work, such as international economic affairs. The Permanent Under Secretary supervises and co-ordinates the work of Directors and is responsible for the formulation of policy and the deployment of resources within 'Command areas'. These fall into three

[5] See www.fco.gov.uk. For in-depth analysis see Sir John Coles, *Making Foreign Policy: A Certain Idea of Britain* (London: John Murray, 2000), chapter 4.

broad categories: geographical (for example Europe, Africa and Commonwealth); functional (for example international security, overseas trade) and administrative (for example resources, personnel and security).

There is a great deal of continuity in the conduct of foreign affairs: Prime Ministers and Foreign Secretaries come and go, but civil servants in the Foreign Office and in embassies and consulates overseas have far more permanence. Britain maintains diplomatic missions in 188 countries. It is from these bases around the world that intelligence passes to the Foreign Office, and from there to the Prime Minister, Foreign Secretary and Cabinet. For the most part there is also much party political consensus on foreign relations issues. When major threats to international security emerge or localized wars or disasters strike, however, there must be a swift reaction from states which, whether through historical links or perceptions of necessity, can defuse actual or potential disturbances in the international order. Similarly, it falls to international organizations, such as the United Nations and the North Atlantic Treaty Organization, to strive for peace and to bring relief to civilian casualties through the provision of humanitarian aid. Neither Parliament nor the general public exert much influence on foreign policy, save where opinions are heightened through major developments which have a direct impact on citizens' lives.

It is from the embassies around the world that intelligence is gathered on local matters and transmitted to London. On these missions and their relationship with the FCO, Sir John Coles writes:

The debate between overseas posts and London headquarters is a crucial part of the making of foreign policy. The input of overseas missions varies widely from immediate analysis of, and urgent advice on, sudden crises and events to deeper analysis of political and other trends of the country concerned . . .

At the London end the practical manifestation of all this activity in posts across the world is the morning's crop of telegrams and e-mail messages, supplemented by a steady flow of letters and reports dealing with less immediate policy issues.[6]

---

[6] *Making Foreign Policy*, pp. 88–9.

The Joint Intelligence Committee (JIC)[7] has the responsibility for assessing threats to British interests. Much of the data also comes via the Government Communications Headquarters (GCHQ) which monitors signals intelligence around the world, to be sifted and analysed by the JIC. The JIC reports directly to the Prime Minister and senior colleagues and a Weekly Digest of Intelligence (the Red Book) provides a synopsis of issues relevant to British interests.[8]

Despite the network of embassies and consulates and the flow of information to London, there have in the past been some significant failures to predict emergencies. There was a failure to foresee the nationalization of the Suez Canal in 1956, Ian Smith's intention to sever links between Rhodesia (as it then was) and Britain by issuing a Unilateral Declaration of Independence in 1965, the Argentinian invasion of the Falkland Islands, the collapse of Communism and the break-up of the Soviet Union in the 1990s and the developing crisis in the former Yugoslavia.[9]

Current aims and objectives of foreign policy

The Mission Statement of the Foreign and Commonwealth Office issued in 1997 states that the underlying objective of foreign policy is 'to promote the national interests of the United Kingdom and to contribute to a strong world community'. As has always been the case, a healthy economy is developed and sustained through trading relations with other nations and is dependent upon good international political relations. In its 2001–4 Statement,[10] the FCO lists the following objectives:

I.   A secure United Kingdom within a more peaceful and stable world.

II. Enhanced competitiveness of companies in the UK through over-

---

[7] On which see further Chapter 8.

[8] See Sir Percy Cradock, *In Pursuit of British Interests: Reflections on Foreign Policy under Margaret Thatcher and John Major* (London: John Murray, 1997), chapter 6.

[9] See Coles, *Making Foreign Policy*, chapter 2, but cf. Cradock, *In Pursuit of British Interests*, chapter 6.   [10] October 2000.

seas sales and investments; and a continuing high level of quality foreign direct investment (through British Trade International, shared with the Department of Trade and Industry).

III. Increased prosperity for the UK through a strengthened international economic order.

IV. A strong international community; leading to an improved quality of life worldwide.

V. Pivotal influence worldwide over decisions and actions which affect UK interests; positive foreign perceptions of the UK; authoritative comprehensive information on foreign issues for UK decision-takers.

VI. A strong role for the UK in a strong Europe, responsive to people' s needs.

VII. Effective Consular services to British nationals abroad.

VIII. Regulation of entry to, and settlement in, the UK in the interests of social stability and economic growth (shared with Home Office).

IX. Secure and well-governed United Kingdom Overseas Territories enjoying sustainable development and growing prosperity.

Each of these objectives is subdivided into related aspects and allocation made to specific FCO departments. Under the first objective, for example, the FCO aims to contribute towards stability in the Balkans, the Middle East, the Gulf, Eastern Europe and Central Asia, Africa, the East Mediterranean, the Asia-Pacific region and in Latin America and the Caribbean region. Also included is the need to modernize NATO and to work towards an enlarged Security Council of the United Nations.[11] In relation to the European Union, the FCO intends to work towards having an EU 'military crisis management capacity', and to have in place a 50,000–60,000-strong EU military force capable of reacting to crises and providing peace-keeping personnel. The FCO is also committed to improved effectiveness of the UK's contribution to conflict prevention in those areas where the UK can make an impact, a joint target shared with the Ministry of Defence.

[11] On which see pages 519 ff. below.

THE CHANGING NATURE OF INTERNATIONAL RELATIONS

The geopolitical position of Britain – a small island off the north-west coast of continental Europe – has had profound implications for Britain's relations with the rest of the world. Originally, her island status dictated the need both to establish maritime trade-routes and to consolidate Britain's defence against potentially predatory peoples and nations. By the seventeenth century Britain had mastered the seas of the world. The talent for adventure and exploration began in the reign of Elizabeth I (1558–1603). Historically, however, as Britain expanded her trading relations with nations far and wide, she also exhibited greedy imperialist ambitions. Not only did Britain enter trading relations internationally, but she also extended her political power across the globe, if necessary by force. One by one, countries with less well-developed defences fell under British sovereignty. From Asia and India to North America and the West Indies, the British Empire grew. Competition with England's old opponent, France, extended to ousting the French from their colonial territories. In 1763 French Canada became a British possession. The first rebellion against British imperialism came from the American colonies. On 4 July 1776 the colonies issued their Declaration of Independence, but it was not until 1783 that peace was finally secured and the independence of the future United States ensured. In 1770 Captain Cook seized New South Wales, Australia, as British territory. Napoleon's defeat at Waterloo in 1815 and the subsequent peace accord further enhanced Britain's global reach with territories stretching from the Cape of Good Hope to Singapore and Malaya. By the reign of Queen Victoria (1837–1901), large swathes of the global map were painted with British Imperial pink. Across the globe, Britain had secured bases from which to defend her interests, some – as in the case of Hong Kong, the Falklands Islands and Gibraltar – having little rationale beyond their strategic positions.

As will be seen in Chapter 12, however, the nineteenth century witnessed the steady march from imperial rule to semi-independence for colonial territories in terms of the right to legislate for the territory. Dominion status, implying equality rather than subservience in the relationship between Britain and her dependent territories, was gradually assumed, by Canada in 1867, Australia in 1901, New Zealand in 1907 and South Africa in 1910. The Empire was being translated into a Commonwealth of Nations, united by mutually advantageous trading relations, a common language, administrative and legislative institutions, a legal system conferred by Britain and common allegiance to the British Crown. Independence for British colonies, whether inside or outside the Commonwealth, was, however, still some way in the future.

Two World Wars left Britain free and victorious but economically savaged: the post-war years being characterized by Britain's 'descent from power'.[12] The defeat of Germany in the First World War expanded Britain's Empire further with Iraq and Palestine coming under British control as protectorates. Britain's navy remained powerful and intact. New forces were, however, emerging. The Russian Revolution of 1917 had ushered in a potential new enemy: Communism. In the East, Japan exerted her power, invading Manchuria in 1931. Economic recession in the West fuelled German nationalism and smoothed the path for Adolf Hitler and the Nazi Party to take power in 1933. Germany, in contravention of the 1918 peace settlement, was rearming. In 1938 Germany invaded Austria. In March 1939 Germany seized Czechoslovakia and Poland and subsequently turned her attention to Russia. Once again Britain went to war. Globally, the war left fifty million dead. Even as the Second World War raged, however, the allied leaders – Prime Minister Winston Churchill of Britain, President Roosevelt of the United States of America and Stalin of the USSR – were planning for lasting world peace.

By 1945 Britain's position in the world had changed for ever. Two new superpowers emerged from the Second World War: the United States of America and the Communist Soviet Union. Although Britain continued to regard herself as a world leader, the balance of power had permanently shifted. Within two decades most of Britain's Empire had been lost. Colonialism was no longer a politically acceptable or viable concept in the new emerging post-war climate. Self-determination and

[12] The phrase is that of F. Northedge, *Descent From Power: British Foreign Policy 1945–1973* (London: Allen & Unwin, 1974).

independence from all colonial powers, including Britain, was firmly on the global agenda. Nor could Britain afford to maintain her colonies. The armed services were run down and conscription was abolished. As the government gave priority to improving the lot of citizens at home, through the introduction of the Welfare State and the National Health Service, so defence assumed lower priority. Britain was, however, as a result of the peace settlement, responsible for more territories than ever before – extending from Hong Kong and Malaya to Egypt and Palestine and Africa.

In 1947 new threats emerged. The alliance between Britain, the United States and the Soviet Union collapsed. The Soviet Union in effect closed off Eastern and Central Europe from the West: the Iron Curtain had descended. The allied division of Germany into four zones, with the Americans, French and British in Western Germany and the Soviets in Eastern Germany, consolidated the Soviet Union's domination of Eastern Europe. The Cold War began, pitching the ideologies of Communism and capitalism against each other. In the Middle East, following Britain's withdrawal from Palestine, the new state of Israel was established and Arab nationalism intensified.

In 1948 Winston Churchill described British foreign policy as being one of three interlocking 'circles': globalism, Atlanticism and Europeanism. Churchill, however, still insisted that Britain was at the 'point of conjunction', at the centre of world politics.[13] Internationally, however, notwithstanding her wide-ranging economic, trading and political relations across the globe, Britain's power and influence was waning. Increasingly dependent on the United States, not least for military support, Britain sought to establish a 'special relationship' with successive American administrations. If it ever was a 'special relationship' it was very much one in which Britain was the junior partner. In 1962 the former United States Secretary of State, Dean Acheson, stated:

Great Britain has lost an empire and has not yet found a role. The attempt to play a separate power role – that is a role apart from Europe – based on a

---

[13] Speech to the Conservative Party Conference, 1948. See A. Shlaim, 'Britain's Quest for a World Role', *International Relations* (1975), pp. 840–41.

'special relationship' with the United States – on being the head of a 'Commonwealth' which has no unity, or strength – this role is about played out.[14]

Nevertheless, Britain remained important to the United States. The United States' former isolationism in world politics had been breached by her (albeit reluctant) involvement in two World Wars. As the now-major Western superpower, the United States had no desire to assume the role of international policing and dispute-settlement. Shared language, legal systems and traditions, plus Britain's geographical position, made co-operation between the United States and Britain a matter of mutual benefit in questions of defence, intelligence and security.[15]

In 1947 India, Pakistan and Ceylon secured independence from Britain. In Malaya a Communist uprising caused Britain to engage in a long, costly and bloody campaign of guerrilla warfare. In 1950 the Korean War erupted, to which Britain had to commit naval forces and contribute to the United Nations' effort. Around 45,000 British soldiers fought under United Nations' command, with a loss of 1,078 men. With the Communists having taken over in China in 1949, the West feared Communist expansion into Korea, Japan and other Asian areas. Britain was obliged to support the Americans in protecting South Korea from the North Korean invasion in 1949. In 1950 China sent troops to support North Korea. The threat of conflict escalating into another global war was clear.[16]

In 1956 a crisis developed in the Middle East which changed for ever Britain's role and influence east of Europe. In 1954 Colonel Gamal Abdel Nasser ousted the previous military government in Egypt and appointed himself Prime Minister. Refused increased arms supplies from the West, Nasser purchased from Czechoslovakia. Nasser was anti-British, and from a British perspective, was intent on ending British influence in the Middle East. Fears were heightened in 1956 when Nasser

---

[14] *Keesing's Contemporary Archives*, vol. 14 (Bristol: Keesing's Publications Ltd., 1963–4), quoted in R. C. Macridis (ed.), *Foreign Policy in World Politics* (Englewood Cliffs, NJ: Prentice-Hall, 8th edn., 1992), p. 7.

[15] As evidenced by the positioning of American military hardware, including nuclear weapons, on British soil and the sharing of signals intelligence between the British Government Communications Headquarters (GCHQ) and the American National Security Intelligence Agency which has a base at Nemwith, Yorkshire.

[16] It was not until 2000 that Britain reopened diplomatic links with North Korea.

recognized Communist China. Nasser then nationalized the Suez Canal Company. The bulk of the Company's stocks were in British and French hands. Britain regarded the Canal as vital to Britain's route to the Gulf and the Far East. Britain and France, supported by Israel, planned to take the Canal by force. The Americans, under President Eisenhower, would not support armed action against Egypt. None the less, the British destroyed the Egyptian air force and soon Anglo-French forces were in place. The Egyptians, however, severed the oil pipeline to Syria, on which Britain was dependent for fuel. The campaign was a disaster for Britain. She was opposed by most United Nations' members; the Soviet Union threatened to attack Britain and France and to send support to Egypt. The United States blocked an application for a much-needed loan to Britain from the International Monetary Fund and threatened oil sanctions against Britain. The United Nations General Assembly called for a ceasefire and the removal of all foreign troops from Egypt, the reopening of the Suez Canal and for United Nations troops to be despatched to the Canal. The British and French withdrew, humiliated. In 1957 Prime Minister Anthony Eden resigned, to be replaced by Harold Macmillan, whose task it was to rebuild a relationship with the United States.

It was Macmillan who perceptively understood the changing role of Britain in a post-colonial era. In 1960 he delivered his 'Winds of Change' speech,[17] predicting the independence of African colonial states. Ghana achieved independence in 1957, Nigeria in 1960, Sierra Leone in 1961, Uganda in 1962, Tanzania, Zambia and Malawi in 1964, and the Gambia in 1965. In 1965 the white government of Rhodesia (as it then was, now Zimbabwe), under Prime Minister Ian Smith, issued a Unilateral Declaration of Independence from Britain. Britain reasserted her sovereignty over Rhodesia,[18] but it was an act of futility. Economic sanctions were imposed, but largely failed. Above all, the Rhodesian situation illustrated the sometimes difficult transition from colonialism to independence. It was to be a recurring problem in Harold Wilson's and James Callaghan's premierships.[19] As Harold Macmillan had recognized in 1960, African national consciousness had become a political fact: the

---

[17] To the South African Parliament in Cape Town.
[18] Under the Southern Rhodesian Act 1965. [19] 1964–70, 1974–9.

age of white minority rule in Africa was over. Ian Smith's government, however, attempted to withstand the forces of nationalism, and the attendant terrorism which reflected its demands. By the late 1970s his government had lost both authority and support. In 1979 a black government had been elected, but Smith still clung to power. Only in 1979 was a constitutional settlement reached under which the state of Zimbabwe was born, in April 1980, and white rule ended.

From 1945, then, Britain's international relations became an increasingly complex web of intersecting circles. Britain's diplomatic and trading relations had for centuries been international, albeit focused on the Empire and later the Commonwealth of Nations. With the ending of the Second World War in 1945, however, there was perceived to be a need for co-operation between nations for peace and security, the prevention of war and the promotion of the self-determination of formerly colonial peoples, and a need for the better protection of individual rights and freedoms – irrespective of geopolitical boundaries. However, as the Cold War evolved, the developed world found itself divided, not just by political boundaries, but by conflicting ideologies. In Europe one ideology found expression in the domination of the Soviet Union and its closure of Eastern Europe to the influences of the West. As conventional weaponry gave way to the development of biological, chemical and nuclear weapons – the weapons of mass destruction – so the threat of international conflict changed from the threat to individual lives, whether military or civilian casualties of conventional war, to the threat of the very annihilation of states. The final paradox of human development was the capacity for wholesale human destruction. The nation-state alone could no longer provide its own protection. Mutual security required mutual co-operation. The United Nations, the North Atlantic Treaty Organization (NATO), the Council of Europe and the incipient European Union all emerged from the horrors of war to provide for international and regional co-operation in the pursuit of peace. The idea of the independent isolated sovereign state, maintaining its individual security alone and defending its interests abroad through the maintenance of dependent colonies, had passed into history.

As discussed in Chapter 4, in 1951 the six founder members of the embryonic European Union formed the European Coal and Steel

Community, designed to remove from the control of nation-states the raw materials of war. Supranational control of atomic energy followed with the introduction of the European Atomic Energy Community in 1957, which together with the European Economic Community, was designed to establish an internally tariff-free common market for member states' goods. While Britain had expressed enthusiasm for the idea of a united Europe, she remained outside, fearful of the implications of Europe for her national sovereignty and the impact that membership of Europe would have on Britain's traditional trading partners, the Commonwealth states, and her relationship with the United States. There was also an official underestimation of the capacity of other European nations to achieve their objectives, which while initially modest included ambitious long-term plans for greater economic and political union. However, recognizing that the formation of the European Economic Community would have an adverse effect on British trade, Britain sought an alternative European market. This it found in 1959 in the European Free Trade Area, EFTA, joined also by Austria, Denmark, Norway, Portugal, Sweden and Switzerland, designed to provide a common market, but without a common external tariff, and thereby preserving the favoured position of Britain's Commonwealth trading partners. An alternative to the European Economic Community, it was thought by Harold Macmillan likely to enhance British influence with the United States, by establishing an alternative economic power bloc within Europe. He was wrong, for it soon became clear that the American government supported the European Economic Community, and favoured Britain's membership of it as contributing to a strong American-European alliance.

By 1960 it was becoming clear that the European Economic Community was not only viable, but thriving. Britain had to reassess her position. But having earlier rebuffed France's and Germany's initially positive stance towards British membership, the British government was now on insecure ground. In 1961 Prime Minister Macmillan embarked on renewed negotiations and announced to Parliament that Britain intended to join, provided the terms were acceptable. Edward Heath, future Prime Minister and firm pro-European, was put in charge of negotiations. While Britain now accepted the need for a common external tariff and common agricultural and commercial policies, she nevertheless sought to secure special terms for Commonwealth food imports. Although she was largely successful in this, a blow was delivered in 1963 when French President Charles de Gaulle, despite several summit meetings with Macmillan both in France and England, vetoed British membership.

Now rejected by Europe, Britain maintained her trading alliances with the EFTA bloc and her Commonwealth partners. However, the Commonwealth was changing, and Britain's reliance on historical and political ties did not translate into continued economic ties. Sentiment for the Commonwealth remained high in government circles, and notwithstanding changing relations, official policy under Macmillan was to encourage greater Commonwealth trade. However, Commonwealth exports to Europe were increasing, and those to Britain declining. Exports to the Commonwealth were also falling. Canada looked increasingly to the United States market, while Australia was developing links in the emerging markets of Asia. India was becoming increasingly influenced by the Soviet Union, and many African states now achieving independence and black majority rule were forging alliances among themselves and also looking to the Soviet Union for support.

In 1964 the Labour Party returned to power, under the apparently anti-European leadership of Harold Wilson. Europe was not a major interest, except for the purpose of forging closer trading links. Wilson was preoccupied with matters at home, most pressingly the need to reinvigorate a flagging economy. None the less, officials were monitoring the impact of Britain's exclusion from the Common Market, and the decreasing trade with the Commonwealth. The cost of defence was seen by Wilson as something which could not be sustained: in 1967 the intention of withdrawing Britain from positions east of Suez was announced, to the dismay of Australian and Asian Commonwealth leaders. As seen above, in 1965 the government was beset by a further problem: that of Rhodesia's Unilateral Declaration of Independence from Britain. Wilson began to revise his views on Europe, and in 1967 embarked on a tour of Europe. Soon, he announced the intention to reapply for membership. President de Gaulle, however, was still in power, and while he remained Britain could not negotiate acceptable terms for membership. When de Gaulle resigned in 1969, a powerful obstacle to Britain's entry was removed.

Meanwhile at home the 1970 general election returned the Conservative Party to power. Edward Heath had a deep commitment to Europe, one which had been nurtured since his teenage years. Heath was single-minded in his objective of taking Britain into Europe: all other objections, such as the transatlantic relationship and the position of the Commonwealth, retreated into the background. While Heath secured a favourable deal for New Zealand exports, the terms of entry were otherwise unfavourable. Nevertheless, their significance paled beside the possibility that the objective of entry by 1973 would not be achieved. In 1971 the deal was done and in October 1971 the House of Commons voted in favour of membership – Heath returned to Downing Street to celebrate by playing J. S. Bach.

For Margaret Thatcher, the longest-serving Prime Minister of the twentieth century, three issues dominated: the Argentinian invasion of the British Falkland Islands, relations with Europe and the return of Hong Kong to Chinese sovereignty. In 1982 Argentine forces invaded the Falkland Islands. A British possession for nearly 150 years, and of strategic importance, the Falklands had a population of less than 2,000. Negotiations between Britain and Argentina over the future of the Falklands had stalled, but Britain was entirely unprepared for the invasion, and had cut back its naval defences in the region. The Falklands campaign lasted just two months: the recovery of the islands cost 255 British deaths, 777 injured, the loss of six ships, and a total of some £5 billion. But victory was Thatcher's, and from a position of lessening electoral support in the face of difficult economic conditions, Thatcher went on to win the 1983 general election with a commanding majority.

Europe overshadowed Thatcher's premiership. When Britain negotiated entry under Edward Heath, it was from a position of weakness, and the unfavourable terms of entry gave little scope for immediate improvement. Two principal sources of dissatisfaction existed. The first was the Common Agricultural Policy (CAP) which in part provided for guaranteed prices and the control of output, and favoured the inefficiencies of scale of French farming while penalizing the more efficient agricultural production of British and German farming. The CAP took up the largest part of the Community budget, and its major beneficiaries were French farmers, a powerful political lobby in France. The second issue was that of Britain's contribution to the Community budget. Harold Wilson had sought to renegotiate the level of Britain's contributions, but secured no rebate. By 1980 Britain's contribution was set at £1,000 million and due to increase. Margaret Thatcher demanded, stridently, 'our [*sometimes*, my] money back'.[20] In 1984, at Fontainebleau, the matter reached its head: and Thatcher won, although at an incalculable cost to Britain's relations with her European partners. Like so many other Prime Ministers before her, Edward Heath excluded, Thatcher had an ambivalent attitude to Europe. Superficially, she presented a sceptical face, determinedly protecting British interests, as she perceived them, against a necessary but objectionable 'foreign' power. On the other hand, it was Thatcher who signed Britain up to the greatest integrationist treaty to date – the Single European Act 1986.

The European Economic Community had established the Common Market: internally a tariff-free zone, externally having common tariffs. There remained, however, many other obstacles to the free movement of persons, goods, capital and services: the original 'four freedoms'. Under the Commission presidency of Jacques Delors (soon to be seen as the bad man of Europe), the move towards a truly free and single market began. Arthur Cockfield, in 1982 Secretary of State for Trade, set to work, with Margaret Thatcher's approval, identifying the obstacles to the single market and planning to eliminate them by 1992. For the objectives to be achieved, it was necessary to make the system of voting in the Council of Ministers more flexible, and hence a considerable extension of qualified majority voting (QMV) was required.[21] An intergovernmental conference was convened in 1985 – against British wishes – and six months later the Single European Act came into being. The principal aim of the Single European Act was the attainment of the single market. That, however, entailed other matters of a far more contentious nature. European monetary union, for many years an aspiration, found its first formal expression in the Act. The Act also proclaimed the aim of moving towards European unity. Qualified majority voting was extended, and the European Assembly was formally renamed the European Parliament. The Court of Justice – the highest

[20] See M. Thatcher, *The Downing Street Years* (London: HarperCollins, 1993), especially chapter 3.
[21] QMV limits the ability of individual member states to block Community initiatives: see the discussion in Chapter 4.

court in the European Community (now Union) – was given jurisdiction to rule on the Act, thereby ensuring consistency in its application within member states. Plans to develop a common approach to immigration foundered with Britain's insistence on retaining controls of her island boundaries. With the treaty signed, the European Communities (Amendment) Bill was presented to the House of Commons; it passed all its legislative stages within six days and was approved by a hefty majority. The momentum towards the European Union, to become a reality in 1992, had been formalized.

The third issue with which Margaret Thatcher had to grapple was that of Hong Kong. The island of Hong Kong had been ceded to Britain in perpetuity. The New Territories, however, which bordered the People's Republic of China, and in which a majority of Hong Kong's workers lived, had been granted to Britain on a ninety-nine-year lease which was due to expire in 1997. China intended to reassert its rightful sovereignty of the New Territories but also laid claim to Hong Kong. In 1984, Thatcher signed a Joint Declaration in which Hong Kong would be permitted to remain a capitalist society retaining its legal system for a guaranteed period of fifty years from 1997, within the People's Republic, as a Special Administrative Region. The notion of one nation, two systems, was crystallized. Confidence in the 'guarantees' given to the people of Hong Kong waned. The Thatcher government offered 250,000 British passports to selected Hong Kong residents. Emigration from Hong Kong accelerated. When the pro-democracy movement in China was brutally crushed at Tiananmen Square in 1989, the prospects for Hong Kong's Western liberal society looked increasingly uncertain. The task of bolstering democracy in Hong Kong prior to the hand-over of the territory fell to John Major's premiership, and to the last Governor of Hong Kong, the former Conservative Party Chairman, Chris Patten.

Margaret Thatcher resigned from office in November 1990; her successor John Major inherited her external relations legacy: the 'problem' of Europe, the hand-over of Hong Kong and relations with the former Soviet Union once the collapse of Communism, in its infancy in 1985, took hold and the Iron Curtain – which for over fifty years had divided Europe and the world into two opposing ideological camps – was finally lifted.

THE EMERGENCE OF INTERNATIONAL ORGANIZATIONS

The United Nations

The League of Nations had been formed in 1916 as a commitment to solving disputes through negotiation under the auspices of a truly international organization dedicated to peace. With the ending of the First World War, a Peace Conference convened in Paris, the product of which was the Treaty of Versailles, which incorporated the Covenant of the League of Nations. Ironically, although President Woodrow Wilson was one of the principal forces in the peace settlement, the United States Senate later rejected American membership of the League. Under the League, colonies and territories which had been under the sovereignty of Germany and Ottoman Turkey were transferred to the victors of war on the basis of trust. The mandated territories went principally to Britain and France.[22] A Permanent Mandates commission was established to advise on all questions relating to the mandates, and reported to the Council of the League.

The League of Nations, however, failed.[23] In 1931 Japan invaded and occupied Manchuria, part of the Chinese Empire. In 1933 Italy planned to attack Abyssinia. Although the League imposed sanctions on Italy these proved worthless, and Abyssinia became an Italian possession. In Spain, civil war broke out, fuelled by Nazi support for Franco's Fascist Party. Although a Non-Intervention Committee had been formed, it was clear that not only Germany but also Italy and Portugal had intervened, while the Soviet Union had supplied aid to the government. Despite the League, no action was taken to stop the German and Italian interventions. The ideals behind the League, however, remained and in the aftermath of the Second World War the United Nations was born. In 1946 the League Assembly met for the purpose of transferring its

[22] Britain assumed responsibility for Palestine, Tanganyika, Transjordan and Iraq. French rule extended to Syria and Lebanon. Britain and France shared the mandate for the Cameroons and Togoland.

[23] See D. Hurd, *The Search for Peace: A Century of Peace Diplomacy* (London: Warner Books, 1997), chapter 1.

powers and functions to the United Nations, and the League's existence terminated.

In 1941 Churchill and Roosevelt met off Newfoundland and agreed the principles which would regulate post-war settlements.[24] In 1942 representatives of twenty-six nations met and signed the United Nations Declaration. In 1943 Churchill, Roosevelt and Stalin held a conference at Tehran. In 1944 the Bretton Woods Conference, held in New Hampshire, saw the birth of the International Monetary Fund and the World Bank,[25] the headquarters of which were to be located in Washington DC. Also in 1944, representatives of the United States, Britain, the Soviet Union and China met at Dumbarton Oaks in Washington to formulate the basis of an organization dedicated to lasting international peace. In 1945 came the Yalta conference, attended by Roosevelt, Churchill and Stalin, at which the demand for unconditional surrender from Germany was restated and further consideration given to the proposals for a United Nations organization. While the United Nations' Charter is committed to the principle of the sovereign equality of all,[26] in practice it was to be the victorious Allied superpowers who were to dominate the organization, a matter which caused disquiet among smaller nations. There was to be a General Assembly,[27] analogous to a parliamentary assembly, at which all members were represented. However, it was the Security Council which would have true executive power, and of its membership, only five superpowers were to have permanent seats: the Republic of China, France, the Soviet Union, the United Kingdom and the United States of America.[28] Decisions in the Security Council required a unanimous vote: any permanent member therefore had a power of veto. A further six nations – now ten – would have seats on the Security Council for two-year terms. The final stage on the road to the United Nations was the San Francisco conference of 1945, at which the Charter of the United Nations was signed. Controversially, the United Nations Headquarters was to be situated in New York, not in Europe, psychologically representing a shift in the focus of international power and placing the United States centre-stage.

[24] Resulting in the Atlantic Charter.
[25] Originally the International Bank for Reconstruction and Development.
[26] Article 2(1) of the UN Charter.   [27] Ibid., Article 9(1).
[28] Ibid., Article 23(1).

Aims and objectives

Article 1 of the United Nations Charter states that the principal purposes of the United Nations are:

1. To maintain international peace and security, and to that end: to take effective measures for the prevention and removal of threats to the peace, and for the suppression of acts of aggression or other breaches of the peace, and to bring about by peaceful means, and in conformity with the principles of justice and international law, adjustment or settlement of international disputes or situations which might lead to a breach of the peace;
2. To develop friendly relations among nations based on respect for the principle of equal rights and self-determination of peoples, and to take other appropriate measures to strengthen universal peace;
3. To achieve international co-operation in solving international problems of an economic, social, cultural, or humanitarian character, and in promoting and encouraging respect for human rights and the fundamental freedoms of all without distinction as to race, sex, language, or religion; and
4. To be a centre for harmonizing the actions of nations in the attainment of these common ends.

The United Nations now comprises 189 countries, each of which accepts the obligations of the UN Charter which defines the UN's role.

The principal organs of the United Nations

Six principal organs were established under the Charter: the General Assembly, the Security Council, the Secretariat headed by the Secretary-General, the International Court of Justice, the Economic and Social Council and the Trusteeship Council. In addition to the World Health Organisation and International Monetary Fund, there also exist numerous specialist non-governmental organizations (NGOs), many of which have consultative status in relation to the principal organs.[29] The NGO system is co-ordinated by the NGO Committee which is responsible for considering applications for consultative status and any realignment

---

[29] See P. Willetts (ed.), *The Conscience of the World: The Influence of Non-Governmental Organisations in the UN System* (London: Hurst & Co, 1996).

in an NGO's status,[30] and is a permanent standing committee of the Security Council. Over 1,500 NGOs have consultative status with the Economic and Social Council (ECOSOC).

In addition to NGOs are the United Nations related agencies, as illustrated below:

Major specialized agencies

FAO	Food and Agriculture Organization of the United Nations
ILO	International Labour Organization
UNESCO	UN Educational, Scientific and Cultural Organization
WHO	World Health Organization

Technical specialized agencies

ICAO	International Civil Aviation Organization
IMO	International Maritime Organization
IFAD	International Fund for Agricultural Development
ITU	International Telecommunication Union
UNIDO	United Nations Industrial Development Organization
UPU	Universal Postal Union
WIPO	World Intellectual Property Organization
WMO	World Meteorological Organization

Financial specialized agencies

IMF	International Monetary Fund
IBRD	International Bank for Reconstruction and Development
IDA	International Development Association
IFC	International Finance Corporation

[30] NGOs are classified into Category I and Category II, Category I indicating a basic interest in most of the activities of the Security Council, Category II being those with special competence in some field of UN activity.

Other UN-related agencies

IAEA	International Atomic Energy Agency
ISBA	International Sea-Bed Authority
UNCTAD	United Nations Conference on Trade and Development
WTO	World Trade Organization.[31]

The work of the United Nations[32]

Since its birth, the United Nations has striven to resolve inter-state conflicts and to reach settlements to international crises through peace-making, peacekeeping and humanitarian assistance. In 1960 the General Assembly adopted a *Declaration on the Granting of Independence to Colonial Countries and Peoples*, and since that time some sixty former colonial territories have attained independence. The United Nations was instrumental also in ending the system of racial segregation – apartheid – in South Africa. The Iran–Iraq War ended with a UN-sponsored peace settlement in 1988. In former Yugoslavia, United Nations peacekeepers sought to bring peace to Croatia, to protect civilians in Bosnia and Herzegovina and to ensure that the former Yugoslav Republic of Macedonia was not drawn into the war. In relation to the Middle East, the United Nations has worked for decades, and through five wars, to seek to bring peace to the region. Wherever conflict and war erupt, the United Nations will work towards peace.

In its peacekeeping role, it is the Security Council which defines the scope of operations and mandates. Peacekeeping may involve military personnel establishing buffer zones to separate warring parties while negotiations for peace take place, or the use of civilian police and other personnel to help monitor elections or human rights standards, or to monitor peace agreements. Some operations may be swift, others protracted: UN peacekeepers have been in Cyprus since 1964, and the operation maintaining a ceasefire line between India and Pakistan has been in place since 1949. Since 1948, some 118 countries have provided more than 750,000 military and civilian police personnel. In the year

[31] Source: Willetts, *The Conscience of the World*, table A.4, p. 284.
[32] Space and the sheer scale and number of United Nations operations preclude anything other than a sampling of the UN's role.

2000 some 35,400 military and civilian police personnel were deployed in fifteen operations world-wide.

International human rights standard-setting and monitoring is another key concern of the United Nations. In 1948 the Universal Declaration of Human Rights was proclaimed by the General Assembly of the United Nations, setting international standards, *inter alia*, for the right to life, liberty and nationality, to freedom of thought, conscience and religion, the right to work and be educated and to participate in government. Two international covenants, the Covenant on Economic, Social and Cultural Rights, and the Covenant on Civil and Political Rights, supplement the Universal Declaration. Since its introduction, the Declaration has provided the base for over eighty conventions and declarations on human rights, some subject-specific, such as conventions to eliminate racial and gender discrimination, the rights of children, the rights of refugees. Others are directed more broadly: examples include declarations on the self-determination of peoples and the right to national development. Human rights endeavours are co-ordinated by the High Commissioner for Human Rights; the UN Commission on Human Rights reviews the record of states in promoting rights and has the power to appoint independent experts to examine human rights.

The control of weapons of mass destruction (WMD) is also a UN concern, as is the elimination of landmines which claim thousands of victims world-wide each year, whether by death or mutilation.[33] In 1968 the Nuclear Non-Proliferation Treaty was signed; in 1996 the Comprehensive Nuclear-Test-Ban Treaty. Treaties have also been signed prohibiting the development, production and stockpiling of chemical weapons and bacteriological weapons.

The provision of humanitarian aid in emergencies and natural disasters – whether through flood, drought, earthquakes or conflict – is another United Nations concern. To combat and reduce the impact of disasters, the United Nations raises money from international donors to help fund humanitarian relief. In 1997–8 the United Nations assisted more than fifty-one member countries to deal with over seventy-seven natural disasters; in 1999 more than $1.4 billion was raised to provide aid to some 26 million people. The United Nations High Commissioner

---

[33] In 1997 over a hundred nations signed the Ottawa Convention outlawing landmines.

for Refugees (UNHCR) is central to assisting refugees and displaced persons. In 1999 there were some 22 million people in need of UNHCR aid, including some 2.5 million Afghan refugees, 1 million in the former Yugoslavia and, in Central Africa, some half a million refugees. Civil wars are estimated to have separated a million children from their parents in the past decade, and to have made 12 million more homeless and left 10 million 'severely traumatized'. The United Nations Children's Fund (UNICEF) seeks to protect such children and to provide food, clean water, medicine and shelter. Not only is such work costly, and often logistically difficult, but it is also dangerous. The United Nations records that since 1992 over 180 UN civilian staff have been killed and 178 taken hostage while serving in humanitarian operations.

Limitations on United Nations effectiveness

The United Nations is not a form of world government: it depends on the co-operation of its members and their willingness to comply with UN standards and operational requirements. The United Nations has no military arm, it is dependent for its operations on military and civilian personnel supplied by its member states. United Nations operations are costly: it is dependent upon the prompt payment of contributions from its members to meet administrative and operational costs. Permanent members of the Security Council can apply a veto against UN operations, a power statistically most used by the former Soviet Union and the United States of America, less so by Britain, China and France. The permanent members of the Security Council were fixed nearly sixty years ago, determined by the then powerful allied states. Despite the reordering of power on the world stage, there has been no reordering of the membership of the Security Council. Accordingly, there is no seat for the European Union (but one each for two of its members, Britain and France). Nor do two of the world's now most powerful economies – Germany and Japan – have permanent status.

The British government is committed to the United Nations system. The United Kingdom is the sixth largest contributor to the United Nations Regular Budget (general fund), the fifth largest contributor to UN peacekeeping budgets and one of the largest voluntary contributors to UN funds and programmes and Specialized Agencies. Britain's contribution in 1998 amounted to over £330 million. Of this, over £35 million went to the Regular Budget, over £29 million to UN peacekeeping operations, over £51 million to UN Specialized Agencies, and Britain's voluntary contributions amounted to over £204 million. Not all member countries are so co-operative: at the start of the Gulf War, the United States owed some $451 million; in 1992 it owed $757 million.

The United Nations has also, inevitably in a multi-national quasi-governmental organization, found itself hampered by politics. Since its origins, decisions in the General Assembly have been reached on the principle of equality – one nation, one vote – and by a simple majority. However, the statement of principle masks extensive degrees of alignment between nations – on regional or ideological bases. Plenary sessions of the General Assembly convene in the autumn each year to debate the most important items of the agenda. Other matters are decided in one of the several main committees. However, the work of the General Assembly is ongoing. Member nations have delegations in New York.[34] The United Nations headquarters is far more than a parliamentary building at which formal meetings are held: less formal interactions take place daily between diplomats in the lounges, lobbies and dining-rooms. Meetings of the principal United Nations organizations also take place almost daily, with representatives participating as delegates and others as observers. Furthermore, while the Security Council Permanent Members wield the greatest power, the Security Council also has ten elected representatives from the regional groups, who are elected by the General Assembly. Broadly, the recognized regional groupings are Africa and Asia, Eastern Europe, Latin America, Western Europe and other states. These groupings, however, do not truly respond to geographical groupings, nor do they recognize the considerable economic, linguistic, political and religious diversity within the group. It is the Security Council and not the General Assembly which makes the major decisions relating to United Nations initiatives and operations. A veto on the part of one of the Permanent Members leads to inaction.

Under the Charter the Council is required to be so organized as to 'function continuously' and to meet every fortnight, although this is

[34] The United Kingdom's Mission comprises the Ambassador and Permanent Representative and thirty-four other staff.

not always applied. While non-members of the Council may ask to be allowed to participate in debate, they may not vote. The political problem with the Security Council lies in both its composition and the veto-power accorded to the Permanent Members. As noted above, permanent membership was determined initially in accordance with those who were the victors in war. Notwithstanding shifts in power – the demise of Britain as a world power and global domination by the United States, especially since the end of the Cold War – there has been no reform of Security Council membership. The power of veto is something which has been used to great effect, especially by the former Soviet Union and the United States. To take just two examples: for decades the United States has imposed an embargo on trade with Cuba, a position strengthened in 1992 when the then President signed the Cuba Democracy Act to prevent US subsidiaries trading with Cuba from third countries.[35] The United States has maintained this position, notwithstanding General Assembly votes condemning American policy, the effect of which is to deny to the Cuban people, who no longer receive aid from Russia, the materials to maintain their infrastructure, medical supplies and foodstuffs. Cuba still pays with the well-being of its people for the implacable hatred of the US for Castro's regime, despite the fact that it was brought about by popular revolution and has endured since 1959. A second example comes from Iraq. The Iran–Iraq War erupted in 1980 and was to continue for nearly a decade. In 1990 came Iraq's invasion of Kuwait, a dispute resolved only by international military force led by American and British troops. In 1990 the United Nations Security Council adopted a Resolution condemning the invasion and demanding the immediate withdrawal of Iraqi forces and that Iraq and Kuwait begin negotiations for peace. Of the many Resolutions which followed, the most damaging was Resolution 661 which imposed sanctions on Iraq following its failure to withdraw from Kuwait. All overseas Iraqi assets were effectively frozen, Iraqi oil sales were banned as were exports to Iraq. Under pressure, the United States and Britain subsequently lifted the embargo on medical supplies and foodstuffs. The use of international force against Iraq

---

[35] See G. Simons, *United Nations: A Chronology of Conflict* (Basingstoke: Macmillan, 1994).

appeared to be sanctioned by Resolution 678, from which China abstained[36] and which Yemen and Cuba, non-permanent members without a veto, voted against. The Resolution authorized member states 'to use all necessary means' to implement 660 (Iraqi withdrawal), but did not specifically authorize the use of force, although it was so interpreted by the United States which dominated the military action carried out under the aegis of the United Nations. The United States effectively blocked international opposition through the use of financial clout. Turkey received $8 billion worth of military equipment and low-cost loans worth £1.5 billion through the International Monetary Fund and World Bank; Syria was offered arms; Iran received substantial World Bank loans; a $15 billion Egyptian debt was waived; Ethiopia was offered an investment package. Yemen, which voted against the Resolution, was penalized through the suspension of a $70 million aid programme, the World Bank and International Monetary Fund blocking Yemeni loans.[37] The Resolution against Iraq remains in force: in 2000 the British Foreign Secretary stated that the Resolution remained in force as a result of Iraq's failure fully to comply with United Nations requirements.

The North Atlantic Treaty Organization (NATO)

In 1949 the United States of America, Canada and ten European nations signed the North Atlantic Treaty, bring together an alliance dedicated to maintaining each other's defence. The total membership of NATO is now nineteen.[38] The Treaty derives its legitimacy from the United Nations Charter. NATO members are committed to maintaining and developing their defence capabilities and providing the basis for collective defence planning. Consultations between member countries take place when one or more considers that its security is at risk. The Treaty refers to the right of collective self-defence, as laid down by the UN

[36] An abstention does not amount to a veto, but to a concurring vote.
[37] See Simons, *United Nations*, chapter 7.
[38] Belgium, Canada, Czech Republic, Denmark, France, Germany, Greece, Hungary, Iceland, Italy, Luxembourg, Netherlands, Norway, Poland, Portugal, Spain, Turkey, United Kingdom and United States of America.

Charter, and an attack on one member country is regarded as an attack on all. With the ending of the Cold War, the end of Communism and of ideological divisions in Europe, the role of NATO expanded to encompass truly trans-European co-operation in the search for peaceful settlements of disputes. Towards this end, a 'Partnership for Peace' Programme has been established to promote co-operation among the NATO allies and twenty-six partner countries. The political framework for Partnership for Peace is the Euro-Atlantic Partnership Council (EAPC), which includes forty-six countries and which met in 1999 following the NATO summit, represented by heads of state and government from member countries.

Originally, decisions were reached through infrequent meetings of Foreign Ministers of member countries in the North Atlantic Council. In 1951 a civilian body of Council Deputies was created to carry out Council directives and co-ordinate the work of subordinate bodies. The Council Deputies became a permanent body in 1952. The permanent Council, comprising ambassadors, generally holds regular weekly meetings. Meetings at ministerial level, attended by Foreign and Defence Ministers, are held at least every six months. Occasional meetings are also held at the level of heads of state and government. Summit meetings – the highest level of decision-making – occur less frequently. In 1999, the fifteenth formal meeting of the Council at Summit level took place in Washington, commemorating the fiftieth anniversary of the Alliance.

BRITAIN AND EUROPE

Continental Europe has always been central to Britain. Historically it was a relationship characterized more by war than by peace. With Europe the site of global conflagration in 1914 and 1939, and Britain the defender of European liberty from attempted German hegemony, and ultimately – with her allies from around the globe, most significantly (albeit belatedly and reluctantly) the United States – the victor, Britain's future relations with Europe were always to be complex. Nevertheless, it was Winston Churchill who called for a United States of Europe after the Second World War.[39] While that was rejected by Britain, and British entry to the European Community (now Union) was delayed until 1973, Britain nevertheless played a full part in reconstructing legal and political relations in Europe. In 1949 the Council of Europe was born, out of which came the European Convention on Human Rights and Fundamental Freedoms setting pan-European standards for the protection of individual rights against the power of governments and public authorities.[40]

THE MOVEMENT TOWARDS COMMON EUROPEAN FOREIGN AND SECURITY POLICIES

While the founding fathers of the European Communities[41] envisaged a 'United States of Europe', the origins of the Communities were far more modest. Removing control of the raw materials of war from the nation-states and bringing it under a supranational authority, and providing for a tariff-free trading bloc of European nations was the primary objective, and the idea of a European Union – as it now exists with its three 'pillars' of common Foreign and Security Policy and Justice and Home Affairs alongside the European Community – lay far in the future.

The idea of closer political co-operation, which would facilitate a common stand against the rest of the world and which would ultimately lead to the evolution of a common Foreign and Security Policy, was however on the agenda. In 1970 the *Luxembourg Report* recommended that Foreign Ministers meet twice-yearly in order to promote the idea of Europe 'speaking with one voice' and demonstrating that 'Europe has a political mission'.[42] With this the Political Committee, made up

[39] Speech at the University of Zurich, 19 September 1946.
[40] For details, see Chapter 7.
[41] The original three Communities: the Coal and Steel Community, Atomic Energy Community and European Economic Community (Common Market): now the European Community and Union. See further Chapter 4.
[42] *First Report of the Foreign Ministers to the Heads of State and Governments of the Member States of the European Community of 27 October 1970.*

of Directors of Political Affairs, was established, enabling ministerial meetings to be held four times a year. European Political Co-operation (EPC) is headed by a presidency which rotates on a six-monthly basis, reflecting the pattern of the Community as a whole. In 1974 the European Council was established, through which heads of states and government meet twice a year, and which accords the highest level of leadership to policy issues such as foreign policy. Since 1981 the European Commission has become fully involved in EPC. In 1986 the Single European Act brought EPC within the framework of the Treaties.

The institutional structure of decision-making in relation to foreign and security policy is complex and multi-faceted. It is also a deeply political matter on which member states of the Union may not agree, either on principle or in relation to specific issues, and about which other states and international organizations – principally but not exclusively the United States of America, the United Nations and NATO – have strong views. Additionally, individual EU member states participate separately and severally within the World Trade Organization (WTO), until 1995 the General Agreement on Tariffs and Trade (GATT), the Organization for Economic Co-operation and Development (OECD)[43] and G8. At G8 summit meetings, the membership comprises the United States, Canada, Japan, Russia and four EU nations, France, Germany, Italy and the United Kingdom. Over and above such forms of international co-operation are the interests of each individual country in the development and preservation of its own foreign relations with other states. Each state is thus operating within a broad spectrum of interconnecting, overlapping concentric circles.

Within the European Union, European Political Co-operation (EPC) has evolved alongside, but not precisely paralleling, trading relations between the Union and other nations and blocs and the granting of aid to developing nations. The responsibility for Europe's external trade lies principally with the European Commission, which, under the Treaties, is empowered to negotiate agreements with non-EU states on behalf of member states. For example, the Lomé Convention, signed in 1975, unites seventy-one developing countries in Africa, the Caribbean

[43] The membership of which includes Japan, Australia, South Korea, Poland, New Zealand and the Czech Republic.

and the Pacific (ACP states) in a 'trade and aid agreement' with the Union, and opens up the Community market to ACP agricultural and industrial products. The General Agreements on Tariffs and Trade, succeeded by the World Trade Organization, came into being in 1948, conceived as an independent agency of the United Nations. GATT had responsibility for regulating international trade, lowering tariffs and the resolution of disputes, and member states were responsible for about 90 per cent of world trade. The successor to GATT, the World Trade Organization, with a base in Geneva, has a total membership of 132 members with a further twenty-nine countries having observer status. All member states of the European Union belong to the WTO. Under the Treaty of Rome [44] the European Commission represents the member states in trade negotiations. Over half of Britain's trade is with European Union partners, operating under the European Single Market, dedicated to the four freedoms of free movement of goods, persons, services and capital. The Single Market opens up a market for goods comprising 380 million consumers and accounts for 40 per cent of world trade. An Internal Market Council, on which each member state is represented, operates the Single Market.

The Organization for Economic Co-operation and Development (OECD) was founded in 1948 as the Organization for European Econ-omic Co-operation (OEEC) principally to oversee the implementation of the Marshall Plan, the post-war programme for European Economic Recovery. The founder-members of the OECD were Austria, Belgium, Denmark, France, Greece, Iceland, Ireland, Italy, Luxembourg, the Netherlands, Norway, Portugal, Sweden, Turkey, the United Kingdom, and the British, French and American zones of occupied Germany. In 1949 the Federal Republic of Germany joined, and the United States and Canada became associate members in 1950. Spain joined in 1959. In 1960 the United States and Canada became full members and the OECD took over from the OEEC. In 1964 Japan was admitted, to be followed by Finland in 1969, Australia in 1971 and New Zealand in 1973. Its membership now also includes Mexico, the Czech Repub-lic, Hungary, Poland and South Korea. The OECD operates on an

---

[44] Article 113. See also Article 229 which confers responsibility on the Commission to maintain 'appropriate relations' with the WTO.

intergovernmental model, decisions being taken on the basis of unanimity within its Council. The European Commission co-operates with the OECD on development issues through a Development Assistance Committee.

As Europe developed from the original European Coal and Steel, European Atomic and European Economic Communities – or Common Market – to the European Union, so too its aims and objectives extended far beyond its original aims. The Union created in 1992[45] was committed not only to mutually beneficial common trading arrangements but to the development of a common currency, common foreign and security policy, common policies relating to immigration and asylum and co-operation in the field of criminal justice. In relation to defence and security, the Western European Union (WEU), which had been formed in 1955 and had long been regarded as moribund, has been revitalized. The origins of the WEU lie in early attempts to form a European Defence Community in 1954, a proposal blocked by France. The Brussels Treaty which introduced the WEU was originally intended to last for a fifty-year period.[46] The WEU is headed by a Council, comprised of Defence and Foreign Ministers of member countries, and meets twice-yearly at ministerial level and monthly at ambassadorial level. The WEU has a parliamentary body, the Assembly, based in Paris, and meets twice-yearly to debate security issues. The WEU is dependent for operations on forces made available by member states.

In 1991 it was agreed that the WEU's headquarters should be relocated to Brussels, and in 1992 the WEU widened its remit to include peacekeeping, humanitarian and rescue tasks. The WEU has thus emerged as an integral part of the European Union.[47] The WEU does not affect membership of NATO, but supplements such membership. In practical terms, the need to develop mutual consultation between the European Union and NATO has led to informal contacts being established

---

[45] Under the Treaty on European Union 1992, the Maastricht Treaty.

[46] The original membership of the WEU comprised the United Kingdom, France, the Benelux countries, West Germany, Italy, Canada and the United States. Portugal, Spain and Greece subsequently joined. Austria, Denmark, Finland, Ireland and Sweden are observer members. Iceland, Norway and Turkey have associate status. Ten Central and Eastern European countries are 'associate partners'.

[47] Treaty on European Union 1992, Article J4; Treaty on European Union 1997, Article 7.

between the NATO Secretary-General and the EU High Representative for Common Foreign and Security Policy, and discussion of participation of non-EU European allies and practical arrangements for EU access to NATO planning capabilities and NATO's collective assets and capabilities. At NATO's 1999 Washington Summit, Europe's Security and Defence Identity (ESDI) was considered, an essential component of which was the development of the Union's military capabilities. At the Council Meeting of the European Union in 1999, it was agreed that the Union would aim to be able to deploy, by the year 2003, military forces of up to 50,000–60,000 troops to undertake humanitarian and rescue tasks, peacekeeping tasks, and tasks of combat forces in crisis management. The forces would undertake military operations in response to international crises in circumstances where NATO was not as a whole militarily engaged. It was also decided at the 1999 Council meeting that permanent political and military structures would be created. These include a Political and Security Committee and a Military Committee and a Military Staff. The Union also agreed to maintain and develop consultation and co-operation with NATO and with NATO members who are not members of the Union, in relation to European security and defence.[48]

BRITAIN AND THE COMMONWEALTH

The Commonwealth is a unique constitutional entity: it has no formal defining legal text, no treaty regulates it nor do formal legal procedures regulate its intergovernmental relations. Undefined by legal texts, and neither established nor regulated by treaties, the Commonwealth is characterized by 'bonds of common origin, history and legal traditions'.

---

[48] These developments have not been without controversy. While the Secretary General of NATO, Lord Robertson, emphasized that 'more Europe' would not lead to 'less NATO' and that a stronger Union would mean a stronger Alliance, the Conservative opposition in Britain has expressed disquiet. The argument put forward was that the European initiative, supported by Prime Minister Tony Blair, was in some sense motivated by 'anti-American' forces and that Britain's relationship with the United States would be harmed by such a development.

The Commonwealth now comprises fifty-four nations, and has a population of nearly two billion people spanning six continents and five oceans. A quarter of the world's population and land surface are united within the Commonwealth. Among its members are thirteen of the world's fastest growing economies and fourteen of the world's poorest. What sets the Commonwealth apart from other international organizations is its history, its institutional informality and its common bonds of shared language, traditions and values inherited from former colonial times.

In 1971 the Commonwealth was defined as being 'a voluntary association of independent sovereign States, each responsible for its own policies, consulting and co-operating in the common interests of their peoples and in the promotion of international understanding and world peace'.[49] The Commonwealth is founded on the principle of equality of all its members, and accordingly only independent states may become members of the Commonwealth. All members of the Commonwealth (with the exception of Mozambique) have experienced direct or indirect British rule or have been linked to another Commonwealth country. Dependent territories of member countries[50] and self-governing states associated with member countries,[51] while not full members, are regarded as being 'within the Commonwealth' and may participate in Commonwealth affairs and receive Commonwealth assistance. Membership of the Commonwealth has no impact on a member state's sovereignty: each is free to decide its own form of government, policies and relations with other international organizations. However, membership is dependent upon acceptance of, and respect for, the core values and principles of the Commonwealth, as set out in the *Declaration of Commonwealth Principles* issued in 1971 and revised by the *Harare Commonwealth Declaration* of 1991.[52]

The Head of the Commonwealth is Queen Elizabeth II. The reasons for this are historical and lie originally in the British Empire and the transition of its dependent countries from being led by a dominant,

---

[49] Commonwealth Declaration, 22 January 1971.
[50] e.g. Christmas Island, the Australian Antarctic Territory and Coral Sea Islands, which are dependencies of Australia.
[51] e.g. the Cook Islands and Niue, which are associated states of New Zealand.
[52] See further below.

fully sovereign nation, imposing its laws and policies on them, to independence.[53] Throughout the nineteenth century the right to self-governance was increasingly recognized. 'Dominion' status, which was granted to Canada in 1867, Australia in 1901, New Zealand in 1907, South Africa in 1910 and the Irish Free State in 1921, entailed a recognition of independence and equality. In 1926, the Imperial Conference defined Dominions as 'autonomous communities within the British Empire, equal in status, in no way subordinate one to another in any aspect of their domestic or external affairs though united by a common allegiance to the Crown and freely associated as members of the British Commonwealth of Nations'. The movement towards republican governments heralded constitutional change. Hitherto the common bond between members of the Commonwealth had been acceptance of the monarch as head of state. When India decided to become a republic, it also wanted to remain within the Commonwealth, but accepting the monarch as head of state was clearly incompatible with republican status. In 1949, at a meeting of Commonwealth Prime Ministers, it was decided that India could remain as a member, accepting the monarch not as head of state, but rather as a 'symbol of the free association of independent member nations and as such Head of the Commonwealth'. By 2000, of the Commonwealth's total membership, thirty-two states were republics, five had their own national monarchies, while sixteen were constitutional monarchies which recognize the Queen as their head of state. As noted above, membership involves the acceptance of and respect for core Commonwealth values. Where these are not complied with, membership of the Commonwealth may be suspended. In 1995, for example, heads of government decided that Nigeria had violated Commonwealth principles and its membership was suspended, initially for a two-year period. Nigeria's progress towards reintroducing democratic government was monitored by the Commonwealth, and with the swearing-in of a democratically elected civilian President in May 1999 its suspension from membership was lifted. South Africa's membership lapsed when it became a republic in 1961. It was clear that if it reapplied for membership it would be rejected because of its apartheid policies;

---

[53] The movement from Empire to decolonization is discussed more fully in Chapter 13.

it was only accepted back into the Commonwealth following democratic elections in 1994.

Commonwealth principles

Every two years, heads of government meet (at Commonwealth Heads of Government Meetings: CHOGMs) to discuss matters of mutual interest. At the 1971 CHOGM held in Singapore, the Declaration of Commonwealth Principles was agreed which included:

- a commitment to world peace and support of the United Nations;
- commitments to the liberty of the individual, irrespective of race, colour, creed or political belief, and the individual's democratic right to participate in democratic political processes;
- a commitment to combatting racial discrimination and opposition to all forms of colonial domination;
- a commitment to removal of disparities in wealth between nations, working against poverty, ignorance and disease and to raising standards of living; and
- a commitment to international co-operation.

These principles were reaffirmed and supplemented at the 1991 CHOGM in Harare, and taken together represent the core of Commonwealth values. The *Harare Declaration* recognized the changing nature of international relations. The Cold War had ended, decolonization was almost complete and South Africa was then progressing towards dismantling apartheid and introducing democratic, majority-rule government based on racial equality and respect. At the same time, over the previous twenty years, while many Commonwealth countries had made progress in economic and social development, many other member countries remained trapped in poverty, over-population and poor environmental conditions. The *Declaration* committed the Commonwealth as a whole to 'sound and sustainable development' achieved through a redistribution of resources from the developed world to developing countries. Furthermore, the *Declaration* stressed the importance of protecting and promoting democracy, the rule of law and independent judiciaries, human rights, including equal rights and opportunities for all citizens regardless of race, colour, creed or political belief, and in particular the promotion of equality for women. Environmental protection was also emphasized, consistent with principles of sustainable development. Drug trafficking and abuse and communicable diseases were also to be targeted.

In 1995 heads of government met in New Zealand and announced the Millbrook Commonwealth Action Programme ('Commonwealth Ministerial Action Group', CMAG). The CMAG was designed to further the achievement of objectives set out in the *Harare Declaration*. The CMAG has a three-part programme designed to advance fundamental Commonwealth political values, promote sustainable development and facilitate consensus-building between Commonwealth members. Key measures include providing assistance in creating and building institutions to foster respect for Commonwealth principles, providing assistance in constitutional and legal matters with a view to initiating programmes of democratization, including assistance in the conduct of elections and their monitoring. On sustainable development, the CMAG is pledged to increase financial resources, and to work towards a greater flow of investment to developing countries. To ease the debt burden of poor countries, the CMAG is promoting methods of providing debt relief. To bolster compliance with Commonwealth values, the CMAG was empowered to take action, through sanctions, against those countries which violated Commonwealth principles.

At the 1999 CHOGM, the first summit meeting held in the now-democratic South Africa, heads of government addressed the issue of globalization and development. The *Fancourt Declaration* recognized that globalization was 'creating unprecedented opportunities for wealth creation' and the improvement of the human condition, but nevertheless recognized that its benefits were not being felt by all nations. The harsh reality remained that half of the world's population lived on less than $2 per day. The *Declaration* called for action at national and international levels to reduce poverty. In doing so, the *Declaration* insisted that methods of reducing poverty must centre on involving those most affected by ensuring that the poor have a voice in the future of their country. The *Declaration* stated:

We believe that the spread of democratic freedoms and good governance, and access to education, training and health care, are the key to the expansion of human capabilities and to the banishment of ignorance and prejudice.

Recognising that good governance and economic progress are directly linked, we affirm our commitment to the pursuit of greater transparency, accountability, the rule of law and the elimination of corruption in all spheres of public life and in the private sector.

The modern Commonwealth, founded on the principles of equality and mutual respect at the summit meeting of 1951, has reached its fiftieth birthday. A review of the Commonwealth and its future is to be undertaken at the 2001 CHOGM in Australia, focusing on the role of the Commonwealth in the twenty-first century.

Organization of the Commonwealth

The role of Head of the Commonwealth is undefined by legal texts – as is the Commonwealth as a whole. The role is not hereditary. Although Queen Elizabeth II was unanimously accepted by members in 1952 on the death of her father, there is no automatic succession to the office. The Queen attends the bi-annual Commonwealth Heads of Government Meetings (CHOGMs) and gives a formal address. She also meets informally with all heads of state of the Commonwealth.

The Commonwealth is headed by a Secretary General. Under the Secretary General's stewardship, the Commonwealth Secretariat works to achieve Commonwealth objectives. Formed in 1965, the Secretariat has twelve separate divisions. The operational arm of the Secretariat is the Commonwealth Fund for Technical Co-operation, established in 1971, which, at the request of Commonwealth governments, provides 'technical assistance and expert advice on all issues within the Commonwealth's agenda'.[54] Aid to developing states is a key concern. Commonwealth experts advise on national debt problems, economic restructuring and other issues. The Commonwealth Secretariat carries out feasibility studies for small businesses and assists with technical knowledge and with education and training.

---

[54] The Commonwealth Fund for Technical Co-operation has four principal divisions: the Economic and Legal Advisory Services Division; the Export and Industrial Development Division; the General Technical Assistance Services Division; and the Management and Training Services Division.

12

A SKETCH OF THE PAST:
THE MAKING OF MODERN BRITAIN

INTRODUCTION

The British system of government has evolved rather than been planned and systematically constructed: the contemporary system of government is the product of centuries of development. Systems of government and constitutions come in many forms. A constitution may be broadly defined as the set of rules which identify the institutions of government, regulate the exercise of powers of government and set out rights of citizens. It may be written or 'unwritten'; monarchical or republican; democratic or totalitarian; it may regulate a state which is either unitary or federal, characterized by different basic constitutional principles. Whatever form individual constitutions take, they all fulfil the same function: they outline, in greater or lesser detail, the role, functions and powers of the institutions of the state, the relationship between those institutions, and the relationship between the state and its citizens, usually in the form of a constitutional Bill of Rights. The extent to which Bills of Rights are enforceable by the individual vary according to the degree of respect which governments accord to citizens' rights and freedoms.

The constitution of the United Kingdom has never been formally drafted into an authoritative document. In many states around the world there was a point in time at which – whether through revolution or the peaceful gaining of independence from a previously governing colonial power – it became both necessary and desirable to work out the manner in which the state would be run, and to define the rights of citizens in relation to their government. By contrast, apart from a period of constitutional upheaval in the seventeenth century Britain has enjoyed peaceful, and independent, evolutionary development, and has never been in a situation which provided the catalyst for the formal drafting of a constitution. The present-day constitution is the result of this process which has been continuous since the invasion of England by William the Conqueror in 1066. The consequence of this evolutionary process is a system of government which reveals many curious, and some little understood, features. While there is no need to embark on a detailed history in order to understand contemporary arrangements, it is useful to appreciate the major constitutional developments which have occurred at different periods in the past and which continue to exert their influence on the present.[1]

ORIGINS

The island-state of Britain, with its natural coastal defences, has been successfully invaded and completely conquered only twice in its long history, once by the Romans and once by William of Normandy in the eleventh century. In 55 BC Julius Caesar arrived, bringing the primitive island under the power of the Roman Empire. It remained so until the beginning of the fifth century, leaving behind a legacy of classical architecture, sophisticated administration, towns, roads and waterways and the Latin language. London became the administrative capital, where the governor resided, and from which all roads led out to the regions. Only Scotland proved ungovernable. Having conquered it the Romans withdrew, building Hadrian's Wall, eighty miles long, to keep out the warring Scots. Regional government institutions were introduced with each town having a senate and elected magistrates, forming a system through which the commands of the governor could be communicated and enforced. Networks of fortified

---

[1] Appendices I and II list monarchs and Prime Ministers of Britain.

garrisons spread across the land, occupied by legions drawn from other parts of the Empire who had the power to suppress any local discontent. Gilbert Sheldon records that there were three principal periods during the Roman occupation: 'a century of peaceful penetration, three centuries of imperial rule and of increasing fusion, and a century of decay.'[2]

By the fourth century Christianity had become the dominant religion of the Roman Empire. Pagan cults, such as that of the Druids, had been wiped out. Churches were built throughout the country, uniting the people of Britain with the rest of the Empire. Britain, however, was only an outpost of the Empire, and an expensive one to maintain. External threats required either a large standing army in Britain, or the ability to despatch necessary forces from other parts of the Empire to defend Britain. A standing army posed a threat: a popular general might usurp the power of the Empire. On the other hand, despatching troops when required was slow and also disruptive of other campaigns. Frequent and savage raids by barbarians, seeking not to colonize but to plunder, depleted the wealth of the land. When the Roman Empire came under threat in France the legions were recalled, leaving Britain vulnerable to attack from across the northern border and from invaders from across the Channel and North Sea. It is thought that by the year 442 the entire Roman administration had withdrawn from Britain. And the invaders came: Anglo-Saxons arrived to pillage and destroy what remained of Roman civilization in Britain. Britain became a country of warring local leaders.

Christianity, however, did not die out. In the fifth century St Patrick arrived in Ireland. A century later the Pope despatched St Augustine to England, where in Canterbury Christianity became established once more. Churches and monasteries were built across the country. Clashes between the practices of the old English Church and the Roman Church were settled. Civilization again began to grow. But again it was threatened from outside. In the eighth century the Vikings (from Denmark, Norway and Sweden), like the Anglo-Saxons before them, came to conquer the land, destroying churches and monasteries, pillaging

[2] G. Sheldon, *Transition from Roman Britain to Christian England* (London: Macmillan, 1932), p. 32.

whatever wealth they could find and wiping out the Anglo-Saxon kingdoms, with the exception of Wessex, the region comprising what is now Hampshire, Wiltshire and Somerset. King Alfred came to the Wessex throne in 871 and was to rule for thirty years. In 878, in a battle decisive for the future of England, Alfred defeated the Danish king. In 886 Alfred captured London. A Christian king, Alfred the Great reversed the decline in civilization which accompanied the Viking invasions, and built a complex defence system to quell future invaders. Between his accession in 871 and the twelfth century the boundaries between England, Scotland and Wales, already in rudimentary form under the Romans, became more distinct.

1066–1649

In 1066 William the Conqueror, Duke of Normandy, arrived in England, defeating King Harold and his armies at the Battle of Hastings, and claiming the English crown. At that time there was no unified state, nor were Ireland, Scotland or Wales a part of the kingdom seized by William. Rather, England was divided into separate, and often warring, regions under different kings and queens. William's first task was the unification of England under his rule. The process was long and slow, and, under William, mostly achieved by the suppression of opposition through bloody and brutal force. In order to assess the wealth of and in his nation William set about the first national survey: the *Domesday Book* which catalogued every piece of land, its ownership and who occupied it, largely with a view to raising revenues for the Crown. Historian F. W. Maitland describes *Domesday* as a 'geld book', the geld being a tax, although later historians have attributed a wider significance to *Domesday* than a mere record of taxable titles to land. Threats from abroad required both money and an army. *Domesday* revealed who held financial, political and military power in the country and on whom the king could call for support: a shrewd political move which laid the foundations for the centralized state which was to develop. By William's reign the system of counties was already in place: the king's commissioners were charged with the duty to survey each area by summoning juries to give evidence of the wealth in the area. William's arrival also signalled the close relationship between England and continental Europe, a relationship which was to endure, albeit uneasily, until the sixteenth century. Latin had long been the 'official language' of England. Now came a mixture of French and English, or Anglo-Norman, so that in the reign of William three languages effectively existed.

In the reign of Henry II (1154–89) the rudiments of a unified English state with central government and a common legal system were achieved. The legacy in England was one of feudalism under the power of the barons to whom monarchs had granted land in exchange for political and military support. Henry believed in centralized power and administration and set about installing a system of courts – or assizes – staffed by the King's judges and dispensing a common law of England throughout the land. Henry II, like so many kings to follow, fell out with the dominant Church of Rome. Religion played a central role in the formation of the modern state. The Catholic Church, revitalized under Pope Gregory VII (pope 1073–85), insisted that all, including the king, owed a duty of absolute obedience to the Church. The monarch was regarded as appointed by God: the king held office by virtue of God and the Church and could not therefore claim greater authority than the Church. The Archbishop of Canterbury, as premier bishop, held formidable power. It was within his rights to excommunicate anyone in the realm, including the bishops. He controlled vast lands and wealth. Loyalty and obedience, according to the Church, was primarily due to the pope. Should the king pass laws in contradiction to those of the Church, to whom did the duty of allegiance lie? From the perspective of the archbishop it was clearly to God and the pope. Here indeed was a power to rival that of any king.

Thomas Becket became Chancellor of the king's household, and Henry II's friend. When the archbishopric of Canterbury fell vacant, Henry wanted Becket elected. Henry's wish was granted. But rather than a loyal ally who would champion the king's cause against the Church, Becket set about consolidating the power of the Church. The feud resulted in Becket being charged with financial misdealing while Chancellor and with contempt of court. On being found guilty, Becket sought to compensate the king. When his offer was rejected he fled into exile. Six years later, he returned and in 1170 the king and archbishop were reconciled. The peace lasted less than six months. The king received a report that the archbishop had summoned an army, supposedly to challenge royal authority. Becket was murdered by the king's knights in his own Cathedral. That a Christian king – God's deputy on earth – should be involved in the assassination of the archbishop while at prayer in his church, was viewed with horror. The martyred Becket was canonized within two years. But following his public pilgrimages of atonement, Henry gradually restored his popularity with the people and with the Pope, who, in 1171, granted Henry II the 'overlordship' of Ireland following a successful military expedition. Henry died in battle in France in 1189.

Until the English Civil War in the seventeenth century, kings and queens held near-absolute governing power. It had always been the case, however, that the monarch needed revenue to administer the state and to provide security in the form of an army. For revenues to be raised for both purposes, the monarch needed supporters. It is in this practical need that the explanations lie for the still peculiarly English social class system and in particular the inherited titles which entitled peers to sit in the House of Lords. The king would grant 'honours': titles and land to supporters in return for revenue and, when necessary, the personnel for an army. The king's, or queen's, loyal supporters formed his or her closest advisers, in the form of the King's, or Queen's Council, the predecessor of the Privy Council and, with the extension of democratic government, the Cabinet.

In legal as opposed to political terms, it remains the case today that all powers of government formally lie in the hands of the Crown. While the legal system slowly developed, with independent judges, and an incipient Parliament emerged as a debating and legislative chamber, the supreme power lay with the monarch. This power, loosely but inaccurately labelled the 'divine right of kings', represented an actual and potential source of conflict between the monarch, the judges and Parliament. When the Crown claimed 'divine right' it was a claim that monarchical power was derived from God. In constitutional terms, the power of the Crown is an 'inherent' power, a 'prerogative' power: that is to say, the power naturally resides in the office of the Crown. The implication of this was that the power was absolute and unchallengeable by any other person or institution.

As the scale of government grew, the aristocracy made up the first, and original, Parliament in the form of the House of Lords. (The House of Commons, the representatives of the 'common people', was a later supplement.) However, although the Crown's powers were great, they were limited by the practical realities of the need for support. An early conflict between the king and the barons – those supporters on whom the king had conferred titles of honour – gave rise to the first formal limitation on royal power: the Magna Carta of 1215.

The grievances against the king, now King John (1199–1216), centred on the raising of taxation from merchants and others, a right claimed by the Crown, together with the king's right to prevent citizens from leaving the country, and complaints about the criminal justice system administered in the king's courts. Signed at Runnymede on the banks of the River Thames, Magna Carta represented a victory for the barons, the 'upper classes' (as opposed to the ordinary people), against royal power. It is to Magna Carta that the right to trial by jury can be traced.

Nevertheless, Magna Carta had great significance for the ordinary man and woman. The right to trial by jury ensured that royal power would not be abused and that the legal process and that alone would determine a person's right to freedom or otherwise. It also, significantly, proclaimed that the king was under, rather than above, the law and that if the king attempted to set aside or avoid the law the law would step in to control him. Thus the idea of government under law emerged together with an early assertion of the rights of the individual even against the Crown.

Equally significant for the liberty of the individual was the ancient prerogative writ of habeas corpus. In origin, this writ was an order of the court to bring a person before it in order to give evidence in legal proceedings.[3] By the seventeenth century it had come to be interpreted as enabling an individual to petition to have his or her detention tested for its legality.[4]

By the thirteenth century the House of Commons had come into being, albeit in embryonic form and far removed from being a democratic

---

[3] See R. J. Sharpe, *The Law of Habeas Corpus* (Oxford: Oxford University Press, 1976); Jenks, 'The Story of Habeas Corpus' (1902) 18 LQR 64, 65.
[4] See *The Five Knights' case (Darnel's case)* (1627) 3 St Tr 1.

body. In 1265 representatives from English counties and boroughs[5] were summoned by the king to attend Parliament to advise the king on various matters. Previously the king had called on representatives to meet with him in Council for specific but not general purposes. Records show that in 1268 the king summoned the mayor, bailiffs and six representatives from each of twenty-seven selected towns. Those who were to represent the towns were 'elected' from the higher strata of society. By 1275 the king, by writ, instructed sheriffs to send four or six men to Parliament to advise the king. The practice in relation to summoning varied: on some occasions knights from each county were called, on others elected citizens of the larger towns and also burgesses[6] from the boroughs. The City of London was treated differently, with representation in Parliament being drawn from the mayor and aldermen of the city. There was no apparent consistency in terms either of those summoned or of those attending the Parliament.[7] What is clear, however, is that during the reign of Edward I (1271–1307) Parliament was becoming recognized as not just the assembly of lords, barons and bishops (as in the contemporary House of Lords) but also as a body of commoners representing local areas. What we recognize today as the Parliament of Crown, Lords and Commons had become an identifiable part of the constitution by the end of Edward I's reign, and as time progressed these rudimentary Parliaments were to be assembled more frequently, although it was not until the great electoral reforms of the nineteenth century that the franchise was extended to the point where Parliament was a truly representative body.

By Edward III's reign (1327–77), Parliament had assumed a form which is still recognizable today. By now the House of Commons was

[5] Boroughs are towns exercising local government functions which had been established through the grant of a Royal Charter. Their historical origins are obscure. Maitland states that even in the early tenth century there was a distinction drawn between a 'borough' and a 'mere township': see F. W. Maitland, *Domesday Book and Beyond: Three Essays in the Early History of England* (Cambridge: Cambridge University Press, 1897; London: Fontana Library, 1960), p. 214.

[6] A citizen of the borough chosen to represent the borough; later, the elected Member of Parliament.

[7] To offset expenses, the community represented by the knights and burgesses was required to pay a fixed sum of money. Salaries for Members of Parliament were not introduced until 1911.

more firmly established: the knights and burgesses from the counties and boroughs representing the ordinary people. These representatives were elected, not by the people, but by the freeholders of property in the county, although there was little nation-wide consistency in the qualification to participate in the election of representatives. The idea that 'ordinary subjects' should be consulted as to their representatives and play a full role in the political process had not yet been born. Representation was confined to the wealthy and powerful: for the most part, it was wealthy merchants who represented their area and who had a particular interest in trade and national finance. Nor were Parliaments summoned regularly: the need to summon Parliament, and the exclusive right to do so, remained for long the sole and absolute prerogative of the Crown, only to be curtailed by the constitutional settlement of 1689. Abuse or misuse of the Crown's prerogative power by successive kings is one of the main explanations for the Civil Wars of the seventeenth century. It was not the misuse of the prerogative alone, however, which caused constitutional and political disquiet. The history of England during the sixteenth and seventeenth centuries was also characterized by the conflict between State and Church which had first arisen under Henry II.

Until the reign of Henry VIII (1509–47), the prevailing religion was Roman Catholicism. Henry VIII's well-documented marital problems led to a breach with Rome and the Catholic faith, which was to have profound influence on later political events. When Henry wished to end his marriage to Catherine of Aragon, he appealed to the Pope for a declaration that his marriage to Catherine had not been valid in the eyes of the Church. The Pope, however, was not inclined to offer him a way out of the marriage. Henry, finding his intention to dispose of Catherine and marry Anne Boleyn thwarted, declared the religious independence of England from Rome, and proclaimed himself head of the Church of England. To demonstrate his power against the Church of Rome, Henry set about ridding England of Roman influence, destroying monasteries and churches, and – of greater constitutional significance – demanding absolute allegiance on the part of all officers of state to himself as head of the Church of England, and recognition of his supremacy over both Church and State.

The religious conflict between the Church of England and the Church of Rome which began in the reign of Henry VIII, and the conflict between king, Parliament and the judges which had endured with greater or lesser intensity for centuries, culminated in civil war. From the contemporary perspective of a largely secular society it is difficult to comprehend the religious conflicts of earlier centuries, and, especially in England, the significance of Roman Catholicism and the fears and hatred it provoked. Yet Catholicism played a fundamental role in the shaping of British history. Although Henry VIII broke with Rome, and established his authority as head of the Church of England, he never lost his own love for Catholicism. Personal and political necessity motivated Henry, not a form of doctrinal rejection.

A Protestant Reformation was vibrant in Northern Europe, and took hold in Scotland. But England was faced by a Catholic Europe to the south: France, Spain and Italy, long seen as traditional foes with designs on the island nation of Britain, were firmly under papal control. And thus it was, after the Reformation, that Catholicism came to be seen by the common people as not just a rejected religion (by England), but also one which was firmly allied to England's traditional and potential enemies. The problem was exacerbated by the need for kings and queens to find suitable wives and husbands; they frequently used marriage as a means of ensuring a powerful ally within Europe. Henry VIII had first married the Spanish Catholic Catherine of Aragon; his daughter Mary – intent on re-establishing Catholicism in England – married the Catholic Philip of Spain; Charles I married the Catholic Henrietta Maria of France; Charles II married the Catholic Catherine of Braganza (who failed to produce an heir to the Crown, although Charles made up for this through his numerous mistresses, on his death leaving fourteen illegitimate children). His younger brother James, once widowed, married an ardent Catholic princess, Mary of Modena. Small wonder that the royals were under suspicion in relation to their dedication to the established Church of England. Fears of 'popery' ran high for centuries.

It was in Henry VIII's reign that Ireland came firmly under English rule.[8] Although Pope Adrian IV had conferred on Henry II the 'overlordship' of Ireland in 1171, that power was confined to the specific

---

[8] Wales had been conquered by the English in 1282 and from 1284 English law extended to Wales.

purpose of reforming the Irish Church. Henry VII (1485–1509) had raised the issue of English rule over Ireland, although at the time English rule extended only to the Pale, the area to the north and west of Dublin. When Henry VIII broke with Rome, Irish leaders called on the Pope and the Spanish Emperor for support against the king of England. The resulting rebellion was crushed, and in 1541 the Irish Parliament finally recognized Henry as king of Ireland.

Henry was succeeded initially by his sickly son Edward VI who died at the age of sixteen, and then by his daughter Mary, who was devoutly Catholic and virulently anti-Protestant. Mary married Philip of Spain in 1554 – a Roman Catholic and heir to the Spanish throne. Under Henry and Edward suppression of the trappings of Catholicism had been relatively muted. Under Mary, on the other hand, full-scale persecution of Protestants was carried out. Although queen for only five years (1553–8), Mary succeeded in martyring over three hundred Protestant heretics in just four years, in bloody public displays. In the public mind, Catholic rule, in alliance with Catholic Spain, became associated with oppression, violence and the influence of Catholic continental Europe.

Mary died at the age of forty-two, to be succeeded by her sister Elizabeth, who reigned from 1558 to 1603. Elizabeth had been imprisoned by Mary for allegedly being part of a plot to overthrow the Catholic Queen. The Protestant Elizabeth made enemies in Europe, and the Pope absolved Catholics from their duty of allegiance to Elizabeth in 1570. But while Elizabeth insisted on conformity with the Protestant faith, she was tolerant of private religious dissent. Under Elizabeth poetry and drama flourished: Christopher Marlowe, William Shakespeare and Ben Jonson are all products of the Elizabethan age. In terms of British power, Sir Francis Drake expanded British interests through his voyages of discovery while also masterminding the victorious defeat of the Spanish Armada in 1588. This powerful 'Virgin queen' commanded the love and respect of her people in a manner that few other monarchs have accomplished. At the time of her death Elizabeth had restored England to international power, had presided over a civilized and largely tolerant court and had laid the foundations of a society in which art, literature and theatre were to flourish.

The Tudor age ended with the death of Elizabeth, heralding the

Stuart era. James VI of Scotland became James I of England, thus uniting the crowns of England and Scotland.[9] James I of England was not a successful monarch. He inherited a debt from the reign of Elizabeth worth some £100,000. Inflation and the cost of war made monarchy expensive. Personally awkward and ungainly, extravagant and homosexual, James avoided the limelight. Whereas Elizabeth had ruled her people with a common, if firm, touch, and aroused their admiration and support to the point of adoration, James was a solitary king who did little to endear himself to the people and even less to Parliament, although his reign started with goodwill. The problem, as so often, was finance. Short of personal revenue, and lacking essential parliamentary support for the granting of 'supply', James had two choices. Either he could raise the money under the prerogative right of imposition by forced loans, fines and taxes without Parliament's involvement, or he could persuade Parliament to finance government. Initially Parliament was generous, voting him three subsidies, worth nearly £400,000, in 1606. But whereas Elizabeth had been frugal to the point of meanness, James was extravagant and within two years an annual deficit of £100,000 was in place and a debt of over half a million pounds.

James I used the prerogative to issue proclamations, a practice which, though not new, was raised under his son and successor Charles I (1625–49) to new and disastrous heights. But James, unlike Charles, was careful in his use of power and mindful of the need to preserve a balance of power between himself and his Parliament. While viewing himself as above the law, he nevertheless accepted that a good monarch would act according to law. But Parliament increasingly objected to the making of law outside its own precincts. There was a great distinction, in parliamentary eyes, between a king giving his assent to laws passed by Parliament and a king issuing proclamations and thus making law without any parliamentary control. Impositions – finance raised by monarchs without parliamentary approval – remained a problem. The question raised its head once more in 1606 when John Bate refused to

[9] James was the son of Mary Queen of Scots and her second husband, Darnley. He came to the English throne through the Treaty of Berwick signed in 1586 between Elizabeth I and James. The Treaty guaranteed that Scotland and England would be allies, that each would respect the other's crown during their lifetimes and that James would succeed Elizabeth should she remain childless.

pay the required money. Rather than exert royal authority James allowed the matter to go before the Court of Exchequer. The court ruled, in the *Case of Impositions*, in favour of the Crown,[10] distinguishing between the ordinary prerogative which was a matter of common law and unalterable other than by Parliament, and the absolute prerogative of the Crown which conferred unlimited authority on the Crown to act in relation to matters of high policy and government, including matters of import and export, thus confirming that the king could raise money through the imposition of customs moneys. In *Prohibitions del Roy*[11] Sir Edward Coke, Chief Justice of Common Pleas, told the king that while he might attend court he could not give judgment. James also came up against Coke over the right of the Crown to issue proclamations which attempted to restrict the jurisdiction of the courts. In the *Case of Proclamations*,[12] Coke ruled that the king, however learned in other matters, had insufficient knowledge of the law to interfere with its workings. Coke was dismissed by the king.

Charles I came to the throne in 1625. He had married Henrietta Maria, a member of the French royal family and a Catholic. Unlike his father, Charles was a pious and serious man, and there was no room for the licentiousness and bawdiness which had characterized James I's court. But Charles also came into conflict with Parliament over the issue of taxes which Parliament would only grant on the condition that the king get rid of his close adviser and friend the Duke of Buckingham. This was unacceptable to Charles, who then tried to raise the money without Parliament's consent, relying on the royal prerogative. It was Ship Money which caused the greatest offence. In order to raise money to fund the navy and build naval defences, Charles levied tax on the counties, without parliamentary consent. The challenge to his power came in the case of *R v. Hampden*.[13] The court, however, ruled that the king had the sole (prerogative) right to determine the threat to national security and to raise the necessary funds to avert the threat.

The tussle for power between Parliament and the Crown continued, a struggle which ended in civil war. In 1628, fully aware of Charles's view as to the prerogative, Parliament presented the king with the

---

[10] *Bates case* (1606) Lane 22; 2 St Tr 371.   [11] (1607) 12 Co Rep 63.
[12] (1610) 12 Co Rep 74; 2 St Tr 723.   [13] (1637) 3 St Tr 825.

Petition of Right which had four major aspects. The Petition of Right provided that no freeman should be 'restrained or imprisoned' unless there existed lawful cause; that the writ of habeas corpus, which gave the courts the power to test the legality of a person's detention, should be available to all, even those imprisoned by the king; that if there was no legal cause for imprisonment the person should be freed or granted bail; and that freedom of property included the right not to be taxed by the king without the consent of an Act of Parliament. Only when Charles agreed to the Petition did Parliament grant the king his money. Charles then dismissed Parliament (as was his legal right under the prerogative) and reigned for the next eleven years under the prerogative with the assistance of the King's Council.

The need for finance arose, again in relation to a dispute with the Scots. Charles had tried to foist the English Prayer Book on them, and threatened to confiscate Scottish church lands. The Scots rebelled. Charles recalled Parliament. Although the first re-established Parliament lasted only a few weeks, in November 1640 the Long Parliament began which endured for twenty years. Parliamentarians, angry at being ignored for so long by the king, impeached Sir Thomas Wentworth, Earl of Strafford, the king's closest personal adviser. Strafford's 'crime' was to have enforced the king's will, through military force, too ably in both the North of England and later in Ireland.[14] When, however, a Presbyterian uprising occurred in Scotland, Strafford's zeal proved disastrous and the English were routed. The parliamentary leader, John Pym, proposed an Act of Impeachment alleging militarism and tyranny. Strafford defended himself ably. Parliament then proceeded to pass a Bill simply declaring Strafford guilty of treason, and Parliament voted for his execution without any evidence or testimony being given. The decision to execute Strafford fell to the king. Threatened by angry mobs outside Parliament and a hostile establishment, Charles felt obliged to sign the Act of Attainder, only to regret his 'single frailtie' and the abandonment of his friend. Strafford was beheaded on Tower Hill in May 1641. Parliament thus reasserted itself against the king. Soon it became clear that the country was divided between the supporters of Parliament and those who wished to exercise control over the king, his

[14] See R. F. Foster, *Modern Ireland 1600–1972* (Harmondsworth: Penguin 1989), chapter 4.

ministers, the Church of England and the army, and those royalists who supported Charles. Parliament remained dissatisfied with the treatment it had received from Charles, and the perceived abuse of royal power during the long years of personal rule. The Scots were invading from the north. In Ireland rebellion broke out. In January 1642 Charles made the mistake of deciding to prosecute five parliamentarians who opposed his view on the prerogative, and rode with over three hundred swords-men to the House of Commons to demand their surrender. The five had fled, but the uproar at the king's actions caused Charles to flee from London. Negotiations for the restoration of order broke down, and in August 1642, at Nottingham, the king raised the Royal Standard and declared war.

When the Civil War broke out in 1642, the country was split into supporters of the king – the Cavaliers – and supporters of Parliament, the Roundheads (so named because of the Puritan belief that short hair signified purity and godliness). By 1645, following the Battle of Naseby, the king had clearly lost the war. He turned to the Scots for help: he was after all the son of James VI of Scotland. The Scots, however, although they wanted to preserve a Stuart on the English throne, had not forgiven Charles for his attempt to force the English Prayer Book on them. Instead of saving Charles, the Scots handed him over to the parliamentarians, and he was executed in Whitehall on 30 January 1649.[15]

REPUBLICAN RULE 1649–1660

The radicalism of a republican government, headed by Oliver Cromwell and supported by the army, was not to last. Cromwell dissolved Parliament, in order to avoid an election in a time of transition when his government was not yet firmly in control. Instead, a nominated assembly – known as the 'Parliament of Saints' – was formed. This

[15] There were in fact two civil wars between 1642 and 1648, the first involving Charles, the second, 1648–9, essentially a series of pro-royalist uprisings which did not involve the king.

undemocratic experiment did not work, and Cromwell soon realized the need for an authoritative executive to control the legislature. Under the Instrument of Government of 1649, Cromwell became Lord Protector of the Commonwealth of England, Scotland and Ireland, and installed himself in the Palace of Whitehall. For five years he ruled alone with his Council of State until a unicameral elected Parliament was introduced in 1654 with 460 members. Cromwell could not disband the army because of fears of royalist uprisings. When one occurred in 1655, Cromwell imposed direct army rule, dividing the country into eleven districts under army control. Civil unrest and dissatisfaction with military rule was soon felt. Nor were relations between Parliament and the army harmonious.

Cromwell had earlier devised a written, republican constitution, but it was never fully implemented. Republican rule was characterized by Puritanism. Dress was sombre, theatres and entertainments were banned, Sunday became a day of fasting. Immorality was punished harshly, adultery being punishable by death. The failure of Cromwell to gain the love of his people fuelled a desire to return to the old arrangements, with the monarchy restored, along with the House of Lords and the Church of England, and a return to parliamentary rule. With the death of Oliver Cromwell in 1658, plans were put in place for the son of Charles I, now living in exile in France at the court of Louis XIV, to return to England and assume the throne. In 1660, Charles II was restored to the throne.

But the former conflicts could not be forgotten. Having once challenged the power of the king in civil war, and executed him, Parliament was set on establishing its supremacy over the Crown. Or rather, one faction of Parliament was – and again the issue in the background (or was it foreground?) was religion.

RESTORATION OF THE MONARCHY

Charles II, son of Charles I, was born in May 1630. At the age of only eight, Charles was given his own court at Richmond and tutored for kingship. In his childhood he experienced the turmoil of civil war.

When war was declared in August 1642, Charles, aged only twelve, was at the king's side, but when the war went in favour of the Roundheads the king ordered his son to leave the country. In France Charles's education in all matters social and sexual was completed. After the execution of his father, Charles spent the republican years restlessly in exile, although Scotland recognized him as king in 1650, and he was crowned in 1651. In support of the king the Scottish army battled in vain against the forces of Cromwell. In 1652 Charles was forced to flee once more, this time a hunted fugitive, dependent upon loyal Royalist supporters, many of them persecuted Catholics, until he finally escaped as a refugee from his own land.

The restoration of the monarchy, while popular with the people and set to endure to the present day, did not, however, end disputes about the respective roles of the king and Parliament, nor the question of religion. While Charles II, the 'merry monarch' of Restoration England, had the support of the people, conflicts continued over the position of Catholicism in the country, and perceptions that Charles II was sympathetic to religious toleration, including tolerance towards Roman Catholics, caused disquiet. Outwardly dedicated to the Church of England, like his father before him, Charles never lost his sympathy for Catholicism, the religion of his mother and his childhood: on his deathbed he formally converted to Catholicism once more.

Charles II's court was extravagant, more than counterbalancing the restraint of Puritan rule. With the suppression of the senses lifted, architecture, art, literature and theatre flourished. Science also prospered: the Royal Society was established with Charles becoming its official founder in 1662. The Royal Observatory at Greenwich was established on Charles's order in 1675. The country also benefited commercially from the Restoration. Under Charles the largest merchant shipping fleet in Europe developed and trade expanded rapidly with Europe and the Americas. Life for all, even the poorest, became more comfortable as consumer goods became available. The professions expanded to serve the needs of this more affluent and commercially centred society. But all was not sweetness and light. The population of the cities, in particular London, were savaged by the Great Plague of 1665–6, and the City of London itself was largely razed to the ground by the Great Fire of 1666. But out of these disasters came benefits.

Measures for better sanitation and housing standards to minimize the risk of further outbreaks of disease were introduced. Out of the ashes of the Great Fire arose the reconstructed St Paul's Cathedral, one of Wren's greatest masterpieces, and all over the City of London Wren's parish churches were built.

Charles II was a complex character, whose outward demeanour was affable, open, quick-witted, tolerant, and casual to the point of indolence. Yet in politics he was noted for ostensibly pursuing one policy while quietly and secretly pursuing another. His stated aims and objectives were seldom what they appeared to be. His policy in relation to Parliament was to allow it to stand from 1661 until early 1679, one effect of which was to avoid general elections. This 'standing Parliament' became viewed with as much disquiet as a standing army, being perceived as a threat to the liberties of the people. Charles also maintained maximum control through his appointment of ministers of differing political views. There was no chief minister, no co-ordinating force save the king, and by ruling through ministers with no cohesive viewpoint, Charles reserved for himself maximum control and power of decision.

When Charles II assumed the kingship in 1660, he did so with the powers of his father intact. The Convention Parliament – the House of Commons – which recalled the king did not take the opportunity to settle and restrict the king's powers. Disillusionment with the experience of republican rule and the power of the army and the desire for the security of the traditional form of government under the monarch perhaps caused Parliament to be less concerned for the terms of the settlement in their desire for the return of the king. But a fundamental change had occurred. Cromwell's government had abolished the House of Lords and disestablished the Church of England. It had been the Commons alone – under Cromwell and his army – which ran the country. With this experience the Commons grew in confidence. No longer could the king ignore the Commons. And of this Charles II was well aware. Nevertheless, the king retained the right to create new parliamentary boroughs through Royal Charter. This power, which was gradually challenged by Parliament, gave the king the right to determine the representation in the Commons and the method by which representatives would be elected: it was exercised with increasing care by the Crown. Between 1603 and 1660 only eleven boroughs had been created by Royal Charter, with a further twenty-five being established not by the king but by Resolutions of the House of Commons. Nevertheless, the right of enfranchisement left to the king enabled him to increase the membership of the Commons, and to affect the degree of support on which he could rely in the Commons. In 1677, giving way to the increasing hostility of the Commons, Charles abandoned his right, and from 1677 to 1832 the number of Members of Parliament remained at 513.

Notwithstanding this political limitation, Charles still had room to manoeuvre his support in Parliament. Under the Corporation Act of 1661, membership of public office in municipal corporations (local government) were restricted to those who took the sacrament of the Church of England; these officials were removable by the king. Moreover, the king had the power to call in Royal Charters for scrutiny, with the attendant power to remove the Charter or to remodel the boroughs. In part the motivation was to remove from local government the old political and religious factions that remained after the Commonwealth era, and to ensure religious conformity and greater loyalty to the restored monarchy. But through these means Charles, although now unable to create new boroughs, could control the representation in his own favour and limit the extent of opposition to his policies, and most importantly could resist the desire of the Commons to exclude his Catholic brother James from the throne.

The House of Commons also agitated for regular Parliaments to be held, a move which challenged the prerogative right of the king. Although unsuccessful in terms of law, it was clear that Charles II was mindful of Parliament's growing authority. Other than the last four years of his reign, when Parliament remained dissolved, regular Parliaments were held, at intervals of only a few months, whereas in previous reigns there were regularly periods of years before the king or queen summoned Parliament. But if the king was increasingly sensitive to Parliament's demands for regular meetings, and generally compliant, he still maintained significant power in the House of Commons by virtue of his power of appointment. The root of the problem (from the standpoint of democracy) lay in the king's power to control elections and his power of patronage, the combination of which led to the king's Court Party being made up of those who held office under the Crown.

An early but unsuccessful attempt was made by the Commons to exclude from Parliament any Member who either held office under the Crown on election, or was subsequently appointed to such office. The matter was almost resolved in Charles's reign, through a Place Bill, but Charles then dissolved his last Parliament.

Anti-Catholic fever reared its head in most extreme form with the Popish Plot of 1678. The plot – which was pure fiction – was devised by one Titus Oates, an ambitious, mendacious minor cleric of the Church of England. Oates devised a scheme whereby, through careful drafting of various documents and their infiltration into the homes of prominent people, the suggestion would be put abroad of a Catholic plot, implicating Jesuits, Benedictines and Dominicans, to assassinate the king and to overthrow both the Church of England and the government with French help. News of the plot was treated with deep scepticism, but nevertheless Oates was interrogated by the Privy Council. Then Oates struck lucky. A magistrate who had taken Oates's evidence was found murdered. The murder was attributed to the Jesuits, and suddenly Oates had succeeded where otherwise he would surely have failed.

The parliamentarians seized on the Plot as evidence that there were those who would stop at nothing to destroy the king and the Church of England. The Plot led directly to the decision by the parliamentarians under Lord Shaftesbury to attempt to exclude the Catholic heir to the throne, James, Duke of York, from the succession. Here we find the seeds of the two political parties which were to dominate government until the birth of the Labour Party at the end of the nineteenth century. Two main groups emerged – the Court and Country (alternatively known as the Whig[16]) parties – although they were not yet closely defined in terms of either membership or general policies. Political parties need leadership, organization, electoral and financial support and the means to publicize their views, most particularly a free press. On the Country side, there was clear leadership in the form of the Earl of Shaftesbury, both central and local organization and a Whig press. Many of its members were wealthy landowners and support was also drawn from the commercial classes. Thus there was a country-wide base from which

[16] The name is believed to have derived from the term Whiggamores, a label attached to militant Scottish Presbyterians.

the party could operate, whose principal belief was that should the Catholic James succeed Charles II the trust of the people, which conferred sovereignty on the king in Parliament, would be betrayed. The second grouping was the Court Party, later to be the Tory Party.[17] Inheriting its mantle from the Cavaliers in the Civil War, the Court Party believed fervently in the Crown, the divine right of succession and the Church of England. The royal prerogative was divinely conferred. The king's powers were absolute and there was no question of allowing 'the people' to participate in sovereign power. The Court Party was slower to find a parliamentary leader, although certainly Charles II and his ministers represented its first unifying core.

There is no clear-cut picture to be painted of these early political groupings. 'Country' and 'Court' parties are not synonymous with Whig and Tory as the early parties popularly became known. Membership and support varied, according to particular issues. Rather than two parties, four parties were identifiable, and even these revealed different shades of leaning. As Rubini, citing Walcott, puts it: 'One might thus see a full circle of political opinion, in which there is court, court-tory, country-tory, country, country-whig, whig, court-whig, and so back to court, thus making a full circle of political opinion, allowing for a wide variety of alliances.'[18]

The sequel to the Popish Plot of 1678 was the Exclusion Crisis which dominated Parliament from 1679 to 1681 and threatened a constitutional crisis which at least equalled that which was to follow in 1688–9. What was being sought was nothing less than the secularization of the monarchy and the rejection of the established 'divine' right of succession to the Crown. Had it succeeded, which it did not, by excluding James from the succession Parliament would in effect have conferred on itself a choice as to who should succeed. It did not threaten monarchy as such, but rather removed the right of succession and placed the power of appointment, or election, in Parliament's favour. It was in this time of the Crisis, 1679–81, that the Whig Party became an organized and

---

[17] The name is believed to derive from seventeenth-century Irish outlaws who plundered and killed English settlers.
[18] D. Rubini, *Court and Country 1688–1702* (London: Rupert Hart-Davis, 1967), pp. 16–17, citing R. Walcott, 'The Idea of Party in the Writing of Stuart History', *Journ. Brit. Stud.*, 1 (1962), 54–62.

distinctive political party. Not only was it well organized in Parliament, but there was also a network of support throughout the country as Exclusion became a matter of national debate.

Exclusion represented the catalyst for the formation of a distinctive party, although exclusion was not its only objective. Among other areas of concern were greater controls over the powers of the Crown, greater tolerance for those religious dissenters from the established Church of England, and for reforms relating to elections and the franchise. At the heart of Whig philosophy was the idea of the 'sovereignty of the people' as expressed through Parliament. Equally dear to Whig philosophy was the ownership of private property – not just of the wealthy gentry but of all citizens. Shaftesbury's close friend was John Locke,[19] the Whig philosopher whose writings have had enduring influence down the centuries. His *Two Treatises on Government*[20] expounding a radical Whig philosophy was not published until 1690. Although written during the Exclusion Crisis and widely circulated at the time, it represented a justification for the peaceful revolution which occurred with the abdication of James II. Out of the Exclusion Crisis and the peaceful revolution which brought William and Mary to power, there had now emerged the first real political parties, and they were to endure until the late nineteenth century, albeit under different names. Gradually the impact of parties was felt throughout the country, not just in terms of sympathies for one side or the other but also in terms of parliamentary election results.

As a result of the failure of the Whigs to exclude James, he succeeded Charles in 1685. He ruled a mere three years and nine months. Under the Test Act of 1673 Catholics had been prohibited from holding office under the Crown, and those taking public office had to affirm the Protestant faith. The Test Act required that any person holding public office had to swear loyalty to the Church of England. This forced James, when Lord High Admiral under Charles II, into the open and drove him from office. James dispensed with the Act in relation to Catholic army officers whom he had appointed. When challenges arose in the courts, James dismissed the judges who ruled against him. A Catholic chapel was built in the heart of Whitehall Palace. In 1687 three hundred

[19] 1632–1704.   [20] London: J. M. Dent, 1977.

Catholic Justices of the Peace were appointed. In the same year James suspended laws which penalized Catholics.[21] By March 1688 some twelve hundred Catholics had been appointed, James having dismissed the former Protestant incumbents. It was not that James was trying to re-establish Catholicism as the dominant, established church of the state, rather that he was fervently in favour of tolerance of all religious beliefs. A firm believer also in the divine right of kings, James viewed the power of the Church of England as limiting: if he could succeed in breaking down the religious monopoly of public offices, the power of the Church of England would be effectively checked.

As a policy it was the undoing of his reign. The struggle between Protestantism and Catholicism continued, to be complicated further by dissenters from the Church of England proper who formed assorted religious factions. Nor had opposition to James's succession died out and in 1685 Charles II's illegitimate son, the Duke of Monmouth, launched an insurrection, and was defeated at the Battle of Sedgemoor. In revenge James sent Judge Jeffreys to the West Country to stamp out, through harsh penalties, any further opposition to his rule. Monmouth was beheaded. To reinforce his control, James – in the face of parliamentary opposition – began to staff the army with Catholics.

Declarations of Indulgence were issued by James, aimed at securing complete religious toleration. The clergy were ordered to read the Declarations to their congregations. When, in response to a second Declaration, the Archbishop of Canterbury and six bishops petitioned the king to withdraw the order to the clergy, James had them tried for seditious libel. But this act of kingly intolerance and attempted suppression of dissent aroused deep public hostility. The jury acquitted the bishops, the judges having failed to 'direct' the jury to convict.[22]

Concern grew that should James and Mary produce a male heir to the throne, that heir would mark the return of the country to papist rule, at the expense of the now-established, Protestant, Church of

---

[21] The dispensing power was a prerogative right. In effect, named individuals could be exempted from obedience to particular penal laws, and any penal sanction which might follow a breach of the law. See *Godden v. Hales* (1686) 11 St Tr 1166; 2 Shower 275, in which the court ruled that the king had the right to dispense with laws for his own reasons which were a matter for the king alone to decide.

[22] *The Seven Bishops case* (1688) 12 St Tr 371.

England. In 1688 James and Mary had a son: the epitome of anti-Catholic fears. So virulent were these concerns that fantastic propaganda was put about suggesting that the baby had been smuggled into the royal bedchamber in a warming-pan. Ultimately, faced with open revolt from those on whom he was dependent, James fled the country, throwing the royal seal of office into the Thames.

His reign was marked by his abuse of the prerogative to suspend and dispense with laws, his maintenance of a standing army with an increasingly Catholic flavour, his interference with central and local administration through replacing Anglican offices with Catholic incumbents and his attempts to pack Parliament with Members who would support his objectives. While James and his court – and Parliament – were enjoying less than harmonious relations, negotiations had been entered into with James's Protestant son-in-law, Prince William of Orange, with a view to William invading with an army to seize power and to reign jointly with his wife Mary.

During the reign of James II another, and rather different, 'revolution' was taking place, one which was to reach its full significance in the next century: the scientific revolution. Isaac Newton was born during the Civil War. A mathematician, physicist and astronomer, he transformed modes of thought about the world. It might be felt that the scientific revolution has little to do with systems of government: but Newton (and René Descartes before him) brought about a fundamental change in people's perceptions of the world. For centuries, the world had been interpreted either as a 'natural ordering' as in ancient Greek thought, or through the eyes of those interpreting God's divine will. The realization that the world could be rationally understood, without mysticism or superstition, was of prime importance to questions of the relationship between citizen and government and profoundly influential in the evolution of ideas concerning the rationality of the human mind. So radical was the thinking of the early scientists, mainly in Europe, that the Catholic Church condemned scientific explanations of the world. Newton was elected President of the Royal Society in 1705, and knighted in 1707.

THE SETTLEMENT OF 1689

Once James had fled to France, the way was clear for William to enter the country. However, conditions were imposed on William and Mary's rule. It was the Bill of Rights 1689 which defined the respective roles and powers of the Crown and Parliament. It would be incorrect, however, to assume that the Revolution Settlement was a radical departure from the past. More than anything it appears as a document which sought to place limits on the king's powers without attacking his fundamental prerogatives. The Crown's power to summon and dissolve Parliament remained, as did the right of the king to appoint ministers of his own choosing. The prerogative in relation to foreign affairs also remained untouched, a power which was to cause dissent during William and Mary's reign.

The Bill of Rights was intended to lay to rest the threat of resurgent Catholicism in royal circles and to ensure that the powers of the Crown were to an extent better controlled thereafter by the power of Parliament. While Henry VIII had established the Crown as head of the Church of England through the Succession Act, the Act of Supremacy and the Treason Act of 1534, events in subsequent years had shown that Catholicism had an enduring power, even at the level of kingship and state administration. With William's acceptance of the Crown, subject to Parliament's terms,[23] the possibility for future abuse of royal power was curtailed. The Bill of Rights made it clear that the king no longer had any power to suspend laws made by Parliament, nor to raise taxation for the Crown's use without Parliament's consent. Furthermore, the Bill of Rights prohibited the Crown from raising and keeping an army without the consent of Parliament. Parliament's right to regulate its own proceedings also stems from the Bill of Rights, Article 9 of which laid the foundation for the modern concept of parliamentary privilege and the right to absolute freedom of speech in parliamentary proceedings. The right to trial by jury was reaffirmed. It was also provided that Parliament should meet 'frequently' in order to be able to deal with the

---

[23] See the Coronation Oath Act 1688 and Crown and Parliament Recognition Act 1689.

complaints and concerns of citizens. It is from 1689 that the contemporary concept of parliamentary supremacy derives.

The Bill of Rights 1689, however, was not a comprehensive constitutional settlement, still less a form of written constitution. The question of succession to the Crown and the position of the judges was not decided until the Act of Settlement 1701, the principal provisions of which provided that the Crown could only devolve to Protestant heirs, and that in the future no Roman Catholic could inherit the Crown, nor could any king or queen or heir to the throne marry a Catholic. In relation to the judges, their independence was to be guaranteed. In the past, one of the prerogative powers claimed by the Crown was to exercise judicial powers personally, and to suspend the operation of Acts of Parliament. For the future this was denied, and the position of the judges protected from royal interference. The Act of Settlement also provided that judges in the higher courts were to enjoy security of tenure during the judges' 'good behaviour'. The king could no longer dismiss judges as he thought fit: only a successful 'address' to both Houses of Parliament alleging wrongful conduct on the part of a judge could dismiss a judge from office.

The Settlement of 1689 also failed to address the issue of parliamentary representation. During the Interregnum, Cromwell had devised plans for a reformed electoral system, but these were never implemented. With the Settlement of 1689 the landed aristocracy nominated representatives of boroughs for election to the House of Commons. Democracy – in terms of equal representation of areas, whether county or borough – was a long way off, as of course was the right to vote for most of the population.

The reign of William III and Mary II (1688–1702 and 1688–94 respectively) was to lead to significant changes in the practice of government. William and Mary's marriage was in part an Anglo-Dutch alliance, designed to check French ambitions under Louis XIV. But William was not universally liked, nor was his election universally accepted. The Tory party held the succession to be a matter divinely ordained: William was a foreigner, although as a grandson of Charles I he had a right to claim the Stuart throne, as did his wife Mary, the daughter of James II. William was not prepared to see Mary rule on her own, and in any event she was not regarded as politically astute. An early challenge to

William and Mary's rule came in 1690 when the French backed a plan to restore James to the Stuart throne; the threat was raised again in 1694 when a Jacobite plot to assassinate William was discovered. James himself, with the support of the French, was now in Ireland, seeking to reconquer the Protestant areas of Northern Ireland. In 1690 James II and William III met in battle. The Battle of the Boyne, won by William with support from Protestant nations across Europe, still has resonance in the history of Northern Ireland.

William was first and foremost a military man. His single-minded political objective on the European scene was to check the power of France. For thirty years from 1689 England was engaged in war in Europe. Between 1689 and 1697 the Nine Years War raged with the greatest English army ever employed overseas. For at least half the year William was overseas, and in his absence Parliament was not allowed to sit. William's ambition of checking French power was not realized in his lifetime, but his efforts had profound effects. J. R. Jones writes of the Nine Years War that 'this war permanently transformed England, equipping the country with the military, diplomatic and fiscal machinery, and generating the self-confidence, that were to enable it to expand and develop so spectacularly in the next century'.[24] In domestic affairs, a change in the balance of power between the monarch and Parliament was to find expression in the Triennial Act 1694[25] which required that Parliament be summoned every three years, thus curtailing William's prerogative. Greater parliamentary control over royal finances was secured under the Civil List Act of 1698. Parliamentary control over the army was also established under the Mutiny Act of 1688 which authorized the keeping of a standing army for the defence of the realm for a period of one year. The Act also introduced the system of military law which remains today, establishing trial by courts-martial for those subject to military law. In terms of party politics in William's reign, the picture is confused. Clinging to his prerogative, William appointed ministers from both Whigs and Tories, a mixed system which would ensure his maximum control in Parliament. Many Tories viewed

[24] *Country and Court: England 1658–1714* (London: Edward Arnold, 1978), p. 258.
[25] Triennial Acts had been passed in 1640 and 1664, but had been ignored by former kings.

William's succession with suspicion on the basis that he had driven out the legitimate king, while the Whigs, who strongly favoured limited monarchical power and the Revolution Settlement, were not so devoted to the concept of monarchy. William used both to his advantage.

The problem of the royal succession remained unresolved. While it was clear that on the demise of William and Mary, the crown would pass to Princess Anne, the younger of James II's two daughters and a devout Protestant, Anne's only child died in 1700 and it was clear by then that she would have no more children. Parliament resolved that the crown should pass to the grand-daughter of James I, Electress Sophia of Hanover. As noted above, the Act of Settlement 1701 barred any Catholic, or heir married to a Catholic, from the succession.

By 1701, through the Bill of Rights 1689 and the Act of Settlement 1701, the constitutional and political position of the Crown, Parliament and the judiciary was settled in its current form. Judges could no longer be dismissed at the will of the king: their tenure of office was secure during 'good behaviour' and could only be terminated in the future by a successful address to both Houses of Parliament for their removal from office. However, while the powers of the Crown and the independence of the judiciary were to remain unchanged to the present day, Parliament, while given supremacy over both the Crown and the judiciary, remained far removed from its current form. The Bill of Rights, however, did not succeed in dampening conflict within the country over the succession. James II, now in Catholic France, and his Jacobite supporters remained a threat, one which was to manifest itself in the next century.

Political parties – the Whigs and Tories – had evolved in identifiable form as proponents for and against particular principles. In 1695 the restrictions on publications lapsed, thus unleashing unprecedented public political debate. Newspapers developed to carry the news of the country to the people. Governments, however, were not yet of any one political party. It was still for the monarch to elect his or her ministers from wherever he or she chose. The civil service, which had long existed in unorganized form, now started to emerge as a permanent professional, salaried institution serving successive governments. New departments were set up: the Post Office, Navy Office and Customs and Excise date from this period. In 1694 the Bank of England was founded. Finance for the monarchy – which had hitherto been self-supporting save in time of war – was reorganized in 1698 and the Civil List introduced. Any other moneys needed, such as to meet the cost of defence and war, had to be voted by Parliament. The City of London flourished, accompanied by the rise in middle-class professions.

William died in 1702, to be succeeded by Anne. Like her predecessors, Anne, the last Stuart to reign, held firmly to her prerogative. Mindful of the dangers of falling into too close an alliance with either Whigs or Tories, Anne remained aloof from both. But war continued, the War of the Spanish Succession lasting from 1701 to 1713. War in Europe divided public opinion in the country more sharply than before. The Whigs supported the war, the Tories opposed it, each party having a portion of the press behind it. Anne, in the attempt to ameliorate political conflict, turned increasingly to more moderate political figures. She died in August 1714. Her named successor, Sophia of Hanover, had died just two months earlier. The succession passed from the House of Stuart to the House of Hanover under George, Sophia's eldest son.

One issue of the greatest importance was settled in Anne's reign: that of the union of Scotland with England. The history of the two independent nations had been characterized by conflict and war. Despite a Stuart king, James VI of Scotland, succeeding Elizabeth I to the English throne, political union remained unresolved. By the end of William III's reign, the king had become convinced of the need to end the hostilities by securing a lasting union between the two countries. When Anne came to the throne, an Act establishing commissioners to negotiate a settlement was passed. By 1706, terms were agreed under the Union Treaty with Scotland, the union to come into effect in May 1707. For Scotland the primary inducements were economic: there had long been a marked disparity between the wealth of the two countries, the Scottish economy was depressed and Scotland was denied, until the union, access to English colonies and markets. But other large issues were also at stake. Central to Scottish interests were the guaranteed protection of the Presbyterian faith, and the continuance of its separate legal system and laws. Both were guaranteed by the Act of Union, the new British Parliament only having power to alter the private rights of Scottish citizens if that would be for their benefit. The political effect of the union was the abolition of both the formerly sovereign English and

Scottish Parliaments, and the coming into being of a Parliament of Great Britain to govern both Scotland and England.

THE EIGHTEENTH CENTURY

By 1714, Britain had established herself as a world military power, and maintaining the balance of power in Europe became the preoccupation of eighteenth-century governments. The wars – which involved some 120,000 men in the army and led to the expansion of the Royal Navy – were expensive and could only be conducted with the support of the people. Foreign policy could no longer remain the exclusive prerogative of the Crown but had also to have the support of Parliament and the nation.

George I, who reigned from 1714 to 1727, was never a popular king. His grasp of English was poor, he had little understanding or interest in the life of his subjects and had more interest in Hanover where he was born and raised. Supporters of the House of Stuart seized on the opportunity to press once again for Jacobite rule, in the name now of James II's son, James Edward Stuart, Pretender to the throne. They failed, being beaten at the Battle of Preston in 1715. Far from being politically neutral as his predecessors had been, George I allied himself with the Whigs, now led by Sir Robert Walpole. In 1716 a Septennial Act was passed, extending the life of Parliament from three to seven years, thus providing for an unprecedented period of parliamentary stability, and limiting the powers of the king. It became accepted from this time that whoever the king chose as his first minister – the Prime Minister – although not yet necessarily a member of the Commons, had to command the support of the House of Commons. Political power, under this unpopular foreign king, had shifted towards the king's ministers. Sir Robert Walpole dominated the political scene. Becoming First Lord of the Treasury and Chancellor of the Exchequer in 1721, he held office for over twenty years, exercising control over the Commons, and was in effect the first Prime Minister. Not that Parliament was in a contemporary sense democratic. It was dominated by a relatively small, relatively cohesive, elite group, the Whig oligarchy, which ruled the political scene and brought a period of domestic stability after the turbulence of the previous century.

The period which followed the wars in Europe also led to profound changes in society. New outlets had been established for British goods overseas and the vast navy and merchant fleet ensured the delivery of produce to new markets. The needs of army and navy encouraged developments in the manufacture of weapons and ships. The seeds of the industrial revolution had been sown. In the same era structural and demographic change was taking place. In England, formerly characterized by small villages and rural communities, new towns and ports developed around emerging industries and economic activities. Bristol, Plymouth, Leeds, Halifax, Birmingham and Sheffield became centres of commercial activity.

During the reign of George II (1727–60), another recognizable feature of government developed: the Cabinet. While the king met his advisers in his own Council, ministers would meet in Cabinet, without the king. Nevertheless, the king retained central control. All Acts of Parliament, then as now, had to have royal approval; the royal prerogative remained, curtailed since 1689, but still a significant source of power. George II also faced a Jacobite threat, the last in history. In 1745, 'Bonnie Prince Charlie', Charles Edward Stuart, grandson of James II, dubbed the Young Pretender, invaded from Scotland. The Pretender took Edinburgh, Carlisle and Derby, only to be brutally crushed at the Battle of Culloden.

During this era social change, which had been incremental since Tudor times, accelerated at an unprecedented pace. Although by 1760, 75 per cent of the population were still involved in agriculture, new inventions and techniques were transforming farming into a more efficient industry. The growth of new towns and innovations in production resulted in early industrial expansion into areas such as steel-making, metalworking and textiles. Workers became organized in large-scale productive units, headed by the new entrepreneurial managerial class. Efficient means of transport were being developed to meet the needs of new industry and commerce.

For centuries the road system was little more than a system of unsurfaced tracks across the countryside. The duty to keep roads clear of rubbish and reasonably passable fell to the local parish. Local trusts had been introduced late in the Stuart era which were entitled to levy tolls for the use of roads for all except pedestrians. Although great progress was made there was little co-ordination between areas and no centralized supervision of the system.

In 1760 George III, grandson of George II, came to the throne. Unlike his Hanoverian predecessors, George III had been born and raised in England and regarded himself as an Englishman. In 1763, under the Treaty of Paris, the British Empire was enlarged by the acquisition of Canada, parts of south-eastern America and islands of the Caribbean from the French. At home, the Whig oligarchy, which had secured political stability for so long, had fallen from power and the king was faced with a succession of ministries which contributed to instability. Indirect taxation of the American colonies, to subsidize the cost of maintaining British troops – an estimated £225,000 a year – to defend the colonies, was introduced, leading to the cry from the colonies of 'no taxation without representation' and heralding American independence. War erupted in 1776. In 1781 the British surrendered, and in 1783 peace was finally made.

During George III's reign the issue of parliamentary reform was placed firmly on the political agenda. In the late 1760s the majority of the population was not politically aware. The idea of a universal right to vote was as yet unborn. Nor was there much dissatisfaction with the system of government. The settlement of 1689 had conclusively limited the power of the Crown and ensured that Parliament was the sovereign body: that it remained largely unrepresentative of the people was not a primary issue.

To understand the origins of the popular movement for reform of the unrepresentative House of Commons it is necessary to consider the role of John Wilkes. Wilkes was first elected to Parliament in 1757. His career was dominated by his clash with the executive and Parliament. In 1762 he founded the *North Briton*, a daily newspaper generally regarded as a 'scandal sheet'. Believing his political advancement to be hampered by ministers and the king, Wilkes started a scurrilous campaign against Lord Bute, the Prime Minister who had displaced from office Wilkes's hero William Pitt (the Elder). The reaction of the executive to Wilkes's campaign ignited a wave of popular clamour, mostly confined to London, against the government and the perception that the government was unlawfully attempting to subvert individual liberty. 'Wilkes and Liberty' became synonymous. The catalyst lay in the attempt to suppress the *North Briton* through the use of general warrants. In the absence of clear proof that Wilkes was the author of a libellous article, a warrant was issued for the arrest of the authors, publishers and printers of the news-sheet to face charges of seditious libel. Forty-nine people were arrested, Wilkes among them. Wilkes applied for a writ of habeas corpus to test the legality of his detention. The Chief Justice granted it, ruling that Wilkes's arrest was a breach of parliamentary privilege.[26] Parliament in turn decided to expel Wilkes. In 1764 the government then tried to persuade Parliament to reverse the court's decision over the legality of general warrants. However, while the government won Parliament's support, it did so with such a small majority that it was unsafe henceforth to rely on general warrants.

Meanwhile, Wilkes was still wanted for trial over a pornographic verse. He fled the country and lived in exile in France from 1764 to 1768. He was declared an outlaw in 1764. Wilkes's next move, and his most audacious, was to seek re-election to Parliament. He returned to England in 1768, having begged the King for mercy (it was not granted), and stood for election in Middlesex. He was duly elected by a huge majority and wisely the authorities abandoned Wilkes's status of outlaw. However, Wilkes was still wanted in relation to a number of alleged misdemeanours. He was duly arrested and placed in custody awaiting trial. Public reaction was swift and vociferous, and there was rioting in his support. In one riot at St George's Field seven people were killed by police. When Wilkes emerged from custody, he again stood for Parliament, was elected and then expelled from Parliament. Three times the electors expressed their wishes, three times Parliament frustrated them. On the third election, Parliament went too far. Rather than expelling Wilkes again, it voted to overturn the election result and announce that the loser had won. Wilkes agitated outside Parliament for parliamentary reform and for the right of newspapers to report parliamentary proceedings without the threat of prosecution. In 1774 he was re-elected for Middlesex. By then, however, the threat of the American war was in the air, and the reform movement lost its momentum.

[26] On which see Chapter 3.

Holmes and Szechi sum up the Wilkes saga: '[F]or all its puny origins it contained the seeds of future greatness and of ultimately epic change.'[27]

THE FRENCH REVOLUTION AND NAPOLEONIC WARS

In 1789 another threat loomed, one which challenged the very structure of society. The French Revolution swept away centuries of aristocratic rule and the monarchy with it. The reverberations in Britain were felt throughout the land. When in 1793 France declared war on Britain and Holland, even the system of government and society seemed threatened. Invasion by France seemed imminent, and Britain had not only her own shores to protect but her world-wide trading interests. Conflict endured in Europe until 1815, with a quarter of a million men engaged in the British army. In Britain the need for security of the state led to civil liberties being curtailed. Habeas corpus was suspended by the Habeas Corpus Act of 1794, the right to assemble was curtailed through the Treasonable Practices and Seditious Meetings Act 1795 and any combination of workers banned through the Combination Acts of 1799 and 1800. Penalties were harsh. On conviction for a first offence, the offender was liable to three months in prison, or two months' hard labour. Anyone who combined with another for the purposes of seeking improved pay or conditions of work was caught by the Act. When peace came in 1815 nothing in society or politics was ever quite the same again. The horrifying lesson of the French Revolution for the upper classes was that the people could turn against them, that wealth and the power that came with it was no protection against the angry mob. For the classes beneath, the Revolution had demonstrated the real political power of ordinary citizens to change the world around them. Hitherto, the idea that ordinary people could have a role to play in the political life of a nation, and real power, was unknown. Now perceptions changed. Small wonder that the government felt threatened.

The influence of one political philosopher – Thomas Paine – was

---

[27] G. Holmes and D. Szechi, *The Age of Oligarchy* (Harlow: Longman, 1993), p. 315.

profound in the sea-change in political thinking of the time.[28] Paine had early emigrated to America, under the patronage of Benjamin Franklin. While nearly a century before, in *Two Treatises on Government*, John Locke had argued for the sovereignty of Parliament as the representative of the people over the king, Paine in *Common Sense* (1776) and *The Rights of Man* (1791–2),[29] offered a more radical philosophy. Paine's powerful thesis had as its foundation the inherent rights of individuals, rights which no government could take away. Each individual was sovereign, and this sovereignty was something which existed prior to any form of government. Accordingly, the power given to government was conditional upon the respect accorded to citizens. These rights were neither limitable nor removable. If any government abused the trust of the people, the people could, and should, remove that government and replace it with one which respected the terms of the trust. The philosophy propounded by Paine, who was involved in both the American War of Independence and the French Revolution, found expression in the Preamble to the American Constitution, and in the American Bill of Rights proclaiming the constitutionally guaranteed protection of rights and fundamental freedoms.

At home, in the 1790s Britain faced a wave of radicalism and dissent. As E. J. Evans writes, '[T]he French Revolution let the genie out of the bottle', and '[T]he 1790s witnessed the first national political movement since the Civil War which involved the lower orders to a significant degree.'[30] Fired by Paine's *Rights of Man*, radical societies sprang up in Scotland and England. Paine was forced to flee to France, under threat of prosecution for seditious writing capable of undermining the security of the state. Economic failures fuelled the discontent of the working classes. In the navy, mutiny occurred, albeit short-lived and quickly suppressed, representing a critical threat to British success in the war with France. An Act against illegal oaths was passed in 1797, initially in response to the mutiny, but later directed against trade unions. To control the dissemination of hostile comment, in 1798 Parliament passed an Act requiring the registration of newspapers and punishment for

---

[28] On Paine's influence on the concept of rights see further Chapter 7.

[29] ed. H. Collins (New York: Penguin, 1984, repr. 1998).

[30] E. J. Evans, *The Forging of the Modern State: Early Industrial Britain, 1783–1870* (New York: Longman, 1983), p. 66.

the producers of newspapers (and their readers) for publication or possession of unlicensed papers.

The impact of the French Revolution, and notions of freedom and equality, were also felt in Ireland. In 1791 the Belfast Society of United Irishmen was formed, under the leadership of Protestant lawyer and republican Wolfe Tone,[31] seeking parliamentary reform, including the ending of discrimination against Catholics and Catholic representation. In 1792 the British Parliament passed the Catholic Relief Act which allowed Catholics to vote and to practise law, but not to stand for Parliament. However, any measure of relief for Catholics was viewed by the minority (but all-powerful) Protestant community with suspicion, and led inevitably to a hardening of sectarian attitudes. In 1794, in the north of Ireland, the Protestant Orange Order was founded, celebrating the victory of Protestant King William at the Battle of the Boyne. Fears that the United Irishmen would turn to France for support in their republican objectives led, notwithstanding Prime Minister Pitt's sympathy for Catholic emancipation, to repressive measures. A Militia Act and an Insurrection Act both reached the statute book in 1793 and 1796. Fears of civil war were in the air. In 1798 came the expected revolt with the Great Uprising which, far from spreading to a full-scale religious war, was swiftly and brutally crushed by British forces. The leaders of the uprising, McGracken and Monro, were executed.

The need for a solution to the Irish problem nevertheless remained. Britain was in the grip of the war with France: she could not afford to have the threat of an unstable Ireland next door, especially given French support for the Catholic Irish. The solution was deemed to lie in the abolition of the Irish Parliament and full union with Britain, with Irish representation in both the House of Commons and House of Lords. Through a mixture of bribery and persuasion, anti-union members of the Irish House of Commons left politics. The Act of Union became law in 1800. Representation in the House of Commons was set at one hundred Irish members, while twenty-eight Irish peers sat in the Lords. The union was not to last: the strength of republicanism was too strong among the

---

[31] Tone was captured, tried and convicted of treason. Facing the death penalty, Tone hanged himself. By the time an application for habeas corpus had been heard and the warrant granted, Tone was dead. Dicey ironically portrays this as demonstrating the power of habeas corpus in relation to civil liberties.

still discriminated-against Catholic population, and sectarian strife was set to endure. The movement for Home Rule for Ireland was to dominate Irish and English politics until the twentieth century.

Britain emerged from the wars of 1793 to 1815 with the greatest empire of any nation on earth.[32] But the war brought its own toll of misery and acted as a catalyst for change. For the workers at home the period of war was one of economic hardship and repression. Set against this was the dawning of ideas of equality and democracy. There could be no going back to the security of the past. In 1815 the soldiers returned. Hundreds of thousands of men, once soldiers, now returned to face unemployment. Trade had been severely interrupted by the war and an economic depression fell on the country. The people, no longer silent and acquiescent in whatever policies the government might choose to pursue, demanded political reform. Universal male suffrage and a reform of the electoral boundaries and representation were demanded, along with measures to relieve poverty. In Manchester in 1819 a political assembly was dispersed with the death of eleven people at what became known as the Peterloo Massacre. Parliament responded with repressive measures, strengthening anti-sedition and libel laws. It was clear that reform could not be postponed indefinitely.

In George III's reign, which lasted for sixty years, the most profound demographic, economic and social changes occurred. In the early years of his reign London had a population of some 700,000, twelve times larger than the next largest city, Bristol. All roads led to London (as they had since Roman times), carrying fresh and live produce to feed the capital. G. M. Trevelyan records that

A hundred thousand head of cattle and three-quarters of a million sheep yearly walked up to Smithfield for the slaughter, many of them from Scotland or from the borders of Wales.

and that

strangest of all to the modern eye would be the droves of geese and turkeys, two or three thousand at a time, waddling slowly and loquaciously along all the

---

[32] In the course of the war, William Wilberforce (1759–1833) campaigned for and won the fight to eradicate the slave trade. His Bill became law in 1807 under the Abolition of the Slave Trade Act.

roads to London from a hundred miles around, between August and October, feeding on the stubble of the fields through which they passed. On one road, from Ipswich to London, 150,000 turkeys walked over the Stour bridge each year.[33]

Agriculture was changing. Formerly open lands were enclosed, with profound effects on the agricultural labourer and the poor. By 1801 some twenty Enclosure Acts had been passed, minimal compensation being paid which prevented the displaced from establishing their own farms under the new system. While enclosure made production of the food supply more efficient, the wealth it generated went not to the displaced worker but to the landowners.

Workers in the years of the Napoleonic Wars suffered badly: wages fell and many had to accept whatever terms an employer offered. Faced with increasingly repressive laws against any form of trade unionism, the desperate turned to violence, not only rioting but also destroying the production machinery which so damaged employment prospects. Throughout the industrial regions, organized bands of workers – the Luddites – set about economic destruction. Government spies were extensively used to counteract these terrorist operations. Parliament responded once more with repression: those who engaged in breaking weaving-frames (which employers had adapted to increase efficiency at the cost of quality) became liable to the death penalty. Trevelyan records that in Cheshire fourteen death sentences were handed down, two of which were imposed, while in Yorkshire seventeen men were hanged and seven transported for seven years (one for life).[34] The Combination Laws were repealed in 1824.

But economic progress continued. The cotton industry developed, as did the extraction of iron and coal, both now organized as units of large-scale production, with coal for the first time being used for the production of iron. In 1781 James Watt had patented his second steam engine, the impact of which affected every manufacturing process. The factory system was being developed, bringing together large numbers of workers who had previously been engaged in cottage industry pro-

---

[33] G. M. Trevelyan, *British History in the 19th Century and After: 1782–1919* (London: Longman, 1937), pp. 10–11.
[34] Ibid., p. 188.

duction. The population was both growing fast and shifting to meet the demands of the new industrial age. Improvements in sanitation and medical advances led to a decline in infant and child mortality. Trevelyan records that in 1835 the medical journal *The Lancet* estimated that the 'death-rate for children was halved between 1750 and 1830'.[35] While agricultural districts declined, mining areas and the new industrial centres grew in population.

THE GREAT REFORM ACT

George III died in 1820; his eldest son, George IV, reigned ten years, succeeded by his younger brother, William. William IV, 'Sailor Billy',[36] was sixty-four when he came to the throne in 1830, and reigned only seven years. Yet in this time the greatest parliamentary reform ever witnessed was to occur: the Reform Act of 1832. In truth, the Act was not very 'great' from the perspective of the ordinary person, but it was certainly radical at the time. The Act addressed the problem of the rotten boroughs which had existed since medieval times. The problem of these boroughs was essentially that they were represented in Parliament by nominees of the landowners. In turn, the landowners were in informal partnership with the aristocracy sitting in the House of Lords. For centuries it was the aristocracy who therefore controlled those sitting in the people's house, the House of Commons. Probably the worst example of a rotten borough was that of Old Sarum. Long abandoned, the borough nevertheless returned two Members of Parliament, to represent a total of seven electors. Deeply opposed by the Tory House of Lords, it took three Bills, one general election and the threat of the king to create sufficient sympathetic new Whig peers in the Lords for the Bill to become law.

Also entangled in the movement for reform was the issue of Catholic emancipation. Religious discrimination had continued, in the form of the Test and Corporation Acts which excluded Catholics from public

[35] Ibid., p. 137.
[36] So nicknamed because of his career in the navy.

office and membership of Parliament. In January 1828 George IV appointed the Duke of Wellington, hero of the Napoleonic Wars, as Prime Minister. In the Commons was Sir Robert Peel. Wellington and Peel fragmented the Tory party and soon ushered in a Whig government. Nevertheless, to the horror of their party, Wellington and Peel had the Test and Corporation Acts repealed, thus ending centuries of religious discrimination. Wellington's administration collapsed in 1830.

The Representation of the People Act 1832 – the great Reform Act – disenfranchised fifty-six boroughs, and a further thirty boroughs had their representatives cut from two to one. Twenty-two new two-member and twenty new single-member borough constituencies were created. County representation was increased. The qualifications for the right to vote were increased. In county constituencies, adult males owning freehold property worth at least £2 per annum were enfranchised, as were adult males having copyhold land (tenure of land, recognized by the courts, but less than freehold) worth at least £10 per annum. Adult males leasing land worth at least £50 per annum were also enfranchised. In borough constituencies, adult males owning or occupying property worth £10 per annum were enfranchised, on condition that they had been in possession of the property for at least a year and all related taxes on the property had been paid and that they had not received any poor law relief (welfare benefits) in the previous year. In order to throw light on the eligibility of voters, a register of voters was for the first time established.

What effect did the Act of 1832 have? From 1831 to 1833 the overall size of the electorate increased by 78 per cent, to a total of 652,777 voters. The main beneficiaries were the middle class: non-property holders, or holders of less valuable land irrespective of their legal rights over the land, were not enfranchised. Nor of course were women. In terms of those eligible to stand for election, the bias towards the wealthy remained. To stand as a candidate for a borough constituency, there was a property qualification of £300, and for a county candidate £600. What the Act did not do was to extend the vote to all citizens. Those working-class persons who had agitated for electoral reform were left empty-handed. Political rights were firmly tied to property rights.

Between 1800 and 1850 the population of Britain rose by 73 per cent. By the time of the Reform Act 1832, the industrial revolution was in full swing. Modes of production had changed, and transportation now included not only tarmacked roads but a network of canals. The great centres of production developed into great cities: Birmingham, Bristol, Leeds, Liverpool, Manchester and Sheffield all experienced population explosions. The expansion of the railway network from the 1830s speeded up industry and commerce. Economic and industrial advances, accompanied by population shifts towards new forms of production, gave rise to the demand of the 'common man' for better conditions. In the 1830s the conditions of the people differed widely, the starkest contrast being between the city and the rural areas. Labour started to organize into unions. After the ban on unionization was repealed in 1824, workers were swift to form into co-operative units to fight for better pay and conditions. The economic and social changes brought about by the industrial revolution propelled government into unprecedented areas of regulation, in health and sanitation, factories, housing and employment. The civil service multiplied.

Demands for political reform also continued. In 1828 a People's Charter was drafted by Francis Place. Among its demands were universal suffrage for all men, the abolition of property qualifications for Members of Parliament, salaries for Members of Parliament, constituencies of equal size, the secret ballot for all voters and annual Parliaments. Throughout the country a 'Chartist movement' developed, supporting the aims of the Charter. While not a unified national organization, the Chartists represented a nation-wide network of agitators for reform, with rallies attracting thousands of people. Although the movement had withered by 1858, it represented a real and visible focal point for radical dissent. Given that 1848 was the year of revolution in continental Europe, small wonder the government viewed Chartism with suspicion, especially when it threatened public order. Chartism succeeded in attracting greatest support in times of economic hardship. It could not survive, unorganized, fragmented and without funds, as a political force in times of economic prosperity. Symbolically, however, Chartism was fundamentally important in raising issues of constitutional importance with the ordinary people. Its legacy was to find expression in the expansion of the trade union movement, and the political recognition of the working class through the formation of the Labour Party.

The nineteenth century saw a general increase in popular protest. Chartism was not the only political movement under way. Following the Napoleonic Wars, a Corn Law Act of 1815 was passed which protected the domestic market by prohibiting imports of wheat other than where the price of domestic wheat had reached a certain market price. The effect of this on the poor was devastating. Riots had occurred in London when the Bill was going through Parliament, and demands continued that the Corn Law be repealed. In 1838 the Anti-Corn Law League was established as a vehicle for the expression of dissent and demands for reform.[37] Meetings and public lectures took place throughout the country. This was a one-issue campaign, and one which had an uneasy, often antagonistic, relationship with the Chartist movement. The Corn Laws were ultimately repealed in 1846, and the League dissolved. What these two popular movements show, above all, is that nation-wide protest, for parliamentary reform on the Chartist side, and economic reform on the side of the Anti-Corn Law League, was by the 1840s an established means of applying pressure on the still-unrepresentative Parliament on behalf of the people, both franchised and disenfranchised.

THE VICTORIAN AGE

Constitutionally, when Victoria came to the throne in 1837 it was under more restrictive conditions than her predecessors. The shift of power from Crown to Parliament had moved decisively and finally in favour of the latter. Victoria accepted that the role of the Crown was to be outside the cut and thrust of daily politics. The monarch had by now become what Bagehot labelled the 'dignified' rather than the 'efficient' part of the constitution.[38] Eighteen fifty-one was the year of the Great Exhibition: a celebration of the economic and industrial power which Britain had achieved through the commercial and industrial revolutions. Under Victoria the British Empire was at its height.

[37] See L. Brown, 'The Chartists and the Anti-Corn Law League', in A. Briggs (ed.), *Chartist Studies* (London: Macmillan, 1967), chapter 11.
[38] W. Bagehot, *The English Constitution*, 1867 (London: Fontana, 1993).

The years of Victoria's reign (1837–1901) saw an unprecedented rise in state involvement in all aspects of society. In 1834 a new Poor Law Act had been passed, reforming the system of poor relief that had been in place since the reign of Elizabeth I; the Municipal Corporations Act 1835 had established elected borough councils. County councils and county borough councils were established in 1888 and the final and lowest layer of local government, urban district councils, rural district councils and parish councils, in 1894.[39] Local Boards of Health were established in 1848. The state moved into the supervision and control of housing and sanitation, with local authorities empowered to build housing to replace urban slums. Education was to follow, although this was to prove a far more contentious area of state involvement. Cole and Postgate estimate that in 1839, 33.7 and 49.5 per cent of men and women were illiterate.[40] The problem of education provision, as with so much of British history, lay with the claims of the Church. The Church of England regarded education as inextricably linked to the supervision and provision of religious instruction according to the beliefs of the established Church. Others favoured education on non-denominational lines while yet others favoured an entirely secular system. Only in 1870 was an Education Act passed that allowed for state provision to operate alongside the existing voluntary system. In 1876 education became compulsory for all up to the age of twelve years, although there was no state provision for secondary education until 1902.

Electoral reform returned to the political agenda soon after the Crimean War (1853–6). Economic prosperity had enlarged the middle classes. The disenfranchisement of the working class represented a potential threat to economic success. The perceived difficulty, from the perspective of the upper and middle classes, however, was how to extend the franchise without giving political power to the lower classes. From the perspective of more than a century, it is difficult to understand just why the extension of the vote worried those who had achieved it. The entitlement to vote was not regarded as a right, but as a privilege, and one not to be given to others lightly. For the sceptics, the right to vote

---

[39] Under the Local Government Acts 1888 and 1894.
[40] G. D. H. Cole and R. Postgate, *The Common People 1746–1946* (New York: Methuen, 4th edn., 1949), p. 308.

was inextricably linked to education, and education the labourer did not have. Also involved was the perception that if the 'working man' gained the vote, he would gain power – the power of a class which, if united against its 'masters', could spell ruin for that class. The 'working man' was conventionally deferential to his 'betters': he needed no expression of his interests through the vote, because his 'betters' would ensure the best representation on his behalf (the same argument was used in Victorian times to deny women the vote). Walter Bagehot gives these fears expression in the following manner:

no one will contend that the ordinary working man who has no special skill, and who is only rated because he has a house, can judge much of intellectual matters. . . . They [labourers] have no time to improve themselves, for they are labouring the whole day through; and their early education was so small that in most cases it is dubious whether even if they had much time, they could use it to good purpose.

And further:

in all cases it must be remembered that a political combination of the lower classes, as such and for their own objects, is an evil of the first magnitude; that a permanent combination of them would make them (now that so many of them have the suffrage) supreme in the country; and that their supremacy, in the state they now are, means the supremacy of ignorance over instruction and of numbers over knowledge.[41]

Notwithstanding these fears, the Conservative administration of 1867 under Disraeli placed a Reform Bill before Parliament: a move judged by Cole and Postgate as 'one of the most contorted and unexpected portions of parliamentary history, ending in the enfranchisement of a considerable part of the British working class by the party which was controlled by its most resolute and natural enemies'.[42] The Representation of the People Act of 1867 continued the distinction drawn earlier between borough and county constituencies. In the boroughs, the vote was extended to all householders and all those paying £10 in rent. In the counties, the occupational qualification was reduced from £50 to

41 Bagehot, *English Constitution*, pp. 273, 278.
42 Cole and Postgate, *Common People*, p. 390.

£15. The electorate doubled: now two out of five had the vote. But this meant that three out of five did not. Most significant of these were women. Although John Stuart Mill proposed an amendment to the 1867 Bill, it was rejected: women had to wait until 1918 for the right to vote at the age of thirty, and until 1928 for the right to vote at the age of majority on equal terms with men (then twenty-one years). Nevertheless, the 1867 Act was indeed radical. One principal effect was to enhance the power of the ordinary people, at the expense of the aristocracy and elite. The House of Commons now truly had the right to call itself representative. The power of patronage – to control the vote in a constituency in favour of a chosen candidate – was further reduced in 1872 with the introduction of the secret ballot.

The story of the nineteenth century ends with the role of political parties and trade unions and the evolution of the Labour Party. After two further electoral reforms, in 1884 and 1885, the electorate had expanded to include not only urban workers but also many agricultural workers in the counties, provided that they could satisfy the occupation and lodger qualifications then in place. It fell to the Conservative and Liberal Parties, as the old Tory and Whig parties were now known, to ensure that the electorate understood and accepted their competing policies. No longer could it be assumed by political parties that persuading Parliament of what was good 'for the people' was enough: the people themselves had to be consulted. And so the birth of extensive local party administration came into being, to attract members, to organize elections and drum up party support. Nor would candidates standing as independents any longer succeed: each needed a political platform and the support of a party organization in order to ensure electoral success.

By the 1870s and 1880s workers were more organized than ever before: trade unionism and the struggle for decent pay and conditions of work were here to stay. This did not of itself, however, lead to the establishment of a political party directly aimed at representing the interests of workers. A few workers stood for Parliament, but for the most part worker representation in Parliament was through the Liberal Party, either by candidates being adopted by the Party, or less directly by the Liberals defending the workers' interests in Parliament. In the 1880s there were also other forces at work. In 1881 the Democratic

Federation was founded as a radical socialist movement inspired by the writings of Karl Marx. In 1884 it was renamed the Social Democratic Federation (the SDF). Marx and Engels were confident that the conditions in industrial Britain were such that a popular working-class revolution would first occur in England, rather than elsewhere in continental Europe. Allied to working-class conditions, a depression in the 1880s lowered wages. In 1884 also, the essentially middle-class Fabian Society was formed, the influence of which was mainly felt in the next century. Marx's predictions proved false. The popular grass-roots support necessary to generate the revolution that would overthrow the capitalist system was never established. By the late 1880s, the SDF had lost its influence. Nevertheless, the time had come for the formation of a political party specifically to represent the interests of the working class, in its own right, rather than remaining dependent on the largesse of the Liberal Party which had hitherto accommodated working-class parliamentary candidates.

In 1888 Keir Hardie concluded that the Liberal Party would not best defend working-class interests, and founded the Scottish Labour Party. In 1892 three Labour Members of Parliament were elected, including Keir Hardie. In 1893 a gathering of like-minded socialist-orientated delegates met, under the chairmanship of Hardie, and the Independent Labour Party was formed.

Where did this leave the Liberal Party, which for so long regarded itself as the defender of the working man? It appears to have failed the working class in two principal respects. First, in the closing years of the nineteenth century the issues dominating the Liberal government were not working-class interests but rather reform of the House of Lords and the problem of Irish Home Rule, despite the fact that the Liberals had promised a wide range of social and political reforms which would have benefited the working class. While the Liberals were neglecting the working class, pro-working class organizations were springing up outside Parliament. The Social Democratic Federation, the Fabian Society and the Independent Labour Party were the organizational antecedents of the Labour Party. Keir Hardie also mobilized the support of the now-powerful unions for a specifically labour-orientated party seeking representation in Parliament. In 1900, at the Trade Union Congress conference, the Labour Representation Committee emerged:

the original Labour Party. By the 1920s the Labour Party was to be the second largest party in Parliament, and the official opposition to the Conservative Party.

At the dawning of the twentieth century we find in place essentially all the ingredients of government which exist today. The gradual evolution of the constitutional system has progressed from the medieval divine right of kings through to a constitutional monarchy, the legal powers of which remain great, but which in practical terms cannot be exercised other than through the democratically elected government of the day. The United Kingdom exists in the form of England, Ireland, Wales and Scotland. The question of Ireland, the ultimate severing of the counties of the north from the rest of Ireland and the establishment of an independent Republic of Ireland, were problems addressed but not yet settled. The judiciary, once at the mercy of kings and queens, had enjoyed full independence of government and politics since the Act of Settlement 1701. The class structure, dominated by the oligarchy born of property, public school and Oxbridge education, was firmly in place. Monarchy, the House of Lords, the established Church of England, the military, civil service and professions all reflected the bias created by status.

In the nineteenth century there was movement from *laissez faire* state to interventionist state. The idea of social and economic rights, never explicitly formulated, came into being: the individual was no longer a mere subject, but now a citizen entitled to representation in the legislature and to laws securing minimum standards of social welfare. But minimal they were: the welfare state lay nearly half a century in the future. While the idea of freedoms and rights consciously developed out of the American and French Revolutions and the writings of John Locke and Tom Paine, at the turn of the century these remained largely unarticulated and unenforceable in law.

The two-party political system emerged out of the seventeenth century crisis, and although dominated by the Conservative and Liberal parties at the end of the nineteenth century, a new political force, the Labour Party, was born at the end of the century, ultimately to displace the Liberal Party in the next century.

THE TWENTIETH CENTURY

Internationally Britain emerged from the nineteenth century as a powerful nation with a vast empire, with all the economic and commercial advantages that went with its near-global trading relations. The age of decolonization and the self-determination of peoples had not yet been born. But if the eighteenth and nineteenth centuries resulted in Britain's emergence as a world power with an extensive empire, the twentieth century changed all that. The first half of the twentieth century was dominated by two World Wars, 1914–18 and 1939–45. In 1917, as a result of the revolution, Russia withdrew from the allied forces.[43] Following the First World War, the Treaty of Versailles 1919 laid down the future, and imposed harsh penalties on Germany, including the loss of her colonies. The League of Nations emerged as the forerunner to the United Nations, although the refusal of the Americans to join reduced the League's effectiveness.

Between the two World Wars there was world-wide economic depression. In September 1939 the Second World War started, lasting until the capitulation of Germany and Japan in 1945. With the war ended, there was another threat: the Soviet Union which dominated Eastern Europe. Two new superpowers had emerged, the United States of America and the Soviet Union. As part of the peace settlement Germany was divided, the division symbolized most acutely by the division of Berlin into areas controlled by the allied victors and separated by the Berlin Wall. The Cold War lasted for over forty years as Western democracies sought to limit the Soviet Union's dominance of Europe behind the 'iron curtain' and the advance of its dominant ideology, Communism.

In 1945 the United Nations was established, committed to maintaining world-wide peace and raising the standard of human rights throughout the world. In 1949 the North Atlantic Treaty Organization (NATO) was formed, comprising the United States, Britain, Canada, France and other Western European nations. The response of the Soviet

---

[43] Originally, Britain, France, Japan and Russia supported by troops from Australia, Canada, New Zealand and South Africa, and from 1917 the United States.

Union was the formation of the Warsaw Treaty Organization, the Warsaw Pact. Within Europe, the Council of Europe was formed in 1950 mirroring in many respects the aims and objectives of the United Nations in its determination to secure peace and ensure the protection of human rights. Under the Council of Europe, the European Convention on Human Rights and Fundamental Freedoms was drafted, providing a code of civil and political rights which were to be enforceable at a European level through the European Court of Human Rights. Also motivated by the need to avoid future war were the European treaties which were the precursors of the European Union – the European Coal and Steel Community and the European Atomic Energy Community, both of which brought the raw materials of war under 'supranational' control.

In terms of constitutional development in Britain, the first decade of the twentieth century saw conflict arise between the two Houses of Parliament, which was resolved only with the emasculation of the unelected House of Lords. By constitutional convention, the House of Lords gave way to the elected House of Commons on matters of finance, but otherwise enjoyed equal powers in relation to legislation. In 1909 the House of Lords rejected, in breach of the convention, the government's Finance Bill. The government appealed to the king to create sufficient new peers to guarantee the passage of the Bill, but the king insisted that the government first get the mandate of the people. The 1910 general election returned the government to power and the House of Lords then passed the Bill. The Parliament Act 1911 was then passed to curtail the power of the Lords, which was further curtailed under the Parliament Act of 1949.

Women won the right to vote at the age of thirty in 1918: some advance on no vote, but still discriminatory in so far as the age of majority was twenty-one at the time. The participation of women in the war effort between 1914 and 1918 and their general entry into the workforce to offset the shortages created by the conscription of men into the army was to change the role of women for ever. While the 'age of gentility' remained for upper- and middle-class women, for working-class women employment opportunities opened up outside the world of domestic service. The world of politics, for so long dominated by the Conservatives and Liberals, was also changing: the newly formed Labour Party first came to power in 1924. For the first time the working class had its own voice, no longer dependent upon the goodwill of the Liberal Party for the representation of its interests.

Britain emerged from the Second World War with her economy and infrastructure in need of rescue, but her Empire intact.[44] Yet, within a quarter of a century the age of empire had passed, not only for Britain but also for other colonial powers. The age of the self-determination of peoples and the right to independence had been born out of global conflict. One by one former colonies demanded independence: India the earliest in 1947, Malaya in 1957. In 1957 Harold Macmillan, then Prime Minister of Britain, made his prophetic 'winds of change' speech, predicting the overthrow of colonial power throughout the African continent. Ghana achieved independence in 1957, Nigeria in 1960, Uganda in 1962. Nyasaland, now Malawi, and Northern Rhodesia, now Zambia, gained independence from Britain in 1963. In 1965 the government of Southern Rhodesia, as it then was, declared unilateral independence from Britain and proclaimed her own sovereignty: it was not until 1979 that a constitutional settlement was reached which brought an end to white minority rule in what is now Zimbabwe.

As formerly dependent states each claimed their right to complete self-determination, empire vanished, its only echo being the Commonwealth. The relationship between Britain and her colonies had never included direct rule from Westminster or Whitehall; rather the relationships were characterized originally by a British administration established within the territory, English law extending to the legal system of the colony with the Privy Council the ultimate appeal court, and with the allegiance of the colonial government to the British Crown. By the middle of the nineteenth century, the demand for greater clarity in the relationship between Britain and her territories grew, culminating in 1865 with the Colonial Laws Validity Act which confirmed the capacity of colonial legislatures for self-regulation, while affirming the ultimate sovereignty of the imperial Parliament. The Commonwealth of Nations, all members owing allegiance to the Crown, was a recognized entity by

[44] With two exceptions. America had thrown off the yoke of imperialism in 1776. Southern Ireland achieved independence in 1922 and emerged as the Republic of Ireland.

1884. In 1867 Canada became a self-governing Dominion – a status implying equality with rather than subordination to Britain. Australia followed in 1900, New Zealand in 1907 and South Africa in 1910. Four-yearly prime ministerial conferences were established, at which the evolution of self-governance was discussed. In 1931, following an Imperial Conference, the Statute of Westminster was passed, extending the powers of Dominion legislatures to amend or repeal Acts of the United Kingdom Parliament, with the exception of those provisions which related to the Dominion's powers to legislate.

While the original basis of the Commonwealth was the bond of allegiance to the Crown, the movement towards republicanism forced a change in direction for the Commonwealth. Indian independence represented the catalyst for change. India had remained a Dominion[45] until independence in 1947. In 1949 India's desire to become a republic and yet remain within the Commonwealth posed a novel question concerning allegiance. The result was the London Declaration of 1949 which revised the position and enabled India to be the first republican member of the Commonwealth. The position then established, which remains today, is that the British Crown is recognized as the 'symbol of free association and thus Head of the Commonwealth'.

In large measure, it was the Commonwealth which explained Britain's originally ambivalent stance towards membership of the European Community (and now Union), the joining of which was the most constitutionally significant development of the latter half of the twentieth century. While Commonwealth nations enjoyed special trading arrangements with Britain, and successive British governments were committed to the maintenance of close links with the multi-cultural and multi-racial Commonwealth, it was clear that these could not be sustained if Britain joined the European Communities. The Common Market – the key component of the three European Communities – was founded on the principles of freedom of movement of capital, goods, services and people. Central to this endeavour was the abolition of barriers to free trade between the member states of the Community and the acceptance of a common external tariff system. While Britain's trade with the Commonwealth was on the decline, nevertheless these

[45] Under the India Act 1935.

trading relationships required special consideration, and the protection of Commonwealth relations became a central feature of negotiations for British entry to the Community. As discussed in Chapter 4, following Britain's original distrust of the European enterprise, and France's rejection of Britain's belated application to join in 1961, Edward Heath, Prime Minister from 1970 to 1974, eventually secured British entry in 1972, membership which came into effect on 1 January 1973. As the aims and objectives of the original Communities expanded and evolved, moving into areas such as monetary union, the development of common foreign and security policies and policies relating to judicial co-operation, the European Union emerged.[46] 'Europe' was to prove the most contentious aspect of British political life for the duration of the twentieth century, and beyond.

The 1950s and 1960s witnessed an expansion in immigration into Britain from Commonwealth nations – a movement which changed the face of Britain and created its own tensions in society. The Britain of former times, albeit with national identities in its component nations (Northern Ireland, Scotland and Wales) and divided by social class, soon became a truly multi-cultural and multi-racial country. As the extent of racial discrimination became clearer, Parliament acted first in 1965 and subsequently in 1976 to provide mechanisms to eliminate the public manifestations of discrimination and to provide remedies for victims of discrimination.

The systematic organization of labour was also a characteristic of this period as workers united to fight for decent pay and conditions of work. With their power-base in the Labour Party, including block votes at Conference which could dictate Party policy, union power challenged governments of all political persuasions. The 1974 election called by Conservative Prime Minister Edward Heath was fought, unsuccessfully, on the slogan 'who runs Britain?' In 1979 the Labour government under James Callaghan was brought down in part by industrial unrest culminating in the 'winter of discontent' with its interruption of essential services and widespread strikes. The miners' strike of the 1980s was the catalyst for curtailing union power through legislation. The unions'

---

[46] Under the Treaty on European Union 1992, as amended by the Treaty on European Union 1997.

hold over the Labour Party was broken only in the mid-1990s when the then leader of the Party, John Smith, following the initiative of his predecessor, Neil Kinnock, succeeded in removing the unions' power of the block vote and introducing the 'one member, one vote' system for Party Conference decisions.

The 1960s saw a social revolution also in terms of the young: the explosion in fashion and music created its own culture and lifestyle. At the same time, the demand for women's rights was becoming more emphatic. Women were demanding full equality in education and in the work-place in the form of equal pay and equal conditions of work and relief from the tyranny of domesticity. Suddenly, the formerly (however superficially) cohesive society of earlier decades looked very different as different groups sought recognition of their individual identities free from discrimination by the majority population. The latter half of the twentieth century was characterized by the struggle for individual freedoms and rights, a struggle which has not yet ended.

Meanwhile in Northern Ireland the search for a peaceful settlement between the warring Catholic and Protestant factions continued.[47] Civil unrest, bordering at times on civil war, revived in the late 1960s as Catholics voiced their dissent against discrimination in all aspects of life meted out by the politically-dominant Protestant Ulster Unionists. The product of Britain's imperialist past, and long preceding Britain's eighteenth- and nineteenth-century seizures of territory, the 'troubles' in Northern Ireland dominated politics for the last decades of the twentieth century. The seemingly irreconcilable differences and the ingrained hatred and distrust between the two communities within the province led to the loss of thousands of lives – of civilians, of the police and security forces and of members of terrorist organizations. In 1998 a peace settlement was finally agreed, which if all parties complied with its terms, would lead to the devolution of legislative power again to the Northern Ireland Assembly. The requirement that paramilitary organizations, on both sides, decommission their weapons, was breached by the Irish Republican Army, and in early 2000 devolution was suspended, only to be redevolved following concessions by the

[47] See Chapter 5.

Ulster Unionists. The dawning of the new century brought no guarantee of permanent peace in the troubled province.

In 1997, after eighteen years of Conservative rule, a Labour government came into power once more. It did so with a massive parliamentary majority and on a radical programme of constitutional reform. At the dawning of the new century and new millennium Britain is in the midst of constitutional change, the implications of which will not be clear for many years to come.

APPENDIX I:
MONARCHS OF BRITAIN

	Reigned
William (the Conqueror) (1027–87)	1066–87
William II (Rufus) (1056–1100)	1087–1100
Henry I (1068–1135)	1100–35
Stephen (?1097–1154)	1135–54
Henry II (1133–89)	1154–89
Richard I (1157–99)	1189–99
John (1167–1216)	1199–1216
Henry III (1207–72)	1216–72
Edward I (1239–1307)	1272–1307
Edward II (1284–1327)	1307–27
Edward III (1312–77)	1327–77
Richard II (1367–1400)	1377–99
Henry IV (1366–1413)	1399–1413
Henry V (1387–1422)	1413–22
Henry VI (1421–71)	1422–61 (briefly restored to the throne in 1470)
Edward IV (1442–83)	1461–70, 1471–83
Edward V (1470–?1483)	1483
Richard III (1452–85)	1483–5
Henry VII (1457–1509)	1485–1509

Henry VIII (1491–1547)	1509–47
Edward VI (1537–53)	1547–53
Mary I (1516–58)	1553–8
Elizabeth I (1533–1603)	1558–1603
James I (1566–1625)	king of Scotland: 1567–1625; king of England: 1603–25
Charles I (1600–49)	1625–49
Interregnum (1649–60)	
Charles II (1630–85)	1660–85
James II (1633–1701)	1685–8
William (III) and Mary (II) (1650–1702, 1662–94)	1689–1702
Anne (1665–1714)	1702–14
George I (1660–1727)	1714–27
George II (1683–1760)	1727–60
George III (1738–1820)	1760–1820
George IV (1762–1830)	1820–30
William IV (1765–1837)	1830–37
Victoria (1819–1901)	1837–1901
Edward VII (1841–1910)	1901–10
George V (1865–1936)	1910–36
Edward VIII (1894–1972)	1936 (abdicated)
George VI (1895–1952)	1936–52
Elizabeth II (1926–)	1952–

APPENDIX II: PRIME MINISTERS OF BRITAIN

	Party	Dates
Sir Robert Walpole		3 April 1721–11 February 1742
Earl of Wilmington		16 February 1742–2 July 1743
Hon. Henry Pelham		25 August 1743–10 February 1746
Earl of Bath		10–12 February 1746
Hon. Henry Pelham		13 February 1746–6 March 1754
Duke of Newcastle		6 March 1754–26 October 1756
William Pitt (the Elder)		16 November 1756–6 April 1757
Duke of Devonshire		6 April–8 June 1757
Earl Waldegrave		8–12 June 1757
Duke of Devonshire		12–29 June 1757
William Pitt (the Elder)		29 June 1757–5 October 1761
Duke of Newcastle		5 October 1761–26 May 1762
Earl of Bute		26 May 1762–8 April 1763

	Party	Dates
George Grenville		10 April 1763– 10 July 1765
Marquess of Rockingham		10 July 1765– 12 July 1766
William Pitt (the Elder)		30 July 1766– 12 March 1767
Duke of Grafton		12 March 1767– 28 January 1770
Lord North		28 January 1770– 20 March 1782
Marquess of Rockingham		27 March–1 July 1782
Earl of Shelburne		3 July 1782– 24 February 1783
Duke of Portland		2 April– 19 December 1783
Hon. William Pitt (the Younger)	Tory	19 December 1783– 14 March 1801
Henry Addington	Tory	14 March 1801– 10 May 1804
Hon. William Pitt (the Younger)	Tory	10 May 1804– 23 January 1806
Lord Grenville	Whig	11 February 1806– 24 March 1807
Duke of Portland	Tory	31 March 1807– 6 September 1809
Spencer Perceval	Tory	4 October 1809– 11 May 1812
Earl of Liverpool	Tory	8 June 1812– 17 February 1827
George Canning	Tory	10 April– 8 August 1827
Viscount Goderich	Tory	31 August 1827– 8 January 1828
Duke of Wellington	Tory	22 January 1828– 15 November 1830

	Party	Dates
Earl Grey	Whig	16 November 1830– 9 July 1834
Viscount Melbourne	Whig	16 July– 17 November 1834
Duke of Wellington	Tory	17 November– 10 December 1834
Sir Robert Peel	Conservative	10 December 1834– 8 April 1835
Viscount Melbourne	Whig	18 April 1835– 30 August 1841
Sir Robert Peel	Conservative	30 August 1841– 30 June 1846
Lord John Russell	Whig	30 June 1846– 23 February 1852
Earl of Derby	Conservative	23 February– 19 December 1852
Earl of Aberdeen	Coalition	19 December 1852– 1 February 1855
Viscount Palmerston	Whig-Liberal	6 February 1855– February 1858
Earl of Derby	Conservative	20 February 1858– June 1859
Viscount Palmerston	Whig-Liberal	12 June 1859– 18 October 1865
Earl Russell	Whig-Liberal	29 October 1865– 26 June 1866
Earl of Derby	Conservative	6 July 1866– 25 February 1868
Benjamin Disraeli	Conservative	28 February– 3 December 1868
William Gladstone	Liberal	3 December 1868– 17 February 1874
Benjamin Disraeli	Conservative	20 February 1874– 18 April 1880
William Gladstone	Liberal	23 April 1880– 23 June 1885

	Party	Dates
Marquess of Salisbury	Conservative	23 June 1885– 27 January 1886
William Gladstone	Liberal	1 February– 20 July 1886
Marquess of Salisbury	Conservative	25 July 1886– 11 August 1892
William Gladstone	Liberal	15 August 1892– 3 March 1894
Earl of Rosebery	Liberal	5 March 1894– 25 June 1895
Marquess of Salisbury	Conservative	25 June 1895– 12 July 1902
Arthur Balfour	Conservative	12 July 1902– 4 December 1905
Sir Henry Campbell-Bannerman	Liberal	5 December 1905– 7 April 1908
Herbert Asquith	Liberal	7 April 1908– 26 May 1915
Herbert Asquith	Coalition	26 May 1915– 7 December 1916
David Lloyd George	Coalition	7 December 1916– 19 October 1922
Andrew Bonar Law	Conservative	23 October 1922– 20 May 1923
Stanley Baldwin	Conservative	22 May 1923– 22 January 1924
James Ramsay MacDonald	Labour	22 January– 4 November 1924
Stanley Baldwin	Conservative	4 November 1924– 5 June 1929
James Ramsay MacDonald	Labour	5 June 1929– 24 August 1931
James Ramsay MacDonald	National Government	25 August 1931– 7 June 1935
Stanley Baldwin	National Government	7 June 1935– 28 May 1937

	Party	Dates
Neville Chamberlain	National Government	28 May 1937– 10 May 1940
Winston Churchill	Coalition	10 May 1940– 23 May 1945
Winston Churchill	Conservative	23 May 1945– 26 July 1945
Clement Attlee	Labour	26 July 1945– 26 October 1951
Winston Churchill	Conservative	26 October 1951– 5 April 1955
Sir Anthony Eden	Conservative	6 April 1955– 9 January 1957
Harold Macmillan	Conservative	10 January 1957– 13 October 1963
Sir Alec Douglas- Home	Conservative	18 October 1963– 16 October 1964
Harold Wilson	Labour	16 October 1964– 19 June 1970
Edward Heath	Conservative	19 June 1970– 3 March 1974
Harold Wilson	Labour	3 March 1974– 16 March 1976
James Callaghan	Labour	5 April 1976– 28 March 1979
Margaret Thatcher	Conservative	4 May 1979– 22 November 1990
John Major	Conservative	27 November 1990– 2 May 1997
Anthony Blair	Labour	2 May 1997 to present

INDEX